SO-BCA-325

Arguments about Arguments

Systematic, Critical, and Historical Essays in Logical Theory

This book brings together a selection of essays by one of the pre-eminent scholars of informal logic. Following an approach that is empirical but not psychological, dialectical but not dialogical, and focused on interpretation without neglecting evaluation, Maurice Finocchiaro defines concepts such as reasoning, argument, argument analysis, critical reasoning, methodological reflection, judgment, critical thinking, and informal logic. He defends theses about the rarity of fallacies but the frequency of fallacious reasoning; the asymmetry of positive and negative in argumentation, interpretation, and evaluation; and the role of critical thinking in science, among other topics. And he presents extended critiques of the views of many contemporary scholars, while also integrating into the discussion Arnauld's *Port-Royal Logic*, Gramsci's theory of intellectuals, and case studies from the history of science, particularly the work of Galileo, Newton, Huygens, and Lavoisier.

Maurice A. Finocchiaro is Distinguished Professor of Philosophy Emeritus at the University of Nevada, Las Vegas. The author of eight other books, including *Galileo and the Art of Reasoning* and *Gramsci and the History of Dialectical Thought*, he has received major grants and fellowships from the Guggenheim Foundation, the National Science Foundation, the National Endowment for the Humanities, and the American Council of Learned Societies. He is currently president of the Association for Informal Logic and Critical Thinking.

42, principle of charity, N.B

Arguments about Arguments

Systematic, Critical, and Historical Essays in Logical Theory

MAURICE A. FINOCCHIARO

University of Nevada, Las Vegas

2005

Katz:

In this little book I use logic the *informal logic* to develop in detail a simple system of than actual system of formal logic. So, *logic about logic!*

(In Euclidean geom we use *informal logic* on every page, but seldom discuss informal logic. the nature of logic, which is an exciting subject itself.)

CAMBRIDGE
UNIVERSITY PRESS

CAMBRIDGE UNIVERSITY PRESS
Cambridge, New York, Melbourne, Madrid, Cape Town, Singapore, São Paulo

Cambridge University Press
40 West 20th Street, New York, NY 10011-4211, USA

www.cambridge.org
Information on this title: www.cambridge.org/9780521853279

First published 2005

Printed in the United States of America

A catalog record for this publication is available from the British Library.

Library of Congress Cataloging in Publication Data

Finocchiaro, Maurice A., 1942–
Arguments about arguments : systematic, critical, and historical essays in
logical theory / Maurice A. Finocchiaro.
p. cm.
Includes bibliographical references and index.
ISBN 0-521-85327-3 (hardcover) – ISBN 0-521-61853-3 (pbk.)
1. Reasoning. I. Title.
BC177.F565 2005
160–dc22   2004027496

ISBN-13 978-0-521-85327-9 hardback
ISBN-10 0-521-85327-3 hardback

ISBN-13 978-0-521-61853-3 paperback
ISBN-10 0-521-61853-3 paperback

Contents

Preface and Acknowledgments

This book is a collection of selected articles published during the past three decades in various journals, anthologies, and conference proceedings. No substantive alterations have been made in the original text, but many editorial changes have been introduced. For example, not only have typographical errors been corrected, but for the sake of uniformity spelling has been standardized; all bibliographical references are now in the APA style of author, date, and page number(s); and all chapters have been subdivided into sections with numbers and headings. Moreover, to avoid duplication, the individual bibliographies have been combined into one for the whole book; to update the publication information, works that were originally listed as "in press" have been provided with the subsequent actual publication date; and entries by the same author for the same year have been appropriately redesignated.

With regard to the titles of the chapters, I have followed something of a middle course. The original article titles have been left unchanged, except for two things. The first is that the year of original publication has been added in parentheses at the end of each title. The second is that in some cases, in part II, subtitles have been added in order to reflect the two-fold aspect (critical and thematic) of that group of chapters. The original titles and the added dates ensure the unambiguous and easy identification of the original articles from the bibliography, where they had to be listed because of cross-referencing. Thus there is no need to indicate here or in a separate section of this book the places of original publication of the various chapters; readers can simply consult the bibliography.

I considered including summaries of the chapters in the introduction or in another special section of this book, but this would have been superfluous because almost every chapter contains a summary, usually in the last section, headed as summary, conclusion, epilogue, recapitulation, or the like. Thus readers can read such summaries by turning to those concluding sections of chapters.

As the table of contents indicates, the chapters have been grouped into four "parts" of this volume. This grouping is meant to be reflected in the book's subtitle: Part I ("Theorizing about Reasoning and Argument") and part II ("Fallacies and Asymmetries") contain the mostly systematic chapters; part III obviously includes the mostly critical chapters; and part IV includes the mostly historical ones. Such a classification also has a thematic motivation: In part I, the main topics are theories of reasoning and argument; in part II, fallacies and asymmetries; in part III, accounts of philosophical reasoning and argument and dialectical approaches to the study of argument and reasoning; and in part IV, critical thinking in science. However, such a grouping is neither exact nor exclusive, and in fact the introduction explains in more detail the many other themes and approaches that criss-cross the various chapters. At any rate, it should be noted that within each part, the chapters are printed in chronological order.

Finally, some acknowledgments are in order. My appreciation goes to the many scholars who have provided valuable encouragement, support, and suggestions over the past three decades, although the number is so large that I cannot name them all here. I am also grateful to the (three anonymous) Press referees for their enthusiasm, and especially to the one who made the brilliant suggestion to entitle the book *Arguments about Arguments*, instead of using the pedestrian and prosaic title that I had originally proposed. More specifically, Michael Scriven has provided the initial (1967) inspiration and a constant model to emulate, as the introduction makes clear. The late Henry Johnstone became a catalyst for many of my ideas ever since the original publication of chapter 18 (1974) triggered our acquaintance and made us aware of the overlap in our work. Else Barth has been gracious and generous ever since my oral presentation of chapter 2 in 1986 revealed that I had independently arrived at and was pursuing in my own way her program in empirical logic. Alec Fisher, James Freeman, Ralph Johnson, and Harvey Siegel have provided not only the original stimulus for some of the essays collected here, but also friendly encouragement and feedback regarding the compilation and viability of this volume. The University of Nevada, Las Vegas, has continued to provide institutional support even after I decided to retire from formal teaching in order to work full-time on research, scholarship, and writing. Finally, acknowledgments go to the original publishers of the essays, in regard to which the reader can look up the information in the bibliography, under my name, the year, and the title of each chapter.

Introduction

An Approach to a Branch of Logic

When I first began thinking about the issues discussed in this book, some four decades ago, one of the problems I was concerned with was the existence of God. I felt the problem to be of vital importance, as important as anything that was a matter of life and death; indeed that it was a question of *everlasting* life, of eternal salvation or damnation. Thus I tried to learn all I could about the arguments for the existence of God. I wanted to be sure that I knew them all and none escaped my attention; that I understood them properly and did not misinterpret them; and that I could evaluate or assess their correctness, worth, or strength. This concern led me to read the relevant works of classic authors such as Aristotle, St. Anselm, St. Thomas Aquinas, Blaise Pascal, and David Hume,[1] as well as those of contemporary authors like Karl Barth, Antony Flew, Alasdair MacIntyre, John Robinson, and Wallace Matson;[2] and I soon realized that another aspect of the same problem was to learn, understand, and evaluate the arguments *against* the existence of God, such as the objection from evil.

Examples of the questions I happened to think about are the following. The first of Aquinas's arguments begins with the undeniable premise that there is motion in the world and by a series of steps arrives at the conclusion that there must be a prime unmoved mover, which is called

[1] Aristotle 1952, 1: 326–27 (*Physics*, vii, 1, 241b24–243a2), 334–55 (*Physics*, viii, 250b10–267b26), 547–48 (*Metaphysics*, vi, 1, 1025b3–1026a32), 601–95 (*Metaphysics*, xii, 6–9, 1071b3–1075b10); Anselm 1958, 1–34 (*Proslogium*), 35–144 (*Monologium*); Aquinas 1952, 3–152 (*Summa Theologica*, first part, questions 1–26); Pascal 1952, 213–16 (*Pensées*, 233); Hume 1935 (*Dialogues*).

[2] Barth (1963; 1964); Flew and MacIntyre 1955; Robinson 1963; Matson 1965.

God.[3] But a second premise used by Aquinas is the claim that whatever is in motion is moved by something else. Now, whichever other flaws or merits the argument may possess, and whichever support this second premise may have had at the time of Aquinas, one difficulty is that since the seventeenth century, physics – the science of motion – has discovered that it is not motion that needs an external mover, but changes in (the direction or speed of) motion; this is the so-called law of inertia, or the first law of motion, or Newton's first law; so a key premise of Aquinas's first argument is false. I do not want to give the impression that this criticism was the end of the discussion, but rather I mention it to illustrate how this argument about the existence of God provided an occasion to distinguish between conclusion and premises.

By contrast, Aquinas's second argument was an occasion to reflect on the distinction between the acceptability of a premise and the acceptability of an inference from premise to conclusion. The second argument is similar to the first but utilizes the principle of causality, the premise that everything that exists is caused by something else, and it arrives at the conclusion that there must be a first cause, generally called God.[4] Here one issue would be the interpretive question of how exactly this argument differs from the first. Furthermore, evaluatively speaking, the principle of causality could not be questioned as easily, if at all, as the corresponding principle of motion of the first argument. However, to arrive at a first cause, the second argument depends on the idea that the series of causes and effects cannot go back *ad infinitum*. Can we then criticize the argument, as Bertrand Russell did,[5] by objecting that this idea assumes that it is impossible for a series to lack a first term, whereas mathematics tells us that this assumption is wrong because the series of negative integers ending with minus one clearly has no first term?

Or consider Anselm's ontological argument: God must exist because by God we mean a being such that nothing greater can be conceived; that is, by definition God is perfect in every way or possesses all perfections; but if God did not exist that would mean that He lacked existence, and so He would not possess the particular perfection called existence; in short, if God did not exist then He would be perfect in every way.[6] To understand this argument properly, one would have to determine whether and how

[3] Aquinas 1952, 1: 12–13 (*Summa Theologica*, first part, question 2, article 3).
[4] Aquinas 1952, 1: 13 (*Summa Theologica*, first part, question 2, article 3).
[5] Russell 1945, 462.
[6] Anselm 1958, 8–9 (*Proslogium*, chapter 3), 37–41 (*Monologium*, chapters 1–2).

it assumes that existence is a predicate; and one would also want to know how this argument is different from and how it is similar to Aquinas's fourth argument, which also involves the notion of perfection.[7] And to evaluate the ontological argument, one could object that existence is not a predicate; another question would be whether the argument really proves its stated conclusion or something else, namely that *if* God exists *then* he exists necessarily.

As a final example, consider the fact that the existence of God is still a controversial issue, that is, there is no consensus among scholars that the existence of God can be proved by means of conclusive arguments; can one use this very fact as a reason why God does not exist?[8] That is, can one formulate the meta-argument that if God exists, then by now mankind would have discovered the relevant evidence and arguments, because God is supposed to be the creator of the universe and of the human mind, and the human mind is supposed to be rational, and its inability to prove the existence of its creator must be a sign of something? Is this meta-argument an instance of the fallacy of ignorance, or can it escape that criticism?

The arguments for and against the existence of God thus provided my first introduction to an activity which I would now call argument analysis. But these arguments and this activity were not the only things that were leading me into the direction of a cluster of fields represented in this book. For at about the same time, during my college years, I also became interested in the problem of the logical analysis of scientific knowledge. Having started my undergraduate education with the intention of majoring in theoretical physics, I found that besides being interested in the drill and exercise questions and problems that appeared in class discussions, homework assignments, and examinations, I also was asking myself questions that did not seem to have the same kind of straightforward answers and that my professors were not as ready or willing to answer. They were questions like the following.

What is the relationship between the first and the second law of motion? The first, also called the law of inertia, states that every body persists in its state of rest or uniform motion in a straight line unless it is compelled to change that state by an external force; and the second, also called the law of force, asserts that force equals the time rate of change of momentum, or in cases where the mass is constant, force equals mass

---

[7] Aquinas 1952, 1: 13 (*Summa Theologica*, first part, question 2, article 3).
[8] Cf. Scriven 1966, 152–58.

times acceleration.[9] Is the law of inertia just a special case of the law of force, that is the case when the acceleration and force are zero, or does the first law contain information above and beyond that conveyed by the second law? Or is their relationship such that the first law says that if there is no external force acting, then the body will remain at rest or in uniform rectilinear motion, whereas the second law claims that if there is an external force, then the body will undergo an acceleration proportional to it? Such a relationship would amount to their being essentially the converse of one another. Or is the second law a special case of the first insofar as the first is really the biconditional[10] that if there is no force, then there is rest or uniform motion (i.e., no acceleration), *and* if there is a force, then there is acceleration; whereas the second law is just a quantitative reformulation of the same biconditional, to the effect that if there is acceleration, then there is a force proportional to it, and if there is a force, then there is an acceleration proportional to it?

Another problem stems from the fact that physicists often regard the proposition "force equals the time rate of change of momentum" as the definition of force.[11] Now if a definition is an explanation of the meaning of a word or of a concept, how can such a definition be a law of nature, the second law of motion? And if a definition is not an explanation of a meaning, what is it? What is the definition of a definition, or the meaning of meaning?[12] Furthermore, if the second law is a definition, note what happens when it is used to replace the term "force" in the statement of the law of inertia; the latter then reads that every body persists in its state of rest or uniform motion unless it is compelled to change that state by a change in its velocity, namely unless it does not persist in that state;[13] and this sounds like a tautology. But how can a tautology be a law of nature?

Should such problems be solved by interpreting these two laws in a different and less obvious manner? That is, the first law could perhaps be interpreted to mean that the natural state of a physical body is rest or uniform motion, and such a state is natural in the sense that it requires no explanation. The second law could be construed as saying that what

---

[9] Cf. Feynman et al. 1963, pp. 9–1 to 9–2; Kittel et al. 1962, 55–56; Ingard and Kraushaar 1960, 59; Lindsay and Margenau 1957, 85–86; Newton 1934, 13.

[10] The question whether the first law is really a conditional or a biconditional may be regarded as equivalent to the question of the meaning of the connective unless, i.e., whether "p unless q" means "p if and only if not-q" or merely "p if not-q."

[11] See, for example, Ingard and Kraushaar 1960, 59; Lindsay and Margenau 1957, 86.

[12] At the time I consulted Ogden and Richards 1946; and "The Problem of Meaning in Linguistics," in Quine 1961, 47–64.

[13] Cf. Lindsay and Margenau 1957, 86–87; Eddington 1930, 124.

requires explanation is deviations from the natural state, i.e. accelerations; and such explanations should be sought in terms of forces, i.e., by saying that accelerations are the effects of the action of external forces. The two laws would then be two methodological principles of explanation whose roles would be complementary.

While the arguments about God's existence had provided me with an introduction to that type of critical thinking that may be called argument analysis, such questions about the logical structure and status and the methodological import of the laws of physics provided my first introduction to other aspects of critical thinking, such as self-reflective argumentation, critical reasoning, and metacognitive reflection.

A third intellectual source of this book lies in the influence exerted on me in graduate school by the ideas of one of my professors in philosophy of science. Paul Feyerabend introduced me to an appreciation of the history of science and the historical approach to scientific methodology, to the analysis of scientific reasoning from the point of view of rhetoric and persuasion, and to Karl Popper's philosophy of science and the critical approach to science and philosophy (labeled "critical rationalism").[14] To be sure, I did not follow Feyerabend into his epistemological anarchism of "anything goes," which I regard as an iconoclastic excess. Nor did I follow the Popperians too closely into their emphasis on falsificationism, anti-justificationism, and anti-inductivism. Instead, my exposure to the history of science, rhetorical persuasion, and Popperian critical rationalism soon converged to make me focus on the arguments and reasoning that played a crucial role in the Copernican Revolution, especially the arguments for and against the earth's motion around the sun, as recorded and reported in Galileo Galilei's *Dialogue on the Two Chief World Systems, Ptolemaic and Copernican* (1632). Here was a collection of arguments and reasoning comparable to the arguments about the existence of God for their number, variety, accessibility, relevance, and importance.

A fourth source brought me a lot closer to the material in this book. At a slightly later stage of graduate school in philosophy, I was deeply influenced by the ideas of another one of my professors.[15] Through Michael Scriven I became exposed to the philosophy of the social sciences and the problem of their epistemological relationship to the natural sciences; to

[14] At the time the relevant works were Feyerabend (1962a; 1962b; 1963; 1965; 1970a; 1970b; 1970c); later such ideas were systematized and elaborated in Feyerabend 1975.
[15] At the time the relevant works were Scriven (1956a; 1956b; 1958; 1959; 1962a; 1962b; 1966; 1968).

the metascientific concept of explanation and its relationship to deduction, covering laws, inference, and understanding; and to another topic that brings us to the heart of the matter and deserves special attention.

That topic was treated in a seminar entitled "Elementary Reasoning from an Advanced Standpoint," given in the winter quarter of 1967. Scriven's description of the course is sufficiently eloquent, emblematic, and informative as to deserve extended quotation:

The logical structure of actual arguments is still strikingly obscure, a fact which is concealed behind the internal precision, the intricacy and the intrinsic interest of the various formal systems which have been spawned in the attempt to clarify that logical structure. The classical formal accounts, from the syllogism through extensional sentential calculi to the systems S1–S6, are either notoriously or notably deficient, especially with respect to (i) the encoding procedure, (ii) the identification of assumptions and presuppositions, (iii) the circularity of certain definitions of the connectives in terms of the stroke function (or of numbers in terms of iterated quantifiers), (iv) the analysis of implication, (v) the distinction between deductive and inductive arguments and (vi) that between use and mention, (vii) the "paradox of analysis," (viii) the "Achilles and the tortoise" regress, (ix) the nature of argument by analogy and (x) of induction by simple enumeration, (xi) the analysis of "internal" and "external" probability, (xii) general statements, (xiii) "classical" and "criterial" definitions, (xiv) evaluation, etc.

This seminar will examine some well-known proposed treatments of these difficulties, including suggestions by philosophers such as Lewis, Reichenbach, Carnap, Strawson, Ryle, Toulmin, Anderson and Belnap. To provide a basis for such discussions, the seminar will be substantially concerned with the "workshop" task of analyzing elementary arguments with more than usual care. This analysis will be used not only to evaluate the suggestions mentioned, but also to develop a more accurate account of reasoning and a more effective method of teaching the skills involved in it. This will involve some study of relevant psychological data, of innovative elementary texts, and of the relation between psychology and logic. Prerequisite: the capacity to identify 80% of the topics and people mentioned or unusually high motivation and reasoning capacity. Texts: Toulmin, *Uses of Argument* and Strawson, *Introduction to Logical Theory*[16]

Here was a manifesto which I would now reconstruct as follows. The overarching issue may be defined as that of the methodological and epistemological status of the science of logic or logical theory and the status of the science or theory of reasoning and argument. For example, is logic an abstract science that studies entailment, truth functions, the calculus of propositions, predicates, relations, identity, etc.; or is it a special social science that studies the mental activities of reasoning and

---

[16] From a class handout distributed on 31 January 1967 at the University of California, Berkeley.

argument? If the former is the case, how does logic relate to mathematics? Is it just a branch of mathematics? Or does it provide the foundations of mathematics? If logic is a social science, how does it relate to experimental cognitive psychology? In any case, aside from the issue of the meaning to be attached to "logic," there is a thriving enterprise called formal or symbolic logic, and there exists an important human activity consisting of reasoning and argumentation; so we may ask, what is or ought to be the relationship between formal or symbolic logic and reasoning or argument? Moreover, even if we take the point of view of the (empirical) science of reasoning, there is also the question of how such a science would relate to the practical *art* of reasoning. Finally, even if we take the point of view of symbolic logic, there is the nontrivial question of how its principles are to be applied to the analysis of arguments in natural language.

Scriven's recommendation of Stephen Toulmin's book *The Uses of Argument* was a consequential one. However, the primary lesson I derived from Toulmin was not a particular theory of the layout or arguments, which however novel and interesting I did not find especially viable and congenial. Nor did I derive from it a special theory of argument assessment to the effect that principles of evaluation are field-dependent and that there are no universally correct such principles. Rather I adopted from Toulmin what seemed to be his solution to the problem of the epistemology of the science of logic and argument. He seemed to be suggesting a critique of formal or symbolic logic as being insufficiently concerned with actual human reasoning, with nondeductive arguments such as are common in law, with argumentation in natural language, and with practical applications; and he seemed to be making a plea for a logical theory that was more empirical, more general, more natural, more practical, and more historical.[17]

---

[17] Here is one of the most emblematic passages: "Logic conceived in this manner may have to become less of an *a priori* subject than it has recently been.... Accepting the need to begin by collecting for study the actual forms of argument current in any field,... we shall use ray-tracing techniques because they are used to make optical inferences, presumptive conclusions and 'defeasibility' as an essential feature of many legal arguments, axiomatic systems because they reflect the pattern of our arguments in geometry.... But not only will logic have to become more empirical; it will inevitably tend to become more historical. To think up new and better methods of arguing in any field is to make a major advance, not just in logic, but in the substantive field itself: great logical innovations are part and parcel of great scientific, moral, political or legal innovations. In the natural sciences, for instance, men such as Kepler, Newton, Lavoisier, Darwin and Freud have transformed not only our beliefs, but also our way of arguing and our standards of relevance and proof" (Toulmin 1958, 257–58).

The four sources I have elaborated did not immediately and directly lead me to the investigations presented in this book. For about a decade I studied the arguments for and against the existence of God primarily to seek enlightenment about God and religion and not to master argument analysis. Similarly I studied the logical structure and status of the laws of physics to learn primarily about the nature of science and scientific reasoning and not about human reasoning in general. I studied the persuasive force and critical-rationalist aspects of scientific reasoning in the history of science to learn first and foremost about the role of persuasion, criticism, and history in scientific inquiry, and only secondarily to learn about the role of these things in general human reasoning. And I studied the problem of the epistemological and methodological status of the science of logic and reasoning not in order actually to build or develop a viable logical theory or theory of argument, but mostly as a special problem in the philosophy of science, special in three senses: (1) it is a particular one out of many such problems; (2) the science or discipline in question – logic – is especially important; and (3) it encompasses an overarching issue, namely whether logic is or ought to be a mathematical or a social science, and if the latter whether the social sciences are *sui generis* or like the natural sciences.

Thus, in line with the second strand mentioned above, in my undergraduate thesis I examined the problem of the relationship between the laws of quantum mechanics and of classical thermodynamics, by analyzing some of Werner Heisenberg's arguments that the former are essentially similar to the latter; my key aim was a better understanding of quantum physics.[18] And combining the third and fourth strands, my doctoral dissertation and first book examined the methodological and epistemological status of the historiography of science from the point of view of the concept of explanation; I analyzed the logical structure of explanations advanced by historians of science to determine whether they are more like scientific explanations or more like historical explanations, or whether they are special and if so what their special characteristics are; my two-fold aim was to understand better the concept of explanation on the one hand and to understand and improve the discipline of history of science on the other.[19]

In both cases, however, most of my discussion consisted of interpretations and evaluations of arguments, in the former case arguments

---

[18] Finocchiaro 1964.
[19] Finocchiaro 1969; 1973c.

advanced by physicist Heisenberg; in the latter case arguments propounded by philosophers Joseph Agassi (who had pioneered the critical examination of the historiography of science), Carl Hempel, and
Michael Scriven (both of whom had elaborated the theory of explanation), and by historians of science Alexandre Koyré (when explaining
aspects of Galileo's physics) and Henry Guerlac (when explaining aspects of Lavoisier's chemistry).[20] Thus both theses consisted largely of
exercises in argument analysis. The rest amounted to what I would now
call self-reflective argumentation and methodological reflection; that is,
in the constructive parts of those investigations I advanced and defended
some appropriately nuanced claims about the relationship between quantum mechanics and classical thermodynamics, about the nature of the
concept of explanation, and about the status and prospects of the discipline of history of science. In short, although these earlier works were
not yet explicit contributions of the type found in this book, they were
sustained exercises in argument analysis, self-reflective argumentation,
and methodological reflection, and so they were significant experiences
in preparing the ground for those contributions. One other experience
was also crucial; it regards teaching, to which I now turn.

My experience as a teaching assistant in graduate school consisted
largely of assisting in symbolic logic courses, and to a less extent in introductory philosophy courses of both the historical and the problem-
oriented variety. But after I obtained a tenure-track position in logic and
philosophy of science, for several years my teaching experience consisted
mostly of teaching a course in introductory logic that was meant to be
distinct from an introduction to symbolic logic; the course was supposed
to be an introduction to reasoning and critical thinking that would focus
on actual arguments in natural language and on the development and
improvement of students' logical skills. The teaching of such a course
turned out to be a very challenging task. For one thing, at that time
(early 1970s), there were not many appropriate textbooks. Three exceptions were Max Black's *Critical Thinking* (1952), Monroe Beardsley's
Thinking Straight (1966), and Howard Kahane's *Logic and Contemporary
Rhetoric* (1971); but after adopting them, I found them not completely
satisfactory for one reason or another. The difficulty was compounded by
what I had learned from Scriven's "Elementary Reasoning from an Advanced Standpoint" and Toulmin's *Uses of Argument*; for the appreciation

---

[20] See Agassi 1963; Guerlac 1961; Heisenberg 1955; Hempel 1965; Koyré 1939; Scriven
(1958; 1959; 1962a); cf. Finocchiaro (1964; 1969; 1973c).

of the epistemological problem of the status of the science of logic or
reasoning suggested that the material taught in my introductory logic
could and should be not some second-class substitute for introductory
symbolic logic, not some sloppy version of a more rigorous course, but
merely a simplified account of a subject with its own distinctive and high
standards, aims, and criteria.

Fortunately I was not the only scholar struggling with this problem.
Soon more appropriate textbooks began to appear, for example, Scriven's
Reasoning (1976) and Robert Fogelin's *Understanding Arguments: An Introduction to Informal Logic* (1978). Moreover, the field of "informal logic"
began to take root in 1978 in Canada with the first international symposium on the subject; the "critical-thinking movement" began to organize
itself at its first conference in 1981 in California; and the same happened
to "argumentation theory" in The Netherlands in the early 1980s.[21]

In my own case, my exposure to the pedagogical problem of teaching introductory logic and critical thinking had two important effects.
One involved the realization that many problems with the introductory
logic course were the result of its being introductory rather than of my
wanting to focus on actual reasoning and practical skills; for example,
all introductory courses face the problems of the necessity of simplification, the distinction between simplification and oversimplification, and
the relationship between introductory and more advanced courses. This
realization led me to conceive and teach a more advanced course. Entitled "Logical Theory," the course description read: "General study of
the nature of argument; how it relates to reasoning, criticism, deduction,
logical form, induction, and persuasion. Emphasizes both the systematic
development of logical concepts and their application to actual arguments."[22] And in turn, the preparation for this course and the attempt to
create material suitable for it resulted directly in researching and writing
many of the essays that are reprinted in this book.

The second effect was that my teaching introductory logic provided not
only serious pedagogical challenges, but also rich and fruitful material
and motivation to undertake the studies collected in this book. Although
all pedagogical experience has, or should have, some such synergistic interaction with research, the case of introductory logic and critical thinking is special in this regard. Its special character is due to the fact that if

---

[21] Cf., respectively, Blair and Johnson 1980; Paul (1982; 1984; 1985); Barth and Martens
1982; Eemeren et al. 1987.
[22] For more details, see Finocchiaro 2002.

logic is conceived as the theory and practice of reasoning (as the science and art of reasoning), then a classroom is really a privileged laboratory and a kind of field work; students' homework, examinations, and class participation are automatically instances of what is being studied. Clearly nothing of the kind is true when a course is studying numbers, atoms, living organisms, the economy, society, governments, historical events, poetry and literature, or ontological status and metaphysical problems.[23] The teaching of reasoning has a unique self-referential character. Or at least that is what happened in my experience. Thus almost all the following essays have a pedagogical foundation and motivation, although needless to say the connection is neither simple nor direct, and it would be a serious misconception to think that these essays have merely, or even primarily, pedagogical value.

Before describing those essays, it will be useful to describe two other contributions which could not be reprinted here for the simple reason that they are books. Many parts and aspects of these books are indeed discussed, reworked, and elaborated in many of the collected essays, or overlap with them, but no chapters from those books have been simply reprinted. The first book is *Galileo and the Art of Reasoning* (1980), the second is *Galileo on the World Systems* (1997).

I have mentioned above that in the 1960s, mostly under the influence of Feyerabend, I had already discovered and begun to problematize the arguments for and against the earth's motion that played a crucial role in the Copernican Revolution. After the detour and experience of my investigation into the logic of explanation in historiography of science, and with the awareness suggested by Scriven and Toulmin of the importance of the problem of the methodological status of the science of logic or reasoning, and with the motivation supplied by the pedagogical experience of teaching introductory logic and critical thinking, I was ready to systematically study those Copernican and anti-Copernican arguments. That was my main research project in the following decade (the 1970s). An explanation of the book's title and subtitle will provide the needed description here.

[23] Here one might object that, like reasoning, psychology is also special insofar as it studies human behavior, which is also instantiated by students in psychology courses. But one should note that if we are talking about general psychology, the self-referential aspect is minimal because student behavior (other than their intellectual and cognitive activities) is or ought to be irrelevant or at best secondary; if we talking about cognitive psychology, then the self-referential aspect is significant and central and the analogy to logic becomes strong.

In *Galileo and the Art of Reasoning*, the first word refers to the fact that the arguments under scrutiny are those in Galileo's *Dialogue on the Two Chief World Systems*. The "art of reasoning" represents the point of view I am taking in studying that material, and it could also be called the point of view of critical reasoning. The obvious connection between the two parts of the title is the thesis that Galileo is first and foremost a practitioner of the art of reasoning, a critical reasoner, a practical logician, an applied logician, a logician in action. One corollary of this thesis is that, since Galileo is also the "father of modern science," critical reasoning can be regarded as an essential element of scientific inquiry. A second important thesis, grounded in a detailed analysis of Galileo's methodological practice and reflections, is that another essential element of Galileo's science is something I call "judgment": the prudent, impartial, moderate, and balanced synthesis of such opposites as observation and speculation, mathematization and qualitative considerations, causal explanation and phenomenological description, and demonstrative necessity and probable inference. In turn, a corollary of this thesis is that such methodological judgment is also an essential procedure in science. Now, applying the two corollaries to the science of logic or reasoning, we get that a viable program in logical theory is or should be to practice critical reasoning and methodological judgment in dealing with the subject matter in question: reasoning and argument. One consequence of this research program is that formal or symbolic logic can be criticized (as a theory of reasoning) for being excessively apriorist, one-sidedly focused on mathematical or deductive reasoning, and exclusively normative or insufficiently descriptive. But this is just one of several important consequences, and analogous ones follow in regard to the experimental psychology of reasoning, to rhetoric, to traditional inductive logic, and so on. And this brings me to the book's subtitle, *Rhetorical Foundations of Logic and Scientific Method*.

To avoid being misleading I must confess and clarify that the word "rhetorical" here was a rhetorical ploy meant to correct a situation in which rhetorical considerations and factors were neglected. What the book did was to focus on and elaborate those aspects of logical theory and scientific methodology that involved reasoning, argument, judgment, and methodological reflection. I would now subsume such mental activities under the notion of critical thinking, and so the subtitle should be understood to mean "critical-thinking aspects of logical theory and scientific methodology"; and this is as linguistically awkward now as it was then. However, with regard to rhetoric, one important connotation of the word refers to the theory and practice of persuasion. In this sense, the subtitle was describing the fact that the book in part discussed the role of persuasion in logical theory and scientific method and claimed that this role was more important than commonly believed at that time (1960s and 1970s); for example, the class of arguments that aim merely to persuade and the property of persuasiveness had been neglected or ignored in traditional logic and relegated to rhetorical studies. But the subtitle also conveys the impression that persuasive and rhetorical factors are fundamental and can serve to ground logical theory and scientific methodology; and this impression is misleading partly because it is an injudicious exaggeration of the role of rhetoric (and so violates the judgment requirement of scientific method), and partly because (as the book argues at length) the detection and effectiveness of rhetorical factors often depend on logical factors involving reasoning (and so logic is prior to rhetoric in a way in which the reverse in not true). Indeed, as one acute critic (who detected my rhetorical ploy) correctly judged, a more descriptive subtitle would be "logical foundations of rhetoric and scientific method."[24]

The later work, *Galileo on the World Systems: A New Abridged Translation and Guide,* provides a guide to the critical reading of Galileo's *Dialogue.* Since, as noted above, the *Dialogue* is full of arguments and counterarguments, interpretations and evaluations of arguments, self-reflective argumentation, and methodological reflections, such a guide also amounts to a concrete guide to critical thinking. The book consists of a translation of about 40 percent of Galileo's 500-page text; extensive notes providing informative, historical, critical, and scholarly commentary, stressing critical reasoning and methodological reflection; a long historical introduction situating Galileo's work in the context of the Copernican Revolution, the Scientific Revolution, and the Galileo Affair; and a long theoretical appendix that systematizes a number of concepts and principles useful for the understanding and assessment of reasoning and argument in general, and in which I illustrate these concepts and principles by means of Galilean examples.

Thus, clearly, this later book deals with the same material as the earlier one and from the same point of view. However, the later book is more concrete and down-to-earth. Moreover, whereas the earlier one *presupposes* access to and acquaintance with the Copernican arguments, the second book *provides* the texts. Whereas the earlier one focuses on *demonstrating* my various historical, philosophical, and logical claims, the later

[24] Lupoli 1986.

one focuses on *illustrating* them. Whereas the earlier book is engaged in scholarly controversy regarding the various issues about Galileo's science, the Copernican Revolution, logical theory, and scientific methodology, the later book by and large bypasses controversy and mostly presupposes a solution or position (my own) on the issues. Further, because the later book has the benefit of almost two decades of additional reflection and work on the subject, the reconstructions and evaluations of Galilean arguments tend to be crisper and clearer, and the systematization of the theoretical concepts and principles is slightly more complete and adequate. For example, the misleading rhetoric of "rhetoric" of the earlier book is avoided and replaced by what I hope is a more satisfactory presentation as well as a more balanced intrinsic account.

With such considerations in the background, it will now be useful to describe the most important aspects of the essays collected in this book, in particular the methodological approach followed, the theoretical framework adumbrated, the scholarly literature engaged and criticized, and the historical material integrated into the discussion.

Methodologically, my approach is *historical-textual* in the sense that it focuses on the analysis of historically important texts containing reasoning, arguments, and critical thinking. It is a special case of an approach that is broadly empirical but normative, and it may be instructively contrasted not only to the apriorist orientation of formal deductive logic, but also to the experimental approach of cognitive psychology and the inductive-intuitive approach of analytical philosophy. Almost all chapters exemplify this feature, but it is most explicitly discussed in chapters 2–4, 11, 12, and 18–21.

My approach is also *dialectical*, in at least two senses of this controversial concept. One is that in the subject matter studied, I tend to stress counterarguments, objections, criticism, evaluation, potential (and not necessarily actual) dialogue, and the clarification (rather than the resolution) of differences of opinion; this characteristic emerges most explicitly in chapters 13, 15, and 17, and to a lesser extent in chapters 4, 7, 12, and 16. The other sense of dialectical refers to my engagement in dialogue with other scholars, as will be most readily apparent in chapters 4, 6, and 8–17.

Furthermore, my approach is *interpretive* in the sense that it stresses the understanding and reconstruction of arguments (as distinct from their evaluation and criticism) to a far greater degree than is commonly the case. Although all scholars admit that it is important to give an accurate reconstruction before advancing criticism of an argument, usually this requirement turns out to be perfunctory, or functions only as a means to an end. In my approach the interpretation of arguments is intrinsically valuable from a logical and philosophical point of view, and so it is taken much more seriously. This aspect of my approach is most clearly exemplified in chapters 2, 6, 10, and 16–21.

Related to these three methodological traits, there is a fourth one which I call my *self-referential* approach. That is, in doing informal logic and argumentation theory (i.e., in theorizing about arguments and critical thinking), I take very seriously the goal of practicing what one preaches, and so I tend and try as much as possible to treat the views of other scholars as instances of arguments, as well as to engage myself in argumentation in my interpretation and evaluation of those views. In other words, I tend to follow my historical-textual approach not only when I am studying argumentation found in texts by past icons such as Galileo, Newton, Lavoisier, and Huygens, but also when I am studying texts authored by scholarly peers such as Henry Johnstone, Ralph Johnson, Harvey Siegel, and Gerald Massey; on such occasions, I also tend to follow my interpretive approach, and make a serious effort to understand and reconstruct their arguments; at the same time, I am concerned not merely with understanding them, but also with evaluating their arguments, which is to say that I follow a dialectical approach. The self-referential character of my approach is best illustrated in chapters 9–11 and 16–17.

Theoretically, my essays elaborate a conceptual framework as well as a number of claims. The conceptual framework involves the following (theoretical) definitions. *Reasoning* is a special type of thinking that consists of interrelating thoughts in such a way that some are dependent on or follow from others (chapters 1, 3, 4, 12, and 14). An *argument* is an instance of reasoning that attempts to justify a conclusion by supporting it with reasons *or* defending it from objections (chapter 17). *Argument analysis* is reasoning aimed at the interpretation or evaluation of arguments (chapter 5). *Critical reasoning* is reasoning aimed at the interpretation, evaluation, or self-reflective presentation of arguments; that is, critical reasoning consists of either argument analysis or self-reflective argumentation (chapter 5). *Methodological reflection* is a special type of thinking that consists of the formulation, interpretation, evaluation, or application of methodological principles, that is, inexact and fallible rules stipulating useful procedures in the search for truth (chapters 5 and 22). *Critical thinking* is thinking that consists of either critical reasoning or methodological reflection (chapters 5 and 10). *Judgment* is thinking that consists of the prudent, impartial, moderate, balanced, or judicious combination of opposite or distinct requirements or points of view (chapters 12, 14, and 21–23). *Informal logic* is the attempt to formulate, to clarify, to test, to systematize, and to apply concepts and principles for the interpretation, evaluation, and practice of reasoning or argument (chapters 1–3 and 5). And again, although each of these concepts pervades almost all the chapters, it emerges most explicitly in those that are indicated.

With regard to claims, the most salient ones that are defended are as follows. So-called fallacies (so called in textbooks) are typically either nonfallacious arguments, non-arguments, or inaccurate reconstructions of the originals (chapter 6); but many arguments can be criticized as fallacious in various identifiable ways (chapter 7). There seem to be various important asymmetries between the positive or favorable and the negative or unfavorable evaluation of arguments (chapter 8), although one particular alleged asymmetry seems untenable, namely the alleged fact that it is possible to show formal validity but not formal invalidity (chapter 9). One of the most effective ways of criticizing arguments and reasoning is to engage in *ad hominem* argument in the seventeenth-century meaning of this term, namely to derive a conclusion unacceptable to opponents from premises accepted by them (but not necessarily by the arguer); and correspondingly one of the greatest weaknesses of human reasoning is the failure to consider or engage in such *ad hominem* argumentation (chapters 4, 16, and 18). Argumentation and critical thinking play an important and still unappreciated and understudied role in science, as may be gathered by an appropriate analysis of the thought of Galileo, Huygens, Newton, Lavoisier, Einstein, Boltzmann, and the Copernican Revolution (chapters 18–23).

Next, it will be useful to explain more fully the critical dimension of this book by describing the most important examples of work by other authors that is criticized (constructively as well as destructively) in these essays:[25] David Perkins's psychological experiments on the difficulties affecting everyday reasoning (chapter 4); Gerald Massey's thesis that there is an asymmetry between the formal validation and formal invalidation of arguments (chapter 9); Harvey Siegel's 'reasons' conception of critical thinking (chapter 10); L. Jonathan Cohen's metaphilosophical view

---

[25] Insofar as my criticism is destructive, I do not want to convey the impression that it does, can, or should put an end to the discussion; but the examination of such subsequent discussions and their continuation are obviously beyond the scope of this book and this introduction. Still, a few references to some of these further discussions may be useful, e.g., Barth 2002; L. J. Cohen 1991; Finocchiaro 1990b; Krabbe (1998; 2002); Siegel 1990; Walton 2004.

that analytical philosophy consists largely of inductive reasoning in which generalizations about concepts are based on particular intuitions (chapter 11); Antonio Gramsci's views on logic, politics, dialectics, intellectuals, and philosophy (chapter 12); Else Barth and Erik Krabbe's attempt to move logic from an axiomatic to a dialogical approach (chapter 13); James Freeman's dialectical account of the macrostructure of arguments (chapter 13); the logical instrumentalism and the theory of argument in Antoine Arnauld and Pierre Nicole's *Port-Royal Logic* (chapter 14); the account of complex argumentation by the Amsterdam pragma-dialectical school of argumentation theory (chapter 15); Douglas Walton's dialectical account of the distinction between argument and explanation (chapter 15); Henry Johnstone's metaphilosophical view that all valid philosophical arguments are *ad hominem* (chapter 16); Alvin Goldman's moderately dialectical definition of argument (chapter 17); Ralph Johnson's strongly dialectical definition of argument (chapter 17); C. L. Hamblin's account of argument in general and of *ad hominem* argument in particular (chapter 18); Dudley Shapere's account of scientific change and rationality (chapter 22); and Karl Popper's critical rationalism in general and account of scientific rationality in particular (chapter 23).

These essays also have an historical dimension in a sense distinct from the historical-textual approach in the theory of argument and from the critical examinations of alternative theories described above; that is, they incorporate a wealth of historical material that deserves notice. My examination of the *Port-Royal Logic* (chapter 14) is an attempt to identify an historical tradition and find an historical precedent for the current theorizing. My analysis of Antonio Gramsci's *Prison Notebooks* (chapter 12) endeavors to connect to the theory of reasoning and argument a contemporary classic that has never before been viewed in this manner, and thus to broaden and diversify the relevance of both logical theory and Gramsci. And my account of critical thinking in science (chapters 18–23) is obviously a series of case studies in the history of science dealing with past figures and episodes of paradigmatic importance; these chapters belong to a genre that has now become quite common among historically minded philosophers of science, but whereas such case studies often lead such scholars to relativist and evolutionist conclusions, I am led into the almost opposite direction, for my historical scientific case studies are meant to add diversity to the kinds of evidence and data on which my theoretical framework is based.

Although these historical chapters cluster around the topic of critical thinking in science, the diversity of topics extends much beyond this cluster. When we add the more systematic and critical chapters to these historical ones, the diversity seems even greater. However, if one wants to seek a deeper unity underlying such diversity, one can find it at the epistemological and methodological level. That is, the unity of these chapters lies in the fact that they are contributions to a branch of logic that may be characterized as the attempt to formulate, to clarify, to test, to systematize, and to apply concepts and principles for the interpretation, evaluation, and practice of reasoning or argument; and they exemplify a distinctive approach to such a branch of logic, an approach that, as already explained, may be characterized as historical-empirical, dialectical-critical, interpretive, and self-referential. Moreover, such diversity should also be taken as an indication of wealth and fertility, for here is a field that not only consists of the efforts of self-styled representatives of informal logic, critical thinking, and argumentation theory, but that can also use as material for analysis the work of scientists from Galileo to Einstein, and that can also integrate into the field the efforts of such apparent outsiders as Perkins, Massey, Cohen, Johnstone, Goldman, Shapere, and Popper, and even the efforts of such classics as Gramsci and Arnauld.

PART I

THEORIZING ABOUT REASONING
AND ARGUMENT

Informal Logic and the Theory of Reasoning (1984)

1. A Definition of Informal Logic

Informal logic seems to be suffering from an image problem, a bad conscience, and an identity crisis. The image problem derives from the somewhat negative connotations of the term "informal," which often conveys the impression that what we have here is a sloppy, nonserious approach to the study of logical problems.[1] The bad conscience stems from conceiving the field as the theory of informal fallacies, and then taking the notion of "theory" to be such as to imply that a theory worthy of the name is necessarily formal;[2] this would make the label "informal logic" a disguise for the formal theory of those fallacies different from the deductive and inductive ones. These two views are, respectively, a methodological interpretation of informal logic in terms of its alleged approach ("informality"), and a substantive definition in terms of its alleged subject matter ("informal fallacies"); now, since it is not easy to devise alternative interpretations as long as one keeps close to the terminological and verbal level,[3] this may lead to the identity crisis of wondering what on

[1] The first definition given by the *Oxford English Dictionary* for the word "informal" is: "Not done or made according to a recognized or prescribed form; not observing forms; not according to order; irregular; unofficial, disorderly" (1933 edition, vol. 5, p. 273).

[2] Here I am thinking of the interpretation given in Woods 1980. Woods is certainly right to distinguish between two senses of "formal": (1) the use of formal, mathematical, or symbolic techniques, and (2) formalization or the construction of logistic or axiomatic systems (p. 58). He is also correct in noting that, from the point of view of (2), even mathematics is typically *informal*; and so he is merely advocating (1). Nevertheless, it is questionable whether this can escape the present difficulty.

[3] What I mean here is that if we take the label "informal logic" too seriously, and then we try to examine its meaning and uses, we could not ignore the sense given to the term in

earth informal logic is supposed to be. In this chapter I plan to bypass these difficulties by conceiving informal logic as the theory of reasoning. By theory of reasoning I mean the attempt to formulate, to test, to clarify, and to systematize concepts and principles for the interpretation, the evaluation, and the sound practice of reasoning. I claim that the theory of reasoning so defined is a legitimate philosophical enterprise which is both viable and important, and that it corresponds to the central theoretical[4] concerns of those who explicitly identify themselves with the field of informal logic, but that it also suggests certain constructive criticisms and desirable reforms in this discipline.

2. Clarifications

Let me begin by clarifying my definition of the theory of reasoning. First, notice that I speak of reasoning, rather than, for example, argumentation; this is deliberately meant to allow a broader domain, by including, besides the study of arguments, such activities as problem-solving, decision-making, persuasion, and explaining, which cannot be equated with argumentation, but which may involve reasoning in an essential way. The emphasis on reasoning is also meant as a reminder that what is being studied here is a mental activity that actually occurs in the world and which leaves empirical traces (normally in the form of written or oral discourse). This in turn means that the theory of reasoning has an empirical orientation and is not a purely formal or abstract discipline.

Second, you should notice my explicit reference to the *interpretation* of reasoning. This is needed partly for the intrinsic reason that such interpretation aims at the understanding of reasoning, and the understanding of

Ryle 1954. For Ryle informal logic is essentially identical to ordinary-language philosophy, or to be more exact, to the analysis of the "logic" of concepts like pleasure, memory, responsibility, chance; whereas formal logic is the study of concepts such as "all," "some," "not," etc.

4 In speaking of the *theoretical* concerns of "informal logicians," I mean to distinguish them from practical concerns. In fact, as Michael Scriven stressed at the Second International Symposium on Informal Logic, informal logic cannot be equated with the theory of reasoning *simpliciter*, any more than medicine can be equated with the theory of healing; just as medicine includes the activity of actually curing diseases, so informal logic refers to the activity of formulating actual arguments. What this means is that informal logic must be taken to refer both to the theory and practice of reasoning. This, in turn, introduces further complications, some of which will be discussed below, toward the end. For other developments, see Finocchiaro 1980b, especially pp. 299–302, where a different twist is given to Scriven's point, by introducing the notion of *reasoning about reasoning*, as a helpful way of combining the theory and the practice of reasoning.

a phenomenon is obviously an essential concern of any theorizing. However, I also emphasize it in order to correct what I feel is an over-concern with evaluation; this imbalance is shown, for example, by the fact that informal logic textbooks often define logic as the attempt to distinguish good from bad arguments, and by the fact that no explicit mention of interpretation is made in Johnson and Blair's definition given at the First International Symposium of Informal Logic.[5] Therefore, the interpretative dimension needs distinct recognition despite the fact that we would all agree that it is indirectly mentioned by the evaluative dimension, insofar as the proper evaluation of an argument presupposes that it has been properly interpreted.[6]

My third clarification involves the inclusion of concepts and principles for the sound *practice* of reasoning. Notice that I am not talking about important or original reasoning, but merely about correct reasoning. Principles for reasoning well would obviously be related to principles for the evaluation of reasoning. Nevertheless the difference remains since the activity of evaluation would normally come after a certain argument has been produced, whereas the practice of reasoning means simply the construction of actual arguments or the actual involvement in reasoning. In this regard, both interpretation and evaluation have something in common which they do not share with practice; they are both reflection on previous practice, whereas the practice of reasoning is the construction of what can later become the subject of those types of reflection.

Another important feature of my definition is that I speak of *concepts and principles*. Notice that I do not say "universally valid principles," hence it is an open question whether any of them exist. If not, it would be part of the task of the theory of reasoning to tell us that the most we can hope for are principles of restricted application and limited validity, as well as to specify which principles hold in which fields.[7] Moreover, because of the distinction between interpretation and evaluation, my definition also leaves it as an open question whether there are universally valid principles of interpretation, even if it turns out that there are no universally valid principles of evaluation. Additional openness is allowed by my reference to concepts, as well as to principles. In fact, a concept may be useful for interpreting, evaluating, or practicing reasoning, even though

5 Cf. Johnson and Blair 1980, 3.
6 For an explicit discussion of this presupposition, see for example McPeck (1981, 63) and Finocchiaro (1980b, 339–40).
7 As also discussed below, this answers some of the explicit and implicit objections found in McPeck 1981.

there might be disagreement about which principles or which types of principles formulated in its terms are the correct ones. For example, one might agree that the notion of *ad hominem argument* is important at least as a way of classifying certain types of reasoning, but one does not have to agree with Henry Johnstone's metaphilosophical principle of interpretation that all genuinely philosophical arguments are *ad hominem*,[8] nor with the widely accepted principle of evaluation that *ad hominem* arguments are fallacious.

Finally, I should clarify that, in saying that the theory of reasoning aims to formulate, to test, to clarify, and to systematize principles, I am indeed referring to four distinct activities. Obviously, systematization is impossible unless the principles in question have already been formulated and have undergone a certain amount of testing and clarification. Moreover, there is no reason to expect the same degree of systematization that was possible for Euclidean geometry or celestial mechanics. Nevertheless, although one of the greatest temptations to be resisted is that of premature systematization, the idea of systematization is not excluded in principle. The reference to testing reflects the semi-empirical orientation mentioned earlier, and it can mean either confirmation or disconfirmation. A good example of disconfirmation is Professor Hintikka's criticism that the quantification theory of symbolic logic is neither a correct description of nor a correct abstraction from natural-language reasoning with quantifiers,[9] while a good example of confirmation would be L. Jonathan Cohen's demonstration that probabilistic reasoning by juries in Anglo-American courts conforms to a number of principles which embody an inductive, neo-Baconian, non-Pascalian notion of probability.[10] Last, the clarification of principles is distinct from their formulation, as shown for example by the fact that, regardless of who was the first to formulate explicitly the Principle of Charity, additional insights have been provided by Ralph Johnson's recent discussion in the *Informal Logic Newsletter*.[11]

I claimed above that the theory of reasoning so conceived represents a critical systematization of work in the field of informal logic. In order to justify directly this claim one would have to argue that the main concerns of informal logicians can find a place, or can be improved by corresponding investigations, in the theory of reasoning. However, the sketch

[8] Johnstone 1978.
[9] Hintikka 1974.
[10] L. J. Cohen 1977; 1981b.
[11] Johnson 1981a.

just given is sufficient to suggest a considerable overlap between the two; hence I will postpone for the moment a direct comparison, and I will go on to add further indirect evidence for their correspondence by discussing the question of the philosophical legitimacy of the theory of reasoning. This discussion will take the form of answers to various objections.

3. Replies to Four Objections

The most fundamental objection to the theory of reasoning is that the alleged entity which is the subject matter of its inquiries does not really exist.[12] Reasoning is presumably an epiphenomenal illusion deriving from using a general label to refer to a number of disparate activities. A theory of reasoning *per se*, as distinct from theorizing about particular instances or types or fields of reasoning, makes no more sense than a theory of success in general; just as success in one field (say business) is very different from success in another field (say sports), so is the skill of legal reasoning, for example, different from that of scientific reasoning. Even a general-sounding type of success, like Dale Carnegie's winning friends and influencing people, is not truly universal since it is obvious that one could master this art and yet fail at such things as sports, teaching, military strategy, debating, poetry, etc. Hence, even if the entity sometimes labeled everyday reasoning turns out to be theoretically and critically comprehensible (taking this label to refer to reasoning about such practical and fundamental issues that deserve the attention of every educated person), even then the theory of everyday reasoning would not be equivalent to the theory of reasoning *simpliciter*, since the nature of everyday reasoning would be bound to differ from the nature of reasoning in such special domains as science, the law, medicine, business, etc.

My answer to this powerful objection consists of a counter-charge and a constructive suggestion. The counter-charge is that the criticism confuses the interpretation and the evaluation of reasoning, and that in effect it overstresses the latter. This is shown by the tendency of these critics to compare reasoning with such implicitly evaluated entities as success, creativity, constructiveness, and effectiveness,[13] whereas the proper analogue to such nongeneralizable non-entities would be correct reasoning. In

---

[12] McPeck 1981, especially pp. 84–85. McPeck is directly concerned with teaching, and so he might not endorse my adaptation of his criticism to the context of theorizing. The same qualification applies to some of the other objections discussed below which stem from his book.

[13] McPeck 1981, 84–85.

other words, these critics ignore the fact (which they themselves admit[14])
that "reasoning" is both a task and an achievement term; to engage in
reasoning does not necessarily imply to be successful at it. This means
that, at worst, what's impossible is a general theory of correct reasoning,
and not necessarily a general interpretative theory of the structure of
reasoning. However, even the limited pessimistic conclusion seems excessively apriorist, since, given that it would allow for limited theories of
correct reasoning in particular fields, there is no a priori reason to predict that the further generalization and systematization of these limited
theories will necessarily fail. Moreover, the notion of a field of reasoning
is problematic,[15] and the same criticism made against the possibility of
generalizations among fields could be leveled against the possibility of
generalizing within a given field, which after all consists of various subfields. Finally, it is possible that a general theory of evaluation might be
based in part on a general theory of interpretation, whose possibility, as
we have seen, is untouched by the present criticism. But this brings us
to the question of what all types and instances of reasoning have in common, and it is here that my constructive suggestion becomes relevant. I
think that the essential feature of all reasoning is the interrelating of individual thoughts in such a way that some follow from others,[16] and that
the normal linguistic expression of such interrelated thinking involves
the use of particles like 'because,' 'therefore,' etc. However minimal this
conception is, it allows the theory of reasoning to get started by suggesting that we try to understand and to evaluate those discourses having a
high incidence of these logical particles.

If this first objection to the legitimacy of the theory of reasoning threatens to deprive it of a genuine subject matter, a second criticism threatens
to let a discipline other than philosophy lay claim upon that domain. The
objection would now be that there already exists a branch of cognitive
psychology, namely the psychology of reasoning, that theorizes about the
phenomenon in an a posteriori fashion. What then is the difference, if
any, between the psychology of reasoning and the philosophical theory of
reasoning?

Let me begin answering this objection by noting that at a phenomenological level there are certainly some differences. To be specific, psychologists tend to be experimental, to refrain from explicit evaluation, and to

[14] McPeck 1981, 13.
[15] As has been shown by Johnson 1981b.
[16] For more details see Finocchiaro 1980b, especially part III, p. 311.

favor explicit explanations in terms of theoretical models of unconscious mental processes.

Their experimental approach may be viewed as their way of being empirical, and it may be contrasted with the philosophers' historical method, which is another kind of empirical orientation. In other words, psychologists tend to establish contact with the real world of reasoning by making experiments in which human subjects are asked to perform various tasks which involve reasoning in one form or another; on the other hand, philosophers tend to study reasoning that has already taken place and left historical traces, usually in the form of written records. One may question the soundness of the experimental approach since the data thereby collected reflect the artificiality of the experimental situation; that is, the reasoning in which the experimental subjects are led to engage is necessarily artificial since their reasoning is taking place solely as a result of their participation in the experiment and the experimenter's instructions; thus, one may be reluctant to generalize or extrapolate that whichever features human reasoning exhibits during experiments, will also characterize it in real-life situations. Now, this difficulty with the experimental approach might lead one to claim that if psychologists wanted to be properly empirical, then they should adopt the historical approach favored by philosophers;[17] however, such a proposed reform would not obliterate the surface difference that presently exists between the two enterprises.

It is perhaps in order to neutralize this criticism of the experimental approach that psychologists are also inclined to devise models of mental processes that explain the experimental data they collect. I believe the connection would be that if the cognitive performance shown by experimental subjects is the effect of the mental processes postulated to explain it, and if these explanation-providing processes are sufficiently basic and general, then one is entitled to say that the latter processes possess a robust reality, firm enough to prevent variation from an experimental to a real-life situation. In short, if during the experiments what is happening inside the minds of the subjects is of the appropriate sort, then the same things would have to happen outside the experimental situation. Whatever the soundness of these claims, my main concern is to emphasize the difference from the philosophical theory of reasoning. I think the central difference is that the explanatory mental models devised by psychologists normally involve processes of which the human reasoners are not in fact or could not in principle be or become conscious. By contrast,

---

[17] This has been argued in Finocchiaro 1980b, chapter 2.

the philosopher who is trying to understand reasoning does so in terms of conscious or potentially conscious processes; for example, unstated assumptions may be originally overlooked in a given argument, but they are certainly entities that can be brought before the mind as a result of discussion.

The third surface difference between the psychology and the philosophy of reasoning concerns evaluation. It is explicitly included in my definition of the theory of reasoning, and it obviously corresponds to the philosophers' practice of assessing the validity, soundness, or correctness of the reasoning they examine. By contrast, psychologists like to follow a supposedly value-free approach; they pretend that they are merely describing and explaining the cognitive phenomena they observe. Even when they claim to have found evidence that human beings reason in various specific illogical or irrational ways,[18] psychologists adopt a curiously non-evaluative stance, for they treat this alleged irrationality as a fact-to-be-explained, rather than as a condition to be avoided, and they take this irrationality merely to mean an objective discrepancy between the performance of experimental subjects and various abstract principles taken from truth-functional logic, the mathematical theory of probability, etc. Clearly the real difference is one of explicitness, rather than presence or absence, of evaluation.

Actually, this leads to another difference from the point of view of evaluation. Once we see that the real fact established by psychologists is the discrepancy between human reasoning and the principles of traditional formal deductive and inductive logic, there is no reason to prefer an evaluative conclusion about human irrationality to one about the empirical unfoundedness of formal logic. In fact, given an empirical orientation, it seems clear that the discrepancy should be resolved by a negative evaluation of the traditional logical principles. This is precisely what L. Jonathan Cohen has been doing in the domain of probabilistic reasoning, where he has attempted to devise a non-Pascalian theory of probability more in conformity with the actual performance of human beings.[19]

So we may summarize the evaluational differences between the psychology and the philosophy of reasoning by saying that whereas psychologists evaluate reasoning only implicitly and unavoidably, philosophers do so actively and explicitly; moreover, psychologists' evaluations are

---

[18] Wason and Johnson-Laird 1972; Tversky and Kahneman (1971; 1973).

[19] L. J. Cohen (1977; 1981a; 1982). Finocchiaro (1980b) follows a similar approach, though his context is that of the general theory of reasoning.

directed against the performance of their experimental subjects, whereas philosophers' evaluations tend to be directed against traditional formal logic. Together with the difference between an experimental and an historical approach, and between the use of nonconscious and of potentially conscious mental processes, these are certainly sufficient to distinguish the two fields of endeavor. I should end this section by saying that there is no reason, however, why philosophers cannot adopt and appropriate useful facts or ideas examined by psychologists. Besides the discrepancy between actual cognitive performance and formal logic, another very important fact for which there seems to be overwhelming evidence is that in general the content of propositions has a significant effect on how people interpret their logical form, and in particular the concreteness or the abstractness of the subject matter sometimes facilitates and sometimes hinders their reasoning.[20]

Another sweeping criticism that can be leveled against the legitimacy of the theory of reasoning raises questions about "argument analysis as a plausible subject for study."[21] What is called argument analysis in the literature is indeed the heart of the theory of reasoning since it largely corresponds to what I call the interpretation and the evaluation of reasoning. For example, of Michael Scriven's seven steps of argument analysis,[22] the first three obviously pertain to interpretation since they are, respectively, the clarification of meaning, the identification of conclusions, and the portrayal of structure; the last three obviously deal with evaluation since they speak of the criticism of the premises and of the inferences, the introduction of other relevant arguments, and the overall evaluation of the given argument; the fourth step is the formulation of unstated assumptions or missing premises, and I would regard it as being partly an interpretative and partly an evaluative problem. What supposedly undermines the viability of argument analysis are the following three things. First, the three interpretative steps are neither sequential nor discrete since it is clear that each presupposes the other two: for example, one cannot understand the meaning of an argument and of its parts without knowing the identity of its conclusion and how its various components are structured into a whole.[23] Second, it is clear that the articulation of unstated assumptions is a task that requires creativity and imagination,

---

[20] Wason and Johnson-Laird 1972, 54–85, 193.
[21] McPeck 1981, 89.
[22] Scriven 1976, 39–51.
[23] McPeck 1981, 87–89.

and hence the procedure is neither mechanical nor methodical.[24] Finally, the evaluation process presupposes substantive and factual information which cannot be regarded as logical in any sense of the term (including the sense of the phrase "informal logic"); this is obvious from the step that requires criticism of the premises and the one that asks us to introduce other relevant arguments.

I agree with almost all of these points, with one very important exception. The final conclusion of this critical argument simply does not follow, that is the conclusion that argument analysis and the theory of reasoning are not a serious or plausible subject for study. In order to infer this conclusion one would have to assume that the only serious or plausible disciplines are those that possess techniques and procedures that are simple, effective, and mechanical. There are many difficulties with this assumption. Partly it seems to advocate an untenable scientism according to which the only subjects worthy of pursuit are the exact sciences. Partly it seems to leave the door open for the kind of irrationalism that the proponents of the new rhetoric have been reacting against,[25] namely that intellectual respectability is to be equated only with effective decision procedures, and all else is equally worthless. Obviously the proper thing to do, when mechanical methods are not available, is to elaborate the imperfect rules of thumb that are possible. And partly such an assumption seems to ignore even the well-known limitations of mathematics and formal logic stemming from Gödel's theorems; for example, there is no mechanical procedure to construct derivations of theorems in the predicate calculus. In summary, I would say that this objection reflects an inadequate epistemology and philosophy of science.

The last objection I want to discuss is one to which I am not sure I can give an effective rebuttal. It stems from the theory/practice distinction. The difficulty is that, despite its empirical, practical, and contextual orientation, and despite its sensitivity to concrete reasoning in natural language, the theory of reasoning is still a theoretical inquiry whose concepts and principles, however sound and low-level, need to be applied and used in practice in ordinary contexts different from that of philosophical reflection. This is simply an instance in the domain of reasoning of a general difficulty that seems to afflict the most diverse fields. For example, if one looks at science, the greatest exemplars of scientific practice

---

[24] McPeck 1981, 91.
[25] Perelman and Olbrechts-Tyteca 1969, 1–10.

are such people as Galileo, Newton, Lavoisier, and Einstein, whereas the most outstanding theorists of science are such people as Bacon, Peirce, Duhem, Popper, etc.; in politics we find, on the one hand, Pericles, Caesar Augustus, Jefferson, Disraeli, etc., and on the other hand, Aristotle, Machiavelli, Tocqueville, etc.; in morality, one group would include Socrates, St. Francis, Gandhi, etc., the other Aristotle, Kant, Bentham, etc. Why should we expect the situation to be any different in the domain of our present interest?

This difficulty can also be elaborated in another way. From the point of view of reasoning, the theory of reasoning is at best an instance of a special kind of reasoning, namely reasoning about reasoning. What reason is there to think that if one becomes proficient in reasoning about reasoning, one will be also proficient in reasoning about atoms and molecules, torts and contracts, personal and emotional problems, affirmative action and nuclear deterrence, etc.? When expressed in these terms, this objection may be reminiscent of the earlier one about whether there is any such thing as reasoning in general. However, what we have here is a new difficulty, since we are now asking whether there is any significant similarity between, for example, reasoning about reasoning and reasoning about atoms and molecules, whereas earlier we were asking whether there is any significant similarity between such things as reasoning about atoms and molecules and reasoning about torts and contracts. Someone could admit that there are significant similarities among fields at the object level, but not between the object level and the metalevel, or one might think that each field is significantly different from each other, but argue that, for example, object-level reasoning about atoms and metalevel reasoning about reasoning about atoms do not constitute two different fields. But the transference between these two levels is what the present objection questions, or to be more exact, the transference from the higher into the lower level.

In order to begin answering this objection, I would want to say that the divergence between theory and practice mentioned above does not show that the theoretical reflections of the practitioners, or the actual behavior of the theorists, are inadequate, but only that normally they do not excel. Second, even from the point of view of excellence, there are exceptions to this generalization. For example, Socrates is not only a model of moral life, but a brilliant ethical theorist; Galileo is not only "the father of modern science," but also an acute methodological theorist; and both Socrates and Galileo were nonnegligible theorists of reasoning, as well as

effective practitioners of reasoning.[26] Third, I should call attention to one
element of my definition of the theory of reasoning which I have already
mentioned, but without the proper emphasis. I defined the enterprise in
terms of concepts and principles, not only for the interpretation and the
evaluation of reasoning, but also for the "sound practice" of reasoning.
Although the amount of theoretical understanding such principles for
reasoning well provide is in inverse proportion to the ease of their practical applicability, some of them can certainly be formulated in such a
way as to be easily applicable. Fourth, the objection seems stronger than
it is only if we emphasize a necessary connection between proficiency in
theory and proficiency in practice, for it is clear that there is no necessary
connection. However, if we are more realistic and speak in terms of influence, then I think we can say that proficiency in certain kinds or aspects
of theorizing is likely to improve practice, and conversely proficiency in
actual reasoning is likely to produce the desire for theoretical reflection
in order to understand better what one is doing. Finally, theory and practice are not themselves inert, static entities, and so, to the extent that
there is a lack of correspondence, one can demand that they be brought
closer together, that theory be constructed with an eye toward practice,
and that practice be more infused with theory.

4. Summary

To sum up, I have addressed myself to the problem of giving a positive,
constructive, and self-sufficient interpretation of informal logic, by view-
ing it as a philosophical approach to the theory of reasoning. I began
by defining the theory of reasoning in such a way as to avoid apriorism,
excessive evaluationism, dogmatic universalism, and premature systematization. And then I defended the viability, the philosophical character, and
the methodological legitimacy of the theory of reasoning so conceived by
defending it from a number of objections. These were the criticisms that
its defining subject matter – reasoning – is perhaps a fictitious one; that
even if reasoning is not a fictitious subject matter, it can be studied only
by a branch of cognitive psychology; that even if there is a distinct, philosophical way of studying reasoning, this is not a discipline that can be
taken seriously, as the difficulties afflicting argument analysis show; and
finally, that at any rate, the practical import of the theory of reasoning is

[26] The case of Socrates is, of course, well known, while for the case of Galileo the thesis is
demonstrated in Finocchiaro 1980b.

suspect. Both my elaboration of the definition and my methodological justification of the theory of reasoning suggest a considerable overlap[27] with "informal logic." Two other ways of strengthening this suggestion have not been attempted in this chapter. One would be a detailed examination of explicit contributions to the theory of reasoning.[28] A second way of strengthening the suggestion would be to show how contributions to the theory of reasoning can be interpreted as contributions to informal logic, in the sense that they are addressing themselves to topics and issues of explicit concern and interest to informal logicians.[29]

[27] Notice that I speak of overlap, and not of identity, partly because, as clarified earlier, informal logic has a practical component which cannot be completely reduced to the theoretical one, even when the latter is required to include the elaboration of principles for the sound practice of reasoning.

[28] Cf. Finocchiaro 1981, where it is argued that the theories of fallacies prevalent among informal logicians are contributions (of various worth) to the theory of the evaluation of reasoning.

[29] A possible example might be to elaborate the "informal logic" aspect of a work like Finocchiaro 1980b; cf. Johnson and Blair 1985.

2

An Historical Approach to the Study
of Argumentation (1987)

1. Elements of the Historical Approach

The primary purpose of this chapter is to elucidate and illustrate an historical approach[1] to the study of argumentation. I am also interested in justifying this approach and in discussing a number of difficulties that it faces and some fruitful lines of inquiry it suggests. However, space limitations will force me to be rather sketchy and allusive in regard to this justification and discussion, whose details will have to await some other occasion. Nevertheless, I invite reactions to the secondary topics as well as to the central ones.

By way of elucidation, an historical approach is to be understood as a type of empirical approach, empirical primarily in the sense in which this term is contrasted to an apriorist, rationalistic, or intellectualist orientation. In this context, formal logic, or at least the relevant parts of formal logic,[2] may be taken as an example of the apriorist approach, while

---

[1] This may be regarded as being in the tradition of Toulmin, who was explicit that "not only will logic have to become more empirical; it will inevitably tend to become more historical. . . . In the natural sciences, for instance, men such as Kepler, Newton, Lavoisier, Darwin and Freud have transformed not only our beliefs, but also our way of arguing and our standards of relevance and proof" (1958, 257). There are differences, however. For example Toulmin's thesis here is primarily a metalogical claim, whereas mine bypasses issues in the philosophy of logic as such. And his conception of 'historical' here seems to refer primarily to notions of evolutionary development, emergence of novelty, and absence of eternal absolutes, whereas mine emphasizes merely the past, the naturally occurring, and the observational.

[2] Here I am thinking of a work like Kalish et al. 1980, whereas Tarski 1965 may be regarded as a semi-empirical approach to *mathematical* reasoning, and Jeffrey 1967 a relatively autonomous and self-contained investigation.

cognitive psychology[3] may be regarded as an instance of a different type of empirical approach. The main methodological difference between cognitive psychology and the historical approach advocated here is that the former is experimental, while the latter is merely observational. Whether the historical-observational or psychological-experimental approach is preferable is an issue of great interest and importance, which for the moment I merely want to raise rather than discuss, let alone settle.[4] It should also be clear that the historical approach is in no way committed to any sort of naive empiricism, according to which one should observe argumentation with a *tabula rasa* and without any presuppositions; for I do not think such naive empiricism is tenable. Nor is the historical approach committed to an absolute separation between the empirical and the a priori; for what we have instead is a relative and contextual distinction. Finally, it should be pointed out that such orientations are matters of degree, and so what I would advocate is a greater emphasis on empirical studies of argumentation (at least among philosophers[5]), rather than the

[3] See, for example, Wason and Johnson-Laird 1972, Johnson-Laird and Wason 1977, and Evans (1982; 1983c).

[4] In Finocchiaro (1979b; 1980b, 256–72) I argued for the superiority of the historical approach by exploring some difficulties in the otherwise important work in the psychology of reasoning by Wason and Johnson-Laird (1972). In a recent paper, Wason (1983) has replied to some of my criticism and has thrown some new light on the specific experimental phenomenon that had occasioned my criticism, that is the so-called "Wason's four-card problem." Nevertheless, I am not sure that the methodological issue is significantly affected. If we take the issue to be that of experimental versus historical-observational approach, I would now want to strengthen my argument in two ways, which, ironically, would utilize ideas and arguments advanced by other cognitive psychologists.
   One would be what I take to be a central point in Byrne 1983, namely that if we reject the use of subjects' "protocols" as explanations of their performance, and regard them merely as data, then they can function to provide more stringent tests for theoretical claims. Another would be to exploit some of the conclusions found in Evans (1982; 1983b; 1983c). His work is too important and controversial for any one-sentence summary, and it certainly deserves extended critical scrutiny. Nevertheless, at the risk of oversimplification I will say that he criticizes the "rationalist" approach in the experimental psychology of reasoning, and he engages in an impressive constructive attempt to interpret such experimental data along the lines of general cognitive psychology, using notions and activities like perception, memory, and at times even purely statistical scholastic considerations. From this it is a short step to conclude that psychologists' reasoning experiments have not really been testing reasoning and argumentation, but other cognitive activities, so that if it is the study of reasoning and argumentation that we are dealing with, then the experimental approach has been shown to have severe limitations indeed. Needless to say, this methodological issue deserves further discussion, and I will tackle it more fully on some other occasion.

[5] This is not to say, of course, that even among philosophers the empirical emphasis is totally absent. In fact, the recent emergence of what is sometimes called "informal logic"

total exclusion of apriorist, conceptual analyses. In short, the historical study in question is an empirical, not an empiricist approach.

A second needed clarification regards its relationship to the normative approach. Although sometimes the empirical and the normative are contrasted with each other, that is not my intention here. I do not mean to exclude normative considerations. On the contrary, my historical approach to argumentation has normative and evaluative aims in addition to descriptive, analytical, and explanatory ones. The question of the exact relationship between the two sets of goals is another interesting and important issue that could be dealt with in a longer or in a purely methodological investigation. However, in the present one I also want to present some concrete and substantive results, and so these remarks will have to suffice for the moment.

In regard to approaches that might be labeled rhetorical and dialectical, I would begin by delimiting the meaning of these terms as follows. I would take 'rhetorical' in Perelman's sense,[6] as meaning pertaining to persuasion, and I would take 'dialectical' to mean dialogical, that is, pertaining to dialogue. And then I would say that I see no reason to exclude the rhetorical and dialectical aspects of argumentation from the historical approach. Of course, if the rhetorical approach is taken to be the one that studies exclusively the persuasive aspects of argumentation, then it would be incompatible with the historical approach. Similarly, if the dialectical orientation is defined as the approach that examines only the element of dialogue in argumentation, then it would not be possible to proceed both historically and dialectically. So, while I would not attribute the features of 'rhetorical' and 'dialectical' to the historical approach in exactly the same way that I would speak of its being empirical and normative, nevertheless the rhetorical and dialectical aspects of argumentation do come within the purview of my historical approach.

One last clarification is needed before we go on. In many contexts the historical is opposed to the theoretical. I am thinking, for example, of such contrasts as economic theory versus economic history, philosophical theorizing versus the history of philosophy, natural history versus natural

is a sign of greater interest in the empirical study of argumentation among philosophers; for an excellent review of the literature, see Johnson and Blair 1985, and for a more methodological analysis, see Finocchiaro 1984b, which is in part a methodological defense from criticism such as McPeck 1981; this last issue could now benefit from some of the insights in Johnson-Laird 1983a. Other interesting philosophical discussions of the question of empiricism are Barth 1985a and Harman 1984.

6 Perelman and Olbrechts-Tyteca 1958.

philosophy, and more generally of the classification of disciplines into those that deal with particulars and those that deal with generalities. This is not the contrast I have in mind when I speak of the historical approach to the study of argumentation. Rather, one of its central aims is indeed the formulation of generalizations. The historicity refers primarily to the nature of the evidence, data, or sources that are examined in order to reach those generalizations. To what extent it is possible to formulate high-level, systematic, interpretative, and explanatory theories, in addition to low-level principles and approximate rules of thumb, is another one of those interesting and important problems, whose full details are off-limits in the present context.

The historical approach begins with the selection of some important book of the past, containing a suitably wide range and intense degree of argumentation. Many of the classics would fulfill this requirement, for example, Plato's *Republic,* Thomas Aquinas's *Summa Theologica,* Galileo Galilei's *Dialogue on the Two Chief World Systems,* David Hume's *Dialogues Concerning Natural Religion,* Charles Darwin's *Origin of Species,* perhaps Karl Marx's *Capital.* Not all classics would be appropriate; this is easy to see for works of poetry, fiction, and literature. Historical works such as those of Thucydides, Guicciardini, or Burckhardt do contain an occasional argument, but not sufficiently frequently. I do not think that philosophical classics would qualify either, if we are thinking of such works as Aristotle's *Metaphysics,* Descartes's *Meditations,* Kant's *Critique,* or Hegel's *Phenomenology.* The problem with them would not be an insufficient degree of argumentation, but an insufficiently wide range of topic. In other words, they would make good case studies in philosophical argumentation, whereas our present concern is argumentation in general. Analogous remarks apply to mathematical classics such as Euclid's *Elements.* In some cases works other than the classics would serve the purpose, for example collections or selections of judicial opinions of bodies like the United States Supreme Court or the World Court in The Hague.[7]

The first step of the historical approach gives content to the qualification made earlier, to the effect that there is no commitment here to naive empiricism. In fact, it is obvious that such a selection presupposes a notion of what argumentation is. In this sense, there is an element of apriorism. However, this is not to say that one is deciding or assuming in advance what descriptive generalizations or normative principles of

[7] Interesting variations of this textual-analytical discussion of the historical approach may be found in Ennis 1968, Vignaux (1976, 266–326), and Walton (1985, 92–112, 226–36).

argumentation the investigation will reveal. It is quite possible to keep an open mind about them, and hence the authenticity of the empirical procedure remains.

A second step of the historical approach is that the investigator has somehow to acquire mastery of the content and historical background of the chosen text. I am not sure that one has to get to the point of being able to make original contributions to the scholarly subspecialty, defined as the interpretation and criticism of the author in question. But at least one ought to be able to appreciate and understand the work of these scholars. One interesting question at this junction is whether our argumentation theorist has to be able to read the text in the original language. I am not sure about this, but I want to suggest that it is *not* obvious that such linguistic competence is necessary, for it is quite possible, indeed likely, that the theoretically relevant features of argumentation are language-invariant; therefore, while an accurate translation is necessary, it may not be impossible for the argumentation theorist to obtain useful results by studying the translated text. Nevertheless, this is a methodological problem that deserves further exploration.

2. Illustration: A Study of the Arguments in Galileo's *Dialogue*

At this point I will switch from a general elucidation to what I call an illustration of the historical approach. It is a personal illustration in the sense that it summarizes work done by the present author (Finocchiaro 1980b). The book chosen was Galileo's *Dialogue on the Two Chief World Systems*, first published in 1632. This is the book that led, a year later, to the famous trial and condemnation for heresy by the Roman Inquisition, an episode which came to be described by some as "the greatest scandal in Christendom." From a scientific point of view this book represented Galileo's mature synthesis of the new astronomy revolutionized by Copernicus in 1543 and by his own telescopic discoveries, and of the new science of mechanics on which Galileo had been working for more than forty years. His *Dialogue* of 1632 should not be confused with his other famous book, the *Discourse on Two New Sciences*, which was published in 1638 and lays the foundations of mechanics and of engineering and avoids discussion of astronomical and cosmological topics.

In the present context, the important point is that Galileo's *Dialogue* is a 500-page work full of arguments and critiques of arguments on all sorts of topics, ranging from astronomy, mathematics, and physics to philosophy, common sense, and everyday life. There are arguments and counterarguments about such things as the perfection of the universe; the natural motion of bodies; the similarities and the differences between the earth and the heavenly bodies; the role of Aristotle's authority; the causes of the tides; and the location (in the atmosphere or in the heavens) of the nova of 1572. Some of the arguments are about whether the earth's axial rotation is rendered impossible by the empirical evidence from vertical fall, from the experiment of dropping a rock from the top of the mast of a moving ship, from east-west gunshots, from north-south gunshots, from vertical gunshots, from point-blank gunshots, from the flight of birds, and from the extruding power of whirling. Other arguments are about whether the same idea can be refuted by the thought-experiment of dropping a ball from the moon to the earth, by the epistemological principles that all natural phenomena must be explicable and that the senses cannot deceive us, and by the metaphysical principles that each simple body must have one and only one natural motion, that similar substances must have similar motions, and that motion cannot last forever. Still other arguments are about whether the earth's orbital revolution around the sun conflicts with biblical passages and with available astronomical observations concerning the dimensions and distance of the stars, the elevation of the celestial pole and of the stars, the lack of stellar parallax, and the seasonal changes in the sun's apparent motions. Finally, there are arguments about whether the earth's motion is rendered probable by the principle of simplicity, whether it is confirmed by evidence from the relationship of orbital periods and sizes and from the heliocentrism of planetary motions, and whether it is the best explanation of retrograde planetary motion and of the apparent annual motion of sunspots.

By one count there are seventeen[8] main arguments that Galileo gives in support of conclusions he favors, and twenty-nine[9] critiques of arguments he opposes. And I am referring here to main arguments and main subdivisions of the book, and not to the various subarguments that are parts of these; counting the latter would yield a much greater number. Moreover, it is possible to show that all these forty-six main discussions can be integrated into a single argument, since the seventeen main positive conclusions are all part of or steps toward the single cosmological thesis that the earth moves, while the twenty-nine critiques support negative

[8] Finocchiaro 1980b, 32–33, sections IA1, IA2–3, IC2, IC3, IIA2 (nos. 1–8), IIIB1–3, and IV.
[9] Finocchiaro 1980b, 32–33, sections IA4, IB1–3, IIB1 (nos. 1–2), IIB2a–b, IIB3 (a, c, d, e), IIB4, IIB6, IIC1–6, IIIA, and IIIC1–8.

conclusions that undermine the opposite thesis that the earth stands still at the center of the universe.

All this is still relatively preliminary, in the sense that it is the sort of fact that justifies the selection of such a work for an historical case study in argumentation theory. In a sense this fact is immediately obvious even to a casual reader of the *Dialogue*, as long as he has the proper appreciation for argumentation. The articulation of the details of this fact is, of course, another story, and a long story at that; it is part of the spadework required as a precondition for a fruitful investigation in argumentation theory.

The next step was to elaborate a relatively a priori element of my historical approach. It was to find and articulate some principles for the systematic collection of the data. Four ideas were of paramount importance here. First, all data should consist of reconstructed arguments, that is, interpretations of arguments contained in the text, restated in natural language in such a way as to portray them as clearly and accurately as possible, by ignoring extraneous material and adding as many reasoning and argument indicator terms as needed. Second, an argument should be reconstructed with the primary aim of exhibiting its propositional structure, that is, the inferential and ratiocinative interrelations among the various statements or propositions that are its constituent parts; in this context a proposition is taken as the basic unit of acceptance or rejection or as the basic carrier of truth or falsehood, and so the portrayal of propositional structure is an intermediate level of analysis, since it disregards the internal structure of propositions, or to be more exact, it leaves this finer structure to a secondary or subsequent stage of inquiry. Third, the most useful method of describing the propositional structure of an argument turned out to be the technique of root or inverted-tree diagrams, coupled with a numbering system that assigns to each proposition a sequence of numbers which uniquely defines its place in the network: for example, "1-1" and "1-2" would be respectively the first and second premises supporting proposition "1," while "1-2-1" would be a proposition supporting "1-2" and "1-2-1-1" would support "1-2-1."[10] Fourth, the normative and evaluative aim of the project should be addressed by interpreting the book's critiques of arguments as arguments about arguments and reconstructing them in the manner just sketched.

---

[10] Finocchiaro 1980b, 311–26. The first work where I saw this technique explicitly discussed is Angell 1964 and I adapted it from him. Nowadays it is very common, though various authors add various twists to the basic idea; see, for example, Scriven (1976, 41–43) and Eemeren, Grootendorst, and Kruiger (1984, 17–36).

When the text of Galileo's *Dialogue* is studied in accordance with these principles, the forty-six main arguments mentioned earlier generate several hundred reconstructed subarguments, each of which may to some extent be examined by itself. This constitutes a rich and varied data base which one may then analyze in an empirical fashion to determine which interesting conclusions it supports. These theoretical implications will be discussed presently, but first I should like to stress that this data base is neutral vis-à-vis these conclusions, and hence it is to be hoped that other researchers will subject it to their own analysis to test their own theories. In other words, the construction of such data bases, by using other appropriate classics, is a valuable enterprise suggested by the historical approach to the study of argumentation, and I believe that the one I have constructed for the case of Galileo's *Dialogue* will be found to have value independently of the conclusions I shall be drawing from it.

In drawing these conclusions I distinguish two stages of analysis, depending on how far one has moved beyond the information contained in the evidence. I presume it would be possible to go further and deeper than I have done, and so I regard my own conclusions as open to both correction and improvement. The two stages are concept formation and generalization. There are three clusters of concepts suggested by my data base: evaluation categories, evaluation methods, and elements of argumentation. Beginning with the last, the elements of argumentation are its constitutive aspects, in the sense that argumentation is normally a mixture of these activities; there are six activities that seem prevalent: deduction, induction, explanation, evaluation, persuasion, and linguistic expression. The exact definitions and interrelationships of these notions are beyond the scope of this chapter. For now the following will have to suffice. Notice that these notions are not necessarily mutually exclusive or jointly exhaustive: for example, there is probably some overlap between induction and explanation since some inductive generalizations may be viewed as inferences to the best explanation;[11] similarly, justification is an obviously relevant activity, probably related to persuasion, but it is not in the above-mentioned list. The item termed "linguistic expression" refers to the use of such words as 'therefore,' 'so,' 'because,' and 'since,' and such usage might be taken to yield a so-called operational definition of argumentation. Evaluation is in the list not only because the evaluation of an argument itself requires an argument, but also because argumentation often consists of the evaluation of actual or potential arguments

---

[11] See, for example, Ennis 1968.

or counterarguments. The relevant sense of explanation is not that of elucidation or clarification, but that of causal explanation, using a broad meaning of cause so as to count explanations by reasons as one type of causal explanation. Finally, induction here is taken to refer to such activities as reasoning by analogy and the determination of support.

The cluster of evaluation methods consists of techniques that arguers may use for arriving at and justifying various evaluations of arguments. I labeled the six most frequently occurring ones as follows: active evaluation, *ad hominem* argument, explanation of error in reasoning, method of alternative conclusion, method of counterexample, and principle of charity. This list too is partly overlapping and partly open-ended. Active evaluation is the procedure of testing inferential relationships among propositions by becoming actively engaged in the argumentation being evaluated, that is by arguing at the level of, and largely in terms of, the argument being evaluated and checking whether what follows from its premises are the conclusions it draws or other propositions. *Ad hominem* argument is reasoning where the arguer derives a conclusion not acceptable to an opponent from premises accepted by the opponent, but not necessarily generally acceptable.[12] The explanation of an error in reasoning refers to a description of the error in general terms and such that it gives us some insight into why it is erroneous; this is contrasted both with a mere description of the error or with a proof of erroneousness. The method of counterexample is the well-known technique of showing that it is possible for the argument being evaluated to have true premises and false conclusion, by constructing another argument of the same form whose premises are obviously true and conclusion obviously false.[13] The method of alternative conclusion tries to show that a conclusion does not follow from the premises because some other different conclusion follows instead. Finally, the principle of charity is the rule that arguments should be reconstructed in such a way that they are immune to trivial and minor criticism, so that their evaluation can concentrate on important issues.

The cluster of evaluation categories refers to various types of attributes with which one may evaluatively characterize reasoning. There are eleven

---

[12] Besides the discussions in Finocchiaro 1980b, cf. Finocchiaro 1974a; Johnstone (1959; 1978); and Walton 1985.

[13] Here I do not wish to convey the impression that I am unaware of the fact that there is no such thing as *the* form of an argument, and hence the method of counterexample must be handled with care. In fact, I agree with much of Massey 1981a, and I think the consequences of that fact have not been fully appreciated. It may be better to speak of the method of logical analogy, as done in Govier 1985.

relatively common ones: circularity, equivocation, fallacy of composition, groundlessness, incompleteness, infinite progression, invalidity, irrelevant conclusion, question-begging, self-contradiction, and uselessness. Even more than the previous two, this list is in need of analysis and systematization, given the greater number of concepts involved. Notice that all the categories are critical or negative, and so I believe that the analysis might result in a theory of fallacies, or at least a theoretical classification of fallacies.[14] Here, let me simply focus on the less familiar categories. An incomplete argument is one whose premises neglect information relevant to the conclusion. An infinitely progressing argument is one which has no non-arbitrary final conclusion; its explicit conclusion does follow, but so does the denial of the conclusion, and the denial of this denial, and so on without end. A self-contradictory argument is one with inconsistent premises; it thus automatically escapes formal invalidity, but it does not escape other types of inadequacy. And a useless argument is one which is contextually a subargument of a bigger argument such that the final conclusion of the first argument appears as an intermediate proposition of the bigger argument, and a final reason of the first argument is more questionable than the final conclusion of the bigger argument; more simply, a useless argument is one whose conclusion is grounded on a proposition more difficult to ascertain than that conclusion.

The second stage of my theoretical analysis of the Galilean data base was the formulation of some generalizations supported by it. One conclusion here is that argumentation normally consists of critical arguments, that is, arguments whose conclusion expresses an unfavorable evaluation about either a particular claim or a particular argument. I hesitate somewhat in saying "normally," and it might be safer to say, more simply, that *most* argumentation consists of critical arguments. Or one might introduce a distinction between two types of arguments, critical and constructive ones, the latter being arguments whose conclusion is a proposition about some entity or event and not about some claim or argument. Then an even weaker way of stating the conclusion would be that the distinction between critical and constructive arguments is the most important one, much more than the distinction between inductive and deductive, or between truth-functional and quantificational arguments, and so on. Perhaps a more proper formulation would be to say that critical arguments

---

[14] Despite my criticism of some aspects of the fallacy approach in Finocchiaro (1980b; 1981), I stress what I call the negative evaluation of reasoning; thus I am far from rejecting the concept altogether, and objections like those in Govier 1982 miss the main point. The real challenge is to come up with a better theoretical understanding of fallacies.

are more basic than constructive ones. At any rate the direction of this conclusion is clear: it is that critical arguments are much more fundamental than usually thought and deserve much more explicit and direct study than they usually receive.[15]

Analogous remarks apply to what I call complex arguments, as distinct from simple ones. Here a simple argument is one without intermediate propositions between the premises and the conclusion, whereas a complex argument is one containing at least one proposition which is the conclusion of one subargument and a premise of another. The overwhelming fact about my data base is that almost all arguments are complex. Despite the fact that complex arguments obviously consist of simple arguments, I think that the former deserve more explicit and direct theoretical investigation. To use a traditional distinction, one might say that, though simple arguments may be ontologically prior, complex arguments have priority from an epistemological viewpoint. The point is that one ought to treat simple arguments as aspects of, or abstractions from, complex ones, rather than examining the latter as mere strings of the former.

A third conclusion is that arguments normally have an open structure. That is, they are normally susceptible to further enlargement and complication of their structure. Since to speak of their structure refers to their network of interrelated propositions, this openness means that much of the structure is implicit. One could say that normally only part of the argument is given, the part needed in the context to remove doubts and objections.

The fourth and final conclusion is an evaluative one. My data indicate that the most effective way of evaluating argumentation seems to be the techniques of active evaluation. Recall that active evaluation takes the form of arguing that one proposition does not follow from another because what really follows from it is some other proposition different or inconsistent with the first; thus the critic engages in argumentation at the same object level as the argument being evaluated, rather than reasoning only at a metalevel; in short, he produces what might be called a counterargument.[16] In this conclusion I am, of course, deriving the 'ought' from the 'is,' but the latter is value-impregnated to begin with, since it includes the intuitive judgment that Galileo was usually right in his criticism of the Aristotelian arguments he rejected.

[15] See Johnstone 1959 for other arguments in support of a similar conclusion.
[16] In view of the similarities between this "active evaluation" and Johnstone's account of *ad hominem* argumentation, the reader should compare Johnstone (1959; 1978).

3. Summary and Further Problems

To summarize, the historical approach to the study of argumentation may be defined as a type of empirical, normative, theory-oriented, and textual-analysis approach. It may be contrasted to the apriorist approach of formal logic, and distinguished from the experimental method of cognitive psychology and the empiricist approach of naive empiricism. It may be combined with both rhetorical and dialectical orientations. And it may be illustrated by my study of the arguments in Galileo's *Dialogue* of 1632, which has yielded three types of results: a data base of hundreds of reconstructed arguments and of critiques reconstructed as arguments about arguments; three clusters of concepts, namely elements of argumentation, evaluation methods, and evaluation categories, which deserve further systematic analysis; and four general conclusions about the importance of critical arguments, complex arguments, open-structured arguments, and active evaluation, which need further refinement, further empirical testing, and further supporting argumentation or criticism. Other problems worth further inquiry are the exact relationship between an empirical and a normative approach; the relative merits of the historical-textual orientation and the experimental-psychological method; the linguistic dependence or invariance of argumentation; and, finally, one other issue not previously mentioned, but which does deserve the last word. This is the question of the possibility, character, and details of a *science* of argumentation, and of what would be the most scientific approach to follow in this field. As long as we do not uncritically assume either positivism or scientism, the problem may be regarded as an open question. I happen to have an answer ready-made. It is that the approach to argumentation here labeled "historical" is the most scientific approach to the topic. In fact, I have argued the case elsewhere (Finocchiaro 1980b), and it may come as no surprise that my argument amounts to taking Galileo as a model scientist, judiciously extracting from his work the procedures that characterize the scientific approach, and trying to apply them in the study of argumentation. I would still uphold this argument, so much so that I did consider entitling this chapter "A Scientific Approach to the Study of Argumentation." It is an expression of my rejection of positivism and scientism that I chose the more modest title.

3

Methodological Problems in Empirical Logic (1989)

1. Introduction

What I plan to do in this chapter is to elaborate a definition of empirical logic, and then to discuss a number of resulting methodological problems. These involve questions about the relationship among empirical logic so conceived and other orientations in logic, other approaches to the study of reasoning, and different conceptions of the empirical approach. One of the most fundamental of these problems is that of the relationship between empirical logic and the experimental psychology of reasoning, and so I shall focus on that, though not limit myself to it. To be more exact, I should speak of their lack of relationship, for it turns out that the laboratory experiments performed by cognitive psychologists are not really tests of reasoning; consequently, the experimental method will emerge as being of dubious value in empirical logic. If such a logic is to be feasible, it must follow some other approach. The one I find most fruitful is the historical-observational approach.

2. Conceptions of Logic

Empirical logic may sound like a contradiction in terms since by logic one often means the domain of the non-empirical. However, an equally common meaning is that logic pertains to the domain of reasoning, and so an empirical logic becomes possible simply as an empirical approach to the study of reasoning.

Although the empirical study of reasoning is an old, indeed ancient, enterprise, the explicit and self-conscious use of the term "empirical logic" is relatively recent. It is due, I believe, to Arne Naess and Else Barth.[1] It constitutes a much-needed label to designate an approach to the study of reasoning different from those that go under such names as formal, mathematical, symbolic, and philosophical[2] logic. Conversely, empirical logic clearly has considerable affinity with a number of recent movements and proposals that go under such names as informal logic,[3] probative logic,[4] natural logic,[5] ordinary logic,[6] and naturalized logic.[7]

In this context, the empirical is being contrasted primarily to the a priori, and not, for example, to the normative or to the theoretical; thus the empirical, the theoretical, and the normative are regarded as mutually consistent and partly overlapping orientations. Furthermore, I do not wish to equate the empirical and the dialectical or dialogical approaches. However, this is not to deny that many proponents of various versions of empirical logic are also inclined to favor a focus on the dialectical-dialogical aspect of reasoning and argumentation.[8] I myself support this emphasis,[9] but I take the dialectical nature of argumentation as a specific feature which the empirical approach is capable of revealing.

It could also be argued that empirical logic has much in common with several other enterprises whose labels or descriptions do not suggest the connection as readily as the just-mentioned logics. One of these other enterprises is Perelman's well-known new rhetoric.[10] Another is the kind of reasoning about reasoning which L. Jonathan Cohen has recently identified with analytical philosophy, and which he has interestingly characterized as both inductive and based upon intuitions of an empirical sort.[11]

---

[1] Naess (1982a; 1982b); Barth 1985a.
[2] Although the label "philosophical logic" suggests an alternative approach different from mathematical, formal, or symbolic logic, their difference seems to be primarily substantive rather than methodological, so that work in "philosophical logic" usually consists of the application of formal, mathematical, and symbolic methods to the analysis of philosophical reasoning. Here I am thinking, for example, of the sort of contribution which gets published in the *Journal of Philosophical Logic.*
[3] Johnson and Blair (1980; 1985); Finocchiaro 1984b.
[4] Scriven 1987.
[5] Beth et al. 1962; Braine 1978; Lakoff 1970.
[6] Ennis 1969; 1976.
[7] Johnson 1987.
[8] Here I have in mind such works as Barth (1982; 1985b; 1987); Barth and Krabbe 1982; Barth and Martens 1982; Blair and Johnson 1987; Eemeren and Grootendorst 1984; Eemeren 1987; Grootendorst 1987; and Johnson 1987.
[9] Finocchiaro 1980b, 418–21; 1988c.
[10] Perelman and Olbrechts-Tyteca 1958.
[11] L. J. Cohen 1986.

All such connections, the obvious as well as the more problematic ones, deserve extended exploration. However, what I want to do here is to elaborate the definition of empirical logic just given and then to answer a number of methodological difficulties that can be raised against it.

3. A Definition of Empirical Logic

I said that empirical logic may be defined as the empirical study of reasoning. To be more exact, I mean the attempt to formulate, to test, to clarify, and to systematize concepts and principles for the interpretation, the evaluation, and the sound practice of reasoning.

First, notice that I speak of *reasoning*, rather than, for example, argumentation; this is deliberately meant to allow a broader domain, by including, besides the study of arguments, such activities as problem-solving, decision-making, persuasion, and explaining. The emphasis on reasoning is also meant as a reminder that what is being studied is a mental activity that actually occurs in the world and which leaves empirical traces, normally in the form of written and oral discourse. This in turn means that the study of reasoning has an empirical orientation and is not a purely formal or abstract discipline.

Second, you should notice my explicit reference to the *interpretation* of reasoning. This is needed partly for the intrinsic reason that such interpretation aims at the understanding of reasoning, and the understanding of a phenomenon is obviously an essential concern of any theorizing. However, I also emphasize it in order to correct what I feel is an overconcern with evaluation; this imbalance is shown, for example, by the fact that elementary logic textbooks often define logic as the attempt to distinguish good from bad reasoning. Therefore, the interpretative dimension needs distinct recognition despite the fact that we would all agree that it is indirectly mentioned by the evaluative dimension, insofar as the proper evaluation of an argument presupposes that it has been properly interpreted.[12]

My third clarification involves the inclusion of concepts and principles for the *sound practice* of reasoning. Notice that I am not talking about important or original reasoning, but merely about correct reasoning. Principles for reasoning well would obviously be related to principles for the evaluation of reasoning; nevertheless, the difference remains since

[12] For an explicit discussion of this presupposition, see for example McPeck (1981, 63) and Finocchiaro (1980b, 339–40).

the activity of evaluation would normally come after a certain argument has been produced, whereas the practice of reasoning means simply the construction of actual arguments or the actual involvement in reasoning. In this regard, both interpretation and evaluation have something in common which they do not share with practice; they are both reflections on previous practice, whereas the practice of reasoning is the construction of what can later become the subject of those types of reflection.

Another important feature of my definition is that I speak of *concepts and principles*. Notice that I do not say "universally valid principles," hence it is an open question whether any of them exist. If not, it would be part of the task of empirical logic to tell us that the most we can hope for are principles of restricted application and limited validity, as well as to specify which principles hold in which fields.[13] Moreover, because of the distinction between interpretation and evaluation, my definition also leaves it as an open question whether there are universally valid principles of interpretation, even if it turns out that there are no universally valid principles of evaluation. Additional openness is allowed by my reference to concepts, as well as to principles. In fact, a concept may be useful for interpreting, evaluating, and practicing reasoning, even though there might be disagreement about which principles or which types of principles formulated in its terms are the correct ones. For example, one might agree that the notion of *ad hominem argument* is important, at least as a way of classifying certain types of reasoning, but one does not have to agree with Henry Johnstone's metaphilosophical principle of interpretation that all genuinely philosophical arguments are *ad hominem*,[14] nor with the widely accepted principle of evaluation that *ad hominem* arguments are fallacious.

Finally, I should clarify that in saying that empirical logic aims to formulate, to test, to clarify, and to systematize principles and concepts, I am indeed referring to four distinct activities. Obviously, systematization is impossible unless the principles in question have already been formulated and have undergone a certain amount of testing and clarification. Moreover, there is no reason to expect the same degree of systematization that was possible for Euclidean geometry or celestial mechanics. Nevertheless, although one of the greatest temptations to be resisted is that of premature systematization, the idea of systematization is not excluded in principle. The reference to testing reflects the empirical orientation mentioned earlier, and it can mean either confirmation or disconfirmation. Lastly,

[13] This answers some of the explicit and implicit objections found in McPeck 1981.
[14] Johnstone 1978.

the clarification of principles is distinct from their formulation, as shown for example by the fact that, regardless of who was the first to formulate explicitly the Principle of Charity, additional insights are being provided by subsequent discussions in the literature.[15]

I believe that the study of reasoning so conceived represents a critical systematization of work in the field of empirical logic. In order to justify directly this claim, one would have to argue that the main concerns of empirical logicians can find a place, or can be improved by corresponding investigations, in this sort of study of reasoning. However, the sketch just given is sufficient to suggest a considerable overlap between the two; hence, for now I will go on to add further indirect evidence for their correspondence by discussing the question of the methodological and epistemological legitimacy of empirical logic. This will take the form of answers to various objections. The three objections I shall discuss in turn involve the question whether there is such a thing as reasoning in general, whether such a theory of reasoning is practically applicable, and how empirical logic relates to the experimental psychology of reasoning.

4. The Problem of the General Definition of Reasoning

One of the most fundamental objections is that the alleged entity which is the subject matter of empirical logic does not really exist.[16] Reasoning is presumably an epiphenomenal illusion deriving from using a general label to refer to a number of disparate activities. A theory of reasoning *per se*, as distinct from theorizing about particular instances or types or fields of reasoning, presumably makes no more sense than a theory of success in general; just as success in one field (say, business) is very different from success in another field (say, sports), so is the skill of legal reasoning, for example, different from that of scientific reasoning. Even a general-sounding type of success, like Dale Carnegie's winning friends and influencing people, is not truly universal since it is obvious that one could master this art and yet fail at such things as sports, teaching, military strategy, debating, poetry, and so on. Hence, even if the entity sometimes labeled everyday reasoning turns out to be theoretically and critically comprehensible (taking this label to refer to reasoning about such practical and fundamental issues that deserve the attention of every

---

[15] Johnson 1981a.

[16] McPeck 1981, especially pp. 84–85. McPeck is directly concerned with teaching, and so he might not endorse my adaptation of his criticism to the context of theorizing.

educated person), even then the study of everyday reasoning would not be equivalent to the study of reasoning *simpliciter*, since the nature of everyday reasoning would be bound to differ from the nature of reasoning in such special domains as science, the law, medicine, business, and so on.

My answer to this objection consists of a counter-charge and a constructive suggestion. The counter-charge is that the criticism confuses the interpretation and the evaluation of reasoning, and that in effect it overstresses the latter. This is shown by the tendency of these critics to compare reasoning with such implicitly evaluated entities as success, creativity, constructiveness, and effectiveness,[17] whereas the proper analogue to such nongeneralizable non-entities would be *correct* reasoning. In other words, these critics ignore the fact[18] that reasoning is both a task and an achievement term: to engage in reasoning does not necessarily imply to be successful at it. This means that, at worst, what's impossible is a general theory of *correct* reasoning, and not necessarily a general interpretative theory of the *structure* of reasoning. However, even the limited pessimistic conclusion seems excessively apriorist, since, given that it would allow for limited theories of correct reasoning in particular fields, there is no a priori reason to predict that the further generalization and systematization of these limited theories will necessarily fail. Moreover, the notion of a field of reasoning is problematic,[19] and the same criticism made against the possibility of generalizations among fields could be leveled against the possibility of generalizing within a given field, which after all consists of various subfields. Finally, it is possible that a general theory of evaluation might be based in part on a general theory of interpretation, whose possibility, as we have seen, is untouched by the present criticism.

This brings us to the question of what all types and instances of reasoning have in common, and it is here that my constructive suggestion becomes relevant. I think that the essential feature of all reasoning is the interrelating of individual thoughts in such a way that some follow from others,[20] and that the normal linguistic expression of such interrelated thinking involves the use of particles like 'because,' 'therefore,' and so on. However minimal this conception is, it allows the study of reasoning to get started by suggesting that we try to understand and to evaluate those discourses having a high incidence of these logical particles.[21]

[17] McPeck 1981, 84–85.
[18] McPeck (1981, 13) is aware of this fact, but does not realize its importance.
[19] As has been shown by Johnson 1981b.
[20] For more details, see Finocchiaro 1980b, especially pp. 311–31.
[21] See, for example, Smit (1987; 1989; 1992).

5. The Theory versus the Practice of Reasoning

The second objection I want to discuss stems from the theory/practice distinction. The difficulty is that, despite its empirical, practical, and contextual orientation, and despite its sensitivity to concrete reasoning in natural language, empirical logic is still a theoretical inquiry whose concepts and principles, however sound and low-level, need to be applied and used in practice in ordinary contexts different from those of philosophical reflection. This is simply an instance in the domain of reasoning of a general difficulty that seems to afflict the most diverse fields. For example, if one looks at science, the greatest exemplars of scientific practice are such people as Galileo, Huygens, Newton, Lavoisier, and Einstein, whereas the most outstanding theorists of science are such people as Bacon, Peirce, Duhem, and Popper; in politics we find, on the one hand, Pericles, Caesar Augustus, Jefferson, Disraeli, and so on, and on the other hand, Aristotle, Machiavelli, Tocqueville, and so on; in morality, one group would include Socrates, St. Francis, and Gandhi, the other Aristotle, Kant, and Bentham. Why should we expect the situation to be any different in the domain of our present interest?

This difficulty can also be elaborated in another way. From the point of view of reasoning, the study of reasoning is at best an instance of a special kind of reasoning, namely reasoning about reasoning. What reason is there to think that if one becomes proficient in reasoning about reasoning, one will also be proficient in reasoning about atoms and molecules, torts and contracts, personal and emotional problems, affirmative action and nuclear deterrence, and so on? When expressed in these terms, this objection may be reminiscent of the earlier one about whether there is any such thing as reasoning in general. However, what we have here is a new difficulty, since we are now asking whether there is any significant similarity between, for example, reasoning about reasoning and reasoning about atoms and molecules, whereas earlier we were asking whether there is any significant similarity between such things as reasoning about atoms and molecules and reasoning about torts and contracts. Someone could admit that there are significant similarities among fields at the object level, but not between the object level and the metalevel; or one might think that each field is significantly different from each other, but argue that, for example, object-level reasoning about atoms and metalevel reasoning about reasoning about atoms do not constitute two different fields. However, the transference between these two levels is what the present objection questions, or to be more exact, the transference from the higher into the lower level.

In order to begin answering this objection, I would want to say that the divergence between theory and practice mentioned above does not show that the theoretical reflections of the practitioners, or the actual behavior of the theorists, are inadequate, but only that normally they do not excel. Second, even from the point of view of excellence, there are exceptions to this generalization. For example, Socrates is not only a model of moral life, but also a brilliant ethical theorist; Galileo is not only "the father of modern science," but also an acute methodological theorist; and both Socrates and Galileo were nonnegligible theorists of reasoning, as well as effective practitioners of reasoning.[22] Third, I should call attention to one element of my definition of empirical logic which I have already mentioned, but without the proper emphasis. I defined the enterprise in terms of concepts and principles, not only for the interpretation and the evaluation of reasoning, but also for the *sound practice* of reasoning. Admittedly, the amount of theoretical understanding provided by such principles of correct reasoning is in inverse proportion to the ease of their practical applicability; nevertheless, some of them can certainly be formulated in such a way as to be easily applicable. Fourth, the objection seems stronger than it is only if we emphasize a necessary connection between proficiency in theory and proficiency in practice, for it is clear that there is no necessary connection; however, if we are more realistic and speak in terms of likely influence, then I think we can say that proficiency in certain kinds or aspects of theorizing is likely to improve practice, and conversely proficiency in actual reasoning is likely to produce the desire for theoretical reflection in order to understand better what one is doing. Finally, theory and practice are not themselves inert, static entities, and so, to the extent that there is a lack of correspondence, one can demand that they be brought closer together, that theory be constructed with an eye toward practice, and that practice be more infused with theory.

6. The Experimental Psychology of Reasoning

The third and last objection, and the one I shall discuss at greatest length, involves the connection between empirical logic and the experimental psychology of reasoning. We shall see that this exercise will turn from an objection to empirical logic into a wide-ranging criticism of the psychology of reasoning itself.

---

[22] The case of Socrates is, of course, well known, while for the case of Galileo the thesis is demonstrated in Finocchiaro 1980b.

The clarification of this connection is one of the most immediate questions that arise as soon as one has said that empirical logic is to be understood as the empirical study of reasoning. The question would be whether therefore empirical logic is just another name for a thriving enterprise which has already existed for some time, and which is practiced in this subspecialty of cognitive psychology. If it were, then one could question the propriety of the new label; whereas, if it were not, one would want to know what the difference is.

Moreover, it is obvious that in the psychology of reasoning the approach is empirical in the sense of experimental; that is to say, psychologists perform laboratory experiments with human subjects to determine how they reason, why they reason as they do, and whether their reasoning is normatively correct.[23] On the other hand, I would argue that philosophers (like Arne Naess) who are explicitly groping toward an empirical logic are best seen as practicing an historical and observational approach.[24]

We thus seem to have at least three empirical approaches to the study of reasoning: the intuitive-inductive approach of the analytical philosophers (at least as analytical philosophy is interpreted by L. J. Cohen[25]), the experimental-psychological method of cognitive psychologists, and the historical-observational approach (à la Naess). An urgent task facing the empirical logician would seem to be to characterize these three approaches in more detail, to give illustrations of them, and to assess their relative merits.

Since I have recently discussed the historical approach elsewhere,[26] and since the inductive-intuitive approach is eloquently presented, exemplified, and defended in Cohen's recent book, I believe the most fruitful thing for me to do here is to examine the experimental-psychological approach.

7. The Problem of Rationality

Let me begin by admitting that the general cultural and philosophical significance of recent work in the psychology of reasoning is difficult to overestimate. In fact it is very easy and tempting to interpret such work

---

[23] See, for example, Evans (1982; 1983b); Johnson-Laird 1983a; Johnson-Laird and Wason 1977; Nisbett and Ross 1980; and Wason and Johnson-Laird 1972.
[24] Cf. Finocchiaro 1987a, where I illustrate the historical approach by means of Finocchiaro 1980b. Cf. also Naess 1982a; 1982b.
[25] See L. J. Cohen 1986.
[26] Finocchiaro 1987a.

as an experimental demonstration of human irrationality, in the sense that most people allegedly engage in incorrect reasoning most of the time, so that fallacious reasoning is the norm rather than exception. In other words, the psychology of reasoning is often taken to have provided nothing less than an experimental refutation of Aristotle's dictum that man is a rational animal.

Among psychologists there is a wide, though not universal,[27] consensus about this anti-rationalist interpretation. However, among philosophers, as might be expected, the matter is more controversial. Some have indeed welcomed and even strengthened such a conclusion,[28] but many have criticized it on a variety of methodological, epistemological, and even substantive grounds.

For example, Cohen[29] points out that, to arrive at the anti-rationalist conclusion, psychologists have to proceed in accordance with what he calls the "preconceived norm method," according to which they assume a priori the soundness of certain normative principles, then use them to evaluate the performance of experimental subjects, and then explain errors so defined in terms of either faulty programs or temporary malfunctions of the human reasoning apparatus. He contrasts this to what he calls the "norm extraction method," which assumes that subjects normally reason correctly, and then uses their normal performance to derive descriptive and normative principles of reasoning. Cohen then argues for the superiority of the norm extraction method both on general grounds, and on the grounds that the experimental evidence collected by psychologists themselves can be explained better in its terms.

There is little doubt that Cohen is on the right track, though it is equally obvious that the issue deserves greater discussion.[30] In the present context, however, it is sufficient to add the following twist to his criticism. That is, by using the preconceived norm method, psychologists are being insufficiently empirical since they are in effect assuming a priori the soundness and applicability of the principles of standard formal logic, of either the deductive or inductive variety. In other words, they are presupposing that the principles of formal logic are the normative laws of thought, as it were. And this brings us to another issue.

At a more specifically logical level, psychological experiments may be taken to have strengthened the traditional philosophical critique of

---

[27] Examples of exception may be found in Henle (1962; 1978; 1981); Falmagne 1975; and Revlin and Mayer 1978.

[28] Stich (1981; 1985); Stich and Nisbett 1980.

[29] L. J. Cohen 1982; see also L. J. Cohen (1979; 1980; 1981a).

[30] For some related issues, see Finocchiaro 1979b; 1980b, 256–72.

psychologism. I am referring to Frege's criticism of the thesis that the principles of (formal) logic are the (descriptive) laws of thought. The connection is somewhat indirect because what philosophers perceive as psychologism appears to psychologists as logicism. In fact, they are primarily interested in the laws of thought, and their experimental investigations of human thinking have led them to conclude that human beings do not in fact reason in accordance with the principles of (formal) logic; thus, they see themselves as having given an experimental refutation of the logicist thesis that the (descriptive) laws of thought are the principles of (formal) logic.[31]

From another point of view, this recent trend in the psychology of reasoning represents a reaction against the earlier arguments of Piaget and his followers. In fact their theory of formal operational thought is a classical example of the logicist thesis.[32] Nowadays, the evidence against this thesis seems overwhelming, and some time ago Piaget himself qualified his theory in such a way as to concede the essential point of his critics.[33]

Now, such a trend may please some of the philosophical followers of Frege since the anti-logicism of experimental psychologists thus corresponds to the anti-psychologism of formal logicians. However, this should be a source of concern for philosophers and logicians in general since such mutual reinforcement raises questions about the human relevance of formal logic, namely about its empirical relevance to human reasoning. Such relevance could be maintained on the normative and evaluative plane. However, if one questions the epistemological foundations of such normative logical principles, then an apriorist approach would be needed on this plane. Therefore, from the viewpoint of an empirical logic the difficulty mentioned earlier would reappear.

These considerations suggest that the psychology of reasoning may be fairly criticized for being insufficiently empirical in regard to the normative principles it uses in the evaluation of the reasoning of experimental subjects.

8. Explanation Difficulties

The just-mentioned difficulty may be called the problem of rationality, or the problem of the empirical basis of the normative principles used by psychologists to evaluate the reasoning of experimental subjects. Although

[31] Johnson-Laird 1983a, 23–40; 1983b.
[32] Inhelder and Piaget 1958; Beth and Piaget 1966; Piaget 1972b.
[33] Piaget 1972a; for a summary of many of the criticisms, see Evans 1983c, 218–23.

it is perhaps the problem that has received the greatest attention, it is not the only one. There is another cluster of difficulties which have been raised mostly by psychologists themselves, and which from a philosophical viewpoint may perhaps be conceptualized as involving the *explanation* of the observed performance of the experimental subjects.

Occasionally some psychologists have criticized their fellow experimenters for the widespread tendency to neglect the investigation of *why* subjects give the answers they do when performing the experimental task. For example, in a wide-ranging critique of the field, A. Newell once expressed the point by saying that experimenters often fail to explore the method used by a subject to arrive at his answers.[34] And Mary Henle has expressed it by saying that experimenters tend to neglect "*how* people reason," that is, the process whereby subjects obtain the results they do.[35] The point is that experimenters concentrate on such things as describing *what* answers the subjects give, measuring the latency of responding, and computing error rates or success frequencies.

Of course, there are good reasons why experimenters tend to neglect the subjects' rationale. One is that the subjects' underlying reasons are relatively inaccessible, insofar as to determine them would require additional evidence, for example their answers to other appropriately related questions. Moreover, there is often an indeterminacy effect in operation here, such that the attempt to ascertain the subjects' underlying reasons has a tendency to disturb them and change their content and character.[36]

The collection and analysis of so-called protocols provide a good illustration of this inaccessibility and indeterminacy. Protocols are written records produced by the subjects to indicate what they are thinking at various stages of an experiment. Psychologists are aware of the great difference between concurrent and retrospective protocols; they are also aware of the difference between using them as additional data about the subjects and as explanations of their performance; and they are aware of the dangers of the latter type of usage.[37] For example, retrospective protocols, which ask subjects to state the reasons underlying their previous answers, often turn into exercises of rationalization, that is, into attempts to construct a reason that would justify the correctness of the answer previously given by a subject to the experimental task.[38]

[34] Newell 1973.
[35] Henle 1981, 339.
[36] This insight may be found in L. J. Cohen 1981a, 328.
[37] See, for example, Byrne 1983.
[38] Wason 1983, 54–60; Evans 1982, 170–73.

Finally, it must be admitted that psychologists usually do try to explain those features of the subjects' performance which they describe. Such explanations, however, often apply only to the phenomena they are intended to explain.[39] This is another way of saying that they are ad hoc. And in turn, such ad hocness is a type of empirical inadequacy insofar as the mechanism postulated to do the explaining lacks independent supporting evidence.

To summarize this cluster of problems, we may say that the experimental approach to the study of reasoning has the following limitations: (1) it encourages the description of easily detectable and measurable features of reasoning, to the detriment of more enlightening ones; (2) the attempt to obtain more enlightening data normally takes the form of having the subjects write protocols, which is problematic, but at any rate is a step in a direction away from the experimental approach and toward the historical-observational approach; and (3) explanations of experimental data are often ad hoc.[40]

9. Reasoning versus Nonreasoning

The two previous difficulties relate primarily to essential aspects of the evaluation and the explanation of subjects' performance. The next difficulty goes to the heart of the matter since it concerns the question

---

[39] This criticism can be found in Evans 1982, e.g., pp. 42, 98, 105, and 111–12.

[40] It should be repeated that here I am merely stressing and adding my own twist to criticism that has been advanced by psychologists themselves. For example, in a synoptic review of work dealing with sentence verification tasks, Evans concludes: "Some of the earlier studies of sentence verification were criticised for making inferences about comprehension in the absence of a theory of how the tasks are performed. On the other hand the models which specify the strategies in detail *do* seem to be rather artificial and task specific. My objection to the models arises from the fact that they are devised in too precise a manner, to predict data in far too limited situations ... constructed *post hoc* to fit a particular set of results, and thus the specific nature of their predictions is not over-impressive, even when applied to new variations within the same paradigm. What the authors of such models do *not* seem to do is to formulate a general theoretical framework, of which their model is a particular application, and assess its validity across a wide variety of experimental paradigms" (1982, 42). He expresses an analogous complaint about work dealing with syllogisms: "Reasoning errors are reliably and systematically related to the structure of the syllogisms used. *How* performance is related to the mood and figure of syllogisms is well established, and only disputed in matters of fine detail. *Why* these effects occur is much trickier to determine, however. Though reliable, the effects observed are complex in nature, and irritatingly specific to the paradigm used. No simple and general theoretical principles seem to have been discovered which can explain all the major findings" (Evans 1982, 111).

whether the phenomena studied by means of the experimental method are really phenomena of reasoning or of some other kind of mental activity. If there is no significant reasoning involved, then the experimental psychology of reasoning becomes largely irrelevant in the present context, however interesting it may be as a part of cognitive psychology or cognitive science in general.

Before reviewing directly some of the experimental data which cast doubt on the ratiocinative character of psychological experiments, it should be mentioned that some psychologists have shown awareness of the problem. And this has happened on both sides of the rationalism versus irrationalism divide, and on both sides of the debate of answer or result versus method or process. For example, Mary Henle has clearly argued that "presenting a logical problem does not guarantee ratiocination by subjects: they may guess, evaluate the material truth of propositions, apply learned rules, or whatever."[41] And Jonathan Evans is explicit that it should "not be assumed, a priori, that 'reasoning' is necessarily going on in reasoning experiments"[42]; thus, he realizes that "if the task requires access to memory of things which are not presented, then it is not simply a reasoning task,"[43] and that "since all realistic reasoning tasks permit the suggestion that subjects are generalizing learned responses, it can never be established that *reasoning*, in the philosophical sense, is occurring at all."[44] Because of this, he has argued that the so-called psychology of reasoning should become more integrated into general cognitive psychology than it has been. However, needless to say, these psychologists have not stressed these facts to question the methodological status of their discipline. On the other hand, as an outsider to the field, I feel free to do just that.[45]

The amount of experimental evidence suggesting this intrinsic limitation is impressive. Consider experiments with categorical syllogisms,

[41] Henle 1981, 339.
[42] Evans 1982, 5.
[43] Evans 1982, 5.
[44] Evans 1982, 227.
[45] It should be mentioned that there would be another way of interpreting this methodological limitation in a constructive, positive manner, besides Evans's plea for greater integration into cognitive psychology; it would be to formulate an appropriate conclusion about the nature of reasoning, something to the effect that reasoning is not really the type of mental activity we had thought it was. This seems to be the direction favored by Howard Margolis, who "gives an account of thinking and judgment in which – to lay cards immediately on the table – everything is reduced to pattern-recognition" (Margolis 1988, 1), if we in turn interpret this interpretation as meaning that reasoning is a form of perception.

where subjects are given a pair of categorical statements involving three terms, and then they are asked to do one of two things depending on the type of experiment: in one type they are asked to draw a conclusion that follows necessarily from the premises in the form of another categorical statement involving two of these same terms; in the other type they are asked to select the one necessary consequence out of several listed statements. All studies find extremely high error rates, although explanations differ.

One phenomenon, called the "atmosphere effect" relates to the so-called mood of a syllogism. Recall that the mood of a syllogism refers to which of the four types of categorical statement is instantiated by each of the three propositions in a syllogism, so that there are 64 ($4 \times 4 \times 4$) different possible moods. The atmosphere effect is the phenomenon that subjects have a tendency to choose conclusions of the same quality and quantity as the premises, that is conclusions that are either universal or particular, and either negative or affirmative like the premises. For example, they have a tendency to assess as valid not only the actually valid Barbara syllogism "all A are B, all C are A, therefore all C are B," but also the following invalid ones: (1) all A are B, all C are B, therefore all A are C; (2) all A are B, all A are C, therefore all B are C; and (3) all A are B, all C are A, therefore all B are C.[46]

Another phenomenon is called the figural bias or figural effect because it involves the figure of the syllogism. Recall that the figure of a syllogism is defined in terms of the position of the middle term: in the so-called first figure, the middle term is the subject of the major premise and predicate of the minor; in the second figure, it is the predicate of both premises; in the third figure, it is the subject of both premises; and in the fourth figure, it is the predicate of the major premise and the subject of the minor. Now, experimental subjects have a definite preference for the first figure and a definite dislike for the fourth, and they are relatively indifferent to the second and third. The structural details are such that what this means is that subjects have a bias toward drawing conclusions in a definite direction; this is the direction resulting from writing the two premises next to each other so as to have the two occurrences of

[46] For more details, see Evans 1982, 82–98. Of course, complications arise in the case of premises with mixed quality and quantity, and then the phenomenon may have to be redescribed accordingly, for example: "1 If the quantity of at least one premise is particular then the conclusion is particular, otherwise it is universal. 2 If the quality of at least one premise is negative then the conclusion is negative, otherwise it is affirmative" (Evans 1982, 83).

the middle term contiguous, then deleting it, and then formulating a conclusion whose subject and predicate are the remaining terms with the order unchanged. For example, subjects have a tendency to endorse the following invalid syllogism: all A are B, some B are C, therefore some A are C; whereas they are inclined to reject the following valid one: some A are B, all B are C, therefore some C are A.[47]

There is also experimental evidence for what is called a "belief-bias." This is a phenomenon that everyone can probably support with considerable anecdotal evidence, for it consists of the fact that subjects have a tendency to draw conclusions that accord with their prior beliefs about substantive empirical truth or falsehood, and to refrain from doing so when conclusions conflict with those beliefs. In syllogism experiments this tendency is relatively weak,[48] whereas in some studies of conditional reasoning the effect is highly significant.[49] At any rate, this phenomenon would provide the clearest indication that the subjects are not engaged in reasoning in these experiments.

Let us now consider some experimental discoveries involving conditional propositions. The basic types of relevant argument are the valid *modus ponens* and *modus tollens*, and the fallacies of affirming the consequent and denying the antecedent. However, psychologists must be credited[50] with something which an empirical logician ought to be very sensitive to. That is, for each of these four types, they distinguish four subtypes, depending on whether or not an explicit negation occurs in the antecedent or the consequent of the conditional premise; such refinement is a consequence of the realization that negations and negative propositions are psychologically tricky and difficult to handle.

Here one curious phenomenon is that, other things being equal, subjects have a greater tendency to draw a negative than an affirmative conclusion.[51]

Another is what Evans has called the "matching bias," which may be defined as the phenomenon that subjects have a tendency to give answers or solutions involving things mentioned in the statement of the question or problem, independently of or in spite of the logic of the situation; thus what is going on is a kind of matching exercise rather than reasoning.[52]

---

[47] For more details, see Evans 1982, 98–105.
[48] Evans 1982, 105–11.
[49] Evans 1982, 151–55, 180–87; Griggs 1983, 18–29; Wason 1983, 65–71.
[50] Especially noteworthy is the work of Evans 1972a; 1972b; 1982; 1983a; 1983b; 1983c.
[51] Evans 1982, 129–44.
[52] Evans 1982, 139–41; 1983b, 137–42.

The explanation of these facts is controversial. However, the possibilities seem to me to reduce to the following. One possibility is that subjects are reasoning in accordance with incorrect rules and principles, such as the illicit conversion of subject and predicate in connection with some of the syllogism experiments.[53] Another is that the thinking of the subjects is influenced by a number of nonrational or nonlogical factors.[54] Now, there is an interesting irony here. The former type of explanation is favored by scholars who regard themselves and have been regarded as rationalists; whereas the latter type has been favored by purported or self-styled anti-rationalists. My own inclination is toward the nonrational type of explanation, but with the explicit and emphatic proviso that nonrationality and irrationality ought not to be equated. Moreover, I would add that nonrational thinking is so prevalent in psychological experiments that the question must be raised as to whether they are testing reasoning at all. I would go further and argue that the logical relevance of cognitive experiments has been rendered suspect.

Up to a certain point I am, however, willing to concede that the whole effort has not been useless. Rather I am inclined to think that there would have been no way of knowing a priori that the experimental method of studying reasoning has severe limitations. Indeed the empirical logician has to be empirical not only in the specific study of reasoning but also in methodology. Therefore he ought to welcome the empirical exploration of the fruitfulness of various methods. However, the time is now ripe to try to learn from experience, and I believe that the recent history of the experimental psychology of reasoning contains a definite lesson: the lesson is that some other approach should be explored in the empirical study of reasoning.

10. The Observational-Historical Approach

One of these alternative approaches is what I call the historical approach, which, as I conceive it, is empirical in the sense of observational. The historical approach begins with the selection of some important book of the past, containing a suitably wide range and intense degree of reasoning. Many of the classics would fulfill this requirement, for example, Plato's *Republic*, Thomas Aquinas's *Summa Theologica*, Galileo Galilei's *Dialogue on the Two Chief World Systems*, David Hume's *Dialogues Concerning Natural*

---

[53] Cf. Evans 1982, 83–105.
[54] Cf. Evans 1982, 125, 155, 234–57.

Religion, Charles Darwin's *Origins of Species,* perhaps Karl Marx's *Capital.*[55] Not all classics would be appropriate; this is easy to see for works of poetry, fiction, and literature. Historical works such as those of Thucydides, Guicciardini, or Burckhardt do contain an occasional argument, but not sufficiently frequently. I do not think that philosophical classics would qualify either, if we are thinking of such works as Aristotle's *Metaphysics,* Descartes's *Meditations,* Kant's *Critique,* or Hegel's *Phenomenology.* The problem with them would not be an insufficient degree of reasoning, but an insufficiently wide range of topic. In other words, they would make good case studies in philosophical reasoning, whereas empirical logic is meant to deal with reasoning in general. Analogous remarks apply to mathematical classics such as Euclid's *Elements.* In some cases works other than the classics would serve the purpose, for example collections or selections of judicial opinions of bodies like the United States Supreme Court and the World Court in The Hague, or the proceedings of debates in the parliaments of various countries.[56]

At this point I could give a personal illustration of the historical-observational approach in terms of my work on *Galileo and the Art of Reasoning.* However, one version of such an illustration is now available in print.[57] Therefore, I feel it is better to bring this chapter to a conclusion.

11. Epilogue

In summary, I began with the suggestion that empirical logic may be defined as the empirical study of reasoning. I went on to explain this in terms of the formulation, testing, clarification, and systematization of concepts and principles for the interpretation, the evaluation, and the sound practice of reasoning. I then defended this conception from a number of methodological objections. One was whether there is really a unified subject matter called reasoning. Another involved the question of the practical utility of such an empirical logic. The objection which I discussed at greatest length involved its relationship with the psychology of reasoning. However, the examination of this last objection turned into a critique of this potentially competing field.

To summarize that critique, recent work in this field has been interpreted by some as an experimental demonstration that humans are

---

[55] Another good choice would be the one made by P. A. Smit, namely Lenin's *What Is to Be Done?*; see Smit (1987; 1989; 1992).

[56] This would be in line with Walton 1992.

[57] Finocchiaro 1987a.

irrational and that they reason illogically; however, it is better interpreted as showing the unempirical character of the normative principles of evaluation used by experimental psychologists. Another limitation of recent work is that psychologists tend not to explain the reasons for subjects' responses, and when they do their explanations are either ad hoc or suggestive of an historical rather than an experimental approach. A number of experimental phenomena were then described: the atmosphere effect and the figural bias in syllogism experiments; the preference for negative conclusions and the matching bias in experiments with conditional propositions; and the belief bias in all types of experiments. Such phenomena suggest that the subjects are engaged not in reasoning, but in some other type of mental activity. Therefore, experimentation has no role or a problematic one in the empirical study of reasoning.

However, none of this impugns the legitimacy of empirical logic, which remains viable as an historical-observational approach to the formulation, testing, clarification, and systematization of concepts and principles for the interpretation, the evaluation, and the sound practice of reasoning.[58]

---

[58] This chapter corresponds in large measure to the Fourth Evert Willem Beth Lecture which I delivered in 1987 at the University of Groningen and the University of Amsterdam. Parts of it have been previously published in Finocchiaro 1984b, and were presented at the Second International Symposium in Informal Logic (University of Windsor, Canada, 1983) and at the first session sponsored by the Association for Informal Logic and Critical Thinking (Boston, 1983). Other parts were presented at the International Congress on Communication and Cognition (University of Ghent, Belgium, 1987).

4

Two Empirical Approaches to the Study of Reasoning (1994)

1. Introduction[1]

In a number of papers I have advocated a type of empirical approach to the study of reasoning which may be called the historical-textual or informal-logic approach.[2] Here reasoning is conceived as a special type of thinking which consists of interrelating thoughts in such a way that some are dependent on and follow from others. To this abstract definition one may add something of an operational definition by saying that reasoning occurs paradigmatically in written or oral discourse which contains a high incidence of reasoning indicator terms such as therefore, thus, hence, consequently, since, because, and for. What this means is that, while all reasoning is thinking, not all thinking is reasoning, and hence the study of reasoning is only a part of the study of mental and cognitive activities. I am not uninterested, of course, in the relationships between

---

[1] This chapter was also published in German in Finocchiaro 1995c. An earlier version was presented at the Summer Institute on Argumentation, University of Amsterdam, Holland, 25–26 June 1990; I thank Frans Eemeren and Rob Grootendorst for the invitation and David Hitchcock for some valuable comments, which I hope to be able to take into account on some other occasion. Another version was presented at the Interdisciplinary Research Project on "Cognition and Context," Technical University of Berlin, Germany, 4 May 1992; I thank Professors Roland Posner and Bernd Maher for the invitation and encouragement. I also thank the referees of *Informal Logic* for valuable comments, and its editors for being willing to consider an article whose right of first publication belonged to *Zeitschrift für Semiotik*.

[2] See especially Finocchiaro 1984b; 1987a; 1987b; 1989b. This is also in the tradition of Barth (1985a; 1985b; 1987); Barth and Martens 1982; Barth and Krabbe 1992; Blair and Johnson 1980; Johnson 1987; Johnson and Blair 1985; Naess (1966; 1982a; 1982b); and Scriven 1987.

reasoning per se and thinking in general, but my own special focus is on the former.

In this context the empirical is contrasted primarily to the apriorist approach, in regard to which I would give the example that, if and to the extent that we regard formal logic as a theory of reasoning, it would be a type of apriorist approach. On the other hand, I do not mean to contrast the empirical to the normative, and in fact the aim of the historical-textual approach is the formulation of normative and evaluative principles besides descriptive, analytical, and explanatory ones. Another proviso is that the empirical approach ought not to be regarded as empiricist, namely as pretending that it can study reasoning with a *tabula rasa*. I would have no difficulty admitting that various kinds of concepts are presupposed in any empirical investigation, though of course I would insist that the presupposed concepts are not the same ones which are at issue in the given empirical investigation, or at least the form or version of the concept or principle in question is not the same as what is presupposed.

Next, it is useful to say a few words about the variety of empirical approaches. We may distinguish at least three types of empirical orientations. One is the experimental approach, which consists of bringing human subjects (on a paid or volunteer basis) into a laboratory; explaining to them the questions to be answered, or problems to be solved, or tasks to be performed; arranging for them to respond usually by a yes or no, or with a multiple-choice selection, or in some other highly structured fashion; recording such responses; analyzing such recorded data usually by statistical methods; and then drawing some more or less theoretical conclusion, either an inductive generalization extrapolated from the data or an explanatory hypothesis accounting for the data. What I have in mind here is the work of cognitive psychologists such as Johnson-Laird, Wason, Evans, Kahneman and Tversky, and Nisbett and Ross;[3] I do not include Piaget simply because I want to emphasize that, as just explained, I am dealing with approaches to the study of reasoning and not to the study of thinking in general, and my impression is that Piaget's work deals with the more general topic, however suggestive it may be for reasoning as well. Another approach is the one analytical philosophers use when, on the basis of imagined examples, they reach generalizations about concepts such as existence, knowledge, belief, explanation, intentionality, justice, and morality; here I am thinking of the work of philosophers like Quine, Hintikka, Hempel, Scriven, Searle, Rawls, and Harman; this approach has

---

[3] See their works listed in the bibliography.

been analyzed with great insight and originality by L. Jonathan Cohen[4] and characterized as being inductive reasoning in which normative generalizations are based on particular intuitions. The third orientation is the historical-textual approach, which could be equated with informal logic[5] and of which more presently. While sharing the general empirical orientation, I have criticized both the experimental-psychological approach and the inductive-intuitive approach for a number of reasons which cannot be repeated here but which include the argument that often both of these approaches exhibit inadequacies the overcoming of which requires moving in the direction of the historical-textual approach.[6]

With the background of these remarks, what I should like to do here is to focus on a subtype of the experimental-psychological approach which has been used with great skill and insight by David N. Perkins,[7] and which for reasons that will become apparent shortly I shall label the experimental-critical approach. What motivates me to discuss Perkins's work in detail is the surprising fact that some of his own substantive results are amazingly similar in content to conclusions I have reached through the study of very different material and following an historical-textual procedure rather than an experimental one. The similarity of these conclusions, and the fact that they have been arrived at independently of each other, will of course yield some mutual reinforcement, but it will also provide the occasion for exploring more deeply the methodological similarities between the two approaches. There are after all some obvious similarities between them, and perhaps they can be seen to be both special cases of some empirical approach yet to be characterized.

2. Examples of Reasoning Studied

Let us begin by describing what may be called the raw material that has been studied in the two cases. It will be immediately obvious that the subject matter of the reasoning studied could hardly have been more different. Perkins has studied arguments and reasoning which may be labeled everyday or informal, dealing with the following four issues which

---

[4] See L. J. Cohen 1986 and its references to the works of these and other analytical philosophers; cf. Finocchiaro 1991.

[5] See Blair and Johnson 1980; Johnson and Blair 1985; and Finocchiaro 1984b.

[6] See Finocchiaro 1991 for the details of the criticism (but also appreciation) of the inductive-intuitive approach, and Finocchiaro (1979b; 1980b, 256–72; 1989b) for the details about the experimental-psychological approach.

[7] See his works listed in the bibliography.

were relatively current in the United States at the time he conducted his experiment: whether or not a military draft in the United States would increase American influence in the world, whether or not the display of violence on television increases violence in real life, whether or not a deposit of five cents for bottles and cans of soft beverages like Coca Cola would reduce litter in streets and parks, and whether a stack of bricks created by a minimalist artist named Carl Andre is really art. As you can see, these are also polemical issues.

On the other hand, I have studied arguments and reasoning about the motion of the earth, its location in the universe, and the physical and chemical differences between the earth and the heavenly bodies; these are issues which were discussed at various phases of the Copernican Revolution, and which are recorded in Galileo Galilei's book entitled *Dialogue on the Two Chief World Systems, Ptolemaic and Copernican* (1632). In some obvious sense, therefore, these are scientific arguments, scientific in the sense of the history of science, and to be more exact prevalent during the formative period of modern science, if not in the sense of contemporary science.

2.1. The Arguments in the Experimental-Critical Study

It will be useful for our later analysis to give some examples. In regard to the five-cent deposit issue, the question was whether a law requiring a five-cent deposit on bottles and cans would reduce litter. The following argument conveys the idea of what we are dealing with:

The law wants people to return the bottles for the five cents, instead of littering them. But I don't think five cents is enough nowadays to get people to bother. But wait, it isn't just five cents at a blow, because people can accumulate cases of bottles or bags of cans in their basements and take them back all at once, so probably they would do that. Still, those probably aren't the bottles and cans that get littered anyway: it's the people out on picnics or kids hanging around the street and parks that litter bottles and cans, and they sure wouldn't bother to return them for a nickel. But someone else might – boy scout and girl scout troops and other community organizations very likely would collect the bottles and cans as a combined community service and fund-raising venture. I know they do that sort of thing. So litter would be reduced. [Perkins et al. 1983, 178][8]

Consider now the question, "Would restoring the military draft significantly increase America's ability to influence world events?" Here are some typical arguments:

---

[8] As Perkins himself clarifies, this is not an argument that was given by any one of the experimental subjects, but rather each step was given by many.

Yes, because a draft would give the U.S. more manpower in the army. The U.S. would have a bigger stick to wave and foreign nations would be impressed.

Yes, because more manpower would put the U.S. in a better position to fight limited tactical wars. Since everyone is scared of world-wide nuclear war, small-scale wars are more likely and a military well-manned and ready to intervene should provide more influence.

No, because a draft would trigger widespread protests, as it did during the Vietnam war. This internal dissension would be seen as lack of unity and a sign of weakness by foreign observers.

No, because nowadays it's computers, missiles, and the people who design and maintain them that really count. If the U.S. needs anything in the army, it's more smart technical people. But a random draft won't net very many such people. [Perkins 1985, 22]

2.2. *The Arguments in the Historical-Textual Study*

Let us now get a glimpse of the Copernican and anti-Copernican arguments, found in the text of Galileo's *Two Chief World Systems*. One is the so-called a posteriori argument for the earth-heaven dichotomy. It reads quite simply: no heavenly changes have ever been observed; therefore, the heavenly region is unchangeable (Galilei 1953, 46–48).

Galileo counters this argument in at least four ways. One is to point out that in his own time the premise is no longer true, in the light of, for example, the telescopic observations of sunspots and the naked-eye observation of novas. Here it is important to note that, though this criticism is in some obvious sense nonlogical, it is the one that takes Galileo the longest to articulate, since he has to argue every inch of the way through all sorts of controversial issues in order to refute the premise (Galilei 1953, 50–58).

Other Galilean criticisms are based on the contextual distinction of two meanings for the phrase "heavenly changes": a heavenly change can mean the generation or decay of a heavenly body as a whole, and it can mean a partial change within a heavenly body.

When interpreted holistically, the original argument amounts to the following: no one has ever observed any generation or decay of a heavenly body in the heavenly region; therefore, the heavenly region is unchangeable. It is then subject to the criticism that this way of reasoning would lead one to the following absurd argument: no one has ever observed any generation or decay of a terrestrial globe (i.e., the whole planet earth) in the terrestrial region; therefore, the terrestrial region is unchangeable (Galilei 1953, 49–51).

When the argument is interpreted the other way, Galileo objects that it is still wrong for the following reason: no terrestrial changes would be noticeable to an observer on the moon before some particular very large terrestrial change had occurred, and yet terrestrial bodies are obviously changeable and would have been so even before that occurrence (Galilei 1953, 49–50).

The fourth criticism Galileo makes is directed to the more plausible particularistic (second) version and amounts to the following argument: if there were changes in the heavenly bodies, then most of them could not be observed from the earth, since the distances from the heavenly bodies to the earth are very great, and on earth changes can be observed only when they are relatively close to the observer; moreover, even if there were changes in the heavenly bodies large enough to be observable from the earth, then they might not have been observed, since even large changes cannot be observed unless careful, systematic, exact, and continual observations are made, and no such observations have been made, at least not by the argument's proponents (Galilei 1953, 47–50).

The other Galilean example to be considered here mentions centrifugal force to show why the earth cannot rotate. It may be stated thus: if the earth were rotating, objects on its surface would be scattered away from it toward the heavens because rotation has the power of extruding objects lying on the surface of the rotating body; but objects on the earth's surface are not observed to be scattered toward the heavens; therefore the earth does not rotate (Galilei 1953, 187–88).

Galileo counters in at least two ways. He objects that what follows at most from the principle of centrifugal force is not the scattering of objects on a rotating earth but rather either that (a) if the earth had always been rotating then there would not be any objects on its surface now, or that (b) if the earth were to start now rotating then objects already on its surface would be scattered; but the other premise as stated connects with (b) rather than (a); so the final conclusion that follows from the argument as stated is that the earth did not just start to rotate (Galilei 1953, 188–90).

Continuing with the criticism, Galileo is well aware that one could reformulate the argument by restating the second premise to read: there obviously are now loose objects on the earth's surface; then it would connect with the first one of the consequences (a) of centrifugal force, to yield the conclusion derived by the argument's proponents.

Here we see the reason for the qualifying phrase "at most" in the previous criticism. For Galileo objects that a rotating earth would not really scatter its surface bodies toward the heavens, his argument being essentially a quantitative one: though it is true that the cause of scattering increases as the speed when the radius is constant, when speeds are equal the cause of scattering decreases as the radius increases, so that this cause increases directly with the speed and inversely with the radius; thus, perhaps this cause remains constant when the speed increases as much as the radius, namely when equal numbers of rotations are made in equal times; hence, the earth's rotation would cause as much scattering as a wheel which rotated once in twenty-four hours; that is why there would be no scattering on a rotating earth (Galilei 1953, 211–12, 217–18).

3. The Experimental-Critical Case Study

These arguments were meant to convey an idea of the very different subject matter of the reasoning studied respectively by Perkins and by myself. But of course the fact that the content of the reasoning is so very different does not preclude a theoretical similarity in its structure and its evaluation, in terms of descriptive and normative principles at some level of generality; nor does it preclude a methodological similarity in the procedures followed for investigating it. The extent of these theoretical and methodological similarities will be seen presently. Let us begin with Perkins's experiment.

3.1. The Experiment

Perkins examined 320 subjects, divided into eight groups of forty. They were mostly students, partly from high school, partly university undergraduates, and partly graduate students. They also included two groups of adult nonstudents, one with and one without university degrees.

His procedure was to have a one-hour interview with each subject, focusing on two issues. At the beginning of the hour, the experimenter selected one of the above issues and asked subjects to reflect on it with the aim of formulating and justifying a conclusion, or to give reasons for both sides if they could not decide in favor of one or the other conclusion. Then subjects were asked to articulate whichever reasoning they did on either side of the case. Another important step was that, even when subjects had justified a given conclusion, they would be asked by the experimenter to formulate two objections against it. This process was then repeated for a second issue. Each interview was tape-recorded for later analysis.

I believe that Perkins's central interest was the determination of the difficulties in everyday reasoning, as the title of one of his papers explicitly suggests. That is, he wanted to determine what are the shortcomings of everyday reasoning, whether for example it is beset by formal fallacies like affirming the consequent, inductive fallacies like hasty

generalization, or informal fallacies like *ad hominem* argument. One interesting and important aspect of Perkins's work is that, to use his own
language, he decided to "operationalize" this problem by determining "to
what sorts of objections are everyday arguments subject" (Perkins et al.
1983, 180). We might say that he decided to continue to follow an empirical approach in studying the evaluation of reasoning, in exploring how
arguments are actually criticized.

We have already seen that experimental subjects were one source of
these objections since each was asked to criticize his own conclusion in two
ways. However, the data base of objections was expanded much beyond
that as follows. One other source was the interviewer since "depending
on certain decision points in the interview, the experimenter often made
an objection, a standardized one, if applicable, or one conceived on the
spot" (Perkins et al. 1983, 180). A third source was two of the three
experimenters who listened to a large number of the taped interviews.
Altogether this procedure generated about 2,000 objections.

The analysis of these objections involved first devising a classification
system, which was done by the third experimenter who had not listened
systematically to the taped interviews. Then each objection was classified
by each of the experimenters, and those without concurrence by at least
two judges were discarded. Although the system had fifty-five categories,
90 percent of the objections fell into eighteen categories with at least
2 percent each, and a large majority (of much more than half) fell into
just nine categories, which will be explained shortly.

3.2. *Results*
The two most striking first-level conclusions are the following. The first
is that most objections (a simple majority of more than half) involve
categories that are nonlogical, in the traditional sense of either deductive
logic, inductive logic, or the logic of informal fallacies. In other words,
most difficulties with everyday reasoning are nonlogical. Of course, it
remains to be seen what their nature is, or whether the notion of logic
should be expanded to include them, given that we are dealing with
reasoning after all. Second, the most common flaw of everyday reasoning,
that is by far the single most frequent objection, was one which Perkins
calls "contrary consequent."

3.3. *Classification of Objections*
Let us, therefore, begin our review of the most common flaws of everyday reasoning found by Perkins with this category. Contrary consequent

is defined by him as the difficulty of "starting with the same situation . . . and reasoning to a 'contrary consequent,' or one inconsistent with the supposed consequent" (Perkins et al. 1983, 181). In other words, "while the subject argued from A to B, one could alternatively argue from A to not-B . . . by a different line of argument" (Perkins 1989, 180). An example may be drawn from the issue of the American military draft and world influence: "a subject might argue, 'A military draft would strengthen the army and hence impress foreign nations into complying with our policies.' A contrary consequent argument would be: 'But, on the other hand, a military draft might provoke widespread protest, displaying our disunity as a nation, and decreasing our influence on foreign nations'" (Perkins 1989, 180). It is obvious that Perkins is using the term 'consequent' to mean 'consequence' or 'conclusion,' and not to mean the second ('then') clause of a conditional proposition, which is the traditional logical meaning of the term 'consequent'; nevertheless, his meaning is clear, and I see no problems with this category.

A second common difficulty unearthed by Perkins involves a category he labels "contrary antecedent" and defines as follows: "saying the supposed consequent of the argument is not, or not necessarily, a consequent of the argument at all, but instead a consequent of something else" (Perkins et al. 1983, 182). The example he gives is the following: "subjects occasionally argue, 'People are watching more and more television and violence is on the upswing, so television violence increases real world violence.' To this, there is the objection, 'There are many other possible causes for increasing violence – for instance a lax judicial system'" (Perkins et al. 1983, 182).

Some comments are in order here. First, it is obvious that the original argument is an excellent candidate for the classical inductive fallacy of *post hoc ergo propter hoc,* and therefore we must be careful when claiming that the difficulties studied do not involve the classical fallacies, for what may be happening is simply to give a different label for the traditional things. However, rather than pursuing this line of criticism, I should like to make what is perhaps a more constructive suggestion, moving in the direction of reducing this category to the previous one, thus increasing the frequency of contrary consequent even further. The disagreement in this type of polemic involves two causal claims, the one alleged in the conclusion of the original argument, and the one alleged in the objection. That is, the objector is denying that television violence increases real-life violence, and proposing that perhaps the lax judicial system increases real-life violence; in the process, he is not denying the correlation stated in premise of the original argument, but simply suggesting a different line of argument using additional available evidence. We thus have a case of arguing from A to not-B, in response to an argument from A to B, and this was precisely the so-called contrary consequent category. In other words, "contrary antecedent" is the special case of "contrary consequent" when there is a special relationship between the conclusion derived in the original argument and the contrary one derived in the objection: the two conclusions are "contrary" in the sense that one claims that c causes e, the other claims that c' causes e, and c and c' are different. This reduction of the second category to the first would explain why Perkins mentions contrary antecedent only in his first, more preliminary article (1983), and not in his later more definite one (1989).

Be that as it may, let us go on to the next category, which he calls "external factor." In Perkins's words, this "holds that another intervening factor blocks or vitiates the inference, which is not denied as a general tendency, but denied in the case of concern, because of the external factor" (Perkins et al. 1983, 182). His example is that "people arguing the draft issue sometime say, 'We have a large population that would pull through in any military crisis.' Objection: 'A large population used to help, but today modern nuclear weapons can make short work even of a large population'" (Perkins et al. 1983, 182). In regard to this category, Perkins himself points out that it is a special case of contrary consequent, namely the special case where the "contrary consequent" presumably follows due to an external factor, rather than to something intrinsic to the situation mentioned in the premise of the target argument. This explanation suggests to me that we may take the categories of "external factor" and of "contrary antecedent" as special cases of "contrary consequent," namely cases where the contrary consequent is derived from additional considerations of special interest.

Another one of Perkins's categories is that of "neglected critical distinction." Such an objection amounts to charging the following: "That may be true in general, but in this situation you are not distinguishing between certain relevant subclasses. In fact, the critical subclass is one you've overlooked, and it turns out contrary to the generalization" (Perkins et al. 1983, 183). His example is taken from the five-cent deposit issue, in response to the idea that the deposit would motivate people to return the bottles and cans: "many people may do so. But you have to distinguish between people consuming beverages in their homes and people on picnics, or bumming around streets and parks. It's much less convenient for the latter to return the bottles, and they are the ones that do most of the littering anyway" (Perkins et al. 1983, 183). Again, we are dealing with a contrary consequent, in this case due to a so-called critical distinction.

A fifth common difficulty involves what Perkins calls "alternative argument." This is defined as "a certain kind of an objection to an objection. The new objection acknowledges the force of the original objection, but argues that the inference goes through on other grounds in any case" (Perkins et al. 1983, 183). For example, the original argument might claim that five cents will motivate people. An objection to this might be that five cents is not enough. And then one might object to this objection as follows: "Probably not by itself. But a bottle bill and the associated publicity will make people more environmentally conscious, so they will be more careful about litter" (Perkins et al. 1983, 183). It seems clear that this is a special case of contrary consequent when the target argument happens to be itself an objection.

These five categories account for at least 60 percent of Perkins's data base, and we may agree with him that they are relatively nonlogical, in the traditional sense of logic. We may also agree with him that these five categories have something in common, although the exact description and conceptualization of this common element is a more controversial matter. To give a flavor of his type of analysis, we may quote here his words to the effect that these five categories "all involve objections that introduce new causal chains or other major elements into the reasoner's model of the situation" (Perkins et al. 1983, 184), a point we shall discuss later. However, at a lower level of analysis, I believe my account above has already established that these five categories all reduce to the first one, in the sense that the last four are special cases of the first.

Let us now examine the four other categories discussed or mentioned by Perkins which are relatively more logical-sounding. They are labeled disconnection, scalar insufficiency, counterexample, and contradiction.[9] Disconnection, which accounts for a sizable 13 percent of the data, is defined as a difficulty in reasoning "where the reasons seem to have nothing to do, or not enough to do, with the conclusion" (Perkins et al. 1983, 182). This is simply what one might expect from the label, and corresponds to what others would call *non sequitur* or irrelevance.

Counterexample difficulties involved 11 percent of the objections, and the category is essentially what one might expect. Perkins adds, however,

---

[9] Contradiction, which accounts for 7 percent of the objections, was not mentioned in Perkins et al. 1983, but is introduced in Perkins 1989, 180.

that objections stemming from individual cases as well as subsets of cases were treated as involving counterexamples, but that both individuals or subsets had to have some empirical basis in order to be treated as such.

Scalar insufficiency, for which Perkins does not give a percentage, occurs when "there is an insufficient degree of a factor for the consequent to follow, or for it to follow to the expressed degree" (Perkins et al. 1983, 182–83). For example, in regard to the effectiveness of the five-cent deposit law, a common objection was that "five cents isn't enough for people to bother with" (Perkins et al. 1983, 183). Another example which could be subsumed under this category is Galileo's point that the centrifugal tendency on a rotating earth could not be sufficient to counteract the downward tendency due to weight. And in turn, this should be sufficient to suggest that scalar insufficiency is not necessarily a trivial affair.

The category of contradiction accounts for 7 percent of the cases and is defined as one might expect, namely as the charge that the target argument contains some kind of inconsistency (Perkins 1989, 180).

4. The Historical-Textual Case Study

Before proceeding with further analysis, it is best to present the data base and some of the conclusions of the historical-textual investigation[10] to which I wish to compare the experimental study just discussed.

4.1. The Data Base

The historical-textual approach begins with the selection of some important book of the past, containing a suitably wide range and intense degree of reasoning. Many of the classics would fulfill this requirement, for example, Plato's *Republic*, Thomas Aquinas's *Summa Theologica*, Galileo Galilei's *Dialogue on the Two Chief World System*, David Hume's *Dialogues Concerning Natural Religion*, Charles Darwin's *Origin of Species*, perhaps Karl Marx's *Capital*. Not all classics would be appropriate; this is easy to see for works of poetry, fiction, and literature. Historical works such as those of Thucydides, Guicciardini, or Burckhardt do contain an occasional argument, but not sufficiently frequently. I do not think that certain philosophical classics would qualify either, if we are thinking of such works as Aristotle's *Metaphysics*, Descartes's *Meditations*, Kant's *Critique*, or Hegel's

---

[10] This was originally reported in Finocchiaro 1980b, but see Finocchiaro (1987a; 1987c) for additional clarifications and elaborations.

Phenomenology. The problem with them would not be an insufficient degree of reasoning, but an insufficiently wide range of topics. In other words, they would make good case studies in philosophical reasoning, whereas our present concern is reasoning in general. Analogous remarks apply to mathematical classics such as Euclid's *Elements*. In some cases works other than the classics would serve the purpose, for example collections or selections of judicial opinions of bodies like the United States Supreme Court or the World Court in The Hague.

The book chosen was Galileo's *Dialogue on the Two Chief World Systems*, first published in 1632. This is the book that led, a year later, to the famous trial and condemnation for heresy by the Roman Inquisition, an episode which came to be described by some as "the greatest scandal in Christendom." From a scientific point of view this book represented Galileo's mature synthesis of the new astronomy revolutionized by Copernicus in 1543 and by his own telescopic discoveries, and of the new science of mechanics on which Galileo had been working for more than forty years. His *Dialogue* of 1632 should not be confused with his other famous book, the *Discourse on Two New Sciences*, which was published in 1638 and lays the foundations of mechanics and of engineering and avoids discussion of astronomical and cosmological topics.

In the present context, the important point is that Galileo's *Dialogue* is a 500-page work full of reasoning on all sorts of topics, ranging from astronomy, mathematics, and physics to philosophy, common sense, and everyday life. There are arguments and counterarguments about such things as the perfection of the universe; the natural motion of bodies; the similarities and the differences between the earth and the heavenly bodies; the role of Aristotle's authority; the causes of the tides; and the location (in the atmosphere or in the heavens) of the nova of 1572. Some of the arguments are about whether the earth's axial rotation is rendered impossible by the empirical evidence from vertical fall, from the experiment of dropping a rock from the top of the mast of a moving ship, from east-west gunshots, from north-south gunshots, from vertical gunshots, from point-blank gunshots, from the flight of birds, and from the extruding power of whirling. Other arguments are about whether the same idea can be refuted by the thought-experiment of dropping a ball from the moon to the earth, by the epistemological principles that all natural phenomena must be explicable and that the senses cannot deceive us, and by the metaphysical principles that each simple body must have one and only one natural motion, that similar substances must have similar motions, and that motion cannot last forever. Still other arguments are about whether the earth's orbital revolution around the sun conflicts with biblical passages and with available astronomical observations concerning the dimensions and distance of the stars, the elevation of the celestial pole and of the stars, the lack of stellar parallax, and the seasonal changes in the sun's apparent motions. Finally, there are arguments about whether the earth's motion is rendered probable by the principle of simplicity, whether it is confirmed by evidence from the relationship of orbital periods and sizes and from the heliocentrism of planetary motions, and whether it is the best explanation of retrograde planetary motion and of the apparent annual motion of sunspots.

By one count there are seventeen main arguments that Galileo gives in support of conclusions he favors, and twenty-nine critiques of arguments he opposes. And I am referring here to main arguments and main subdivisions of the book, and not to the various subarguments that are parts of these; counting the latter would yield a much greater number. Moreover, it is possible to show that all these forty-six main discussions can be integrated into a single argument, since the seventeen main positive conclusions are all parts of or steps toward the single cosmological thesis that the earth moves, while the twenty-nine critiques support negative conclusions that undermine the opposite thesis that the earth stands still at the center of the universe.

All this is still relatively preliminary, in the sense that it is the sort of fact that justifies the selection of such a work for an historical-textual case study in the theory of reasoning. In a sense this fact is immediately obvious even to a casual reader of the *Dialogue*, as long as he has the proper appreciation for reasoning. The articulation of the details of this fact is, of course, another story, and a long story at that; it is part of the spadework required as a precondition for a fruitful investigation.

The next step was to elaborate a relatively a priori element of my historical-textual approach, for as mentioned above, by empirical I do not mean empiricist. It was to find and articulate some principles for the systematic collection of the data. Four ideas were of paramount importance here. First, all data should consist of reconstructed arguments, that is, interpretations of arguments contained in the text, restated in natural language in such a way as to portray them as clearly and accurately as possible, by ignoring extraneous material and adding as many reasoning indicator terms as needed. Second, an argument should be reconstructed with the primary aim of exhibiting its propositional structure, that is, the inferential and ratiocinative interrelations among the various statements or propositions that are its constituent parts; in this context a proposition is taken as the basic unit of acceptance or rejection or as the basic carrier of truth or falsehood, and so the portrayal of propositional structure is an intermediate level of analysis, since it disregards the internal structure of propositions, or to be more exact, it leaves this finer structure to a secondary or subsequent stage of inquiry.[11] Third, the most useful method of describing the propositional structure of an argument turned out to be the technique of root or inverted-tree diagrams, coupled with a numbering system that assigns to each proposition a sequence of numbers which uniquely defines its place in the network: for example, "1-1" and "1-2" would be respectively the first and second premises supporting proposition "1," while "1-2-1" would be a proposition supporting "1-2" and "1-2-1-1" would support "1-2-1."[12] Fourth, the normative and evaluative aim of the project should be addressed by interpreting the book's critiques of arguments as arguments about arguments and reconstructing them in the manner just sketched. This step is in accordance with another point mentioned earlier to the effect that by empirical I do not mean "value-free."

When the text of Galileo's *Dialogue* is studied in accordance with these principles, the forty-six main arguments mentioned earlier generate several hundred reconstructed subarguments, each of which may to some extent be examined by itself. This constitutes a rich and varied data base which one may then analyze in an empirical fashion to determine which interesting conclusions it supports. These theoretical implications will be discussed presently, but first I should like to stress that this data base is intended to be neutral vis-à-vis these conclusions, and hence it is to be hoped that other researchers will subject it to their own analysis to test their own theories. In other words, the construction of such data bases, by using other appropriate classics, is a valuable element of the empirical study of reasoning, and I believe that the one I have constructed for the case of Galileo's *Dialogue* will be found to have value independently of the conclusions I shall be drawing from it.

[11] Here, I make the same distinction made by Freeman 1991 between the macrostructure and the microstructure of reasoning.

[12] The first work where I saw this technique explicitly discussed is Angell 1964 and I adapted it from him. Nowadays it is very common, though various authors add various twists to the basic idea; see, for example, Scriven (1976, 41–43) and Eemeren and Grootendorst (1992, 73–89). The essential idea was introduced much earlier by Naess in a book first published in Norwegian in 1941, and then translated into English (Naess 1966, especially pp. 106–15).

4.2. *Conclusions*

In the present context the most telling conclusions involve what I call
"evaluation methods," namely techniques used for determining whether
a particular instance of reasoning is correct or incorrect. I labeled the six
most frequently occurring ones as follows: method of alternative conclusion, active evaluation, *ad hominem* argument, method of counterexample, principle of charity, and explanation of error in reasoning. This list
is partly overlapping and partly open-ended, and the three most relevant
methods are alternative conclusion, active evaluation, and *ad hominem*
argument.

See
p. 42

The method of alternative conclusion tries to show that a conclusion
does not follow from the premises because some other different conclusion follows instead; here the alternative conclusion is meant to be
different in the sense that there is some conflict (thought not necessarily
a strict formal inconsistency) between it and the original one. This is not
to say that one criticizes an argument by simply giving a counterargument supporting a conclusion conflicting with the original one, for this
might be a species of irrelevant criticism (if the premises of the counterargument were completely new and had nothing in common with those
of the original argument). Nor is it to say that one shows simply that
the exactly same original premises imply a proposition conflicting with
the original conclusion, for this situation would represent only a special
case. Rather, one starts with the same original premises, but then adds
other contextually appropriate propositions (perhaps in the process sub-
tracting some from the original set), in order to arrive at a conflicting
conclusion in such a way as to utilize some of the original premises in the
new counterargument.

The other two methods are related. Active evaluation is the procedure of testing inferential relationships among propositions by becoming actively engaged in the reasoning being evaluated, that is by arguing
at the level of, and largely in terms of, the argument being evaluated
and checking whether what follows from its premises is the conclusion it
draws or some other proposition. *Ad hominem* argument is not meant in
the present-day sense of the informal fallacy of attempting to discredit an
argument by discrediting the character or motives of the person advancing the argument; rather it is meant in the seventeenth-century sense,
namely as reasoning where the arguer derives a conclusion not acceptable to an opponent from premises accepted by the opponent, but not
necessarily generally acceptable.[13]

---

[13] This is also John Locke's meaning; see Finocchiaro 1974a.

Here I have focused on these three, repeating the original terminology used in the original study, for several reasons. First, all three seem to relate in some obvious sense to Perkins's key category of contrary consequent.[14] Second, although I did not do a specific quantitative analysis, there is no question that these three methods were collectively the most frequent ones. Finally, all three seem to be variations on a common theme, in the sense that both active evaluation and *ad hominem* argument may be thought of as special cases of the method of alternative conclusion.

That is, *ad hominem* argument is the special case where the alternative conclusion is not acceptable to the proponent of the original argument and where the additional premises that yield it are acceptable to him; and active evaluation is the special case where the alternative conclusion is grounded on additional considerations that remain, at least relatively, within the spirit of the framework of the original argument. Using symbols, the explanation might be as follows. Suppose we have the target argument, C because R1 and R2. The alternative-conclusion criticism tries to show that starting with R1 and R2, what really follows is not-C rather than C, because of R3, R4, . . . , and Rn, where the additional propositions R had been overlooked by the original argument. In the general case the additional propositions are simply propositions which are justifiable in the context, whether or not they were known to the original arguer; therefore, the full critical counterargument would have to contain a justification of these additional propositions. What makes such criticism particularly effective is the fact that the critic begins by agreeing with the initial premises of the original argument, but then goes on to point out things the consideration of which leads into a different direction. When the additional propositions are accepted by the original arguer, but are not generally acceptable, we have the case of an *ad hominem* argument in the seventeenth-century sense. When the additional propositions are either relatively uncontroversial, or relatively immediate consequences of the original premises R1 and R2, then we have the case of active evaluation; however, the notion of active evaluation also calls attention to the fact that the criticism is a counterargument, and so in this kind of criticism one becomes actively engaged in reasoning.

---

[14] To be more exact, his classification categories correspond more directly and formally to what I call evaluation categories, but these are in turn related to the methods in the way indicated above, namely that the methods are the techniques to be used to generate evaluations in terms of various specific categories. Moreover, as sketched below, a later stage of theoretical analysis reveals more interconnections among them.

4.3. Galilean Illustrations

For some illustrations, consider the following anti-Copernican argument,[15] called the contrariety argument in favor of the earth-heaven dichotomy: (12) bodies do not change unless there is contrariety; (11) there is no contrariety among heavenly bodies; therefore, (1) heavenly bodies are unchangeable. (The "contrariety" mentioned in this Aristotelian argument refers to such relationships as hot versus cold, light versus heavy, and dry versus wet.)

One of Galileo's objections to this is that the anti-Copernicans should not stop here but go on as follows: (21) bodies which have contraries are changeable, since (211) bodies do not change unless there is contrariety; but (22) heavenly bodies have contraries, since (221) heavenly bodies are unchangeable, (222) terrestrial bodies are changeable, and (223) changeability and unchangeability are contraries; therefore (2) heavenly bodies are changeable. This is an *ad hominem* criticism of the original argument, *ad hominem* in the precise sense defined here; and it is also a case of active evaluation because the criticism is adding very little beyond what the original argument asserted.

Another Galilean objection is the following. (3) It is questionable whether contrariety is absent even within the heavenly region since (31) Aristotle would regard heavenly bodies as the denser parts of the heavens, (32) if heavenly bodies are regarded as the denser parts of the heavens then differences of rarity and density exist in the heavens, and (33) if differences of rarity and density exist in the heavens then a change-producing contrariety exists in the heavens; this is so because (3311) differences of rarity and density give rise to the light/heavy contrariety in the terrestrial region, (3312) this contrariety gives rise to the upward and downward spontaneous motions, and (3313) these motions are allegedly the source of terrestrial changes, and hence (331) differences of rarity and density may be regarded as the cause of terrestrial changes; moreover, (3321) the cause of terrestrial as well as celestial differences of rarity and density is the quantitative difference of more or less matter in a given space, (3322) the cause of terrestrial differences of rarity and density is not the qualitative difference of heat and cold (since [33221] the density of solid substances changes little when their degree of heat changes significantly), and hence (332) the cause of terrestrial differences of rarity

---

[15] For this argument and the ensuing objections to it, see Galilei (1953, 38–47) and Finocchiaro (1980b, 357–72). Note that the propositions are here numbered in accordance with the principles stated earlier.

and density is the same as the cause of celestial differences of rarity and density.

The *ad hominem* element here is the fact that the anti-Copernicans are obliged to admit the presence of contrariety in the heavens (conclusion unacceptable to them), and the fact that they themselves would have to say that heavenly bodies are the denser parts of the heavens (premise accepted by them but not necessarily acceptable). The argument also has an element of active evaluation in the sense that it requires some immersion in the Aristotelian framework to justify the point made in the objection that celestial differences of rarity and density are a change-producing contrariety (proposition 33). And the objection also has an element of general alternative conclusion in the sense that it justifies a number of needed propositions as part of the counterargument.

Referring to the a posteriori justification of the earth-heaven dichotomy, mentioned earlier, we have an example of active evaluation in Galileo's third critical point; it amounts to saying that if otherwise correct, the conclusion to draw would be that the heavenly bodies are unchanged so far (and not that they are unchangeable). His fourth objection to the same argument provides an example of alternative conclusion, since it amounts to saying that what follows is that perhaps the heavens have not been observed carefully and systematically enough (rather than that the observed lack of changes corresponds to reality).

A final example is provided by Galileo's first criticism of the centrifugal force argument, also mentioned earlier; the criticism amounts to saying that the argument as stated only implies that the earth has not just changed its state from rest to rotation (rather than that the earth is not and has never been in a state of rotation).

5. Comparative Analysis of the Two Case Studies

What are we to make of this convergence? Let us begin by trying to characterize it more precisely, and then we can examine its implications. Three points should be noted about the convergence, namely that it is partly substantive and partly methodological, and that it is not total insofar as the above-mentioned common conclusions are embedded in different theoretical frameworks.

5.1. Substantive Similarities
In saying that the convergence is partly substantive I mean that both Perkins's experimental-critical study and my historical-textual one have

arrived at generalizations which make very similar claims. Let us analyze this similarity. One way of stating Perkins's conclusion is that the most common flaw of everyday reasoning is the failure to consider contrary lines of reasoning, that is lines that would arrive at contrary conclusions. And one way of stating the conclusion of my historical-textual study is to say that the most effective way of criticizing reasoning is to apply the method of alternative conclusion, that is to justify a conclusion conflicting with the one under consideration largely on the basis of the same premises. Aside from the question of the proper domain, the two statements are two aspects of the same point. The first stresses a property belonging to reasoning, but the property is a negatively evaluated trait, and so there is a corresponding method of establishing such a trait, which is what the second statement focuses on. We may also say that the first is an evaluative claim about the phenomenon of reasoning, the second is a normative principle about what to do in order to detect the phenomenon or when faced with the phenomenon. Or again, the first is an evaluative judgment upon the situation, the second is a normative principle about what one ought to do. However, there is a correspondence between the two.

By the question of the proper domain I mean the issue of exactly which phenomenon these conclusions deal with. Perkins speaks of everyday or informal reasoning, and contrasts it to formal reasoning best exemplified in mathematics. In my investigation I have dealt with a classic scientific controversy, but I would hesitate to speak of scientific reasoning without qualification because my aim was to focus on some universal and fundamental aspects of the scientific reasoning in question. Here one could speak of revolutionary scientific reasoning, in the sense of Thomas Kuhn's (1962) distinction between normal and revolutionary science, but I am not sure I would want to convey all the connotations that such phraseology would give. A common property of both Perkins's everyday reasoning and the scientific reasoning I have studied is controversy, and so one could speak of controversial reasoning and say that both conclusions apply to controversial reasoning, namely reasoning in controversial situations. One problem with such a focus is that the common result then seems much less striking, for the result reached is really part of the nature of controversy and so was to be expected. Perhaps it would be best to take the domain to be that of informal reasoning, as Perkins himself suggests; but then we must not equate it with everyday reasoning and instead allow it to include scientific reasoning.

5.2. *Methodological Similarities*

In regard to the respective approaches, aside from the empirical orientation, it might appear at first look that doing psychological experiments with human subjects and reading texts in published books are as far apart as any two procedures could be. However, if we scratch under the surface, we begin to see the similarities. To begin with, the experiments were primarily the means to get the subjects to engage in reasoning, and the most immediate product was audiotapes whose content was then studied and analyzed. Thus, it seems to me that the heart of Perkins's data too was texts, though delivered orally and recorded in tapes. More importantly, unlike the traditional experiments in cognitive psychology, Perkins's experiment was designed to produce not merely yes or no answers, or multiple choice decisions, but rather reasons for the answers; in fact, the actual answers were relatively unimportant since the subjects were instructed to explain the reasons on both sides in case they could not decide in favor of one, and in any case they were also asked to formulate objections to two aspects of their own arguments. Moreover, they were given some time to reflect on the issue before explaining their reasoning. Finally, the collection of objections originates in part from two of the three experimenters who listened to a large sample of the tapes. We thus have elements of reflection, ratiocination, and critical discussion of the type that are the heart and soul of scientific and other scholarly research and are then written up in books and articles. Of course, even such experimental data are still a long way from the complexity, richness, and polish of a published scholarly or scientific book, but the difference is merely one of degree, whereas my impression is that the contrast to the data of the usual experiments of cognitive psychology is one of kind. Therefore, besides noting the similarity between the experimental-critical approach practiced by Perkins and what I have called the historical-textual approach, I would also argue that Perkins's approach is much more valid that the usual experiments and provides the only effective experimental means of getting in touch and coming to grips with the phenomenon of reasoning.[16]

In short, the experimental approach of the type practiced by Perkins and the historical-textual approach I have practiced are indeed two variants of the empirical orientation, but what they have in common is much more significant than what distinguishes them. Here, I am making

---

[16] See especially Finocchiaro 1979b; 1989b.

a purely methodological point, for in regard to theoretical framework the situation is different and certainly not so simple. To this we now turn.

5.3. *Theoretical Frameworks and Differences*

By theoretical framework I mean the network of conclusions, ideas, concepts, and principles which Perkins derives from his experiment, but also from other sources, and in the context of which he holds the substantive conclusion mentioned earlier (that the key difficulty in everyday reasoning relates to contrary consequent and its cognates).

Let me begin by saying that I do not disagree with Perkins that even this conclusion is strictly speaking a theoretical claim because each of his classification categories is in a sense a theoretical construct. Nevertheless, I would add that this conclusion, and its mirror image in my account, is relatively low-level and relatively close to the data, and so the theoretical leap is rather small.

After this Perkins goes on to argue that most objections "extend the reasoner's current model of the situation" (Perkins et al. 1983, 183) and that the essential difficulties are under-exploration and bias in "situation modeling" (Perkins 1989, 178–79), a notion he adapts from Johnson-Laird (1983a); and in line with this type of consideration, he advocates a "critical epistemology" as a solution, and then does another experiment suggesting that an intrusive, maieutic, Socratic technique can effectively teach this epistemology and can lead to significant improvement in reasoning (Perkins 1989, 185–88). He also argues that, on the other hand, the impact of conventional education on informal reasoning is negligible (Perkins 1989, 181–83); and that the imagination has an essential role to play in reasoning, informal and everyday, as well as mathematical (Perkins 1985). Another important conclusion he elaborates is that almost all objections involve context-specific considerations (Perkins et al. 1983, 179, 184), and that, as mentioned earlier, most do not involve traditional logical considerations. And in regard to the nature of informal reasoning and its differences from formal, Perkins argues that whereas in informal reasoning premises are not fixed, they are in formal reasoning; that whereas in informal reasoning inferential links are not perfectly reliable, in formal reasoning they are meant to be; that whereas informal reasoning involves many lines of argument, formal reasoning is one-lined;[17] that, whereas

---

[17] E. M. Barth has objected that this is questionable even for axiomatic deduction, given that the latter can be shown to be algorithmically equivalent to both Beth's semantic-tableau method and the dialogical method, and given that the dialogical method involves *lines*

in informal reasoning each line of argument addresses both sides of the issue, formal reasoning is one-sided;[18] and that, whereas in informal reasoning each line of argument is short, formal reasoning consists of long linked chains of argument (Perkins et al. 1983, 177–79; Perkins [1985, 20–21; 1989, 176–78]).

Much of this is interesting, insightful, and acceptable. Moreover, some of these conclusions are similar to ones I have drawn, as is the case, for example, in regard to the importance of context in reasoning and in its evaluation.[19] However, most of these conclusions are not the ones I have drawn from my data. In this context, I can focus on only one possible dissimilarity, disagreement, or divergence. It regards the question of whether or not, or the sense in which, the major difficulties of informal reasoning are logical.

Part of this issue may be a verbal disagreement; that is, the issue hinges in part on what we mean by logic. As mentioned earlier, there is no doubt that both his data and mine show that the faults of informal reasoning are not primarily the fallacies of traditional deductive or inductive logic, or of the traditional logic of informal fallacies. On the other hand, if we take logic to be the theory of reasoning, a conception which can be argued to go back to the father of the science of logic, Aristotle (Johnson 1987), then any theoretically significant phenomenon in this domain would to that extent be of logical interest. Therefore, it may be preferable to approach this issue from another angle.

In my discussion above, for the sake of incisiveness and in order to stress an important substantive similarity, I said nothing about a cluster of concepts suggested by my investigation which are in one sense more closely analogous to Perkins's categories for classifying objections. I call them evaluation categories, and they enable me to classify criticisms of arguments. The cluster is not meant to be exhaustive, and the items

---

of attack and *lines* of defense and thus interprets a formal proof as an interplay between lines of attack and lines of defense (Barth and Krabbe 1982). I agree that one should not accept uncritically the claim that formal reasoning is "one-lined," and that in the light of Barth and Krabbe's work such a claim may well be untenable. To resolve this difficulty, I would want to clarify the notion of a "line of argument"; one question would be whether Barth and Krabbe's concept is the same as the one intended by Perkins in this claim; another question would be the relationship between the notion of a "line of argument" and that of the "side" of an issue, mentioned in the next claim. This problem is both interesting and important, but I cannot resolve it here.

[18] Once again, note that there is a question about the exact meaning of "one-sided," especially in relation to the notion of "one-lined" mentioned in the previous claim.

[19] See, for example, Finocchiaro 1980b, 145–66, 305; 1984b; 1987a; 1987c.

are not meant to be mutually exclusive. In alphabetical order, they are the following: circularity, equivocation, fallacy of composition, ground-lessness, incompleteness, infinite progression, invalidity, irrelevant con-clusion, question-begging, self-contradiction, and uselessness. Especially revealing for some additional similarities with Perkins's work would be the categories of groundlessness, incompleteness, irrelevant conclusion, and uselessness. But that is not what I wish to elaborate here.

Rather the point to reflect on is that the single most frequent category is invalidity, which is reminiscent of Perkins's notion of disconnection. I do not mean invalidity simply in the sense of deductive formal logic, but rather as something of a generalization of it. That is, I wanted a label to refer to a flaw in reasoning which involves the failure to connect properly premises and conclusion, namely a flaw in the inferential link between premises and conclusion. I believe this sense of invalidity to correspond more or less to the ordinary language meaning of the word "invalid" when applied to arguments, but that is another story. It should be stressed that, although such a notion of invalidity overlaps with formal invalidity insofar as it refers to challenges to the premise/conclusion connection which may very well involve bringing in other premises, it still retains the contrast with direct challenges to the simple truth of the explicit premises of an argument.

Now, taking the hint from this empirical fact about the pervasiveness of invalidity in my data, I began a later stage of analysis[20] with this gen-eral notion. That is, I began by defining invalidity as the failure of one proposition to follow from others, so that an inferential step is invalid if and only if the conclusion does not follow from the premises.[21] This is understood in a general sense such that formal deductive invalidity is the special case when this failure comes about for the reason that a counterexample argument exists, namely another argument of the same form with clearly true premises and clearly false conclusion.

The inductive incorrectness of inductive arguments turns out to be in large measure the special case of invalidity when the reason why the conclusion does not follow from the premises is that it does not follow

---

[20] One may usefully distinguish the stages of data collection (or construction of the data base, if you will), concept formation, generalization, and theorizing or theory articulation; cf. Finocchiaro (1980b, 424–31; 1987a; 1987c).

[21] David Hitchcock has suggested that this should be modified to read "if and only if the conclusion is not justified by the premises," an interesting suggestion I have been unable to incorporate in this chapter; in any case, some of his own work is relevant and important, especially Hitchcock (1987; 1989; 1994).

any more likely than some other specifiable proposition. In other words, in such a situation the critic produces another argument which has (or at least includes) the same premises as the original argument but a different conclusion, and which appears to be of equal strength as the original. This occurs primarily with explanatory (or causal) arguments whose conclusion is an explanation of what is stated in the premises, and the criticism amounts to providing an alternative explanation (or cause).

There are four other special cases of invalidity, due again to special situations, involving difficulties either with the logic of some of the informal fallacies, or with rhetorical matters, or with the justification of premises, or with the justification of presuppositions. However, there is no space here even to summarize them. Instead, let me say that it also turns out (or so I argue) that all other ten of my evaluation categories can be interpreted in terms of invalidity, in one or another of its six special cases. Moreover, what I call the evaluation methods, the three discussed above and three others I have not discussed here, also can be connected to this notion of invalidity.[22]

As mentioned earlier, all this involves a later stage of analysis when an attempt is made to interpret the lower-level concepts and generalizations in a theoretically more interesting way. Such theorizing is not meant to undermine or undo the empirical reality of the phenomenon revealed earlier simply in terms of the methods of alternative conclusion, active evaluation, and *ad hominem* argument. However, this does suggest that the similarity with Perkins's work may be rather limited, because it does not extend to the theoretical framework in which the lower-level common generalization is embedded. And this possible theoretical divergence, in the presence of an undeniable substantive similarity, was the main thing I wanted to explain in this context.

One final comment is in order to bring us back to the issue of whether or not the difficulties of informal reasoning are "logical." Whether my theoretical framework built on invalidity is acceptable or not, I believe it could not be denied that it deals with the logic of reasoning because it deals with matters involving the *relationships* of propositions with each other, as contrasted to issues of the relationship between propositions and the world, for example. So, while it is worth repeating that we are not dealing with traditional logic, I would want to claim that there is

---

[22] I do not wish to give the impression that there is a one-to-one correspondence between the six cases of invalidity and the six evaluation methods; the occurrence of the number six in both clusters is fortuitous.

a way of interpreting the difficulties of informal reasoning as "logical" errors. One other point that should not be forgotten is that these are not "logical" errors in the sense that they are invented or conceived a priori, for the empirical credentials of this type of investigation should by now be beyond dispute.[23]

This comparison of Perkins's experimental-critical approach and of my historical-textual approach has revealed that there are important theoretical differences underlying the common substantive conclusion, as well as significant methodological similarities underlying the prima facie different approaches. It would be arbitrary to say whether the methodological similarities are more important than the methodological differences, as it would be to say whether the substantive-theoretical differences are more important than the substantive-theoretical similarities. Nevertheless, by contrast to the traditional experimental-psychological and to philosophers' inductive-intuitive approaches, not to mention the apriorist approach, the substantive and methodological commonalities between the two approaches discussed here give them a research potential which is far from negligible.

6. Recapitulation

In conclusion, reasoning may be defined abstractly as the interrelating of thoughts in such a way that some follow from others, and operationally in terms of linguistic expressions with a high incidence of words like therefore, because, and consequently. The empirical approach is to be contrasted with an apriorist and an empiricist orientation, but not with a normative aim, and so the empirical approach advocated here aims to study mental processes which exist independent of the investigator. There are at least four varieties of the empirical approach, namely the traditional experimental method of cognitive psychologists, the intuitive-inductive method of analytical philosophers, the experimental-critical approach pioneered by David N. Perkins, and the historical-textual approach attempted by the present author. Perkins has studied primarily everyday informal reasoning involving such issues as the advisability of a small deposit on the purchase of bottled and canned beverages in an attempt to reduce litter and whether compulsory military service in the United States would increase American world influence. The present author has

---

[23] We are dealing with "empirical logic," as it were; cf. Barth (1985a; 1985b; 1987); Barth and Martens 1982; Barth and Krabbe 1992; and Naess (1982a; 1982b).

studied primarily informal but scientific reasoning, as it occurred during the Copernican Revolution, and as recorded in Galileo's book *Two Chief World Systems*.

Perkins's experiment interviewed 320 subjects and produced a collection of 2,000 objections, 90 percent of which could be classified into nine categories. Of these, the most common one was that of contrary consequent, which then together with four other related categories accounted for a large majority of the data. These categories are nonlogical in the traditional sense, and so it seems to be a well-established conclusion that most difficulties with everyday informal reasoning involve a failure to appreciate contrary arguments.

The historical-textual study by the present author was a critical examination of Galileo's *Two Chief World Systems*, which created a data base consisting of hundreds of reconstructed arguments about natural phenomena as well as critical of other arguments. Here the inescapable conclusion is that the most effective way of criticizing reasoning is to use what I call the method of alternative conclusion, and its variants active evaluation and *ad hominem* argument in the seventeenth-century sense of this term.

The substantive similarity between the two respective conclusions is striking, and provides additional mutual reinforcement. This coincidence also strengthens the viability and effectiveness of the two respective methods, the experimental-critical approach and the historical-textual approach, and it also points to the large overlap between these two methods. However, neither these methods nor the respective results are identical, and in fact the respective theoretical frameworks, while containing other similarities, contain also important differences. One of the most important of these theoretical differences is the issue of the nature of the concept "logic," and in what sense and to what extent the flaws of informal reasoning are logical. The chapter ended with an elaboration of this difference.

5

Critical Thinking, Critical Reasoning, and Methodological Reflection (1996)

1. Argument Analysis

I want to begin this chapter with a relatively uncontroversial assumption. That is, I regard it as unproblematic that one type of critical thinking is the reasoned interpretation or evaluation of an argument.[1] Note, however, that this really involves two special cases of critical thinking, the reasoned interpretation of arguments and the reasoned evaluation of arguments; for I distinguish interpretation and evaluation along obvious lines that I could elaborate but shall not, for lack of space; on the other hand, if we want a single handy label to refer to one or the other or both, we may speak of the critical interpretation of arguments, or argument analysis. Similarly, note that I speak of the reasoned interpretation or evaluation and not of mere interpretation or evaluation; that is, in these two special cases of critical thinking we must have not only an interpretive or evaluative claim about an argument, but also a justification of the claim by means of reasons. In other words, this first, presumably uncontroversial type of critical thinking is the case of what may be called reasoning about reasoning, or argumentation about argumentation.[2]

2. Informal Logic

This first, prototypical case of critical thinking needs now to be limited in one direction, and broadened in two others. The limitation involves the

[1] For example, this is certainly *part* of Scriven's definition, of which mine may be regarded as a variant; see Fisher and Scriven 1997.

[2] In this chapter I treat reasoning and argumentation somewhat interchangeably, though they could be distinguished, and for many purposes they should.

problem of the relationship between critical thinking and informal logic. For the latter too aims at the interpretation and evaluation of arguments. What then is the difference? I believe the difference is one of generality, systematicity, and conceptual explicitness. If we take the latter to be elements of the mental activity called theorizing, then I can express my point by saying that informal logic is the theory of argument or reasoning. It is obvious, however, that this theory is not value-free or purely interpretive, but also normative; thus we may think of informal logic as the normative theory of argument, as long as we do not go to the other extreme and act as if its normative character deprives it of any descriptive or empirical content, and of an explanatory or interpretive aim. This point can be made more explicit by defining informal logic as the formulation, testing, systematization, and application of concepts and principles for the interpretation, evaluation, and practice of argument or reasoning.[3] This definition also makes more vivid the problem of distinguishing critical thinking in the prototypical sense from informal logic.

I have already said that the difference lies along the dimensions of generality, systematicity, and conceptual explicitness. In regard to generality, if one is engaged in the critical interpretation of a particular argument and reaching a conclusion merely about that argument, then one is engaged in critical thinking; whereas if one is engaged in the critical interpretation of a whole class of arguments or reaching a conclusion about arguments in general, then one is doing informal logic. However, this dimension of generality makes it clear that the difference is a quantitative one of degree rather than a qualitative one of kind.

In regard to systematicity, what readily comes to mind is the Euclidean type of axiomatization. However, just as readily, I would want to add that it is both unrealistic and anachronistic to expect such systematicity in informal logic. But then the challenge becomes that of articulating a different kind of systematicity.

This problem may be expressed differently. Once one has formulated some principles of interpretation or evaluation, one may want to explore the logical relationships among them, logical in the sense of standard formal logic. Certainly the informal logician will want to do some of that. But is that the only kind of systematization one can undertake? If so, we would have the ironical situation that if the informal logician wants to

---

[3] See Finocchiaro 1984b; but this conception largely overlaps with that of Blair and Johnson 1980 and Johnson and Blair 1985.

claim to do something above and beyond the critical thinker, he has to engage in formal logic; if not, the question is what is this other kind of systematization.

At any rate, in regard to the difference between critical thinking and informal logic from the point of view of systematicity, it would seem that on the one hand systematicity is a matter of degree, but that on the other hand if a critical interpretation of an argument becomes systematic to any extent, then one is taking a qualitative step (however small) away from critical thinking as such and toward informal logic.

Conceptual explicitness was the third distinguishing characteristic. It too is a matter of degree. Even the critical thinker can hardly avoid using such terms as argument, premise, conclusion, serial structure, intermediate propositions, linked versus independent reasons, interpretation, evaluation, criticism, objection, counterargument, fallaciousness, and so on. However, in the critical interpretation of a particular argument, many of the subtler ones of these concepts may be only implicit. On the other hand, I take it that part of the business of informal logic is to render more explicit concepts that are implicit in the practice of critical thinking.

There are probably other distinguishing characteristics, besides generality, systematicity, and conceptual explicitness; and even these three require more clarification and analysis than I have provided. Nevertheless, given the aforementioned relatively uncontroversial definitions of critical thinking (in its prototypical sense) and of informal logic, we may say that while they are both meta-argumentative activities concerned with the critical interpretation of arguments, what distinguishes them is that informal logic has a higher degree of generality, systematicity, and conceptual explicitness.

In terms of a slogan, we might say that informal logic is generalized or systematized critical thinking, and critical thinking is applied informal logic. However, to repeat, this refers to the prototypical case of critical thinking. It is now time to expand the concept of critical thinking.

3. Self-reflective Argumentation

The first expansion is in the direction of what I shall call self-reflective argumentation. So far, the prototypical case of critical thinking involves the critical interpretation of already constructed arguments advanced by others. However, sometimes it is proper and advisable to engage in some interpretation and/or evaluation of an argument that one is constructing and advancing. If we subsume self-interpretation and self-evaluation under the notion of self-reflection, then we may say that at such times one is engaged in the self-reflective formulation or construction of one's own argument.

In other words, the prototypical case of critical thinking occurs when the subject matter of our argument is itself an argument. However, the subject matter of most arguments is not arguments, but rather numbers, atoms, human affairs, social institutions, historical events, and so on. In such cases, one may engage in argument in a more or less self-reflective manner.

What is required for reasoning to be self-reflective, and how do we distinguish reasoning which is self-reflective from reasoning which is not? We should not expect that, when we are self-reflectively constructing our own argument, we will analyze and evaluate it with the same degree of explicitness and formality as when we are critically analyzing the arguments of others. But the degree of self-interpretation or self-evaluation cannot be too low, otherwise we would have an instance of mere reasoning and not critical reasoning.

The sensitivity to self-interpretation is normally shown by careful attention to such questions as what are our conclusions and what are our reasons, whether we are advancing just one reason or more than one, and how our reasons are meant to connect with our conclusions. The sensitivity to self-evaluation is normally shown by careful attention to such questions as whether we are advancing a conclusive or very strong or moderately strong or weak argument; this involves the degree of support the reasons lend to the conclusion. It is also shown by paying attention to possible criticism, objections, and counterarguments against our own argument, and to ways of rebutting these. (For an extended example of self-reflective argumentation, see the Appendix to this chapter.)

This expansion of critical thinking from the case of critical interpretation of arguments to self-reflective argumentation involves a relatively small step since what is involved is being willing to include our own arguments as well as the arguments of others when we speak of the critical interpretation of arguments. Moreover, both types have in common the element of reasoning, so much so that they may be subsumed under the handy label of critical reasoning. In this sense, critical reasoning is not equated with critical thinking, but is a special case of it; for critical thinking subsumes at least one special case which involves an expansion of the concept beyond reasoning.

4. Methodological Reflection

In fact, there is an important type of thinking consisting of reflections on what one is doing when engaged in inquiry, the search for truth, or the quest for knowledge; that is, thinking aimed at understanding and evaluating the aims, presuppositions, and procedures of knowledge. Some call this metacognition;[4] I call it methodological reflection. Methodological reflection is another special case of critical thinking. The point of subsuming methodological reflection under the heading of critical thinking is that it corresponds to an important connotation of the notion of criticism, pertaining to reflective awareness of a kind different from the interpretation and evaluation of arguments. Let me explain.

Any inquiry, search for truth, or quest for knowledge about nature and physical reality eventually leads to questions about the nature of inquiry, truth, and knowledge; the focus then temporarily shifts from natural science to methodological reflection. The same happens with any inquiry into any other topic; so these shifts occur in other fields, whether they study numbers, life, human nature, history, society, or the supernatural.

There are many causes for such methodological pauses. Sometimes investigators want to gain a deeper understanding of what they are doing, what their aims are, what procedures they follow, what rules they accept, and what their presuppositions are. Sometimes they are challenged by a critic about one of these things and want to determine whether the criticism is valid. Sometimes important differences arise with fellow practitioners, and their resolution requires that such things be identified, interpreted, and evaluated.

Methodological reflection is concerned with the identification, description, interpretation, and evaluation of the aims, procedures, rules, and presuppositions of inquiry, truth-seeking, or knowledge-gathering. As defined, methodological reflection is essentially context-dependent and practically oriented; it arises in the course of inquiry about other topics and ends when further reflection is no longer relevant. However, it is obvious that it can also be undertaken in a systematic, general, conceptually explicit, and theoretical manner, independent of the contextual and practical origin it had initially; indeed, it has become professionalized into a branch of technical philosophy. We may refer to it as systematic methodology; others may wish to call it systematic epistemology, or just epistemology.

---

[4] Cf. Battersby 1989; Kitchener (1983a; 1983b); Kitchener and Fisher 1990; McGuinness 1990; Meichenbaum 1986; and Paris and Winograd 1990.

This relationship between methodological reflection and systematic methodology is analogous to that between critical reasoning and informal logic. This may be taken to provide another, formal reason for subsuming both critical reasoning and methodological reflection under the notion of critical thinking, for they share a contextual dependence or practical orientation. However, this formal analogy must be seen in the light of the substantive difference between their respective subject matters (arguments versus methodological principles).

A methodological principle is a general rule about the conduct of inquiry, search for truth, or quest for knowledge. Whereas an argument must have at least two propositions one of which is based on the other, a methodological rule is a single proposition. Thus, critical reasoning involves reasoning more directly than does methodological reflection.

Methodological principles are special kinds of propositions, defined partly by their content and partly by their form. I just described their content explicitly by reference to inquiry, truth, and knowledge; this content gives them special importance. I also described their form when I said that they are rules and general statements. To say that they are rules means that they are prescriptions about what we should do or what is desirable to do if we want to arrive at the truth, acquire knowledge, and conduct inquiry properly; this in turn means that they may be obeyed or disobeyed, followed or violated, acted upon or disregarded. Thus, another important point is the *application* of methodological principles, and this element should be added explicitly to the definition: methodological reflection aims at the formulation, interpretation, evaluation, *and* application of rules for the conduct of inquiry. To say that methodological principles are general means that they convey information which can be applied to more than one particular case; it does *not* mean that they are necessarily universal and categorical, or that they convey information about each and every situation.

Let me give some examples of methodological principles. In regard to the role of observation in inquiry, some hold the principle that a theory should be rejected if it conflicts with observation; others hold that if there is a conflict between a theory and an observation, then one should either revise the theory or reinterpret the observation. Another principle states that, if two theories are otherwise equivalent, we ought to prefer the one which can explain more observed facts. The principle of simplicity would state that, other things being equal, a simpler theory is to be preferred to one which is less simple.

Besides contrasting methodological reflection with critical reasoning and systematic methodology, it is useful to contrast it with method, or at least with one meaning of this word. Method is sometimes conceived as a set of rules which are exact, infallible, unchanging, and mechanically applicable, so that use of the method guarantees that we will arrive at the truth or solve the problem at hand. As conceived here, methodology is *not* meant to have this connotation. Instead a methodological principle is an inexact and fallible rule open to reformulation and requiring judgment for its application.

This talk of procedure leads to the distinction between results and method or methodology. A method is a procedure used to arrive at certain results. The results are the conclusions, ideas, hypotheses, theories, or beliefs at which we arrive at the end of a particular investigation, or which we test by means of such an investigation. Thus, a methodological rule is a procedural rule, a rule about a procedure conducive toward truth.

Another important distinction is that between methodological reflection and methodological practice. This is the distinction between what investigators say about the procedures they follow or should follow in their research and what they actually do when engaged in research. This is also called the distinction between theory and practice, between reflective pronouncements and practical involvement, and between words and deeds.

It should be stressed that methodological reflection is a type of critical thinking not, or not merely, or not primarily, insofar as one can argue for and against various methodological principles, and thus engage in the critical interpretation and the self-reflective formulation of methodological arguments. To do this is to engage in critical reasoning; given the controversial nature of methodology, critical reasoning about methodological issues is both common and necessary.

The point to stress is that in methodological reflection there may be critical thinking in the third sense elaborated here even when there is no reasoning to any significant degree. Since the evaluation of methodological principles clearly and inevitably involves methodological arguments, and self-reflective ones at that, the aspects of methodological reflection that need emphasis are those different from evaluation, namely the identification, formulation, interpretation, and application of methodological principles.

5. An Historical Example of Methodological Reflection

I want to conclude with an example of methodological reflection which is relatively short and nontechnical. It is taken from Galileo's *Dialogue on the Two Chief World Systems, Ptolemaic and Copernican* of 1632. This book contains many examples of critical interpretations of physical arguments and of self-reflective arguments about physical reality, which I have elaborated elsewhere and need not concern us here. The passage I have in mind is primarily a comment on open-mindedness and the fact that the Copernicans were more open-minded than the Ptolemaics. It is in the form of a story related by one of three speakers in the dialogue:

I must take this opportunity to relate to you some things which have happened to me since I began hearing about this opinion. When I was a young man and had just completed the study of philosophy (which I then abandoned to apply myself to other business), it happened that a man from Rostock beyond the Alps (whose name I believe was Christian Wursteisen) came into these parts and gave two or three lectures on this subject at an academy; he was a follower of Copernicus and had a large audience, I believe more for the novelty of the subject than anything else. However, I did not go, having acquired the distinct impression that this opinion could be nothing but solemn madness. When I asked some who had attended, they all made fun of it, except one who told me that this business was not altogether ridiculous. Since I regarded him as a very intelligent and very prudent man, I regretted not having gone. From that time on, whenever I met someone who held the Copernican opinion, I began asking whether he had always held it; although I have asked many persons, I have not found a single one who failed to tell me that for a long time he believed the contrary opinion but that he switched to this one due to the strength of the reasons supporting it; moreover, I examined each one of them to see how well he understood the reasons for the other side, and I found everyone had them at his fingertips; thus, I cannot say that they accepted this opinion out of ignorance or vanity or (as it were) to show off. On the other hand, out of curiosity I also asked many Peripatetics and Ptolemaics how well they had studied Copernicus's book, and I found very few who had seen it and none who (in my view) had understood it; I also tried to learn from the same followers of the Peripatetic doctrine whether any of them had ever held the other opinion, and similarly I found none who had. Now, let us consider these findings: that everyone who follows Copernicus's opinion had earlier held the contrary one and is very well-informed about the reasons of Aristotle and Ptolemy; and that, on the contrary, no one who follows Aristotle and Ptolemy has in the past held Copernicus's opinion and abandoned it to accept Aristotle's. Having considered these findings, I began to believe that when someone abandons an opinion imbibed with mother's milk and accepted by infinitely many persons, and he does this in order to switch to another one accepted by very few and denied by all the schools (and such that it really does seem a very great paradox), he must be necessarily moved (not to say forced) by stronger reasons. Therefore, I have become most curious to go, as it were, to the bottom of this business, and I regard myself very fortunate to have met the two of you; without any great effort I can hear from you all that has been said (and perhaps all that can be said) on this subject, and I am sure that by virtue of your arguments I will lose my doubts and acquire certainty.[5]

---

[5] Galilei 1632, 154–55; the translation is my own, as found in Finocchiaro 1997a, 148–49; cf. Galilei 1967, 127–29.

One key claim here is that all Copernicans had previously been Ptolemaics, but no Ptolemaics had previously been Copernicans. Another is that the Copernicans knew the pro-Ptolemaic arguments, but the Ptolemaics did not know the pro-Copernican arguments. Let us take open-mindedness to include at least the following two skills: (1) the ability to know, understand, and learn from the arguments against one's own views, and (2) the ability to reject previously held views and accept opposite views; then these claims can be reformulated by saying either that the Copernicans were open-minded but the Ptolemaics were not, or at least that the Copernicans were more open-minded than the Ptolemaics. A third claim in the passage is that, whenever one abandons a long-held and generally accepted view and adopts a new and unpopular opinion, the arguments for the new view are probably stronger. A fourth claim is not explicit but obviously suggested; that is, the instantiation of this generalization to the case of the Copernicans yields the claim that the Copernican arguments are stronger.

The three explicit claims are intriguing and controversial, but unsupported in the passage. Moreover, there is no suggestion that they constitute an argument. Nor it is obvious what conclusion is to be drawn from the first two claims. When the book was first published, Church authorities received the complaint that this passage contained the argument that Copernicanism is true because the Copernicans are open-minded;[6] but this would be an uncharitable interpretation, since the alleged conclusion is stated more strongly than it needs to be. On the other hand, it would be relatively plausible to argue that Copernicanism was worth pursuing as a research program because the Copernicans were more open-minded than the Ptolemaics.

At any rate, my main conclusion is that, despite its lack of (explicit) argumentation, this passage contains critical thinking of the methodological-reflection variety.

6. Summary

In this chapter I have articulated a notion of critical thinking which subsumes three main special cases and differentiates it from informal logic. The prototypical case of critical thinking is the interpretation and/or evaluation of arguments. A second special case is that of self-reflective argumentation. A third case is methodological reflection, namely the

---

[6] See Finocchiaro 1989a, 222.

formulation, interpretation, evaluation, and application of methodological principles; these are inexact and fallible rules stipulating useful procedures in the search for truth. Informal logic is conceived as the formulation, testing, systematization, and application of concepts and principles for the interpretation, evaluation, and practice of argument. Thus, critical thinking and informal logic are related insofar as the informal logician must practice critical thinking, in its three varieties; but they differ insofar as informal logic aims at a greater degree of generality, systematicity, and conceptual explicitness than critical thinking.

Appendix: An Example of Self-reflective Argumentation

My example of self-reflective argumentation consists of Galileo's argument for the earth's diurnal axial rotation at the beginning of the Second Day of the *Dialogue*.[7] Since the number of propositions is large, and the structure is relatively complex, I shall use the technical apparatus of inverted-tree diagrams to picture the propositional structure of the argument; the labels for the propositions are the ones which I shall be progressively assigning to them as they are introduced in the discussion.[8] It will be easier to follow the discussion by referring to the following diagram:

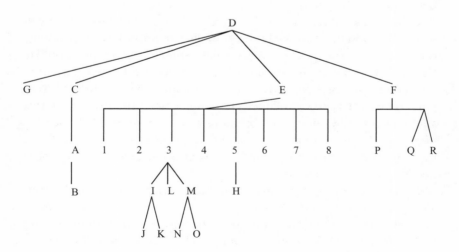

---

[7] Galilei 1632, 139–50; cf. Finocchiaro 1997a, 128–42, and Galilei 1967, 114–24.
[8] See, for example, Finocchiaro 1980b and Freeman 1991.

Galileo begins the discussion with a statement of the principle of the relativity of motion, namely the idea that motion exists only in relation to things lacking it, whereas shared motion has no effect on the relationship of things sharing it; let us abbreviate this proposition by A (and then we will progressively label other key propositions in alphabetical order, unless explicitly labeled otherwise in the text under consideration). In the course of the discussion he gives a partial justification supporting this principle in terms of familiar examples of shared and unshared motion, though he does not stress this justification and regards the principle as relatively uncontroversial; let us label this support B. His primary interest is to apply this principle to the problem of explaining apparent diurnal motion; that is, the relativity of motion is taken to imply that the apparent westward diurnal motion can be explained by saying either that all heavenly bodies revolve westward daily around a motionless earth or that the earth alone rotates eastward on its own axis every day; let C refer to this consequence of the principle.

Given this premise (that diurnal motion can be explained either way), Galileo goes on to argue that therefore (D) terrestrial axial rotation is more likely than universal revolution around a motionless earth because (E) the geokinetic explanation of apparent diurnal motion is simpler than the geostatic explanation, and (F) nature usually operates by the simplest possible means. The argument so far is: A because B; because A, therefore C; and because C, E, and F, therefore D.

Galileo makes it clear that he is asserting the final conclusion only with probability, and that his conclusion embodies an implicit comparison between the two contradictory views which generate the controversy. He also explicitly states that his conclusion needs to be qualified in another crucial way; that is, it depends on the assumption that all other relevant phenomena can also be explained either way, namely the assumption that all the many anti-Copernican objections can be refuted and all the phenomena on which they are based could occur on a moving earth. These Galilean remarks are explicit indications of the self-evaluating element needed for critical reasoning.

Let us label the assumption just mentioned G. The best place for this assumption in the overall economy of this argument is as an additional premise directly supporting the final conclusion, alongside C, E, and F. We might ask at this point the more technical question whether this assumption is a reason linked with or independent of these other three. I would opt for a link on the grounds that it makes a point which is similar to, though of course more general than, the specific claim that diurnal motion can be explained either way (C); moreover, the simplicity considerations made in the other two premises (E and F) apply as much to the general as to the specific point. Note also that this assumption is a generalization about anti-geokinetic arguments, and that the rest of the book supports it by critically examining each in turn and attempting to refute them all. However, in this passage this assumption is unsupported and so constitutes a final reason.

The rest of this passage argues in support of the greater simplicity of terrestrial rotation (E) and in support of the principle of simplicity (F), which so far have just been stated. In its central part, Galileo lists seven numbered reasons why terrestrial axial rotation is simpler than universal geocentric revolution; then at the end he adds an eighth reason, without labeling it as such. That is, the geokinetic system involves (1) fewer moving parts, smaller bodies moving, and lower speeds; (2) only one direction of motion (eastward) rather than two opposite ones; and (3) periods of revolution which follow a uniform pattern, namely that of increasing with the size of the orbit. Moreover, the geostatic system involves (4) a complex pattern for the size and location of the orbits of the fixed stars; (5) complex changes in the individual orbits of fixed stars (due to [H] the precession of the equinoxes); (6) an incredible degree of solidity and strength in the substance of the stellar sphere which holds fixed stars in their fixed relative positions; (7) a mysterious failure for motion to be transmitted to the earth after it has been transmitted all the way down from the outer reaches of the universe to the moon; and (8) the postulation of an ad hoc *primum mobile*.

It is probably best if we leave these numerals alone and let them stand respectively for the propositions supporting the comparative simplicity claim (E). Though each of these eight premises are propositions which implicitly compare and contrast the two alternatives in regard to a particular property, it should be noted that only the first two seem to involve matters of degree, whereas the other six seem to involve discrete properties which one of the two world systems possesses but the other one lacks. An interesting question here is whether these eight reasons are linked or independent. I would say, first, that each strengthens the others, and so the total amount of support they give to their conclusion is a function of all of them taken collectively; this suggests that they may be viewed as linked. However, each reason provides some degree of support independently of the others; moreover, each proposition is a perfectly natural answer to the question whether there is another reason why one should accept the comparative simplicity claim; thus, I am inclined to

regard them as basically independent. Note also that the first proposition has three parts, each of which would need separate support; that
the fifth one is provided a brief justification; and that the third is especially important and is supported by a relatively lengthy, novel, and strong
argument.

As phrased above, proposition 3 states that the periods of revolution
have a uniformity in the Copernican system which they lack in the geostatic one. In the supporting subargument Galileo begins with a claim
which I call the law of revolution: (I) it is probably a general law of nature that, whenever several bodies are revolving around a common center,
the periods of revolution become longer as the orbits become larger. He
then supports this by the well-known fact that (J) the planets revolve in
accordance with this pattern, and by his own discovery that (K) Jupiter's
satellites also follow the pattern. The important point is that, though
this feature of planetary revolutions was known to the Ptolemaics and
incorporated in their system, before the discovery of Jupiter's satellites it
would have been rash to generalize a single case into a general law; however, the completely different and unexpected case of Jupiter's satellites
suggested that this was not an accidental coincidence but had general
systemic significance; thus, while this inferential step ("J, K, so I") is not
conclusive, it cannot be dismissed.

Given the law of revolution (I), Galileo goes on to combine it with
the claim that, whereas (L) the earth's diurnal motion in the Copernican
system is consistent with the law of revolution, (M) the diurnal motion of
the universe in the Ptolemaic system is not. The point would be that this
difference gives the Copernican system a uniformity or regularity lacking in the Ptolemaic system, which is what is asserted by Galileo's third
reason (proposition 3) why the former has greater simplicity than the
latter (proposition E). He considers the consistency between Copernican diurnal motion and the law of revolution to be sufficiently obvious
to need no support. The argument would be that in the Copernican
system the diurnal motion is the axial rotation of the earth, and this axial rotation is not an orbital revolution and does not involve a member
of a series of increasingly large orbits; thus, the law is not even meant
to apply to terrestrial rotation. To justify the inconsistency between the
law of revolution and Ptolemaic diurnal motion, he explains that (N) in
the geostatic system the diurnal motion corresponds to the revolution
of the outermost sphere (whether stellar sphere or *primum mobile*) around
the central earth, but (O) this outermost sphere involves both the largest
orbit and the shortest period. This completes the subargument supporting the greater Copernican uniformity in regard to periods and orbits of

revolution (proposition 3), namely the argument *from* the law of revolution, for short.

At the end of the passage, there is a discussion of the principle of simplicity (F), which was a crucial premise directly supporting the final conclusion about the greater likelihood of terrestrial rotation (D). Though there might be some question how this principle should be formulated, let us focus on the interpretation adopted above, namely that nature usually operates by the simplest possible means. When so stated, Galileo in part suggests what might be called a teleological justification for the principle of simplicity, namely the teleological principle that (P) it useless to do with more means what can be done with fewer. However, he also recognizes that (Q) the principle of simplicity is subject to the following theological objection: given a God who is all-knowing and all-powerful, God can create and operate a more complicated system as easily as a simpler system, and so a more complex world system is as likely to exist as a simpler one; in other words, it is false that nature usually operates by the simplest possible means because nature was created by an infinitely powerful God and such a God would be as likely to use more power to operate a more complex universe as to use less power to operate a simpler world. Galileo tries to address this objection directly, though I do not find his answer too relevant or convincing; however, his presentation of this objection indicates the kind of self-evaluation which is part of critical reasoning. Finally, let us simply label his answer R, and let us note that we have labeled by the simple propositional label Q the whole admission of the existence of the theological objection, including a statement of its details as part of proposition Q; in terms of these labels, the last subargument has the structure "F because P, and because Q and R."

This leads to a final comment about this instance of self-reflective argumentation. That is, though we have imposed some structure onto Galileo's argument for terrestrial axial rotation, his presentation of the argument is sufficiently self-reflective to make its overall structure relatively clear.[9]

---

9 Shorter versions of this chapter were presented at the Conference 95 on Critical Thinking and Informal Logic, George Mason University, Fairfax, Virginia, 15–18 June 1995; at the 15th Annual International Conference on Critical Thinking and Educational Reform, Sonoma State University, Rohnert Park, California, 30 July to 2 August 1995; at a session sponsored by the Association for Informal Logic and Critical Thinking, meeting in conjunction with the American Philosophical Association, Seattle, 3–6 April 1996; and at the International Conference on Formal and Applied Practical Reasoning, Bonn, Germany, 3–7 June 1996. In the proceedings of the latter conference, my contribution (Finocchiaro 1996b) contains a different but overlapping discussion of the topics discussed in this chapter.

PART II

FALLACIES AND ASYMMETRIES

6

Fallacies and the Evaluation of Reasoning (1981)

1. The Fallacy Approach

The evaluation of reasoning is perhaps the central practice in philosophical scholarship, yet theoretical discussions of it are very rare. To be sure, the theory of validity in formal logic is in a sense a theoretical analysis of the evaluation of reasoning, insofar as formal validity is supposedly the fundamental concept expressing a positive, favorable evaluation of an argument, while an argument is supposedly the fundamental unit of reasoning. In the present context, however, the relevance of formal validity does not seem to go very far; moreover, insofar as it is relevant, it faces the difficulty stemming from the well-known fact that formal validity is neither a sufficient nor a necessary condition for the favorable evaluation of an argument.[1] It is not sufficient because it excludes neither question-begging arguments nor self-contradictory ones (i.e., argument with inconsistent premises). It is not necessary partly because of the Toulmin-type objection that most good arguments most of the time (in the empirical sciences, legal contexts, humanities, and everyday life) are not formally valid,[2] and partly because formal validity presupposes fully reconstructed arguments,[3] which in human reasoning are the exception rather than the rule.

The theory of fallacies may be interpreted as a more relevant contribution to the evaluation of reasoning. This applies to the somewhat informal

---

[1] See, for example, Johnstone 1959, 57ff.

[2] Toulmin 1958.

[3] Cf. Johnstone's point (1959, 58ff.) about the difficulty of separating premises and conclusions in a philosophical argument. I believe that the difficulty is more general, insofar as it exists outside philosophical argumentation, and insofar as it relates to the full reconstruction of arguments. Cf. Finocchiaro 1980b, chapter 17.

accounts of fallacies found in many logic textbooks, rather than to theories of fallacies. For, on the other hand, the theory of *formal* fallacies is
conceptually indistinguishable from the theory of validity, since, as the
textbooks point out, a formal fallacy may be regarded as any (formally)
invalid argument, and hence we would not have here an alternative approach to our problem, different from the problematic theory of validity.
On the other hand, formal theories of fallacies[4] need to be applied in
order to be useful for the evaluation of reasoning, and such application
is neither discussed by the proponents nor likely to be any easier than
the informal evaluation of the reasoning under consideration.

By contrast, informal accounts of fallacies are potentially more promising since they seem to deal directly with the evaluation of reasoning. Unfortunately, before one can appreciate the merits of the fallacy approach,
one must expose the demerits of the textbook accounts, to which we now
turn.

2. Criticism of Textbook Accounts

It is impossible to read the accounts of fallacies given in introductory
logic textbooks without a deep sense of frustration and dissatisfaction.
These accounts usually contain four elements: a general definition of the
concept of a fallacy, a description of various practices which are categorized as fallacies, a classification of fallacies into various groups, and an
illustration of the descriptions of fallacies with examples.

As concerns the concept of a fallacy, there is a tendency to regard
any logically incorrect argument as a fallacy. But then, either explicitly
by giving a definition of a more specific notion, or implicitly by limiting
the discussion to only certain kinds of logically incorrect arguments, the
concept of a fallacy effectively becomes that of a type of common but
logically incorrect argument.

The things which are categorized as fallacies include such practices
as appeals to force, to pity, to authority, *ad hominem* arguments, begging
the question, *dicto simpliciter*, converse accident, equivocation, amphiboly,
composition, division, *post hoc ergo propter hoc*, hasty induction, affirming
the consequent, and denying the antecedent.

The classification of fallacies usually divides them into four major
groups. One group is made up of fallacies variously called linguistic,
verbal, semilogical, or of ambiguity; a second group is variously called

---

[4] E.g., Hamblin 1970, especially pp. 253–303. Textbook accounts have been criticized in
Hamblin's book, pp. 9–49, primarily to provide a motivation for his formal theory of
fallacies.

psychological or of irrelevance; a third group is made up of so-called deductive, logical, or formal fallacies; and a fourth group consists of so-called inductive or material ones.

The fourth element of such accounts, the examples of the various types of fallacies, is usually rather meager. It consists mostly, if not exclusively, of more or less artificially constructed examples for the purpose of illustrating the various descriptions of fallacies. Examples of fallacies actually occurring in the history of thought or in contemporary investigations and controversies are rare.

What is wrong with such accounts of fallacies? One problem concerns the paucity of actual examples, just mentioned. It is in fact puzzling that logic textbooks shouldn't be able to come up with more examples of fallacies actually committed given that fallacies are supposed to be *common* errors in reasoning. One gets the suspicion that logically incorrect arguments are not that common in practice, that their existence may be largely restricted to logic textbook examples and exercises.

If someone doubts the fact being referred to, let him consult some textbooks.[5] Let him consult Wesley C. Salmon's *Logic*[6] and discover that

---

[5] The books mentioned in my text are, I believe, a representative cross-section of books that have been traditionally well known, widely used, and influential. Most recently (in the 1970s) a trend has emerged toward more realistically oriented textbooks. The best such books, however, de-emphasize the fallacy approach: for example, Scriven 1976, which has probably the best discussion of the evaluation of actual, everyday arguments, avoids the concept of fallacy altogether; Fogelin 1978, which probably has the best collection of actual, classic selections of arguments, emphasizes analysis and understanding, rather than criticism. On the other hand, the fallacy-oriented textbooks tend to define so many types of fallacies that most of what they call "fallacies" involve faults and problems other than errors of *reasoning*; the result is an unacceptable amount of violence to the fundamental distinction between an argument and a non-argument; this is bound not only to cause confusion to the student, but also to affect the author's own judgment of what is an argument and what isn't. For example, Howard Kahane (1971, 28) misinterprets an insult as an error of reasoning when he gives as an example of "the fallacy of *ad hominem* argument" Spiro Agnew's famous remark that "a spirit of national masochism prevails, encouraged by an effete corps of impudent snobs who characterize themselves as intellectuals." [For an analysis of some actual and nonfallacious *ad hominem* arguments, see Finocchiaro 1974a.] Another example is the invitation by Engel (1976, 63–64) to treat as a "fallacy of ambiguity" an explanatory remark found in John Maynard Keynes's *Treatise on Money*: "It is enterprise which builds and improves the world's possessions. If enterprise is afoot, wealth accumulates whatever may be happening to Thrift; and if enterprise is asleep, wealth decays whatever Thrift may be doing." [For a significant and fallacious argument exploiting ambiguity, see Finocchiaro 1973b; for a significant but nonfallacious use of ambiguity in reasoning, see Finocchiaro 1977b.] It is obvious that the cavalier way in which these admittedly realistically fallacy-oriented authors dispose of highly controversial issues can only encourage the kind of superficiality which I argue below to lie at the root of the problem of the fallacy approach.

[6] Salmon 1973.

no actual example is given for any of the fallacies mentioned above. Let him consult Robert J. Kreyche's *Logic for Undergraduates*[7] and find the same desert in his text discussion of fallacies. Let him consult Cohen and Nagel's *Introduction to Logic and Scientific Method*[8] and discover that, though their account of what they call "abuses of scientific method" may be interpreted as containing some actual examples, their account of formal, verbal, and material fallacies does not. Let him consult Fearnside and Holther's *Fallacy: The Counterfeit of Argument*[9] and discover that, though the examples are more numerous, better, and less artificial than in more standard logic texts, it is not clear how many of them would remain fallacious when put in the mind or mouth of actual persons in an actual situation.

Let him consult Monroe Beardsley's *Thinking Straight*,[10] which is more practically oriented than most books. He will find that, though the exercises often concern actual examples, these are usually either prejudicially edited or inadequate illustrations of the various fallacies and argument forms. If these exercise examples had been illustrations, one would find the author giving more actual examples in his textual discussion, whereas one finds only one example of the fallacies mentioned above. On p. 217 (3rd edition, 1966) one finds a passage which may have been somewhat edited, since no reference to the source is given. Even so, the passage is not a very good example of an *ad hominem* fallacy, since for this purpose the author is forced to misinterpret the argument being advanced, which is actually an argument from analogy. Be that as it may, the point here is that even in such a practically oriented textbook as this one, one finds *only one* alleged example of a fallacy actually committed.

Finally, let him consult what is perhaps the most ambitious, popular, and widely acclaimed introductory logic textbook, Copi's *Introduction to Logic*.[11] He will find there in the author's account of fallacies only three actual examples. The historical question that Stalin is reported by Harry Hopkins to have asked Churchill at Yalta, "And how many divisions did you say the Pope had available for combat duty?", is given as an example of the fallacy of appeal to force.[12] The second example, which is supposed to illustrate the fallacy of appeal to pity, is part of the plea to the jury made by

[7] Kreyche 1970.
[8] Cohen and Nagel 1934.
[9] Fearnside and Holther 1959.
[10] Beardsley 1966.
[11] Copi 1972.
[12] Copi 1972, 74.

the famous lawyer Clarence Darrow at the trial of Thomas I. Kidd.[13] The third one, and in Copi's own words a "considerably more subtle example" of the appeal to pity fallacy, is Socrates' refusal in Plato's *Apology* to make an appeal to pity.[14] This example is perhaps too subtle. And rather subtle, one will find practically all of the eighteen or so quotations included in the exercises among a larger number of less subtle but more artificial examples.[15]

The conclusion I wish to draw from such "consultations" is not that errors in reasoning are probably not common in real life, but that there probably are no common errors in reasoning. That is, logically incorrect arguments may be common, but common types of logically incorrect arguments probably are not.

The problem I wish to raise here is, do people actually commit fallacies as usually understood? That is, do fallacies exist in practice? Or do they exist only in the mind of the interpreter who is claiming that a fallacy is being committed?

The next problem I wish to raise concerns the classification of the fallacies. It does not concern the question of the various groups into which fallacies should be subdivided, which is a problem often mentioned in textbooks and which actually turns out to be just a question of what names to give to the various groups. The problem is that a given alleged fallacy cannot be understood to be a fallacy unless it is classified as belonging to a certain group. In fact, the various groups derive from the various reasons why various given practices are fallacies. In other words, the inadequacy of the classification of fallacies can derive only from the inadequacy of the justification of their fallaciousness. Hence, since the arbitrariness of the classification is usually admitted, the arbitrariness of the justification should also be admitted.

In other words, the real problem here is whether any given alleged fallacy is really a fallacy and why, and not what the various kinds of fallacies are. In fact, if a fallacy is defined as a type of common but logically incorrect argument, the various types would have to be the following: (1) arguments claiming to be deductively valid but which are actually invalid;

[13] Copi 1972, 78.
[14] Copi 1972, 78–79.
[15] Copi (1972, p. vii) claims that in the fourth edition of his *Introduction to Logic* "thanks largely to the useful criticisms by Professor C. L. Hamblin in his book *Fallacies*, some corrections have been made in Chapter 3." A comparison with Copi's third edition will show, however, that the "corrections" really amount to nothing more than cosmetic changes; see, for example, Copi 1972, 73, 78, and 82.

(2) arguments claiming to be inductively strong but which are actually inductively weak; (3) arguments claiming to have *some* inductive strength but which have none.

The problem then, with this element of logic textbooks' accounts of fallacies, is the failure to recognize that the problem is not one of classifying a disputed practice which can be shown to be a fallacy on other grounds, but one of showing that it is a fallacy. For there is no way for an argument to be a fallacy without falling into one of the three above-mentioned classes. This makes one suspect that many of the disputed practices usually regarded as fallacies may be either not fallacies or not always fallacies.

To investigate this in more detail, let us examine the second element of textbook accounts of fallacies, the description of various devices which I wish to call by the neutral term of "disputed practices." One problem with these descriptions is that they are usually prejudicial in the sense that their fallaciousness is built right into their description. There would be nothing wrong with this were it not for the fact that they then become logician's fictions or at best practices seldom found in reality (actual life). There is a pattern in these biased descriptions, and it is the following. If the disputed practice is a type of inductive argument, namely one claiming that the conclusion is only strongly, but not conclusively, supported by the premises, then the practice will be described as a type of deductive argument, namely one claiming that the conclusion is conclusively supported by the premises. If the disputed practice is a type of what might be called a partial argument, namely one claiming that the conclusion is only partly, but not too strongly supported by the premises, then the practice will be described as a type of allegedly inductively strong argument. One might think that the pattern runs out of material here, but it can be extended as follows: if the disputed practice is a type of non-argument, namely not an attempt to support one proposition with others, then it will be described as an argument claiming that certain propositions provide at least some support for another (the conclusion). Finally, if the disputed practice is an argument having as conclusion a special type of proposition, then it will be described as an argument having another conclusion; the pattern (or shall I say the fallacy?) is that of exaggerating the strength of the connection claimed between various assertions or of creating one where none is claimed.

The pattern can be illustrated by considering some of the disputed practices which textbook writers find most abhorrent. One of these is the so-called fallacy of affirming the consequent. I need not remind the reader that this fallacy is defined as that committed when a proposition is inferred from a conditional of which it is the antecedent and from the consequent of the conditional. But though it may be that all the textbook examples of arguments having the form "If P, then Q; Q; so P" are indeed fallacious, that does not mean that actual arguments having this form are *normally* fallacious.

In order to declare such an argument fallacious the logician must interpret it to be a deductive argument, namely an argument that claims to be formally valid. In other words, when the argument giver says, "If P then Q; Q; therefore, P," the logician must interpret this to mean "P → Q; Q; therefore, as a necessary consequence of them alone, P."

But the argument could also mean: "Q; the fact that P would explain the fact that Q; therefore, no other explanation of Q being available, we may presume that P." Under the second interpretation, there is nothing logically wrong with the argument. Hence it is not arguments having the form of affirming the consequent that are fallacies, but deductive arguments having that form. That is, to show that the actual argument is a fallacy, the logician has to argue that it is deductive. This will usually be a difficult, if not insurmountable, task, since most such arguments are inductive; and evidence for this is the fact that the textbook writer usually does not even attempt to show that the argument does claim to be formally valid.

Another alleged fallacy beloved of textbook writers is the *post hoc ergo propter hoc* manner of reasoning. This is described in W. C. Salmon's *Logic* as "concluding that *B* was caused by *A* just because *B* followed *A*" (1973, 101–2) and in Copi's *Introduction to Logic* as "the inference that one event is the cause of another from the bare fact that the first occurs earlier than the second" (1972, 82). No justification is given why these interpretations are preferable to the following: "concluding that *B* was caused by *A partly because B* followed *A*" or "the inference that one event is the cause of another from the fact, *among others*, that the first occurs earlier than the second." These latter interpretations should be preferred because they are more accurate in the sense that they correspond more closely to a type of reasoning in which people actually engage.

Included in a third group of fallacies are usually appeal to force and appeal to pity. A typical description of the first is "appealing to force or the threat of force to cause acceptance of a conclusion" and of the second "appealing to pity for the sake of getting a conclusion accepted."[16]

[16] Copi 1972, 74, 77.

These descriptions are prejudicial in their reference to a conclusion, since a conclusion is by definition a proposition which is part of an argument and which is being supported by other parts of the argument called premises. Hence appealing to force or pity to cause acceptance of a *conclusion* means giving an argument in which the conclusion is supported not by appealing to evidence but by appealing to force and pity. Of course *these* arguments are fallacies of irrelevance, but irrelevant are also those notions of appeal to force and to pity to actual appeals to force and pity. These could nonprejudicially but along the same lines be described as "appealing to force or to pity to cause acceptance of a certain proposition or to cause a certain action." When so described, they can be seen to be methods, among others, of which giving an argument is one, in order to cause acceptance of a certain proposition. And the appropriateness of the method depends on the context. What does not depend on the context is the truth of the claim that it is a category mistake to regard typical actual appeals to force and to pity as fallacies; being non-arguments, they cannot be logically incorrect arguments.

3. Constructive Lessons

Turning this discussion into a more positive direction, my critique may be interpreted to support and to be supported by two traditional philosophical doctrines, that evil is unreal and that the real is rational.

To establish a connection with the doctrine of the unreality of evil it suffices to regard fallacies as logical sins, or erroneous reasoning as logical evil. This in turn involves the idea that truth, logical correctness, validity, and rationality are values like goodness, beauty, and utility; the most recent historical appearances of this idea were perhaps in the philosophy of Benedetto Croce and of John Dewey. My discussion would then be giving a meaning to the unreality of logical evil and would be indicating the sense and extent to which it is true: actually occurring logically incorrect arguments are not very common because, to find one, the logician usually has to exaggerate the strength of the logical connection between premises and conclusion being alleged by the argument giver.

The real, which in this context the rationalist would claim to be rational, is the actual reasoning practiced by people in their various activities. The rationalist is a priori skeptical about whether fallacies are as common as introductory logic textbooks would want to make him believe. The realist, on the other hand, that is to say the one who has a sense of reality, feels (a posteriori) that people are simply not as irrational as those textbooks would lead one to believe. The rationalist will try to find ways of interpreting actual arguments so that they are logically correct; the realist will try to find as accurate a reconstruction of actual arguments as possible. In so doing, the realist discovers that actual arguments do not tend to be logically incorrect as much as textbooks lead one to believe; that is to say, he discovers that the rationalist is right. Realism and rationalism in this case coincide.

Of course, a thoroughgoing rationalist may be inclined to go to the absurd extreme of claiming that no actual argument is ever fallacious. Absurd, if for no other reason than that would mean that the usual logic textbook accounts supporting their concept of a fallacy are logically correct. To be sure, the rationalist might in his quest try to find evidence that those accounts are not arguments, and hence not logically incorrect for categorial reasons. He may find rationality in them by categorizing them differently. I personally don't know what this category would be, but I doubt very much that the rationality involved would be pedagogic or rhetorical rationality. The realist in me prevails here and parts company with the rationalist.

Without abandoning such realism, one may strive for fairness and attempt to find valuable elements and lessons. I believe that one central insight of the fallacy accounts is the recognition of the importance of negative, unfavorable evaluation, for the search for fallacies is a search for faults of reasoning. Now, negative evaluation is intrinsically more instructive than positive evaluation because the justification of one's negative evaluation automatically involves a contrast that the justification of positive evaluation does not, namely the contrast between the (allegedly) good argument supporting the negative evaluation and the (allegedly) bad argument being evaluated. Thus, negative evaluation is methodologically more significant.

This corresponds to conclusions reached by other philosophers in other contexts. For example Karl Popper and his followers have stressed the primacy of falsification and criticism as opposed to confirmations and justification in science;[17] Henry Johnstone, Jr. has argued that, in philosophy, critical arguments are more fundamental than constructive ones;[18] and Imre Lakatos has stressed the methodological importance of refutation in mathematics.[19]

---

[17] Popper 1959; Bartley 1962; Agassi 1963; Lakatos and Musgrave 1970.
[18] Johnstone 1959, 79, 82.
[19] Lakatos 1963–64.

Third, there is a lesson one can learn indirectly from accounts of fallacies, by analyzing the fundamental reason of their inadequacy, exhibited
above. I think it is obvious that this is the failure to understand properly
the reasoning being evaluated, that is, the failure to reconstruct *accurately*
the arguments under evaluation.

Now the requirement of accuracy in the reconstruction of arguments
is equivalent to requiring good or sound reasoning about the arguments
being evaluated, namely requiring the (informal) validity of the higher-
level meta-arguments going from the actual, unreconstructed arguments
to the reconstructed ones. Hence, the superficiality of the usual accounts
is a logical error, or "fallacy": this fallacy would be analogous to the inconsistency between what one preaches and what one practices; logic textbooks preach good arguments, but they practice bad arguments about
arguments. Once this point is understood, the remedy becomes obvious:
it is a more practical or reality-oriented study of argumentation.

This is analogous to conclusions reached on other grounds by Stephen
Toulmin and Michael Scriven. Toulmin speaks of a reform of logic to
make it more empirical, historical, and anthropological, and less of an a
priori subject.[20] Scriven speaks of the ethics and of the effectiveness of
argument analysis and formulates a Principle of Charity,[21] according to
which one should reconstruct an argument so as to contain its unstated
assumptions, but that

the assumptions you identify mustn't be too strong or they will be an unfair
reconstruction of the argument, since they will be fairly easily refuted even though
the argument might still be perfectly sound. On the other hand, the assumptions
mustn't be too weak, or they won't connect the stated premises to the conclusion.
(Or they won't support an independent part of the conclusion that has so far
received no support.) The assumption mustn't be a triviality of definition or
fact – since it then isn't worth mentioning. Nor can it be a mere assertion of
the fact that the arguer thinks this is a sound argument, since that's not worth
mentioning. It must be something new, but on the other hand, it must still be
true [i.e., plausible] and relevant.[22]

Fourth, the above critique of fallacies suggests another important principle for the theory of reasoning. We have seen that understanding (in the
sense of accurate reconstruction) is a necessary condition for an adequate
negative evaluation. Now, if it can be argued that such understanding is

[20] Toulmin 1958, 254–59.
[21] Scriven 1976, 71–73.
[22] Scriven 1976, 173–74.

not necessary for an adequate positive evaluation, then there would be an asymmetry between the justification of a negative evaluation, and the justification of a positive one, for an adequate evaluation may be viewed as one with a sound justification. I believe the just-mentioned antecedent condition does in fact hold, since an adequate positive evaluation is an adequately justified claim that the argument being evaluated is good; even if this argument has been inaccurately reconstructed, as long as this inaccurate reconstruction is justifiably a good argument, then something of logical value has been achieved. In other words, when the reconstructed argument is intrinsically valuable, it does not matter if it is inaccurate.

Does this involve attributing merit to something (the original argument) or someone (the arguer) that does not deserve it? If the context is an evaluation or second-order one, as distinct from a purely creative one, then at least the causal assertion is true that the original argument was instrumental in the creation of the one that has intrinsic value; hence, the original argument has at least this heuristic or methodological value. Thus, there is no misplaced merit.

This conclusion corresponds to a point made by Richard Montague in the context of the problem of applying formal semantics to natural languages. He speaks of the difference between symbolic interpretation (of natural arguments) which are formally valid and those that are formally invalid.[23]

In summary, textbook accounts of fallacies are basically misconceived, partly because their concept of fallacy is internally incoherent, partly because the various alleged fallacious practices have not been shown to be fallacies, partly because their classification of fallacies is unsatisfactory, and partly because their examples are artificial. However, from the point of view of the problem of the evaluation of reasoning, they are instructive: they are a more relevant attempt at solving it than the theory of formal validity; they point in the right direction of emphasizing unfavorable evaluation; they can lead to an appreciation of the important problem of the accurate reconstruction of arguments, and to an appreciation of the asymmetry between negative and positive evaluation.

4. Woods and Walton on *Post Hoc*

It might be objected that this critique of fallacies has only pedagogical but not theoretical significance because it is grounded on textbook

[23] See Montague's comments in Staal 1969, 275.

accounts. In order to answer this objection it will now be argued that similar problems arise in nontextbook contexts. Let us begin with a very recent discussion of *post hoc ergo propter hoc* by two connoisseurs and serious theorists of fallacies, who are otherwise well aware of what they call "the inchoations and banalities of the 'Standard Treatment' offered in introductory logic texts."[24] In an otherwise enlightening article, Woods and Walton define seven types of causal fallacies, but they fail to illustrate them properly.

They begin with arguments "concluding that ψ was caused by φ just because ψ temporarily followed φ" (p. 583). Their first example for this is: "I took a dose of Sinus Blast and a couple of days later my cold cleared up. The suggested conclusion, namely that taking Sinus Blast *caused* the cold to disappear, is fallacious" (p. 583). The example is clearly artificial, and this fact is recognized by the authors when they call it "a stock example" (p. 583).

Their second example of this type of argument is taken from D. H. Fischer's *Historians' Fallacies*: "On the fatal night of Doria's collision with the Swedish ship Grisholm, off Nantucket in 1956, the lady retired to her cabin and flicked the light switch. Suddenly there was a great crash, and grinding metal, and passengers and crew ran screaming through the passageways. The lady burst from her cabin and explained to the first person in sight that she must have set the ship's emergency brake" (p. 584). It is not clear whether this is an actual historical report or not. It could be merely an artificial example embedded in an actual event. But let us assume that it is an actual report. The woman's argument is being reconstructed as:

Immediately after I flicked the light switch, there was a great crash.
So, my flicking the light switch caused the great crash.
So, my flicking the light switch caused the activation of the ship's emergency brake.

This reconstruction is no more accurate than the following:

Immediately after I flicked on the light switch, there was a great crash.
So, my flicking the light switch *may* have caused the great crash.
So, if my flicking the light switch caused the activation of the ship's emergency brake, *then* my flicking was the cause.

---

[24] Woods and Walton 1977a. In the rest of this section, subsequent references to this article will be made in the text in parentheses.

There is nothing very obviously wrong with the argument when so reconstructed.

The next type of argument discussed by Woods and Walton is one "concluding that ψ was caused by φ just because there was a positive correlation between some previous instances of φ and instances of ψ" (p. 584). Their example is taken from H. L. Labaree's *Reliable Knowledge*: "Near perfect correlations exist between the death rate in Hyderbad, India, from 1911 to 1919, and variations in the membership of the International Association of Machinists during the same period" (p. 584). As they point out, it would be fallacious to conclude that the first situation causes the second. However, I would add, that is why no one ever gave such an argument. What we have here is, as they admit, another "stock example" (p. 584).

Third, we have the fallacy of "reversing cause and effect" (p. 584). Their example is taken from D. Huff's *How to Lie with Statistics*: "The people of the New Hebrides have observed, perfectly accurately, over the centuries, that people in good health have body lice and people not in good health do not. They conclude that lice make a man healthy" (p. 584). This does sound like an historical report and does constitute an actual example. Woods and Walton suggest that it is good health that causes lice in the sense that "whereas lice were the norm among this people, when anyone took a fever and his body became too warm for comfortable habitation, the lice departed" (p. 584). Unfortunately, what this means is that it is *bad* health that causes *lack* of lice, which is not an example of reversal in the sense intended by Woods and Walton. For their meaning is that in this fallacy one concludes that φ causes ψ, when in fact ψ causes φ (pp. 580, 589); however, in the example given, the conclusion is that φ causes ψ, when in fact lack of ψ causes lack of φ. We may still have a problem here, but it is doubtful that we have a "fallacy," since if both health and body lice were the norm among this people, then they probably would not be concerned with the cause of either, but rather with the cause of deviations from the norm. They would be committing the fallacy in question if they had concluded that lack of lice causes bad health; of course, they may have drawn this conclusion, but that is not what they are being reported as having done. Given the example as it is, it may be these authors who are committing a causal fallacy when they suggest an analysis in terms of reversal of cause and effect. For such an *analysis* presupposed that health causes lice, which may be an instance of either the second type of fallacy discussed by them and mentioned above, and/or of their seventh one mentioned below, which involves the overlooking of negative correlations (health and no lice).

Their fourth type of fallacy is an argument "concluding that φ is the cause of θ when both are the effect of a third factor, ψ" (p. 585). The first example they give is given by them for the sake of contrast and not as an instance of the fallacy in question. The example involves the causal sequence "getting married $\rightarrow$ more housework $\rightarrow$ more absenteeism" (p. 586), where "we have a genuine causal relation mediated by a third factor" (p. 586). The other example is the following: "It was found that married persons ate less candy than single persons. A second look at the data showed that if married and single persons of equal age are compared, the correlation between marital status and candy consumption disappears. Here it would be misleading and incorrect to conclude: getting married $\rightarrow$ eating less candy. The correct conclusion is that getting older is the operative factor in both increased likelihood of marriage and decreased candy consumption" (pp. 586–87). The authors are not claiming that anyone drew the fallacious conclusion, only that "it would be misleading and incorrect to conclude. . . ." Hence, we have an artificial example.

The fifth type is "confusing causation and resemblance" (p. 588), for which they give the following example from Fischer's *Historians' Fallacies*: "The Picts constructed brochs and souterrains that were small, dark, and mysterious. Therefore, the Picts themselves were small, dark, and mysterious" (p. 588). Later, in another section of their article, Woods and Walton qualify their discussion of this fifth fallacy by saying that "although it is a kind of causal fallacy, we do not regard it as essential to *post hoc*, but rather as a kind of fallacy of resemblance or analogy" (pp. 589–90). I regard this qualification as an intimation that this fallacy is more likely being committed by someone who *analyzed* this example as a fallacy of confusing resemblance and causation, rather than by the argument giver. Be that as it may, it must be also be pointed out that in this example there is nothing very obviously wrong with the part of the argument pertaining to smallness, whereas the part pertaining to darkness and mysteriousness reminds one of textbooks' "inchoations and banalities" rightly lamented by Woods and Walton themselves.

The sixth fallacy is defined as "citing a pragmatically otiose necessary condition" (p. 589) and illustrated by: "Smith drowned because he did not learn to swim when he was young" (p. 589). This is clearly an artificial example, and moreover it is not an argument.

The last fallacy is defined as "overlooking or suppressing information that may run counter to the apparent trend of the correlation" (p. 589).

The example is: "It is easy to show by figures that the more it rains in an area, the fuller and better the wheat grows. Conclusion: rain is good for the crops" (p. 589). Suffice it to say that this is an artificial example.

My conclusion is that Woods and Walton's otherwise excellent discussion of *post hoc* is no more realistic in its examples nor more careful in argument reconstruction than the textbook accounts.

5. Letters to the Editor by Professional Philosophers

Let us look at other fallacy allegations by philosophers. The context here will be one which, if not philosophical in the sense of pure philosophical theorizing, is philosophical in the sense of exhibiting philosophers in action attempting to clarify issues and present arguments by employing philosophical concepts. Thus, the discussion will be instructive from the point of view of the rhetoric of philosophy, besides being so from the point of view of the philosophy of rhetoric in the sense of general theory of reasoning. Moreover, it so happens that the discussion pertains to the *post hoc* fallacy.

In the June 1971 issue of *Commentary*, Samuel McCracken published an article entitled "The Drugs of Habit and the Drugs of Belief" (pp. 43–52), and the article and the issues discussed therein were the subject of a favorable editorial in the same issue by Norman Podhoretz (pp. 4–6). One main argument in this editorial should be reconstructed as follows:

Marijuana is a harmful and dangerous drug for several reasons.

First, it is addictive and habit-forming in its own right since (1) there are people who are dependent upon it, use it every day, would be distressed and even frantic if it suddenly became unavailable, and would have the greatest difficulty in getting accustomed to its absence; (2) the fact that many of its users do not become addicted to it or can take it in moderation is irrelevant because this fact means only that marijuana is not necessarily habit-forming, it does not mean that it is never habit-forming; and (3) the fact that, unlike alcohol and cigarettes, no connection has yet been established between marijuana and any physical ailment is also irrelevant because it took a very long time before the case against cigarettes could convincingly be made, and (life being what it is) lovers of marijuana have to expect that a similar fate will befall their own drug as the use of it spreads and more data becomes available to statistical examination.

Second, marijuana can and does lead to heroin in a substantial number of cases, the number being roughly equal to the number of heroin addicts among us, since there are a very few heroin addicts to be found who did not begin by smoking marijuana, often at a relatively early age.

Third, marijuana only sometimes, not necessarily, leads the user into the use of heroin, and this quality of uncertainty makes it dangerous in a sneaky and seductive manner because if marijuana possessed the inexorable power to drag everyone who ever used it into the hell of heroin, then the pool of potential heroin recruits would diminish drastically in size and with it the total amount of harm done (this would happen because in that case marijuana would lose its effectiveness as a titillation and a lure, due to the fact that it would be feared as greatly as heroin itself); but, the way things are, marijuana promises delight and keeps the promise often enough to maintain its credibility.

In passing from the first of these reasons to the second one, Podhoretz had asserted:

If it is true that marijuana is not necessarily habit-forming, it is also true that marijuana does not necessarily lead the user into the use of heroin (which can serve here as a stand-in for all the harder drugs of habit). But of course it is equally true that there are very few heroin addicts to be found – not to mention users of the hallucinogens – who did not begin by smoking marijuana, often at a relatively early age. What this means is that marijuana can and does lead to heroin in a substantial number of cases – the number being roughly equal to the number of heroin addicts among us – and what this means is that marijuana is a dangerous drug.[25]

Now, in the October 1971 issue of the magazine, a letter to the editor by Professor Heidelberger, a philosopher, objected to the passage just quoted with these words:

If this argument instructs us on the dangers of marijuana, it can also teach us about other, seemingly more innocent substances. If it is true that water is not necessarily habit-forming, it is also true that water does not necessarily lead the user into the use of heroin (which can serve here as a stand-in for all the harder drugs of habit). But of course it is equally true that there are very few heroin addicts to be found – not to mention users of the hallucinogens – who did not begin by drinking water, often a relatively early age. What this means is that water can lead to heroin in a substantial number of cases – the number being roughly to equal to the number of heroin addicts among us – and what this means is that water is a dangerous drug.[26]

Professor Heidelberger's criticism was discussed by Podhoretz who labeled it "a sophomoric sophistry."[27] McCracken called it "a chestnut going back at least to Mark Twain."[28] McCracken also argued that

the point is that . . . the correlation between the use of marijuana and the use of heroin . . . is more than statistical. First there is the human tendency, widespread

---

[25]   *Commentary*, June 1971, p. 6.
[26]   *Commentary*, October 1971, pp. 12–14.
[27]   *Commentary*, October 1971, p. 22.
[28]   *Commentary*, October 1971, p. 20.

if not universal, to satiety and consequent escalation of pleasures. Second, some of the assumptions which make marijuana look good are also persuasive for the other drugs; once the assumptive leap has been made for marijuana, the jump to heroin is the less.... [Finally] there is such a thing as dependency on drugs *in general*, satisfied by marijuana when possible [i.e., available], by more dangerous drugs when necessary.[29]

It is clear that McCracken is taking Professor Heidelberger's objection to be a charge of "*post hoc ergo propter hoc*" (with elements of the first and second types in the classification of Woods and Walton). And, it is equally clear that this charge is effectively refuted by McCracken's pointing out that it is a misleading oversimplification (inaccurate reconstruction) to think that Podhoretz's "*propter hoc*" conclusion is being asserted "just because" of the "*post hoc*" promise. Or, to use Scriven's terminology, Professor Heidelberger is violating the Principle of Charity.

However, there is another way of interpreting Professor Heidelberger's objection. In the December issue, a letter to the editor by Professor Judith Jarvis Thomson came to Heidelberger's defense by claiming that his objection was an "elegant"[30] demonstration of the formal invalidity of Podhoretz's argument by the well-known method of counterexample, consisting of an argument having the same form as Podhoretz's argument, but having true premises and false conclusion.[31]

In reply to Professor Thomson's defense, McCracken stated that it did not occur to him to consider such an interpretation of Heidelberger's criticism "because it did not occur to me that this was all he was saying... [for] Professor Heidelberger's imputation of such a blunder is, *pace* Professor Thomson, quite as insulting as any remark made in rejoinder to it... [and] none of this [Podhoretz's] argument, to be sure, is meant to demonstrate conclusively that marijuana does lead to heroin use, merely to suggest the possibility that it can."[32] McCracken is saying that Podhoretz's argument is obviously an inductive argument, so that a charge of deductive invalidity is true but not worth making; hence the charge of deductive invalidity (meant as serious criticism) is a greater violation of the <u>Principle of Charity</u> and presupposes a more inaccurate reconstruction than the charge of *post hoc*.[33] In turn, it was more charitable

See p. 42

[29] *Commentary*, October 1971, p. 20.
[30] *Commentary*, December 1971, p. 32.
[31] *Commentary*, December 1971, p. 32.
[32] *Commentary*, December 1971, p. 34.
[33] The inductive/deductive *terminology* is nowhere used by McCracken; my claim is one about the *concepts* behind the words. As a matter of fact, at the *verbal* level McCracken

(to Professor Heidelberger) to interpret his objection as McCracken did in his first reply, rather than as Professor Thomson suggests in her letter.

It should also be pointed out that the charge of formal invalidity also faces the following problem, not mentioned by McCracken. Professor Heidelberger's counterexample is not a proper one due to the premise "of course it is equally true that there are very few heroin addicts to be found – not to mention users of hallucinogens – who did not begin by drinking water, often at a relatively early age." This proposition is not true since the term "begin" in the context means "begin their drug experiences"; for such is the meaning in Podhoretz's original argument which is referring to marijuana. Of course, this problem is related to the well-known fact that formal analysis presupposes constancy of meaning and is incapable of dealing with the effects of shifts in meaning. But to say this is not to justify the charge of formal invalidity; rather, it is to suggest another one of its limitations.

Professor Heidelberger may have been led to a charge of formal invalidity by interpreting the passage on which he focuses his attention (quoted above) as a two-step argument with the unstated final conclusion that marijuana is necessarily habit-forming. One step of the argument would then be an instance of denying the consequent, having the first sentence in the above quoted passage as the conditional premise, and having as second premise the proposition that marijuana necessarily leads to heroin. This proposition would also be the conclusion of the second step of the argument, grounded on the marijuana-heroin correlation. This would explain and partly justify Professor Heidelberger's deductivist interpretation. Unfortunately it would do so at the cost of an impermissible abstraction of the present passage from the rest of the editorial, which makes it clear that Podhoretz is asserting that (1) marijuana is *not necessarily* habit-forming, and (2) it does not *necessarily* lead to heroin. In short, the first sentence of the passage analyzed by Professor

speaks of "*post hoc ergo propter hoc*" and says that the attribution of this fallacy to Podhoretz would be more insulting than the attribution of what he (McCracken) had earlier interpreted Professor Heidelberger to be alleging. Since McCracken's earlier critique of Professor Heidelberger had been a defense of the causal connection suggested by Podhoretz, then in fact it was earlier that the *post hoc* problem was first discussed. The inductive *post hoc* problem (at the *conceptual* level) is discussed again in McCracken's second letter, *after* he dismissed the deductivist critique as "insulting," in the passage just quoted, and as a charge of "so classically an example of the fallacy *post hoc, ergo propter hoc*" (*Commentary*, December 1971, p. 34), in a sentence omitted from my quotation for the sake of clarity.

Heidelberg is not a genuine hypothetical proposition, but an unprosaic way of expressing the *conjunction* of (1) and (2), above.

In summary, this discussion indicates very vividly how philosophers' charges of fallacy are often themselves fallacious, in the sense of being the result of uncharitable and/or inaccurate, and hence rhetorically ineffective, reconstructions. There is no need, however, to yield to the temptation of defining a "fallacy of inaccurate reconstruction," so as to have a handy label to characterize the central flaw of discussions of fallacies whether by textbooks, or in theoretical discussions, or in rhetorical contexts. In fact, I have emphasized that there is nothing simple about such an error. For one thing, one would have to speak of "inaccurate reconstruction in negative evaluation," because of the asymmetry mentioned earlier. Moreover, in order to exhibit the inaccuracy of reconstruction, one has to produce a reconstruction which is more accurate than the one being questioned; this would normally be a more complex reconstruction. Thus, my critique of fallacies can escape the *tu quoque* charge.

7

Six Types of Fallaciousness

Toward a Realistic Theory of Logical Criticism (1987)

Like Mt. Everest and the moon, fallacies are challenging simply because they exist. Though it is not exactly true that if they did not exist someone would have to invent them, they do seem to possess the uncanny power deriving from the principle that likes attract each other, and so a number of authors have recently complained about such things as "the fallacy behind fallacies" (Massey 1981a), the prevalence of "some fallacies about fallacies" (Grootendorst 1987), and "how philosophers' charges of fallacy are often themselves fallacious" (Finocchiaro 1981, 22).

Be that as it may, the phenomenon of error in general, and of fallacies in particular, is too much a part of the human condition for us to give up the study of them simply because this study, like any other human activity, is itself liable to error and to fallacy. So, instead of trying to articulate and classify the various errors (be they actual, potential, or imaginary) that characterize the study of fallacies, it is preferable to begin by briefly mentioning a number of approaches that are possible and that are to some extent followed by different scholars. This is especially true in the present context, where the only appropriate attitude is one of live and let live.

1. Methodological Considerations

It is useful to distinguish three main approaches to the study of fallacies, the third being the one to be pursued here. In the first, one takes the essential problem to be that of devising various formalisms of either classical or nonclassical mathematical logic that are meant to represent the various fallacies which philosophers have named and discussed. Here fallacies are taken to be self-subsisting entities that have their own abstract existence independently of human thinking. This is the approach which is perhaps best exemplified by the work of Woods and Walton.[1] The full description and evaluation of this approach is admittedly a long story and cannot be attempted here. Thus, with all due respect to the practitioners of this approach, and with the proviso that if they were not doing this I would be tempted to do it myself, allow me to state briefly my disagreement. I find this approach excessively abstract and formalistic and insufficiently empirical and practical, and I believe that at the root of this approach lie two things: a mathematical-formalist bias, and an obsession with philosophers' conceptualizations of fallacies rather than with the actual fallacious thinking by ordinary people.

At the opposite extreme of the methodological spectrum we find the empirical approach of experimental psychologists (e.g., Wason and Johnson-Laird 1972, Nisbett and Ross 1980, and Evans 1982). No less than the formalist approach, this second one would deserve extended discussion as well as rigorous pursuit in the spirit of both methodological pluralism and the economic maximization and exploitation of resources at one's disposal.[2] Here I can only dogmatically state the reasons for my skepticism. Partly I feel that it represents an empiricist excess; in part it displays a curious "value-free" attitude, as if the attribution of fallacies to people's thinking were not an evaluative enterprise; it also tends to be uncritical vis-à-vis the epistemological basis of the logical theories it uses to define the fallacies experimentally attributed to humans;[3] and finally it faces some internal problems of a sort suggesting that its experimental results are not really phenomena of reasoning, but rather involve other cognitive activities like perception.[4]

---

[1] See, for example, Woods and Walton (1977b; 1982) and Walton (1981; 1985). Their individual and joint publications are too numerous to list here, as one can see from the partial list in Walton 1985, 293–95. In all fairness it should also be mentioned that some of their work is not at all formalist but comes close to the third approach mentioned below, an example being Walton 1987.

[2] I am here referring to such methodological suggestions as the pluralism advocated by Feyerabend 1975, and the at least temporary "normal-science" closed-mindedness of Kuhn's (1970b) theory of scientific revolutions.

[3] L. J. Cohen is perhaps the leading exponent of this sort of criticism, which may be found, for example, in L. J. Cohen 1982. A different type of methodological criticism may be found in Finocchiaro (1979b; 1980b, 256–72), to which a reply was attempted by Wason (1983).

[4] Here I am referring to the work of Evans (1982; 1983b), though it must be said in all fairness that this methodological point represents *my* interpretation of his criticism, a matter elaborated in more detail, if still insufficiently, in Finocchiaro 1987a, n. 4.

Elements of the third alternative approach have been emerging for some time. One clue can be traced at least as far back as Strawson's *Introduction to Logical Theory* and his notion of "the logician's second-order vocabulary" (1952, 15); I would include "fallacy" terminology here, since it ordinarily occurs when someone wants to comment about some logical feature of a first-order expression of reasoning. This means that the best place to begin with in the study of fallacies, or at least a crucial phenomenon to examine, is allegations that fallacies are being committed. An analogous, though slightly different suggestion is being made by Grootendorst when he says that "*fallacy* is a theory-dependent concept. That is, something is only a fallacy within the framework of a properly articulated theory of fallacies."[5] My point amounts to a slight twist on this. I am saying that fundamentally we have a fallacy only within the framework of a given practitioner's conception of the argument he is commenting upon. That is, we have "theory" in the sense of reflection upon practice.

A second feature of this approach involves the realization that the study of fallacies is part of what Johnson and Blair call "the theory of criticism" (1980; 1985, 186–87), or what I elsewhere have called the problem of the evaluation of reasoning (Finocchiaro 1981). What this amounts to is that a fallacy-allegation or fallaciousness-claim is to be treated as a special case of criticism or evaluation and thus studied in the context of criticism or evaluation in general. Moreover, we can thus easily incorporate an important element of the dialectical approach, since the fallaciousness of an argument is not seen as an objectively verifiable fact but rather as the result of the intersubjective interaction of the persons engaged in dialogue.[6] Finally, this point is beginning to be appreciated even by scholars who are otherwise proponents of the formalist approach, as shown by what is undoubtedly the most comprehensive available account of *ad hominem* argument, namely a work by Walton (1985) where he properly treats both an *ad hominem* argument and the claim that a given argument is *ad hominem* as types of criticism.[7]

---

[5] I quote from p. 8 of the typescript of Grootendorst 1987.

[6] Cf. Grootendorst (1987), who, in illustrating the dialectical approach by means of the example of the argument from authority, says that "a second difference is that in other approaches the expert's expertise is seen as an objectively verifiable fact, whereas in the dialectical analysis it is regarded as the intersubjective agreement of the discussants" (p. 16 of the typescript).

[7] Unfortunately he is not always consistent in this, though I am not sure whether at the root of this inconsistency lies his formalist bent; for more details see Finocchiaro 1987b, which is a review of Walton 1985.

Besides being sensitive to the second-order vocabulary, and oriented toward the evaluation of argument, a proper approach must, I believe, recognize the negativity of the evaluations expressed by "fallacy" second-order terminology. In other words, fallaciousness-claims are obviously an unfavorable type of evaluation of an argument. This point is so obvious that its significance is easily missed. And yet when the nature of positive logical evaluation is compared with the nature of negative logical evaluation, certain asymmetries emerge.[8] The existence, origin, and avoidability of these asymmetries is a fascinating problem in itself and deserves much more discussion than it has so far received in the literature. In the present context it will have to suffice to note that negative evaluations are more frequent, much lengthier, much fuller of complexities, and much more interesting than positive evaluations of arguments. Hence we can take advantage of this phenomenon by studying the wealth of data that exist when our task is conceived in the manner mentioned above, that is, given that the study of fallacies is conceived in terms of the various ways in which one can find logical fault with arguments.

The next issue that needs to be decided in such an approach is how literal one wants to be about studying fallacies. That is, should we examine only those reflective judgments that use the particular term "fallacy"? This might seem advisable since semantic intuition suggests that a fallacy is a particular type of logical error, or if you will, that to charge a fallacy is to express a special kind of second-order negative evaluation; the point here would be that there is something especially seriously wrong with an argument that commits a fallacy, or alternatively that to characterize an argument as a fallacy is to devalue it to an especially low degree. To this one might reply that what we are exploring is not the semantics of "fallacy" but the logic of fallacy, and so to be too literalistic would be self-defeating. Moreover, even a semantics of "fallacy" would have to admit other cognate terms like "fallacious" and "fallaciousness," as when one says that such and such an argument is fallacious; but once the term "fallacious" is allowed inside the field, then we are really in the domain of the general theory of logical error or general theory of negative evaluation, since this term

---

[8] Cf. Massey 1981a; Finocchiaro (1980b, 332–42; 1981); and Richard Montague's remarks in Staal (1969, especially p. 275). Though Massey's articles on fallacies are commonly viewed, perhaps even by himself, as undermining what is sometimes called informal logic, it seems to me that this is not so, any more than my own (Finocchiaro 1981) points in the direction of what is claimed by someone like Govier (1982). I believe that the full import and significance of Massey's thesis for informal logic remains to be appreciated and exploited. Cf. also Bencivenga 1979; George 1983; and Massey (1975a; 1975b; 1981b).

does not seem to possess the finality and annihilating connotation that the word "fallacy" does. Finally, when one characterizes an argument as a fallacy (in the literal sense), he must be able to specify what special kind of fallacy it is, because otherwise the claim only means that there is something wrong with the argument, and this would bring us back to questions of degrees of fallaciousness, varieties of logical error, and so on; now, if one cannot be literalistic about fallacy, without being literalistic about particular nameable special cases of fallacy, then the literalistic approach is simply too narrow and constricted, and ultimately it leads to studying philosophers' "fallacy" talk, rather than negative judgments of arguments by ordinary experienced arguers.[9]

Finally, mindful of the above-mentioned criticism of the first two approaches, the one we are proposing tries to steer a middle course between abstract theory and uncritical experimental data. To what extent we are successful is, of course, something that the reader must judge for himself. A good, if short, example of a balanced, negative, evaluative, and reflection-oriented examination of a particular type of logical criticism is Govier's (1985) study of the technique of criticism by logical analogy. In my own exposition, to emphasize this attempt at a balanced synthesis of the other two approaches, I shall proceed in a bidirectional sort of way by alternating and counterposing theoretical and empirical considerations (sections 2 and 3, respectively), and then by alternating within the latter what may be called the element of data collection and the element of analysis of data; this is aimed at ensuring both that my theorizing is not empty and that my "observing" is not blind.

2. Theoretical Considerations

Let us proceed then to an abstract conceptualization of *fallacious* arguments, or types of logical *fallaciousness*. I focus on these terms in part because they are cognate to the word "fallacy" but are weaker, in accordance with the preceding considerations. I could have chosen the term "invalidity,"[10] but only at the risk of confusion and deviance, given the traditional definition of validity. The term "unsound" would have also

---

[9] It is interesting that in one of his latest papers on the topic, presented at the First International Congress on Argumentation (Amsterdam, 3–6 June 1986), Douglas Walton argued for a weakening of the literalistic, finalistic conception of fallacy. Whether this involves a movement away from the earlier formalistic approach for which he is famous and toward the one advocated here, is difficult to say. Cf. Walton 1987.

[10] This is the term I used in Finocchiaro (1980b, 424–31), a term that misled myself, in the sense that I did not realize fully the pertinence of the theory of invalidity elaborated there to the theory of fallacy.

violated well-established conventions and created confusion, though admittedly the phrase "unsound inference" is less ambiguous and confusing than the attribute "unsound argument," and in fact it comes close to the notion of fallaciousness I am trying to articulate. The word "incorrectness" would be too weak as a description of the logical error involved, and too inclusive of all sorts of nonlogical error. By contrast the notion of fallaciousness seems quite inclusive of all the various degrees of logical error; it also seems to exclude automatically nonlogical errors, for, though it is very proper to speak of a fallacious belief (and thus apply the label to a single proposition, rather than to an argument), when this is done there is a connotation that the incorrectness of the belief is due largely to the impropriety of the reasons on which it is based.

It seems to me that fallaciousness is essentially the failure of one proposition to follow from others: that is, an argument is fallacious if and only if the conclusion does not follow from the premises. Starting with this basic definition, I plan to explore the main reasons why a conclusion might not follow from premises, and each such reason will yield a distinct type of fallaciousness. Notice that to formulate the problem this way immediately places us into the Strawsonian second-order level, or into what might be called the level of "reasoning about reasoning."[11] For we are then trying to think of the various ways in which we would go about justifying the claim that a particular conclusion does not follow from particular premises.

It might seem that this is a hopeless task since we are talking about the absence of a relationship between premises and conclusion, the relationship of consequence, and this relation either holds or it does not, and there is only one way of characterizing this absence. However, we are trying not to describe the different absences, but to catalogue the different grounds for the absence.

The typology we want should be analogous to, but different from and richer than, the twofold classification commonly discussed in elementary textbooks about how the justification of a claim may fail, or how the conclusion of an argument may turn out to be untenable: that is, the conclusion may not follow from the premises, or at least one of the premises may not itself be true. The difference is that we have already excluded the latter flaw, as textbooks themselves frequently are quick to do. The standard justification for this exclusion is that the individual truth or falsity of a proposition involves questions of its relationship to the world, and hence falsity of premises is a material, nonformal, or nonlogical flaw.

[11] Cf. Finocchiaro 1980b, 301.

However, it can be easily argued that the examination of the correspondence between a proposition and the world ordinarily reduces to the examination of the relationship between this proposition and others. Even if one accepts this, the intended distinction could still be made in terms of whether or not the proper relationship holds among the *given* propositions, that is, the statements explicitly made in the argument; we could then say that an argument is logically flawed if and only if the *stated* conclusion does not follow from the *stated* premises. But, assuming we are dealing with natural language argumentation, the question of whether or not the consequence holds usually cannot be decided without subjecting to various transformations the conclusion as originally stated and the premises as originally stated. This really amounts to an examination of the relationship between the original propositions and others, and though the latter may be relatively general principles involving various logical and linguistic concepts, they obviously have to be learned, and so it is not clear that logical evaluation as ordinarily understood can remain faithful to the idea of restricting oneself to relationships among the originally given propositions. However, what I want to conclude from this discussion is not that logical flaws or logical evaluations do not essentially involve questions of the interrelations of propositions, but rather that we cannot totally exclude other propositions of an appropriate sort. Since what I am here calling fallaciousness is by definition the basic logical flaw of reasoning, then it is also true to say that fallaciousness must indeed involve interrelationships among propositions, but not merely among the propositions explicitly stated. So I am conceiving the failure of the conclusion to follow from the premises quite generally, in such a way that the failure may originate from the way that these propositions relate among themselves and/or to others.

Let us begin with an analysis of the most familiar case of fallaciousness, invalidity. That is, it may be that the conclusion of an argument does not follow from the premises because it is possible for the premises to be true while the conclusion is false. Such possibility would normally be shown by constructing an argument with the same form or structure as the original one, but having obviously true premises and obviously false conclusion. Such an argument is called a counterexample. So in this first type of fallaciousness the conclusion does not follow because an appropriate counterexample exists. Other well-known ways of describing the situation would be to say that the conclusion does not follow because it does not follow *necessarily,* or because it does not follow in virtue of the *form* of the argument, or because it does not follow ("analytically") in virtue of the meaning of the terms involved, or because it does not follow in virtue of the rules of *deductive* inference. Correspondingly, this first type of fallaciousness could be labeled formal, analytic, or deductive fallaciousness, or as we said earlier simply invalidity.

A second reason why one might be entitled to say that the conclusion does not follow from the premises is that it may not follow any more likely than some other specifiable proposition. In other words, in such a situation the critic produces another argument which has the same premises as the original argument but a different conclusion, and which appears of equal strength as the original. This occurs primarily with explanatory arguments whose conclusion is an explanation of what is stated in the premises, and the criticism amounts to providing an alternative explanation. Occasionally it may happen that the explanandum occurs because of both factors mentioned in the two conclusions, but the point is that a given explanation has no force if there is no reason to prefer it to some other alternative. This may be called explanatory fallaciousness; since it is obviously reminiscent of inductive incorrectness, it may also be called inductive fallaciousness. Still, since the connection between explanation and induction is problematic, it may be advisable to avoid the latter label.

These first two types of fallaciousness are relatively well known, and so what we have done here is primarily to embed well-known facts into a (presumably) novel conceptual framework. Our other types involve a greater departure from well-trodden paths.

To appreciate the third type of fallaciousness we need to underscore the fact that we are dealing with natural language argumentation as it occurs in ordinary circumstances, and that such arguments are always incompletely stated and have many missing assumptions or tacit presuppositions. With this in mind, it is easy to see that a reason why the conclusion does not follow from the premises may be that one of the presuppositions is false. What does this falsity mean in this context? I believe it really amounts to the existence of some ("sound") argument constructible in the context, whose conclusion is the denial of the presupposed assumption. Even the groundlessness of such a presupposition would create trouble for the original argument, at least as long as such a groundlessness is not merely asserted but demonstrated, that is, as long as one gives contextually sound arguments to show that there seems to be no good reason to assert the assumption in question. This third type may be called presuppositional fallaciousness.

Let us notice now that a pattern is beginning to emerge here. In fact, the first type was grounded on the construction of an appropriate

counterexample, the second on the production of an alternative explanation, the third on the construction of a presuppositional criticism, and
all three of these entities are arguments different from but appropriately
related to the original. This pattern allows us to define a fourth type of
fallaciousness where the conclusion does not follow because what does
follow from the premises is some specifiable proposition inconsistent
with it. Such a proposition would naturally be called a counterconclu-
sion, and the new argument a counterargument. Normally such a counterargument will have as premises not only the premises of the original
argument, but other propositions which are independently justifiable
or contextually acceptable. For lack of a better term, this type may be
called positive fallaciousness, to underscore the fact that the criticism
here contributes something positive since it shows what does follow from
the premises, and not merely what does not.

The fifth type of fallaciousness may be called semantical, and is meant
to take care of equivocations. This is the case when the conclusion does
not follow because the premises contain a term which has two meanings
such that, if it is used in one sense, one of the premises is false (though
they would imply the conclusion), whereas if the term is used in the other
sense, the premises do not imply the conclusion (though admittedly the
previously problematic premise becomes true); in short, in the context
the conclusion cannot follow from true premises. The discussion below
will show that semantical fallaciousness is very intimately related to presuppositional fallaciousness, since the semantical ambiguity in question
is normally not a self-subsisting property of a term, but rather something
that needs to be argued in the context on the basis of the inferential relationships affecting the term. Nevertheless, it is useful to have a special
term for this phenomenon.

Finally, our sixth and last type refers to the flaw of begging the question
and circularity. This too will be seen to involve presuppositional fallaciousness, but could be given the special name of persuasive fallaciousness. In
such cases the conclusion does not *follow* from the premises because it *is*
one of the premises.

We have thus defined six types of fallaciousness: formal, explanatory,
presuppositional, positive, semantical, and persuasive. They all involve arguments whose conclusion may be said not to follow from the premises,
and thus logical evaluations of the relationships among propositions;
moreover, in each case the reason for the fallaciousness involves the construction of some other argument, or some other part of the original
argument, to make the point. The exact meaning and interrelationships

of these six notions need more analysis and exploration. This cannot be done here, or at least not at this juncture, since it is now time to focus on some empirical data. To these we now turn, keeping in mind that they are not mere examples of the concepts just defined, but data which partly illustrate them, and partly possess a life of their own, on which some light may be thrown by means of these concepts.

3. Data: Empirical and Analytical Considerations

One of the richest collections of arguments available anywhere is found ✓ in the works of Galileo Galilei. Any argumentation theorist who is able and willing to overcome whatever free associations the title of "Father of Modern Science" may bring to mind, will find as much food for thought as scientists and scientific methodologists have found in regard to questions and topics that interest them. The fact is so striking and overwhelming that argumentation theorists can appreciate the point and exploit the material without any technical involvement in the specialty of Galilean scholarship. This is even more true for the study of fallacies, at least as conceived here, namely as the study of negative evaluations of arguments, for the scientific revolution which Galileo fathered was essentially dependent not only on the reasoned adoptions of new physical and cosmological ideas, but also on the reasoned rejection of many long-standing physical and cosmological arguments on which the older ideas were based. So let us briefly summarize some of the classical arguments in favor of the conclusion that the earth stands still at the center of the universe, and Galileo's criticism of them.[12]

This conclusion may be conceived as addressing two questions, one about the earth's state of rest or motion, the other about its location at or off the center. The two questions are distinct at least insofar as it is possible that the earth might have been located at the center and yet have a daily axial rotation. Moreover, the question of location was contextually equivalent to whether the annual revolution along the ecliptic orbit belongs to the sun (which would correspond to geocentrism) or to the earth (which would correspond to heliocentrism). Some of the arguments against heliocentrism were those that supported the earth-heaven dichotomy, according to which the universe is divided into two

---

[12] The arguments and the criticism are found in the *Dialogue Concerning the Two Chief World Systems* (Galilei 1632; 1953). Feyerabend 1975 and Finocchiaro 1980b contain analyses of many of Galileo's critiques.

radically different regions: a terrestrial region which is the domain of change and where things are made of the four elements (earth, water, air, and fire), and a heavenly region in which bodies consist of the fifth element aether and which is devoid of any physical or chemical changes (other than regular circular motion). Given the earth-heaven dichotomy, it is impossible for the earth to have an orbital revolution around the sun and be a heavenly body. Four arguments are particularly instructive for our purpose: two for the earth-heaven dichotomy, and two against the earth's axial rotation.

The so-called a posteriori argument grounds the earth-heaven dichotomy on observation. It reads quite simply: no heavenly changes have ever been observed; therefore, the heavenly region is unchangeable (Galilei 1632, 71–72; 1953, 46–48).

Galileo criticizes this argument in at least four ways. One is to point out that in his own time the premise is no longer true, in the light of, for example, the telescopic observations of sunspots and the naked-eye observation of novas. It is interesting to point out that, though this criticism is in some obvious sense nonlogical, it is the one that takes Galileo the longest to articulate, since he has to argue every inch of the way through all sorts of controversial issues in order to refute the premise (Galilei 1632, 75–82; 1953, 50–58).

The other Galilean criticisms are based on the contextual distinction of two meanings for the phrase "heavenly changes": a heavenly change can mean the generation or decay of a heavenly body as a whole, and it can mean a partial change within a heavenly body.

When interpreted holistically, the original argument amounts to the following: no one has ever observed any generation or decay of heavenly bodies in the heavenly region; therefore, the heavenly region is unchangeable. It is then subject to the criticism that this way of reasoning would lead one to the following absurd argument: no one has ever observed any generation or decay of terrestrial globes in the terrestrial region; therefore, the terrestrial region is unchangeable (Galilei 1632, 74–75; 1953, 49–51).

When the argument is interpreted the other way, Galileo objects that it is still wrong because: no terrestrial changes would be noticeable to an observer on the moon before some particular very large terrestrial change had occurred, and yet terrestrial bodies are obviously changeable and would have been so even before that occurrence (Galilei 1632, 74; 1953, 49–50).

What are we to make of these second and third Galilean criticisms? It seems to me that we can say, at least provisionally, that they are trying to establish the invalidity or formal fallaciousness of the two versions of the a posteriori argument. The technique used is that of the construction of counterexamples, namely arguments of the same form but with true premises and false conclusion. It should be noticed that, despite the ambiguity mentioned by Galileo, he is not (correctly) charging any equivocation here, as he does for some other arguments to be examined presently.

At this point someone might interject that the very fact that this particular argument was called the a posteriori argument indicates that it was meant to be an "inductive" rather than a "deductive" argument, and hence the criticisms just made might be true but of dubious force or relevance. It is perhaps to anticipate such an objection that Galileo has another criticism that can be taken to address precisely this issue.

The fourth criticism Galileo makes is directed to the more plausible particularistic (second) version and amounts to the following argument: if there were changes in the heavenly bodies then most of them could not be observed from the earth, since the distances from the heavenly bodies to the earth are very great, and on earth changes can be observed only when they are relatively close to the observer; moreover, even if there were changes in the heavenly bodies large enough to be observable from the earth then they might not have been observed, since even large changes cannot be observed unless careful, systematic, exact, and continual observations are made, and no such observations have been made, at least not by the argument's proponents (Galilei 1632, 72–74; 1953, 47–50).

This criticism is interpreting the original argument as an explanatory argument; that is, it presents the conclusion about heavenly unchangeability as the explanation of the observational absence mentioned in the premise. Two other ways of explaining the fact are being suggested: it may be due to the great distance between the earth and the heavenly bodies, and/or to the lack of sufficiently careful observations of the heavenly bodies. These alternative explanations do not *refute* the Aristotelian *explanation* but the Aristotelian *argument*; that is, this criticism does not prove the conclusion of the original argument false, but rather *weakens* the inferential link between premise and conclusion, since there is no reason to prefer the Aristotelian explanation to the Galilean one. Therefore, the point being made is a logical criticism. The logical flaw being charged is explanatory or "inductive" fallaciousness. The technique being used is the construction of an alternative explanation.

Another argument in support of the earth-heaven dichotomy was the contrariety argument: (12) bodies do not change unless there is contrariety; (11) there is no contrariety among heavenly bodies; therefore, (1) heavenly bodies are unchangeable.[13]

One of Galileo's criticisms of this is the following. The major premise (12) would have to be supported on the basis of the alleged fact that: (121) there is a correlation between the changes among terrestrial bodies and such pairs of contraries as upward and downward motions, hot and cold, and dry and moist; therefore, in the major premise the term "bodies" means parts of whole worldly globes. But the minor premise is supported by the following argument: since (1121) there are three types of simple motions (straight-toward, straight-away from, and around the center), and (1122) the two straight motions are contraries, but (1123) one thing can only have one contrary, it follows that (112) circular motion has no contrary; but (111) heavenly bodies have circular motion; therefore, (11) there is no contrariety among heavenly bodies. Therefore, in the minor premise the term "bodies" means whole worldly globes. Therefore, if this term has the first meaning then the minor premise is groundless, and if it has the second meaning then the major premise is groundless. However, if the conclusion is to follow, this term must be used with the same meaning in both premises. Therefore, if the conclusion follows, one of the premises must be groundless; or again, if both premises are grounded then the conclusion does not follow (Galilei 1632, 69–71; 1953, 44–47).

What does this criticism amount to? It obviously charges some kind of equivocation or semantical fallaciousness. But this is not the same as invalidity or formal fallaciousness, since we are not saying that if the original premises are *true* the original conclusion may be *false*. On the other hand, it may be that when we consider the fuller argument into which the original has been embedded, we then do have invalidity for some steps of the fuller argument. To explore this, let us focus on its two subarguments reconstructed to support the two premises of the original argument. The groundlessness of each of the original premises [(11) and (12)] given the meaning of the term "bodies" associated with the other, amounts to the invalidity of the respective subarguments for those two premises given the correctness of the other. If this is typical of equivocations or

---

[13] Galilei (1632, 62–63; 1953, 37–39). Here and in what follows the numbering of the various propositions in an argument is designed to explicitly reflect its inferential structure, as suggested in Angell (1964, 369–93) and in Finocchiaro (1980b, 314–15). The gist of the rules is to add a digit (in the order 1, 2, 3, etc.) to whatever number designates a given conclusion, in order to designate a reason supporting this conclusion.

semantical fallaciousness, then we see that what is involved is a type of presuppositional criticism; for we have constructed the argument that might be said to be *presupposed* by the original, and such a longer presupposed argument is using a particular term illegitimately with different meanings in different places.

In the Galilean text we find a second criticism. It is this. If one accepts the contrariety argument, then one would have to accept the following self-contradictory argument: (21) bodies which have contraries are changeable, since (211) bodies do not change unless there is contrariety; but (22) heavenly bodies have contraries, since (221) heavenly bodies are unchangeable, (222) terrestrial bodies are changeable, and (223) changeability and unchangeability are contraries; therefore (2) heavenly bodies are changeable (Galilei 1632, 65–67; 1953, 40–43).

This argument is self-contradictory insofar as the conclusion (2) asserts what premise (221) denies. But such self-contradiction may be more apparent than real. Assuming there is nothing else wrong with it, then the gist of the argument is that if (211) and (221) are both true, then so is (2). This means that if (211) is true and (2) is false, then (2) is true. Or, if (211) is true, then if (2) is false then (2) is true. So, if (211) is true, then so is (2). If this is correct, then this is really a contextual argument supporting (2).

Now, from the point of view of the original argument this is what may be called a counterargument, that is an argument whose conclusion is a proposition inconsistent with the original conclusion (and whose premises include the original premises). Insofar as the counterargument is correct, the original one is fallacious in the positive sort of way mentioned earlier, which points out what does *not* follow by showing what *does* follow. What makes this particular charge of positive fallaciousness seem special is the fact that the counterargument contains so little above and beyond the original, and so is relatively elegant; usually more is needed.

Let us now go on to examine the first of two arguments against the earth's axial rotation, namely the vertical fall argument. It may be stated as follows: (3) the earth does not rotate because (31) bodies fall vertically, and (32) this could not happen if the earth rotated; for (321) if the earth rotated and bodies fell vertically, then falling bodies would have a mixture of two natural motions, toward and around the center, (322) which is impossible because (3221) every body can have only one natural motion, and because (3222) on a moving ship a rock dropped from the top of the mast falls behind and lands away (stern) from the foot of the mast (Galilei 1632, 164–69; 1953, 138–43).

The first Galilean criticism here is that if the phrase "vertical fall" is taken literally and at its face value, then the argument begs the question, because it presupposes the conclusion that the earth is motionless. The literal meaning of vertical fall is downward motion in a straight line along an extended terrestrial radius, i.e., perpendicular to the earth's surface. This may be called actual vertical fall and should be distinguished from apparent vertical fall, which means fall that to an observer on the earth's surface appears to be vertical, as when a rock is dropped from the top of a tower and lands at its foot directly below with no deviation. The two would coincide on a motionless earth, but an important point, which could be agreed upon by both sides of the controversy is that *if* the earth were in axial rotation then the two would *not* coincide, since the appearance of vertical fall would imply an actually slanted path and thus an actual nonvertical fall.

So this first criticism begins by noting that premise (31) of the original argument "appears" to be talking about *actual* vertical fall, and there is no problem with the first inferential step from premises (31) and (32) to the conclusion (3), since we have an instance of denying the consequent. Then the critic asks how the argument's proponents know that bodies do indeed fall vertically, i.e., that premise (31) is true. The answer would be: because (311) bodies are *seen* to fall vertically, i.e., because of apparent vertical fall. Now the truth of this observation is undeniable, but the critic next asks how actual vertical fall follows from apparent vertical fall. This is a legitimate question since, as pointed out above, on a rotating earth apparent vertical fall would not imply actual vertical fall. It seems that the only way to justify the needed implication (or conditional proposition) is to assume that we are on a motionless earth. But this is precisely what the original argument is trying to prove.

Thus if in the initial subargument of the original argument vertical fall means actual vertical fall, then it presupposes the following argument: (4222) the earth does not rotate, and (4221) if the earth does not rotate then apparent vertical fall implies actual vertical fall, so (422) apparent vertical fall implies actual vertical fall; but (421) bodies do appear to fall vertically; so (42) bodies do actually fall vertically; but (41) if the earth rotates then bodies would not (actually) fall vertically; so (4) the earth does not rotate. The argument from (42) and (41) to (4), which is equivalent to the original one from (31) and (32) to (3), begs the question because the question is (4222) [which is the same question as (31)], the fuller argument to (4) is being presupposed, and the identity of (4222) and (4) yields a circle.

However, perhaps the original argument was speaking of apparent vertical fall. In that case the issue would reduce to the tenability of the impossibility of mixed motions, i.e., to proposition (322). In the argument as stated, this proposition is already supported with reasons, and so its tenability largely depends on whether or not the corresponding subarguments involve any fallaciousness. Galileo has criticisms of both these subarguments.

Consider first the argument that (322) it is impossible for a falling body to have two natural motions, toward and around the center (i.e., vertical and horizontal) because (3221) every body can have only one natural motion. As you might expect, Galileo elsewhere[14] explicitly questions the empirical correctness of this premise, but that does not concern us here; the only thing to note is that, once again, the empirical issue requires argumentation. However, he also implicitly objects that the two "natural" motions of falling bodies on a rotating earth would be "natural" in different senses: the downward fall would be natural in the sense of spontaneous (not potentially everlasting), whereas the rotational motion would be natural in the sense of potentially everlasting (not spontaneous). Now the premise (3221) here may be perfectly true of each of these two kinds of natural motion, but it would imply only that a body cannot have two kinds of spontaneous motion or two kinds of everlasting motions; it clearly does not imply that it cannot have one kind of one, and one kind of the other.[15]

This criticism is obviously an equivocation charge, and its fuller analysis is left as an exercise for the reader.

Consider now the argument that (322) a mixture of natural motions is impossible because (3222) on a moving ship rocks dropped from the top of the mast fall behind. Again, besides arguing that this alleged ship experiment does not in fact happen this way, he objects that the unwillingness of the rock to move simultaneously in two directions is not the only possible explanation of the alleged fact. It might happen because the horizontal motion imparted by the ship to the rock is forced motion, which might be dissipated after the rock is left to itself. It might also happen because of air resistance, which would oppose the horizontal motion acquired by the rock (Galilei 1632, 166–69; 1953, 140–44).

---

[14] Galilei (1632, 281–89, 423–42; 1953, 256–64, 397–416).
[15] This criticism is not that explicit in the text, but it can be derived from Galilei (1632, 38–57; 1953, 14–32); cf. Finocchiaro 1980b, 349–53, 389.

This is a charge of explanatory fallaciousness, of the type also illustrated earlier; and it is supported by the technique of alternative explanation.

The last argument to be considered here mentions centrifugal force to show why the earth cannot rotate. It may be stated thus: (52) if the earth were rotating, objects on its surface would be scattered away from it toward the heavens because (521) rotation has the power of extruding objects lying on the surface of the rotating body; but (51) objects on the earth's surface are not observed to be scattered toward the heavens; therefore (5) the earth does not rotate (Galilei 1632, 214; 1953, 187–88).

Galileo criticizes this argument in at least two ways. He objects that what follows at most from the principle of centrifugal force (521) is not the scattering of objects on a rotating earth (52), but rather either that (a) if the earth had always been rotating then there would not be any objects on its surface now, or that (b) if the earth were to start now rotating then objects already on its surface would be scattered; but the other premise as stated, proposition (51), connects with (b) rather than (a); so the final conclusion that follows from the argument as stated is that the earth did not just start to rotate (Galilei 1632, 214–16; 1953, 188–90).

What comes to mind to conceptualize this criticism is the Aristotelian *ignoratio elenchi*, or irrelevant conclusion, or more simply irrelevance. In terms of the conceptual framework being developed here, we seem to have a case of positive fallaciousness.

Continuing with the criticism, Galileo is well aware that one could reformulate the argument by restating premise (51) to read: there obviously are now loose objects on the earth's surface; then it would connect with the first one of the consequences (a) of centrifugal force, to yield the conclusion derived by the argument's proponents.

Here we see the reason for the qualifying phrase "at most" in the previous criticism. For Galileo objects that a rotating earth would not really scatter its surface bodies toward the heavens, his argument being essentially a quantitative one: though it is true that the cause of scattering increases as the speed when the radius is constant, when speeds are equal the cause of scattering decreases as the radius increases, so that this cause increases directly with the speed and inversely with the radius; thus, perhaps this cause remains constant when the speed increases as much as the radius, namely when equal number of rotations are made in equal times; hence, the earth's rotation would cause as much scattering as a wheel which rotated once in twenty-four hours; that is why there would be no scattering on a rotating earth (Galilei 1632, 238, 244; 1953, 211–12, 217–18).

One term that Galileo himself uses to characterize the fault being charged is incompleteness. This is a fairly good conceptualization since the criticism points out that linear speed is not the only effective variable, though it is the only one considered in the original argument. I believe such incompleteness corresponds to positive fallaciousness, for the criticism points out what does really follow when the neglected factor is taken into account.

4. Conclusion and Further Problems

In this chapter we have reported and analyzed Galileo's main logical criticisms of four important anti-Copernican arguments. His criticism of the a posteriori argument for the earth-heaven dichotomy tries to show that it is both formally and inductively fallacious; two counterexamples are given to support the former charge, and an alternative explanation to support the latter. In his criticism of the contrariety argument for the earth-heaven dichotomy, one charge is that this is semantically and presuppositionally fallacious because of an equivocation with the term "bodies"; and he also charges that the argument is positively fallacious by constructing an elegant counterargument. The vertical fall argument (in its actual vertical fall version) is criticized as begging the question by constructing the presupposed argument and pointing out the circularity of the latter; the apparent vertical fall version is criticized for equivocating with the term "natural" at one point, and thus being semantically fallacious, and also for containing an explanatory fallaciousness, exhibited by means of an alternative explanation of the alleged ship experiment. Finally, he objects to the centrifugal force argument for being irrelevant as ordinarily stated, and for being incomplete when properly rephrased, such irrelevance and incompleteness being subtypes of positive fallaciousness.

Our analytical review encountered two cases of formal fallaciousness (in the a posteriori argument), two cases of explanatory fallaciousness (in the a posteriori and vertical fall arguments), two cases of semantical fallaciousness (in the contrariety and vertical fall arguments), three cases of positive fallaciousness (in the contrariety and centrifugal force arguments), and one case of persuasive fallaciousness (in the vertical fall argument). Thus we have had nine specific instances of fallacious arguments.

In the light of our earlier theoretical considerations, some of these logical flaws are what may be called subtypes of fallaciousness: equivocation, circularity, incompleteness, and irrelevance. On the other hand, some of them constitute main types: formal, explanatory, presuppositional, and positive. Incompleteness and irrelevance are subtypes of positive fallaciousness, equivocation and circularity subtypes of presuppositional fallaciousness.

Our four historical cases and nine specific instances of fallacious arguments may be said to provide empirical content and concrete illustrations for the four general types and four common subtypes of fallaciousness proposed in our theoretical considerations. However, this relationship merely reflects our order of exposition, or "context of justification," so to speak. It would be equally true to say that our types and subtypes of fallaciousness are meant to help us make sense of a classic controversy in the history of thought; for example, the distinction between general types and common subtypes does not emerge clearly until the end of our analytical data review. This second relationship is the one that reflects more closely the "context of discovery."[16]

This mutuality and contextuality of the epistemological relationship between data and theory in turn reflects our methodological orientation, discussed at the beginning of this paper. It is perhaps the other side of the coin of another feature of our approach, namely the attempt to follow a judiciously realistic course between formalist and empiricist extremes. More positively viewed, our approach tries to build upon a number of recent trends, so that our effort here could be seen as being part of a developing tradition; basically it is the result of the attempt to formulate the problem of the nature of fallacy in terms of the logic of the negative evaluation of argument, that is, in terms of a theory of logical criticism.

Much more work remains to be done. At the methodological level it would be useful to have more sustained comparative discussion of our negative-evaluation approach, the formal orientation (of scholars like Woods and Walton), and the experimental method of psychologists (like Wason and Johnson-Laird, Nisbett and Ross, and Evans). For example, is it really fair to attribute to them tendencies to excess that turn the formal into the formalist, and the empirical into the empiricist? Is not the approach advocated here equally liable to excess, the main liability being theoretical poverty or theoretical disorientation? Is it really correct to equate the formal approach and the history-of-philosophy approach, according to which the central problem to solve is to make sense out of philosophers' conceptualizations of fallacies in the course of history? In regard to the negative-evaluation approach per se, we need to explore the

[16] This can be seen from the order I followed in Finocchiaro 1980b.

exact nature and status of the asymmetries mentioned earlier between validity and invalidity, and favorable and unfavorable evaluation. And what is the exact connection between this approach advocated here and the dialectical orientation? Are there not many more similarities than the one briefly mentioned earlier, and are there not also differences? Could one argue that the negative-evaluation approach is after all a special case of the dialectical one, since the emphasis on evaluation is simply a way of introducing dialectical considerations?

At the theoretical level we need clearer and more precise definitions of the various types of fallaciousness, of their mutual interrelationships, and of their relationship to other concepts such as validity, induction, rhetorical persuasion, and criticism. We also need to explore whether there are more of what we have called main types, and of what we have called common subtypes. And exactly what theory of (the structure of) argument is presupposed by the theory of criticism adumbrated here? Should a theory of argument have been developed before any attempt at a theory of criticism? Could a theory of argument be developed from the theory of criticism sketched here? Is one prior to the other, or are they on an equal status?

At the empirical level, one would like to explore whether other historical controversies or classic collections of arguments and criticism can be enlightened by some of the ideas developed here, and confirm or disconfirm them. And it would also be interesting to see whether any of them can shed light on some of the experimental data psychologists have collected, or perhaps even to devise and carry out new experiments in their terms.

At the pedagogical level, one would like to know how beginning students would react to appropriate presentations of the varieties of fallaciousness discussed here.

Finally, if any of the additional problems for future research mentioned here are found to be fruitful and worthy of pursuit, then one could add fruitfulness to the other reasons favoring the approach, the theoretical framework, and the particular theses advanced here.[17]

[17] Parts of this chapter were researched and written while the author was on sabbatical leave (fall 1986) from the University of Nevada, Las Vegas, and during his tenure as Barrick Distinguished Scholar (1986–87) at the same institution. I hereby express my gratitude and acknowledge the support.

8

Asymmetries in Argumentation and Evaluation (1992)

1. The Problem

A number of scholars in a variety of fields have elaborated the existence of various cognitive asymmetries relating in one way or another to the practice and theory of argumentation. The purpose of this chapter is to call attention to the problem and to begin examining the nature and implications of these phenomena explicitly from the viewpoint of the theory of argumentation.

2. Massey: Formal Validation versus Invalidation of Arguments

One of the most gripping of these problems has been discussed by Massey and his critics (Massey 1975a, 1975b, 1981a, 1987; Bencivenga 1979; Finocchiaro 1994a; George 1983; Johnson 1989; McKay 1984, 1987).[1] Their concern has been the question of asymmetry in the evaluation of arguments from the viewpoint of formal logic, namely in assessing the formal validity or formal invalidity of arguments, or in short, in the formal validation and formal invalidation of arguments. Massey has elaborated the thesis that whereas formal logic does provide techniques for proving arguments formally valid, it does not provide any techniques for

---

[1] Though Massey himself has often presented this thesis as a direct attack on informal logic, his conception of informal logic equates the field with the study of fallacy in general and so-called informal fallacies in particular, but the field has now advanced beyond that (Finocchiaro 1984b; Johnson and Blair 1985); moreover, his attack has been ably criticized by Johnson (1989). Massey has recently credited Oliver 1967 with the discovery of the asymmetry thesis; so one should perhaps label this alleged phenomenon the Oliver-Massey asymmetry.

proving arguments formally invalid; thus there is a fundamental asymmetry between formal validation and formal invalidation, the asymmetry being that the former is feasible but the latter is not. Using argument-theoretical language, and echoing the title of one of Massey's papers, one might say that while it is possible to give good arguments that good arguments are good, it is not possible to give good arguments that bad arguments are bad.

Massey's rationale is as follows. To show that a given natural-language argument is formally valid, it suffices to show that it has a valid argument-form. However, to show that a given argument is formally invalid, it is not enough to show that it has an invalid argument-form; rather one has to show that there is no valid argument-form which the original argument instantiates, and formal logic cannot do this since it is essentially the never-ending search for new valid argument-forms.

This asymmetry has been criticized from two directions: Bencivenga (1979) has objected that the formal validation of arguments is as questionable as their formal invalidation, and McKay (1984; 1987) has objected that formal invalidation is not as hopeless and arbitrary as Massey makes it sound.

Adopting these criticisms, I am inclined to conclude the following (Finocchiaro 1994a). Formal validation depends on the determination of the validity of argument forms, which in turn depends on the discovery and invention of proofs, which is ultimately an informal process; and formal validation also depends on the translation or interpretation of the original natural-language sentences involved, which depends in turn on linguistic intuitions about the synonymy of various natural-language sentences; and the latter is an inherently informal process. Similarly, formal invalidation depends partly on the claim that a given argument form reflects all relevant logical details of the argument in question, which is best regarded as an inductive generalization; and formal invalidation also depends on the comparison between the argument in question and a proposed counterexample argument, and such comparison is best regarded as an instance of analogical reasoning, with all the advantages and the pitfalls pertaining thereto. Thus, strictly speaking, formal validation and invalidation are equally unfeasible; whereas informally speaking, they are equally feasible. In any case, they stand on an equal plane, and the asymmetry disappears.

A basic flaw in Massey's argument for his asymmetry thesis is, I believe, an over-emphasis on one aspect of the total process of argument evaluation; this is the step of comparing the given natural-language

Fallacies and Asymmetries

argument with known argument-forms. There is indeed an asymmetry at this juncture, involving the relationship between arguments and argument-forms; it is important to remember that if an argument instantiates a valid argument-form the argument is thereby valid, but that if an argument instantiates an invalid form the argument is not thereby invalid. What this means is that the property of instantiating a valid form is crucial to an argument, whereas the property of instantiating an invalid form is not. However, if one looks at the rest of the evaluation process, this asymmetry loses its significance. For example, it is balanced by at least one other asymmetry of a reverse kind. That is, in the evaluation of an argument form, to show its invalidity it suffices to find a specific counterexample argument; but to show that the argument form is valid, it is not enough to find a specific example argument or to fail to find a counterexample; we must show that no counterexamples exist.

It should also be obvious that Massey's thesis is relevant to the evaluation of only the inference of an argument, and not other aspects such as the acceptability of the premises. Similarly, he is discussing only what may be called deductive evaluation, rather than other weaker forms of support by the premises to the conclusion. While these two limitations are perhaps less serious than the more internal flaw mentioned in the previous paragraph, nevertheless, from the point of view of the evaluation of arguments all three difficulties point in the same direction. That is, if what we have in mind is realistic evaluation of realistic arguments, then Massey's asymmetry involves merely *one* step of *one* type of evaluation of *one* aspect of arguments.

3. Popper: Empirical Verification versus Falsification of Scientific Ideas

Formalist-inclined scholars are not the only ones who have sensed some kind of cognitive asymmetry; a similar asymmetry is a well-known part of Popper's epistemology (Popper 1959, 1962; Bartley 1982, 1984; Miller 1987).[2]

The relevant Popperian thesis may be expressed by saying that, whereas the empirical verification of a scientific generalization or hypothesis is not feasible, empirical falsification is, and in this sense there is an asymmetry

---

[2] See also Klayman and Ha (1987), who distinguish the distinction between confirmation and disconfirmation from that between positive and negative strategy, implying that a stress on refutation is consistent with a positive strategy.

between empirical verification and falsification. The supporting argument is that an empirical generalization with an indefinite or potentially infinite domain can never be conclusively verified because we can never observe all its instances; however, observing a single counterinstance will falsify the generalization. Similarly, in evaluating a theoretical hypothesis by testing its empirical consequences, the non-occurrence of a single consequence will falsify it by means of *modus tollens*, whereas the occurrence of however many consequences will not prove its truth, on pain of committing the fallacy of affirming the consequent. Popper is obviously speaking primarily of individual claims rather than arguments. How can his point be translated into argument-theoretical terminology?

Suppose we begin focusing on *the arguments* in support of scientific generalizations or hypotheses, for example inductions by enumeration or hypothetico-deductive explanations. What is Popper saying about such arguments? Presumably he is saying something more than that all such arguments are to be evaluated as being formally or deductively invalid; this is true, but uninteresting and unsurprising. Using the term "induction" in a sense different from Popper, we might say that perhaps what he means is that all such arguments are even *inductively* incorrect; but this would lead to the terminological contradiction that no inductive arguments are inductively correct, and so it would be preferable to express the Popperian point differently. I believe Popper also means to claim that empirical-scientific arguments (like inductions by enumeration and hypothetico-deductive explanations) are probabilistically weak; that is, according to the traditional conception of probability, all these arguments are such that the conclusion is rendered highly improbable by the premises; therefore, they are all to be evaluated negatively, and none positively. The essential reason for the probabilistic weakness of such arguments is the following: the conclusion contains more information than the premises, and so the probability of the conclusion is the product of the probability of the premises and the probability of the additional information; since probabilities are numbers between zero and one, such a multiplication yields a number less than the original numbers; that is to say, the probability of the conclusion is less than the probability of the premises, and so the conclusion has been rendered less probable.

If there is an asymmetry here, it is that no positive evaluations of inductive arguments are possible, only negative evaluations of them; that is, favorable verdicts of inductive arguments are never justifiable, whereas unfavorable verdicts are easily, indeed trivially, justifiable. When expressed in this manner, in terms of arguments, the Popperian asymmetry does not sound like a genuine asymmetry, and so let us go back to his initial point about the falsification and the verification of generalizations and hypotheses.

From this viewpoint, Popper's thesis seems analogous to Massey's. However, there is a reversal of sorts. Indeed, the two asymmetries look like opposites since what is impossible for Massey is unfavorable formal evaluation and for Popper favorable empirical evaluation, whereas the type of feasible evaluation is the favorable one for Massey and the unfavorable one for Popper.

Actually, the analogy between Massey's and Popper's asymmetries extends further, in that the latter is subject to the same type of difficulty as the former. That is, Popper too is overstressing a single step in the overall process of evaluation. As his critics have pointed out, the empirical falsification of generalizations or hypotheses presupposes the verification of the particular statements describing the counterinstances or the non-occurred consequences; these statements provide the minor premises of the refutation by *modus tollens*. However, the verification of these minor premises presupposes that we assume *other* generalizations or hypotheses, and so empirical falsification is really a process of inter-theoretical comparison where one generalization or hypothesis is judged worse than another. Now, empirical verification is merely the other side of the coin of this process, where one claim is judged better than another. It follows that the alleged asymmetry evaporates.

4. Experimental Psychology: The Pollyanna Principle and the Negativity Effect

A phenomenon of asymmetry has also been studied by social and cognitive psychologists. They have found overwhelming experimental evidence for the existence of a positivity bias in evaluations (Matlin and Stang 1978). That is, humans presumably have a tendency to evaluate favorably themselves, other people, and objects and situations in general. For example, in evaluating students, teachers have a tendency to give a better than average grade to the average student; and the same happens in student evaluations of teachers (Matlin and Stang 1978, 1–2, 179–82). This has come to be called the "Pollyanna Principle," after the child heroine in Eleanor Porter's story. Though I know of no experiments testing the relative frequency of positive evaluations and negative evaluations of arguments, this principle would predict that subjects would give positive evaluations more frequently than negative evaluations, in ways not entirely accountable on the basis of the actual correctness or incorrectness of arguments. This imbalance between negative and positive evaluations is not, however, what psychologists call the asymmetry in question; rather they call it simply a bias.

On the other hand, there is considerable psychological evidence for a negativity effect at another level. This involves the fact that negative information is given greater weight than positive information (Kanouse and Hanson 1971; Peeters 1971). Now, the weighting of information is an instance of evaluation, so we are dealing with the evaluation of evidence; and negative evidence refers to information suggesting something bad about the entities under consideration; so the phenomenon is that arguments from negative evaluative premises to negative evaluative conclusions are regarded as stronger than arguments from positive evaluative premises to positive evaluative conclusions. In short, negative arguments are evaluated more positively than positive arguments.

Psychologists refer to both the positivity bias and the negativity effect taken together as the "positive-negative asymmetry." Though the two phenomena seem to contradict each other, several interpretations have been devised to make them compatible. For example, Peeters (1971; 1974; 1986; 1987) has argued that because of the positivity bias people have a general presumption that things are good; because of this presumption, when something bad happens the contrast makes it stand out, and so more weight is attached to it. Another illustration of their compatibility is provided by an experiment done by Czapinski (1980; 1982; 1986), in which he asks students in university or pre-university classes to name the fellow students they like most and those they dislike most; the positivity bias shows itself insofar as the number of students liked is significantly greater than the number of students disliked, while the negativity effect shows itself insofar as the intensity of disliking is much greater than the intensity of liking, where intensity is measured by such things as the average number of negative selections received by unpopular students and the total number of negative selections received by the most unpopular ones.

5. Constructive versus Destructive Interpretations of Texts

I believe this is the proper point at which to bring up a phenomenon to which I have myself called attention elsewhere (Finocchiaro 1979a; 1980b, 332–41; 1981, 17–18; 1988c, 28–29, 121–22, 141, 245–48). Here, let me begin with what seems to be a brute socio-historical fact: in scientific and scholarly investigations the unfavorable evaluation of arguments seems much more prevalent than their favorable evaluation. This is readily apparent at scholarly conferences, symposia, and congresses. We are all acquainted with the fact that commentaries have a strong tendency to pick out the negative points of the paper being commented upon, whereas positive remarks tend to be either absent or very brief.

The same thing happens in the domain of scholarly activity consisting of book reviewing. In the category of negative evaluation outstanding examples would be Kaufmann's critique (1951) of Popper's *Open Society and Its Enemies*, Chomsky's attack (1959) on Skinner's *Verbal Behavior*, and Shapere's review (1964) of Kuhn's *Structure of Scientific Revolutions*. But I cannot think of comparable instances of positive evaluations.

Extending our scope somewhat, I do not think one could easily find positive analogues for the following negative evaluations: Galileo's critique of geostatic arguments in the *Dialogue on the Two Chief World Systems*; Hume's critique of theistic arguments in the *Dialogues Concerning Natural Religion*; Popper's criticism of historicist arguments in *The Poverty of Historicism*; Wittgenstein's criticism of the private language argument; Scriven's critique (1959; 1962a) of Hempel's deductive-nomological account of explanation (1965); and Jonsen and Toulmin's critique of anti-casuistry arguments in *The Abuse of Casuistry* (1988).

It could be said, in line with psychologists' discussions of the negativity effect, that what is happening here is that such negative critiques stand out against a background of favorable evaluations and so are more easily remembered. However, I do not think it is just a matter of memory; even diligent research would not reveal significant cases of positive evaluations. What we would probably discover is that most scholars do indeed evaluate most of each other's arguments positively most of the time, but that they do so casually, summarily, cursorily, briefly, and implicitly. Only rarely do they make an extended or explicit evaluation, and when they do the results are usually negative. Therefore, some kind of asymmetry remains. That is, negative evaluations of arguments are either much more common or much more explicit than positive evaluations.

The next point to notice is that the more extended and more explicit character of negative evaluation may be interpreted as resulting from the fact that negative evaluations tend to include a substantial justification for the negative conclusions, whereas positive evaluations tend to be merely stated with little or no justification. Therefore, it is better to express this asymmetry in terms that involve justification: the point would be that negative evaluations of arguments tend to be accompanied by a justification, whereas positive evaluations tend to be given without justification.

If we now ask why this should happen, we may speculate as follows (Peeters 1971; Finocchiaro 1980b, 1981, 1988c; Lewicka 1988). First, expressions of negative evaluations are potentially more damaging than their positive counterparts, and so it makes sense that one would feel the need to require that negative evaluative claims be not merely stated but substantiated. Second, the justification of a negative evaluation is more instructive than the justification of a positive evaluation because the former involves a contrast that the latter does not, namely the contrast between the presumably good argument supporting the negative evaluation and the presumably bad argument being evaluated. Therefore, we may say that the justification of negative evaluations is desirable and valuable in ways that the justification of positive evaluations is not.

6. Harman: Positive versus Negative Undermining of Beliefs

One other problem involves the question of what Harman (1986) has called positive versus negative undermining of beliefs. He argues that beliefs need not be abandoned just because one cannot produce a justification, that is, just because they are negatively undermined; on the other hand, they should be abandoned when their justifying reasons are positively known to be bad, that is when those beliefs are positively undermined. His argument is a *reductio ad absurdum* of the principle of negative undermining: the crucial point is that people do not keep track of the justifications for a belief, even if they originally acquired it on the basis of reasons; hence, if this lack of justifications would require us to abandon those beliefs, we should abandon almost everything we believe, which is absurd.

Let us see how this point could be translated into argument-theoretical terminology. The positive undermining of a belief amounts to being able to produce the arguments supporting that belief, evaluating the correctness of those arguments, and concluding that those arguments are incorrect; that is, the positive undermining of a belief means abandoning a belief on the basis of negative evaluations of the arguments supporting that belief. Now, since abandoning a belief may be conceived as a negative evaluation of a belief, then we may say that the principle of positive undermining is requiring that negative evaluations of beliefs be grounded on negative evaluations of the arguments supporting that belief. On the other hand, the principle of negative undermining involves the negative evaluation of a belief in the absence of a negative evaluation of the supporting arguments; the belief is evaluated negatively simply because it lacks supporting arguments. This is perhaps like short-circuiting the evaluation process by trying to say that a belief is wrong because it is unjustified, which is itself wrong because in order to be wrong a belief must have something positively wrong with it; being actually grounded on an incorrect justification would be an instance of a definite fault, but the lack of any actual grounding would not be.

Harman's positive undermining should not, of course, be equated with actual refutation, namely with producing an argument (presumably a correct one) whose conclusion contradicts the belief under scrutiny. Actual refutation is certainly a stronger type of criticism than positive undermining, which in turn is stronger than negative undermining. Nevertheless, the difference between negative and positive undermining is a plausible one, and so their asymmetry apparently remains.

7. Scriven: Favorable versus Unfavorable Evaluation of Products

One final asymmetry has been mentioned by Scriven (1989).[3] It involves a significant difference between the negative evaluation and positive evaluation of products. He has pointed out that there is an important class of evaluation situations where the identification of a particular flaw is sufficient to justify the rejection of a product; for example, demonstrably unsafe brakes would certainly disqualify an automobile from consideration for possible buying. On the other hand, a product can be deemed acceptable only when it possesses a whole list of necessary qualities. This suggests that negative evaluative conclusions are easier to justify than positive ones; or, in argument-theoretical terminology, we may say that good arguments with negative evaluative conclusions are easier to construct than arguments with positive evaluative conclusions.

It might be objected that this asymmetry is more apparent than real because there are positive analogues to Scriven's "disqualifiers"; they might be called "pre-emptors." For example, *X* might be a producer of high-quality automobiles, and therefore any automobile produced by *X* would

---

[3] I rely on my memory of the plenary lecture he gave at the Third International Symposium on Informal Logic, University of Windsor, June 1989, and personal discussions and correspondence; I have been unable to obtain a copy of his text, and indeed do not know whether he plans to include this point in his written paper.

have a high probability of being excellent and could be safely evaluated positively. The answer to this objection is that the positive evaluation is relative to the purchaser's interests in a way in which the negative evaluation is not. That is, for example safe brakes are a necessary condition for a good automobile in general, but the excellence of a Mercedes automobile is not a sufficient condition for it to be worthy of purchase by a consumer in general, because of considerations of cost, aesthetics, etc.

Nevertheless, this asymmetry deserves further study partly to determine its exact nature and partly to determine its exact relationship to the others. For example, its direction seems to go against that of some of the other asymmetries because here the justification of negative evaluations seems easier than the justification of positive ones, whereas the methodological asymmetry suggested above seemed to involve the reverse. Moreover, Scriven himself has discussed the case of evaluative arguments whose inferential soundness is not affected by the falsity of some premises; in these cases no one quality can outweigh the cumulative effect of all the others, and therefore even the present type of asymmetry may not apply.

8. Epilogue

We may summarize this survey of cognitive asymmetries as follows. Massey has elaborated an asymmetry in the evaluation of arguments from the viewpoint of formal logic between their formal validation and formal invalidation. Popper and his followers have articulated an asymmetry in the empirical evaluation of scientific hypotheses and generalizations between their empirical verification and empirical falsification. Experimental psychologists have tried to combine the Pollyanna Principle and the negativity effect into an asymmetry between the psychological acceptance of positive and of negative evaluations. In a number of writings I have mentioned the asymmetry between the justification of constructive textual interpretations and the justification of destructive textual interpretations. Harman has underscored the asymmetry between a negative and a positive undermining of beliefs. And Scriven has mentioned the asymmetry between the favorable and the unfavorable evaluation of products.

All these asymmetries seem to involve evaluation more directly or explicitly than argumentation. Argumentation comes into the picture primarily by way of the evaluation of arguments or the justification of evaluations. The asymmetries also seem to involve, or stem from, in one way or another the distinction between positive or favorable and negative or unfavorable evaluation. Further study is needed to determine more exactly what such asymmetries have in common and what they derive from.

It remains to be seen whether these apparent asymmetries are real. I mentioned above and have argued elsewhere that the Massey asymmetry is more apparent than real. And the Popperian asymmetry has been questioned by philosophers of science. Are the others equally questionable? It seems hard to believe that an illusion should occur in so many different contexts. Therefore, the conclusion we have to reach for now is, once again, that the phenomenon deserves further study.

9

The Positive versus the Negative Evaluation of Arguments (1994)

1. Introduction

The problem I should like to explore is the question of whether there are significant differences between the positive and the negative evaluation of arguments, what is the nature and origin of these differences, and what are their implications for theory, practice, and teaching. Because this is a relatively novel problem, most of my discussion will have to be concerned with a formulation and clarification of the issues. Nevertheless, I hope to be able to focus on a few details, and perhaps suggest some fruitful lines of inquiry for the resolution of some of these issues.

2. Preliminary Conceptual Clarifications

Evaluation is here something I would distinguish from the construction and the interpretation arguments, without however separating these three activities. In other words, the construction, the interpretation, and the evaluation of arguments are interrelated, but that is not to say that they are the same. In short, the distinction is meant to avoid confusion and conflation, not to establish a separation or bifurcation. At the terminological level, I think it would be proper to refer to what I have in mind by means of other labels such as appraisal, assessment, and judgment. I am reluctant to add the term "criticism" to this list of near-synonyms because I think criticism tends to have a negative connotation, in the sense of negative evaluation; nevertheless, to the extent that this connotation can be avoided, I would have no objection to speaking also of criticism.[1]

---

[1] For a discussion of some nonnegative aspects of "criticism," see Bailin 1988.

My distinction between negative and positive evaluation is meant to refer to the difference between good and bad arguments, or right and wrong, correct and incorrect, sound and unsound, valid and invalid, logical and illogical, convincing and unconvincing, plausible and implausible, erroneous and not, fallacious and not, and the like. One could also speak of the difference between favorable and unfavorable evaluation, approving and disapproving, appreciative and depreciative, or constructive and destructive. Of course, at a subsequent and more refined level of analysis one may want to explore the differences among all the pairs just mentioned. I do not mean to pre-empt the possibility of such refinements; all I am saying is that they do not significantly affect the issue I am concerned with here.

Similarly, I do not mean to deny the propriety of discussing whether the evaluation of arguments is a viable and feasible activity.[2] To be sure, I am inclined to think that the anti-evaluation stance is ultimately untenable, partly because it is itself the evaluative expression of a thesis about evaluative arguments, and partly because I am too realistically and empirically minded to be blind to the fact that arguments are getting evaluated all the time. However, for the purpose of the present discussion I am simply taking for granted that there is such a thing as the evaluation of arguments and that many examples exist. On this assumption, I then want to explore the nature of the difference between two types of evaluative verdicts.

One other preliminary clarification is in order. Much of what claims to be, or is often taken to be, evaluation of arguments is really evaluation of individual claims, theses, beliefs, theories, hypotheses, and the like. Here, my point is that I want to be strict and literal, so that by the evaluation of an argument I do not mean simply the evaluation of a claim, but rather the evaluation of a claim together with the supporting reasons or justifying premises. This point is worth stressing despite the fact that one type of evaluation of a claim would consist of examining whether it is justified, and to do the latter one would have to evaluate actual or potential justifications of the claim, namely arguments; the reason is that I want to deal with the evaluation of arguments directly and explicitly, not indirectly and implicitly. In other words, in evaluating an argument favorably, scholars and laymen often advance some other argument in support of the conclusion of the original argument; and analogously, in evaluating an argument unfavorably, they often give a refutation of the original conclusion, namely a counterargument, namely another argument whose

[2] For some insightful discussions of this cluster of issues, see Willard 1983.

conclusion is a denial of the original conclusion. The study of the evaluation of individual claims is certainly instructive in itself and would have to be part of a general theory of evaluation; and it is relevant to the present problem because there are important relationships between the evaluation of arguments and the evaluation of the conclusions of arguments. But, again, relationships ought not to be turned into confusing conflations, any more than distinctions should become bifurcating separations.

Finally, one last distinction will allow us to go to the heart of the problem, and not merely enable us to clarify a different aspect of the matter. The evaluation of arguments may be conceived as involving two main things: an evaluative claim about some argument, and the articulation of the rationale for the evaluative claim, namely a metalevel argument about the original argument. Now, we could not go very far in understanding the nature of the evaluation of arguments without understanding how one justifies such evaluations. In other words, we need to study the logic of a special class of arguments, namely evaluative arguments, and in particular evaluative arguments about arguments; and the question we want to examine is whether these meta-arguments exhibit a significant difference when their conclusions express favorable verdicts from when they express unfavorable verdicts.

3. The Problem of Formal Validation versus Formal Invalidation

In what follows I focus on a special case of the general problem which has been discussed by Gerald Massey and his critics.[3] Their concern has been with evaluation from the point of view of formal logic, namely with assessing the formal validity or the formal invalidity of an argument; thus one could speak here of the formal validation and the formal invalidation of arguments. Massey has elaborated the thesis that whereas formal logic does provide techniques for proving arguments formally valid, it does not provide any techniques for proving arguments formally invalid; thus there is a fundamental asymmetry between formal validation and formal invalidation, the asymmetry being that the former is feasible, but the latter is not. Using argument-theoretical language, and echoing the title of one of Massey's papers, one might say that while it is possible to give

[3] Massey (1970, 93–94; 1975a; 1975b; 1976; 1980; 1981a; 1981b; 1987); Bencivenga 1979; George 1983; McKay (1984; 1987). Another noteworthy criticism of Massey is Johnson (1989), who focuses on the question of the viability of informal logic and of fallacy theory; these are important issues, and Johnson's critique is incisive and well founded, but they are different from the present focus.

good arguments that good arguments are good, it is not possible to give good arguments that bad arguments are bad.

Massey himself has occasionally presented this thesis as a direct attack on informal logic. However, the conception of informal logic presupposed in that polemic is the one which equates the field with the study of fallacy in general, and of so-called informal fallacies in particular. Now, whatever justification there may have been in the past for such a conception, the field has lately advanced much beyond that,[4] and so we need not say anything more about that aspect of the polemic.

Massey's primary objective has really been to exploit the asymmetry in order to motivate and justify his own program for a philosophical linguistics which would simultaneously unify logic and grammar and provide what could plausibly be called a "natural logic":[5] this program is meant to provide principles for the analysis of the formal structure of natural language argumentation, and such that formal validity and formal invalidity would be consequences of grammatical-logical well-formedness and the failure of well-formedness. Despite the attractiveness of this empirical bent and of this emphasis on natural language argumentation, the formalism of the program is so ambitious that in this context we need not discuss further this alleged consequence of the asymmetry.

At any rate, the asymmetry has been criticized from both directions. That is, Ermanno Bencivenga (1979) has objected that the formal validation of arguments is as questionable as their formal invalidation, and Thomas McKay (1984; 1987) has objected that the formal invalidation of arguments is not as hopeless and arbitrary as Massey makes it sound. In the one case, formal validation and invalidation are equally unfeasible, strictly speaking; in the other case, they are equally feasible, loosely speaking. But in both cases they stand on an equal plane, and the asymmetry disappears.

Massey himself has recently credited to someone else the discovery of the asymmetry thesis, that is, to the lead paper in the October 1967 issue of *Mind*, by American philosopher James W. Oliver (1967). Therefore, Oliver's contribution should also be taken into account.

It might seem that this topic is unimportant for informal logic given that it concerns formal validation and invalidation, given that the existence of the asymmetry is questionable, and given that its alleged implications are in the direction of formalism. However, I believe the problem

---

[4] See, for example, Doss 1985; Finocchiaro (1980b; 1984b); and Johnson and Blair 1985. See also the criticism in Johnson 1989.

[5] Massey (1975a, 74–76) regards this as being partly in the tradition of Lakoff 1970.

is extremely important and relevant because it involves an appreciation of some of the limitations of formal logic, and these point in the direction of informal logic. Moreover, this type of asymmetry seems to be a special case of a general phenomenon or cluster of problems which have been studied from many quarters and which cannot be easily dismissed.[6] It should also be kept in mind that the literature on formal validation versus invalidation has prima facie an added, self-referential relevance to our general problem insofar as it constitutes for us something of a case study of the problem: we have Oliver's original argument; then Massey's argument could be regarded as a positive evaluation of that original argument; on the other hand, the objections by Massey's critics (Bencivenga, McKay, and George) could be regarded as negative evaluations of Oliver's argument.

4. Oliver on Formal Invalidation

Let us now focus on Oliver's argument since, as Massey (1987) himself has pointed out, it antedates Massey's account by about a decade. Oliver's

---

[6] For more details on this, see Finocchiaro (1980b, 332–41; 1981, 17–18; 1988c, 28–29, 121–22, 141, 245–48; 1990a; 1992a). Here one should add two other apparent asymmetries which emerged in discussions at the Third International Symposium on Informal Logic, University of Windsor, Canada, 15–18 June 1989, where parts of this chapter were first presented. One was hinted at in the panel discussion on legal reasoning, and it involves situations where considerations of the burden of proof are important; it seems that in Anglo-Saxon jurisprudence guilty verdicts must be proved more stringently than innocent verdicts, that is, legal proofs of guilt are more easily criticizable than legal proofs of innocence. Another type of asymmetry was mentioned by Michael Scriven (1989) in his plenary lecture, and it involves a significant difference between the negative evaluation and the positive evaluation of at least products. He pointed out that there is an important class of evaluation situations where the identification of a particular flaw is sufficient to justify the rejection of the product (for example, demonstrably unsafe brakes in an automobile), whereas the product can be deemed acceptable only when it possesses a whole list of necessary qualities; this suggests that negative evaluative conclusions are easier to justify than positive ones; or, in argument-theoretical terminology, we might say that good arguments with negative evaluations as conclusions are easier to construct than arguments with positive evaluative conclusions. This type of asymmetry certainly deserves further study, partly to determine its exact nature, and partly to determine its exact relationship to the others. For example, its direction seems to run counter to that of some of the other asymmetries because here the justification of negative evaluations seems easier than the justification of positive ones, whereas the asymmetry suggested above seemed to involve the reverse. Moreover, in his lecture Scriven himself discussed the case of what he called evaluative arguments whose inferential soundness is not affected by the falsity of some premises; in these cases no one quality can outweigh the cumulative effect of all the others, and therefore even the present type of asymmetry does not seem to apply.

main conclusion is that there is one and only one rigorously correct method of showing that an argument is formally invalid: it is to show that its premises are true and that its conclusion is false. This claim has two parts, one negative the other positive. The positive part asserts that

(1) showing that the premises are true and the conclusion false is a rigorously correct method of showing that the argument is formally invalid.

The negative part asserts that

(2) there is no other rigorously correct method of showing that an argument is formally invalid.

Oliver's argument in support of the positive part of his thesis is brief and uncontroversial. It is based primarily on the following definition of formal validity:

(1.1) a formally valid argument is one which instantiates a valid argument form; and
(1.2) a valid argument form is an argument form which has no counterexamples; where
(1.3) a counterexample to a given argument form is an argument which instantiates that form and has true premises and false conclusion.

The rest of the argument would be the following: whatever forms the given argument instantiates, none of those forms is valid because they all have a counterexample, namely the given argument in question.

These definitions and this argument are only a slightly more pedantic manner of saying the following: a formally valid argument is one such that it is impossible for its premises to be true and its conclusion false; now if the given argument has true premises and false conclusion, then it is obviously possible for its premises to be true and its conclusion false. QED.

Oliver's argument in support of the negative part of his thesis (2) is more roundabout, and ultimately can at best be only inductively correct since it depends on an empirical or imaginary examination of various methods together with a disqualification of each as not being rigorously correct. His examination consists of three types of considerations:

(2.1) no method is rigorously correct if it depends on the false principle that
(2.11) a formally invalid argument is one which instantiates an invalid argument form;
(2.2) all apparently rigorous methods, such as truth tables, syllogistic rules, and Venn diagrams, are methods for showing the invalidity (or validity) of various argument forms rather than of arguments;

(2.3) if one examines the textbooks, none of the methods one finds is in fact rigorously correct: they either use the false principle (2.11) just mentioned, or they equivocate between arguments and argument forms.

Let us focus on this principle (2.11) that a formally invalid argument is one which instantiates an invalid argument form, for which we may adopt the elegant label of "pseudo-principle of illogical form" given to it by Massey (1987). Now, as Oliver points out, the first thing to understand about this principle is that, although it looks equivalent to the definition of formal validity, it really is not. That is, it looks like one can obtain this principle by starting with the definition and replacing the term "valid" by the term "invalid." The two principles are indeed isomorphic transformations of each other, with the terms "valid" and "invalid" interchanged. However, such a transformation is itself invalid. In particular, the invalidity pseudo-principle does not follow validly from the definitional principle of validity. In other words, the following meta-argument is not formally valid:

(3) a formally valid argument is one which instantiates a valid argument form,
(4) so, a formally invalid argument is one which instantiates an invalid argument form.

Whatever plausibility this argument has, it stems from the fact that it appears to instantiate an argument form such that the premise is a biconditional and the conclusion is another biconditional whose two components are denials of the components of the former. That is, the premise may be interpreted as the biconditional that

(3.1) an argument is valid iff it instantiates a valid argument form;

and the conclusion may be interpreted as the biconditional that

(4.1) an argument is invalid iff it instantiates an invalid argument form.

And then it looks as if the transition from the premise to the conclusion instantiates the form:

(3.2) p iff q, so (4.2) not-p iff not-q,

or at least the form:

(3.3) (x)(Fx iff Gx), so (4.3) (x)(-Fx iff -Gx).

However, such instantiations do not work out. For example, if "Gx" symbolizes the expression "x instantiates a valid form" then "-Gx" would symbolize the expression "x does not instantiate a valid form," and the latter is by no means synonymous with the expression "x instantiates an in-valid form." The difference between these two expressions is that the first means that there is no valid form instantiated by x, whereas the latter means that there is an invalid form instantiated by x. Now, going back to the argument in question, what this shows is that it does not instantiate either one of the two valid forms mentioned. But this does not prove its invalidity, since to do this one would have to show that the argument does not instantiate any valid form. What this analysis does do is to explain the semblance or appearance of validity.

At this point it would be natural to try to find a form which the argument does instantiate. The premise is an instance of the form:

(3.4) (x){if Ax then [Vx iff (Ey)(Fy & Ixy & Vy)]},

which may be read as:

(3.5) an argument is formally valid iff there is some argument form such that the argument instantiates it and this form is valid.

And the conclusion instantiates the form:

(4.4) (x){if Ax then [-Vx iff (Ey)(Fy & Ixy & -Vx)]},

which may be read as:

(4.5) an argument is not formally valid iff there is some argument form such that the argument instantiates it and this form is not valid.

Now, this meta-argument form is itself invalid, but to conclude from the invalidity of this form that the original argument is invalid would be to commit the error which Oliver is trying to expose.

Therefore, he resorts to what he regards as the only correct method of proving invalidity, mentioned above. He first points out that the premise is true by definition, and then he refutes the conclusion by giving some counterinstances, that is, instances of arguments which instantiate invalid forms but are valid. One of these is the following instance of affirming the consequent:

(5) "If something is red, everything is red.
Everything is red.
Therefore, something is red" (Oliver 1967, 463).

In regard to the apparently rigorous methods of proving invalidity, for the cases of truth tables and Venn Diagrams, it is obvious that they refer to argument forms and not to arguments, and that therefore the gap remains between the invalidity of the forms and the invalidity of the original natural language arguments. The case of the syllogistic rules is not so obvious. Oliver's argument here is that there are many syllogisms which instantiate invalid forms but are valid. Consider for example:

(6) "Some men are non-self-identical.
Some Parisians are non-self-identical.
Therefore, no Parisians are men" (Oliver 1967, 471).

This instantiates the syllogistic form:

(7) some A are B; some C are B; so, no C are A,

which violates all the main rules of the syllogistic theory. Yet the original argument is formally valid because the premises are both logically false. Or consider the argument:

(8) "Nothing that is blue or not blue is square.
Nothing that is red or not red is square.
Therefore, something that is red or not red is blue or not blue" (Oliver 1967, 472).

This syllogism instantiates the form:

(9) no A is B; no C is B; so, some C is A,

which is obviously invalid and violates several rules. Yet the original argument is formally valid because the conclusion is logically true.

5. Massey's Asymmetry

Although in his latest paper on the topic Massey (1987) has credited Oliver with having anticipated the asymmetry thesis, Oliver does not in fact speak of asymmetry. Indeed, he says almost nothing about methods for proving validity, and so he is making no comparison and contrast on the basis of which he might have inferred an asymmetry. This contrast and this inference were Massey's own contributions in his *earlier* papers on the topic.[7] Working at that time independently of Oliver, Massey did three main things. He explained how the definition of formal validity

---

[7] I emphasize *earlier* because in his latest paper on the topic, Massey (1987) seems to abandon the asymmetry thesis and to focus on the indeterminacy of translation, which he claims applies to both formal validity and formal invalidity; however, he claims (1987, 6) that the indeterminacy of translation applies asymmetrically to the cases of validity and invalidity, and so a new version of his asymmetry thesis emerges. The examination of this new alleged asymmetry is beyond the scope of this chapter.

yields a viable method for proving that arguments are valid: this is the familiar technique of finding a form which the argument may be said to instantiate and which is valid. He strengthened Oliver's conclusion that there is one and only one method of proving formal invalidity, namely the combined verification of premises and falsification of conclusion, which Massey (1975a, 64) labels "the trivial logic-indifferent method."[8] And then on the basis of these two theses he explicitly drew the conclusion that there is a fundamental asymmetry between formal validation and invalidation.

Massey's strengthening of the point about the difficulties with formal invalidation is as follows. As we have already seen, the basic definition of formal validity is essentially a biconditional one side of which states that

(10) if an argument instantiates a valid argument form, then it is formally valid;

the other side may be stated as saying that

(11) if an argument does not instantiate a valid argument form, then it is formally invalid.

The latter principle could be regarded as providing a method of showing invalidity by showing that the argument fails to instantiate a valid form.

The essential difficulty with this is that the class of valid argument forms is not closed; that is, we cannot provide a complete list of all valid argument forms. Formal logic is an open-ended science, and formal logicians are constantly adding to the known list of valid argument forms. This is illustrated even in the pedagogy of formal logic, which usually proceeds from truth functions, to monadic predicates, to relational predicates, to identity theory, and so on. Thus, if a valid syllogism is symbolized merely with the resources of the truth-functional calculus, it will fail to instantiate any valid form, but that will not render it invalid, but merely *truth-functionally* invalid. Similarly, if a valid argument whose validity depends on identity is analyzed with the resources of predicate calculus without identity, it will fail to instantiate a valid form, but that will not render it invalid.

---

[8] Massey also provided the following more elegant counterexample to the pseudo-principle of formal invalidity: "If something has been created by God, then everything has been created by God. Everything has been created by God. [Therefore,] Something has been created by God" (1981a, 492).

Further, in the context of logical theorizing, Massey gives two interesting examples. Consider the argument:

(12) John took a walk by the river; so, John took a walk.[9]

This argument is indeed intuitively valid, and could even be shown to be valid with the help of some meaning postulates. However, its *formal* validity was in question until Davidson (1968) devised an argument form which this argument instantiates. Now, if the above principle had been taken to refer to known logical forms, before Davidson's analysis it would have declared this argument invalid. Similar remarks apply to an argument first shown valid by Leonard and Goodman (1940) by devising a calculus of individuals to enrich ordinary predicate calculus. The argument is:

(13) Tom, Dick, and Harry are partners; so, Tom and Harry are partners.[10]

Here the essential point is that, just because one has not found a valid argument form, one cannot be certain that someone else will not find it, or that someone else will not invent some new logical system which will allow us to devise an appropriate form.

6. Weakening the Formal Validation of Arguments

Criticism of the Oliver-Massey thesis has tried to show that on the one hand formal validation is not as rigorous as they make it sound, and that on the other hand formal invalidation is more rigorous than they make it sound.[11] Let us begin with formal validation.

One criticism is that the formal validation of an argument depends on the existence of valid argument forms, but the validation of the latter is a less rigorous affair than it may seem.[12] Recall that to say that an argument form is valid is to say that it has no counterexamples. Now, although finding even one counterexample will invalidate the form, not finding it may be due to lack of ingenuity. Of course, one will have a validation if one finds a proof in a consistent and sound logical system, but many logical systems (including relational predicate calculus) are not decidable, and

---

9 Massey 1981a, 495; cf. Massey (1987, 7–8) and Davidson 1968.
10 Massey 1981a, 495; cf. Massey 1976 and Leonard and Goodman 1940.
11 This useful classification is due to Massey himself (1987). There is also the criticism of George (1983), objecting that Massey presupposes an untenable concept of argument.
12 This point is similar to one made by Bencivenga (1979, 249–50).

so finding a proof is not a mechanical task. In other words, in special cases of decidable logical systems like the truth-functional calculus, the validation of an argument form is a mechanical procedure; but in general, since many logical systems are undecidable, the validation will depend on the construction of a proof in a sound and consistent system. Such a construction will provide a rigorous validation, but finding it is not a rigorous process.

The plausibility of Massey's thesis about formal validation derives partly from the simplicity and triviality of his examples. One of these involves an argument of the form "P & Q; so, Q,"[13] another the form "all A are B; x is A; so x is B."[14] The issue could have been much more difficult if we were dealing with a form like the following:

(14) -(Ex)(Ey)(Fx & Gy & Hxy);
(x)[if Fx then (Ey)(Fy & Hxy)];
(x)(y)(if Hxy then Hyx);
so, -(Ex)(Fx & Gx).[15]

Another criticism of the above-mentioned thesis about the formal validation of arguments involves a fact admitted by Massey himself (1980, 321), and exploited by him for other purposes. That is, the validation of *arguments* involves linguistic intuitions to the effect that certain statements are synonymous with certain others. This applies even to the trivial example referred to in the previous paragraph. The original argument was:

(15) Sam and Sue are doctors; therefore, Sue is a doctor.[16]

Here the premise must be intuited to be synonymous with the statement that "Sam is a doctor and Sue is a doctor"; only then can we regard it as an instance of the conjunction "P & Q." The crucial importance of linguistic intuition is clearly and vividly shown by another example given by Massey where the same translation would be wrong: "Tom and Dick weigh 200 kilograms" (1980, 320). This obviously does not mean that Tom weighs 200 kilograms and Dick weighs 200 kilograms.

[13] Cf. Massey 1975a, 63.
[14] Cf. Massey 1975a, 64–65.
[15] See Kalish, Montague, and Mar 1980, 249, 261, where this form is instantiated by the argument: no teacher is married to a student; every teacher is married to a teacher; marriage is a symmetrical relationship; so, no teacher is a student.
[16] Cf. Massey 1975a, 63.

7. Strengthening the Formal Invalidation of Arguments

Let us now consider some criticism of the Oliver-Massey thesis about formal invalidity. As mentioned before, this criticism tries to show that formal invalidity can be justified without reliance on the non sequiturs and equivocations they are bent on exposing.

It will be useful to focus on the argument we examined earlier, which goes from the definition of formal validity to the pseudo-principle of illogical form. The meta-argument was as follows:

(16) an argument is formally valid iff it instantiates a valid argument form;
so, an argument is formally invalid iff it instantiates an invalid argument form.

Earlier, following Oliver, we invalidated this argument by pointing out that the premise is true and the conclusion is false. Moreover, it certainly would be formally invalid to argue that this argument is invalid *simply because* it instantiates the following invalid form:

(17) (x){if Ax then [Vx iff (Ey)(Fy & Ixy & Vy)]}
so, (x){if Ax then [-Vx iff (Ey)(Fy & Ixy & -Vy)]}.

However, as Thomas McKay has argued, "instancehood" is not their only relationship, for we can also show that the form "represents all details likely to be relevant to the validity of the argument" (McKay 1984, 99). Notice that this is something that would not be true if we were to interpret a valid syllogism by the mere resources of the sentential calculus, which would yield the argument form:

(18) P; Q; so, R.

Notice also that this is a form also instantiated by every argument with two premises and one conclusion. Similarly, recall that earlier we mentioned an argument which is valid even though it instantiates the form of affirming the consequent; that form did not represent all relevant logical details.

Therefore, the pseudo-principle of illogical form should be modified to read:

(19) an argument is formally invalid iff it instantiates an invalid argument form *and* this form "represents all details likely to be relevant to the validity of the argument."[17]

Now, this modified rule of formal invalidity is not as neat as the pseudo-principle, and its satisfaction is both a matter of degree and subject to

---

[17] Again, the quoted clause is from McKay 1984, 99.

revision. However, all that this means is that the formal invalidation of an argument is an empirical, pragmatic, or informal business.[18] It remains true that by using such a rule arguments cannot be formally invalidated by means of formally valid meta-arguments, but it is equally true that their formal invalidation *can* be justified. We might add that this difficulty with this part of the Oliver-Massey thesis is that they were restricting themselves to what might be called deductive arguments, in a situation where all we can ever hope for is inductive arguments.

A second criticism would involve a reappraisal of what is called the "method of counterexample" by some (Salmon 1984, 21) and the technique of "refutation by logical analogy" by others.[19] This is the technique of invalidating an argument by formulating another argument with the same logical form as the first and with obviously true premises and obviously false conclusion. Oliver (1967, 469–70) explicitly criticizes this technique by interpreting it as being identical to the technique of using the pseudo-principle of illogical form. I suppose he is thinking that to say that two arguments have the same form is to say that the two arguments instantiate the same form. On this interpretation, his criticism would indeed follow.[20]

However, this technique ought to be interpreted as a way of bypassing the problem of having to deal with a logical form to attribute to the arguments in question and to be instantiated by them. The really important thing would be the counterexample, which is another actual argument. Talk of the same form of two arguments thus would be a way of saying that they are formally isomorphic or analogous, that is, that there is a one-to-one correspondence between various elements of the two arguments; it would not be a way of saying that each of the two arguments has some unique logical form and that the logical form of each is identical.[21]

[18] Bencivenga (1979) also reaches conclusions that point in a pragmatic and empirical direction.

[19] Oliver 1967, 469; Copi (1986a, 187–90; 1986b, 289–91); Govier 1985. McKay (1987) also discusses this same technique, although without using the label.

[20] Oliver's interpretation was perhaps partially justified since the target of his criticism seemed to be Copi, who does indeed have that in mind. In fact, although Oliver (1967, 469) deliberately omits a specific bibliographical reference for the quotation he is criticizing, and although he must have been using an earlier edition of Copi's book, even the seventh edition of the latter reads almost exactly like Oliver's quotation; cf. Copi 1986b, 289.

[21] The move I am suggesting is analogous to Quine's move about meaning and sameness of meaning: the latter need not presuppose the existence of mysterious entities called meanings which words have, but may be conceived as a relationship of pairs of linguistic expressions, which may be labeled synonymy; see Quine 1961, 11–12, 22, 48. I also

Let us apply the technique to the same meta-argument discussed above. When presented with this argument, one could respond that it is no more valid than the following argument, which is obviously invalid:

(20) a person is a doctor iff he has received a doctoral degree;
so, a person is a nondoctor iff he has received a nondoctoral degree.[22]

This argument is obviously invalid because its premise is obviously true, whereas its conclusion is obviously false: a nondoctor is a person who has not received *any* doctoral degrees, whereas doctors usually receive other nondoctoral degrees before their doctoral one.

Now, let us ask why they could be said to have the same logical form. Clearly it would be incorrect to say that the original argument (16) and the counterexample (20) have the same logical form because they instantiate the same argument form; we have already seen that, for example, all syllogisms may be said to instantiate the form "P, Q, so R," but this does not even begin to give them the same form. Equally obviously, it would be correct to say that these two arguments have the same form because they instantiate the same argument form (17) *and* this form represents all the details likely to be relevant to their validity; however, this type of consideration would merely repeat the point made earlier, when we modified the pseudo-principle of illogical form into a workable rule for formal invalidity.

If we want to make a different point, perhaps we could say something like the following. In each of the two arguments one is moving from a biconditional premise to a biconditional conclusion, and in the process a particular term which appears in both clauses of the premise is replaced by a contradictory term in both clauses.

think that my move is practically identical to the one suggested by George (1983), although I am not sure because his argument is unnecessarily complicated. Working in the context of Bolzano's logical theory, George argues that for Bolzano the form of an argument is a set of arguments generable from it, and that this avoids Massey's asymmetry because "the fact that invalid forms can have valid arguments as elements is a matter of no significance, since the only form we look to in assessing validity or invalidity is that generated from the argument itself" (George 1983, 321). Moreover George criticizes Massey by arguing that his examples are not well-formed arguments, since there is more to defining an argument than specifying a ({premise}, conclusion) pair, namely a third element amounting to "understanding what the argument is"; in short, Massey's examples are examples of ambiguous arguments from the point of view of Bolzano's theory. It should be mentioned that Massey (1987) takes George's criticism into account and ends up partially agreeing with him.

[22] Another example would be: a homeowner is a person who owns a home; so a nonhomeowner is a person who owns something which is not a home.

Let us see why this sort of consideration would not apply for the case of the valid instance of affirming the consequent discussed earlier. Oliver's example was:

(21) "If something is red, everything is red.
Everything is red.
Therefore, something is red" (Oliver 1967, 463).

Suppose we tried to invalidate this argument by advancing the following alleged counterexample:

(22) if Ronald Reagan lives in San Diego, then he lives in California;
Ronald Reagan lives in California;
so, Ronald Reagan lives in San Diego.

These two arguments have many similarities, but also one crucial difference: in the original argument the conclusion is a special case of the second premise, but this is not so in the alleged counterexample. We may conclude that in order to have the same form, two arguments must share *all* relevant structural details, and not just some.[23]

More generally, we may say that two arguments have the same form iff whenever the first instantiates a given form so does the second and vice versa; that is, two arguments have the same form iff there is no argument form which one of them instantiates but the other does not. For example, in the two arguments just discussed, (21) and (22), the following form is instantiated by the first but not by the second:

(23) if $(Ex)Rx$ then $(x)Rx$; $(x)Rx$; so, $(Ex)Rx$.

Similar remarks would apply to the above-mentioned valid syllogisms which instantiate invalid forms. For example, argument (8) could not

---

[23] Incidentally, one consequence of this would be that some instances of the same conditional argument forms would not really have the same form. For example, the following are traditionally regarded as having the same form because they both instantiate *modus tollens*: (A) if Richard Nixon lives in Florida then he lives on the East Coast; Richard Nixon does not live on the East Coast; so, Richard Nixon does not live in Florida; (B) if Richard Nixon lives in Florida then he does not live in New York; Richard Nixon lives in New York; so, Richard Nixon does not live in Florida. In general, each of the four types of conditional propositional argument would have four subtypes, depending on the occurrence or non-occurrence of negations in the antecedent or the consequent. This corresponds to the way such arguments are experienced at the psychological level, as experimental psychologists have demonstrated (Evans 1972a; 1972b; 1982; 1983a; 1983b; 1983c).

be invalidated by advancing the following alleged counterexample:

(24) no man is a woman;
no inanimate object is a woman;
so, some inanimate object is a man.

Both this argument and the earlier one (8) instantiate many forms, but the following is instantiated only by the earlier one (8) and not by this one:

(25) no A or not-A is a B;
no C or not-C is B;
so, some C or not-C is A or not-A.

However, this is still too formalist.[24] I believe that ultimately we should take more seriously the suggestion implicit in the label which refers to analogy. That is, ultimately this method of invalidation should be conceived as analogical reasoning about arguments,[25] that is, as a meta-argument which concludes that the given argument is invalid because the counterexample argument is invalid and the two arguments are analogous. Then the alleged analogy could be discussed in the usual ways, by examining the extent and nature of the similarities and the dissimilarities between the two arguments. Here too we would have a type of inductive reasoning about deductive or formal arguments, or to be more exact, inductive reasoning about the formal and the deductive evaluation of arguments.

Our conclusion is, again, that although the formal invalidation of arguments is not an easy matter, it is a task which can be justified to a greater or lesser degree. This was also found to be the case for formal validation, though we arrived at such a conclusion by approaching from the other side, that is by criticizing the thesis that formal validations were generally susceptible of rigorous demonstration. Therefore, the two processes seem to be more similar than dissimilar, and the asymmetry alleged by Oliver and Massey evaporates.

8. Epilogue

More importantly and more positively, we have seen that even the formal validation and invalidation of arguments involve what may be called

---

[24] Further formalist developments could perhaps be articulated by adapting some of the ideas contained in the paper Hitchcock (1989; 1994) presented at the Third International Symposium on Informal Logic.

[25] I owe this idea in part to Govier (1985), who comes close to saying just this, and to Copi (1986a), who very suggestively includes the technique of refutation by logical analogy in the chapter on analogical reasoning.

informal argumentation. Formal validation depends on the determination of the validity of argument forms, which in turn depends on the discovery and invention of proofs, which is ultimately an informal process; and formal validation also depends on the translation or interpretation of the original natural language sentences involved, which depends in turn on linguistic intuitions about the synonymy of various natural language sentences; and the latter is an inherently informal process (*pace* Massey). Similarly, formal invalidation depends partly on the claim that a given argument form reflects all relevant logical details, which is best regarded as an inductive generalization; and formal invalidation also depends on the comparison between the argument in question and a proposed counterexample argument, and such comparison is best regarded as an instance of analogical reasoning, with all the advantages and the pitfalls pertaining thereto.

Further informal-logic implications stem from the case-study aspect of our analysis. Once one reconstructs Oliver's account as an argument trying to show the formal invalidity of justifications of typical invalidity-verdicts, Massey's own account becomes primarily a second argument using Oliver's main conclusion as a premise to arrive at the further conclusion of asymmetry, rather than a positive evaluation of Oliver's original argument accompanied by a supporting justification. Moreover, I presented two criticisms of the Oliver-Massey argument by adapting and adding to the objections raised by Bencivenga, McKay, and George; and these criticisms were negative evaluations of Oliver's main conclusion about formal invalidation and of Massey's conclusion about formal validation. Now, it is perhaps debatable whether or not these criticisms were directed at the arguments rather than at the conclusions, but it is clear that the negative evaluations were not simple invalidity-verdicts, if at all; for the criticisms were that the formal validation of arguments is a less formal affair than the Massey asymmetry thesis claims, and that the formal invalidation of arguments is a less hopeless affair than Oliver's thesis claims. All of this is, I believe, typical of philosophical argumentation, which goes to show that the latter is not significantly governed by formal-logical considerations even when the topic involves concepts of formal logic.

Of course, this general positive conclusion ought to be no surprise to the informal logician; the most it may do is to give explicit articulation to his basic intuitions. However, from a pedagogical point of view, a perplexing problem emerges from our exercise of evaluating the Oliver-Massey argument. Given, as we have seen, that the actual arguments on which one bases verdicts of formal validity or invalidity are typically formally invalid, is it proper to pretend to teach students how to argue formally about the subject matter that makes up the usual examples of formal-logic textbooks? Would it not be better to begin arguing formally about such concepts as validity, invalidity, argument form, and the like? I believe this can be done only by completely mathematizing the subject and teaching formal logic purely as a branch of mathematics. But there is another way, which turns out to be another way to teach informal logic. It is to teach about such concepts as formal validity and invalidity, argument form, and so on, by emphasizing the nonformal, informal, and inductive considerations discussed above. To do this would be to teach the informal logic of formal logic, as it were; to teach informal logic by using formal logic as substantive content. But then the question arises whether or in what contexts such a substantive content is appropriate. How does it compare with current events, newspaper reports and magazine articles, classic texts in the history of thought, and so on?

PART III

CRITIQUES

Metaphilosophical Views and Dialectical Approaches

10

Siegel on Critical Thinking

Reasoning versus Rationality versus Criticism (1989)

1. The 'Reasons' Conception of Critical Thinking

Although the practice of critical thinking goes back at least to the time of Socrates, and the theory of it at least to 1941 with the publication of Edward M. Glaser's *An Experiment in the Development of Critical Thinking*, the phenomenon has now acquired some of the trappings of a "movement," and in fact some of its leading exponents do not hesitate to speak of it by using this label (Paul 1985). Interest in critical thinking has always had, and continues to have a strong pedagogical orientation (Ennis 1962, 1980, 1981; McPeck 1981; Paul 1982, 1984, 1985), but recently the phenomenon has begun to receive epistemological and methodological scrutiny. An excellent example of this relatively novel approach to critical thinking is Harvey Siegel's book *Educating Reason: Rationality, Critical Thinking, and Education* (1988). This work moves the discussion of critical thinking to a qualitatively higher level of sophistication, and it does so with intelligence, breadth of preparation, and a touch of inspired zeal. We therefore have two sets of reasons for paying attention to this work.

The focus of Siegel's book is the notion of critical thinking, which gives it the following structure. He begins with an account and constructive criticism of three conceptions of critical thinking, those of Robert Ennis, Richard Paul, and John McPeck. These lead to Siegel's own account, which he calls the 'reasons' conception, and which he articulates primarily in terms of reason assessment and the practice of the critical spirit. He then gives several arguments to justify the pedagogic value of critical thinking so conceived: one involves respect of students as persons, another individual autonomy, a third one the Western cultural tradition, and a fourth one democratic institutions. In what are perhaps the most cogent parts of the book, he then answers two criticisms: the ideology objection according to which the justification of critical thinking, like everything else, presupposes a prior ideological or political commitment; and the indoctrination objection which holds that education for critical thinking is impossible because all education is indoctrination. Siegel then applies his conception to two issues. One is the problem of minimum competency testing and the relativity of standards; he seems to be against minimum competency testing, but I found the details of his argument hard to follow. The other issue is science education, in regard to which he criticizes the anti-critical ideal which some attribute to or derive from the works of Thomas Kuhn; this is interesting and important, so that Siegel's line of argument deserves a more extended summary.

Siegel gives an account of Kuhn's view of science as being anti-critical through and through. "Normal science" is, of course, easily seen as anti-critical, along lines that were indicated long ago by Popper and his followers (Popper 1970; Watkins 1970). However, Siegel develops the anti-critical interpretation of Kuhnian science in other ways as well: revolutionary science is no less anti-critical, though for a different reason, namely because of the alleged incommensurability of competing paradigms; Kuhn's view of scientific knowledge is supposedly anti-critical because it is relativistic; and science education for Kuhn becomes a case of "dogmatic indoctrination" (Siegel 1988, 95). Then Siegel objects to the type of science education suggested by this Kuhnian view by questioning its practical viability, practical effectiveness, morality, and philosophical soundness. For example, Siegel questions whether there is any a priori reason or empirical evidence that Kuhnian education is effective; he also argues that the so-called distortion of the history of science fostered by normal-scientific textbooks violates students' moral dignity and autonomy. Adapting some of the ideas found in Schwab (1962), Siegel would favor a scientific education which would emphasize reasoning, and this could be done by focusing on pluralistic scientific theorizing, the reflective philosophical understanding of science, and the difference between science and pseudo-science.

To this Kuhnian exegesis and critique, I would want to add my own qualifications, arguments, and examples (Finocchiaro 1973a; 1973c, 180–98; 1980b, 145–223). However, I think that Siegel provides a useful and incisive survey.

Despite the obvious merits of Siegel's book, the purpose of my remarks is primarily critical. This will give us an opportunity not only to engage in some critical thinking about critical thinking, but also to call attention once more to the well-known phenomenon that negative criticism is in general much more prevalent than positive evaluation. I mention this fact not only as a justification of the prevalent tone of my remarks, but also to bemoan the fact that this phenomenon is very much neglected as a topic of theoretical reflection and analysis. Although I have mentioned this problem before (Finocchiaro 1980b, 332, 338–41; 1988c, 28–29, 35–36, 121–22, 245–48), and although this is not the occasion to attempt to contribute something to its solution, its general neglect is such that it is entirely appropriate to exploit every opportunity to raise the awareness of the problem.

Actually, it will turn out that my criticism will also be constructive, in an indirect sort of way. But this will not become apparent until the end of my discussion.

2. Critical Thinking = Reasoning = Good Reasoning = Rationality?

The first two sentences on page 1 of Siegel's book read as follows: "There is at present an unprecedented interest in critical thinking. National Commissions on the state of education decry the lack of emphasis on the development of reasoning ability in schools and call for the inclusion of reasoning in the curriculum as the fourth 'R'" (p. 1).[1] He goes on to give other evidence for the unprecedented interest in critical thinking, but that need not concern us here. For these sentences are sufficient to reveal a central thesis on which I want to focus; this thesis is the main missing premise or unstated assumption in the passage just quoted, when the passage is interpreted as an argument. If the content of this unstated assumption is not immediately apparent, little doubt should remain after considering an equally revealing passage which happens to occur in the last paragraph of the last page of the last chapter:

My final (transcendental) argument . . . is for the proposition that critical thinking is, at a minimum, "first among equals" in the pantheon of educational ideals. Why should critical thinking be the ultimate, if not the only, educational ideal? Consider a case in which that ideal conflicts with some legitimate other. In such a case one might argue that the other should override critical thinking in this

---

[1] Subsequent references to Siegel 1988 will be given without the numeral "1988," as done here.

instance. And perhaps so it should. But it requires rational argument, and appeal to reason, in order to make the case for the preferability of the rival ideal to that of critical thinking. And such an appeal is, of course, an appeal to, and an honoring of, the latter ideal. [p. 137]

Let us reconstruct and simplify both of these arguments for the sake of clarity and incisiveness. The second one may be construed as claiming that the ideal of critical thinking is the most fundamental one because the ideal of reasoning is self-justifying in a way that no other educational ideal is. Similarly, Siegel's initial argument may be interpreted as claiming that there is an unprecedented interest in critical thinking because there is an unprecedented interest in reasoning. My reconstructions should make obvious the content of the idea assumed in both arguments: it is the claim that critical thinking is to be identified with reasoning, that reasoning and critical thinking are the same thing.

As a matter of fact, Siegel is so explicit about this claim throughout his book that there would have been no need for me to be as round-about as I have been in introducing it, were it not for the fact that the two passages just quoted will also serve other purposes, as will appear shortly. Siegel's explicitness is apparent from the very label he gives to his account, namely "the 'reasons' conception of critical thinking" (pp. 32–47). His equation of reasoning and critical thinking is also apparent from the following entirely typical assertion: "A critical thinker is one who appreciates the importance, and [convincing] force, of reasons. When assessing claims, making judgments, evaluating procedures, or contemplating alternative actions, the critical thinker seeks reasons on which to base her assessments, judgments, and actions" (p. 33).

Thus, there seems to be no doubt that Siegel is equating reasoning and critical thinking. To make matters more confusing, there are two other things to which he also equates critical thinking. One of these seems to be *good* reasoning.[2] This is suggested in part by a statement he makes so often that after a while it acquires the status of a slogan

---

[2] This is the impression conveyed by the book, for reasons given below, and from many other indications in it. However, I am puzzled by this, which suggests a failure to distinguish reasoning *per se* and good reasoning. In fact, elsewhere Siegel (1985) explicitly makes a distinction which seems equivalent to the present one; there he explicitly distinguishes the question of what scientific rationality consists of, which he answers in terms of commitment to reasoning, and the question of what is to count as a good reason in science, which is much more difficult and which he leaves unanswered in this article. In other words, in his 1988 book, Siegel seems to speak as if he held the thesis that reasons must be rational, to use the formulation adopted by Levin (1988), and to suggest that the latter's criticism of this thesis would not apply here.

or aphorism, namely the assertion that a critical thinker is one who is appropriately moved by reasons (e.g., pp. 2, 23, 32). Here I want you to note the reference to appropriateness. If the claim were merely that a critical thinker is one who is moved by reasons, then we would have merely an expression of the previously mentioned equation of reasoning and critical thinking. However, the point of the reference to appropriateness must be to identify critical thinking with appropriate reasoning, or good reasoning, or correct reasoning.

The other entity brought into the equation is rationality. This occurs when Siegel criticizes McPeck's limitation of critical thinking to reasoning where the reasons or evidence are especially problematic. Siegel's words are very explicit:

> The distinction McPeck draws here between critical thinking and rationality is I think untenable.... Once one rejects this limitation on the range of critical thinking, the distinction between critical thinking and rationality collapses. Critical thinking is coextensive with rationality... rationality and critical thinking are both "coextensive with the relevance of reasons." The connection between rationality and reasons is as tight as it can be.... In so far as rationality consists of believing and acting on the basis of good reasons,... we must perforce regard critical thinking not as a dimension of rationality, but as its equivalent.... [p. 30]

Note that Siegel here seems to identify not only critical thinking and rationality, but also rationality and reasoning, as we would expect from his previously mentioned assumption.

Finally, at the beginning of his elaboration of his own conception of critical thinking, Siegel claims that "there is...a deep conceptual connection, by way of the notion of reasons, between critical thinkers and rational persons... critical thinking involves bringing to bear all matters relevant to the rationality of belief and action; and education aimed at the promulgation of critical thinking is nothing less than education aimed at the fostering of rationality and the development of rational persons" (p. 32).

3. Rejection of This Equation

Thus there are four things that Siegel seems to be equating: critical thinking, reasoning, good reasoning, and rationality. I believe that all these equations are problematic. Some of the difficulties can be seen by reflecting on the passages quoted above from Siegel's own book. Recall his initial evidence supporting the existence of an unprecedented interest in critical thinking, and his final argument in favor of the supremacy of the educational ideal of critical thinking. Whether or not one agrees with these conclusions or the supporting reasons, these are obviously instances of reasoning. However, they are clearly not instances of critical thinking, since nothing is being criticized; neither the reasons nor the conclusions are critical of anything. Moreover, they are not, in my opinion, instances of good reasoning since, as pointed out earlier, both arguments assume the identification of reasoning and critical thinking, and this equation seems to me to be untenable. Therefore, to that extent they are also not instances of rationality. On the other hand, consider Siegel's criticism of McPeck's distinction; it is indeed an instance of critical thinking, but as my quotation reads, there is no reasoning in it, since the reasons for Siegel's criticism are not included; a fortiori, the question of its being an instance of either good reasoning or rationality would not even arise. Fourthly, Siegel's claim about the alleged deep conceptual connection between critical thinking, reasoning, and rationality is not only not an instance of reasoning, but not even of critical thinking; this is, of course, no criticism of that particular claim, but it is a reminder that there is or ought to be nothing wrong with thinking which is neither critical nor ratiocinative.

These counterexamples, and the consequent difficulties, are meant to raise the issue, rather than settle it. In fact, once the issue has been raised, we can get more deeply involved in reasoning and/or critical thinking, by engaging in another element of it, which is admittedly crucial. I am referring to what Siegel calls the reason assessment component, concerning which I agree with him that it is an essential part of critical thinking. It will emerge, however, that here I would want to add my own twists to this thesis by amplifying it and by giving a different justification.

The main one of my amplifications emerges very readily. For, now that we have agreed about the importance of assessing Siegel's reasons for his equations, it becomes obvious that we have to find or identify those reasons first. In other words, we have to get involved in what may be called reason identification; this may be regarded as an element of critical thinking distinct from, but related to, the element of reason assessment; and it may also be regarded as a sub-element of reason assessment insofar as it is a necessary precondition for the latter. I would prefer the former interpretation since I feel there is in the field too much emphasis on evaluative judgments, and too little on analysis, interpretation, and understanding. Be that as it may, let us see why Siegel wants to equate critical thinking with the things he does.

Finding such arguments is not easy. And here it should be stressed that I am not looking for Siegel's arguments in favor of critical thinking as an educational ideal, in regard to which they are both explicit and generally convincing. For, once critical thinking is conceived in terms of reasoning and rationality, the justification of the value of critical thinking turns out in reality to be a justification of the value of rationality and reasoning. Now, at least to a rationalist like myself, such a justification will be relatively straightforward. Rather, what I am looking for are arguments why critical thinking should be equated to reasoning and rationality.

4. The Conceptual Argument

One clue to the existence of one argument is given at the end of chapter 1, where Siegel summarizes its content and previews the next chapter, stating among other things that he will "provide an underlying rationale for the reasons conception in terms of the conceptual connections between critical thinking, rationality, and reasons" (p. 31). And, in fact, the first section of chapter 2 (pp. 32–34) mentions these three things in its title and begins by declaring, as we have seen, that "there is ... a deep conceptual connection, by way of the notion of reasons, between critical thinkers and rational persons" (p. 32). The connection is provided by *principles* in the sense that they are essentially connected with both reasoning and rationality. The connection between principles and reasoning is one of presupposition: whenever one gives A as a reason for B one is committed to some generalization to the effect that A's warrant B's. And the connection between principles and rationality is that one meaning of rationality involves principles: "in fact, they define a general concept of rationality. A rational man is one who is consistent in thought and in action, abiding by impartial and generalizable principles freely chosen as binding upon himself."[3]

This conceptual argument strikes me as unconvincing for the following reasons. First, the question of the connection between critical thinking and either reasoning, rationality, or principles has not been addressed, and thus the gap between the main topic and these other things remains. In other words, this argument is still assuming without justification that critical thinking is the same thing as reasoning or rationality. Therefore, the most that would follow is not Siegel's conclusion that "there is then

[3] Siegel 1988, 33, quoted from Scheffler 1973, 76.

a deep conceptual connection, by way of the notion of reasons, between critical thinkers and rational persons" (p. 32), but rather that there is a deep conceptual connection, by way of the notion of principles, between reasoners and rational persons, between reasoning and rationality.

Second, there is the difficulty that even the more restricted conclusion would follow only if the principles involved were of the same type. However, the relevant principles to which one is committed in reason-giving are principles specifying what kind of conclusion one may draw from what kind of premise. Some of these principles may be subject-specific, and some subject-neutral, as Siegel correctly argues in some of his criticism of McPeck. But such principles of reasoning are different from the principles of rationality in question. Even the principles of rationality mentioned by Siegel show this. In fact he refers to the principle of consistency in thought and action, and the principle of impartiality according to which similar cases ought to be treated similarly. Now, consistency of thought and action is a principle about the relationship between thought and action, whereas principles of reasoning are about the relationship between one thought and another. And the principle of impartiality is really a principle about using similar principles in similar cases, and thus a principle about principles; applying this very principle to the case at hand, it yields the conclusion that principles of reasoning ought to be handled differently from principles about principles. In short, principles of reasoning may be one sub-type of principles of rationality, but the latter include other sub-types.

Thus, my conclusion is that Siegel's conceptual argument does not provide an adequate justification for his identification of critical thinking, reasoning, and rationality; in fact, it provides no reason at all for equating critical thinking to either one of the other two things, whereas the reason advanced for equating reasoning and rationality is insufficient or irrelevant.

5. The Critical Argument

Siegel does have another argument, found at the end of his critique of McPeck's views. This critical argument is an attempt to show that McPeck's distinction between critical thinking and rationality is untenable (pp. 28–30).

One strand of this argument is that this distinction is incompatible with the idea that reason assessment is a central component of critical thinking. Since, as mentioned above, I agree about the centrality of reason assessment, this incompatibility would provide a very effective reason. But is there really such an incompatibility? Recall that McPeck's distinction, at least as interpreted by Siegel (1988, 29–30; cf. McPeck 1981, 12), is one in terms of the problematic character of the reasons involved; that is, critical thinking is the special case of reasoning when the reasons are perceived to be especially problematic. The best sense I can make of Siegel's criticism here is that he is saying that from the point of view of reason assessment there is no important difference. In Siegel's words: "the reason assessment component of critical thinking extends to *all* reasons, not just 'meta-reasons' concerning the constitution, relevance, or appropriateness of 'ground-floor' reasons" (p. 29). This criticism seems to me to reduce to objecting that the distinction is untenable because it cannot be made from the viewpoint of reason assessment, that is, by distinguishing sub-types of reason assessment. However, this misses the mark because McPeck's point is that the distinction can be made in terms of sub-types of thinking, the defining characteristic being whether or not reason assessment is present; that is, critical thinking would be the special type of thinking which is accompanied by reason assessment. Therefore, I do not think McPeck's distinction is incompatible with the centrality of reason assessment; on the contrary, it is a direct consequence of making reason assessment so central as to be the definitional criterion of critical thinking.

McPeck's distinction does presuppose that there can be cases of thinking or reasoning which are not accompanied by (explicit or reflective) reason assessment. This brings us to the second strand of Siegel's critical argument. It reduces to the following:

On McPeck's construal of critical thinking as a subset of rational thinking, a person who properly utilized available evidence in order to solve some problem or come to some belief, e.g. one who planned a trip route by carefully examining maps, noting terrain, balancing time demands against the goals of the trip, etc. – in short, one who planned the trip rationally – would *not* count as having engaged in critical thinking while planning it. This . . . seems absurd on its face. [pp. 29–30]

Well, I see nothing absurd in this. Siegel finds it so because he is equating reasoning and critical thinking, and thus sees every instance of reasoning as being also an instance of critical thinking. This emerges explicitly a few lines thereafter when Siegel declares that "we must perforce regard critical thinking not as a dimension of rationality, but as its equivalent. . . . Otherwise, we are forced to regard instances of believing and acting on the basis of good reasons as non-instances of critical thinking" (p. 30). However, the issue now is precisely whether we can equate rationality or reasoning with critical thinking, and so here Siegel is providing no reason for this equation.

Therefore, I am inclined to say that Siegel's critical argument for identifying critical thinking and reasoning or rationality also fails: the first strand misses the target, and so McPeck's distinction remains unrefuted; the second strand provides no actual reason for that identification.

6. Other Arguments

Besides what I have called the conceptual and the critical arguments, which are relatively explicit, there are other considerations of a more implicit sort which could be made in defense of Siegel's identification, especially of the equation of reasoning and critical thinking.[4]

For example, the book may be said to contain an historical argument insofar as the 'reasons' conception of critical thinking is made to emerge from a constructive criticism of the three main available conceptions of critical thinking, advanced by Robert Ennis, Richard Paul, and John McPeck. The answer to this is as follows. In regard to Ennis, his conception has evolved, and the evolution shows a shift from talking about "critical thinking" to talking about "rational thinking" (Ennis 1962, 1980, 1981); now, this shift represents a recognition that the claims being made are unjustified if intended as an analysis of the notion of "critical thinking"; and this recognition presupposes a significant difference between this notion and that of "rational thinking" or reasoning. In regard to McPeck, as we have seen, the difference between reasoning and critical thinking represents a difference between his views and those of Siegel. On the other hand, Paul's views do coincide with Siegel's on this point, but an appeal to them would in this context become a questionable argument from authority.

It could also be argued that the expression "critical thinking" does have a meaning that encompasses reasoning, for persons who may be said to belong to the critical-thinking movement. This is indeed true, and the fact may be even significant from the point of view of the sociology of knowledge and culture, but here we are questioning whether this movement is justified in understanding the expression the way it does. Therefore, one cannot appeal to this fact on pain of begging the question.

---

[4] These were suggested by Siegel himself at a discussion of his book, held at the Eighth Annual and Sixth International Conference on Critical Thinking, Sonoma State University, Rohnert Park, California, 7–10 August 1988, where a shorter version of this chapter was first presented.

Perhaps Siegel could say that his equation of critical thinking and reasoning is a stipulative definition. This would be a recognition that his claim departs from common usage. But then the question would become whether this stipulative definition should be accepted, and especially in the context of Siegel's articulation of critical thinking as a general intellectual ideal, this question could not be dismissed.

Next, an attempt might be made to shift the burden of proof by challenging the critic to show what is wrong with Siegel's equation(s), to explain what is the difference between reasoning and critical thinking, and to say why the two should be distinguished. In my view this would be a proper request, but the reason for this propriety may not be consistent with Siegel's view. In fact, to justify the propriety of the request one would have to appeal to some such principle as that it is rational to continue to accept a belief as long as there is no special reason to reject it.[5] However, this principle runs counter to Siegel's approach which views rationality in the more usual fashion, namely in accordance with the principle that it is rational to continue to accept a belief if and only if one has a special reason to do so. Therefore, in the context of this critical review the burden of proof remains with Siegel.

And this brings us to one final countermove. This would be to say that this dispute is a verbal one, since it is not clear that it makes any difference whether or not one equates critical thinking, reasoning, and rationality the way Siegel does. To this one could reply that the dispute is no more verbal than any other philosophical disagreement about the nature of and relationship among concepts, such as whether knowledge and justified true belief, or justice and fairness, or explanation and deduction are related in this manner or that. More importantly, the issue is a consequential one because, by uncritically equating the things he does, Siegel is prevented from grasping the key role that criticism and critical thinking have in reasoning and rationality. I am not saying that this deep fact[6] is either obvious, or established, or well known, but only that one is bound

---

[5] This corresponds to what Harman (1986, 46) calls the "*Principle of Conservativism*: One is justified in continuing fully to accept something in the absence of a special reason not to."

[6] This view of rationality corresponds to the recent elaboration by Harman of the difference between the positive and the negative undermining of beliefs, and between the coherence and the foundational approach to reasoning (1986, especially pp. 32–42). It also corresponds to the older attempts by some of the Popperians to emphasize falsification, refutation, and criticism in epistemology (e.g., Agassi 1963; Bartley 1964; Koertge 1974; Popper [1963, 369–96; 1972, 1–31]; Settle et al. 1974). See also Finocchiaro 1980b, 418–31.

to miss it by proceeding as he does. Nevertheless, the difference between the two principles mentioned in the preceding paragraph is obviously significant and pregnant with consequences, and it seems to me that their difference could be conceptualized in terms of critical thinking as follows: the first principle (not espoused by Siegel) is saying that to think "critically" about beliefs, in the usual and negative sense of criticism or negative evaluation, is the essential component of rationality; whereas the second, more traditional principle (accepted by Siegel) is saying that the positive justification of beliefs by supporting reasons is the essential component. In short, for all his talk of critical thinking, Siegel does not really show that much appreciation for it.

Now, although Siegel's book is full of arguments on other related topics, I find no other arguments supporting the equations I have focused on. Therefore, my general conclusion is that the book has not adequately justified the thesis that critical thinking is coextensive with reasoning and with rationality.

7. Summary

My critical conclusion does not mean, of course, that this thesis is either unjustifiable or false. A different argument would be needed to show that critical thinking, reasoning, and rationality differ, and how. I have not constructed such an argument. What I hope to have done is the following. I have formulated the problem of the relationship between critical thinking, reasoning, and rationality, and I feel that my critical argument is sufficient to show that there is a problem. I believe I have also shown that Siegel has not solved this problem. Moreover, I have engaged in an exercise in critical thinking, and the exercise is such that a number of theoretical claims are illustrated or reinforced: not only the thesis that reason assessment is central to critical thinking, but also the complementary thesis that reason identification is also important, and indeed that conclusion identification is equally crucial; in fact, my detailed analysis began by identifying several important claims made in the book, then went on to identify the supporting reasons, and then assessed these reasons. Finally, although my discussion does not solve the problem of how critical thinking, reasoning, and rationality relate and how they differ, I hope my exercise provides material and suggestions for its solution.

11

Induction and Intuition in the Normative Study of Reasoning

Cohen on Inductive Reasoning in Philosophy (1991)

1. Introduction

In the contemporary philosophical scene, the work of L. Jonathan Cohen[1] stands out in several ways. One stems from the significance, range, and combination of topics on which he focuses, which are primarily reasoning and rationality, induction and probability, metaphilosophy, philosophy of science, and philosophy of law. Another relates to the character of the approach he follows in his investigations, and which I would describe as both theoretically deep and practically relevant, both insightful and well argued, rigorous without being pedantic, and original without being cranky. Cohen's work also deserves admiration and emulation because of the particular stand he takes on the issues and the particular conclusions he arrives at in regard to the topics studied; and here I have in mind his defense of human rationality from the attacks of experimental psychologists, his defense of democratic values and principles in regard to the use of lay juries in jurisprudence, and his defense of pluralism, open-mindedness, and dialogue in analytical philosophy.

In the light of all this, it is obvious that my remarks here cannot do full justice to the depth and variety of Cohen's work. I shall limit myself to some issues in his latest book (1986), and even in regard to them I feel that all I can do is to provide what may serve as the beginning of a potential dialogue, rather than a full analysis and resolution of them.

---

[1] See, for example, L. J. Cohen 1966; 1970; 1977; 1981a; 1986.

2. Reasoning in Analytical Philosophy and
the Inductive-Intuitive Method

The cluster of issues I want to focus on involves the nature of one type of argument in analytical philosophy, its connection with inductive reasoning, and the question of its viability and correctness in general. The topic is, I feel, especially promising in two ways. First, it is simply a socio-historical fact that the amount of work in the field of analytical philosophy is considerable; this is the work of philosophers like Ayer, Carnap, Davidson, Hempel, Hintikka, Quine, Rawls, Ryle, and Scriven, and their followers. Given the sheer quantity of writings, and the fact that they obviously contain reasoning and argument, the field demands serious attention by any serious theorist of reasoning. One could say that its presence is so robust that reasoning in analytical philosophy deserves to be studied simply because it is there, if for no other reason.

The second reason for the special relevance of the topic stems from the fact that Cohen claims that a great deal of analytical-philosophical argument is (1) about reasoning, specifically about (2) norms of reasoning, and consists of (3) inductive reasoning (4) based on intuitions. If he is right, then we may say that there exists a distinctive approach to the study of reasoning, an approach which may be labeled the intuitive-inductive approach. His account would therefore deserve the attention of anyone concerned with the methodology of the study of reasoning, whether he is an advocate or a critic[2] of the experimental approach prevalent in cognitive psychology, or an advocate or critic of the apriorist approach prevalent in formal logic. In fact, Cohen may be taken to have identified, elaborated, and defended a different approach.

Therefore, in his latest work, Cohen's contribution is at least two-sided, metaphilosophical and methodological; metaphilosophical, insofar as it advances a thesis about the nature of reasoning in that particular domain of human inquiry which is analytical philosophy, and methodological insofar as it articulates an approach to the study of reasoning which is worthy of serious consideration in general.

If from the viewpoint of significance Cohen's contribution has this double dimension, from the viewpoint of content it is striking in three ways.

First, there is his emphasis on the importance of induction in philosophical thought. Now, although this sort of recognition goes back at

---

[2] The present author has advanced his own criticism of the experimental method as practiced by cognitive psychologists; see, for example, Finocchiaro (1980b, 256–72; 1987a; 1987c; 1989b).

least to Aristotle's interpretation of Socrates's definitions as the result of inductive arguments,[3] such an inductivist viewpoint goes against the prevailing view that all philosophical argumentation is deductive.[4] And here it should be added, by way of clarification, that Cohen attaches his own special meaning to the notion of induction:[5] on the one hand, he does retain the contrast with deduction, and the idea that inductive reasoning proceeds from the particular to the general; however, he emphasizes that what is particular and what is general is something that depends on the context (p. 82)[6] and more importantly that what he has in mind is not the enumerative but the eliminative type of induction, according to which generalizations are tested by reference to relevant variations in kinds of instances rather than merely being inferred from a multiplicity of instances (p. 69).

Second, there is Cohen's recognition of the importance of singular intuitions as the basis for philosophical conclusions, and here it is important to understand what he means by intuition. He does not mean the infallible apprehension of essences, or a heuristic faculty that is part of the creative imagination, but rather a fallible inclination of judgment originating from a system of tacit rules rather than from any conscious or explicit inferential or causal process (pp. 73–82).

Third, Cohen's central thesis has normative content in the sense that he is attributing a normative aim to analytical philosophy. His critique of naturalized epistemology, and his plea for a normative epistemology and for a normative study of reasoning, make it clear that he is concerned with the normative principles of reasoning.

So far then we might attempt to formulate Cohen's central thesis as saying that analytical philosophers support norms of reasoning by means of inductive reasoning based on singular intuitions. However, there is another dimension of Cohen's thesis that needs elaboration for a fuller appreciation. To see this let us ask whether he is claiming that this is what analytical philosophers are in fact doing, or what they ought to be doing, or both; in other words, are analytical philosophers essentially right in engaging in this type of reasoning?

---

[3] Aristotle, *Metaphysics* 1078b, 29–32; cf. L. J. Cohen 1986, 136–37.

[4] This view is so common that it hardly needs documentation; L. J. Cohen (1986, 67) mentions Passmore (1961, 6).

[5] This, of course, corresponds to ideas he has elaborated in L. J. Cohen (1970; 1977).

[6] From here on, references to L. J. Cohen 1986 will be given in parentheses in the text by mentioning just the page numbers.

It is obvious that Cohen's thesis has a second normative dimension, at the metalevel; that is, his own thesis is primarily a normative principle of philosophical reasoning, a normative principle about the intuitive and inductive basis of norms of reasoning. This is obvious partly from the parts of the book concerned with vindicating the essential correctness of this inductive-intuitive method, and also from the self-referential requirement that his own metaphilosophical exercise is meant to be a piece of analytical philosophy and therefore subject to the same principles being attributed to the latter.

The normative status of Cohen's own metaphilosophical thesis does not, however, undo its factual, descriptive, and explanatory content. So what I am saying is that a full appreciation of it needs to recognize both its normative, evaluative force and its factual, descriptive content. In other words, for Cohen a chief involvement of analytical philosophers *is and ought* to be inductive reasoning based on singular intuitions and supporting norms of reasoning.

These two aspects of the thesis could also be stated as generalizations about norms of reasoning: for example, that norms of reasoning may be properly supported by inductive reasoning based on singular intuitions, and that norms of reasoning are supported in this manner in analytical philosophy. When so stated these two aspects seem to correspond to the above-mentioned methodological and metaphilosophical aspects.

3. Reasoning versus Nonreasoning

Let us now turn into a more critical direction. The first difficulty I should like to raise involves the distinction between reasoning about reasoning and reasoning about nonreasoning. The question is whether the subject matter of analytical-philosophical reasoning is reasoning or something else. This question is different from the one concerning whether or not analytical philosophers are engaged in reasoning when they study whatever it is they are studying. My point is that it is not immediately obvious that, for example, when Hempel (1965) is engaged in analyzing the concept of explanation or when Gettier (1963) is engaged in analyzing the concept of knowledge, they are dealing with the same subject matter as Harman (1986) when he is analyzing the notion of reasoning. Or to give an example from Cohen's own work, when he is engaged in clarifying the concept of intuition (pp. 73–83) or the concepts of belief and acceptance (pp. 91–97), he seems to be dealing with a subject matter significantly different from the case when he is engaged in reconstructing how subjects solve the taxicab problem (pp. 159–64).

I believe Cohen is addressing this issue when he points out that in the analysis of explanation a central concern is whether or not "the inclusion of statements in such-and-such a relationship to one another or to the world at large counts as a reason for calling some given string of sentences an 'explanation'" (p. 73). So in general we may say that in the analysis of concepts philosophers are studying how ordinary people, or the relevant group of practitioners, as the case may be, reason when they apply the concept. Some clarifications are in order here.

First, if we distinguish between the word and the concept, between lexicography and philosophy as it were,[7] then the paraphrase of Cohen's quotation I have just given may be incorrect. I should have said that analysts are studying how people reason when they apply the word, how they would justify the application of a word. To be more exact, we should speak of how people reason when they apply the word correctly. Moreover, a concept may be in someone's mind even without the proper word, and so we would have to say that analysts also study how people would reason if they were to apply the word correctly.

However, it may be objected that the degree or intensity of reasoning here is too weak, that the ratiocination is not sufficiently explicit to be called "reasoning." Moreover, all such reasoning would have a metalinguistic or metaconceptual character that would render suspect its claim to being typical or representative of human reasoning. Finally, in the analysis of the concept of reasoning as such, a philosopher would be examining not only the reasoning involved in the proper application of the notion of "reasoning," but also the more explicit reasoning constituting the content of the argument in question.

In other words, the investigation of what X is (where X stands for a term like explanation, belief, knowledge, intuition, argument, and reasoning) is also an investigation of the reasoning whereby a person judges that this is an X. In fact, the justification of the judgment that this is an X one would require some such reasoning as: this is an X because this is A, B, C, D, etc., and X is anything which is A, B, C, D, etc.[8] Therefore, the explication of X (produced by the analysis of X) serves as the major

---

[7] In view of his critique of the linguistic interpretation of analytical philosophy, Cohen would be the first one to do so.

[8] For a nontrivial example of this type of reasoning, see Finocchiaro 1988c, 197–211, where I reconstruct Hegel's Preface to the *Phenomenology of Spirit* as the argument that philosophy is dialectical because it is pluralistic, conceptual, concrete, self-reflective, spiritual, systematic, negative, and self-referential, and because it sublimates the opposition between truth and falsity, method and result, change and permanence, form and content, and subject and predicate.

premise of such arguments; it is in a sense the principle of reasoning connecting the minor premise and the conclusion. It follows then that the analysis of concepts practiced by analytical philosophers is indeed the investigation of the principles of reasoning in such arguments. Therefore, I would conclude by saying that there is a sense in which one may analyze analysis as reasoning about reasoning.

However, I have a lingering dissatisfaction with this. Since any statement may become part of reasoning when it becomes a premise of an appropriate argument, it appears that in Cohen's account the study of anything would become the study of reasoning, namely of the reasoning involving that something. And then we would want to introduce a distinction between explicit and actual reasoning and merely implicit and potential reasoning.

4. Norms

Another point of difficulty concerns the part of Cohen's thesis claiming that the focus of analytical-philosophical reasoning is the *norms* of reasoning.[9] We may agree with him that "if the normative study of reasoning did not already exist, it would have to be invented" (p. 63).

However, this thesis would not be correct if it meant that whenever reasoning is the subject matter of philosophical reasoning, the relevant aspect of that subject matter is normative principles of reasoning. A common concern of analytical philosophers is the nature of reasoning as reflected in its structure and as expressed by descriptive generalizations about reasoning.

For example, in the analysis of explanation, it seems to me there is a great difference between the question of the structure of scientific explanation and the question of the conditions under which a scientific explanation is acceptable, or preferable to another. Part of Hempel's account claims that scientific explanations have a deductive and nomological structure, and that their logical structure is identical to that of predictions. But then, within the class of scientific explanations so defined, Hempel tries to distinguish various subclasses depending on various virtues or degrees of merit they may or may not possess, involving such questions as whether or not such explanations are true, or highly

---

9 See, for example, his assertion that "if we examine seriatim the problems that actually puzzle analytical philosophers we shall find that the problems of analytical philosophy are all normative problems connected in various ways with rationality of judgment, rationality of attitude, rationality of procedure, or rationality of action" (L. J. Cohen 1986, 49).

confirmed, or sketchy, or ad hoc, or self-evidencing, etc. And he also formulates what he calls "a general *condition of adequacy for any rationally acceptable explanation of a particular event.* That condition is the following: any rationally acceptable answer to the question 'Why did event *X* occur?' must offer information which shows that *X* was to be expected – if not definitely, as in the case of a D-N explanation, then at least with reasonable probability" (Hempel 1965, 367–68). I believe it might be useful to think of generalizations about the logical structure of scientific explanations as principles of *interpretation*, and of generalizations about their various degrees of merit as principles of *evaluation*.

One question I have is how Cohen's norms of reasoning fit into this scheme. The principles of interpretation just mentioned correspond, I believe, to the explications of concepts mentioned earlier. That discussion above was limited to identifying a role in reasoning for such principles, the context being that of the reconstruction of the rationale for a judgment such as that this is a scientific explanation. Now we can add that in certain other contexts those major premises would have normative force, and thus might be regarded as normative principles of reasoning; these would be contexts where one is engaged in the construction of the original argument, namely in the original reasoning arriving at the original judgment.

My initial comment here would be that this normative force of interpretative principles is rather meager in comparison with the normative force of the evaluative principles. In the latter the normative force is full-blown and explicit. But although this distinction between interpretation and evaluation is thusly analogous to our earlier one between reasoning and nonreasoning, the effect on Cohen's discussion is here, I believe, the reverse of the earlier one. What I mean is that here Cohen does properly focus on explicitly normative questions; or to be more exact, when he shows how analytical philosophers engage in the normative study of reasoning, the norms of reasoning in question are of the explicit full-blown variety. This is as it should be if one wants to call attention to the normative dimension of epistemology.

However, this leads me to the criticism that Cohen is not paying sufficient attention to the descriptive, interpretative dimension of analytical philosophy; to the fact that an equally important aim of analytical philosophers is the study of the structure of reasoning and of interpretative principles, independently of their normative dimension or their normative connections. To repeat, one does not have to deny the connection between descriptive and prescriptive principles, nor the implicitly normative dimension of descriptive principles of reasoning. The point is merely to admit the distinct status and philosophical significance' of descriptive principles of interpretation.

To conclude this section, it is best to add an example from Cohen's own practice to the one from the theory of explanation already given. His work is in a sense, as he subtitles it, "an analysis of analytical philosophy." And a main result of this analysis is that "the unifying force in analytical philosophy is its engagement with the reasoned investigation of reasons at that level of generality (varying in accordance with subject-matter) where no conclusions can be taken as universally granted" (p. 57). Another is that "a great deal of reasoning in modern analytical philosophy is inductive, not deductive" (p. 67). These are important generalizations about analytical-philosophical reasoning, but their primary import is descriptive and interpretative rather than normative; and I believe their very significance would be diluted to the extent that we were to construe them in normative terms.

5. Induction

Next I should like to focus on that part of Cohen's thesis which is in many ways the most striking and the most exciting, namely the part which attributes an inductive character to analytical-philosophical reasoning.[10]

The difficulties I feel in this regard concern the relationship between inductive reasoning and (1) deduction, (2) the empirical approach, and (3) what Cohen himself calls "inductivism."

To begin with, it is useful to stress that Cohen is not denying that a great deal of philosophical reasoning is deductive (pp. 66–67), and that he himself points out (p. 144) that the writings of analytical philosophers normally contain a mixture of both deductive and inductive reasoning. How does the metaphilosopher distinguish the two?

Cohen states that "in deductive reasoning our conclusion must be true if the premises are true. Through inductive reasoning – of the kind relevant here – we may acquire some level of justified confidence in a generalization if we accept reasons for supposing that the generalization holds good in certain varieties of instance" (p. 67). These

---

[10] I should also say that my hesitation is greatest here, for in view of Cohen's long-standing and brilliant contributions to the study of induction I cannot help but feel that he must have thought about these questions and must have ready answers for them. Now, although this makes any criticism on my part rather risky, perhaps I can adopt the attitude that, if I can motivate him to provide the answers, the general gain will be considerable.

look to me like definitions of deductively *valid* reasoning and of inductively *correct* reasoning, for they seem to exclude the possibility of deductive arguments which happen to be invalid and of inductive reasoning which happens to be inductively faulty. And I am sure Cohen does not want to allow this consequence. That is, when as examples of deductive reasoning he gives "Descartes's proof of an external world...Spinoza's *Ethics*...transcendental argument" (p. 67), I am sure he does not mean that all these arguments *actually* have the property that "the conclusion must be true if the premises are true" (p. 67). And in regard to the various inductive arguments by analytical philosophers he mentions, I am sure he does not mean that all these arguments actually confer the requisite level of justified confidence in the generalizations being supported. However, if the definitions given really make a distinction between two *types of evaluation* of an argument, how is the distinction between *argument-types* to be made?[11]

In regard to the connection with empiricism, I should like to raise the question whether the inductive approach is a type of empirical approach, and I should like to explore the possibility of an affirmative answer. To be sure, I have no problem grasping the point, which Cohen wisely never tires of reiterating, that inductive reasoning cannot be equated with reasoning based on observation or experiment, and that the latter is only one species of the genus (pp. 67–73). But in my view this does make the inductive approach non-empirical; in fact I would not want to equate the empirical with the observational or experimental, partly because experimentation often contains a priori elements, partly because I am inclined to regard the historical approach as a type of empirical approach,[12] and partly because I would want to analyze the empirical in terms of open-minded fallibilism.[13]

It may also look like Cohen is driving a wedge between induction and empiricism when he says that "the choice between deductive and inductive patterns of argument can be quite independent of any preference for rationalist or empiricist epistemology" (p. 135). However, his meaning turns out to be such as to dispel this initial impression. What he means is that philosophers sometimes use deductive argumentation in the service of an empiricist epistemology, a classic example being Hume's attitude

---

[11] I should mention that I have a hunch that the answer may lie in Cohen's theory of probability as the gradation of provability, which he develops in chapter 2 of L. J. Cohen 1977, but I am not sure.

[12] See, for example, Finocchiaro 1987a; 1987c.

[13] For example, along the lines of Shapere 1984.

toward his epistemological principle that every simple idea is a copy of a previous impression.[14] Similarly, philosophers sometimes use inductive arguments in support of rationalist epistemologies, Cohen's example being Whewell's historical arguments to justify his Kantian epistemology (pp. 135–36). However, I think this merely means that many philosophers are not completely consistent, and that their own philosophical practice often belies the general conclusions they preach, that their general principles often run into self-referential difficulties.

Thirdly, it looks like Cohen is advocating at least the *compatibility* between inductive reasoning and apriorism in view of the fact that some of his most frequent examples of analytical philosophy come from the work of Carnap and Hempel, and yet their theories of confirmation and of explanation are clearly cases of excessive apriorism in the procedure they followed in their own work,[15] a fact which Cohen himself recognizes (p. 126).

However, perhaps all that Cohen is saying is that apriorism is a species of *faulty* inductive reasoning. For on the one hand he regards these philosophers as part of "the curious tendency that existed for a while in modern analytical philosophy to treat certain kinds of scientific problem as philosophical rather than scientific issues" (p. 118), and he criticizes this as a "mistakenly a priorist tendency" (p. 121). On the other hand, he later diagnoses their problem by saying that they "invoked intuitions in relation to certain problems about confirmation, explanation, etc. that are really part of the domain of scientific inquiry . . . in order to achieve an a priori global resolution for issues that in fact require empirical determination in local contexts" (p. 126); and he goes on to suggest that "what is necessary instead is to discern the appropriate domain for philosophical generalization about scientific reasoning – i.e. to discern the level of abstraction or generality at which the analysis of this reasoning is possible" (p. 126). Thus, Cohen's point may be that their reasoning did indeed have an inductive character, but that it was unsound in the sense of being excessively apriorist. Therefore, their work would be instantiating both induction and apriorism, but in a harmless manner.

However, a new difficulty arises at this point. Why should one describe their theories of confirmation and of explanation as examples of faulty inductive reasoning (faulty because apriorist or "hasty") rather than as

---

[14] Hume 1911, 13–14; cf. L. J. Cohen (1986, 132–33, 135) and Finocchiaro (1988a, 314).
[15] For such a critique of Hempel's theory of explanation, see, for example, Finocchiaro 1973c, 17–56.

an example of objectionable *deductivism?* For that is how Cohen describes Chisholm's theory of inductive evidence (p. 140), which seems to me to be an exactly parallel case since Cohen's complaint is its lack of (sufficient) empirical content.[16]

Finally, I am not exactly clear about the connection between inductive reasoning and what he calls "inductivism" in the context of a discussion of "deductivism and inductivism as alternative strategies in analytical philosophy" (pp. 129–47). Obviously, inductivism is partly the strategy of employing inductive arguments, and deductivism the strategy of employing deductive arguments. However, he also draws the contrast in terms of, respectively, a critical[17] versus a conservative orientation, a localized versus a globalist orientation, and an interest in traditional philosophical problems versus an interest in problems stemming from contemporary nonphilosophical areas.

In this section the most striking feature of the discussion is Cohen's judiciousness. For he admits that "within analytical philosophy, both deductivism and inductivism may run into characteristic perils if allowed to dominate excessively" (p. 133); and he recognizes that "in practice, of course, inductivism and deductivism often complement one another in a single text" (p. 144); and he argues that "the thesis that both inductive and deductive reasoning are admissible in any branch of analytical philosophy is a categorical and inductive one, in that intuitively recognizable examples of both kinds of reasoning are cited in support of the thesis" (p. 147).

One comment I have here is that it seems plausible to include all these features under the label of "inductivism." I do see their family resemblance to one another and to the employment of inductive arguments, in the more or less technical sense of induction intended by Cohen. However, I am not sure I see how all of them could be reduced to the technique of employing inductive reasoning, whose possibility is suggested by his choice of the label "inductivism." Another question would be why the empirical orientation is not included in the list.

6. Intuition

Appeal to intuition is certainly one of Cohen's central themes. As mentioned above, it is important to understand that he is talking about fallible

---

[16] Cohen is referring to Chisholm 1970.
[17] This is my own word; L. J. Cohen (1986, 129–35) speaks of "sceptical" conclusions.

inclinations of judgment. It should be mentioned that he argues conclusively, in my estimation, in favor of the primacy of singular intuitions. It is also clear that singular intuitions are seen as providing the data on which inductive reasoning in analytical philosophy is based.

The only issue I should like to raise here is a question about the relative importance of intuitions about imagined artificial examples and intuitions about actual historical cases, which relates to the question whether such intuitions are a priori or empirical.

Let us begin by asking what such intuitions are about. For Cohen they are "about what should be inferred, judged or meant in such-and-such a context" (p. 73), as distinct from what is in fact inferred; they are about "what *is* a reason for what, not ... what is taken by scientists, lawyers, or others to be a reason for what" (p. 77). This is in accordance with the rest of his account which makes these intuitions the basis of inductive reasoning in support of *normative* principles. In short, the relevant intuitions are intuitions about normative issues in particular cases. We might speak of normative singular intuitions.

Are the particular cases merely imagined or empirically real? Are they artificially contrived or historically reconstructed? I feel that this is an important question because its answer determines whether or not the intuitive-inductive method advocated by Cohen is empirical. I believe he is somewhat ambiguous on the matter.

In fact, on the one hand we can find explicit and clear statements of the superiority of real or historical examples over imagined and artificial ones. For example, while discussing this issue as it emerges in the different fields of moral philosophy, grammatical theory, and epistemology he says:

No doubt it is better to rely on real-life decisions of conscience if one can, just as a grammarian may prefer to rely on real-life utterances if he can: there is less risk that the intuitions may be biased, or otherwise influenced, by the preferred theory. But some recourse to intuitions about imaginary situations or utterances may be unavoidable. Similarly a philosopher of science needs to take his examples from the history of science whenever this is possible. But he may not be able to dispense altogether with appeals to avowed intuitions about imaginary cases or his own thought-experiments. [p. 88]

Moreover, Cohen's own examples from the writings of analytical philosophers are almost always actual, historical, and "real-life"; therefore, in his own metaphilosophical theorizing he is certainly practicing what I would call an empirical, historically oriented method.[18]

---

[18] If it should be thought that this is unavoidably so in metaphilosophy, I would give the counterexample of Johnstone (1959; 1978). His metaphilosophical theory focuses on

On the other hand, most of these examples are from analytical philosophers who tend to give imagined and artificial examples, thus shunning the empirical method in their own practice and engaging in some form or other of apriorism. Further, at one point Cohen declares explicitly that an intuition that *p*, in his sense of intuition, is a priori, while admittedly not analytic.[19]

There is no problem with the denial of analyticity, which I take to be another way of stressing the fallibility of the kind of intuitions he is talking about. But the attribution of an a priori status is puzzling. The reason Cohen gives for it is that such intuitions are "not checkable by sensory perception" (p. 75), and do not depend on a "form of introspection" (p. 75). However, it seems to me that the crucial issue would be whether they depend on some form of experience. Now, while I would agree with Cohen that such intuitions do not depend *consciously* or *deliberately* on education, it seems to me that they cannot fail to depend at least *unconsciously* on education, as Cohen admits that they may (p. 77).

In conclusion, while his claim about the a priori status of intuitions is likely to be untenable, there can be no question that he is ambiguous in regard to this whole issue.

It may be that Cohen's partial inclinations toward apriorism stem, at least in part, from his rejection of the experimental-psychological approach to the study of reasoning. The latter is certainly a species of empiricism, but I share Cohen's deep concerns about it, and have advanced some objections of my own.[20] Therefore, it should be clear that I for one am not advocating the substitution of his inductive-intuitive approach by the experimental method of cognitive psychology.

7. Conclusion

In summary, I began this chapter by calling attention to the significance of Cohen's work in general. Then I focused on his latest book, which contains two interrelated themes. One is a metaphilosophical, descriptive, and interpretative account of the nature of reasoning in analytical

---

the process of *ad hominem* argumentation, and I have elsewhere pointed out its many merits (Finocchiaro 1980c); however, without suggesting that this is a major criticism, I would say that his examples *tend* to be imagined and artificial.

[19] "Nothing positive is implied thereby about the specific nature of *p*'s content, where *p* is the intuited proposition. Certainly *p* need not be concerned with non-natural facts or essences. But also, though the judgment that *p* is obviously classifiable as a priori (because not checkable by sensory perception), it need not be analytic" (L. J. Cohen 1986, 75).

[20] See, for example, Finocchiaro 1980b; 1987a; 1987c; 1989b.

philosophy; here his thesis is that a chief aim of analytical philosophers is to elaborate normative principles of reasoning in the various object domains by means of inductive reasoning based on normative singular intuitions. The other theme is the methodological, normative, and evaluative one that this inductive-intuitive-normative method of studying reasoning is a viable one, being preferable, for example, to the experimental method of cognitive psychology.

I am impressed by the originality and fruitfulness of both theses, and my primary aim has been to provide, or ask for, a number of needed clarifications. For example, I have suggested that the study of explicit instances of reasoning has priority over the study of implicit instances, and that much analytical philosophy focuses on non-explicit reasoning. I have also argued that the study of reasoning ought not to be restricted to the study of the norms of reasoning, and that the work of Cohen himself and of many other analytical philosophers is in fact not so restricted, but rather advances important and insightful descriptive interpretations about the nature and structure of reasoning as such. Thirdly, I have attempted to add to the value of the inductive approach to the study of reasoning by relating it to an empirical anti-apriorist approach, and I have suggested the connection needs further elaboration. Finally, I have stressed the importance of distinguishing between two types of appeals to singular intuitions, and I have suggested that if we want to avoid objectionable apriorism the intuitions in question should be about actual or historical cases rather than imagined or contrived ones.

12

Logic, Politics, and Gramsci

Intellectuals, Dialectics, and Philosophy in the Prison Notebooks (1992)

1. Introduction

The aim of this chapter is to explore the ways in which the work of Antonio Gramsci may be fruitful for a proper understanding of the nature and relationship of logic and politics.

First, without denying the existence of other conceptions, I would want to advocate conceiving logic as the judiciously empirical study of reasoning and argument. As long as we do not equate the notion of the empirical with the excesses of empiricism or with the experimental method of cognitive psychologists, I believe this to be a very fruitful approach.[1] In this enterprise which corresponds in large measure to what is called "empirical logic" by some[2] and "informal logic" by others,[3] one may follow an historical approach in which one studies reasoning and argument as these occur in some appropriately chosen book such as Galileo Galilei's *Dialogue on the Two Chief World Systems* or Lenin's *What Is to Be Done?* or Spinoza's *Ethics*.[4] From the viewpoint of such an historical approach to empirical or informal logic, the potential fruitfulness of Gramsci becomes apparent once one realizes that he is the author of a modern classic of political and social thought, namely the *Prison Notebooks*.[5] This means that his work becomes susceptible of being studied in order to determine what

---

[1] See, for example, Barth (1985a; 1985b; 1987); Finocchiaro (1980b; 1984b; 1987a; 1989b); Johnson and Blair 1985; and Naess (1982a; 1982b).

[2] This label is due to Barth 1985a.

[3] Finocchiaro 1984b; Johnson and Blair 1985.

[4] See Finocchiaro (1980b; 1987a) for Galileo; Smit 1989 for Lenin; and Naess 1982a for Spinoza.

[5] See Gramsci 1971; 1975; 1985; 1988.

logical patterns it exhibits, to what extent these patterns are generalizable
to political thought in general, and how they compare and contrast with
other patterns of reasoning in other fields.

The apparent fruitfulness of Gramsci as a case study in the historical-
empirical approach to logic is enhanced by another circumstance. This
is the fact that, due to reasons to be mentioned presently, his work has
become the subject of an enormous and labyrinthine secondary literature.[6] Since the serious student of Gramsci has at some point to come
to terms with this literature, it may be taken to provide a second level of
data and material for logical analysis.

This is still very general in the sense that this kind of potential relevance belongs to any serious work of political thought. However, for the
case of Gramsci there exists at least one study undertaken in large measure from this point of view, and therefore what one may do now is to
formulate more explicitly the lessons implied by such an exercise. What
I mean is that about ten years ago, after completing an empirical-logical
analysis of Galileo's *Dialogue*,[7] I undertook a similar analysis of Gramsci's
Prison Notebooks.[8] It turned out that the concept of argument was not as
useful for the understanding, reconstructing, and evaluation of Gramsci's
thinking, as it had been for Galileo's. That is, almost every proposition
in Galileo's 500-page book can be assigned a place in the overall argument concluding that the earth moves, and hundreds of subarguments
of this main argument can be identified, reconstructed, and theorized
about; whereas nothing even remotely approaching that turned out to
be possible for Gramsci.[9] What did emerge was another concept, labeled
the "dialectic," which enables one to give systemic unity to a work like
his *Notebooks*. In this context, the dialectic is taken to mean a manner of
thinking which avoids one-sidedness by "finding the real identity beneath
the apparent contradiction and differentiation, and finding the substantial diversity beneath the apparent identity."[10] The elaboration of this
sort of theoretical lesson from the empirical-logical analysis of Gramsci
cannot be done at this point because at the moment I want to present it
in a preliminary sort of way as one of two main lines of inquiry involving
logic, politics, and Gramsci.

[6] See, for example, Finocchiaro 1984c; 1986a; 1988d.
[7] Finocchiaro 1980b.
[8] Finocchiaro 1988c; 1988d.
[9] Needless to say, this should not be taken to mean the *total* absence of argument in
     Gramsci.
[10] Gramsci 1988, 389; cf. Gramsci 1975, 2268.

The other one would be the critical examination of Gramsci's ideas on the subject. For it so happens that he did discuss it more or less explicitly in the context of a number of subtopics.

One of these clusters includes such questions as the nature of formal logic, the question whether or not formal-logical competence is innate, its role in education, and its connection with grammar and with oratorical eloquence.[11] This is not a frequent topic of discussion for Gramsci, nevertheless it arises on more than one occasion. Ultimately the connection between these Gramscian views and the central issue of the logic-politics nexus will have to be determined on its own merits in terms of the actual content of those views and in terms of exactly what Gramsci is saying about formal logic. Nevertheless, the initial and preliminary point that can be made is that the views on formal logic advanced by him can be expected to be something other and more than an abstract philosophy of formal logic; they can be expected to be something of political relevance, because of his deep political involvement. That is, politics was indeed for him the central focus of his life and thought, and so if he found the occasion to express some views on formal logic, we can expect them to be views on *politics and* formal logic. However, so far I have said nothing about Gramsci's political involvement, and therefore even the preliminary justification of the present point is incomplete until some account, however brief, is given of his life. This is something needed for other reasons as well, and so it will be done presently.

By contrast with his reflections on formal logic, his thoughts on intellectuals and philosophy are much more frequent and much more central.[12] Indeed he is notorious for his theory of intellectuals, which some have regarded as a contemporary version of the Platonic ideal of philosopher-kings. For this topic, the political relevance is relatively obvious, but the logical import less so. From the viewpoint of the logic-politics

---

[11] Subsequent references to Gramsci 1975 will be made by prefixing the page numbers by "Q" (short for *Quaderni*), as in the following: Q113, Q135–37, Q439–40, Q441–42, Q1055–56, Q1459–67 (especially Q1462–66), Q1540–50 (especially Q1549–50), Q1889–93, Q1948–49, Q2267. Some of these passages are available in English translation in Gramsci (1971; 1985; 1988), and when appropriate in what follows I will give references to both the original Italian and the English translation. It should be mentioned, however, that Finocchiaro (1988c, 249–53) contains a concordance between the pagination in the critical edition of Gramsci's *Notebooks* (Gramsci 1975) and the two major English-language collections (Gramsci 1971; 1985); this ought to be consulted when double references are not explicitly given.

[12] In fact they also occur in some of the most polished and longest essays in the *Notebooks*: Q1375–95, Q1406–11, Q1513–51, Q2259–69.

nexus, what needs to be elaborated is the connection between logic and what Gramsci calls intellectuals and what he calls philosophy. By way of anticipation and summary, I would say that for Gramsci an intellectual is a practitioner of argument who tries to steer clear of both the superficialities of eloquent oratory and the abstractions of mathematical deduction.[13] Similarly, philosophy for him is essentially the systematic avoidance of incoherence or contradiction.[14]

As a final preliminary, I would say that the question of the relationship between logic and politics is a version of the problem of the relationship between theory and practice, or thought and action, and the latter is certainly a frequent topic of Gramsci's reflections.[15] These views of his have a prima facie connection with our topic because politics may be plausibly regarded as a paradigm example of practical action, and logic as a paradigm example of theoretical reflection.

2. Gramsci's Political Appeal and Relevance

Antonio Gramsci was born on the Italian island of Sardinia in 1891 and died in Rome in 1937. He is an important case in modern political and intellectual history because his life and writings lend themselves to interpretations which appeal to the most diverse persons and groups: Marxists, anti-Marxists, and uncommitted political and social theorists. For example, Trotskyites tend to see him as one of their own because he never adhered to Stalinism. During the heyday of what came to be called Eurocommunism, its followers regarded him as the founder of the movement. Critics of communism often see him as their worthiest opponent, seeking to understand him in order to refute him more effectively. Other anti-communist critics find him a uniquely instructive case of someone whose life and thought embody the internal contradictions and external difficulties which are said to demonstrate how and why communism does not work.[16] Many continue to regard him as the "patron saint of the Left,"[17] even though this label was coined about two decades ago when geopolitical conditions were very different. And anyone can read his *Prison Notebooks* and see that they are full of insightful analyses of such

---

[13] See Q1551.

[14] See Q1375–95.

[15] The most relevant notes are those on Q1050–51, Q1385, and Q1780; see also the references and the analysis given below.

[16] The best example of this type of analysis is Del Noce 1978.

[17] Clark 1975.

topics as: the nature of politics and its relationship to culture, religion, and economics; the nature of revolution and its relationship to tradition, reform, democracy, and classes; and the nature of governments, parties, intellectuals, bureaucracies, and journalism.

One of the latest examples of this kind of ambivalent and polymorphous appeal is a column in *Forbes* magazine by American philosopher Michael Novak. Published on March 20, 1989, and revealingly entitled "The Gramscists Are Coming," it is meant as a warning. Novak is certainly right to contrast Gramscism to the usual Marxism which tries to bring about the socialist dream by economic means (such as central planning and the nationalization of industrial production). It is also important to realize, as Novak does, that the means employed by Gramscism are peaceful and cultural (such as education, communication, and persuasion). And it is perceptive of him to note that Gramscism has a special attraction for a segment of American academia.

There is some irony, however, when he advises die-hard academics to "take into account the rambling wrecks of actual Marxist societies"[18] and to study the American system. The irony is that this corresponds in large part to what Gramsci himself ended up doing in the last ten years of his life, from 1926 to 1937: a key background concern was the attempt to learn from the general failure of Bolshevik revolutions in Western Europe from 1917 to 1926, and a central focus of his *Prison Notebooks* was the phenomenon of what he called "Americanism and Fordism."[19] Even in his moments of youthful and high revolutionary zeal, Gramsci's ideal bears an astounding resemblance to the one which Novak quotes from one of the American founding fathers, James Madison. Novak makes an eloquent plea for realism and anti-utopianism and quotes Madison as saying that a "cool and candid people will at once reflect, that the purest of human blessings must have a portion of alloy in them, that the choice must always be made, if not of the lesser evil, at least of the greater, not the perfect good."[20] In fact, we can easily find Gramsci in 1917 asserting that "we conceive life as always revolutionary, and thus tomorrow we will not declare the world we have built to be final, but rather we will always leave the road open toward betterment, toward better harmonies."[21]

[18] Novak 1989, 54.
[19] See Q2137–82 and Gramsci 1971, 277–320.
[20] Quoted in Novak 1989, 54.
[21] Gramsci 1958, 126, from a newspaper article in *Il grido del popolo*, 18 August 1917. All translations from Gramsci are my own unless otherwise noted.

I am not saying that the conclusions reached by Gramsci then are the same as the ones Novak thinks one should reach now. Rather, I would argue that, if by Gramscism one means the pursuit of the usual Marxist ends by cultural peaceful means, then Gramsci was no more of a Gramscist than Marx was a Marxist. The main difference is that Marx lived long enough to feel the need himself to clarify "Moi, je ne suis pas Marxiste," whereas Gramsci's premature death gave him no opportunity to oppose, and indeed triggered, the construction of the myth of Gramscism. This myth was largely contrived by Palmiro Togliatti, the leader of the Italian Communist Party for about forty years, from 1926 to 1964.[22] The real Gramsci remains to be discovered.

3. Gramsci's Life and Its Aftermath

To add plausibility to these suggestions, I would sketch Gramsci's life and its aftermath as follows. In 1917 he welcomed the Bolshevik Revolution as a "revolution against *Capital*."[23] He meant that, rather than being the overthrow of capitalism, it was a refutation of the deterministic interpretation of Marx's *Capital* according to which socialism could come into being only by the gradual evolution of capitalism, and a confirmation of the possibility of the willful radical transformation of social institutions. Partly because of this, in the next few years he took a leading role in the unrest which followed the end of World War I in Italy; the biennium 1919–1920 came to be known as the Red Years, witnessed the workers' occupation of the factories, and climaxed with the essential defeat of the workers.

Being historically oriented and empirically minded, Gramsci always tried to learn from experience. He concluded that a major cause of this defeat was inadequate *political* leadership by the Italian socialist party. Therefore, in 1921 he favored the creation of a new political party to provide the proper leadership; this was the beginning of the Italian Communist Party. However, the new party was no more successful than the old one; in fact, in the following year the Fascists staged the March on Rome, gained control of the government, and arrested the leaders of the new party. Gramsci was one of the few who escaped arrest because he was then in the Soviet Union as the representative of the party to the Communist International. Nevertheless, the new defeat called for a new

---

[22] See the essays and lectures collected in Togliatti 1979.
[23] Gramsci 1988, 32; 1958, 149.

diagnosis, and so Gramsci located a major source of the problem in the undemocratic and sectarian character of the just-founded party.

He soon had the opportunity to begin acting on this new lesson. In 1924 parliamentary elections were held in Italy, and while still abroad he was elected on the Communist Party slate. As a member of parliament enjoying immunity from arrest under Italian law, he returned to Italy. He was selected the new leader of the party, and from this new position in the next two years he tried to reorganize the party to make it more democratic and give it more mass appeal, especially among peasants. This task was a difficult one, partly because the Fascists were consolidating their rule, and so the Communist Party had to operate in a semi-clandestine manner. There were other reasons for this difficulty, but Gramsci did not perceive them until later, after another setback forced him to more rethinking.

In 1926, as a result of special laws for the defense of the state, the Fascists outlawed all opposition parties and arrested their leaders. Gramsci was one of the few who had not gone into exile or underground, and so he was arrested in November. He would spend the rest of his life in various states of imprisonment, dying in 1937 as a result of ill health from which he had always suffered, but which was aggravated by prison conditions.

It was to be expected that in prison Gramsci would reflect on the causes of his latest setback and on the nature of communism in general. There is general agreement that he did just that. And it is a fact that he filled more than a thousand pages in twenty-nine notebooks with notes varying in length from a few lines to chapter-length essays but left essentially unedited by him. Therefore, the *Notebooks* have always posed a major interpretive challenge.

The most widespread interpretation stems from Palmiro Togliatti, Gramsci's fellow college classmate, his successor in the leadership of the Italian Communist Party, and an important figure in his own right. After the fall of Fascism and the end of World War II, Togliatti read into Gramsci what came to be known as the "Italian road to socialism": a strategy for bringing about the traditional Marxist goals of the classless society and the nationalization of the means of production by the use of cultural means, such as education and persuasion; by contrast to Bolshevism, the idea was that one had to first conquer social institutions, and then control of these would yield the desired changes in economic and political institutions. An essential part of the rationale was that, in Gramsci's words, "in the East the state was everything, civil society was primordial and gelatinous; in the West there was a proper relation between state and civil society, and when the state trembled a sturdy structure of civil society was at once revealed."[24]

This strategy was extremely successful for about thirty years, during which the party experienced constant growth. The popularity of Gramsci's writings grew accordingly, spreading gradually but steadily outside Italy. However, beginning about fifteen years ago, "Gramscism" has been in constant decline in Italy, using this label to denote Togliatti's interpretation of Gramsci just sketched. The decline has several causes, not the least of which is the Gorbachev phenomenon, which in so many ways represents a repudiation of many traditional Marxist-Leninist tenets. One of these causes is cultural: in 1975 a critical edition of the *Notebooks* was published, and since then Togliatti's interpretation has come to be seen as less and less defensible. No new consensus has emerged yet, nor is it likely to emerge soon, since it would have to be based on interpretive and analytical spadework of a sort that has barely begun. The present inquiry is in part a contribution to this effort.

The key issue in that wider type of investigation will be to explore whether Gramsci, in his latest and most sustained revision of his thinking in prison, did not limit himself to revising the means but was inevitably led to question the ends he had previously taken for granted. This will involve learning to appreciate the democratic implications of Gramsci's emphasis on the "educator who must be educated";[25] the project will also involve learning to appreciate the pluralism inherent in his manner of thinking; an essential feature of this thinking is the attempt "to find the real identity beneath the apparent contradiction and differentiation, and to find the substantial diversity beneath the apparent identity."[26]

4. Interactionism and Anti-Reductionism

A great temptation for anyone who is even mildly fascinated by the topic of logic and politics is the rationalistic tendency of wanting to interpret politics in terms of logic and reason; even when rationalism admits that political phenomena do not in fact obey the laws and principles of logic, it often retains the pretension that ideally they ought to do so.[27] At the opposite extreme is the cynical temptation of delighting in exposing political arguments as essentially rationalizations of decisions originating

---

[24] Gramsci 1988, 229; cf. Q866.
[25] Q1300; cf. Gramsci 1988, 193.
[26] Q2268; cf. Gramsci 1988, 389.
[27] Here I have in mind such thinkers as Plato, Hobbes, Spinoza, and Locke.

from other causes and of results brought about by other factors.[28] In a sense, the first tendency tries to reduce politics to logic, while the second tries to reduce logic to politics; therefore, they are both reductionistic.

Now, as I have already stated, Gramsci belongs in part to the Platonic rationalistic tradition. However, he has even deeper roots in the tradition of political realism traceable to Machiavelli. In fact, I feel one of the most important things for a proper understanding of Gramsci is to appreciate a general feature of his approach, consisting of the concern with avoiding both types of reductionism. It will be useful to get a flavor of Gramsci's language, terminology, and conceptual framework.

One of the most frequent labels used by Gramsci to refer to his views is "philosophy of praxis." This reflects his concern both with practice, especially political practice, and with that type of systematic reflection aimed at avoiding incoherence which is philosophy.[29]

Another one of Gramsci's favorite phrases is that of "the art and science of politics." In a sense, he was very much concerned with elaborating an art and science of politics. Here art would be the practice of politics, the practical application of principles articulated by the science of politics. And science would be the theoretical understanding of the phenomenon.[30]

Gramsci is also constantly advocating what he calls an "intellectual and moral reform."[31] He always qualifies the reform he has in mind with both predicates, intellectual and moral, never with just one. He seems to have adapted this notion from the Frenchman Ernest Renan, and Gramsci's talk of reform or reformation raises difficulties for those interpreters who want to view him as first and foremost a revolutionist. Be that as it may, his double concern with both thought and action is obvious.

And this brings us to a central thesis in Gramsci, that is, the so-called unity of theory and practice. This is so explicit in his work, and the connection with the logic-politics nexus is so obvious, that I think one can easily adapt Gramsci's more general remarks to our present case. The unity of theory and practice was and is a topic that easily lends itself to reductionism and one-sidedness, and he is very explicit about wanting to avoid that.

---

[28] Here I have in mind such thinkers as Hume, Marx, Pareto, and Croce.
[29] See, for example, Q977–78 and Q1568–70; Gramsci 1971, 136–38; and Finocchiaro 1988c, 133–34.
[30] See, for example, Finocchiaro 1988c, 134–36.
[31] See, for example, Q1560; and Gramsci 1971, 132.

The three Gramscian subtheses to which I wish to call attention are the claims that the unity of theory and practice is a criterion of evaluation, that it is an historical becoming, and that it is a critical act. As a criterion of evaluation, it would enable us, for example, to distinguish great political ideas from vague ones and statesmen of quality from planners of the wordmonger type. In Gramsci's own words:

Ideas are great inasmuch as they are actualizable, that is, inasmuch as they clarify a real relationship which inheres in the given situation; and they clarify this inasmuch as they show concretely the series of actions through which an organized collective will brings to light that relationship and creates it, or else brings it to light and destroys it by replacing it. Great planners of the wordmonger type are such precisely because they are incapable of seeing the ties between the supposedly great idea put forth and concrete reality, incapable of determining the real process of actualization. The statesman of quality intuits simultaneously the idea and the real process of actualization; he compiles the plan and at the same time the regulations for its execution. The planner of the wordmonger type proceeds by doing and undoing, and of his procedure one says that his doing and undoing are all the same. . . . Corollary: every great politician cannot not also be a great administrator, every great strategist a great tactician, every great theorist a great organizer. This indeed may be regarded as a criterion of evaluation.[32]

Gramsci's point about the unity of theory and practice being an historical becoming is very similar. In calling it an historical becoming, Gramsci is contrasting it to its being a brute fact, or as he calls it, a mechanical fact. I believe what this turns out to mean is that, rather than theory and practice being *in fact* united, they *ought to be* united; that is, individuals ought to strive to achieve a correspondence between their thinking and their actions. The unity of theory and practice is thus, again, a normative or evaluative principle.[33] Again, let us hear Gramsci speak for himself:

The average worker acts practically, but does not have a clear consciousness of this [which is both] interacting with and understanding of the world; indeed, his theoretical consciousness can be *de facto* in opposition to his actions. In other words, he has two theoretical consciousnesses, one implicit in his actions and which ties him *de facto* to all his collaborators in the practical transformation of the world, and the other an explicit and superficial one which he has inherited from the past. In such cases, the practical-theoretical situation cannot not become "political," namely a question of hegemony. The consciousness of being part of a

---

[32] Q1050; this passage has apparently not been included in translations such as Gramsci (1971; 1985).

[33] I should add that I think this also corresponds to the Socratic ideal of wisdom, and the Socratic principles that virtue is knowledge and that the unexamined life is not worth living.

hegemonic force (which is to say, political consciousness) is the first step in the subsequent and progressive self-awareness, namely in the unification of practice and theory. Thus the unity of theory and practice is not a mechanical given or act, but an historical becoming. . . . [34]

Many of these Gramscian points are made more explicit in the next and last passage on this topic. This is the note where he calls the unity of theory and practice a critical act, or to be more specific a critical act whereby one strives to make theory more practically effective and practice more theoretically grounded. Gramsci's words leave no doubt about his interactionism and anti-reductionism:

If there is a problem about identifying theory and practice, it is this: to build upon a particular practice a theory which, by coinciding and identifying itself with the decisive elements of the practice in question, would accelerate the ongoing historical process by rendering the practice more homogeneous, coherent, and efficient in all its aspects, namely by eliciting its greatest potential; or else, given a certain theoretical position, to organize the practical elements indispensable for its actualization. The identification of theory and practice is a critical act by which practice is shown to be rational and necessary or theory is shown to be realistic and rational.[35]

Let us now go back to our special topic of the logic-politics nexus. It would seem that a Gramscian approach to this question would be to develop an account which would try to make politics more logical and logic more political, without confusing the two with each other or trying to reduce one to the other. In attempting to make politics more logical, one had better use a conception of logic sufficiently rich so as to make the project a realistic one, and not one characteristic of planners of the wordmonger type. That is, one should also try to make logic more political, at least in the sense of making a serious effort to take political behavior and discourse on its own terms; one should also be sensitive to the possibility that politics may have its logic that logic does not know.

5. Formal Logic

Gramsci's notes on formal logic are a good example of a group of notes which are not easily reconstructible into, or criticizable as, a single unified argument. However, that will not be our primary concern here because their substantive content automatically gives them a logical relevance,

[34] Q1041–42; cf. Q1385 and Gramsci (1971, 333; 1988, 333–34).
[35] Q1780; cf. Gramsci 1971, 364–65.

and so we need not try to give them the additional logical import which would accrue to them as an example of or as material for a case study in empirical-historical logic. Our primary task will be to understand and discuss their political import.

Let us begin with a very intense note which contains many of the themes Gramsci also discusses elsewhere:

> Formal logic or abstract methodology may be compared to "philology." Philology too, together with erudition, has a genuine instrumental value. The mathematical sciences have an analogous function. Conceived as having instrumental value, formal logic has its own meaning and its own content (its content lying in its function), just as tools and instruments of labor have their own value and their own meaning. That the tool which we call "file" can be used indifferently to file iron, copper, wood, various metallic alloys, and so on, does not mean that it is "without content," purely formal, and so on. Similarly, formal logic has its own history, undergoes its own development, and so on; it can be taught, enriched, and so on.[36]

The main point being made here is that formal logic has an objectivity and universality which render it independent of political interests and social conditions. This is what Gramsci means when he attributes to it a genuine instrumental value. The objectivity and universality of formal logic in turn imply that both sides of a political struggle use and need it. In particular, this means that it would be wrong to think that formal logic is a capitalist tool used to exploit the proletariat, or more generally a tool of the upper classes to dominate the lower classes. It follows further that the lower classes need to become proficient in formal logic if and to the extent that they are not.

The same idea is suggested by Gramsci's analogy with what he calls "philology." This is a term he adapts from the Italian historicist tradition of Vico and Croce which means simply the objective determination of the historical facts. Elsewhere Gramsci frequently uses the phrase "the methods of philology and criticism"[37] to convey the same idea. It is obvious that he does not think philology is impossible.

The analogy with mathematics should neither be exaggerated nor misunderstood. In this passage this analogy is claimed only from the point

---

[36] Q1461. I have translated the *e* of the first sentence *si può accostare la logical formale e la metodologia astratta alla "filologia"* as *or* rather than *and* in the light of the earlier version of this note (Q1055–56) where Gramsci says that *la logica formale o metodologia astratta è la "filologia" della filosofia.*

[37] E.g., Q1599; cf. Finocchiaro 1988c, 136, 146.

of view of their objectivity and universality. Elsewhere,[38] Gramsci compares them also from the point of view of abstraction. However, he then elaborates a very important difference between them. That is, unlike the situation in mathematics, in formal logic the tendency to abstraction is checked by a self-referential character absent in mathematics: the principles of formal logic are expressed in a language which suggests that they be applied to the very linguistic formulations being used.

It should also be noted that Gramsci is conceiving logic as methodology, as methodology of reasoning to be exact. This gives logic a second type of instrumental value, as we might call it, different from what Gramsci is calling instrumental value. This involves a practical sense of instrumentality, for a methodology of reasoning is a theory about how to reason, how to practice reasoning. This also suggests that formal logic conceived as abstract methodology has an internal tension that renders it problematic, because of the two conflicting tendencies toward abstraction and toward practice.

The metaphor of a file is interesting but puzzling. In the case of the file it is easy to see what the content of the instrument is. But what is the content of formal logic? Is it its development and history, as Gramsci in part suggests? Could we also say that the content of formal logic is its own technicalities? He also says that its content is its function. But what is its function?

From other passages, we gather that Gramsci seems to have three functions in mind: the control of the logical sloppiness characteristic of grandiloquence and oratorical verbosity; the acquisition of basic knowledge which is not innate; and the learning of discipline and diligent work habits. In regard to grandiloquence, Gramsci states the following:

It is certain that for a very long time the process of becoming intellectually civilized has occurred primarily in an oratorical and rhetorical manner, namely with very little or no help from writing; the recollection of notions heard in an oral exposition was the basis of all education. . . . A new tradition began with Humanism, which introduced the "written assignment" in the schools and in teaching; but we can say that already in the Middle Ages, with Scholasticism, there was an implicit criticism of the pedagogical tradition based on oratory and an attempt to provide the mnemonic faculty with a firmer and more permanent skeleton. Upon reflection, the importance given by Scholasticism to the study of formal logic was in fact a reaction against the argumentative grandiloquence of the old cultural methods. Errors of formal logic are especially common in spoken argumentation.[39] . . . The

---

[38] Q1892–93.
[39] Q1890–91; cf. Gramsci (1985, 382; 1988, 376).

study of the "old formal logic" has nowadays been discredited and partly for good reason. But the problem of having people do an apprenticeship in formal logic as a check against the argumentative grandiloquence of oratory reappears as soon as one takes up the fundamental problem of creating a new culture on a new social basis which lacks traditions like those of the old intellectual class.[40]

A second reason to study formal logic is to learn a way of thinking which is not innate, and which common people of the lower classes would not acquire without explicit study and effort. In Gramsci's own words:

... the rules of formal logic... must be studied because they are not something innate but must be acquired through labor and reflection.[41]

[Now,] this fundamental requirement... is all the more urgent the more the implicit reference is not to the intellectuals and to the so-called educated classes, but to the uneducated popular masses; these have yet to achieve the mastery of formal logic, of the most elementary grammar of thinking and of language.... Therefore one must underscore the importance which the methodology of thinking has in the construction of pedagogical programs.... The methodology of thinking, elaborated as such, will certainly not produce great philosophers, but it will provide criteria of evaluation and of control and will correct the distortions of the ways of thinking of the popular mind.

It would be very interesting to make a comparative examination of the ways of thinking of the popular mind, of the philosophy of the man in the street, and the ways of thinking of reflective and coherent thinkers.[42]

A third reason for studying formal logic is to learn the discipline and the proper habits required in a modern industrial society. As Gramsci puts it:

The child who sweats at *Barbara, Baralipton* [and so on] is certainly performing a tiring task, and it is important that he does only what is absolutely necessary and no more. But it is also true that it will always be an effort to learn physical self-discipline and self-control; the pupil has, in effect, to undergo a psychophysical training. Many people have to be persuaded that studying too is a job, and a very tiring one, with its own particular apprenticeship – involving muscles and nerves as well as intellect. It is a process of adaptation, a habit acquired with effort, tedium and even suffering.[43]

Gramsci is aware of the difficulties, for he concludes by saying that "if our aim is to produce a new stratum of intellectuals, including those capable of the highest degree of specialization, from a social group which

---

[40] Q1892; cf. Gramsci (1985, 383; 1988, 377) and Q1843.
[41] Q1549.
[42] Q1464; cf. Q2267–68.
[43] Gramsci 1988, 319–20; cf. Q1549.

has not traditionally developed the appropriate attitudes, then we have unprecedented difficulties to overcome."[44]

In summary, then, according to Gramsci, formal logic is an abstract methodology of reasoning, and it is politically neutral. It deserves to be studied partly because it provides a good remedy for the ratiocinative sloppiness of oratorical grandiloquence; partly because it is not innate and so it is needed by the popular masses to give them a mastery of the basic grammar of thinking; and partly to teach (especially to people from economically underdeveloped areas) the proper discipline and work habits required in a modern industrial society.

6. Intellectuals, Philosophy, and Logic

The most relevant parts of Gramsci's views would be his theory of intellectuals and of philosophy. It is impossible to analyze the details in this chapter, but we can examine how and why these views are connected with our present theme.

It is well known and readily apparent that Gramsci expands a great deal the notions of intellectuals and of philosophy. This is also to be expected and hardly surprising given that his theory of intellectuals and philosophy is really a theory of intellectuals, philosophy, *and* politics, a *political* theory of intellectuals and philosophy, as it were. However, the focus of the present discussion is *logic* and politics, and so it would seem that the required relevance could be elaborated only by narrowing the scope of those notions, given the obvious point that logic is just one branch of philosophy and that a logician is at most only a special case of an intellectual.

The resolution of this difficulty lies in an expansion of the notion of logic. In the present context, we are not equating logic with formal logic, but are conceiving it as the theory and practice of reasoning, and the theory of reasoning is meant as a quasi-empirical practically oriented theory. In such a view, the notion of logic has been expanded and formal logic is regarded as only a part of logic.

The required relevance is suggested by our own expansion of the notion of logic and Gramsci's expansion of the notions of intellectuals and philosophy. The great promise and fruitfulness of the present inquiry lie precisely in the fact that Gramsci expanded those notions in a direction analogous to that of our own expansion.

[44] Gramsci 1988, 320; cf. Q15§50.

To see this, let us quote his basic definition of philosophy and get a glimpse of the inspiration which animates his remarks on this particular topic:

> It is necessary to destroy the very widespread prejudice that philosophy is something very difficult due to the fact that it is the intellectual activity characteristic of a particular category of specialized scholars or systematic and professional philosophers. Thus it is necessary to show in a preliminary way that all men are "philosophers," by defining the limits and the characteristics of this "spontaneous philosophy" which is practiced by "the whole world." This philosophy is contained: (1) in language itself... (2) in "common sense" and good sense; and (3) in popular religion and in... "folklore."
> Having shown that everyone is a philosopher, even if in their own way and unconsciously,... we go on to the second step, the step of criticism and awareness, namely to the question: is it preferable "to think" without a critical awareness of it, in an incoherent and occasional manner,... or is it preferable to elaborate one's own world view with awareness and critically... ?[45]

For Gramsci this is a rhetorical question, and so what we have here is his own way of making a point which philosophers since Aristotle (and Socrates for that matter) have not tired of making. In fact, after having interconnected philosophy with the things just mentioned, he goes on to make the systematic search for coherence the main distinguishing feature between philosophy on the one hand and religion and "common sense" on the other: "Philosophy is an intellectual order, something which neither religion nor 'common sense' can be.... Philosophy is the criticism and the superseding of religion and of 'common sense,' and in this way it coincides with 'good sense' as opposed to 'common sense'.... Religion and 'common sense' cannot constitute an intellectual order because they cannot be reduced to unity and coherence even in the individual consciousness, let alone the collective consciousness."[46] Here, the only thing I would want to add is to connect this with logic as understood in the present context. In fact, it is obvious that there is a large overlap between the systematic search for coherence and logic as understood here.

---

[45] Q1375–76; cf. Gramsci (1988, 324–25; 1971, 323). It is important to note that here and elsewhere Gramsci uses the Italian equivalent of "common sense" (*senso comune*) to mean common belief (whether right or wrong), as distinct from common sense (which has a positive connotation in English). In other words, what is called "common sense" in English corresponds more closely to what Gramsci calls "good sense." However, I have adopted a literal translation (as other scholars have), and when appropriate I have signaled the different meanings by using quotation marks as scare quotes.

[46] Q1378; cf. Gramsci (1988, 327; 1971, 325–26).

In regard to the notion of intellectual, Gramsci's expansion of the concept is well known.[47] It is well known that he wants to include organizers and administrators under the label. This was implicit above, in the previous discussion of the unity of theory and practice where we saw Gramsci require that great politicians or statesmen be also good organizers. However, that was not at all an inadvertent remark, and elsewhere he is very explicit. For example, in the context of a discussion of the role of intellectuals in European history, he asserts: "the study I have made of intellectuals is conceived very broadly.... After all I extend a great deal the notion of an intellectual and do not limit myself to the current notion which refers to great intellectuals."[48] And in the context of a discussion of Italian history he reiterates: "By 'intellectuals' must be understood not only those groups commonly referred to by this label, but in general the whole social stratum which exercises organizational functions in a wide sense, either in the field of production, or in that of culture, or in that of public administration; they correspond to NCO's, officers and junior officers in the army, and also to those higher officers who have risen from the ranks."[49]

This may look *prima facie* like an expansion of the notion of intellectuals so broad that nothing is left of the original connotation of the term. However, this is not Gramsci's intention, and in a more central passage, already alluded to at the beginning of this paper, he defines his notion in terms of permanent persuasion which attempts to steer a proper balance between the two extremes of grandiloquent oratory and abstract mathematical deduction:

The problem of creating a new class of intellectuals thus consists of the critical elaboration of the intellectual activity that exists in everyone at a certain degree of development, modifying its relationship with the muscular-nervous effort towards a new equilibrium, and ensuring that the muscular-nervous effort itself, in so far as it is an element of a general practical activity which is perpetually innovating the physical and social world, becomes the foundation of a new and integral conception of the world. The traditional and vulgarized type of the intellectual is given by the man of letters, the philosopher, the artist.... In the modern world, technical education, closely bound to industrial labor even at the most primitive and unqualified level, must form the basis of the new type of intellectual.... The mode of being of the new intellectual can no longer consist in eloquence, which is an exterior and momentary mover of feelings and passions,

---

[47] See also Q1519, Q2041, and Gramsci (1965, 481).
[48] Gramsci 1965, 481.
[49] Q2041; cf. Gramsci 1971, 97n.

but in active participation in practical life, as builder, organizer, "permanent persuader," for he is not a pure orator and yet is superior to the abstract mathematical
spirit; from technique-as-work he proceeds to technique-as-science and to the historical humanistic conception, without which one remains a "specialist" and does
not become a "leader" (specialist + politician).[50]

There are two other important indications that Gramsci's "intellectuals" may be taken to correspond in large measure to our "logicians."
One is that in the context of a discussion of intellectuals he formulates
a thesis about the non-innate character of intellectual skills which is formally analogous to his thesis about the non-innateness of logical skills,
which we examined earlier. It's as if Gramsci was using these two terms
interchangeably (logical skill and intellectual skill). In fact, in regard to
so-called intellectuals he asserts:

It is a very widespread error to think that every social stratum elaborates its
consciousness and its culture in the same way, with the same methods, namely
the method of professional intellectuals. Intellectuals are skilled professionals
who understand the operation of their own specialized "machines"; they have
their own system of apprenticeship and their own Taylor system. It is puerile
and illusory to attribute this acquired and non-innate skill to all men, just
as it would be puerile to think that every manual laborer can be a train en-
gineer. It is puerile to think that when a clear and distinct idea has spread
widely, it becomes part of different persons' judgments with the same organizational effects; this is an illuministic error. A professional intellectual typically
can skillfully combine induction and deduction, can generalize without engaging in empty formalism, can transfer various criteria of discrimination from
one domain of judgment to another by adapting them to new conditions, and
so on; this is a specialty, a qualification, not a given of popular and common
belief.[51]

---

[50] Q1551; my translation here is an emendation of the one found in Gramsci (1971, 9–
10) and in Gramsci (1988, 320–21). It should be noted that the English translation
of this passage is somewhat inadequate in Gramsci 1971 and is somewhat corrected in
Gramsci 1988; unfortunately the latter leaves out parts of a sentence, presumably due to
some typographical error. The new concept of intellectual which Gramsci adumbrates
here should not be confused with his notion of a "new" intellectual, in which "new" is
contrasted to "crystallized" (Q1406–11); such new intellectuals are new in the sense of
being the spokesmen of some new social class, and Gramsci is quick to add that they
cannot fail to contain elements of the old, such as language and other "instrumentally"
valuable things such as formal logic (Q1407–8). On the other hand, it seems to me that
the new type of intellectual in the sense of "permanent persuader" might or might not
be new in the other sense, that is, he might be simultaneously of the "crystallized" type;
therefore, I feel that the conception of intellectual as permanent persuader is much
more radical than the conception of intellectual as noncrystallized.

[51] Q2267–68.

The other indication comes from a discussion of his conception of culture in general. The passage occurs in a newspaper article written by Gramsci in his early career, in 1917 to be exact. Although this is a long time before the *Notebooks*, the clarification is so relevant and so suggestive that it is proper to cite it here. In fact, Gramsci states explicitly that by culture he means the practice of reasoning and labels his conception Socratic. In his own words:

To me culture has this meaning: the exercising of thinking, the learning of general ideas, the habit of connecting causes and effects. For me, all persons are educated because all can think and all can connect cause and effect. But this is so only empirically and primordially, not organically. Therefore, they waver, become disoriented, and become either tame or violent, intolerant, and litigious, depending on the case and the circumstance. To explain it better, I have a Socratic conception of culture: I think it consists of thinking correctly, whatever one thinks, and thus acting well, whatever one does.[52]

7. Logical-Theoretical Lessons

It is now time to discuss explicitly possible theoretical lessons derivable from an empirical-logical analysis of the *Notebooks*. This is needed partly as an articulation of one of the two previously mentioned lines of inquiry into our present theme, that is the line of inquiry of analyzing the work of a political activist and theorist like Gramsci as a case study in empirical logic.

As already mentioned, the present author has already completed a critical examination of the *Notebooks* which may be taken as a case study in empirical logic of the type being considered here.[53] One main conclusion implicit in that work is that there exists an unduly neglected manner of thinking consisting essentially of distinguishing-and-relating, distinguishing without separating and relating without conflating, seeking diversity within unity and unity within diversity. This corresponds to an assertion made by Gramsci which I have already quoted twice and am now going to quote again slightly more fully than before: "finding the real identity beneath the apparent contradiction and differentiation, and finding the substantial diversity beneath the apparent identity, is the most delicate, misunderstood and yet essential endowment of the critic of ideas and the historian of historical developments."[54]

[52] Gramsci 1982, 519 (24 December 1917).
[53] Finocchiaro 1988c.
[54] Gramsci 1988, 389; cf. Q2268.

It is useful to have a label for this manner of thinking, although in the present context the exact label is relatively unimportant. It turns out that this is an essential component of Hegel's and Marx's conceptions of dialectic, as well as of Croce's and Gramsci's conceptions. Therefore, I feel justified in speaking of the "dialectic" or the dialectical manner of thinking.[55]

Admittedly, this is a very low-level theoretical lesson, I mean my claim about the existence of such a manner of thinking and its deserving further study. However, I am inclined to think that the dialectic so conceived has great potential importance. This is so partly for the methodological and epistemological reason that Gramsci may very well be right in his larger claim just quoted, that is the claim that the dialectical manner of thinking so understood is the most important endowment of critics and historians. At the moment I am not endorsing this larger thesis, but I wish to point out merely that this thesis would make the dialectic an essential methodological component of the social and human sciences.

Another reason was mentioned earlier when I said that this notion of dialectic allows the interpreter and critic of texts to make sense of much material that would otherwise be extremely baffling. My experience with the critical examination of the *Notebooks* is a witness to this.[56] In other words, Gramsci's own larger claim seems to receive some confirmation in regard to that field of endeavor which may be called hermeneutics and consists of the interpretation and criticism of texts.

The dialectic so defined is also important because it seems to be distinct from and irreducible to the concept of argument or inference, though the two are related. Indeed, it would seem to be an exercise in self-consistency to want to engage in the activity of distinguishing-and-relating about this very activity. Their difference is perhaps obvious if an argument is defined as a series of propositions one of which, called the conclusion, is made more acceptable by means of others, called premises, than it would be in their absence. Argument so conceived has a unidirectionality which is not present in the dialectic. However, the dialectic as defined here is certainly a species of reasoning, if we define reasoning as the interrelating of thoughts in such a way that some are dependent on others. What this means is that one interrelationship between dialectic and argument is that they are both instances of reasoning. Another interrelationship

---

55 For more details, see Finocchiaro 1988c, 147–230.

56 I have also found this concept of dialectic fruitful in making sense of such other texts as *The Communist Manifesto* (Finocchiaro 1983), the passage on the fetishism of commodities in *Capital* (Finocchiaro 1989d), and even physicist Christiaan Huygens' *Discourse on the Cause of Gravity* (Finocchiaro 1980a).

may be definable in terms of the premise-conclusion distinction, which is of course an essential part of argumentation; argument could then be conceived as dialectical thought involving the premise-conclusion distinction.

Another interesting question would be how this concept of dialectic relates to the other meanings and traditions of dialectic. How, for example, does it relate to the dialogical conception of dialectic (and of argument)?[57]

Such purely conceptual and analytical questions need to be pursued, but that cannot be done here. Rather, going back to Gramsci, one of the results of my critical examination of the *Notebooks* is that, besides groping toward and to some extent articulating such a concept of the dialectic, his work provides at least one comprehensive and over-arching illustration of the concept. The basic point of the illustration may be conveyed by describing it as a dialectic of Marxist criticism. That is, we have a dialectical approach to the question of the interpretation and the evaluation of Marxism.

In his account, Gramsci avoids both a totally negative and a totally positive attitude toward Marxism. He is favorable toward it when he tries to defend it from Croce's objections. He is negative toward it when he raises objections against Nikolai Bukharin's Marxist sociology. And he is more or less neutral toward it when he tries to extract from Machiavelli a conception of political activity which may be called Marxian, though not Marxist in the usual sense. Gramsci is also very sensitive to the need to distinguish various aspects within Marxism: its religious element, its scientific aspect, its political component, its philosophical dimension. I would argue on my own part that a proper critical understanding of Marxism needs to distinguish and to interrelate these different aspects. And Gramsci's own work can be in part understood and in part criticized as a dialectical approach to the problem of the interpretation and criticism of Marxism.

Another important and instructive example of a dialectical approach in Gramsci's work is worth mentioning. It is his thesis of the so-called unity of theory and practice. I have already alluded to it indirectly when I discussed this topic above and explored its implications for the question of the logic-politics nexus. It should now be clear that his interactionist and anti-reductionist approach to the question of theory and practice is an instance of his dialectical approach. And my suggested extension of that

---

[57] In regard to the dialogical-dialectical conception of argument, I am referring to such works as Barth and Krabbe 1982 and Blair and Johnson 1987.

interactionism and anti-reductionism to the question of the logic-politics nexus may also be taken to provide an instance of how one may learn from the Gramscian examples as well as from his general conception.

The identification, articulation, and illustration of the notion of dialectical reasoning is not the only "theoretical" lesson implicit in my empirical-logical case study of Gramsci. Another one involves some suggestions about the hermeneutics of negative evaluation and the existence of an asymmetry between the favorable and the unfavorable interpretation of texts. But here I will have to be much briefer partly for lack of space, partly because of the complexity of the details, and partly because the connection with Gramsci is less direct.

The thesis is that negative or unfavorable judgments of authors need to be justified by means of stronger arguments and better documentation than is the case with positive or favorable judgments. That is, we may think of a negative judgment here as consisting of two claims: (1) the interpretive claim that author X said Y, and (2) the evaluative claim that Y is wrong or incorrect. And we may conceive the positive judgment as consisting of, first, the same interpretive claim as before and, second, the evaluative claim that what author X said is right or correct. My thesis really has two parts. The first is that there may be logically important differences and asymmetries in the justification of the second members of such pairs of claims, namely the purely evaluative claims.[58] Second, regardless of this first asymmetry, the interpretive claim needs a stronger documentation in the first context than in the second, that is, in the context of the negative judgment than in the context of the positive one.

Such logical principles need further discussion, elaboration, proof or refutation, and testing, namely confirmation or disconfirmation. Here, I can only discuss the connection with Gramsci's *Notebooks*. The connection stems from the fact that one of the most important strands in the work consists of a series of evaluations of authors, such as Croce, Bukharin, Machiavelli, Marx, Engels, and Hegel. Now the logically oriented reader of Gramsci wants not only to determine, identify, and understand Gramsci's conclusions in such evaluations but also his reasons and his supporting arguments, as well as to evaluate the correctness and cogency of these supporting reasons and arguments. Further, besides burying oneself into the actual details of this sort of critical interpretation and evaluation, if one were engaged in the exercise also from the point of view of empirical-historical logic, then one would obviously want to reflect on what one had done, in order to derive possible general or theoretical lessons. Now,

[58] See Finocchiaro 1994a and the references given there.

when I did this in the context of my own critical examination of the notebooks, the above mentioned asymmetry principle suggested itself.[59]

One other question that should be raised involves the connection between such dialectical reasoning and evaluative asymmetry and politics. That is, even if the above-mentioned theoretical lessons do indeed follow from the critical examination of Gramsci, and even if they are otherwise plausible, what do they tell us about politics?

Let us distinguish the latter into political thought and political action. Then, in regard to political thought one might say that, if one is trying to understand it as thought, then one would certainly want to determine the extent to which dialectical reasoning is present in it, which would require further empirical investigation; similarly, to the extent that the principle of evaluative asymmetry is generally plausible, then political thought can be evaluated in accordance with it, unless some special argument is given as to why it constitutes an exception to the general rule.

Now, in regard to political action and behavior, analogous though slightly different remarks would apply. First, one could say that one should make one's behavior conform to one's thinking, and so the relevance of the above-mentioned lessons is that political behavior should be guided by those principles. However, I would not want to stop here, for to stop here would involve precisely a type of one-sidedness which dialectical reasoning tries to overcome. What I mean is that, as we saw Gramsci remarking earlier, we should also try to ensure that our thinking is realistic, and so political thought should also be guided by political practice. In the present case, this would involve the study of appropriate instances of political behavior to determine what kind of thinking it reflects, and how such thinking compares with the dialectic and the evaluative asymmetry.[60]

8. Epilogue

This chapter has examined three sets of Gramscian views relevant to the question of logic and politics, and two logical-theoretical lessons

[59] See Finocchiaro 1988c, especially pp. 28–29, 121–22, 141, and 245–58. For other possible lessons, see also Finocchiaro 1988d, though the emphasis in the latter is more on the methodology than on the logic of criticism.

[60] These considerations now motivate me to take Gramsci's active political life more seriously than I have done previously. I would want to do this myself first-hand, even though there do exist works by others which study Gramsci's active political life and detect in it elements of the type of dialectical thinking I have detected in the *Notebooks*; see, for example, Paggi 1984 and the comments on this book in Finocchiaro 1986a, and Femia 1981 and the relevant comments in Finocchiaro 1984c. See also Adamson 1980, Finocchiaro 1984a, and Germino 1990.

suggested by a case study of his work in accordance with the historical-empirical approach to logic.

In Gramsci's *Prison Notebooks* we have found an account of the unity of theory and practice which advocates a nonreductionistic and interactionist approach to the question of the relation of logic and politics. We have also found an interpretation of formal logic which, on the one hand, attributes to it a universality which makes it politically neutral; on the other hand, he thinks the study of formal logic has three functions: to help correct the sloppiness of oratorical grandiloquence, to teach a skill (the grammar of thinking) which is not innate, and to teach proper discipline and work habits to young people in underdeveloped societies, where modern industry has not had the opportunity of accomplishing that. And we have also seen that Gramsci's notions of philosophy and intellectuals are analogous to the notion of empirical, practical logic advocated here. An interesting and important project for future investigation would be the reconstruction and evaluation of the full details of Gramsci's theory of intellectuals.

A second and more indirect relevance of Gramsci's work involved a case study in empirical logic consisting of a critical examination of his *Prison Notebooks*, advanced elsewhere by the present author. One logical-theoretical lesson implicit here is that there exists a type of thinking consisting of avoiding one-sidedness by seeking unity within diversity and diversity within unity, that such thinking is a type of reasoning, that it is important, that it is irreducible but related to argumentation, and that it may be labeled "dialectic." Further, two interesting illustrations of such dialectical reasoning are Gramsci's approach to the problem of the evaluation of Marxism and his approach to the question of the unity of theory and practice. Another implicit lesson involves the formulation and illustration of a principle about the asymmetry of favorable and of unfavorable evaluation of texts; that is the principle that in the context of an unfavorable evaluation of the content of a given text, the interpretation of the text needs a stronger justification than in the context of a favorable evaluation.

Many problems remain for future investigation. The serious critical analysis of Gramsci's works has barely begun; we need to explore whether in prison Gramsci revised merely his tactics or also his goals, and the full details of his theory of the intellectual need to be re-examined. The concept of dialectic needs further clarification, especially in relation to the concept of argument and reasoning.

13

The Dialectical Approach to Interpretation and Evaluation

From Axiom to Dialogue (Barth) and from Structure to Dialogue (Freeman) (1995)

1. Motivation

This chapter is part of a project designed to understand what exactly is meant by the dialectical approach[1] and to evaluate its fruitfulness. The context and rationale for this undertaking are as follows.

One motive is that I should like to understand better the relationship of the dialectical to the empirical and the informal-logic approaches. The latter two are approaches toward which I am myself inclined and which I have advocated both in theory and in practice. On the other hand, in regard to the dialectical approach, my attitude has been more ambivalent, for I have not explicitly advocated it and yet I have studied material and problems and reached conclusions which bear a close relationship to the dialectical approach.[2]

---

[1] Here I have in mind the work of such authors as Barth and Krabbe, Freeman, Johnson and Blair, Eemeren and Grootendorst, and Walton.

[2] For example, I have studied (Finocchiaro 1980b) the arguments which were controversial during the Copernican Revolution, as they are recorded in an historical document written in dialogue form, namely Galileo Galilei's book *Dialogue on the Two Chief World Systems*. This has led me to advance the theoretical claim that "an argument is a defense of its conclusion from actual or potential objections" (Finocchiaro 1980b, 419), and this is a claim which may be taken to bring dialogue into the heart of argumentation. I have studied (Finocchiaro 1988c) the problem of whether any sense can be made of the concept of Hegelian dialectic, by analyzing and evaluating several examples of such dialectic as practiced and of how it is theoretically articulated. This has led me to the interpretive claim that Hegelian dialectic is a manner of thinking which emphasizes such practices as the avoidance of one-sidedness, the balance of extremes, and the search for diversity within unity and unity amidst diversity; this, of course, is very different from the concept of dialectic others have attributed to Hegel, but it suggests some obvious connections with dialogue.

Moreover, it turns out that some exponents of the dialectical approach also advocate an informal-logic approach; and here I am thinking of Blair and Johnson. It also happens that some advocates of the dialectical approach have a clear empirical orientation; and here I have in mind Eemeren and Grootendorst. The question that arises here is whether such overlap is a mere coincidence, or whether there is a natural affinity between the informal-logic and the dialectical orientations and between the empirical and dialectical viewpoints.

A third background motive is the following. It stems from the fact that the dialectical approach to argumentation theory has become the dominant one. Now, whenever a given approach in any field becomes dominant, there is always the danger that it will lead to the neglect or loss of insights which are easily discernible from other orientations, and this in turn may even prevent the dominant approach from being developed to its fullest as a result of the competition with other approaches. Thus, I would hold that whenever a given approach becomes too dominant in any field, it is always a good idea to pause, try to identify or think of alternative approaches, and undertake a critical comparison and comparative evaluation of the different methods. Applied to the current status of argumentation theory, this principle suggests that it would be of some value to try to determine exactly what the dialectical approach is and how it relates to others.[3]

Finally, I would argue that the proponents of the dialectical approach have a special methodological duty to undertake a critical dialogue with the exponents of other different approaches. For the dialectical approach, such a task would seem to be required by self-consistency or self-reference or meta-theoretical awareness. Or at least the requirement would follow if we agree that the study of argumentation should consist

---

[3] The methodological principle just stated and applied holds, I believe, quite generally, both in scientific and scholarly disciplines and other areas of human endeavor; it has, in fact, been upheld under a variety of labels. For example, Paul Feyerabend (1975) has advocated what he suggestively calls methodological pluralism or the principle of proliferation. In a social and economic context, Vilfredo Pareto (1925) would, I think, speak of the desirability of a certain kind of equilibrium. In a political domain, James Madison held that the highest goal is the avoidance of tyranny, which he defined as a situation in which a single entity (be it a person, a class, or an institution) holds absolute power and lacks any external check to limit its power (Dahl 1956, 1–19). Finally, in one of the pioneering works of modern political theory, Gaetano Mosca (1939, 428–29) advanced a piece of advice about political action, which one commentator (Meisel 1965, 3) has appropriately dubbed the counterrevolutionary principle; the advice is to try to counteract the current which has achieved predominance.

not only of theorizing about argumentation but also of practice of argumentation, of argumentation about argumentation, as it were.

In accordance with this framework, what I plan to do is to examine some important examples of dialectical orientation in argumentation theory. My choice will be necessarily limited, but a more exhaustive treatment can be undertaken later after a start is made. Similarly, my selection may be idiosyncratic, but I do not think it is arbitrary, for the value and importance of the works being considered will be obvious.

2. Barth and Krabbe: From Axiom to Dialogue

There is much which is valuable, acceptable, and fruitful in Barth and Krabbe's treatise entitled *From Axiom to Dialogue*. However, it is beyond the scope of this chapter to discuss such details or to praise its many merits. Here, I can only focus on the key theme of what they mean by the dialectical approach.[4]

Barth and Krabbe begin with the fundamental notion of a conflict of opinions, in which a proponent and an opponent share a number of concessions but disagree about a particular thesis, in the sense that this thesis is accepted by the proponent but challenged by the opponent. In order to resolve the disagreement, the two parties engage in a dialogue governed by strict rules, the violation of any one of which leads to the disqualification of the party committing the violation and/or to its losing the debate. The aim of the proponent is to defend, and the aim of the opponent is to criticize, the thesis in accordance with the rules. A party wins when the other is forced to violate a rule or exhausts all possibilities for making a move. In a given conflict of opinion, a winning strategy exists for one of the parties if and only if that party can win in a finite number of moves, regardless of what the other party does. An argument is valid (meaning, dialectically valid) if and only if there is a winning strategy for a proponent of the conclusion relative to the premises as concessions.

One of Barth and Krabbe's central technical accomplishments is to devise formal systems of such rules for various formal languages containing propositional connectives and various propositional variables and propositional constants. Such languages are formal in the traditional sense of

---

4 Similarly, although Barth and Krabbe are very explicit in expressing their indebtedness to the work of Beth, Lorenzen, and Lorenz, I will not be concerned with the question of how the contribution of the former pair is a refinement and development of the contributions of the latter trio. .

referring to the syntactical structure of well-formed formulas; this is a sense of formal which the authors call formal$_2$. On the other hand, their system of rules of discussion is formal also in the sense of forcing a regimentation of the dialogue; they call this formal$_3$.[5]

Their central conclusion is that their system of formal dialectics is equivalent to other more traditional and well-known systems, such as those of axiomatization, natural deduction, deductive tableaux, model-theoretical semantics, and semantic tableaux. By the axiomatic approach is meant the approach stemming from Frege according to which one takes a few self-evident propositions as axioms and then other logical truths are derived as theorems, based on the initial axioms, on previously proved theorems, and one or a few rules of inference such as *modus ponens*. By the system of natural deduction is meant an approach stemming from S. Jaskowski and G. Gentzen which does not assume any axioms but uses a relatively large number of rules of inference, as many as are needed for the introduction and the elimination of each logical constant. By the approach of the deductive tableaux is meant an approach which starts with the question of whether a certain conclusion is derivable from certain premises; then systematically reduces this problem to a simpler one by replacing the premises and conclusion of the original problem by correspondingly simpler premises and conclusion; and then repeats this process until one arrives at a premises-conclusion set such that the derivation of the conclusion from the premises is immediately obvious. By model-theoretical semantics is meant the approach stemming from Wittgenstein and Tarski which focuses on defining a valid inference as one which is truth preserving in the following sense: that the conclusion is true in every model in which the premises are true, or equivalently that there is no model in which all the premises are true and the conclusion is false. By the system of semantic tableaux is meant the approach stemming from Beth whose relationship to model-theoretical semantics is analogous to that of deductive tableaux to natural deduction; that is, the question of whether a given argument is valid is reduced to the question whether there exists a model which is a counterexample, and then this problem is reduced to simpler and simpler ones by replacing the original premises and conclusion by corresponding component propositions.

Now, the key conclusion of Barth and Krabbe (1982, 306) is that to say that (a) there is a winning strategy for the proponent of a conclusion

---

5 They also distinguish a notion of formal$_1$ which relates to Platonic forms but which need not concern us here (Barth and Krabbe 1982, 14–15).

relative to an opponent who concedes the premises is equivalent to saying that (b) there is a closed deductive tableau for the same premises-conclusion pair; further, that the latter (b) is equivalent to saying that (c) there is a natural deduction of the conclusion from the premises; that, in turn, claim (c) is equivalent to saying that (d) the corresponding conditional (constructed by saying if all the premises are true then the conclusion is also true) is a theorem in an appropriate axiomatic system; that claim (d) is equivalent to saying that (e) there is no model which is a counterexample for the argument; and finally that claim (e) is equivalent to saying that (f) there is a closed semantic tableau for the argument. These equivalences are established by a circular chain of entailments whereby it is shown that (a) entails (b), that (b) entails (c), that (c) entails (d), that (d) entails (e), that (e) entails (f), and that (f) entails (a). Thus any one of these claims entails any other, and the converse is also true.

This is an impressive accomplishment, and I have no objection to the technical details of the proofs. However, I do want to focus the discussion on three things: the exact import of this conclusion, the logical structure of the supporting argument, and the epistemological character of the procedure used.

In regard to the import of the conclusion, the most important question is whether it amounts to saying what is suggested in the title of Barth and Krabbe's treatise. To suggest that one ought to move from axiom to dialogue is to suggest that the dialectical approach is somehow superior to the axiomatic (and other traditional) approach(es). However, their demonstrated equivalence suggests that neither is more fundamental than the other, but that they are different ways of saying or doing the same thing; that is, they are alternative ways of approaching the study of argumentation, but ultimately they do not conflict and neither can be claimed to be more important than the other.

This situation should be contrasted to the situation which would obtain if all that had been proved was that the system of formal dialectics entailed the axiomatic system but not conversely. If this converse entailment did not hold, then we would be in a situation where formal dialectics could accomplish all that axiomatics could, but also other things which axiomatics could not; this would show that axiomatics would in principle be dispensable, and so the dialectical approach would have some kind of logical or epistemological priority over the axiomatic approach. In other words, in a sense Barth and Krabbe prove too much. By proving the equivalence between axiomatics and dialectics, they show that each approach can do what the other one does, and so neither is more powerful than the other.

In saying this I do not mean to deny that there may be other ways of showing that the dialectical approach is preferable. In fact, Barth and Krabbe's own book is interspersed with a number of epistemological considerations and informal arguments supporting this preference. And many of these arguments are plausible and such that I would be prepared to accept them. However, in this book these are relatively secondary matters, and its emphasis is on elaborating the formal details of the dialectical approach and on examining its relationship to the other systems.

My first point is thus that the central technical accomplishment of Barth and Krabbe does not constitute a justification of a move from axiom to dialogue. My next criticism is somewhat stronger than this. It depends on a feature of the argument they use to support their main conclusion: their main supporting argument is a good example of an axiomatic deduction, or to be more precise, it is an informal version of a natural deduction. In fact, what I have called their main conclusion is what they label "theorem 29" (the last one) in their work, and most of the previous theorems are used in the proof of this last theorem; furthermore, in the proof of most theorems, subsidiary lemmas are usually used. Moreover, the book is also full of a much larger number of formal stipulative definitions and formal postulates stating various substantive rules; finally, the book's own metalinguistic terminology makes liberal use of set-theoretical terminology, so that in a sense set theory is presupposed. In short, the book's main line of argument is essentially an axiomatic or natural deduction of the above-mentioned equivalence theorem.

Now, I believe this is an obvious and undeniable feature of their argument. What is perhaps more controversial is to say that this indicates that the axiomatic or natural-deduction method is treated by the authors themselves as being in some sense primary vis-à-vis the dialectical approach. Of course, if the authors' key theorem is true (as indeed it appears to be), then it would be possible to reformulate their own metatheoretical argument in a dialectical "garb" (to use their own expression). However, this is not done directly and explicitly in the book. Instead, the book's main argument takes the form of a monological derivation of a particular metatheoretical proposition, based on formal definitions, assumptions, and proofs. Thus the apparent priority of the axiomatic (or rather, deductive) method remains.

This axiomatic-deductive logical structure of the argument goes hand in hand with what seems to be a relatively apriorist and non-empirical procedure followed. What I mean is that the material providing the content and illustrations for the various theoretical concepts and principles of their formal dialectics is artificial, abstract, and far removed from actual argumentation in natural language. Most of this material consists of symbolized expressions of well-formed formulas in various propositional languages; the closest they come to realistic empirical material is to consider various truth functions of the following three atomic propositions: there is matter, there is mind, and God exists (Barth and Krabbe 1982, 41–48, 66–67). Natural language argumentation is not treated as possessing an independent reality with which the logician must come to terms by trying to systematize, analyze, and understand it. In other words, if one were to ask for an application of their formal dialectics to actual instances of argumentation and argumentative discourse, the application would be a very long and problematic story in which the focus of the investigation would become questions about how to interpret and apply their theoretical concepts and principles. In this regard, the approach is analogous to that of traditional formal logic.

To be sure, this apriorist approach is in a sense the result of the key task Barth and Krabbe set for themselves, namely to devise a system of formal dialectics and examine its relationship to the traditional logical systems and approaches. In the light of such an aim, such an approach ought not to be surprising. But this is simply another way of describing the apriorism of their approach; such a description does not change or lessen the apriorism.

Similarly, it should be noted that Barth and Krabbe (1982, 75) do discuss the question of whether their rules are natural, namely whether they are accepted by and acceptable to most people; and they do claim that this is so. However, the only supporting argument I find in this work[6] for this claim involves claiming that their rules are intuitively plausible. Now, I would agree that most of their rules are intuitively plausible and that such plausibility makes them in a sense acceptable; but this is not to say that they are accepted in the sense of actually used in ordinary argumentation. Since they point out that there can be no rigorous formal proof, but only persuasive arguments, that a system of formal rules is "natural," I hasten to add that I am not requiring a formal proof but only a persuasive argument; I am asking for an empirical argument providing evidence that their rules are natural in the sense of actually used.[7] As things stand, their rules are natural essentially in the sense in which the

---

[6] However see also Barth 1982.

[7] Krabbe has objected that even this request of mine is excessive since their sense of "natural" is different from mine and they do show that their rules are natural in their sense.

rules of the various systems of natural deduction are natural; and this brings out in another way the analogy of formal dialectics to traditional formal logic.

The Barth-Krabbe dialectical approach to argumentation theory seems to pertain primarily to the evaluation of arguments because it is principally concerned with defining a concept of dialectical validity and with showing that dialectical validity so defined is equivalent to other more traditional concepts such as axiomatic-deductive validity; and I take validity to be a key evaluative notion. By contrast, I now want to examine an instance of the dialectical approach (Freeman 1991) which is explicitly directed toward the interpretation of arguments because it is concerned primarily with articulating a theory of the structure of arguments, and I take structure to be the key interpretive notion. That is, Barth and Krabbe claim that the validity of an argument has a dialectical nature insofar as validity reduces to there being a winning strategy for a proponent of the conclusion engaged in a dialogue with an opponent who concedes the premises but questions the conclusion; whereas Freeman wants to show that the structure of an argument has a dialectical nature insofar as argument structure originates from the answers given by a respondent to the questions of a challenger.

3. Freeman's Dialectical Analysis of Macrostructure

The precise meaning of Freeman's central thesis will be elaborated presently. However, before this elaboration a preliminary clarification is needed to indicate the importance, depth, and radical character of Freeman's project. He is not just redefining argument or argumentation as a discursive exchange between two interlocutors engaged in a dispute. Such a redefinition would indeed make an argument a dialectical process, but the connection between argumentation and dialectics would thereby be immediate; an argument would have a dialectical character simply because the term would denote a phenomenon the existence of which presupposes a dialogue between two persons. Such a redefinition is not without interest, and it may be taken to constitute an additional species of the dialectical approach with its own promise and agenda, which lies perhaps in the direction of social epistemology (Goldman 1994). However, this is not Freeman's approach.

In one sense, Freeman retains the traditional definition of an argument as a series of statements meant to establish a conclusion on the basis of evidence, reasons, or premises. His main point is then to interpret arguments (so defined) as the result of a process of dialogue between a proponent or respondent and an opponent or challenger. In fact, Freeman frequently uses the term "argument" to refer to both the process and the product, and whenever an ambiguity might arise he adds these qualifications and speaks of "arguments as products" and of "arguments as processes"; and he also uses the phrase "argumentative texts" to refer to arguments as products. Then his main point is not the tautological claim that arguments as processes are dialectical, but rather the interpretive thesis that arguments as products are dialectical insofar as they are complex entities which have the parts they do, and whose parts interrelate as they do, because of how they originate from arguments as processes.

The details of Freeman's dialectical interpretation are as follows. To begin with, the simplest possible argument is a pair of propositions, one of which is the conclusion while the other is the reason or premise. Such an argument is the result of an initial, fundamental why-question. For any claim made by a speaker, a challenger may ask why that claim should be accepted or believed. If the challenge is taken up, the respondent's answer provides a reason. The full text, "C because R," is the argument (as product). From this point of view, one may say that Freeman is defining an argument as an answer to a why-question, namely why accept a given claim.

Given such a simple argument, there are three "basic dialectical questions" (Freeman 1991, 38–39) which the challenger may ask. First, one may ask an acceptability question about the reason. Suppose the initial reason is labeled R_1; then one may ask, "Why should R_1 be accepted?" The answer may be labeled R_{11}. We then have generated a so-called "serial" argument, consisting of two simple subarguments: "C because R_1, and R_1 because R_{11}"; or alternatively, "R_{11}, so R_1; so C."

A second "basic dialectical question" one may ask about the argument "C because R_1" is the relevance question, "How is R_1 relevant to C?" In other words, how does R_1 support C? How does one get to C by starting from R_1? How does one infer C from R_1? What is the connection between R_1 and C? Here the answer usually requires giving other reasons R_1', R_1'', R_1''', and so on, such that the original reason R_1 together with these additional reasons can be (more) easily seen to imply or support C. This would generate a so-called "linked" argument structure. That is, the supporting reasons (R_1, R_1', R_1'', and R_1''') need to be linked to one another in order to provide support for or entail C.

When faced with "C because R_1," instead of or in addition to asking the acceptability or relevance questions, a challenger may think that R_1

is insufficient or insufficiently strong to make the conclusion acceptable, and may ask for another reason. This is one of the so-called "adequacy" questions. The answer, "C because R1, because R2, because R3, and so on," generates the so-called "convergent" argument structure, namely an argument where the various reasons (R1, R2, and so on) independently support the conclusion. Of course, the opponent may then go on to challenge the acceptability or relevance of these other reasons (R2, R3, and so on), but then the previously mentioned processes would be repeated.

Another adequacy question the challenger may ask about the simple argument "C because R1" is how the reason can adequately support the conclusion in light of some specifically described counterevidence, objection, or rebuttal. The answer has to provide a so-called counterrebuttal. The argument now gets expanded to "C because R1 and because CR1." This also generates what is essentially a convergent argument structure, except that a way has to be found to keep track of and distinguish directly supporting reasons and counter-rebutting ones.

In Freeman's account, the last two questions are grouped under the heading of "ground adequacy questions"; these also include a third question, which generates modal qualifiers (such as "probably" and "certainly") as a distinct element of argument structure, and which is adapted from Toulmin; but this is beyond the scope of the present discussion. Moreover, what I have mentioned first and called the initial, fundamental why question is not included in what he formally labels the three "basic dialectical questions"; but, from other parts of his account, it is clear that he recognizes that these three questions presuppose the initial question.

The important point is that the five questions I have mentioned are crucial in critical discussions and argumentative dialogues. That is, they are crucial questions in the process of argumentation, in arguments as processes. It is equally important to recognize that Freeman applies and exploits these five questions to construct a successful argument in support of his central thesis. Recall that this is the claim that argumentative texts (arguments as products, or arguments as ordinarily defined) can be understood to have the structure they do because they are the product of a dialogue during which one or more of the basic dialectical questions were asked and answered. The main question I want to explore is what is so dialectical about these questions.

Before answering this question several other features of Freeman's account must be discussed. First, one of its central themes is that of how to construct appropriate tree-like diagrams to picture the various distinct elements of arguments and their interrelationships. In fact, this theme is so dominant that it would be no exaggeration to say that Freeman seems to be primarily concerned with the visual representation of argument structure. It is as if his main thesis was the claim that argument texts have a visualizable structure. Now, I would not want to deny that visual representation definitely has a pedagogical value, and perhaps some theoretical value. However, I do not think there is anything especially dialectical or dialogical in tree-like diagrams which can be visualized, drawn, and printed. Therefore, in the present investigation this gives us one reason to question whether the central thrust of Freeman's project is indeed dialectical.

A second important aspect of his work is that it consists in large measure of a critical examination of other accounts, primarily Toulmin's theory of the layout of arguments, but also Stephen Thomas's (1986) account of argument structure and tree diagrams. In other words, much of Freeman's work is a critical dialogue with such authors, whose views he partly adopts, partly rejects, and partly uses to motivate his own discussion or to strengthen his own arguments. What this means is that Freeman is using something of a dialectical approach in argumentation theory, something we saw above was not the case for Barth and Krabbe's theory; that is, Freeman's own practice is dialectical, in at least a loose but legitimate sense.

On the other hand, it is clear that Freeman does not employ in his own exposition any of the various systems of regimented rules in terms of which his theory analyzes and interprets argumentation (1991, 19–20). For example, one of these rules, which will be further discussed presently, stipulates that the proponent only makes assertions and the challenger only asks questions. Freeman could be excused from the requirements of his own argumentation theory if it were claimed that he was not engaged in argumentation; but presumably this claim would be incorrect. Or one could claim that Freeman's own arguments could be reconstructed in accordance with the principles of his own general theory, and that this would be sufficient because his theory does not claim that actual arguments always originate from dialectical interchanges but only that they can be so reconstructed (Freeman 1991, 21). At this point the question would arise whether his reconstructability-claim is or implies a normative one to the effect that arguers ought to proceed in accordance with his dialectical rules. If so, then the author could be criticized to the extent that he does not practice his own norms. If not, then the reconstructability-claim is a purely theoretical claim; this would not render it either illegitimate or worthless, but it would diminish its importance and would raise some of the usual epistemological and ontological questions about the status of the various elements and structures so diligently studied by the author.

Third, I want to call attention to an implication of Freeman's main thesis which renders his account dialectical in another sense, which is an important one but not explicitly recognized by him. To say that arguments as products are normally the result of arguments as processes means that they are seen as dynamic rather than static entities, as entities having a genesis which leaves structural traces in the product. Now, insofar as the notions of the dynamic and the dialectical have often been associated, this gives argumentation and argument structure another dialectical dimension. However, this is not the conception of dialectic stressed by Freeman, and he does not really exploit the full potential of the dynamic view of arguments, although he does hint at it in his concluding remarks hinting at an extension of his dialectical approach from structural analysis to evaluative appraisal (Freeman 1991, 255–58).

However, the question I want to pursue more deeply is that of what is so dialectical about Freeman's own basic dialectical situations and basic dialectical questions. I have several difficulties with them. The first stems from the fact that his paradigm example of a dialectical exchange is one where the respondent and the challenger have strictly limited roles; that is, the respondent makes assertions but asks no questions, whereas the challenger asks questions but makes no assertions (Freeman 1991, 19–20). This in turn is tied to the idea that the challenger is a so-called rational judge whose "role is simply that of constructive interlocutor, trying to draw out from the proponent the most cogent argument of which he is capable" (Freeman 1991, 18).

I would object that these roles are so limited they constitute not just a simplification, but an oversimplification. My point would be that, while the constructive character of the challenger and the cooperative character of the effort are otherwise admirable, they represent self-defeating limitations; for in this scheme both interlocutors have the same aim of constructing the same argument to strengthen the same conclusion, and the only advantage would seem to be that deriving from the fact that two heads may be better than one. While one can admit such an advantage, it is unclear why a single person cannot also play the role of challenger and ask the basic dialectical questions about his own claim or argument.

Here one can reverse Freeman's point that monologues "where one person questions himself about the acceptability of a view are just special basic dialectical situations where one and the same person plays the proponent and challenger roles" (Freeman 1991, 21); for one could claim that the paradigmatic dialectical situation involves an unnecessary multi-plication of interlocutors, by having two people do what one alone could do just as easily. In other words, given the constructive and cooperative nature of the situation, the division of labor between respondent and challenger is as significant or insignificant as the fact that the role of challenger is *not* split even further in terms of the several different types of basic dialectical questions.

A clue to the insignificance of the distinction between proponent and challenger as envisaged in the paradigm case of the basic dialectical sit-uation lies in the fact that later Freeman allows a role reversal in order to handle more complex situations. These are the cases of defended re-buttals, conditional reasoning, and *reductio ad absurdum*; to picture these cases and to handle the construction of the corresponding arguments, Freeman has the proponent of the original claim become the challenger of, for example, a rebuttal, so that the challenger of the original claim can construct the strongest possible argument in support of a rebuttal to the original argument. I am not questioning the intrinsic plausibility of such role reversal, or its necessity in Freeman's account; I am merely saying that it is a sign that the two roles are artificial constructs of little real significance, and that they can be easily played by one and the same person. To that extent, any significant dialectics or dialogue which would be contrasted to a monologue is hard to see.

I would argue that the simplest possible genuinely dialectical situation is one in which one interlocutor advances one argument and the other interlocutor advances either a counterargument or a critical argument; here, by counterargument I mean an argument whose conclusion is in-consistent with the conclusion of the first argument, and by critical argu-ment I mean an argument whose conclusion is a proposition questioning either a premise of the original argument or one of its inferential steps. I believe that anything simpler than this fails to capture the real dialectics of the situation, for this situation defines the minimal conflict. The point is that in Freeman's paradigmatic dialectical situation there is no real conflict, and hence (I say) no real dialectics.[8]

---

[8] My point may correspond to the conception of dialectics in the informal and persuasive arguments in Barth and Krabbe 1982, although I am not sure. The correspondence seems somewhat clearer to a more recent work in progress by Barth, where she distinguishes dialectics$_1$ from dialectics$_2$, and where the latter is such that "to argue is to try to justify an opinion or statement towards a verbally active audience or to try to refute it against a verbally active advocate." I quote from p. 65 of the manuscript of her forthcoming *Introducing Empirical Logic: A Short Lexicon of Logical Categories, Their Development, and Their Interrelatedness.*

To this Freeman might object that "dialectical situations where several persons are arguing for distinct claims could in principle be reduced to the basic dialectical situation" (Freeman 1991, 21). In other words, my minimal real-dialectical situation might be analyzed as consisting of two of Freeman's paradigmatic dialectical situations: in the first, interlocutor *A* plays the role of respondent for the original claim and interlocutor *B* acts as the (constructive) challenger of this claim; and in the second, interlocutor *B* plays the role of respondent for a second claim (which is inconsistent with the original one or critical of some aspect of *A*'s argument) while interlocutor *A* acts as the constructive challenger of this second claim. The question is whether such a role reversal would be possible or feasible, for this would require interlocutor *A* to act as constructive challenger of a claim which criticizes his own argument, namely as destructive critic of his own argument. So I am not sure that my minimal real-dialectical situation is reducible to a combination of Freeman's paradigmatic basic dialectical situations.

One final difficulty deserves mention. That is, Freeman's "basic dialectical questions" are really evaluative or critical questions. This is something he himself admits at the conclusion of his work (Freeman 1991, 256) in order to point in the direction of an inquiry into the evaluation of arguments, to be undertaken after this one into the interpretation of their structure. I believe this is both correct and important. Indeed, in his account, "the challenger asks these questions only because she recognizes a logical deficiency in the argument. We can view an argument text, then, as the product of an attempt to propound some thesis together with answering the anticipated challenges of a rational critic" (Freeman 1991, 256).[9] However, he does not seem to recognize the implications of this fact for the dialectical nature of argumentation. For given the above-mentioned oversimplification of the two roles, given the need for their reversal, given their cooperativeness and lack of real conflict, what is important about what he calls the basic dialectical questions is not the fact that they are asked by someone other than the proponent, but rather the fact that the latter (the challenger) is asking critical, evaluative questions. Thus it seems that Freeman's dialectics reduces to evaluation.

---

[9] As mentioned above, I have elsewhere advanced the view that "we may then say that an argument is a defense of its conclusion from actual or potential objections" (Finocchiaro 1980b, 419); this looks like a mere linguistic variant of Freeman's claim, but occurs in the context of elaborating the critical rather than the dialectical nature of argument; this coincidence and this difference reinforce the point I am making in this paragraph, namely the evaluative nature of the dialectics examined by Freeman.

What he has elaborated, and he has done so eloquently and convincingly, is the evaluative basis of argument structure. That is, he has elaborated the thesis that reasoning is really a form of evaluation.[10]

4. Conclusion

Much more remains to be done in regard to the project announced at the start of this chapter; further work will have to wait for other occasions. Here I have begun the attempt to understand, criticize, and elaborate the dialectical approach to argumentation theory by a critical examination of two leading works, one dealing primarily with the evaluation of arguments, the other primarily with the interpretation of arguments. The nature and the specificity of the dialectical approach have turned out to be more elusive than anticipated. Barth and Krabbe's demonstration of the equivalence of the methods of axiomatics, natural deduction, and formal semantics to formal dialectics works both ways, so that the former acquire the merits of the latter, and the latter the limitations of the former. Freeman's demonstration that the structure of arguments as products derives from the process of argumentation strikes us as insufficiently dialectical insofar as it involves a conception of dialectics in which dialogue is easily dispensable, and insofar as it suggests that argument structure is rooted more in an evaluative process than in a process of dialogue between distinct interlocutors.[11]

[10] For a different argument pointing in this same direction, see Finocchiaro 1980b, 424–31. This is perhaps a good occasion to mention a third coincidence between these two works, namely their emphasis on the importance of what they both call "macrostructure" as distinct from what they both call "microstructure"; cf. Finocchiaro 1980b, 432–33.

[11] I thank Erik Krabbe for his comments, which provided several clarifications and a few corrections of misunderstandings or technical errors on my part. At the Third International Conference on Argumentation, Amsterdam, 21–24 June 1994, James Freeman commented that he felt we were in substantial agreement, and that our differences were semantical; I am not satisfied with this analysis and plan to pursue a dialogue with him in the future.

14

The *Port-Royal Logic*'s Theory of Argument

Instrumentalism in the Philosophy of Logic (1997)

1. Introduction

The *Port-Royal Logic* is the common title given to a work first published in French in 1662. The original title translates into English as *Logic or the Art of Thinking*. Its principal author was Antoine Arnauld, a priest, theologian, and philosopher who was born in 1612 and died in 1694. A secondary author was Pierre Nicole, and there were other lesser but unknown contributors. They all belonged to that intellectual and religious movement known as Port Royal, which for a time included Pascal. Besides a large number of theological works, Arnauld also authored two other books which are worth mentioning here: the *New Elements of Geometry*, which was a philosophical reworking of Euclid; and the *General and Rational Grammar*, which became known as the *Port-Royal Grammar*.

The *Port-Royal Logic* has recently been called "the most influential logic from Aristotle to the end of the nineteenth century" (Buroker 1996, p. xxiii). And an earlier reader, pupil of Sir William Hamilton and professor of logic at the University of St. Andrews, claimed in 1850 that the *Port-Royal Logic* "has never been superseded" (Baynes 1850, p. xx). Although these judgments are perhaps exaggerated, it is an incontrovertible fact that the work has had a spectacular success as a long-lasting and international best-seller. For example, in French there were five editions and a total of fourteen printings during Arnauld's own lifetime, and at least forty-nine editions and reprints since his death (Clair and Girbal

1965, 4–7). Additionally, there have been five English translations, published in 1674, 1717, 1850, 1964, and 1996.[1]

On the other hand, it must be admitted that the *Port-Royal Logic* is held in low esteem by scholars who are attracted to formal, symbolic, or mathematical logic in the tradition of Frege. They regard it as part and parcel of a counterrevolution in logic (Bochenski 1961, 256–58; Mates 1972, 223–25).

What are we to make of such conflicting judgments? For me, this divergence of opinion is primarily an indication of the gap that separates the field of formal logic from that other field which may be labeled informal logic and/or argumentation theory. In using the locution "informal logic and/or argumentation theory," I am deliberately trying not to distinguish between the two subfields of informal logic on the one hand and argumentation theory on the other; instead I aim to consider a key common area of overlap, and I believe that the following definition represents such an overlap. The field I am talking about is a branch of scholarship whose aim is the formulation, testing, systematization, and clarification of concepts and principles for the interpretation, analysis, evaluation, and practical improvement of reasoning and argument.[2] This field is an enterprise

---

[1] Dickoff and James (1964, p. xl) state that the first English translation appeared in 1674, whereas the first entry in the list by Clair and Girbal (1965, 9) has a publication date of 1685. The relatively large number of English translations is in part due to the fact that they have tended to be relatively inadequate, although it is unclear why this should have been so. For example, Baynes, who did the 1850 translation, motivated the need for a new translation by criticizing previous translations: he claims that the first English translation reads as if it had been done by people with little knowledge of English, French, philosophy, or good taste; one of the most glaring but typical errors he reports involves the French sentence "le Pape qui est vicaire de Jesus-Christ," which means "the Pope who is the representative of Jesus Christ"; in the first English translation, this is rendered as "the Pope who is Antichrist" (Baynes 1850, p. xxxix). Similar inadequacies beset the 1964 translation, which was a volume in the "Library of Liberal Arts" and is now no longer in print (Dickoff and James 1964 = Arnauld and Nicole 1964). It is not surprising, then, that a new and much better translation has just been published (Buroker 1996 = Arnauld and Nicole 1996). In what follows, I shall quote primarily from this latest translation; however, on a few occasions I found that the penultimate translation (Arnauld and Nicole 1964 = Dickoff and James 1964) was preferable; occasionally, I felt neither was satisfactory and I have quoted from other translations or referred directly to the critical edition (Arnauld and Nicole 1965 = Clair and Girbal 1965). In citing the various editions and translations of the *Port-Royal Logic,* I have abbreviated the authors' names to just their initials ("A&N") to make the reading easier on the eye. Occasionally, to emphasize issues of translation or interpretation, I cite these various editions and translations by using the editors' or translators' names, rather than Arnauld and Nicole.

[2] This definition is adapted from Finocchiaro (1984b; 1987a) and Johnson and Blair (1985; 1994). To such an abstract conception, one might add an ostensive definition by pointing

which is partly normative, partly descriptive, and partly analytical; empirically oriented, but not in the sense of experimental psychology nor in the sense of tabula-rasa empiricism; and theoretically oriented, but not in the apriorist sense of formal logic. In what follows, however, I avoid this clumsy locution and use the shorter phrase "informal logic" or "argumentation theory" to refer to the area of overlap just defined.

I thus approach the *Port-Royal Logic* with the following question in mind: I want to explore whether this work can be regarded as a precursor of the contemporary field of informal logic and/or argumentation theory, or alternatively, whether this recent field can be regarded as a development in a tradition having such a classical antecedent. My investigation reveals that this question can be answered in the affirmative.

My approach to the *Port-Royal Logic* may be contrasted with more abstract perspectives which read it from the point of view of post-Fregean formal logic and seek to ascertain its contributions and limitations from that point of view (Buroker 1993; 1994). My approach also differs from more historical perspectives which seek to understand the relationship between this work and other works, thinkers, and movements of the period (Hacking 1975, 73–80; Mancosu 1996, 100–102). I have no objection to such alternative approaches, which have their merits and are perhaps complementary. I merely wish to clarify that my approach should not be confused with these others.

2. Logical Principle versus Practice

The *Port-Royal Logic* has four parts, dealing respectively with increasingly complex categories of thinking. The simplest kind of thinking is called conceiving or conception and consists of the mental representation of what are called ideas; grammatically speaking, ideas correspond to words. The next type of thinking is called judging or judgment and involves the interconnection of ideas so as to affirm or deny some relationship between them; the grammatical analogue is, of course, sentences. The third species of thinking is called reasoning and amounts to interrelating judgments in such a way that the truth of one derives from the truth of others; the linguistic expression of reasoning is done by means of arguments. The last category of thinking is called by Arnauld ordering or method and consists of the systematic organization of ideas, judgments,

to the following works: Toulmin 1958; Hamblin 1970; Scriven 1976; Fisher 1988; Walton 1989a; and Eemeren et al. 1996.

and arguments in such a way as to yield knowledge; this definition makes it clear that this fourth type of thinking corresponds to what nowadays we might call theorizing, or searching for truth, or seeking knowledge, or scientific inquiry (A&N 1996, 23–24).[3]

The correspondence between the *Port-Royal Logic* and informal logic involves primarily some substantive details of the doctrine of reasoning and the doctrine of method, which will be discussed later. However, the correspondence also involves a more general epistemological feature, which is a type of instrumentalism in the philosophy of logic, and which involves the issue of the conception of logic and the issue of the nature of the examples used. To these issues we now turn.

The first one stems from the work's title. I have already mentioned that the official title of the *Port-Royal Logic* is *Logic or the Art of Thinking*. This title embodies a philosophy of logic, that is, the thesis that logic is the art of thinking. There are two parts to this philosophy of logic, the first suggested by the word "art," the second by the word "thinking." Here, the intended contrast to art is science, and the suggested meaning is that logic is a practical enterprise, that it consists of skills which are developed and improved through practice, and that its principles need to be applied. The word "thinking" suggests that logic has a quasi-empirical orientation toward a mental activity; that it deals with processes occurring in the human world rather than with abstract entities; and that it is a kind of psychology (though of course, not a mere psychology, so that any undesirable psychologism can and should be avoided).

The second issue stems from the concreteness and interdisciplinarity of Arnauld's examples; it is best discussed by focusing on a passage occurring in a second preface added to the book in the second edition published in 1664. This second preface was meant to answer several objections raised against the work since its first publication in 1662. One of these objections questioned the propriety of discussing so many examples from other fields, such as rhetoric, ethics, theology, metaphysics, physics, and geometry.[4] Arnauld criticized this objection at length since it involved the heart of the matter.

---

[3] This abbreviated reference follows the convention explained in a previous note; that is, the various editions of the *Port-Royal Logic* will be given in parentheses in the text and in a shortened form, by abbreviating the authors' last names to just their initials.

[4] "To what purpose, they say, this patchwork of rhetoric, ethics, physics, metaphysics, and geometry? When we think we are dealing with precepts of logic, all of a sudden the authors carry us off into the loftiest sciences without knowing whether we have learned them. Should they not assume, to the contrary, that if we already had all this knowledge we would not need this logic? Would it not be better to give us a pure and simple logic

I focus on it because this is indeed a feature of informal logic. That is, informal logic has a general aim insofar as it wants to study reasoning and argument in general, rather than just in a particular field, be it philosophical argument or mathematical reasoning. And informal logic has a concrete, practical, or applied character insofar as it wants to use examples and material which are realistic rather than artificial. Accordingly, informal logic criticizes formal logic on the grounds that the latter tends to use contrived and unrealistic examples, and tends to take its examples from philosophy and mathematics.

Arnauld gives several reasons to undermine the objection. One is that the concrete interdisciplinary examples had the purpose and have had the effect of rendering the book sufficiently appealing to be read by many people.[5] This reason involving popular appeal might be taken to be making at best a rhetorical point and at worst an irrelevant one. However, it does have some epistemological merit insofar as it raises issues in the sociology of knowledge which, while admittedly secondary, are of epistemological relevance; one issue is that of the cognitive value of the diffusion of knowledge.

At any rate, popular appeal is not the only purpose for the diversity of examples; another one is pedagogical effectiveness. Here Arnauld's claim is that if one learns logical principles with the help of natural and realistic examples, one will retain and remember them much better.[6]

A third reason advanced by Arnauld goes deeper because it involves explicitly what may be called his instrumentalist conception of logic, namely, the view that "logic . . . exists only to serve as an instrument for other sciences" (A&N 1996, 16). From this point of view, the artificial examples of

---

text which explains the rules by everyday examples rather than one complicated by all this material that smothers them?" (A&N 1996, 15).

[5] "A book can hardly have a greater fault than not being read, since it is useful only to those who read it . . . if we had followed their thinking and had produced a completely dry logic text with the usual examples of animals and horses, however exact and methodical it might have been, it would only have added to the many texts filling the world which are never read. On the contrary, it is just this collection of different examples that has given some vogue to this logic and causes it to be read with a bit less irritation than others" (A&N 1996, 15).

[6] "Of a thousand young persons who learn logic, there are not ten who know anything about it six months after they have finished the course. Now it seems that the real cause of this widespread forgetfulness or neglect is that all the material treated in logic, which is itself quite abstract and removed from practical matters, is on top of that combined with uninteresting examples that are never discussed elsewhere. So, grasping these subjects only with difficulty, the mind has no basis for retaining them, and easily loses hold of its ideas of them because they are never reinforced by practice" (A&N 1996, 15–16).

conventional logic reinforce the wrong conception of logic, that is, the idea of logic for logic's sake: "because students are never shown any real use of logic, they never put logic to any real use" (A&N 1964, 21). By contrast, Arnauld and his collaborators want "to combine it with established knowledge by means of examples so that the rules and the practice can be seen simultaneously" (A&N 1996, 16).

Such logical instrumentalism raises issues analogous to those raised by the problem of realism versus instrumentalism in epistemology. For example, Arnauld often speaks as if he is denying that logic could have both aims, that it could be both an instrument for inquiry in other fields and a discipline in its own right. However, perhaps he merely wants to emphasize the instrumental aim more than the separate disciplinary status, without denying the partial legitimacy of both. Aspects of his own practice certainly suggest such a more inclusive conception, although admittedly the contrast would then be diluted.

Finally, Arnauld argues that his examples are not taken at random from the various disciplines, but are well chosen to illustrate rules and principles which are suggestive for the discovery of other truths whose discussion could not be included in the book.

This criticism of a common objection to the book's first edition is reminiscent of the sort of thing an informal logician would say. I have discussed it to support and illustrate my claim about the correspondence between the two logics.

3. Syllogisms and Fallacies

We now come to Arnauld's doctrine of reasoning, which will enable us to glimpse at another cluster of features the *Port-Royal Logic* shares with informal logic in addition to logical instrumentalism and interdisciplinary concreteness. This discussion will in part illustrate the issue raised by the just mentioned objection and by Arnauld's reply to it. The discussion will also provide the basis for clarifying the distinction between reasoning and method.

Arnauld's doctrine of reasoning deals with five main topics: syllogisms, enthymemes, nonsyllogistic arguments, the classification of arguments, and fallacies.[7] His treatment of syllogisms is essentially Aristotelian, but with some interesting modifications. One of his key concerns is the

---

[7] This subdivision corresponds, respectively, to the following chapters of part III: 2–13, 14, 15–16, 17–18, and 19–20.

systematization of the various rules for determining syllogistic validity which specify how the various syllogistic terms are to be distributed. His main motivation for this systematization appears to be a concern for understanding what one is doing in applying the various distribution rules and for being aware of why they are correct. The climax of this effort is "a general principle by which the validity or invalidity of every syllogism can be judged, without any reduction to figures and moods" (A&N 1996, 162). This general principle states that a syllogism is valid if and only if "the conclusion is contained in one of the premises and . . . the other premise makes this containment evident" (A&N 1964, 212–13).

Arnauld's brief discussion of enthymemes is simply a reiteration of the point that "enthymemes are, then, the way people usually express their arguments" (A&N 1996, 176). This is an extremely important point in any approach to logic that stresses practice and application. It is very much in line with Arnauld's misgivings about the practical value of the theory of the syllogism.[8] It is also in line with a recurrent theme in the *Port-Royal Logic* about an inherent limitation for any formal theory of reasoning. That is, most human errors are due to the acceptance of false premises rather than to incorrect reasoning from true ones; moreover, "those who could not recognize a fallacy by the light of reason alone would usually not be able to understand the rules behind it, much less to apply them" (A&N 1996, 135; cf. A&N 1996, 9).

There is also a brief discussion of nonsyllogistic arguments, which fall into two groups. One group consists of arguments with more than two premises, such as dilemmas. The other group comprises arguments with more than one step in reasoning such that the conclusion of one step is used as a premise of another step. Here Arnauld does not discuss a point analogous to the one he made for the case of enthymemes, namely that nonsyllogistic arguments are the norm rather than the exception in common reasoning.[9]

The problem of the classification of arguments corresponds to what was called "topics" in traditional logic and rhetoric. The classification in question here is different from the one which has been implicitly used so far and which gave rise to such distinctions as that between syllogisms and nonsyllogisms. The present classification refers primarily to the content

---

[8] At the beginning of part III, chapter 3, Arnauld states that this chapter and the following nine contain "subtle points necessary for speculating about logic, but having little practical use" (A&N 1996, 138).

[9] This point is, however, stressed in contemporary informal logic (Finocchiaro 1980b, 413–21; Freeman 1991).

of the various premises of arguments; for example, whether some premise asserts something about some linguistic or metaphysical issue, or what it asserts about the genus or species under discussion. Thus, traditionally the discussion of such "topics" was deemed to provide a method for the discovery of arguments. On the whole, Arnauld is skeptical about the usefulness of "topics," especially for finding arguments. One of his supporting reasons is that "we sin much more by excess than by defect . . . it would be much more useful to teach [people] to remain silent than to speak, that is, to suppress and cut out their base, common, and false thoughts, rather than to produce as they do a confused mass of good and bad arguments" (A&N 1996, 184).[10]

A large part of the doctrine of reasoning deals with fallacies, on the grounds (still echoed by many informal logicians) that "examples of mistakes to be avoided are often more striking than the examples to be imitated" (A&N 1996, 189). This part is sufficiently long, complex, and theoretically interesting that it would merit separate treatment. However, that is beyond the scope of the present chapter. Here, the following sketch will have to suffice.

Bad arguments are subdivided into two main groups. One group is called sophisms and includes mostly the traditional fallacies stemming from Aristotle, such as begging the question, equivocation, composition, and division. The other group consists of "fallacies committed in everyday life and in ordinary discourse" (A&N 1996, 203); it includes problems stemming from self-love, self-interest, passion, various kinds of excesses, and bad faith; and it includes another miscellaneous series of problems involving such practices as unwarranted inductions, improper reliance on authority, and violations of what Arnauld calls "the greatest precept of rhetoric" (A&N 1996, 224). This precept states that "if we love truth sincerely, we ought not propose it in an offensive manner so as to gain for truth men's hatred and aversion" (A&N 1964, 291).

The discussion of one particular fallacy is worth summarizing here. The fallacy of begging the question is defined in a standard manner, namely, assuming as true the conclusion one is trying to prove. A reference is made to Aristotle as the originator of this definition. Then several illustrations are given. The first one of these involves a passage from the First Day of Galileo's *Dialogue* (A&N 1996, 190).[11] The passage contains

[10] In this quotation, I have changed the translator's *them* to *people.*
[11] For more details, see Galilei (1632, 59–61; 1967, 34–37) and Finocchiaro (1980b, 353–56).

one of Galileo's criticisms of one of Aristotle's empirical arguments for geocentrism; the criticism is that the argument begs the question. The fallacious argument in question is the following: the natural motion of heavy bodies is straight toward the center of the universe since their natural motion is opposite to that of light bodies, and the natural motion of light bodies is toward the circumference of the universe; but the natural motion of heavy bodies is also straight toward the center of the earth; therefore, the center of the earth coincides with the center of the universe. The *Port-Royal Logic* approvingly summarizes Galileo's criticism that the first step in this argument assumes that the opposite of a direction "toward the circumference of the universe" is a direction "toward the center of the universe"; that this assumption holds only if the phrase "toward the circumference of the universe" is understood to mean "in a direction which intersects the circumference of the universe at right angles"; and that, when so understood, we can know that light bodies move naturally in that direction (the corresponding premise of the argument) only if we know that the earth is at the center of the universe (the argument's conclusion).

Now, I am inclined to concur with Arnauld and Galileo that the featured argument begs the question. I am not saying that Galileo's interpretation of the relevant Aristotelian text is necessarily correct. My main point is to give a prominent example of the kind of nontrivial argument used in the *Port-Royal Logic* to illustrate logical concepts and principles.

4. Analysis and Synthesis

The so-called doctrine of method comprises about one-fourth of the *Port-Royal Logic*. Recall that by "method" Arnauld means the systematic organization of ideas, judgments, and arguments in such a way as to yield knowledge. This conception of method immediately suggests that his doctrine of method can be expected to be in large measure a part of the theory of argument, namely that part dealing with principles for the systematic organization of arguments. This initial impression is reinforced by the fact that the discussion of method begins with an account of the relationship between method and reasoning which uses the notion of demonstration as a bridging term: "it seems appropriate to discuss demonstration not apart from but in connection with [method]; for the demonstration of a truth consists more often in a series of arguments than in a single argument, and convincing demonstration requires an arrangement of thoughts which uses what is clearly and evidently known to discover the less obvious" (A&N 1964, 293).[12] Again, the focus is on groups of arguments that establish a conclusion, and so we are not leaving the theory of argument but rather focusing on a special part of it. Important details of Arnauld's doctrine of method point in the same direction, and to them we now turn.

The first order of business is a criticism of skepticism designed to establish that there is such a thing as knowledge. The discussion is fundamentally Cartesian and focuses on the certainty and priority of mental operations. Some limitations are readily admitted in regard to questions about infinity. At the end of the chapter some revealing assertions are made about a priori and a posteriori reasoning. First we have a clear definition; that is, "when the mind reasons from causes to effects, the demonstration is called a priori; when from effects to causes, the demonstration is called a posteriori" (A&N 1964, 301). Then Arnauld adds the qualification that "to classify every demonstration as either a priori or a posteriori requires a broader use of these terms than is commonly made" (A&N 1964, 301); I take this to be a recognition that this distinction between a priori and posteriori is not exhaustive and that one would have to stretch these terms to make it exhaustive. However, he qualifies this qualification with the remark that "it is good to indicate them in passing so that we may understand them and will not be surprised to see them in books or in philosophical discourse" (A&N 1996, 233).

These qualifications are important because I believe that they would also apply to the two main methods which Arnauld proceeds to discuss, namely the methods of analysis and synthesis. To be sure, Arnauld does not explicitly argue that the analysis-synthesis distinction is unimportant. However, he does implicitly suggest it by his remark that ultimately "these two methods differ only as the route one takes in climbing a mountain from a valley differs from the route taken in descending from the mountain to the valley" (A&N 1996, 237–38). I believe this is an eloquent and essentially correct image. Moreover, after a single chapter on analysis, the rest of his discussion of method occurs in the context of synthesis.

It is in part for these reasons that we should take with a grain of salt the following declaration with which the detailed discussion of method begins:

The art of arranging a series of thoughts properly, either for discovering the truth when we do not know it, or for proving to others what we already know, can generally be called method.

---

[12] In this quotation, I have changed the translators' *ordering* to *method.*

Hence there are two kinds of method, one for discovering the truth, which is known as *analysis*, or the *method of resolution*, and which can also be called the *method of discovery*. The other is for making the truth understood by others once it is found. This is known as *synthesis*, or the *method of composition*, and can also be called the *method of instruction*. [A&N 1996, 233]

In this passage, we have not only a distinction between analysis and synthesis, but also the introduction of the equivalent terminology of resolution and composition, as well as a conflation of this distinction with the distinction between the contexts of discovery and of justification. Although I am aware that such a conflation was common in the seventeenth century,[13] this fact does not render it any more plausible for me.

Nor do I find Arnauld's concrete illustration and general description of analysis any more plausible. His concrete example is an account of the immortality of the soul (A&N 1996, 237). However, its details need not detain us because I would question whether his account fits with his own general description. On the other hand, his general description is worth quoting because it will help us understand what analysis is and what it is not:

We are now in a position to understand the analysis done by geometers. Once a question is proposed to them – a theorem of whose truth or falsity they are ignorant or a problem about whose possibility or impossibility of solution they are uncertain – they assume the proposal is true and then examine what follows from this assumption. They conclude that what is assumed is in fact true if during the course of their examination they arrive at some clear truth from which the assumption can be inferred as a necessary consequence. And then beginning with these clear truths at which they had arrived, they demonstrate – using the method of composition – what they had assumed. If, however, in the course of their examination they find as a necessary consequence of their assumption an absurdity or impossibility, the geometers then infer that what is proposed to them is false or impossible. [A&N 1964, 308]

There is a key difficulty here. The typical problem of analysis is to find some true propositions which entail a given proposition whose truth is in question. There is no general method or procedure which enables us to do this. To assume that the given proposition is true and then examine what follows from this assumption is a recipe for finding the consequences of the given proposition, not for finding the propositions of which it is a consequence. It is true, of course, that if among the consequences of the

[13] See, for example, Galilei (1632, 75–76; 1967, 47–58). Of course, the history of the methods of analysis and synthesis is a long story; for some useful accounts, see Jardine 1976 and Naylor 1990.

assumed proposition we find some false proposition, then we can infer with necessity the falsity of the assumption. It is also correct that if among the consequences we find some truths which entail it, then we can assert an equivalence; but there is no recipe for finding those entailing truths. At any rate, there is no reason for compounding the original analytical problem with the equivalence problem; the analytical problem is one-half of the equivalence problem, and we cannot solve the former by first solving the latter; on the contrary, the solution of the latter depends on the solution of the former.

In conclusion, I would say that analysis and synthesis are indeed the reverse of each other. But they are two contexts rather than two methods. Despite my apparent criticism, I would reiterate that I am not really deviating much from Arnauld's actual practice. For he discusses only briefly the analysis-synthesis distinction, and then goes on to discuss what is ostensibly the method of synthesis but could be described as a number of principles for the evaluation of deductive and mathematical arguments.

5. Truth versus Intelligibility

The methodological high point of the *Port-Royal Logic* comes in a chapter with the ambitious title "the scientific method reduced to eight main rules" (A&N 1996, 259). However, it turns out that Arnauld is thinking primarily of the science of mathematics and of the method of axiomatic deduction. In fact, the rules stipulate such things as the following: (1) to define all terms which would otherwise be obscure or equivocal; (2) to use in definitions only terms which are either perfectly understood or already defined; (3) to take as axioms only propositions which are self-evident; (4) to regard as self-evident only propositions which require no more than moderate attention to be seen as true; (5) to use in proofs only definitions, axioms, and previously proved propositions; (6) to avoid equivocation by never forgetting the definitions of the terms used; (7) to treat the more general before the particular and the genus before the species; and (8) to subdivide a genus into all of its species. Thus, for example, Arnauld criticizes Euclid's definitions of angle, ratio, and proportion and Simon Stevin's definition of number as violating, misusing, or misunderstanding rules (1), (2), and (6) (A&N 1996, 240–45). And Euclid is also criticized for not following rules (7) and (8) because, for example, "after treating extension in the first four books, he has a general discussion of the proportions of all kinds of magnitude in the fifth book. He takes up extension again in the sixth, and treats numbers in the seventh, eighth and ninth, to begin again in the tenth by speaking of extension" (A&N 1996, 256).

On the other hand, it is obvious that it is easier to formulate such rules than to apply them. This problem may be seen to emerge from Arnauld's own illustration of rules (3) and (4) (A&N 1996, 250–51). He gives a list of eleven "important axioms that may be used as principles of great truths" (A&N 1996, 250). Some of these are, indeed, unobjectionable; for example, the axiom that "nothingness cannot be the cause of anything" (A&N 1996, 250). But others cannot be taken as really axiomatic; for example, the proposition that "no body can move another body if it is not itself in motion" (A&N 1996, 251).

For these reasons, I find such a list of rules somewhat anti-climactic. However, there is another cluster of issues that raise a more interesting, important, and controversial topic. I shall call it the problem of truth versus intelligibility. This problem does relate to rules (7) and (8), insofar as these speak not only of the proper ordering of genus and species, but also of something which Arnauld calls the "natural order," a notion which so far I have avoided. However, this notion is central in what I would regard as some of his more telling criticisms of mathematicians in general and Euclid in particular. These are the objections that (a) they pay insufficient attention to intelligibility (as distinct from certainty), (b) they make an excessive use of proof by *reductio ad absurdum,* and (c) they make excessive use of roundabout or far-fetched demonstrations. Let me explain.

In regard to the contrast between certainty and intelligibility, Arnauld does not really deny that certain truth is the primary aim of geometry, and thus it can and ought to take precedence over intelligibility. His point is that certain and intelligible truth is better than merely certain truth, and so intelligibility is desirable and ought to be sought whenever it can be added to certainty (A&N 1996, 254, 258). As far as I can tell, this moderate appreciation of intelligibility seems to be a (plausible) departure from Cartesianism, which tends to conflate certain truth with clear and distinct ideas. But in saying this, I am equating Cartesian clarity and distinctness with what I am calling intelligibility, and my equation in turn raises the issue of what exactly Arnauld is talking about in discussing this contrast.[14]

---

[14] The history of the problem of intelligibility versus truth is a long, complex, and fascinating one; see, for example, Buchdahl (1970a; 1970b; 1973).

Arnauld elaborates the contrast in terms of the difference between "convincing" the mind and "enlightening" it (A&N 1996, 254). Conviction involves coming to know that something is true, whereas enlightenment involves coming to understand why something is true. Thus, the distinction between certainty and intelligibility is largely the distinction between knowing that and understanding why.

However, it must be added that this understanding is a deep one, based on "reasons taken from the nature of the thing itself" (A&N 1996, 254). The thing in question here is the thing in regard to which we are convinced with certainty *that* it is true and we want to understand *why* it is true.

Furthermore, intelligibility or enlightenment requires that one pay the proper "attention to the most natural way to convey truth to the mind" (A&N 1996, 258). That is, our knowledge must be in accordance with "the nature of the mind" (A&N 1996, 258). In short, our knowledge must follow a "natural order," to use Arnauld's phrase mentioned earlier, a phrase which we can now see refers specifically to the nature of the knowing subject, to human nature so to speak. Obviously, this sense of natural should not be confused with the other sense, which refers to the nature of the known object; but knowledge should be natural in both senses in order to qualify as enlightenment.

Thus, on the one hand we have certainty, truth, knowledge, and conviction; on the other, we have intelligibility, understanding, enlightenment, and "natural" knowledge. As Arnauld himself suggests (A&N 1996, 254), this general contrast is related to his two other criticisms of mathematicians, to which we now turn.

One of these other complaints is the excessive reliance on proofs by *reductio ad absurdum* (A&N 1996, 255–56). It should be clear that Arnauld is not questioning the logical validity of such proofs; he is not objecting to their ability to establish truth and certainty. His reservation is simply that such proofs produce conviction but not enlightenment; they give us knowledge that but not an understanding of why. I find this to be an interesting comment on the epistemological status of *reductio ad absurdum*; it is a plausible point; and it would be worth further exploration.

Arnauld's other complaint regards demonstrations which he labels "roundabout" or "far-fetched."[15] By such demonstrations he means

---

[15] Arnauld's French locution is *demonstrations tirees par des voies trop eloignees* (Clair and Girbal 1965, 329). "Roundabout" is the translation given by Dickoff and James (1964, 330–31); "far-fetched" is the rendering given by Baynes (1850, 334–35); Buroker (1996,

proofs like Euclid's proof of the Pythagorean theorem (proposition 47 of book I of the *Elements*) and his proof of the theorem that the base angles of an isosceles triangle are equal (proposition 5 of book I); they involve artificial and complex constructions and a relatively large number of steps in reasoning. For example, the most direct and "natural" way of proving the Pythagorean theorem is by drawing the altitude from the right angle to the hypotenuse, and then comparing the similar triangles thereby generated to arrive at the relationship that the square of the hypotenuse equals the sum of the squares of the two legs. However, in the Euclidean proof, one first constructs three squares on the three sides, then one draws some lines from the vertices of the triangle to the opposite sides of the squares, thereby generating a number of rectangles and additional triangles; and then one proceeds to make several comparisons involving several of these figures.

It is hard not to sympathize with Arnauld's complaint. It cannot be denied that such unnatural proofs are hard to remember, and it is probable that they are hard to remember because they are unnatural. That is, they do not proceed in accordance with the nature of our minds. Or again, they produce certainty and conviction, but not enlightenment and understanding.

In conclusion, Arnauld's reflections on the problem of truth versus intelligibility are one of the most important aspects of his theory of method. They are partly Cartesian insofar as they stress intelligibility above and beyond mere truth. But they are also partly non-Cartesian insofar as they exhibit a judicious and balanced attitude which admits the secondary role of intelligibility, does not conflate it with truth, and only objects to the total or excessive disregard of it. Although these remarks are explicitly elaborated in the context of a discussion of method, science, and mathematical proof, they can be easily interpreted as the elaboration of an ideal of intelligibility which can serve to evaluate an aspect of all arguments.

6. Contingent Events versus Probable Reasoning

The other main cluster of issues is discussed by Arnauld under the heading of "some rules for directing reason well in beliefs about events that depend on human faith" (A&N 1996, 262). They deal mostly with questions about ascertaining the occurrence or non-occurrence of historical events.

256) opts for a literal translation, namely, "demonstrations derived by routes that are too remote."

One maxim asserts that the mere possibility of an event occurring is not a sufficient reason for believing in its occurrence and the mere possibility of an event not occurring is not a sufficient reason for believing in its non-occurrence (A&N 1965, 340; cf. A&N 1996, 264). This, of course, sounds like a trivially true principle. However, I believe its formulation by Arnauld is a way of signaling that in this part of his work he is going to deal with the investigation of matters which are neither necessary nor impossible but contingent, so that the relevant evidence and arguments are not conclusive or deductively valid, but rather more or less probable or inductively correct. In fact, in this part of the book, he is frequently engaged in considerations of probability.

A second rule is advanced as an exception to this first maxim. The exception is that, when an event is otherwise well supported, a mere possibility does provide a sufficient reason for dismissing or explaining away apparent counterevidence (A&N 1965, 341; cf. A&N 1996, 265). Let us use his own illustration, which will also give us a flavor of the kind of example used in this part of the book, and an introduction to the fact that these examples involve mostly ecclesiastical history. That is, Arnauld states that there is well-attested testimony that St. Peter visited Rome. But some heretics have objected that this claim seems to conflict with the fact that in his epistles from Rome, St. Paul does not mention St. Peter. Arnauld states that it is obviously possible that St. Peter was away from Rome when St. Paul was there, and this possibility is enough to answer the objection.

A third rule is this (A&N 1996, 264). To determine whether an event occurred, one should examine the circumstances that were present: if such circumstances are usually accompanied by the occurrence of such an event, one may believe that the event probably occurred; if such circumstances are usually accompanied by the non-occurrence of such an event, one may believe that the event probably did not occur. Here Arnauld is explicit that this is proper because we are not dealing with metaphysical certainly or mathematical necessity, but with moral certainty or high probability. This rule may be called the principle of circumstantial evidence.

To appreciate its significance, a contrast will be useful. Arnauld contrasts such circumstantial reasoning to reasoning based on generalities or stereotypes.[16] For example, in regard to the issue of whether any miracles have occurred, he criticizes both credulity and skepticism; that is, both

---

[16] Part IV, chapter 14. Arnauld's French term is *lieu commun* (Clair and Girbal 1965, 342–47); "generalities" is the translation in Dickoff and James (1964, 344–50); "stereotypes" is my term; Buroker (1996, 265–70) translates it sometimes as "banalities" and sometimes as "platitudes."

the tendency to uncritically accept claims about the occurrence of miracles, and the tendency to reject all miracles. Arnauld argues that both attitudes are instances of the same logical or methodological flaw, namely the attempt to decide the issue in an apriorist and deductivist manner, by relying on apparently unassailable propositions. The uncritical believers start from the premise that God is all-powerful; the unbelieving critics, for example Montaigne, start from such premises as that "the truth and the lie have similar faces, a similar demeanor, flavor, and appearance."[17]

The next two rules are clarifications of the third. The fourth one stresses that in using the principle of circumstantial evidence, we must consider *all* relevant circumstances and combine them with each other (A&N 1996, 269–70). This corresponds to what nowadays is called the requirement of total evidence (Hempel 1965, 63–67; Salmon 1984, 96–97). Its justification is clearly stated by Arnauld: "it often happens that a fact that is improbable in relation to a single circumstance usually indicating falsity, should be deemed certain with respect to other circumstances. By contrast, a fact that might appear true in relation to a certain circumstance that is usually connected with the truth, should be judged false according to others that weaken that circumstance" (A&N 1996, 270).

The fifth principle stresses that such circumstantial reasoning is nonmonotonic. Arnauld does not use this term, but the concept is unmistakably in the text. That is, if a possible event is accompanied not only by circumstances which usually accompany its occurrence, but also by some special circumstance which usually accompanies its non-occurrence, then we must either suspend judgment or compare the probabilities (A&N 1996, 270). His example is as follows: suppose a contract has been countersigned by a notary; in the absence of other evidence, we are entitled to infer that it was dated correctly and not post-dated, with a probability whose value is something like 999/1,000; suppose we later learn that the notary stood to gain from post-dating the contract; then the conclusion inferred earlier is weakened; suppose we learn later that the notary made a sudden profit of 20,000 crowns, and that this could have resulted from a knowledge of the existence of the contract prior to the recorded date; then we are entitled to reject our earlier conclusion and conclude instead that the contract was probably post-dated.

Finally, Arnauld discusses a principle which involves probability even more centrally than anything mentioned above. The principle refers to the problem of choosing some course of action based on a comparison

---

[17] Quoted from Montaigne's *Essays* in Buroker (1996, 266).

of the gains and losses resulting from various alternatives. This includes not only betting situations and games of chance, but also precautions to be taken to preserve life and health and avoid death and other risks. Arnauld's point is that one must "consider not only the good or harm in itself, but also the probability that it will or will not occur" (A&N 1996, 273–74). He finds violations of this principle everywhere. One is provided by whoever plays a lottery which does not return all collected bets to the players but uses a portion thereof for overhead expenses or profit. Arnauld also feels that his principle is what is needed to "set straight those people who take extraordinary and bothersome precautions to safeguard their life and health, by showing them that these precautions are a greater harm than the danger of such a remote accident as the one they fear" (A&N 1996, 275). And he ends his book with the following version of Pascal's wager:

> The greatest of all follies is to use one's time and life for something other than what may be useful for acquiring a life that will never end, since all the goods and harms of this life are nothing in comparison to those of the other life.... Those who draw this conclusion and who follow it in the way they lead their lives are prudent and wise, however inexact they are in reasoning about scientific matters. Those who do not draw it, however exact they are in everything else, are treated in Scripture as foolish and senseless persons, and they misuse logic, reason, and life. [A&N 1996, 274]

7. Epilogue

It has emerged that the *Port-Royal Logic* of 1662 contains a substantial theory of argument which has interesting and important connections, suggestions, and implications for the contemporary field of informal logic and/or argumentation theory. This relevance involves several points.

The *Port-Royal Logic* preaches and practices a logical instrumentalism according to which logic is primarily an art rather than a science; it is not a discipline in its own right but an instrument for understanding, evaluating, and improving the arguments and reasoning of other disciplines. Correspondingly, the subject matter studied and examples used have a character that may be labeled interdisciplinary concreteness; that is, it is important that the examples used should come from many different disciplines rather than just mathematics or philosophy; and they should be realistic rather than artificial or contrived.

Arnauld's most sustained theoretical effort is the systematization of syllogistic theory. It is aimed at simplifying the theory in such a way that its user can more readily understand the rationale for the various rules about the distribution of syllogistic terms. However, it is carried out with an awareness that its chief value is not practical but theoretical, which is to say that it provides understanding of why those rules work. Now, this concern with understanding is in part a good example of the stress on intelligibility which Arnauld elaborates in the fourth part of his work. In part it is also a good example of informal logic, whose definition (given in the introduction above) explicitly includes systematization and implicitly includes understanding when it speaks of the interpretation of reasoning. The point is that informal logic is not averse to systematization, but rather requires that systematization should be motivated properly and not be undertaken for its own sake; should not be taken too far, that is, too far removed from the material under consideration; and should not be regarded as the only or the most important task, but be balanced with the others.

The *Port-Royal Logic* also devotes considerable attention to the identification and analysis of fallacies; indeed, its doctrine of fallacies is long and complex enough as to merit further critical examination.

The doctrine of method is in large part a discussion of other issues in the theory of argument. A priori reasoning and a posteriori reasoning are defined simply as special types of argument. The methods of analysis and synthesis turn out to be complementary contexts of argumentation.

About half of the doctrine of method in the *Port-Royal Logic* discusses the problem of the relationship between truth and intelligibility, namely between knowing-that and understanding-why. Arnauld's complaints about geometers' overemphasis on conviction, *reductio ad absurdum*, and roundabout demonstrations, and his pleas for more concern with enlightenment, direct proofs, simple proofs, and the natural order are essentially evaluations in terms of the ideal of intelligibility.

Most of the second half of Arnauld's doctrine of method deals with principles of reasoning relevant to the discovery and justification of contingent truths. This is the context where we are dealing with arguments and evidence which are not completely valid or completely invalid, but rather more or less strong; that is, their strength is susceptible of various degrees of probability between the extremes of zero and one. And the context is also one where the arguments are such that expanding the given set of premises may have opposite effects on the strength of the argument; this strength may be increased or decreased. Here we are then in the domain of contingent argument, probable inference, and nonmonotonic reasoning.

15

A Critique of the Dialectical Approach, Part II

The Amsterdam School and Walton on Complex Dialogues (1999)

1. Introduction

This chapter is part of a project designed to explore the nature of the dialectical approach in argumentation theory, its relationship to other approaches, and its methodological fruitfulness. The main motivation underlying this project stems from the fact that the dialectical approach has become the dominant one in argumentation theory; now, whenever a given approach in any field becomes dominant, there is always the danger that it will lead to the neglect or loss of insights which are easily discernible from other orientations; this in turn may even prevent the dominant approach from being developed to its fullest as a result of the competition with other approaches.

In a previous paper (Finocchiaro 1995b), I undertook a critical examination of two leading examples of the dialectical approach. I argued that Barth and Krabbe's (1982) demonstration of the equivalence of the methods of axiomatics, natural deduction, and formal semantics to formal dialectics works both ways, so that the former acquire the merits of the latter, and the latter the limitations of the former. I also argued that Freeman's (1991) demonstration that the structure of arguments as products derives from the process of argumentation is insufficiently dialectical insofar as it involves a conception of dialectics in which dialogue is easily dispensable, and insofar as it suggests that argument structure is rooted more in an evaluative process than in a process of dialogue between distinct interlocutors.

In this chapter I plan to examine the ideas of other authors who have written on or have used the dialectical approach. I shall use as a guide the following three working hypotheses suggested by the just stated conclusions reached in my previous paper. The first is the claim that if one takes the point of view of formal dialectics, the formal dialogical approach is not essentially different from the monological approach, but rather the two approaches are primarily different ways of talking about the same thing. The other two working hypotheses involve informal rather than formal dialectics. The second working hypothesis is that perhaps there are two versions of the informal dialectical approach, depending on whether one emphasizes the resolution of disagreements or their clarification. The third working hypothesis is that the dialectical approach is fundamentally a way of emphasizing evaluation, a way of elaborating the evaluative aspects of argumentation.[1] These are working hypotheses in the sense that I shall be concerned with testing their correctness, namely with determining whether they are confirmed or disconfirmed by other actual instances of the dialectical approach. Since I shall be examining only examples of the informal dialectical approach, I will be dealing primarily with the second and third working hypotheses.

2. Johnson on the Dialectical Approach

In their paper entitled "Argumentation as Dialectical," Blair and Johnson (1987, 90–92) claimed that to say that argumentation is dialectical involves four things: (1) we should emphasize the process as well as the product; (2) the process involves two roles, that of questioner and that of answerer; (3) the process begins with a question or doubt, perhaps only a potential question or doubt; and (4) argumentation is purposive activity, in which there are two purposes corresponding to the two roles. In his latest paper, Johnson (1996, 103–15) speaks more generally of a pragmatic approach and restricts the dialectical component to just one of three elements, the others being the teleological and the manifestly rational. The most basic feature is that argumentation is teleological in the sense that its aim is rational persuasion. For Johnson, the dialectical aspect of argumentation now becomes largely a consequence of the fact that it aims at rational persuasion. For now by "dialectical" Johnson means that argumentation must include answering objections and criticism. His own words are worth quoting: "That argumentation is dialectical means

---

[1] In their new work, Fisher and Scriven (1997) elaborate an account of critical thinking which they label the "evaluative" conception. I am inclined to think their work could be utilized to add further support to this hypothesis.

that the arguer agrees to let the feedback from the other affect her product. The arguer consents to take criticism and to take it seriously. Indeed, she not only agrees to take it when it comes, as it typically does; she may actually solicit it. In this sense, argumentation is a (perhaps even *the*) dialectical process *par excellence*)" (Johnson 1996, 107). Johnson then goes on to argue that, because argumentation is teleological and dialectical, it needs to be manifestly rational; that is, not only must it be rational, but it must be so perceived by the participants.

It is beyond the scope of the present remarks to discuss Johnson's account more fully. Here, the main thing I want to stress is his conception of the dialectical nature of argumentation. It obviously refers to a critical or evaluative element. He seems to be saying that arguing for a conclusion has two aspects: that of providing reasons and evidence in support of the conclusion, and that of taking into account counterarguments and counterevidence. Moreover, since this taking into account can take the form of either refuting the objections or learning something from them, it is clear that what is involved is not merely negative criticism of the objections but also positive evaluation, as the case may be.

Although Johnson's notion of the dialectical is clear, there is an aspect of his discussion which is not so clear. The difficulty stems from the fact that he plausibly finds it useful to distinguish argument and argumentation, and on the basis of this distinction he seems to say that what is dialectical is argumentation, not argument. In his own words: "Although it seems clear that if the process of arguing is to achieve its goal, the arguer must deal with the standard objections, it is not clear that we would be wise to take this same view of the argument itself – else a great many arguments (which many times fail to deal with objections) would *ipso facto* have to be considered defective – this consequence seems unduly harsh" (Johnson 1996, 104–5).

The issue here is whether we want to make dialectics – or evaluation in my terminology – an integral part of the process of arguing. Perhaps this issue could be described as involving two versions of the dialectical approach, in a strong and in a weak sense. The strong dialectical approach would make the evaluation of objections an essential part of the process of arguing, whereas the weak dialectical approach would make it only a part of a complete evaluation of an issue or claim. This is reminiscent of my distinction between the weak and strong dialectics discussed in my earlier paper.

Be that as it may, my conclusion here is that Johnson's account is such as to support my working hypotheses, primarily the one about the evaluative nature of dialectics, and secondarily the one about the existence of two versions of the dialectical approach.

3. An Example of the Pragma-dialectical Approach

My next example of a dialectical approach is Snoeck Henkemans's (1992) account of complex argumentation. I take her work to be an excellent application and elaboration of the pragma-dialectical approach of the Amsterdam school. Examining her work can also serve here as a good substitute for examining the general framework of van Eemeren and Grootendorst's approach because she deals with a relatively concrete and specific problem. The aim of her doctoral dissertation (Snoeck Henkemans 1992) was to give a pragma-dialectical analysis of complex argumentation, and in particular of the difference between multiple and coordinatively compound argumentation. Having used these terms, I should give some terminological clarification.

By "complex argumentation" is meant argumentation where a conclusion is supported by more than just a single reason, either in the sense that two or more reasons are given to support the conclusion, or in the sense that the reason which directly supports the conclusion is itself in turn supported by another reason. When two or more reasons support the same conclusion, the reasons may be completely independent of one another or inter-related to some extent. Snoeck Henkemans, following the Amsterdam school, speaks of "multiple" argumentation when the two or more reasons are completely independent. This case corresponds to what other scholars call convergent or independent reasons. When the two or more reasons are inter-related, she speaks of "coordinatively compound" argumentation; this corresponds to what others call linked, interdependent, cumulative, or complementary. When a reason that supports the conclusion is itself supported, she calls this case "subordinatively compound" argumentation; it corresponds to what others call serial structure or chain arguments. As if such terminological confusion were not enough, it ought to be remembered that the Amsterdam school also speaks of a "standpoint" to refer to a conclusion, and of an "argument" to refer to a reason.

One of Snoeck Henkemans's (1992, 85–99) main accomplishments is to examine how these various structures result from various kinds of dialogue in which the proponent is involved in answering various kinds of criticism. In particular, multiple argumentation results when the proponent accepts some criticism of a premise and offers a new reason for the conclusion. Subordinatively compound argumentation results when the proponent tries to answer criticism of the acceptability of a premise. Coordinatively compound argumentation results when the proponent tries to answer criticism of the sufficiency of a premise. The case of criticism of the relevance of a premise generates subordinatively compound argumentation in which a reason is given for the unexpressed premise linked to the explicit reason.[2]

This analysis is for the most part interesting, intelligent, and plausible. But I want to offer some critical observations. First, I would say that the upshot of Snoeck Henkemans's analysis is to show primarily that and how complex argumentation is an attempt to overcome criticism of the conclusion, understanding that the criticism may be actual or potential. Now, I believe this thesis to be essentially correct, but it seems to me that it advances the evaluative approach more than the dialectical one. That is, it tends to show how argumentation is essentially a form of evaluation. I do not deny the presence of the dialectical element in the sense of dialogue, but I wish to stress that the purpose of the dialogue is to elicit evaluation. Thus, if the evaluation can be elicited by the proponent's imagining of potential objections, then the dialogue is not essential. Of course, one may then speak, and the proponents of the dialectical approach do speak, of an internal dialogue, but that is just a manner of speaking.

Another striking aspect of Snoeck Henkemans's analysis is that it exploits the notions of acceptability, sufficiency, and relevance of a reason or premise. In a sense what she is doing is to take these notions as relatively unproblematic, and to analyze complex argumentation in their terms. Although this is valuable, there is a difficulty here stemming from the fact that it is not always clear whether a given criticism is directed at the acceptability, or the sufficiency, or the relevance of a premise. This in turn implies that, despite its theoretical elegance, this theoretical framework is not too useful as a practical instrument for the analysis and understanding of actual argumentation.

A related difficulty stems from the artificiality of the dialogical situations examined. These dialogues are artificial in the sense that they are too atomistic. That is, like other proponents of the dialectical approach, Snoeck Henkemans tends to consider dialogues where the interchange involves bits of discourse that are too small to be realistic. The more

---

[2] Although Snoeck Henkemans criticizes the account advanced by James Freeman in some of his earlier papers, her own account is more similar to the one advanced in Freeman's (1991) book on the topic.

realistic situation is one where the basic unit of discourse in a dialogue is already an instance of complex argumentation and the interlocutor's criticism is itself another complex argument. To determine how the two relate requires that we begin with a nondialogical analysis of each discourse, along the lines of what proponents of the dialectical approach would label a structural approach. This suggestion will be illustrated presently.

The critical conclusion suggested here is that Snoeck Henkemans's analysis is not primarily dialectical but evaluative insofar as it is correct, and it is inadequate insofar as it is primarily dialogical.

4. Walton on the Dialectical Approach

In his latest book entitled *Argument Structure: A Pragmatic Theory*, Douglas Walton (1996) offers many insights which are beyond the scope of the present chapter. One line of argument is, however, directly relevant; it is found in the first two chapters of his book. There, Walton seems to argue that the dialectical approach is needed in order to properly distinguish argument from reasoning on the one hand and from explanation on the other.

He begins by admitting that argument is a special case of reasoning, namely reasoning which fulfills the probative function consisting of premises supporting a conclusion. But he claims that such probative reasoning must be viewed in a dialectical context. Doing this requires understanding that the probative function can be fulfilled in several different types of dialogue: critical discussions, negotiations, inquiry, deliberation, quarrels, and information seeking. In Walton's own words, "what is characteristic . . . in all these contexts, is the existence of a proposition that is unsettled, that is open to questioning or doubt, and open to being settled by a dialogue exchange between (typically) two parties" (Walton 1996, 26).

Similarly, in regard to the distinction between argument and explanation, Walton aims to improve the best textbook definitions by adding a dialectical element. He regards as basically right the criterion advanced by Copi and Cohen (1990) which says the following about an expression of the form "Q because P": "If we are interested in establishing the *truth of Q* and P is offered as evidence for it, then '*Q because P*' formulates an argument. However, if we regard the truth of Q as being unproblematic, as being at least as well established as the truth of P, but are interested in explaining *why Q is the case*, then '*Q because P*' is not an argument but an explanation" (Copi and Cohen 1990, 30). Walton objects that this applies only to critical discussions, and that in order to generalize the test one must ask two questions about the proposition at issue, namely: "1. Does the respondent doubt it or disagree with it, implying an obligation on the part of the proponent to support it with premises that provide reasons why the respondent should come to accept it as a commitment? 2. Is the proposition one the respondent is prepared to accept (or at least not to dispute), but desires more understanding of why it is so, or lacks clarification about it?" (Walton 1996, 62).

It might seem as if there is an irreducible dialogical element here. This is especially true for those troublesome cases which have been advanced by various scholars as instances of reasoning which can be both arguments and explanations. However, Walton himself makes a number of qualifications the upshot of which is to suggest that the dialectical context is not that important after all, but may be mere window dressing on probative reasoning (for the distinction between reasoning and argument) and on the questionability of Q (for the argument-explanation distinction). In Walton's own words:

Although this dialectical test focuses on the presumed attitude of the respondent (according to the evidence of the text of discourse in the given case), what is basic is the underlying type of conventionalized speech act and type of dialogue both participants are supposed to be engaged in. It is not the proponent's, or the respondent's, purpose that is the key to the argument-explanation distinction. It is the goal of the type of dialogue they are supposed to be engaged in, as a conventional type of social activity which has normative maxims and principles.

Explanation is one type of activity, argument another. But the key to testing in a given case is to look for the element of unsettledness . . . as indicated by the context of the discourse. [Walton 1996, 63]

My conclusion about Walton's work is that his primary interest seems to be dialogues: to study their nature, structure, types, and so on. It is not surprising that such a study exhibits a deep dialectical component. Nor is it surprising that it leads Walton to study the relationship between dialogues and other things such as arguments, fallacies, and so on, and thus to study the dialectical elements of these other things. But such dialectical elements are things seen when one is wearing dialogical glasses. One can choose to wear monological glasses, and then, for example, argument becomes probative reasoning, and the difference between argument and explanation becomes a matter of whether in "Q because P" the truth of Q is contextually problematic. This conclusion, of course, supports my first working hypothesis.

5. Examples of Concrete Argumentation

As a further test of my working hypotheses, I now want to examine some actual cases of argumentation. They are taken from *The Federalist Papers*, a work which is certainly well known as a crucial document of American history and as a classic of political theory, but which is largely unappreciated and little studied as a source-book of argumentation and material for argumentation theory. Yet, I would go so far as to say that it has few rivals in this regard as well.

There is no question, of course, that the context is one of a critical discussion, the main issue being whether or not the U.S. Constitution should be ratified. The essays were written in 1787–1788, immediately after the constitutional convention in Philadelphia had written a constitution, which was then being considered for ratification by each of the original thirteen states. There is also no question of the dialogical, and to that extent dialectical, context in which pro-constitution arguments contained in *The Federalist Papers* were being advanced. However, to what extent the various ideas of the proponents of the dialectical approach are applicable remains to be seen.

Let us also readily admit that the authors of the federalist essays (Alexander Hamilton, James Madison, and John Jay) behave as good arguers in Ralph Johnson's sense discussed above. That is, the federalists not only advance reasons and evidence favoring the ratification of the constitution, but they examine, criticize, and try to do justice to the objections and counterarguments. But this same fact also shows that they are taking evaluation seriously, that they conceive their task of arguing for the constitution as involving inference, but also as involving evaluation. They know that to be effective they have to discuss the arguments on both sides; rather merely "present" the arguments, they have to evaluate them.

We can also agree with Johnson that this evaluative (or "dialectical") requirement has to be used with care, and that there would be contexts in which it may be too harsh to apply it. A beautiful illustration of this problem is provided by what is perhaps one of the most ingenious of the federalist arguments, namely Madison's argument that a large republic is more likely to control the harmful effects of factions and the tendency for a tyranny of the majority. Madison's own words are worth quoting:

The other point of difference is [a] the greater number of citizens and extent of territory which may be brought within the compass of republican than of democratic government; and it is this circumstance principally which renders [b] factious combinations less to be dreaded in the former than in the latter.

[c] The smaller the society, the fewer probably will be the distinct parties and interests composing it; [d] the fewer the distinct parties and interests, the more frequently will a majority be found of the same party; and [e] the smaller the number of individuals composing a majority, and the smaller the compass within which they are placed, the more easily will they concert and execute their plans of oppression. [f] Extend the sphere and you will take in a greater variety of parties and interests; [g] you make it less probable that a majority of the whole will have a common motive to invade the rights of other citizens; or [h] if such a common motive exists, it will be more difficult for all who feel it to discover their own strength and to act in unison with each other. [i] Besides other impediments, it may be remarked that, where there is a consciousness of unjust or dishonorable purposes, communication is always checked by distrust in proportion to the number whose concurrence is necessary.

Hence [j] it clearly appears that the same advantage which a republic has over a democracy in controlling the effects of faction is enjoyed by a large over a small republic – is enjoyed by the Union over the States composing it. . . . [k] In the extent and proper structure of the Union, therefore, we behold a republican remedy to the diseases most incident to republican government. [Rossiter 1961, 83–84]

Suppose someone were to criticize this argument by objecting that it is flawed because it does not even mention the problem that, for example, the constitution (allegedly) violates the principle of the separation among branches of government (insofar as federal judges are appointed by the executive branch). The latter objection was, of course, an argument against ratification, and the federalists did answer it in another paper (no. 47). However, what would be the point of criticizing this particular argument for this reason? The only thing such a criticism would accomplish would be a reminder that there are other issues that need to be examined besides the advantageous effects of size in regard to factions and majorities. In other words, the criticism would remind us that the argument in question is not conclusive, that by itself it does not establish the conclusion beyond any reasonable doubt. But this limitation would be easily granted by the federalists; indeed, it is implicit in the context. Thus, we may say that the criticism would be too weak, almost worthless.

This passage is also a good illustration of the problem of distinguishing explanation and argument. For this purpose, let us begin by noting that the argument supports its conclusion by explaining how and why the situation it describes would come about from the situation described in the premises. The passage basically examines the effects of a republic's size on the composition and behavior of factions and majorities, arguing that a large size produces greater justice and less abuse of power. This is similar to, though more complex than the two examples from Stephen

Thomas which Walton discusses. I believe that unlike Thomas, Walton would regard the passage as an argument and not an explanation. And I would agree with Walton. Despite the presence of explaining in the arguing, we do not have an explanation. And we do not have an explanation because the context is such that the issue is precisely whether or not large size has this claimed beneficial effect. On the other hand, despite the debate over ratifying the constitution which is in the background, I do not think we need to appeal to any dialectical or dialogical principles to arrive at this interpretation of the passage.

Finally, the passage can also serve as an illustration of the relative merits of the "structural" and the dialectical approaches in analyzing the complex structure of an actual piece of argumentation. It might seem that the question whether the passage is an instance of single or multiple argumentation would be easiest. If we try to apply any dialectical principles of analysis, such as those of Snoeck Henkemans discussed above, the first thing we realize is that we need to have identified a conclusion. Next, we need to identify at least two other propositions, each of which in some sense supports the conclusion. Then the dialectical questions would be whether the proponent accepts criticism of one but not of the other(s), or is trying to answer criticism of the sufficiency of each premise. Now, in the passage quoted above, in order to make any progress at this point, we would have to consider the first full sentence (a–b) as a conclusion and the second full sentence (c–d–e) and the third full sentence (f–g–h) as being each a single proposition supporting the first (despite the fact that they each contain three clauses); and then the dialectical questions could plausibly be answered by saying that each full sentence is open to a potential charge of insufficiency. Thus the second and third sentences constitute coordinatively compound reasons supporting the first. The fourth sentence (i) might be taken as anticipating criticism of the acceptability of the third one; thus the two of them constitute a "subordinatively compound" structure. In regard to the fifth (j) and sixth (k) sentence, the most natural thing to say would be that (j) is a further conclusion supported by (a–b) and (k) a further conclusion supported by (j). However, in Snoeck Henkemans's dialectical terminology, we would have to say that (j) answers or anticipates a criticism of the acceptability of (k), and (a–b) answers or anticipates a criticism of the acceptability of (j). Such dialectical terminology might be taken to be passably adequate. However, I suspect that such terminology can be seen to make sense only after the fact, namely to justify an analysis arrived at by other, more structural means.

In any case, one may also raise questions whether the rules are even passably adequate. The following passage can illustrate this point. It comes from the first federalist paper, where Hamilton outlines his plan for supporting the ratification in the subsequent essays. At one point he gives the following summary of the arguments to be developed:

> My arguments will be open to all and may be judged by all. They shall be at least offered in a spirit which will not disgrace the cause of truth.
>
> I propose, in a series of papers, to discuss the following interesting particulars: – [l] The utility of the UNION to your political prosperity – [m] The insufficiency of the present Confederation to preserve that Union – [n] The necessity of a government at least equally energetic with the one proposed, to the attainment of this object – [o] The conformity of the proposed Constitution to the true principles of republican government – [p] Its analogy to your own state constitution – and lastly, [q] The additional security which its adoption will afford to [q1] the preservation of that species of government, to [q2] liberty, and to [q3] property.
>
> In the progress of this discussion I shall endeavor to give a satisfactory answer to all the objections which shall have made their appearance, that may seem to have any claim to your attention. [Rossiter 1961, 36]

What is the structure of this reasoning?

First let us note that the conclusion is not explicitly stated in this passage, but it is easily formulated; it is that the constitution should be adopted. To make a long story short, I would say that (m) and (n) are coordinatively compound; that (l) and (m) are linked, and so are (l) and (n), that is, each pair is more intimately interdependent than is the case for coordinative compounding; and that there are five independent reasons, namely (l–m–n), (o), (p), (q2), and (q3).

In other words, here we have a case of "multiple argumentation," where several independent arguments are given to support the ratification of the constitution. Yet the Amsterdam dialectical rules do not apply. It would be incorrect to say that the federalists accept (as valid) any criticism of the reasons given; they rather are aware of such criticism and try to answer it. Several distinct reasons are given not because the federalists think that any of them is invalid, but because none of them is sufficient. Why then, Snoeck Henkemans might ask, not regard the whole passage and the whole case in favor of the constitution as an instance of coordinatively compound, rather than multiple, argumentation?

There are two reasons for this. First, the five distinct arguments seem to me as different from each other as any arguments are which support the same conclusion. Thus, if this is not multiple argumentation, I doubt any would be. Second, even if we regarded the whole argument as a single one, and the various reasons as merely coordinatively compound, then we would need to make distinctions among different kinds of coordinative compounding. One kind would be that illustrated by the relationship among (l–m–n), (o), (p), (q2), and (q3); another would be illustrated by (m) and (n), or to be more precise by (l–m) and (l–n); a third one by (l) and (m) and by (l) and (n). Regardless of the labels used, the three kinds of relationships are different.

6. Conclusion

There seem to be theoretical-conceptual difficulties, as well as practical ones, with the dialectical approach. The theoretical difficulties cluster around such questions as the following. What is the relationship between actual and potential dialogue? Is actual dialogue really necessary for a dialectical approach? Is potential dialogue sufficient? Must we not make a distinction between atomistic dialogue consisting of an exchange of small units of discourse such as sentences or words, and more realistic dialogue consisting of the exchanges of relatively long pieces of structured discourse? If and to the extent that the latter is primary, does not the structuralist alternative to the dialectical approach acquire primacy? What is the role and importance of the resolution of disagreements, as contrasted with their clarification?[3] What is the role of criticism and evaluation in the dialectical approach? What is the role of evaluation in argumentation? Is argumentation anything more than inference-cum-evaluation? Is an argument anything more than the defense of a claim from actual or potential objections?

The practical difficulties with the dialectical approach are that its application to actual argumentation suffers from many limitations. This appears to be true even when such argumentation occurs in the context of actual debates, dialogues, and controversies.

None of this is meant to suggest that the dialectical approach should be abandoned. On the contrary, this criticism is offered in the hope that by taking it into account, the dialectical approach can become better and stronger.

---

[3] This type of issue is similar to that treated by Tannen (1998) under the label of "debate versus dialogue."

16

Valid *Ad Hominem* Arguments in Philosophy

Johnstone's Metaphilosophical Informal Logic (2001)

1. Introduction

The aim of this chapter is a critical examination of the thesis that valid philosophical arguments are *ad hominem*. This thesis was advanced by Henry W. Johnstone, Jr. and constitutes a highly original contribution, a brilliant idea, and a constant theme of his half a century of philosophical effort.[1] In general, his work was a pioneering effort in the informal logic of philosophical argument and included other related themes, such as metaphilosophy and the role of rhetoric and of formal logic in philosophy. In focusing on this thesis, I do so because it is probably his key contribution and is emblematic of both the rest of his work and of the informal logic of philosophy. I shall first discuss several clarifications, then a concrete illustration, then some supporting arguments, and finally several objections.

2. Clarifications

The thesis can be expressed in several ways: that "all valid philosophical arguments are *ad hominem*" (PA81);[2] that in philosophy only *ad hominem* arguments are valid (PA3; VR56); that the validity of philosophical arguments lies in the property of being *ad hominem* (PA57–92); that *ad hominem*

---

[1] In this chapter I shall take no account of the evolution of Johnstone's thinking, for that would complicate and lengthen it beyond acceptable limits. However, this limitation does not undermine the primary aim of this chapter.

[2] Because of the many references to Johnstone's two main books, subsequent references will be given in parentheses in the text, using the abbreviations "PA" for *Philosophy and Argument* and VR for *Validity and Rhetoric in Philosophical Argument*.

argument "is the only valid argument in philosophy" (VR134); and that in order to be valid philosophical arguments must be *ad hominem.*

To prevent misunderstandings, the most immediate clarification needed is that Johnstone is not taking the term "*ad hominem* argument" in the sense of contemporary logic textbooks, i.e., as the fallacy of concluding that some claim is false or some argument incorrect on the basis of premises attacking the character, motives, interests, or circumstances of the person advancing it. Instead, Johnstone is using the phrase in its traditional historical meaning, which may be found in Galileo, Locke, Thomas Reid, and Richard Whately (cf. PA73 n. 12; Finocchiaro 1974a). Thus, Johnstone often quotes Whately's definition that "in the *argumentum ad hominem,* the conclusion which actually is established, is not the absolute and general one in question, but relative and particular, viz. not that 'such and such is the fact,' but that '*this* man is bound to admit it in conformity to his principles of reasoning, or consistency with his own conduct, situation,' &c." (Whately 1838, 196). Johnstone rephrases this by saying that "*argumentum ad hominem . . .* is precisely the criticism of a position in terms of its own presuppositions" (VR134), in which he subsumes both propositions and arguments under the label of "position." Elsewhere he states that (in philosophy) an *ad hominem* argument is "an argument against a philosophical thesis [attempting to] exhibit that thesis as inconsistent with its own assertion or defense, or with principles that must necessarily be accepted by anyone who maintains the thesis" (VR45). Finally, these formulations are meant to be equivalent to a still different one using the notion of a "self-defeating" position, as can be seen from Johnstone's following definition: "an argument that [purportedly] shows that a statement or argument defeats its own purpose is, to my way of thinking, precisely an *argumentum ad hominem*" (PA82).

It is equally important that by "validity" Johnstone does not mean formal (or deductive) validity. A key reason for this is that the latter is independent of the truth of the premises, whereas he takes validity to refer not only to the proper relationship between premises and conclusion but also to the truth of the premises; that is, by validity he means something analogous to what is usually called soundness. Here I speak of analogy rather than identity because Johnstone avoids speaking of soundness or truth of premises. Instead, one term he uses is *cogency,* according to which a cogent argument is one that is formally valid and has premises which are impossible to doubt because they are exactly what the doubter holds (VR26). He contrasts cogent arguments to *rigorous* arguments, which he defines as arguments that are formally valid and have premises which are impossible to doubt because to doubt them is to miss the whole point of the argument (VR26). It follows that "mathematical proofs, then, are rigorous; and some philosophical arguments are cogent" (VR26).

Other terms Johnstone uses to clarify his concept of validity are *relevance* and *force*. He does not give an explicit definition or elaborate analysis of these two notions but takes them in an intuitive and ordinary sense. However, his discussion is helpful when he compares valid arguments, criticisms, objections, passports, and contracts, and when he suggests a common core meaning: "These two notions of relevance and force are, I shall maintain, the root ideas common at least to valid arguments, criticisms, objections, and judgments, even if not to valid passports or contracts" (PA62). Helpful is also his discussion that relevance is a necessary but not sufficient condition for force: "It seems clear that no argument lacking relevance can have force. On the other hand, an argument could have relevance without having force. These two statements summarize all that I have discovered about the relationship between relevance and force" (PA62–63).

Johnstone's concept of validity may also be clarified by noting that it is for him essentially synonymous with *effectiveness* or *success*. These two notions focus on actually accomplishing an aim. Since the aim of argument is to support or establish a conclusion, an effective or successful argument is one that actually supports or establishes its conclusion. When the conclusion is not a categorical statement but the conditional claim that there is an internal inconsistency in the position advanced by an arguer (which is the case for conclusions of *ad hominem* arguments), then an *ad hominem* argument is effective, successful, or valid insofar as it really shows that there is such an internal inconsistency. In Johnstone's own words, "an *argumentum ad hominem*, like any other argument, will be valid when it establishes the conclusion it claims to establish, and invalid when it establishes a conclusion independent of this" (PA73).

This explicit definition makes it clear that Johnstone is *not* equating effectiveness or success with persuasiveness, i.e., mere persuasiveness pertaining to rhetoric in the pejorative sense of this word. It is indeed true that his view of the importance of rhetoric and its role in philosophy underwent an evolution, from an initial dismissive to a final appreciative position, according to which rhetoric in the good sense of the word does indeed provide an essential feature of philosophical argument and of its validity (VR81–85). However, I have no space in this chapter to discuss this aspect of Johnstone's views, and the following point about persuasiveness must suffice. In line with his way of thinking, one could say that persuasiveness has two meanings: a persuasive argument could be one which as a matter of empirical fact persuades people; and it could be one which ought to persuade an appropriately relevant group of people. If we understand persuasiveness in the latter normative sense, rather than in the former descriptive sense, then we could equate an effective, successful, or valid argument with a persuasive one; no harm would follow and this connection would provide an additional helpful clarification (cf. Finocchiaro 1997a, 369–71).

We now come to the third key term in Johnstone's thesis, the term "philosophical." Part of what he means can be glimpsed by examining his writings and noting that the concrete historical examples discussed most often are the following: the egalitarian argument that all men are created equal and the teleological argument for the existence of God (PA25–39); Plato's simplicity argument for the immortality of the soul (PA58–59); Aristotle's criticism of Eudoxus's argument that pleasure is the chief good (PA64–67); Berkeley's criticism of the materialist argument that external bodies provide the causal explanation of our ideas (PA67–69); a self-reference objection to naturalist epistemology (PA69–75); Mill's "proof" of the principle of utility (PA77–79); eight of Hume's arguments concerning causal necessity (PA93–104); various realist, antirealist, functionalist, and anti-functionalist arguments in the philosophy of logic (VR45–52); a self-reference objection to Norman Malcolm's claim that ordinary language is the only correct language (VR53–56); Berkeley's argument that to be is to be perceived (Johnstone 1989, 8–10); and Parmenides's argument about the nature of being and Aristotle's refutation of it (Johnstone 1989, 11–12). Although these arguments are not always explicitly discussed in the context of the question of their validity and *ad hominem* character, they do convey a flavor of what Johnstone is talking about; furthermore, even when he discusses them in the context of other issues, those other discussions connect indirectly with this question.

The general impression is that Johnstone is studying arguments characteristic of certain particular branches of philosophy. Clearly these are such branches as metaphysics, theory of knowledge, ethical theory, and logical theory; collectively considered, these could be labeled first philosophy, systematic philosophy, speculative philosophy, or theoretical philosophy. It is equally clear that he is not referring to arguments common in other parts of philosophy; for example, in the historiography of philosophy, scholars often advance arguments that are straightforwardly historical and inductive, involving questions of factual accuracy, causal connection, genetic origin, empirical consequence, and cultural evolution; and they also engage in philological arguments concerning the linguistic integrity of texts, the correct meaning of passages, and the etymology of words. It would be arbitrary to disqualify such arguments from being "philosophical," but it would be uncharitable to advance them as counterexamples to Johnstone's generalization. Let us say they do not fall within its scope and thus do not falsify it; he is simply talking about other kinds of arguments.

Analogous remarks apply to arguments prevalent in various branches of applied philosophy, e.g., philosophy of science, of religion, and of art. On one occasion where Johnstone seems to talk about the nature of science, he is quick to point out that, appearances to the contrary, he does not intend to get involved in questions of the philosophy of science, and that his references to it are merely illustrative and not substantive (PA22). A similar caution regards analytic philosophy, for I agree with L. Jonathan Cohen's (1986) thesis that typical arguments in analytic philosophy are inductive (cf. Finocchiaro 1991). These qualifications are crucial in order to appreciate the strength and weakness of Johnstone's thesis; without such qualifications, one might raise irrelevant objections to it, irrelevant because based on a misunderstanding of his meaning. That is why I regard my remarks above as part of a clarification of his thesis. He is talking about arguments in systematic philosophy.

3. A Concrete Illustration

To understand better Johnstone's thesis, it is useful to give an illustration. Consider the view that ordinary language is the only correct language in philosophy, which is a presupposition of the school that goes by such labels as ordinary-language philosophy or linguistic analysis. As Johnstone indicates, the view can be found explicitly stated in an essay by Norman Malcolm (1942, 357). Now, suppose one were to criticize Malcolm's view by arguing that the history of philosophy readily shows that great philosophers were typically using words in ways that deviate from ordinary language; for example, when Plato speaks of *eidos*, Kant of *Ding*, Croce of *spirito*, Whitehead of *actual occasion*, and Sartre of *projet*, they are not using these words in their ordinary sense. This objection would be ineffective against Malcolm because his position denies the correctness of these philosophers' language, and so these cases do not provide counterinstances consisting of correct language which is non-ordinary; the objection begs the question.

After pointing this out, Johnstone asks us to consider the following criticism. In stating his position, Malcolm is not using the phrase "ordinary language" in the ordinary sense. To use the phrase in an ordinary sense would be to use it in a context like this: suppose a reporter from the popular media interviews a Nobel Prize winner in physics to convey to ordinary people a sense of what kind of person he is and what his discoveries amounted to; suppose also that the physicist is able to explain himself clearly and comprehensibly in a down-to-earth manner, without using scientific jargon and uncommon sentence constructions; in this case it would be proper to say that during the interview the physicist used the most ordinary language. However, Malcolm's "ordinary language" is not equivalent to this because for him technical talk among physicists would also be "ordinary," and so would also be technical talk among artists and art critics. Thus, appearances to the contrary, Malcolm's phrase is itself not ordinary language; since this context is philosophical, by his own principle, his language is not correct. In short, as Johnstone puts it, Malcolm's motto "seems to impugn its own correctness" (VR54).

Next, Johnstone points out that, unlike the first criticism, this second one is valid, in the sense that it succeeds in establishing that Malcolm's thesis (as originally formulated) must be abandoned. To be sure, the thesis could be "revised," for example by saying that in philosophy only "ordinary language is correct language, and pronouncements about ordinary language can also be correct" (VR56). But this revision would underscore the fact that the criticism hits the mark and establishes the critical conclusion that it is not true that in philosophy only ordinary language is correct.

The final point to understand in this illustration is that this successful criticism is an *ad hominem* argument. Applying Whately's definition, the criticism tries to show that Malcolm, in accordance with his principles, is bound to admit that non-ordinary language can be correct. Using Johnstone's definitions, the criticism tries to prove that Malcolm's thesis is inconsistent with its own assertion or defense, that it defeats its own purpose.

4. Justification

Let us now examine Johnstone's justification of his thesis. In an important passage (PA81–82), he suggests there are three main arguments in its favor: an historical empirical argument involving cases of famous arguments from the great philosophers; an abstract theoretical argument involving his conceptions of argument, validity, *ad hominem*, and philosophy; and an intermediate argument involving a classification of philosophical criticisms.

Johnstone's empirical argument is essentially an induction by enumeration in which several typical instances of philosophical argument are examined and each is shown to be both valid and *ad hominem*. In the context where he explicitly elaborates this argument (PA57–80), he considers Aristotle's argument against Eudoxus's conclusion that pleasure is the chief good; Berkeley's argument against the materialist claim that material bodies are the likely causes of our ideas; and a self-reference objection to naturalism. However, as indicated earlier, various aspects of all the arguments in that earlier longer list are used to amplify this set of three.

For my purpose here, I shall focus on Berkeley's anti-materialist argument, found in paragraph 19 of his *Principles of Human Knowledge*:

> But, though we might possibly have all our sensations without them, yet perhaps it may be thought easier to conceive and explain the manner of their production, by supposing external bodies in their likeness rather than otherwise; and so it might be at least probable there are such things as bodies that excite their ideas in our minds. But neither can this be said. For, though we give the materialists their external bodies, they by their own confession are never the nearer knowing how our ideas are produced; since they own themselves unable to comprehend in what manner body can act on spirit, or how it is possible it should imprint any idea in the mind. Hence it is evident the production of ideas or sensations in our minds, can be no reason why we should suppose Matter or corporeal substances; since that is acknowledged to remain equally inexplicable with or without this supposition. If therefore it were possible for bodies to exist without the mind, yet to hold they do so must needs be a very precarious opinion; since it is to suppose, without any reason at all, that God has created innumerable beings that are entirely useless, and serve to no manner of purpose. [Berkeley 1929, 134; cf. PA67]

My own analysis[3] of this passage is that Berkeley is trying to show that it is not even likely that material bodies exists (having earlier argued that it is not necessary that they do). His argument is that there is no good reason for this likelihood, while there is one against it. The reason against it is the theological and teleological claim that material bodies would be useless

---

[3] My analysis differs slightly from that given by Johnstone, but I do this in order to better explain in my own words his key point that this argument of Berkeley is both valid and *ad hominem*. I find Johnstone's own account oversimplified to the extent of making it more difficult to see how Berkeley's argument provides evidence in support of Johnstone's thesis.

creations. He supports his claim that there is no good reason in favor of the likely existence of material bodies by arguing that the only reason is provided by the following "materialist" argument, and this argument is inconclusive. The materialists argue that it is likely that material bodies exist because their existence would provide the simplest explanation of our ideas and sensations. Berkeley objects that this argument is inconclusive because those who try to explain our ideas on the basis of material bodies also believe that it is incomprehensible how matter acts on mind, and so their explanation does not really succeed.

Let us focus, as Johnstone does, on only part of Berkeley's overall argument, namely on what I have called his objection to the materialist explanation of our ideas (the last sentence of the preceding paragraph). The argument is *ad hominem* insofar as it shows, not that there is no explanation of our ideas in terms of external bodies, but that *the materialists* can provide no explanation (given that in their position it is a mystery how matter acts on spirit). That is, Berkeley is criticizing materialism in terms of its own presuppositions; or again, he is trying to show that its thesis of the probable existence of material bodies is inconsistent with its other assertion about how matter can act on spirit. We may also agree with Johnstone that Berkeley's criticism is valid since it aims to show the incoherence of the materialist position, and this incoherence is indeed established.

As stated before, for this and many other arguments Johnstone's historical justification tries to show they are both valid and *ad hominem*. To be fully convincing Johnstone would also have to show that these arguments are valid *because* they are *ad hominem*, and/or that they are valid insofar as they are *ad hominem* and invalid insofar at they are not *ad hominem*. But I do not wish to criticize his historical argument on this basis because to attempt to show such claims would introduce theoretical considerations, which would turn his historical argument into the theoretical justification; and although he does not discuss these considerations in the context of the historical argument, he does discuss them elsewhere, as a separate justification of his thesis. So let us go on and discuss his theoretical argument.

Johnstone first argues that, unlike the situation in natural science where truth and falsity are independent of the supporting evidence, the truth or falsity of a philosophical statement is relative to the argument that proves or disproves it. By this he means that a philosophical statement is one such that "it is impossible to think of the statement as true without at the same time thinking of an argument in its favor, and it is impossible to think of it as false without at the same time thinking of an argument against it" (PA23). The essential reason for this metaphilosophical claim is that "*the argument for a philosophical statement is always a part of its meaning.* Furthermore, . . . *the argument against a philosophical statement is always a part of its meaning*" (PA32). But

> if the truth or falsity of any philosophical statement is relative to the argument that establishes or disestablishes it, then, unlike the truth or falsity of a scientific statement, it is not relative to objective facts. Hence there is no *argumentum ad rem* to establish or disestablish any philosophical statement. This leaves open only the possibility of an *argumentum ad hominem*. But any valid *argumentum ad hominem* will be found to have the same characteristics as each of my examples has been found to have. It will exhibit the self-defeating nature of an argument or statement that it attacks. It will be directly relevant to this argument or statement. It will borrow its force from the energy with which what it attacks is asserted. [PA76]

One could object here that Johnstone's initial metaphilosophical premise is not true, by focusing on a paradigm example of a philosophical statement, namely the existence of God. But I believe this objection would distract us from the main thread I want to develop in this essay. So let me note a sense in which Johnstone's argument has some plausibility. That is, let us apply these ideas to Johnstone's own thesis that valid philosophical arguments are *ad hominem*. Earlier I clarified the meaning of this thesis by explaining the notions of validity, philosophy, and *ad hominem*. However, it should also be noted that once one has explained what Johnstone means by these terms, one has gone a long way toward establishing the correctness of the thesis. One could say that the thesis is almost analytically true, given the meaning of the terms involved. Of course, this is not the whole story because the thesis also has applications to historical reality and normative implications regarding philosophy. On the other hand, the analytic aspect of Johnstone's thesis is part of the story. So his position does have a considerable amount of coherence and self-consistency.

As regards Johnstone's third argument (PA81–92), there is no space to elaborate it here, but it is so original and suggestive that it deserves a few comments. This argument is intermediate between abstract and empirical. On the one hand, it analyzes the notion of a statement or argument "defeating its own purpose" and identifies several ways in which this can happen. On the other hand, it articulates a classification of philosophical criticisms and several subtypes are distinguished; these are all arguments that charge some other argument or statement with the following flaws: unintelligibility (e.g., tautological emptiness, occultness, ambiguity, or inconsistency); dogmatism; *tu quoque*; "throwing out the baby with the bathwater"; denial of one's own presuppositions; and self-contradiction. Then Johnstone tries to show that there is a one-to-one correspondence between such philosophical charges and the various types of "defeating its own purpose." Now, recall that an *ad hominem* argument is one claiming that some statement or other argument defeats its own purpose; then it is easy to see that this intermediate justification amounts to an attempt to show the equivalence between types of critical arguments and subtypes of *ad hominem* arguments. To the extent that Johnstone's classification of philosophical criticism and his subdivision of *ad hominem* argument are exhaustive, he may be taken to have shown that all philosophical *criticism* is *ad hominem*, and consequently that all valid philosophical criticism is *ad hominem*. Whether this is equivalent to showing that all philosophical *arguments* are *ad hominem* depends on whether all philosophical arguments are critical. And this brings us to a major criticism of Johnstone's thesis, by contrast to some of the minor ones already mentioned, which were not stressed but were rather regarded as suggestions for clarifying the thesis.

5. Criticism

In fact, my main objection to Johnstone's thesis is going to be that, although it appears to be essentially true of critical arguments in philosophy, it is not really true of arguments that are noncritical and may be labeled constructive. But before we come to that, let us consider other objections, which although they are also major, can be handled more briefly. Johnstone anticipated almost all these objections, and so the issue is whether he answered them satisfactorily.

One objection was advanced by Warren J. Hockenos (1968; cf. VR56–61). He argued that, by Johnstone's own definitions, a valid philosophical argument is one which establishes the conclusion it claims to establish (PA73); and an *ad hominem* argument is one which concludes that a given thesis is inconsistent with its own presuppositions (VR45, 134). Hence, if a philosophical argument is both valid and *ad hominem*, it establishes that there is an inconsistency between a thesis and its presuppositions. But if this is so, if an inconsistency is really established, the philosophical argument is "*ad rem*" because such an inconsistency would be an objective fact (albeit a logical one); if the argument is *ad rem*, it is not *ad hominem*; therefore, if valid philosophical arguments are *ad hominem*, they are not *ad hominem*. It follows that it is not true that valid philosophical arguments are *ad hominem*.

Johnstone admitted this objection is essentially valid when he confessed that "it is criticisms of the kind that Hockenos makes, whether actually expressed by others or myself, that have caused me, over the years, gradually to modify my conception of the nature and purpose of philosophical argumentation" (VR56). Thus, Johnstone partly undertook a rethinking of his distinction between *ad hominem* and *ad rem* arguments, reconsidering whether these two classes are jointly exhaustive and mutually exclusive (VR57–58), and wondering whether to admit that some valid arguments are *ad rem*. He also tried to show that the arguments mentioned by Hockenos are *ad hominem* after all; for the inconsistency proof would depend on whether the criticized argument and the critic shared the same concept of inconsistency; if they did not, the position under criticism would accept an alleged inconsistency only when demonstrated on the basis of its own concept of inconsistency, i.e., only when the inconsistency criticism was *ad hominem*.

It is important to note that Hockenos's criticism is itself an *ad hominem* argument. This feature may account for its at least partial effectiveness. In a paradoxical sort of way, the criticism may thus reinforce Johnstone's thesis.

This raises an issue from which a second objection can be made to Johnstone's thesis. The question is whether his own argument is *ad hominem*. Since, as we have seen, he has three supporting arguments, this question is threefold. However, it is obvious that the real crucial case involves the theoretical argument. His historical argument is not even a candidate, being instead a good example of the inductive arguments typical of the historiography of philosophy, which we noted earlier fall outside the scope of his thesis. Regarding his argument from the classification of philosophical criticisms, we have not said enough about it to fruitfully pursue the question.

This second objection could be articulated as follows. Johnstone's (theoretical) argument should be *ad hominem*, if we apply the thesis to itself, and there seems to be no reason why we should not. But if his argument is *ad hominem*, then two difficulties follow, an evaluative and an analytical one. The evaluative difficulty is that, despite the fact that by now it should be obvious that the term *ad hominem*, far from being pejorative, is actually favorable (in Johnstone's scheme), still the implication is that it is not "an objective" fact that valid philosophical arguments are *ad hominem*, but rather that it is true only in his own system. The analytical difficulty is that he needs to explain how his theoretical argument does have the property of being *ad hominem*; how its conclusion is critical of some other position and how its premises involve the presuppositions of that other position.

Johnstone was aware of this possible criticism (VR135, 139). Although he did not address the evaluative difficulty, he did respond to the analytical difficulty. But he did not respond in a sustained manner, and the only relevant passage is insufficient:

> my argument does not, at least in any obvious way, miss the point of anyone who might contend that philosophical statements can be true or false independently of the arguments used to establish or disestablish them. It acquires its force precisely from the force of this contention; for the contention can only take the form of an argument, and this very argument will at once serve as a further illustration of the thesis that I have been advocating. Since it exposes the self-defeating character of what it attacks, my argument to the effect that all valid philosophical arguments are *ad hominem* – clearly itself a philosophical argument, and one that I am claiming is valid – is itself also *ad hominem*. [PA81]

To reinforce my criticism that Johnstone's response is insufficient, I shall now articulate a third related objection. One could object that, to be effective, to establish its conclusion, an argument must be formally valid and have premises that are unquestionable; but any philosophical claim is questionable because this is true almost in virtue of the definition of "philosophical"; thus the premises of a philosophical argument are always questionable. However, philosophical premises are *de facto* unquestioned in those circumstances where they happen to coincide with what a person accepts; that is, philosophical premises are not questioned by persons who happen to accept them. Therefore, for persons who accept the premises, and only for them, a philosophical argument (if it is formally valid) will establish its conclusion, will be effective, will be "valid" (in Johnstone's sense). Now, such an argument is easily shown to be *ad hominem* in Whately's sense for it proves, not that the conclusion is a fact or that everyone must accept it, but only that those persons are bound to accept it who accept the premises. But does this yield Johnstone's thesis, whose unpacked meaning is that valid philosophical arguments are those whose conclusion criticizes some statement or other argument in terms of the latter's own presuppositions? Because we are dealing with philosophical claims, the conclusion of a valid philosophical argument is also the denial of some alternative philosophical claim, and so it criticizes some alternative philosophical position; so far so good. But for such philosophical criticism to be *ad hominem*, the argument's premises must be the presuppositions of the alternative position; yet we have seen that these premises are propositions accepted by the argument's proponent; so we have a valid argument criticizing a thesis on the basis of alternative presuppositions and thus lacking the property of being *ad hominem*. It follows that valid philosophical arguments are not *ad hominem*.

This objection reaches a conclusion critical of Johnstone's position, but does so by utilizing many ideas that are part of that position. So it is essentially an *ad hominem* argument. Now, I really see no way of evading this criticism. Thus, here we have a second occurrence of the paradox that Johnstone's thesis is criticized by means of a valid philosophical argument that is *ad hominem*, i.e., by means of an instantiation of that thesis.

But let us leave the dizzying atmosphere of such paradoxes and come down to a last and down-to-earth criticism of Johnstone's thesis. This objection points out that although his thesis has much plausibility when the arguments in question are critical arguments, it seems to be off the mark when we consider "constructive" arguments, which Johnstone might call "*ad rem*"; these are arguments that are not about statements or other arguments, but about things different from statements or arguments. An example is Plato's simplicity argument for the immortality of the soul found in the *Phaedo*, which Johnstone himself discusses (PA58–59), although in connection with other issues. One could add the other classic arguments for the immortality of the soul; the arguments for the existence of God; and the arguments supporting free will.

When faced with such alleged counterevidence, Johnstone could respond, although he did not stress it, in a manner analogous to Malcolm's reply to alleged instances of non-ordinary language that is correct. That is, Johnstone could reply that constructive arguments are seldom if ever valid; here it is worth stressing that the subject term of his generalization is "valid" philosophical arguments and that validity to him means success in establishing the conclusion. Few would be prepared to hold that the just mentioned constructive arguments are valid in this sense. However, Johnstone responded primarily by arguing that such constructive philosophical arguments are critical and *ad hominem* after all (PA35–37, 76–80; VR28, 45).

This Johnstonian argument is articulated by examining Mill's "proof" of the principle of utility:

The only proof capable of being given that an object is visible, is that people actually see it. The only proof that a sound is audible, is that people hear it; and so of the other sources of our experience. In like manner, I apprehend, the sole evidence that it is possible to produce that anything is desirable, is that people do actually desire it. If the end which the utilitarian doctrine proposes to itself were not, in theory and in practice, acknowledged to be an end, nothing could ever convince any person that it was so. No reason can be given why the general happiness is desirable except that each person, so far as he believes it to be attainable, desires his own happiness. [Mill 1965, 221; cf. PA77–78]

The standard criticism of Mill's argument is this. He argues that happiness is desirable because it is actually desired by people. This argument assumes that whatever is actually desired is desirable. But this assumption is false because desirable means "worthy of being desired" and not "actually desired."

Johnstone criticizes this criticism. He begins by stating that Mill's argument should be given the following more sophisticated reconstruction: (a) happiness is desirable because (b) it is actually desired; and (c) whatever is actually desired is desirable because (d) whatever is actually desired is capable of being desired, (e) whatever is capable of being desired is worthy of being desired, and (f) whatever is worthy of being desired is desirable. Moreover, continues Johnstone, instead of dogmatically declaring (e) to be false, one should understand that Mill had a justification for it, namely that it is true because (g) "capable of being desired" does mean "worthy of being desired," and this is so because (h) otherwise one would have a way of knowing worth independent of capability, and (i) this would be unacceptable apriorism (*à la* Kant). In other words, the standard criticism begs the question; whereas Johnstone's reconstruction makes it clear that Mill's argument is directed against Kant and is trying to provide an alternative to it.

Unfortunately, and this is my criticism of Johnstone's account, although Mill's argument is directed against Kant, it is not *ad hominem* against him; for in Johnstone's reconstruction, Mill's argument is based on an alternative to Kant, rather than on Kant's own presuppositions. As Johnstone himself says, Mill's argument is really an argument "to himself." But to say this is to admit that the argument is not *ad hominem*. The difference between oneself (one's own system) and someone else (an alternative system) is not insignificant, *pace* Johnstone, despite the argument advanced in the following passage: "A constructive philosophical argument, when valid, is very much like a valid *argumentum ad hominem*. The only important difference is that the philosopher using a constructive argument considers what he himself is bound to admit, in conformity to his own principles of reasoning or in consistency with his own conduct or situation, rather than considering what someone else is bound to admit. The constructive argument is thus essentially an *argumentum ad seipsum*" (PA79).

6. Epilogue

My conclusion is that, on the strength of Johnstone's arguments, it is probably true that all valid philosophical *criticism* must be *ad hominem* (in his sense of these terms); and this claim is important, insightful, and suggestive. But, for the objections discussed above, this claim should not be equated either with the thesis that all valid philosophical *arguments* must be *ad hominem*, or the thesis that *all philosophical* arguments are *ad hominem*.

17

Dialectics, Evaluation, and Argument

Goldman and Johnson on the Concept of Argument (2003)

1. Introduction: Critique of the Dialogue Model

For several years I have been exploring the nature of the dialectical approach to argument, its relationship to other approaches, its methodological fruitfulness, and its limitations. Although the precise meaning of the dialectical approach is part of the problem, I can say immediately that I mean it in the sense in which it is distinguished from monological or monolectical approaches, and not in the sense it is distinguished from logical and rhetorical approaches; for these two distinctions crisscross each other, as is obvious from the work of many scholars that is both dialectical and logical (Barth and Krabbe 1982; Blair and Johnson 1987; Woods and Walton 1989). My main motivation stems from the fact that the dialectical approach has become the dominant one in argumentation theory.[1] Now, whenever any approach in any field becomes dominant, there is always the danger that it will lead to the neglect or loss of insights which are easily discernible from other orientations; this in turn may even prevent the dominant approach from being developed to its fullest as a result of the competition with other approaches.

Let us begin with a review of some background results from the relevant literature. One of the best examples of the dialectical approach is a work entitled *From Axiom to Dialogue* by Else Barth and Erik Krabbe (1982;

---

[1] The increasing strength of this trend may be seen from the fact that we have now seen the emergence of articles that attribute "dialectical" thinking to scholars whom one would not have expected to be so regarded, for example, Hilary Putnam; cf. Cummings 2002. And the trend is not only international, but also inter-linguistic, as one may gather from Cattani 2001.

cf. Barth and Martens 1982). A critical examination of this work reveals that their achievement is not really to demonstrate the necessity to move from the axiomatic to the dialectical approach, by reducing the former to the latter; instead the structure of their proof is to demonstrate the equivalence of the methods of axiomatics, natural deduction, and formal semantics to the method of formal dialectics. However, as I have argued elsewhere (Finocchiaro 1995b), the proof works both ways, so that the former methods acquire the merits of the latter, and the latter the limitations of the former; and the unintended consequence is that there is no logical difference between the axiomatic and the formal-dialectical method, and their difference will have to be located in some other domain.[2]

Another extremely important result is due to James Freeman's (1991) work on *Dialectics and the Macrostructure of Arguments* and Francisca Snoeck Henkemans's (1992) work on *Analysing Complex Argumentation*. They have independently provided a dialectical analysis of complex argumentation, namely arguments where a conclusion is supported by more than just a single reason, either in the sense that two or more distinct reasons are given to support the conclusion, or in the sense that the reason which directly supports the conclusion is itself in turn supported by another reason. Their main accomplishment is to interpret arguments as the result of a hypothetical dialogue between a proponent or respondent and an opponent or challenger, a process during which the opponent asks various kinds of questions. However, as I have also argued previously (Finocchiaro 1995b, 193–94; 1999, 195–96), the questions asked are by and large evaluative questions, and so besides explicitly providing an illustration of the power of what might be called the informal-dialogical method, these authors have also implicitly suggested the evaluative dimension of complex argumentation. They may also be seen as having stressed the importance of complex argumentation and suggested that the usual emphasis on simple arguments is an undesirable oversimplification.[3]

---

[2] For a good, brief, and instructive example of translation of monological problems into dialogical terminology, see Krabbe 1998.

[3] I believe this double-edged nature of Freeman's and Snoeck Henkemans's work has been recognized by an exponent of the dialectical approach: Erik Krabbe has recently stated that the dialectical "obligation to handle objections can, in solo argument, be dealt with within the structure of a basic argument" (Krabbe 2000, 3), a basic argument being his (Walton and Krabbe 1995) label for what here I am calling complex argument. Similarly, he has suggested that "when studying more complex dialogues in which fallacy criticism is undertaken, not by an external evaluator, but by the participants themselves, profiles [i.e., sequences] of dialogue can again be used as a heuristic device" (Krabbe 2002, 155).

A move in this direction (toward evaluation and complexity) has also been independently made by J. Anthony Blair. In a paper entitled "The Limits of the Dialogue Model of Argument" (Blair 1998), he has distinguished thirteen levels of complexity of dialogues depending on the complexity of the argument allowed at each turn of the dialogue; the thirteenth level is the one which is the norm in a scholarly paper or commentary. Blair also distinguishes between what he labels "solo" arguments and "duet" arguments: in solo arguments the respondent and audience are physically absent; their identity may not be known or fixed; and the norms of the discussion are not settled but open to dispute. Then he argues plausibly that to speak of dialogues for complex or solo arguments is metaphorical at best and probably distorting. Blair concludes with some theses that embody a nondialogical conception of both the dialectical approach and solo arguments. His words are worth quoting at length:

> It would be nice if the term "dialectical" were reserved to denote the properties of all arguments related to their involving doubts or disagreements with at least two sides, and the term "dialogue" were reserved to denote turn-taking verbal exchanges between pairs of interlocutors. Then I could use this terminology to express the points that (1) all argumentation is dialectical, but by no means is all argumentation dialogical, and (2) the dialectical properties of dialogues, and the norms derived from the dialogue model, do not apply to non-dialogical argument exchanges, even though the latter are dialectical too. In other words, both duet arguments and solo arguments are dialectical, but only duet arguments are dialogues. [Blair 1998, 10][4]

One final explicitly critical contribution deserves mention. Chris Reed and Derek Long have stressed the importance and pervasiveness of what they call "persuasive monologue." A persuasive monologue is not merely a soliloquy, which is "a record of a chain of reasoning" (Reed and Long 1998, 2); nor an internal dialogue, "in which the speaker plays both roles" (ibid.); nor a "turn in dialogue" (ibid.). Instead persuasive monologue has two main characteristics: "firstly, the intuitive 'case building' of presenting arguments in support of the thesis" (Reed and Long 1998, 3); and "secondly, there is the more complex technique of presenting counterarguments to the thesis propounded, and then offering arguments which defeat those counterarguments" (ibid.). Although these authors' main interest seems to be the formal analysis and the computerized modeling

---

[4] Blair's clear distinction between (what he calls) the dialogue conception and (what I am calling) the evaluative conception of dialectics suggests the need to explore their relationship to other notions of dialectics, such as the classical Hegelian concept (cf. Finocchiaro 1988c) and, more recently, Hilary "Putnam's dialectical thinking" (Cummings 2002).

of persuasive monologues, the point I would want to stress is that the second clause of their definition refers to replying to objections, and such criticism of counterarguments is a feature which many would not hesitate to call dialectical, in a sense of this word distinct from dialogical.

The upshot of these preliminary remarks is as follows. Proponents of the dialectical approach tend to presuppose a particular concept of dialectics, pertaining to dialogue or turn taking; and they have produced results implicitly suggesting that dialogue may be dispensable (in favor of either deductive axiomatization or argument complexity and evaluation). Critics of the dialectical approach tend to stress monological argumentation, but in so doing they are quite sensitive to an aspect of argument which is dialectical in a sense other than the dialogical one (a sense pertaining to doubting with two sides and defeating counterarguments). With this literature and these reflections in the background, I now want to examine a particular problem, to try to understand the difference (if any) between a dialectical and a nondialectical approach to this problem, and the implications (if any) of the respective solutions to the question of the relative merits of the two approaches. The problem is that of how argument is to be conceived.

2. Concepts of Argument

Let us begin with what may be called the traditional conception of argument, or to be more precise, a version of the standard textbook definition. As many authors have done (Walton 1990, 408–9; Johnson 2000a, 146; Hansen 2002, 264), I too find it useful to quote Copi's definition: "An argument, in the logician's sense, is any group of propositions of which one is claimed to follow from the others, which are regarded as providing support or grounds for the truth of that one" (Copi and Cohen 1994, 5).[5]

However, although many of the same authors (e.g., Johnson 2000a, 148) take this to be a structural definition, I find it improper and misleading to speak of structure here because the structure involved is too insignificant to merit the name. The traditional concept does indeed define an argument as an ordered set of propositions, but the order introduced is simply that of designating one of the propositions as the conclusion; in other words, a distinction is made among all the propositions in the set,

---

5 This definition has remained essentially unchanged at least since the third edition of this classic textbook, which had "evidence" (Copi 1968, 7) in place of "support or grounds."

a distinction between the conclusion and the premises. However, such a single partition does not really yield a genuine structure, which for my sensibility would have to have at least two partitions; that is, the minimal order I would want before calling it a structure is three propositions interrelated in such a way that one is supported by the second, which is in turn supported by the third. Instead of calling it structural, one might call this aspect of the traditional definition relational.

A second important feature of Copi's definition is the reference to the intention or purpose of the arguer. Again, although many commentators (e.g., Johnson 2000a, 148) have denied such a teleological character, it seems obvious to me that when Copi says that the conclusion is claimed to follow from the premises, he is saying that the arguer claims this. And when he says that the premises are regarded as providing support or grounds for the conclusion, he is saying that the premises are so regarded by the arguer; that is, the arguer intends to use the premises to support the conclusion. In short, the purpose of the argument is to justify the conclusion by means of supporting reasons.

I am stressing that according to Copi's version of the traditional definition, an argument has function but no structure.[6] I believe there is a term that conveys both features, namely the term *illative*, which I adopt from Ralph Johnson (2000a, 150), who adopted it from Blair (1995). This traditional definition may thus be called the illative conception of argument. Illation is the special relationship that holds between premises or reasons and conclusion or thesis; it is not a purely abstract relation, but one that subsists in the mind of the arguer and of anyone trying to understand or evaluate the argument.

Two other versions of the traditional definition are worth mentioning, one more and one less abstract than the illative conception. The more abstract one avoids any reference to purpose and defines an argument simply as an ordered set of propositions partitioned into two subsets. For example, in *Choice and Chance*, Brian Skyrms stipulates that "an *argument* is a list of *sentences*, one of which is designated as the conclusion, and the rest of which are designated as premises" (Skyrms 1966, 1–2).[7] Those scholars who deny the teleological character of the traditional definition

---

[6] This is almost the reverse of Johnson's (2000a) view, as it will emerge below.

[7] See also Kalish and Montague (1964, 13), quoted in Johnson (2000a, 123): "an argument, as we shall understand it, consists of two parts – first, a sequence of sentences called its premises and secondly, an additional sentence called its conclusion"; see also Angeles (1981, 18), quoted in Walton (1990, 408): it defines argument as "a series of statements called *premises* logically related to a further statement called the *conclusion*."

are probably thinking of this version, although of course it should not be equated with other versions such as Copi's.

The less abstract (or more concrete) version of the traditional definition adds a rhetorical condition to the illative conception, namely an element of persuasion. This conceives an argument as an attempt to persuade others that a conclusion is true by giving reasons in support of it. An example of such a definition comes from Michael Scriven's book *Reasoning*: "The simplest possible argument consists of a single premise, which is asserted as true, and a single conclusion, which is asserted as following from the premises, and hence also to be true. The *function* of the argument is to persuade you that since the premise is true, you must also accept the conclusion" (Scriven 1976, 55–56).[8]

These three versions of the traditional conception are importantly different, and constitute a sequence of increasingly more complex and narrow[9] definitions (as one moves from the purely abstract one through the illative one to the rhetorical). But they also share some very important features. All three lack any reference to a complex structure, or structure worthy of the name, as I have already mentioned. And all three lack any reference to dialectical matters, which will be our focus. Thus, let us now turn to what we may call the dialectical conception of argument.

The most natural version of the dialectical conception simply adds an element of criticism of objections to what I have called the rhetorical definition. We thus get that an argument is defined as an attempt to persuade someone that a conclusion is acceptable by giving reasons in support of it *and* defending it from objections. The best known example of this is the definition found in Johnson's book *Manifest Rationality*: "An argument is a type of discourse or text – the distillate of the practice of argumentation – in which the arguer seeks to persuade the Other(s) of the truth of a thesis by producing the reasons that support it. In addition to this illative core, an argument possesses a dialectical tier in which the arguer discharges his dialectical obligations" (Johnson 2000a, 168).

---

[8] Cf. Epstein 2002, 5: "We're trying to define 'argument.' We said it was an attempt to convince someone, using language, that a claim is true.... An *argument* is a collection of claims, one of which is called the **conclusion** whose truth the argument is intended to establish; the others are called the **premises**, which are supposed to lead to, or support, or convince that the conclusion is true." Cf. also Govier 1989, 117.

[9] Although these three definitions are increasingly more complex and narrow, they are not necessarily increasingly more adequate, for as I shall argue below, the move from the "justification" of the illative definition to the "persuasion" of the rhetorical definition may not yield an increase in adequacy.

There is no space here for me to repeat or summarize the various clarifications that have been made to Johnson's definition by Johnson (2002a; 2003) himself as well as by Trudy Govier (1998; 1999b; 2000), David Hitchcock (2002a), Hans Hansen (2002), and others (Groarke 2002; Leff 2000; Tindale 2002; Rees 2001; Wyatt 2001), although I will say a little more below in the context of my analysis of Johnson's argument (section 6, below). However, I have already implicitly incorporated many of these clarifications when I gave my own formulation, before exemplifying it with Johnson's definition. In any case, a few remarks are in order and may be relatively novel.

One thing I would want to point out is that by calling illative *core* the complex of conclusion and supporting reasons, Johnson suggests that the illative core is more fundamental than the dialectical tier. Now, this may very well be true; but it may not be. I would regard it as an open question. Of this more presently. However, in order not to beg this question, I shall speak of the illative *tier* or *component* rather than *core*.

Another question I would want to ask is, why call *dialectical* tier or discharge of dialectical obligations such things as examination of alternative positions and reply to objections? What is the concept of dialectics inherent in such a terminological decision, and how is such a conception to be justified? Is it enough to do some hand waving in the direction of Plato's dialogues? Johnson's concept of dialectics is the one inherent in the following explicit statement: "that argumentation is dialectical means that the arguer agrees to let the feedback from the other affect her product. The arguer consents to take criticism and to take it seriously. Indeed, she not only agrees to take it when it comes, as it typically does; she may actually solicit it. In this sense argumentation is a (perhaps even *the*) dialectical process *par excellence*" (Johnson 1996, 107; cf. Johnson 2000a, 161; Finocchiaro 1999, 195).

Third, besides Johnson's references to written text, argumentative practice, purpose, persuasion, and truth, it is important to note the reference to both the illative and dialectical components or tiers. This implies that a text with an illative tier but without a dialectical one is not strictly speaking an argument (as some of Johnson's critics have pointed out, thus yielding an alleged *reductio ad absurdum* of his definition); but Johnson himself prefers to say that such a text "does not fit the paradigm case of argument" (Johnson 2002a, 316).

In the present context, however, the point I want to stress is that there is a natural way to moderate Johnson's double requirement by disjoining the two conditions, in the sense of inclusive disjunction. We thus get the following conception: an argument is an attempt to persuade someone that a conclusion is true by giving reasons in support of it *or* defending it from objections. This is a weaker dialectical conception than Johnson's definition, but it still is importantly dialectical because it does call attention to the potential need to discharge one's own dialectical obligations, and because the inclusive disjunction obviously allows for cases where the argument contains both illative and dialectical tiers.

Such a more moderate dialectical conception has in fact been advanced by some scholars.[10] If I understand him correctly, I believe Alvin Goldman does this in his book *Knowledge in a Social World.* He explicitly allows for what he labels monological argumentation besides dialogical argumentation, as can be seen from this passage: "If a speaker presents an argument to an audience in which he asserts and defends the conclusion by appeal to the premises, I call this activity *argumentation.* More specifically, this counts as *monological* argumentation, a stretch of argumentation with a single speaker.... I shall also discuss *dialogical* argumentation in which two or more speakers discourse with one another, taking opposite sides of the issue over the truth of the conclusion" (Goldman 1999, 131). And for Goldman, a crucial principle governing dialogical argumentation is this: "when there are existing or foreseeable criticisms of one's main argument, a speaker should embed that argument in an extended argumentative discourse that contains replies to as many of these (important) criticisms as is feasible" (Goldman 1999, 144).

We thus have two versions of the dialectical conception of argument, a stronger one exemplified by Johnson that regards the dialectical or critical tier as necessary for any argument, and a moderate one exemplified by Goldman that makes the dialectical or critical tier essential for one type of argument but not for all. Although these two versions of the dialectical conception are the most common and natural ones, there is actually a third version that deserves discussion and may be regarded as more strongly dialectical than Johnson's conjunctive version. This hyper dialectical conception would define an argument as an attempt to justify a conclusion by defending it from objections. According to this conception, replying to objections is both a sufficient and a necessary condition to have an argument; whereas for Johnson's strong dialectical

---

[10] Besides Goldman, Reed (2000, 1) may be attributed this concept when he says, "The most fundamental problem facing the designer of an argument is premise availability: do there exist premises which can support a given conclusion or which can rebut or undercut some counterargument?"

conception, replying to objections is necessary but not sufficient; and for Goldman's moderate dialectical definition, replying to objections is sufficient but not necessary.

Unintuitive as it may sound, the hyper dialectical conception has been advanced by some scholars. In a 1980 book by the present author, entitled *Galileo and the Art of Reasoning*, in the context of a number of theoretical considerations, we find the following theoretical definition: "We may then say that an argument is a defense of its conclusion from actual or potential objections" (Finocchiaro 1980b, 419). More recently, in her review of Johnson's *Manifest Rationality*, Agnès van Rees has criticized his definition of argument for being insufficiently dialectical. Here are her revealing words: "According to this definition, producing reasons and discharging one's dialectical obligations are two different things. But in actual fact, if the notion of argument is indeed to be rooted in the dialectical practice of argumentation, the two should coincide. In a truly dialectical account, argument *per se* would be defined as an attempt to meet the critical reactions of an antagonist, that is, to take away anticipated objections and doubt" (Rees 2001, 233).[11] And besides these two explicit formulations, the hyper dialectical definition has a memorable, emblematic, and brilliant illustration; that is, an argument by Alan M. Turing published in 1950 in the journal *Mind*, advocating that machines can think based primarily on a critique of nine objections to this conclusion.[12]

Once again, however, despite the differences among these three versions of the dialectical conception, my focus will be on what they have in common. Their common element is an emphasis on replying to objections or to criticism. It is such a dialectical component that provides an instructive contrast to the illative conception. And it is this dialectical tier that I want to understand better and evaluate. With such an aim, the next step will be to examine various arguments that have been advanced in favor of the dialectical conception of argument.

3. Arguments for the Dialectical Definition

What we are faced with now is an exercise in informal logic and critical thinking, for what we want to do is to identify, interpret, reconstruct,

[11] She makes it clear that she is speaking from the "pragma-dialectical" point of view of the Amsterdam school of argumentation studies, and indeed one can find statements to this effect in such works as Eemeren and Grootendorst (1992, 73); Snoeck Henkemans (1992, 179); and Eemeren et al. (1993, 12, 14).

[12] I first learned of this collector's piece from Reed and Long (1998, 3).

analyze, evaluate, and criticize the arguments for the dialectical conception of argument. I shall focus explicitly on arguments advanced by Johnson and by Goldman, but implicitly underlying my examination will be arguments suggested by the present speaker in the above-mentioned 1980 book, and by John Stuart Mill in his essay *On Liberty*. There will be no time or space for me to elaborate my 1980 arguments for the hyper dialectical conception, or to search for Rees's argument for the same conception, or to examine Mill's arguments, which will have to be done on some other occasion. However, one additional remark on Mill is worth making.

Mill has already been injected into this discussion by an insightful interpretive hunch of Hansen (2002, 271), when he spoke of Mill's "dialectical method" and quoted a crucial passage from Mill's essay *On Liberty*. This reference led me to read Mill, and I discovered that the second chapter of his essay contains some of the strongest and most instructive arguments. Mill is ostensibly arguing for the thesis that freedom of expression of opinion is essential in the quest for knowledge and search for truth, but the connection with our topic becomes evident when we see that a key part of freedom of expression involves the freedom to express dissenting opinions, which in turn involves the toleration (and indeed the encouragement) of counterarguments; thus truth and knowledge require the understanding and criticism of counterarguments. We can get a glimpse and flavor of the relevance and importance of Mill's considerations from the following striking assertion: "When we turn to subjects [such as] morals, religion, politics, social relations, and the business of life, three-fourths of the arguments for every disputed opinion consist in dispelling the appearances which favor some opinion different from it" (Mill, *On Liberty*, ch. ii, par. 23; 1965, 286–87).

For now, let me focus on an argument that has been advanced by Goldman, or at least which I extract from Goldman; it deserves discussion because of its novelty. What he intends to justify is "a general thesis about critical argumentation and the probability of acquiring truth . . . that lively and vigorous debate is a desirable thing" (Goldman 1999, 144), desirable in the sense that it "has positive veritistic properties" (Goldman 1999, 146). In other words, critical argumentation is likely to lead to the truth. The connection between this conclusion and the dialectical conception of argument may be elaborated as follows. Goldman (1999, 132) says that "critical argumentation is an attempt to defeat or undercut the proffered argument," and he contrasts it to "proponent argumentation [which] is a defense of the asserted conclusion by appeal to the cited premises" (Goldman 1999, 132). To this I add that if critical argumentation is a veritistically good thing, then it will also be desirable for the special case when the proffered argument is a critical argument, and so a reply to the critical argument is called for. Such a reply is precisely what the dialectical conception of argument stipulates.

Next, Goldman distinguishes at least three subtypes of critical argumentation, one that denies the truth of a premise, a second that questions the link between premises and conclusion, and a third one which he calls "presenting a defeater" (Goldman 1999, 140). Then he formulates his argument for the special case of the latter, which is a notion he adopts from John Pollock (1986, 33–39; cf. Goldman 1999, 138–39, 139 n. 11, 144–45) and may be explained as follows. Given an argument with premises P-1 through P-n and conclusion C, a defeater is a critical argument with the same premises plus one additional special premise D and conclusion not-C. A simple example given by Goldman himself is this: consider the argument that it will probably rain tonight because it was so stated last night in the local weather forecast of a reliable news medium; a defeater of this argument would be the counterargument that it will probably *not* rain tonight because although it was so stated last night in the weather forecast of a reliable local news media source, it was also stated this morning by the same source that the forecast had changed and the new prediction was fair weather tonight.

I will label Goldman's argument the "truth-in-evidence" argument because it is based on a premise which he himself calls the truth-in-evidence principle (TEP); it asserts the following: "a larger body of evidence is generally a better indicator of the truth-value of a hypothesis than a smaller, contained body of evidence, as long as all the evidence propositions are true and what they indicate is correctly interpreted" (Goldman 1999, 145). He points out that this principle is an epistemic version of the requirement of total evidence discussed in a methodological context by Rudolph Carnap (1950, 211) and Carl Hempel (1965, 64–67). Goldman also says that the principle is a generalization of Bayes' theorem. Although these are reasons of sorts, and although the principle has some inherent plausibility, Goldman (1999, 145–46) confesses that "I have no proof of this postulate."

But how does this principle support his conclusion that critical argumentation, or at least defeater presentation, is conducive to truth? Clearly, a defeater argument does encompass a larger body of evidence than the argument being criticized. So, Goldman's premise is indeed relevant.

But is it sufficient? He attempts to articulate such sufficiency by commenting on the two provisos incorporated into the principle. The

condition of truth for the evidence propositions could be somewhat re-
laxed (he says) by requiring merely that they be justified. The other
condition was that what the evidence propositions indicate be correctly
interpreted; this seems to mean that it be correct to claim that the
premises of the defeater argument imply or support the denial of the
conclusion of the original argument. And Goldman himself suggests that
in real-world cases such an implication would be itself controversial. The
upshot of his articulation seems to be that in order for a defeater argument to have positive veritistic properties in accordance with the truth-in-
evidence principle, the defeater has itself to be a good argument, namely
have true or justified or acceptable premises, and these premises have to
really support its own conclusion; but in realistic situations such goodness
would be controversial.

Goldman seems to be aware of such difficulties, for despite his articulation and elucidation, what he claims about the premise-conclusion
link of his argument is very modest. He says: "Suppose . . . that (TEP) is
correct. May we derive from it the veritistic desirability of engaging in
defeater argumentation? In other words, does (TEP) imply that defeater
argumentation usually has positive V-value? Although I shall not attempt
to prove it, I suspect that this does follow" (Goldman 1999, 146).

Another difficulty that could be raised stems from the fact that Goldman intends his argument, which is specifically formulated in terms of
defeater arguments, to apply to other cases of critical argumentation.
However, its relevance to these other cases is questionable.

But to end on a more positive note, there are other valuable aspects of
an argument besides such properties as truth of premises and validity of
inference, or acceptability, relevance, and sufficiency of premises. Some
of the additional values are what might be called suggestiveness or fruitfulness and novelty or originality.[13] And along these dimensions, I would
rate Goldman's truth-in-evidence argument very highly.

4. Johnson's Argument: Its Illative Tier

Let us now examine Johnson's argument for the dialectical conception.
As one would expect, his argument possesses an illative component as

---

[13] This point about novelty is, of course, not novel. Johnson anticipates it to some degree
(2000a, 336) and discusses it implicitly in replying to the objection that his own definition
of argument is similar to Toulmin's notion of rebuttal (Johnson 2000a, 173–74). See
also section 6 below.

well as a dialectical tier, and the latter contains both replies to objections and criticism of alternative positions. The main alternative is what he calls the structural definition of argument, which (as suggested above) is not really structural and should rather be labeled the illative conception of argument.

One of Johnson's key supporting reasons I locate in passages where he makes statements such as the following: "Philosophers and others for whom argumentation is the principal methodology routinely include in their own arguments a section in which they voice and then deal with objections to their position.... If ... we look at the best practices of those who have the most at stake in this process, philosophers and logicians who have a vested interest in this practice, we will find that their arguments always take account of the standard objections.... Arguments with a dialectical tier are found in nonacademic discourse as well" (Johnson 2000a, 165–66). Here we have an empirical argument, which some would call an induction by enumeration, and others more simply a generalization argument or an inductive generalization. Although in his book Johnson does not himself categorize this argument in this manner, I am encouraged to advance this interpretation by the fact that in one of his papers he does speak favorably of the "empirical turn" (Johnson 2000b, 14–15). Moreover, such a strand of argument is also found in other dialectically inclined authors. For example, Goldman, after defining an "extended argumentative discourse" as a series of nested arguments that present and answer objections, states that "in science, scholarship, law, and other polemical realms, extended argumentative discourses are the norm. Scholars are expected to report existing findings and literature that form the basis of predictable objections" (Goldman 1999, 144).

Also reminiscent of such an empirical argument is Mill's assertion, quoted earlier, that three-fourths of arguments involving human affairs consist of attempts to reply to objections.

If and to the extent that Johnson's case for the dialectical conception of argument includes an empirical inductive generalization, then its evaluation would have to deal with questions such as the following. For example, if indeed the best examples of arguments by philosophers have a dialectical tier, should our conclusion be that *good* philosophical arguments have a dialectical tier, or that *all* philosophical arguments have a dialectical tier? In other words, that all philosophical arguments *ought* to have a dialectical tier, or that they *do* have a dialectical tier? Can our conclusion be that good arguments *in general* (whether philosophical or not) have a dialectical tier; in other words, from a sample containing information about philosophical arguments, how can we reach a conclusion about arguments in general? Do we not also need data about the characteristics of arguments in other disciplines, such as science and the law, as Goldman indicates? But if we gather such data about, for example, science, such scientific arguments that thus have a dialectical tier may happen to be those in special domains of scientific activity, such as in the context of peer discussion at the frontiers of research or in periods of scientific revolution; what are we then to say about other domains such as the context of scientific justification or the context of pedagogy or periods of normal science? And if indeed, as Mill states, three-fourths of arguments have a dialectical tier (indeed only this tier), should not the conclusion be qualified to make it a statistical rather than a universal generalization? And what are we to say about the other one-fourth of arguments? Finally, if we take seriously the possibility of an empirical inductive confirmation of the dialectical conception of argument, does not the above-mentioned evidence appear as merely anecdotal? Should we not attempt to devise more systematic and controlled tests or data gathering?

Some scholars have indeed undertaken such attempts. I am thinking of Hitchcock's (2002b) sampling of scholarly arguments to test his theory of inference; of David Perkins's (1989; Perkins et al. 1983) studies of the difficulties in everyday reasoning; and of the present author's examination of arguments in Galileo's *Dialogue on the Two Chief World Systems* (Finocchiaro 1980b; 1994b). I believe that by and large the relevant parts of such inquiries do support the thesis of the dialectical nature of argument. In fact, it was in the context of such an empirical investigation that the present writer drew the conclusion mentioned earlier and labeled the hyper dialectical conception of argument, namely "that an argument is a defense of its conclusion from actual or potential objections" (Finocchiaro 1980b, 419).

Although such an empirical approach has also been appreciated or advocated by other philosophers (Barth 1985a; Krabbe 2000, 4), it is unlikely that most philosophers will have much interest in using such empirical argumentation to support their theories of argument; so let us go on to more theoretical and conceptual considerations, especially since we find such supporting reasons in Johnson's book.

A second supporting reason in Johnson's illative tier is a premise about the nature of the process of arguing. He states that "the process of arguing includes, by its very nature, feedback from the Other. Nor does the process of arguing end there. Also included as part of the process must be the response by the arguer to those objections and criticisms, as well as any revisions made by the arguer" (Johnson 2000a, 157). If we recall that for Johnson an argument is the so-called "distillate of the practice of argumentation" (Johnson 2000a, 168), then the relevance and sufficiency of this premise becomes obvious. What about its acceptability? Here we have to remember that Johnson is talking about one of several meanings of the word *argue* or *arguing*; and certainly for this particular meaning it is unobjectionable and true that the process of arguing does have such a dialectical component.

However, this claim about the nature of the process of arguing is almost analytically true. So an unfriendly evaluator[14] might at this point raise the possibility that Johnson's argument from the nature of the process of arguing begs the question. But a more friendly critic might point out that the function of this particular argument is to articulate a necessary connection between the process of arguing and the concept of argument, and the articulation of such analytic relations is a normal part of any theorizing; thus it is no defect of a theory of argument that at some point it has to explain the links among various elements of its conceptual structure. However, such friendly criticism may have a consequence that suggests some possible revision by the arguer. That is, some arguments do not have rational persuasion as their telos, but rather the analytic elucidation of conceptual relations; and this is one of those arguments. But if we defend this argument in this manner from the criticism that it begs the question, then one has to revise the teleological rhetorical aspect of Johnson's definition. This could be done by stating the definition by saying that an argument is an attempt to justify a conclusion instead of saying that it is an attempt to persuade others that a conclusion is true.

Another way out might be to say that here both the friendly critic and the unfriendly evaluator are committing the fallacy of straw man, when they interpret these considerations about the nature of the process of argument as an argument in support of Johnson's definition; after all, he does not himself explicitly label them an argument. This denial of argumentative status would by itself be unproblematic, but it would begin to weigh if added to the previous unfriendly evaluation that

---

[14] In this sentence and the next one, I am (for the sake of the argument) using Johnson's distinction between evaluation and criticism, although it seems to me that the concept of evaluation is broader than he allows and thus includes the concept of criticism as a special case; cf. Johnson 2000a, 217–23.

Johnson's empirical inductive generalization was anecdotal. For one reply to that evaluation might have been that his empirical considerations
should not be interpreted as a real or full-fledged empirical argument
susceptible of evaluation in terms of the adequacy, variety, and represen-
tativeness of the sample used; and then we would be saying that neither
the empirical considerations nor the conceptual ones were arguments.
However, this consequence would not be fatal because there is at least
one passage in Johnson's book that seems to advance a supporting reason as explicitly as the practice of argumentation allows. To this we now
turn.

This is the passage where Johnson tries to ground the dialectical tier on
the telos of rational persuasion. In his own words, "because the practice
exists to achieve rational persuasion of the Other as a rational agent,
the practice must also be dialectical" (Johnson 2000a, 160). To avoid
straw-man problems, I quote this argument verbatim:

Because the arguer's purpose is rational persuasion, a second tier is required
as well. Why? I have shown that the practice of argumentation presupposes a
background of controversy. The first tier (the illative core) is meant to initiate
the process of converting Others, winning them over to the arguer's position.
But they will not easily be won over, nor should they be, if they are rational. The
participants know that there will likely be objections to the arguer's premises.
Indeed, the arguer must know this, so it is typical that the arguer will attempt to
anticipate and defuse such objections within the course of the argument. If the
arguer does not deal with the objections and criticisms, then to that degree, the
argument is not going to satisfy the dictates of rationality; more precisely, to that
very degree the argument falls short of what is required in terms of structure –
never mind the content; that is, the adequacy of the response to those objections.
For those at whom it is directed, those who know and care about the issue, will be
aware that the argument is open to objections from those who disagree with its
reasons, conclusion, and-or reasoning. Hence, if the arguer wishes to persuade
Others rationally, the arguer is obligated to take account of those objections and
opposing points of view. To ignore them, not to mention them, or to suppress
them – these could hardly be considered the moves of someone engaged in
the process of rational persuasion; thus, the process of persuasion must include
a second – dialectical – tier in which objections and criticism are dealt with.
[Johnson 2000a, 160, cf. 165]

This is a plausible argument, but I should like to point out that there are
two, and not just one, final premises: the claim that the purpose of the
argument is rational persuasion, and the claim that the process of argumentation occurs in a context of controversy. And the latter claim is both
crucial and independent of the first. But as John Stuart Mill (*On Liberty*,
ch. 2, par. 23; 1965, 286) pointed out, in Euclidean geometry rational

persuasion is achieved with just the illative tier, without any need of dealing with objections. Hence, the dialectical tier is not a consequence of
just the telos of rational persuasion, but of this telos plus the controversial
origin of argumentation.

In other words, Johnson gives the impression that the third reason of
the illative tier of his argument for the dialectical conception of argument
is the telos of rational persuasion. This impression is misleading because
if this reason were the only premise it would be insufficient and because
in fact Johnson himself combines it with the premise about controversial
origin.

I suspect that Johnson's reaction to this criticism would be to insist
that controversy is presupposed by all argumentation and to regard geometrical proofs as not arguments but mere inferences or entailments.
This move would strike me as arbitrary insofar as Euclidean geometrical
proofs are typically attempts to persuade oneself or others of the truth of
the theorem in question by rational means. Moreover, the move would
be questionable from the point of view of Johnson's own principle of
vulnerability because the restriction of the domain to that of controversial situations tends to make the conclusion true by definition; that is,
the dialectical tier becomes necessary as an immediate consequence of
the controversial context. Then this third reason of Johnson's illative tier
would basically reduce to his second reason.

I believe the way to remedy this difficulty would be to revise the conclusion of Johnson's argument by weakening the requirement of the dialectical tier. For example, instead of being regarded as a necessary condition
to have an argument, the dialectical tier might be regarded as a sufficient
condition. This would amount to replacing the conjunctive version of the
dialectical conception with the disjunctive one mentioned earlier.

5. Johnson's Argument: Its Criticism of Alternative Positions

So far we have examined the illative tier of Johnson's argument for his
dialectical conception of argument. We have identified, analyzed, evaluated, and criticized three supporting reasons. Let us now go on to examine the dialectical tier of his argument. This tier consists of two parts,
criticism of the alternative traditional conception of argument, and explicit replies to explicit objections to his definition. The criticism of alternatives can be easily subsumed under the notion of reply to objections,
by regarding that criticism as a reply to the objection that the traditional
conception of argument is adequate (and constitutes an alternative to the

dialectical conception);[15] but it is useful to treat the two parts separately, as Johnson does explicitly in his book.

Let us begin with a criticism which I have implicitly already examined and so can be dealt with relatively briefly. According to Johnson, "argument has its structure (reasons in support of a thesis, or premises plus conclusion) because of the purpose it serves – rational persuasion. A significant limitation of the structural view is that it ignores this important aspect – purpose or function. The moral of the story is that if a satisfactory conceptualization of argument is to be developed, the purpose or function of the discourse must be referred to" (Johnson 2000a, 148, cf. 167). But earlier I pointed out that, although the purely abstract version of the traditional definition does lack any teleological aspect, the illative conception (such as Copi's) is teleological insofar as it does make the aim of argument the justification of the conclusion by means of supporting reasons. Although justification is indeed different from persuasion, this only means that the illative conception attributes to argument a purpose different from the purpose attributed to it by Johnson's dialectical conception. Now, this conception (and even the rhetorical one) may very well be correct that the purpose is persuasion, and the illative conception incorrect that it is justification, but it seems unfair to criticize the latter for conceiving argument as purely structural without function.

A second criticism advanced by Johnson (2000a, 147) is that "the traditional view ... must ultimately fail because it does not distinguish argument from other forms of reasoning." He discusses three problematic forms of reasoning: explaining, instructing, and making an excuse. This criticism would be relevant and strong if this claim of confusion were true. But it is not. An analysis of Johnson's supporting critical argument will show this.

---

[15] This only means that any alternative position generates an objection, not that any objection yields an alternative position. Indeed, as Govier (1999b, 226–27) has argued, many objections do not involve alternative positions; for example, counterexamples to generalizations are objections but do not constitute alternatives. At times Johnson (2000a, 206–9) speaks of the dialectical tier as having a third part, namely dealing with undesirable consequences or implications of one's position; elsewhere he (Johnson 1998, 2) seems to accept Govier's (1998, 7–8) friendly critical revision that this is a special case of replying to objections; in still other places, Johnson (2002b, 3–4) speaks of *four* types of dialectical material, namely objections, alternative positions, criticism, and challenges. Such discussions suggest that more work is needed to clarify the concept of objection; indeed some scholars (Finocchiaro 1997a, 314–18; Govier 1999b, 229–32; Johnson [2000b; 2002b]; Krabbe 2002, 160–62) have undertaken this task, but much more remains to be done.

Johnson (2000a, 146) says, "I offer reasons in support when I explain, 'The reason that your car won't start is that you have a dead battery, and also the starter is defective.' Here I am supporting one claim (your car won't start) by another (you have a dead battery) and another (your starter is defective)." This example and others given by Johnson involve a misconception of the notion of support used by the illative definition. In this example, the supporting reasons are not the ones mentioned but rather the observational reports (not mentioned) that after turning the ignition key nothing happened; the mentioned reasons are the causes offered to explain the observed fact. Correspondingly, in the quoted text, the claim that your car won't start does not function as a conclusion but rather as a presupposition or premise of an argument aiming to support the causal claim.

Besides this misunderstanding or misrepresentation of the notion of support used by the illative conception, Johnson's critical argument may involve an equivocation on the term *reason*. Admittedly a reason can mean a premise helping to establish a controversial conclusion in an argument, or it can mean a cause or explanation helping to account for why a given noncontroversial claim is true. So it would be correct to say that one offers reasons when one explains, in one sense of *reasons*, but not that one offers reasons in support when one explains. Thus, here it may be the critic (and not the proponent of the illative view) who is failing to distinguish argument from explanation.

Johnson's remarks about the other forms of reasoning suffer from similar difficulties. He says, "I offer reasons when I instruct, 'If you want to get the best light for this shot, you are going to have to use a XDX-1000 filter combined with. . . .' Here I offer a reason (you are going to have to use a XDX-1000 filter) as support for the claim (if you want to get the best lighting), but the function of the discourse is not to persuade anyone that the claim is true" (Johnson 2000a, 146). Once again, there is no relationship of illative support between the two clauses, and there are not even two distinct claims; rather we have a single claim about a means-end connection between two things.

Johnson (2000a, 146) also says that "I offer reasons when I make an excuse, 'I can't go to the show tonight because I have to study for my exam tomorrow.' Here we have the structure of an argument as defined, but that is not sufficient to qualify it as an argument." I would counter that here we are in the domain of motivation, which is subsumable under the general concept of explanation, although it is also useful to treat it as an important special case. That is, one meaning of reason is that of motivation for an action. Clearly the quoted example is an explanation (of the speaker's not going), not an argument trying to persuade anybody that the speaker is not going. But this is an interpretation reached in the light of the illative conception, which clearly has the resources to say that the need to study is the motivating reason *why* one is not going, not the evidence proving *that* one is not going.

A third criticism advanced by Johnson is really a particular case of the second but deserves separate discussion and special attention. It claims that the illative conception presupposes an inadequate conception of a particular kind of reasoning, namely inference. This inadequacy has three overlapping aspects. First, the illative conception tends to conflate three forms of reasoning that ought to be distinguished, namely implication, inference, and argument (Johnson 2000a, 93–95). Second, it conceives the illative core in terms of a model that ought to be discarded, namely what Johnson calls "the (P+I) model, the view that an argument should be seen as consisting of a set of premises, plus an inference from them to the conclusion. The inference is typically represented as a bridge or a link from the premises to the conclusion" (Johnson 2000a, 166–67). Third, it fails to properly distinguish between argument and inference (Johnson 2000a, 177–78).

Much of this criticism is insightful and raises important issues. The key merit is to point out that the illative conception of argument has not been embedded in a wider theory of reasoning that would define, distinguish, and interrelate such concepts as reasoning, argument, inference, implication, and explanation. However, the effectiveness of this criticism is limited by the fact that the dialectical conception of argument, or more generally, Johnson's own pragmatic theory of argument, has also not been embedded within a more comprehensive theory of reasoning. He himself constantly reminds us that the aim of a theory of argument is more narrow than that of a theory of reasoning, and that while the articulation of a theory of reasoning remains a desirable goal, it was not within the scope of his work on the theory of argument. Thus the crucial question is whether the theory of reasoning groped toward or adumbrated by Johnson's dialectical conception is more adequate than that presupposed by the traditional illative conception.

With this aim in mind, I would point out some inadequacies in Johnson's account, besides the ones discussed in connection with the previous criticism involving the relationship among argument, support, reasoning, and explanation (which would also be relevant to the present point). Johnson (2000a, 94) defines implication as "a logical relationship

312 Critiques

between statements or propositions, in which one follows necessarily from the others"; and he gives the following paradigm example: if it is true that if P then Q and that if Q then R, then it is true that if P then R. He gives this definition and illustration in a passage where he also defines and illustrates inference and argument, with the aim of showing how to distinguish and interrelate these three forms of reasoning. However, it seems to me that implication so defined is not a form of reasoning at all; it is an abstraction and not a form of mental activity. He is not defining implication as what might be called deductive reasoning, which instead is subsumed under his definition of inference as a special case; instead he is defining implication in a way that places it outside the domain of reasoning altogether.

In another passage, where he focuses merely on the distinction between inference and argument, he seems to come close to placing argument itself outside the domain of reasoning. In a summary extolling the advantages of the pragmatic approach, he says that one of these advantages is that "we can begin to get a handle on differentiating between arguments and inference. Arguments, as I have shown, are outcomes within the practice that are dialectical in nature and characterized by manifest rationality. What is an inference? In Chapter 4, I presented inference as in one important sense something that happens in the mind, an activity perhaps spontaneous, perhaps calculated, by which the mind moves from one thought to another" (Johnson 2000a, 177–78). After pointing out some similarities, he stresses the following difference: "an inference can be what it is while remaining within the mind of the inferrer; this is not true of argument. One way of drawing this contrast is to say that inferring is monolectical, whereas arguing is a dialectical process. Moreover, argument must be seen within the practice of argumentation, but no comparable requirement exists for inference" (Johnson 2000a, 177–78). The only point I want to make here is that by conceiving an argument as a dialectical process that subsists within the practice of argumentation and cannot remain within the mind of the arguer, Johnson seems to be saying that argument is not a form of reasoning; to be sure it originates in reasoning, but to become argument it has to metamorphosize into nonreasoning. Now, all this may be adequate, sound, and correct from various points of view, but it is clear that we need more than a theory of reasoning; the theory of argument would need to be embedded in something like a theory of action, or a theory of speech acts, or a theory of social interaction.

There is at least one other criticism which Johnson advances against the illative conception, namely its "failure to give an adequate representation of the dialectical character of argumentation" (Johnson 2000a, 165). I hesitate to include this point under the heading of criticism of alternatives, in the dialectical tier of Johnson's own argument; for there seems to be some circularity or question-begging in objecting to a position P by saying that it fails to describe the matter at hand the way its alternative Q does; in fact this failure is guaranteed by P's being an alternative to Q and is an immediate consequence of that fact. In short, to point out this sort of thing is part of the clarification or elucidation of the two positions. However, Johnson is explicit that he regards this as a "limitation" of the traditional conception of argument, and so it deserves some attention. Moreover, it will turn out that the examination of this criticism is useful from a methodological, meta-logical, or meta-theoretical point of view.

As one might expect, to justify this criticism Johnson elaborates an argument trying to show that arguments must have a dialectical tier. But this argument is and can only be one of the positive reasons supporting his dialectical conception; that is, one of the elements of the illative tier of his argument. In fact, he repeats the third reason discussed above, namely the one trying to establish that the telos of rational persuasion implies the necessity of the dialectical tier. Clearly, here I need not repeat my own criticism of that reason. Instead, I want to elaborate a meta-theoretical point.

I want to stress that a positive reason of the illative tier has become a critical reason of the dialectical tier. I believe this could always happen. In fact, consider the illative tier R-1 through R-n of an argument whose conclusion is P; and consider that part of the dialectical tier consisting of various criticisms C-1 through C-n of alternative Q. Now, if and insofar as any one supporting reason is relevant and sufficient, then it would be more or less true to say that, for example, if R-n is true then P is also true. Moreover, if and insofar as the various criticisms are cogent, then it would be approximately correct to claim that, for example, if C-n is true then Q is false; indeed any particular criticism of Q can be phrased in this manner, for that is what makes it a criticism. Next, note that the fact that P and Q are alternatives means that they are at least contraries (though they need not be contradictories), so that, for example, if P is true then Q is false. Finally, putting together the three claims expressed in my last three sentences, we get that if R-n is true then Q is false, and hence that R-n is a criticism of Q; but R-n was one of the supporting reasons in the illative core, and so any such reason can generate a criticism in the dialectical tier.

My final comment here is that not all criticisms of alternatives are or need be dialectical rephrasings of illative supporting reasons. For

example, Johnson's first three criticisms are not like that. Thus in discharging one's own dialectical obligations, it seems important to distinguish between criticisms that are independent of the illative tier and
criticisms that are not. Only the independent criticisms would seem to
add anything new to the argument, whereas the dependent ones may be
useful rhetorically or pedagogically but add little to the logical strength of
the argument. And this was the methodological, meta-theoretical lesson
I wanted to elaborate.

6. Johnson's Argument: Replies to Objections

I have been analyzing Johnson's argument in favor of the dialectical conception in light of his own definition. To complete the analysis there
remains to examine the second part of its dialectical tier, consisting of
his explicit replies to objections. In his book *Manifest Rationality*, he lists,
numbers, and discusses five objections.

The first objection (Johnson 2000a, 169–71) is that the definition
is too restrictive because it disqualifies from the category of arguments
discourses that lack a dialectical tier. Johnson's reply is that his definition
is indeed restrictive insofar as it does imply this disqualification, but it
is not excessively restrictive because this restriction is quite proper. The
restriction is proper because it focuses attention on the paradigm and
central instances of argument, rather than on the derivative cases that
might be called "proto-arguments."

My criticism of this reply is that Johnson's definition is indeed too restrictive because the desired redirection of focus can be accomplished
equally well by the moderate, disjunctive version of the dialectical conception. Recall that that conception states that an argument is an attempt
to justify a conclusion that gives reasons in support of it and/or defends
it from objections.

The second objection (Johnson 2000a, 171–73) is that the dialectical
tier is unnecessary in the definition of argument because the work it does
could be accomplished in other ways: for example, one could make the
dialectical tier part of the normative requirements of a good argument;[16]
or part of the definition of such more complex discourses as extended

---

[16] Johnson (2000a, 171 n. 20) attributes this objection to Blair in Blair and Johnson 1987;
one can also find it in Govier 1998. This objection was also implicitly raised above in
my criticism of Johnson's inductive generalization argument, when I asked whether the
conclusion should be formulated as saying that all arguments have a dialectical tier, or
that all good arguments have it.

arguments, or cases, or supplementary arguments, or full-fledged arguments, and the like, as distinct from mere arguments or ordinary arguments. Johnson's reply is that the first criticism would have difficulties distinguishing between arguments that are bad insofar as they lack a dialectical tier, and arguments that are bad insofar as their dialectical tier fails to reply effectively to objections. Similarly, the second criticism would lead to the question, when is it enough to give an ordinary argument and when is it necessary to present an extended argument?

I agree that it is important to distinguish between the factual existence of a dialectical tier and the evaluative adequacy of it, and so it may be impossible to go through with the suggestion that the question of the dialectical tier belongs wholly to the theory of assessment, and can be removed from the theoretical problem of definition. However, regarding extended, supplementary, or full-fledged arguments, I do not see any difficulty, and that part of this objection seems to me to reinforce the moderate, disjunctive definition.

The third objection is that the definition is circular because it defines argument in terms of argumentation, among other things (Johnson 2000a, 173; cf. Hitchcock 2002a, 289). Johnson replies by admitting that there is a slight circularity, but claiming that the circularity is not vicious or objectionable. I agree with him, in part because I would add that the reference to argumentation is not necessary. In fact, my formulation of the three versions of the dialectical conception avoids such reference, without I believe any loss of generality, at least from the point of view of the contrast between the illative and the dialectical conceptions.

However, another comment is in order. Even if we eliminate mention of argumentation in the wording of the dialectical conception of argument, this eliminates only a potential internal circularity; but this does not avoid what might be called a potential external circularity, that is a circularity in the justification of the definitional claim. In fact, we saw earlier that one of Johnson's supporting reasons in the illative tier of his argument was the one based on the nature of the process of arguing; that that argument could be criticized as begging the question; that that criticism could be answered only by making a revision in the definition; and that the revision was to broaden the concept to include justifications that did not aim at rational persuasion but at conceptual clarification.

The fourth objection is that the definition is not novel because it is similar to that advanced by Stephen Toulmin, who used the notion of rebuttal (Johnson 2000a, 173–74; cf. Toulmin 1958, 101). Johnson replies that his definition is indeed similar to Toulmin's, but has some novelty insofar as it is a generalization of it. I agree that Johnson's definition has considerable originality, vis-à-vis Toulmin's. Thus, we might say that the objection is false. However, I believe another issue needs to be raised here.

That is, is this objection relevant? And if it is, why is it relevant? Neither the dialectical nor the illative conception of argument says anything about novelty. Nor do the traditional or Johnson's theories of assessment. In particular, his definition speaks of the truth of the conclusion, and it is the conclusion's truth that needs to be supported with reasons and dialectically defended from objections; it is not the conclusion's novelty or originality. In short, if this fourth objection were true, namely, if Johnson's definitional conclusion were not novel, why would that be a problem? I do not have an answer to this question, although my intuition tells me that such an objection is relevant, that novelty is important, and so that this is an important question.

The fifth and last objection discussed in Johnson's book is that the problem addressed by the definition is one of "just semantics" (Johnson 2000a, 174–75) because the word "argument" has many meanings, and so it is arbitrary to choose or invent one particular meaning. Johnson replies that although the problem motivating the definition is in a sense semantical, it is not "just semantics" in the sense of being unimportant. In the course of his reply, Johnson probably admits too much when he concedes some force to this objection and declares that his conception is a stipulative definition. For as Hansen (2002, 272–73) has argued and as Johnson himself (2002a, 313–14) later admitted, Johnson's thesis is really a theoretical definition; that is, a claim that is part of a theory of argument aiming to provide concepts and principles for the identification, understanding, interpretation, analysis, evaluation, and criticism of arguments.

Besides these replies to these five objections, contained in the book *Manifest Rationality*, since the book was published several scholars have advanced other objections and Johnson has replied to them (Govier 1998, 1999b, 2000; Groarke 2002; Hansen 2002; Hitchcock 2002a; Leff 2000; Tindale 2002; Rees 2001; Wyatt 2001; cf. Johnson 2002a, 2003). Thus a complete account or an extended discussion of Johnson's argument would have to include these additional objections and replies. However, my aim here is theoretical rather than historical, and so my discussion of them here will be guided by their relevance to the problem under discussion, namely the nature and adequacy of the dialectical approach in general vis-à-vis the nondialectical approach, and in particular the relative merits of the illative and dialectical conceptions of argument.

To begin with, some of the objections raised after publication had been anticipated by Johnson. This applies to the objections that his definition is too restrictive, that the dialectical tier is unnecessary, and that the definition is circular. However, needless to say, after the book's publication, new nuances and clarifications have emerged from these discussions.

In regard to other objections, I wish to reiterate something I stated at the beginning of this chapter. That is, when I introduced the dialectical conception of argument (section 2), I first gave my own formulation, and then I quoted Johnson's definition as an illustration. I also claimed that in giving my own formulation, I had attempted to incorporate the most important clarifications and most telling objections that had emerged from post-publication discussions. One example will have to suffice.

Both Hansen (2002, 269–70) and Hitchcock (2002a, 289) have independently objected that Johnson's definition, as he words it, states or implies that to be an argument (at least in the paradigm sense of the concept) a discourse must contain *all* (and not just some of) the reasons that support the conclusion; plus *only* those reasons that *actually* support it, as contrasted to those that are intended to support it; plus replies to *all* objections and criticisms, and not just to some; and *only actual* replies, rather that attempted replies. Thus, they have suggested that when Johnson says that an argument presents "the reasons that support it [the conclusion]" (Johnson 2000a, 168) the definition should instead speak of "reasons in support of the conclusion" or "reasons that attempt to support the conclusion." And when he says that in the argument's dialectical tier "the arguer discharges his dialectical obligations" (Johnson 2000a, 168), the definition should instead say that the arguer attempts to discharge some dialectical obligations.

These revisions also take care of the infinite-regress objection advanced by Govier (1998, 8; 1999b, 232–37). This is the objection that if all arguments must have a dialectical tier, then a reply to an objection must also have a dialectical tier, since such a reply is or should be an argument; thus, a reply to an objection to the original conclusion must contain replies to the objections to the reply, and so on *ad infinitum.* Johnson's best reply to this objection involves "pointing out the parallel between the illative core and the dialectical tier. That is, the same line of reasoning that prevents an infinite regress in the illative core can also be deployed to prevent the exfoliation of the dialectical tier" (Johnson 2003, section 3a).

Johnson does not elaborate. I suppose what he has in mind is the following traditional difficulty: if an argument must have an illative tier containing "the" reasons that support the conclusion, it must contain not only all the reasons that directly support it (which is already an indefinitely long process), but it must also contain all the lower-level reasons that directly support those direct reasons and so indirectly support the original conclusion; but such indirect reasons must themselves be supported by further reasons, and so on *ad infinitum.* This well-known infinite regress is usually stopped by saying that the illative tier need contain only those reasons that seem appropriate in the given context.

The situation with the dialectical tier is analogous: one replies only to those objections that seem appropriate in the context. At the level of the formulation of the definition of argument, elimination of the definite article I believe does the trick: if we say that an argument is an attempt at justification which gives reasons in support of a conclusion or defends it from objections, this clearly means that it gives one or more reasons in support of the conclusion and/or defends it from one or more objections.

7. Conclusion: A Moderately Dialectical Conception

To recapitulate, Johnson's argument for the dialectical conception of argument is complex and multi-faceted. It has an illative tier that advances at least three supporting reasons: empirical support reminiscent of an inductive generalization; the argument from the nature of the process of arguing; and the argument from the telos of rational persuasion. Johnson's argument also has a dialectical tier consisting of two main parts, criticism of alternatives and replies to objections. He criticizes the traditional conception of argument in at least four ways: that it conceives argument as having structure but no function; that it fails to distinguish argument from other forms of reasoning, especially explanation; that it presupposes an inadequate conception of inference; and that it fails to give an adequate account of the dialectical nature of argumentation. Furthermore, he replies to at least six objections that allege the following charges: excessive narrowness of scope, dispensability of the dialectical tier, vicious circularity, lack of novelty vis-à-vis Toulmin, triviality beyond semantical issues, and infinite regress.

In light of this interpretation, reconstruction, and analysis of Johnson's argument, it is obvious that it satisfies its own definition. And given the stringent requirements of this definition, this satisfaction represents a considerable merit. In the course of my discussion, I have also assessed, evaluated, and criticized that argument. It would be too tedious to recapitulate these assessments, but it is important to point out that they have been partly negative, unfavorable, and destructive, and partly positive, favorable, and constructive. That is, they have been partly critical (in the ordinary sense of criticism connoting negativity), and partly critical in Johnson's (2000a, 217–23) own sense (connoting fruitful constructiveness). To add a further dimension to such constructiveness and to try to provide a synthetic overview of the forest after our long journey through its trees, I would suggest that the upshot of my assessments is that Johnson's argument is cogent insofar as it justifies the following thesis, and implausible otherwise. The thesis is the claim that an argument is an attempt to justify a conclusion by giving reasons in support of it *or* defending it from objections.

I further claim that this is a moderately dialectical conception and that I have provided an argument in favor of this conception. A question now arises. What kind of argument have I provided? Is it self-referentially consistent? That is, does my argument fit my own definition? Is my argument an instance of its own conclusion? I believe it is. It may be viewed primarily as a defense of this moderately dialectical conception by means of criticism of Johnson's alternative strongly dialectical conception. Such a defense would suffice to make it an argument (in the sense of the moderate definition), even though it is obvious that I have not explicitly defended the moderate conception from the other alternatives, namely the hyper dialectical, the illative, the rhetorical, and the purely abstract conception. But I have presumed that in the present context no such defense was needed. If this is correct, this point would further reinforce the moderate conception. On the other hand, my initial remarks about the dialogical model of argument may be seen as an explicit, if summative and sketchy, defense of the same moderate conclusion from the dialogue model.

Moreover, although my moderately dialectical conception of argument does not require every argument to possess an illative tier, my argument may be taken to have such a tier, consisting of two supporting reasons. One is provided by my interpretation, reconstruction, and appropriation of Goldman's truth-in-evidence argument; the other consists of my suggested replacement for Johnson's empirical argument, namely my more systematic version based on the data base from Galileo's *Dialogue.*

Finally, does my argument include replies to objections? I have already pointed out that the criticism of an alternative can be conceived as a reply to the objection that there is no reason to prefer the given conclusion to the alternative. This link is of course what enables my previous considerations to instantiate the moderately dialectical conception of argument. Furthermore, incidentally and in passing, these considerations also contain replies to possible objections. I would have to admit, however, that so far I have not presented explicit replies to explicit objections. I can also say that I welcome objections, although I do so with some hesitation. In fact, such welcoming leads to a paradox.[17]

The arguer's welcoming of objections is certainly important. And Johnson (2000a, 161, 165) has written eloquent words in this regard. But if this open-mindedness is to be more than a desirable psychological trait, one would have to say that a good argument *should* elicit objections; indeed that an argument is good (in part) if and insofar as it generates objections. An argument should not fall on deaf ears; if it does, more than being a sign of its conclusiveness, it is probably a sign of its sterility. Of course, to be really good, an argument should also have the resources to answer or refute subsequent objections. So it is not really the existence of objections or the possibility of generating them that adds value to an argument. It is its ability to elicit refutable, implausible, or invalid objections. It is these that I welcome with open arms.

To encourage this process, I end by volunteering some of these objections myself. The first one may be formulated as follows. It is undeniable that there is a difference between the conjunctive and the disjunctive dialectical conceptions: it is one thing to say that an argument is an attempt to make a conclusion acceptable by means of both reasons in support of it and replies to objections; and it is another to say that an argument is an attempt to make a conclusion acceptable by means of either reasons in support of it or replies to objections. But this is a very small difference: *sub specie aeternitatis*, they are both dialectical conceptions; and even in the less Olympic earlier presentation of various conceptions of argument, both of these conceptions were treated as special cases of the dialectical conception and were regarded as having much more in common than they had differences, especially vis-à-vis the various versions of the traditional conception. So it is unclear what all the fuss is about; the difference is so minor as to approach triviality.

My reply to this objection is that even the eternal gods who view these matters from Olympus need to cultivate their powers of discrimination

---

[17] This paradox is a version of the problem discussed by Johnson (2000a, 223–36) in connection with his principle of vulnerability and his argument that no argument is conclusive. Mill (1965, 293–95 = *On Liberty*, ch. 2, par. 31–33) also discusses a version of this problem.

and their ability to make fine distinctions. So there is no good reason to ignore the difference between conjunction and inclusive disjunction. The important point is that differences should not be magnified or exaggerated, but the other side of this coin is that they should not be minimized or underplayed. However, such balance has been precisely what I have stressed in this chapter, by beginning to point out that these two definitions were versions of the dialectical approach, and by ending with the conclusion that the disjunctive conception seems to be preferable to the conjunctive one.

A second objection one could raise is a criticism from the point of view of what I have called the hyper dialectical conception. This is the view that an argument is a defense of its conclusion from actual or potential objections. From the point of view of the hyper conception, the moderate definition is a step in a direction opposite to what is needed: presumably one should further strengthen Johnson's strong conception rather than weakening it into the moderate conception. And the important reason to take a step toward the hyper conception is the following: given any claim that has been asserted, one could always raise the question, what reasons if any there are in support of the claim? This question may be regarded as the prime or minimal objection to any claim. If one anticipates it, one constructs the illative tier and gives the supporting reasons even before the objection has actually been raised. Or one can wait until after the objection has been explicitly raised. In either case, the illative component can be interpreted as a part of the dialectical tier.

To answer this objection, I would begin by pointing out that if it cannot be satisfactorily answered, then I for one would have no difficulty with revising my conclusion by modifying the moderate into the hyper conception. But before resorting to this revision, I would want to try the following reply. That is, in a way analogous to how this objection attempts to interpret the illative component in terms of the dialectical tier, one can perhaps try to do the reverse and reinterpret the dialectical tier in terms of the illative component.

Consider an argument whose illative component consists of premises P-1 through P-n and conclusion C. And suppose the argument also has a dialectical tier with objections O-1 through O-k, respectively answered by replies R-1 through R-k. Now consider the conjunction of an objection and its corresponding reply, (O-j & R-j), or some appropriately reworded phrasing of it that might be needed for grammatical propriety. It seems to me that such a conjunction would constitute a reason supporting the conclusion C. It would be like saying that one reason for accepting the conclusion is that if one objects to it in such and such a way, such an objection would be incorrect; or collectively considered, one reason for accepting conclusion C is that all objections against it fail, i.e., that there are no objections to it. In other words, an objection to a conclusion C may be seen as a reason against it, a reason for claiming not-C; and if a reason R for not-C is a bad reason, then the claim that R is a bad reason for not-C may be seen as a reason for C. Of course, such a reason would not be a conclusive reason, and to claim such conclusiveness would be to commit a damaging version of the fallacy from ignorance; indeed I have already suggested that for conclusiveness or deductive validity, the question of objections does not even arise. But we are clearly dealing with reasons that, however strong, fall short of conclusiveness, and for such cases the explicit refutation of an explicit objection may be viewed as a supporting reason.

The upshot of these considerations is that while the presentation of supporting reasons may be regarded as a reply to a weak or minimal objection, the refutation of objections may be regarded as a weak or minimal supporting reason. There thus seems to be a symmetry between the illative and the dialectical tiers, and this is perhaps another reason for giving them separate mention in the definition of argument, as the disjunctive conception does.

A third objection to my argument involves Johnson's notion of manifest rationality, by which he means the attempt not only to be rational, but also to look and appear rational. The objection would allege that in my reconstruction of his argument I have ignored the following element of its illative tier: that an argument must have a dialectical tier because "argumentation [is] more than just an exercise in rationality" (Johnson 2000a, 163), it is also an exercise in manifest rationality; and "manifest rationality is why the arguer is obligated to respond to objections and criticisms from others" (Johnson 2000a, 163–64). This argument is hard to miss since it is being referred to in the title of Johnson's book; since it is given in the body of the work when the idea of manifest rationality is explicitly discussed (Johnson 2000a, 163–64); and since elsewhere (Johnson 2000b, 3) he explicitly presents it as an additional line of justification, besides the argument from the telos of rational persuasion. Moreover, the argument is apparently important because if it is cogent it would justify the strongly dialectical conception of argument, but not the moderate definition.

My response to this objection starts with a criticism of the argument from manifest rationality. In regard to its premise that argument is an exercise in manifest rationality, it may be deemed acceptable, but I do wonder whether its acceptability exceeds that of the conclusion. Moreover, I agree that the premise is more or less relevant, but I question whether it is sufficient. One reason for questioning its sufficiency is that, as we saw in the case of the argument from the telos of rational persuasion, an additional interdependent premise is needed, namely a proposition about the controversial origin of argumentation; otherwise, as proofs in Euclidean geometry suggest, rationality can be achieved without replying to objections.

A more specific and important reason for questioning the sufficiency of the present premise of manifest rationality is that it is unclear that it really adds anything to the argument from the telos of rational persuasion. Johnson's key point here seems to be that whereas rationality as such might be taken to require that one answer only objections that are really relevant, manifest rationality requires that one answer objections that appear to be relevant, even if in reality they are not. But I would point out that the inclusion of apparent, as distinct from real objections, is required by the telos of rational persuasion, for it would not be persuasive to neglect objections that are believed (even if incorrectly) to be forceful. In other words, in Johnson's own account the two operative notions are manifest rationality and rational persuasion, and these seem to me to be two sides of the same coin, rather than two distinct concepts. Although similar considerations have led Hitchcock and Hansen[18] to conclude that Johnson's notion of manifest rationality is rhetorical after all, my own conclusion here is that this argument from manifest rationality has no force above and beyond the argument from the telos of rational persuasion.

There is another conclusion I would want to draw. I originally did not include this supporting reason in my reconstruction of the illative tier of Johnson's argument because I judged it to be devoid of the additional force just mentioned. In doing so, I was operating, I believe, from the point of view of strict rationality, as distinct from manifest rationality. I was telling myself that, appearances to the contrary, and despite Johnson's own explicit statements to the contrary, he really had no distinct argument; so also using the principle of charity, I decided it was better to neglect these considerations, rather than interpreting them as an argument and then criticizing the argument as worthless. In that sense and to that extent, my previous neglect was justified, and hence the present objection has no force.

<hr/>

[18] Hitchcock 2002a, 7; Hansen 2002, 273–74; cf. the reply in Johnson 2002a, 327–29.

However, in discussing this objection now, I was taking the point of view of manifest rationality at the metalevel. That is, given all the appearances (at the object level) that manifest rationality is one of Johnson's reasons in support of the dialectical tier, I explored whether these appearances correspond to reality; whether this reason, besides being meant to support his conclusion, does really support it. If and insofar as my doing so has added to the persuasive force of my own argument, then perhaps I have come closer to achieving my present aim of rationally persuading you that the moderate conception is preferable. Furthermore, such rational persuasion has perhaps been enhanced by the fact that I explicitly included at least one objection which for me did not have even prima facie plausibility, but which might be plausibly advanced by Johnson or anyone taking his point of view; and this in turn may be taken to enhance the practical value of manifest rationality, practical in the sense of the practice of argumentation, even if it remains true, as I would hold, that theoretically speaking manifest rationality is an aspect of rational persuasion.

A final objection now comes to mind. It is one from the point of view of the illative conception, and it is based on my criticism of Johnson's criticism of this conception. That is, if it is inaccurate to object, as Johnson does, that the illative conception lacks a teleological aspect and fails to attribute a telos to argument; and if it is inaccurate or unfair to object that the illative conception fails to properly distinguish between argument and other forms of reasoning such as explanation and inference; and if it is circular to object that the illative conception ignores the dialectical nature of argument; then does it not seem that the illative conception can survive Johnson's criticism, and is perhaps adequate? In other words, even if my critique of Johnson's illative tier and of his explicit replies to explicit objections shows that my moderate conception is preferable to his strong one, it does not show that the moderate conception is superior to the illative definition, especially when we recall my criticism of Johnson's criticism of the illative conception. Does not my argument need one other component, namely a criticism of the alternative illative position?

Part of my answer to this objection lies in stressing two arguments discussed earlier: my reconstruction or appropriation of what I have called Goldman's truth-in-evidence argument and of what I have called Johnson's empirical inductive generalization. Insofar as they support my moderate version of the dialectical conception, they do not support the illative conception. I would also want to exploit my claim about the symmetry of the illative and dialectical tiers; insofar as that claim is correct, it suggests that even if the illative conception were otherwise acceptable, the moderately dialectical re-description of the situation would be more encompassing and therefore better.

And this suggests that perhaps the best line of defense here is to question whether the illative definition of argument is really an alternative to the moderately dialectical conception. One reason to see that they are not really alternatives is to stress that the moderately dialectical definition as I phrased it and am defending it here at the end of my discussion speaks of justification rather than persuasion. This is a revision of the dialectical conception required by the difficulties that emerged when I discussed Johnson's argument from the nature of the process of arguing; that argument could not be regarded as a successful attempt at persuasion (since from the point of view of persuasion it may be begging the question), but it was better regarded as a justification (insofar as it is an analytical conceptual elucidation in the context of theorizing). This move from persuasion to justification raises the question of the precise relationship between these two notions, but this issue cannot be elaborated here; suffice it to say that I conceive justification partly as a weakening of the notion of proof, and partly as a requirement for rational persuasion. Thus my moderate conception incorporates an element of the illative definition.

To be sure they are not identical, but they are not inconsistent either. In a sense, the illative conception entails the moderately dialectical one, since the latter is a disjunction of which the former is the first disjunct. But although this entailment ensures their formal consistency, it perhaps points in a misleading direction because it suggests that the moderate conception is a special case of the illative one, whereas the opposite is more nearly correct. That is, the moderate conception is more general than the illative one, in the sense that it can subsume under itself all the particular instances that the illative conception subsumes, plus others that the illative conception does not subsume. If then, the proper relationship between the moderately dialectical and the illative conceptions is not one of competition or inconsistency, but rather compatibility or species and genus, then in arguing for the moderately dialectical conception one need not reject the illative definition, but one should rather incorporate it.

In short, the moderately dialectical conception of argument may be seen as a synthesis of the illative conception and of the strongly dialectical definition. And if the latter two alternatives are dubbed thesis and antithesis, then I may be allowed to end my analysis on this dialectical note. Of course such an ending is dialectical in a sense that is perhaps not in accordance with some people's idea of dialectics, but it is nevertheless suggestive of further work needed to clarify the meaning of the concept of dialectics.[19]

[19] I am of course referring to the Hegelian view of dialectic as the synthesis of a thesis and an antithesis. My reference is made partly in jest, for I am aware that it is questionable whether this triadic interpretation of Hegelian dialectic is anything more than a vulgar oversimplification and has anything more to do with the dialectical philosophy of Hegel than the *terza rima* has anything to do with the poetry and art of Dante's *Divine Comedy*; cf. Findlay (1964, 353) and Finocchiaro (1988c, 183).

PART IV

HISTORICAL ANALYSES

Critical Thinking in Science

18

The Concept of *Ad Hominem* Argument
in Galileo and Locke (1974)

1. Introductory Considerations

There is an activity which, in the world of thoughts and ideas, can be as rewarding and as exciting as literacy criticism is in the world of images and impressions. It is the critical understanding of actual reasoning and may be called "logical criticism." It is partly with this attitude that I undertake the reconstruction of certain arguments found in Galileo's writings.

I say "partly" because this analysis is more than a mere exercise in logical criticism; it is part of a new interpretation of Galileo which, by emphasizing the logical skills and sophistication he displays, would make "the father of modern science" first and foremost a logician. At any rate, since the technique under consideration is very frequently used by him and has often been misunderstood, it is very important to become clear about it by studying the contexts where he is explicit about its use – by himself or by others.

Moreover, it so happens that these passages provide new evidence for the history-of-philosophy thesis of a Galilean origin of Locke's ideas.

Finally this investigation constitutes a chapter in the rather interesting history of the notion of *ad hominem* argument. Part of it has been studied by C. L. Hamblin in his *Fallacies.*[1] He distinguishes two conceptions of *ad hominem* argument. The one prevalent among contemporary logic books is described by him as reasoning such that "a case is argued not on its merits but by analyzing (usually unfavorably) the motives or

[1] Hamblin 1970.

background of its supporters or opponents."[2] The other is an older conception for which Locke is the first known writer in English to have given a formulation when he said that "to press a man with consequences drawn from his own principles or concessions . . . is . . . known under the name of *argumentum ad hominem*."[3]

Several important questions are raised by Hamblin in the course of his analysis. Is the contemporary *ad hominem* really a fallacy?[4] How exactly did the contemporary conception originate? Where did Locke get the term from?

Hamblin has interesting and plausible things to say concerning all of these questions. He suggests that the contemporary conception arose in the nineteenth century through a misinterpretation of the term,[5] though he confesses he does not know exactly how.[6] Moreover, he points out how the question of the fallaciousness of the contemporary *ad hominem* cannot be answered without a careful analysis of the concept of argument;[7] and in his own analysis the nature of argument turns out to be dialectical in an Aristotelian sense which has some correspondence with the old *ad hominem*.[8] This suggests the existence of a more profound connection between the two conceptions than the historical and etymological one already mentioned: the two versions may be conceptually related insofar as the contemporary *ad hominem* is, and must be, *an argument* and all arguments are "really" *ad hominem* in the old sense.

In the light of all this, the search for explicit pre-Lockean discussions of *ad hominem* arguments acquires additional importance: besides being relevant to the historical question of the sources of Locke's terminology, and to the elucidation of the original concept of *ad hominem* argument, the search can indirectly help us understand the general concept of argument.

Hamblin's suggestion that Locke's term comes indirectly from Aristotle[9] is unobjectionable insofar as it goes. It would be desirable, however, to analyze discussions which are both more explicit and closer to Locke's time. In Galileo's writings we find at least three such discussions.

[2] Hamblin 1970, 41.
[3] Locke 1959, 2: 411.
[4] Hamblin 1970, 42.
[5] Hamblin 1970, 157, 175.
[6] Hamblin 1970, 175.
[7] Hamblin 1970, 224.
[8] Hamblin 1970, 241.
[9] Hamblin 1970, 161.

2. Galileo's Argument from the Concave Side of the Lunar Sphere

The first series of references to *ad hominem* arguments occurs in *The Assayer*[10] at the place where Galileo defends one of his arguments from unfair criticism by pointing out that his argument was *ad hominem*. The discussion occurs in the context of a controversy over the nature of comets.

Aristotle's theory of the comets presupposed that the motion of the sky carries along around the earth the air and exhalations making up the part of the terrestrial world contiguous with the celestial region.[11]

In criticism of this presupposition, Galileo had given the following argument.[12] It is not true that this air and these exhalations within the lunar sky are carried around by its revolution because the lunar sky must be attributed the prefect shape of a sphere, and the exhalations consist of a tenuous and light substance, and such exhalations are not swept along by their mere contact with the smooth surface of the revolving (lunar) sky that encloses them. Now,

experiment shows this, for if we cause a concave circular vessel of very smooth surface to revolve about its center with as great a velocity as we wish, the air contained within it will remain at rest. This may be clearly demonstrated by the tiny flame of a little, lighted candle held inside the hollow of the vessel; the flame will not only fail to be extinguished by the air contiguous to the surface of the vessel but it will not even be bent, though if the air were moving so swiftly it ought to put out a much larger flame. Now if air does not participate in this motion, still less would some other lighter and more subtle substance acquire it.[13]

Galileo's argument had in turn been criticized as follows.[14] It is highly doubtful, to say the least, that the concave surface of the lunar sky is spherical and smooth, for several reasons. First, the primary support for this proposition would have to be that otherwise its motion would be retarded; but this Aristotelian justification has no force since our case concerns the concave surface of the lunar sky, and the only things that would slow its motion would be air and fire which possess no retarding power.

Second, it is silly to argue: the concave surface of the lunar sky must be smooth and round because the Moon is a noble body and a round

[10] Galilei 1890–1909, 6: 316, 317, 319, 321; 1966, 276, 279, 280.
[11] Galilei 1890–1909, 6: 53; 1966, 28–29.
[12] Galilei 1890–1909, 6: 53–54; 1966, 29–30.
[13] Galilei 1966, 29–30.
[14] Galilei 1890–1909, 6: 151–54, cf. 316–22; 1966, 105–8, cf. 275–82.

shape is what befits noble bodies; it is as silly as to say that the human body, which is even more noble than the Moon, ought to be round.

Third, the concave surface of the lunar sky is probably rough because this would interconnect all movable bodies through the effect of that roughness on the motion of the upper parts of the terrestrial sphere.

Fourth, according to Galileo himself, by his own alleged astronomical discoveries, the surface of the moon is rough like that of the earth, and the sun itself has imperfections consisting of dark spots near its surface; hence the concave surface of the lunar sky is likely to have imperfections and roughness.

Although Galileo gives cogent detailed replies to this criticism, he does so out of courtesy rather than methodological duty; for, he points out, *his own original argument was ad hominem.* Not once, but four times, in a discussion of four or five pages does Galileo characterize his original argument as *ad hominem:*

Our saying that the concave surface of the lunar sky is perfectly spherical, smooth, and polished is not due to the fact that such is our opinion, but to the fact that so claims Aristotle, against whom we argue *ad hominem.*[15] ... It was said that the lunar hollow is perfectly spherical and smooth not because such we believe it to be, but because such was regarded by Aristotle, against whom we dispute *ad hominem.*[16] ... Before I proceed any further, I again reply to Sarsi that it is not I who wants the sky, as a most noble body, to have a most noble shape, such as the perfectly spherical; it is rather Aristotle himself, against whom we are arguing *ad hominem.*[17] ... Merely *ad hominem* and by arguing *ex suppositione,* and having even made assumptions which are surely false, ... do we inquire whether the lunar hollow, if hard and smooth, which it certainly isn't, when it turns, which is another falsehood, sweeps with it the element of fire, which perhaps isn't there either.[18]

That is why, addressing his critic, Galileo says: "Quite vain, then, is all the remainder of your argument in which you do your best to prove that the lunar hollow must be wavy and rough rather than smooth and polished. It is idle, and does not oblige me to make any reply; still I prefer to let gentlemanly strife prevail between us, as the great poet says, and I shall consider the strength of your proofs."[19]

---

[15] Galilei 1890–1909, 6: 316, my translation; cf. Galilei 1966, 276.
[16] Galilei 1890–1909, 6: 317, my translation; cf. Galilei 1966, 276.
[17] Galilei 1890–1909, 6: 319, my translation; cf. Galilei 1966, 279.
[18] Galilei 1890–1909, 6: 321, my translation; cf. Galilei 1966, 280.
[19] Galilei 1966, 276; cf. Galilei 1890–1909, 6: 317; the verse is from Ariosto, *Orlando Furioso,* XXIII, 81.

What is the conception of *ad hominem* argument inherent in this discussion? It certainly is not the modern conception: Galileo categorizes *his own* argument as *ad hominem* in order to *defend it.* He uses the proposition that the concave surface of the lunar sky is smooth and spherical as a premise in an argument whose conclusion is that the upper air and the exhalations above it could not be carried around by the revolution of the lunar sky. The conclusion conflicts with Aristotle's theory but the premise is accepted by him. On the other hand Galileo rejects the premise simply because he doesn't believe in the existence of the various crystalline spheres. The feature of *ad hominem* must be such as to make irrelevant the arguments questioning the acceptability of the premise. Galileo's argument is in fact a beautiful example of Locke's notion: pressing a man with consequences drawn from his own principles. Galileo is criticizing Aristotle by deriving consequences drawn from Aristotle's own principles. This kind of *ad hominem* argument does not seek to establish the truth of its conclusion but rather the fact that its conclusion follows from certain propositions, which are either unacceptable or not accepted by the arguer, but accepted by the person against whom the argument is directed. From this point of view, and formalistically speaking, an *ad hominem* argument is one that attempts to establish a counterfactual conditional whose antecedent is one or more of the premises, and whose consequent is the conclusion of the argument; in the present case we have: if the concave surface of the lunar sky were smooth, then the upper air and the exhalations would not be carried along with it around the earth. Hence, Locke is right when he remarks that "nor does it follow that another man is in the right because he has shown me that I am in the wrong,"[20] but he is wrong in denying that an *ad hominem* argument "brings true instruction with it and advances us in our way to knowledge,"[21] for conditional knowledge is still knowledge.

At any rate, because of the coincidence between Locke's abstract formulation and Galileo's concrete application, I am led to suggest that Locke's term and concept originate historically from Galileo. This suggestion is and must here remain a conjecture, though one surely worthy of being tested, both because the testing seems rather straightforward and because its corroboration might throw new light on the historical origin of Locke's philosophy, whose distinction between primary and secondary qualities constitutes after all another coincidence with Galileo.

[20] Locke 1959, 2: 411.
[21] Locke 1959, 2: 411.

3. Galileo on Aristotle's Argument against the Vacuum

Be that as it may, there exists another reference by Galileo to *ad hominem* argument. The context is here much less complicated than the previous one and may be adequately supplied by the following passage from *Two New Sciences*:

SAGREDO. I quite agree with the peripatetic philosophers in denying the penetrability of matter. As to the vacua I should like to hear a thorough discussion of Aristotle's demonstration in which he opposes them, and what you, Salviati, have to say in reply. I beg of you, Simplicio, that you give us the precise proof of the Philosopher and that you, Salviati, give us the reply.
SIMPLICIO. So far as I remember, Aristotle inveighs against the ancient view that a vacuum is a necessary prerequisite for motion and that the latter could not occur without the former. In opposition to this view Aristotle shows that it is precisely the phenomenon of motion, as we shall see, which renders untenable the idea of a vacuum. . . . He assumes that the speeds of one and the same body moving in different media are in inverse ratio to the densities of these media; thus, for instance, if the density of water were ten times that of air, the speed in air would be ten times greater than in water. From this . . . supposition, he shows that, since the tenuity of a vacuum differs infinitely from that of any medium filled with matter however rare, any body which moves in a plenum through a certain space in a certain time ought to move through a vacuum instantaneously; but instantaneous motion is an impossibility; it is therefore impossible that a vacuum should be produced by motion.
SALVIATI. The argument is, as you see, *ad hominem*, that is, it is directed against those who thought the vacuum a prerequisite for motion. Now if I admit the argument to be conclusive and concede also that motion cannot take place in a vacuum, the assumption of a vacuum considered absolutely and not with reference to motion, is not thereby invalidated.[22]

It is not easy in this case to formulate the notion of *ad hominem* argument being used by Galileo since it is not immediately apparent what is the argument to which that notion is being applied. For, on the one hand, Sagredo's speech and the beginning of Simplicio's would indicate that its conclusion is a simple denial of the vacuum; on the other hand, the "argument" at the beginning of Salviati's speech might plausibly refer to the one given at the end of Simplicio's speech, whose conclusion is the impossibility of a vacuum being "produced by motion," i.e., being necessary for motion; and finally, the argument being hypothetically admitted as conclusive, in the second half of Salviati's speech, has for conclusion the proposition that motion cannot take place in a vacuum. In other words, in the allegedly *ad hominem* argument, it is unclear whether what is being

---

[22] Galilei 1914, 61–62; cf. Galilei 1890–1909, 8: 105–6.

concluded to be impossible is: (1) a vacuum *per se*, (2) the necessity of a vacuum for motion, or (3) motion in a vacuum.

Let us solve the difficulty by assuming that Galileo's concept of *ad hominem* is the same here as the one he used in *The Assayer*. If we can then construct an argument which is *ad hominem* in that sense, and if there is textual evidence supporting this interpretation, then our assumption will be confirmed.

An argument which is definitely present in the passage can be re-constructed as follows: since the speed of motion in different media is inversely proportional to the density of these media, since the density of a vacuum is infinitely smaller than that of any material medium how-ever tenuous, and since in any such medium the speed of motion has a finite value, it follows that motion in a vacuum would be instantaneous; but instantaneous motion is impossible; therefore, motion in a vacuum is impossible.

Although Galileo will criticize this argument by refuting its first premise,[23] in the passage under consideration he merely remarks (through Salviati) that if we concede its conclusion what we are con-ceding is not something about a vacuum *per se*, but about its relation to motion: motion and a vacuum are incompatible, i.e., if there is motion then there is no vacuum, i.e., if there is a vacuum then there is no mo-tion. There is no way in which this argument could be *ad hominem* in the relevant sense; for it is being attributed to Aristotle, who is supposed to accept both the premises and the conclusion; it would be *ad hominem* only if he did not accept the first premise but accepted the conclusion, and was directing it to someone who accepted the premise but not the conclusion.

A second argument which is also present in the passage is just like the previous one, except that it concludes that "it is therefore impossible that a vacuum should be produced by motion." In fact, this is the argument which is literally at the end of Simplicio's speech. The conclusion seems to mean[24] that it is impossible that there should be a vacuum as a conse-quence of there being motion, i.e., impossible that a vacuum is necessary for motion.

When this is understood, the previous argument about the vacuum becomes a part of the present one, in the sense that the previous con-clusion represents an intermediate step toward the present conclusion.

---

[23] Galilei 1914, 65–68; 1890–1909, 8: 110–13.
[24] Cf. Galilei 1890–1909, 8: 106.

The way in which this previous argument is being expanded is as follows: since motion in a vacuum is impossible, if there is motion there can be no vacuum; this means that it is the *absence* of a vacuum that must be necessary for motion; hence the *presence* of a vacuum *cannot* be necessary for motion, i.e., it is impossible that a vacuum should be necessary for motion.

This conclusion denies the "ancient view" mentioned by Simplicio at the beginning of his speech, and so this argument seems to be the one described by Salviati as "directed against those who thought the vacuum a prerequisite for motion." However, though the argument *can* be so directed, it is not directed *ad hominem* against those people, since the premises do not contain any of their principles or concessions. The Aristotelian *ad hominem* argument against them would have to be one having as a premise the necessity of vacuum for motion which they do accept but Aristotle does not; and the conclusion would have to be an idea that they would be likely otherwise to reject and that Aristotle presumably accepts on other grounds. The following argument satisfies these conditions: since there obviously is such a thing as motion, given (your view) that motion without a vacuum is impossible, since (it can be shown that) motion *in a vacuum* is impossible, we may conclude that a vacuum is an impossibility.

The argument could be reconstructed thus:

(1) There is motion.
(2) If there is motion, then the vacuum exists.
(3) If there is motion, then the vacuum does not exist.
(4) Therefore, the vacuum does and does not exist.
(5) Therefore, the idea of a vacuum is a chimera.

Given that (1), (2), and (3) are all true the argument seems valid.

But whether valid or not, this is the only argument that can be reconstructed from the passage and that is *ad hominem* in the same sense in which Galileo's own argument in *The Assayer* is. The argument must then be the one he had in mind when, in an index to *Two New Sciences* entitled "Table of the More Notable Topics," he formulated the entry: "Aristotle's argument against the vacuum is *ad hominem*, p. —."[25]

It might seem at first that, in characterizing this Aristotelian argument as *ad hominem* Galileo is criticizing it; more exactly, that he is objecting to its soundness as regards the premise that a vacuum is necessary for

---

[25] Galilei 1890–1909, 8: 314.

motion; for he would be saying that the argument establishes the impossibility of a vacuum only if one were to accept that premise (as the ancient atomists presumably did). But for Galileo to do this would be to commit the error of his critic (Sarsi) when he criticized Galileo's own *ad hominem* argument against the motion of the exhalations. And that is why *Galileo does not proceed to argue against the proposition that a vacuum is necessary for motion*, though he does proceed to argue against the premise about the impossibility of motion in a vacuum, in order to exhibit the unsoundness, in that respect, of Aristotle's argument. In other words, in pointing out the *ad hominem* character of an argument the perceptive critic is thereby asserting that it would be inappropriate to criticize *the argument* by objecting to the problematic premise, since the argument giver did not himself accept that premise.

4. Galileo on Tycho's Argument against Copernicus

It should be mentioned that there exists a third Galilean reference to an *ad hominem* argument. This occurs in the *Dialogue Concerning the Two Chief World Systems*[26] and is, I believe, the only other explicit use of the term in Galileo's major works. This *ad hominem* argument is one advanced by Tycho Brahe and his followers against Copernicus and pertains to stellar distances, sizes, and apparent positions. The argument itself, the context in which it is given, and Galileo's criticism of it are each rather complicated, and therefore its analysis is beyond the scope of the present investigation. Moreover, in this *Dialogue* passage, the logical work accomplished by the term and the concept behind it is much less than for the passages I have analyzed, in that its use seems somewhat incidental.

Interestingly enough, there is a literary-rhetorical value in the usage of the notion in the *Dialogue*. In fact Galileo, having indicated how the Tychonians argue *ad hominem*, comments: "I believe that they argue against the man more in defense of another man than out of any great desire to get at the truth."[27] This is a beautiful logical image, one of the many that make the *Dialogue* such a great work of art. This book, however, is also full of reasoning, and so is the passage where our term occurs, and moreover the Galilean comment just quoted is also expressed incidentally by him; finally there is obviously no conflict between a term having literary value and its having logical value. So the question of the logical

[26] Galilei 1890–1909, 7: 399; 1953, 372.
[27] Galilei 1953, 372.

function of the notion of *ad hominem* argument in this *Dialogue* passage could not be dismissed. But because of its more incidental occurrence, it would have to be investigated by testing the working hypothesis that the concept occurring there is the one I have shown to be inherent in the more clear-cut passages studied here.

5. Concluding Remarks

This has been an exercise in what I called above "logical criticism." It should now be clear in what sense this enterprise is similar to literary criticism: its fundamental aim is the critical understanding of a concrete passage for its own sake. It should also be clear in what sense such an activity is philosophical: it is an application of the philosopher's instrument *par excellence*, logical analysis.

It has emerged that the original concept of *ad hominem* argument, formulated by Locke but of unknown origin, was consciously used by Galileo on at least three different occasions, once in each of his three major works, the *Discourse*, the *Dialogue*, and *The Assayer*. The occurrence of such "logician's second-order vocabulary"[28] is evidence that Galileo was a logician of sorts, at least a logician-in-action. Moreover, to the extent that such reasoning, which is *ad hominem* in the sense specified, is a dominant feature of Galileo's work, the suggestion arises that his success was due to his ability to think in terms of his opponents' points of view. And this would have obvious consequences for the methodology of science as well as for philosophical pedagogy.

If this investigation suggests the possibility that Locke got the term "*ad hominem* argument" from Galileo, it also leads one to the question, Where did Galileo get it from? Such questions are, of course, the stock-in-trade of the history of ideas.

Finally, the importance for logic of the concept of argument has been emphasized by Toulmin[29] and Hamblin,[30] among others. But, whether or not one equates logic with the theory of argument, the concept of argument has its own philosophical importance. From the point of view of Hamblin's logical theories, this investigation throws some light on the concept of argument. The relevant element of his views is what he calls his dialectical criteria for a good argument,[31] namely that (1) the premises

[28] Strawson 1952, 15.
[29] Toulmin 1958.
[30] Hamblin 1970, especially chapter 7.
[31] Hamblin 1970, 245.

must be accepted; (2) the passage from premises to conclusion must be of an accepted kind; (3) unstated premises must be of a kind that are accepted as omissible; and (4) the conclusion must be such that, in the absence of the argument, it would not be accepted or would be less accepted than in its presence. These he contrasts to alethic and epistemic criteria. The examples of *ad hominem* arguments I have analyzed make it plausible that it is inappropriate to object to the factual truth of their crucial premise, the one accepted by the opponent but not (necessarily) by the arguer; in other words, the worth of such arguments is independent of the truth of the crucial premise. This is what one would expect if such *ad hominem* arguments are to be genuine arguments, in accordance with Hamblin's criteria.

19

Newton's Third Rule of Philosophizing

A Role for Logic in Historiography (1974)

1. A Logical Approach

Newton's Third Rule of Philosophizing has recently been investigated from several points of view: by studying the vicissitudes of its metamorphosis from "hypothesis" to "rule,"[1] the fact of its augmentation by four sentences in the third edition of the *Principia*, the Aristotelian and neo-scholastic flavor of some of its language,[2] the scholarly significance of its editorial history.[3] All these investigations have been carried on with relatively little concern for the actual intellectual content of the rule itself. The following analysis is intended to supplement and not to replace the studies previously undertaken. The supplement, however, is a necessity, not a luxury, and the historian can neglect it only at his own loss.

What does the rule actually say? Here too the discussion will start with a quotation of the standard English translation, but that will *not* be followed by a comparison with previous English translations, other language translations, the Latin text of the third edition, that of the second, that of the first, the various drafts of it that can be found among Newton's private papers, and other analogous rules and principles formulated by Newton's contemporaries, predecessors, and successors. Instead I shall proceed to *analyze* the rule logically, which too could be regarded as a comparison of sorts, a comparison with certain ideals and universals present in the human mind. In my view this kind of comparison – logical analysis – is

[1] I. B. Cohen 1966.
[2] McGuire 1968.
[3] I. B. Cohen 1971, 21–26.

prior to all the others. In fact, the force of the following query is that of a rhetorical question: how can the standard English-translation text be compared with the innumerable other texts mentioned above unless one first possesses a critical understanding of the content of that text?

Of course, one might admit this question and yet claim or pretend that the standard text can be understood without any elaborate analysis, because there is not anything conceptually problematic about it. In order to answer such claims and pretensions, I will, immediately after quoting the text, state a number of problems which the logically sensitive reader of Newton ought to feel. I shall then try to solve these problems.

Rule III

The qualities of bodies, which admit neither intensification nor remission of degrees, and which are found to belong to all bodies within the reach of our experiments, are to be esteemed the universal qualities of all bodies whatsoever.

For since the qualities of bodies are only known to us by experiments, we are to hold for universal all such as universally agree with experiments; and such as are not liable to diminution can never be quite taken away. We are certainly not to relinquish the evidence of experiments for the sake of dreams and vain fictions of our own devising; nor are we to recede from the analogy of Nature, which is wont to be simple, and always consonant to itself. We no other way know the extension of bodies than by our senses, nor do these reach it in all bodies; but because we perceive extension in all that are sensible, therefore we ascribe it universally to all others also. That abundance of bodies are hard, we learn by experience; and because the hardness of the whole arises from the hardness of the parts, we therefore justly infer the hardness of the undivided particles not only of the bodies we feel but of all others. That all bodies are impenetrable, we gather not from reason, but from sensation. The bodies which we handle we find impenetrable, and thence conclude impenetrability to be an universal property of all bodies whatsoever. That all bodies are movable, and endowed with certain powers (which we call the inertia) of persevering in their motion, or in their rest, we only infer from the like properties observed in the bodies which we have seen. The extension, hardness, impenetrability, mobility, and inertia of the whole, result from the extension, hardness, impenetrability, mobility, and inertia of the parts; and hence we conclude the least particles of all bodies to be also all extended, and hard and impenetrable, and movable, and endowed with their proper inertia. And this is the foundation of all philosophy. Moreover, that the divided but contiguous particles of bodies may be separated from one another, is matter of observation; and, in the particles that remain undivided, our minds are able to distinguish yet lesser parts, as is mathematically demonstrated. But whether the parts so distinguished, and not yet divided, may, by the powers of Nature, be actually divided and separated from one another, we cannot certainly determine. Yet, had we the proof of but one experiment that any individual particle, in breaking a hard and solid body, suffered a division we might by virtue of this rule conclude that the undivided as well as the divided particles may be divided and actually separated to infinity.

Lastly, if it universally appears, by experiments and astronomical observations, that all bodies about the earth gravitate towards the earth, and that in proportion to the quantity of matter which they severally contain; that the moon likewise, according to the quantity of its matter, gravitates towards the earth; that, on the other hand, our sea gravitates towards the moon; and all the planets one towards another; and the comets in like manner towards the sun; we must, in consequence of this rule, universally allow that all bodies whatsoever are endowed with a principle of mutual gravitation. For the argument from the appearances concludes with more force for the universal gravitation of all bodies than for their impenetrability; of which, among those in the celestial regions, we have no experiments, nor any manner of observation. Not that I affirm gravity to be essential to bodies: by their *vis insita* I mean nothing but their inertia. This is immutable. Their gravity is diminished as they recede from the earth.[4]

2. Logical Analysis: Five Problems

The text of the rule itself, exclusive of the comments that follow it, seems to say: if two things are true of any quality of bodies, namely (1) that it admits neither intensification nor remission of degrees, and (2) that it belongs to all observed bodies, then it may be regarded as a universal quality of bodies.

This statement is followed by: three distinct reasons intended to justify it; five more or less uncontroversial examples illustrating the rule; a discussion of divisibility whose function is not immediately apparent; the example of gravity as a special example of the rule; and a qualification to the effect that the quality of gravity, though universal, is not essential.

The first argument justifying the rule seems to have the following structure:

1. Qualities whose presence is universal among observed bodies should be regarded as universal (since qualities of bodies are known only by experiments).
2. Qualities not susceptible of being decreased cannot be lost by bodies that have them (this is obvious).

---

[4] Newton 1934, 398–400.

3. Therefore, qualities which are not attributable to a greater or lesser degree and which are present in all observed bodies should be regarded as universal qualities of all bodies.

This argument is rather puzzling, and the reasoning seems to contain gaps; hence our first problem is whether this reasoning is sound, and if so, why.

The second reason in Newton's justification of the rule is a pragmatic one: it is not good policy to rely on what we can imagine instead of what we have experienced. The third reason is that we should not ignore Nature's example: since she is simple and uniform, we should follow the principle of simplicity (of which the present rule is presumably an instance).

Newton then proceeds to illustrate the rule with more or less uncontroversial examples of universal qualities. They are in turn extension, hardness, impenetrability, mobility, and inertia. What is striking about these examples is that the illustrations completely disregard one of the two conditions mentioned in the rule and in its justification, namely that the quality under consideration should "admit neither intensification nor remission of degrees." In other words, these examples do not seem to be proper illustrations of the rule as stated *and as justified* by Newton, and this is our second problem. To this we might add, If they are not illustrations, what are they?

Next comes a very curious statement: "And this is the foundation of all philosophy." Such a strong and categorical assertion cannot be ignored, even though eventually one might want to take it with a grain of salt. The obvious problem is: *What* is this foundation of all philosophy? Is it the stated rule? Or the (presumed) fact that extension, hardness, impenetrability, mobility, and inertia are universal properties of bodies (including particles of bodies, which are also bodies)? Or is the foundation the universality of inertia? This at least would correspond to the actual practice of Newton himself and his contemporaries, who did in fact use the law of inertia as the foundation of their natural philosophy.

Next comes a passage about infinite divisibility which ends by saying that the present rule would validate a certain inference if we had the appropriate knowledge. Newton is here applying the rule to a new case – divisibility. It is not known or agreed that divisibility is a universal quality, so there is no question of *illustrating* the rule by means of it. But can we *use* the rule to try to determine whether divisibility is universal? How could one do it?

The second paragraph of Newton's explanatory remarks begins with consideration of a special quality – gravity. The first half of that paragraph has all the appearance of an application of the rule to prove that gravity is a universal quality. The proof amounts to a recitation of the presence of this quality in all observed bodies: bodies near the surface of the earth, the moon, the sea, planets, and comets. Once more, as in the case of the uncontroversial examples, Newton does not use the condition stipulating that the quality in question "admit neither intensification nor remission of degrees." Hence the question arises whether, by his own stated criteria, gravity is indeed a universal quality. Or, in case we want to invert matters, given that we want gravity to be a universal quality, does the stated rule capture whatever it is that makes it universal; that is, does it correctly formalize the notion of universality of a quality? And if not, can we formulate a rule that does?

The final three sentences in the second paragraph can be reconstructed as follows. Gravity is not an essential quality of bodies, as inertia is, because whereas the latter is an immutable property, the strength of the former decreases with distance. Newton is presupposing immutability as a criterion for a quality to be essential. This argument has all the tone of a qualification intended to dispel misunderstanding, and since no other connection with the rest of the passage is immediately apparent, at this stage it does not generate any significant problem. It is true we could ask whether this inference is valid and whether its premises are correct, but such logical questions are not always historically important. The situation here provides an instructive contrast with the case of Newton's first justification of the rule; there the soundness of the argument was crucial, and it became the subject for the formulation of our first problem.

The problems that have emerged and that need to be solved if we want to understand the intellectual content of Newton's third rule are these:

1. Is Newton's rationale for the rule adequate?
2. Are the five uncontroversial examples proper illustrations of the rule, or alternatively does the rule properly formulate the universality of the given examples?
3. What is the "foundation of all philosophy"?
4. What is the real function of the discussion of divisibility?
5. Is Newton's proof of the universality of gravity successful by his own criteria, or alternatively does his rule properly formulate the universality of gravity?

3. Reconstruction: Newton's Mixture of Two Rules

Clearly these problems are no less important and no less historical than those concerning whether the rule was in E_1 or in $E_1 a$ or in $E_1 i$ or whether the last three sentences were added in E_3.[5] These five problems dealing with logical processes are nevertheless historical problems because the logical processes are those of historical agents. Nor can the problems be solved basically by looking at other places, and other editions; they can be solved only by (further) logical analysis, to which we now turn.

In his main justification of the rule, Newton is trying to establish universal qualities on empirical evidence. But this is only part of his argument. He is making the universality of a quality dependent also on the impossibility of its being decreased. For there are *two* premises in Newton's argument, the first referring to empirical evidence, the second to possibility of diminution. The question of the soundness of the argument is really the question of the sense, if any, in which it is correct to ground the universality of a quality on the two stated conditions.

The argument might be elaborated as follows. If a certain quality is such that it makes no sense to attribute it to a greater or lesser degree, then it is not susceptible of being decreased when present in a certain object, and so it cannot be taken away from those objects to which it belongs. Hence if all observed bodies have a certain quality which is not attributable in degrees, then there is no way to take that quality away from those bodies. If so, then possession of that quality becomes part of our idea or concept of *body*, and entities not having that quality would not be *bodies* any more than entities like light rays, or thoughts, or numbers are bodies. Hence, with respect to bodies we are assured of the universality of the quality. That is, if there is no way to take a certain quality away from any observed body, then non-observed bodies must be conceived as having that quality; that is, the quality is a defining property of bodies, an essential quality of bodies, thus universal in the sense of essential.

This reconstruction is an intrinsically plausible one, but is it what Newton had in mind? In deciding this, it should be first pointed out that the real question is what Newton had in mind *in this passage*. Hence

---

[5] Using Cohen's terminology, E_1 designates the first edition of the *Principia*; $E_1 a$ designates Newton's annotated copy of E_1, formerly in his personal library, now among Newton's books in Trinity College Library; $E_1 i$ designates an interleaved copy of E_1 that contains Newton's alterations on both printed pages and interleaves, formerly in Newton's personal library, now in the Portsmouth Collection of the University Library, Cambridge; cf. I. B. Cohen 1971, 25–26.

it is largely irrelevant, or to be more exact, it is definitely irrelevant on a first approximation, that in other passages Newton did not equate universal qualities with essential ones and essential ones with defining ones. I am not here attempting to construct a general Newtonian theory of essential qualities, rather I am seeking a critical understanding of his Third Rule. If this reconstruction helps to make sense of it, then it should be accepted unless a better interpretation is provided. Now, this reconstruction renders directly comprehensible what I have called Newton's first justification of the rule. Moreover, it establishes, through the term-concept *essential*, a connection with his final qualificatory remarks, which had appeared irrelevant on our first reading. Finally, it provides the key for the solution of the other problems formulated earlier.

We had noted that Newton does not in fact give an adequate proof of the universality of gravity, adequate in the light of his own rule, any more than he gives adequate illustrations by means of the uncontroversial examples. What was lacking in all such cases was a reference to the first condition mentioned in the rule being satisfied. This is all very well now, since what it means is that gravity has not been shown to be universal in the sense of essential. And since such examples as extension and hardness are *illustrations*, there is no question of their losing the status of universal-essential qualities, only the question of their impropriety.

What we have so far is this: a rule containing two distinct conditions, a sound justification for it, a number of improperly presented illustrations, and an attempt to show that gravity is universal but not in the sense of being essential. That is, the last two elements which we distinguished in our earlier analysis, and which are contained in the second paragraph of Newton's explanatory remarks, are best combined into one element: a clarification of the sense in which gravity is universal. And we can also see that the criterion of immutability, used by him to disqualify gravity from being essential, corresponds to the first condition stipulated in the rule.

Now can the illustrative character of extension, hardness, etc. be rectified? The problem here is not so much that Newton did not mention that they satisfy the first condition mentioned in the rule; the problem is that it is not at all obvious that they do. In fact, it would seem that of the five, only inertia and impenetrability do not admit degrees; whereas extension, hardness, and mobility can be present to varying degrees. Now one could interpret them so that they would admit neither intensification nor remission of degrees – extension as the quality of occupying (some) space, hardness as being solid, and mobility as being capable of motion. But then hardness-solidity would no longer satisfy the second condition and so presumably would no longer be a universal quality. Moreover, and more seriously, the interpretation is illegitimate, since this maneuver would allow any property to be interpreted as admitting of no degree: for example, let gravity be the quality of having *some* weight in the sense of experiencing *some* acceleration in the presence of other bodies. Thus the examples of extension, hardness, and mobility are not merely improper illustrations of Newton's rule as stated, they are not universal qualities in the present sense of being essential.

What must be done then, in order to solve all these problems, is to distinguish *two* rules, corresponding to one of the following two ideas behind the term "universal quality": (A) essential quality; and (B) quality present universally, that is, present throughout the universe, present in unobserved bodies as well. We then get:

Rule IIIA: A quality is an essential quality of a certain class of objects only if (1) it makes no sense to attribute it to a greater or lesser degree, and (2) it belongs to all of those objects that have been observed.

Rule IIIB: A quality is to be regarded as present throughout the universe, or as present universally, or (simply) as universal, if it belongs to all observed objects.

IIIA is a conceptual or epistemological rule, and IIIB is a methodological one; that is, IIIA says something about the conceptual structure of our knowledge of the world, and IIIB is a policy to follow in the investigation of the world. Clearly a quality can be essential (IIIA) without being universally present (IIIB) and vice versa. Moreover, some qualities may be both essential and universal, and some may be neither.

How does this distinction help us to understand the content of the Newtonian text? What I have called the first and main justification of the rule becomes the only justification of IIIA; whereas the second and third reasons given justify IIIB. Extension, hardness, and mobility become illustrations of IIIB; impenetrability and inertia, illustrations of IIIA. To the special example of gravitation, IIIB applies and IIIA does not.

To understand the passage on divisibility one must first distinguish, as Newton does, mathematical from physical divisibility. Then one must realize that the problem concerns not mathematical but only physical divisibility. And the problem is that the only bodies within the reach of experiment that we know to be physically divisible are those that have actually been divided. To determine whether a not-yet-divided body is divisible requires performance of the division. So we do not really have any evidence that undivided particles are physically divisible. Hence we cannot use Rule IIIB to ascribe that property to all particles whatsoever. If, *per impossibile*, we had even one experiment showing that an undivided particle did have the quality, this would mean that the quality had been found to belong to all observed cases (of undivided particles), and Rule IIIB would allow us to conclude that all particles whatsoever are divisible.

The same lack of evidence, together with Rule IIIA, prevents physical divisibility from being an essential quality. The claim that physical divisibility is a universal quality (IIIB) may be equated with the doctrine of infinite divisibility. Hence what Newton is doing here is showing that his rule cannot be used to justify that doctrine.

Finally, what is the "foundation of all philosophy"? My inclination is to say that Newton is claiming that IIIB, not IIIA, is the foundation. But I have really no way of showing this. As indicated before, an analysis of Newton's *practice* would probably come up with the result that the principle of inertia is the foundation. So we cannot dogmatically assume that an investigation of the rest of the *Principia* would tell us what Newton means here. It may be best to regard it as a casual expression and not attach too much importance to it.

4. Confirmation and Further Consequences

The consequences of this interpretation extend beyond the present text. First one can formulate some hypotheses about the original Latin and the adequacy of the standard translation and then test these hypotheses by looking at the other sources. The ambiguity that our logical analysis has revealed in the rule is not something that can be detected in its verbal statement in the standard Motte-Cajori translation, for the phrase used there – "are to be esteemed the universal qualities of all bodies whatsoever" – may be somewhat redundantly repetitive, but it is not linguistically ambiguous (*per se*). Hence there is a certain tension between the statement of the rule and its elaboration, a tension which is created because the rule as stated is not a very good statement of what is being elaborated in the explanatory remarks. In brief, if, as has been shown, there is an ambiguity in the explanatory remarks, then one would expect that the rule too would have been ambiguously expressed. Or alternatively, if the rule is really unambiguously stated, as it seems to be, then it is difficult to believe how Newton could have proceeded to give such an ambiguous elaboration. Hence, either the original writer or the translator is at fault. The choice between those two is obvious. And so we are led to hypothesize and look for a linguistic ambiguity in the original which the translators were wrong not to retain.

Since the translation quoted above is Cajori's revision of Motte's, we ought to first examine Motte's own translation. A comparison shows that though Cajori replaced the term "intention" by "intensification," the phrase "are to be esteemed the universal qualities of all bodies whatsoever" is also present in Motte's translation. The Latin text is the following: "*Regula III: Qualitates corporum quae intendi & remitti nequeunt, quaeque corporibus omnibus competunt in quibus experimenta instituere licet, pro qualitatibus corporum universorum habendae sunt.*"[6] Here the phrase *pro qualitatibus corporum universorum habendae sunt* does have the expected tendency to ambiguity. Of course, there is no grammatical or syntactical ambiguity; *universorum* does not apply to *qualitatibus*, and hence Newton is not talking about a special type of qualities, the "universal" ones, which might be taken to mean the "essential" ones. And yet he is using a term less clearcut than *omnium*, since the adjective *universus* sometimes means "all" and sometimes "pertaining to all." Hence, though Newton is not saying anything ambiguous in the statement of the rule, he is using an adjective which is such that it makes sense to apply to a quality. It is thus not surprising to find him *implicitly* applying it to qualities in the reasoning that follows the statement of the rule.

An adequate English translation is that given by I. Bernard Cohen: "are to be taken as the qualities of bodies universally."[7] The possibility of letting "universally" apply to either "bodies" or "qualities" allows this translation to capture the subtle ambiguity of Newton's expression, an ambiguity which obviously should be retained in a good translation.

One can now make two predictions and leave their testing to future research projects. First, it is conjectured that a scholarly examination of the Latin text of the explanatory remarks for Rule III will find either philological evidence suggesting our analysis or else further evidence of the deficiency of the Motte-Cajori translation. Second, it is conjectured that likenesses of the two rules that we have distinguished, IIIA and IIIB, exist among Newton's manuscripts relating to Rule III.

---

[6] Newton 1726, vol. III, pt. 1, p. 3.

[7] I. B. Cohen (1966, 173–76; 1971, 25). Professor Cohen (1971, 25 n. 7) does *notice* the peculiarity of Newton's language but seems to view the fact as a semantic eccentricity and linguistic aberration, for he relegates his comment to a footnote. Moreover, he regards as "permissible" what is basically Alexandre Koyré's translation in his "Newton's 'Regulae Philosophandi,'" namely "are to be taken as the qualities of all bodies" (Koyré 1965, 267), which is however insufficiently vague and too definite to be acceptable. At any rate Cohen's main concern is to contrast the *habendae sunt* of E_3 and E_2 with the mere *sunt* of $E_1 a$, $E_1 i$, and $E_1 l$, as we may designate the copy of E_1 given by Newton to Locke in the early 1690s, now found in the Trinity College Library (see I. B. Cohen 1971, 24).

Logic and Rhetoric in Lavoisier's Sealed Note

Toward a Rhetoric of Science (1977)

1. The Role of Argument and Rhetoric in Science

The interrelations among argument, rhetoric, and philosophy are well known in rhetorical circles, at least in the sense that they are widely discussed and argued about.[1] The same cannot be said of the interrelationships among argument, rhetoric, and science.[2] This question has, however, had been recently touched upon by philosophers of science.[3] The context has been the problem of scientific rationality and the question of whether the transition from one scientific theory to another can be made in a rational manner. The problem arose from the realization that, in the case of very fundamental scientific developments such as the Copernican revolution and the transition from classical to modern physics, purely logical considerations, rational argumentation, and appeals to the rules of scientific method are not enough to make a scientist change his mind. This realization was then generalized to conclude that the same limitation applies to all, or at least most, or at least the important and interesting, scientific developments. The generalization is I believe illegitimate,[4] but it has generated a lot of discussion and confusion. The

---

[1] See, for example, Johnstone 1959 and Natanson and Johnstone 1965.

[2] Johnstone's discussion of the distinction between science and philosophy does consider the role of argument in science, but not the role of rhetoric. Moreover, he makes it clear that the "science" he is talking about is not (or not necessarily) actual, historical science, but a clearly definable type of activity considered solely for the purpose of offering a contrast to what he takes philosophy to be.

[3] See, for example, Kuhn 1970b, especially pp. 144–60; Lakatos and Musgrave 1970, esp. pp. 1–24, 91–196, 197–278; and Feyerabend 1975, esp. chaps. 1, 12, 16, and 17.

[4] As I have argued in 1973c, 180–98.

more conservative philosophers of science, feeling that the rationality of science was being threatened, have tended to counterargue that transitions from one theory to another *can* be and have historically been made in a logical manner, using as evidence the admittedly less problematic minor transitions or at least the less problematic aspects of the major transitions. On the other hand, the more revolutionary philosophers have tended to reiterate their arguments. Moreover, these latter philosophers have drawn further conclusions from their generalizations about the limits of arguments in scientific changes. Some have concluded that the only sense in which science is rational is that the occurrence of scientific developments is explicable, that is that we can see how and why it comes about that one theory is abandoned and another one emerges in the scientific community. Other philosophers have concluded that the only sense in which science is rational is that scientific changes can be justified after the fact, in terms of an abstract ahistorical scheme which shows how and why the later theory is an improvement of the older one. Some other philosophers have simply concluded that science is an irrational enterprise, or at least no better than myth, magic, or witchcraft.[5] It is possible, however, in fact preferable, to draw the following conclusion.[6] In addition to argument, rhetoric is sometimes crucial in science; and hence, rhetoric has an important role to play in scientific rationality and the rhetorical aspects of science should not be neglected.

Let me illustrate some of what I have in my mind by reference to Galileo, who is a classic instance of the interplay between logical and rhetorical factors, and concerning whom Professor Feyerabend has recently gone so far as to suggest that his scientific success derives from the brilliance of his rhetoric, rather than from the strength of his arguments, which allegedly leave much to be desired.[7] Though the last part of this claim is not well founded, there is no question that Galileo's success is

---

[5] These three approaches are discussed in detail in Finocchiaro 1973a.

[6] Another very interesting conclusion to draw would be to say that important segments of actual, historical science exhibit features of what Johnstone calls "philosophy." The coincidences are, in fact, remarkable: for example, Johnstone speaks of conflicting philosophical statements lacking the property of being "logically commensurate," whereas Kuhn and Feyerabend speak of scientific theories being incommensurable; Johnstone (1959, 32) holds that the arguments for and against a philosophical statement are part of its meaning, whereas Kuhn and Feyerabend speak of meaning variance and hold that the meaning of scientific terms is theory dependent. This opens the way for vindicating the rationality of scientific revolutions by making use of Johnstone's theory of philosophical argumentation.

[7] Feyerabend 1975, chapters 6–12, especially pp. 81–92 and 141–61.

due partly to his rhetoric, but there is no conflict between good rhetoric and good logic (as Feyerabend seems to assume), and the more judicious conclusion is that his success was due to the combination of his rhetoric and logic.

In fact, Galileo's struggle for Copernicanism is a rhetorician's gold mine, and one hopes that scholars with an interest in both science and rhetoric will not neglect the opportunities it offers. Though this is not the place for a rhetorical analysis of Galileo's work, let me indicate some of these opportunities, by way of some questions. Let us restrict ourselves to the *Dialogue Concerning the Two Chief World Systems*,[8] the book he published in 1632 and for which he was tried and convicted by the Inquisition. Should the book be regarded as a rhetorical failure because of the fact that Galileo obviously failed to convince the Church to liberalize its attitude toward Copernicanism? Is the book a rhetorical failure in the light of the fact that, in writing a book on the prohibited topic of the earth's motion, Galileo failed to get away with it? Could it be that this type of rhetorical failure is due to the book's *logical success*, in the sense that, though not proving the earth's motion beyond any reasonable doubt, the book effectively demonstrates that there is no evidence or sound objection against the earth's motion, while there are *some* evidence and arguments in its favor? Since the book became very popular in the scientific circles of the time, and since Copernicanism eventually triumphed, was the book in *this* sense a rhetorical *success*? What are the logical and rhetorical connections between these three different points of view, from two of which the book appears a failure, and from the third of which it appears a success? Do the facts (1) that the book was written in Italian rather than Latin, and (2) that it was written in dialogue form, have a purely rhetorical function, or do they also have a logical function? What rhetorical difference did the change of title have, from *Dialogue on the Ebb and Flow of the Sea*, which Galileo initially suggested, which would have described only the fourth "Day" of the book, and which would have referred explicitly to one of Galileo's arguments in favor of Copernicanism, but which would have avoided any reference to the troublesome "World Systems"? What *exactly* are the roles of the book's three interlocutors, Salviati, Sagredo, and Simplicio? Does the considerable literary brilliance of the *Dialogue* have a rhetorical or logical function, or is it pure poetry? Can one formulate rhetorical principles which inhere in the way the material is arranged, this material being as rich as life itself?

[8] Galilei 1953; 1967.

If the rationality of scientific change and the rhetorical aspects of Galileo's work provide easy ways of coming to appreciate the problem of the interrelations among logic, rhetoric, and science, they are by no means the only way. The study of the logic and rhetoric of "sealed notes" is another avenue, and the one I wish to emphasize here. The practice whereby a scientist submits a sealed note to a scientific society was inaugurated by Robert Boyle (1627–1691) and followed by such individuals as Antoine Laurent Lavoisier (1743–1794) and Michael Faraday (1791–1867). Sealed notes are quite interesting from a rhetorical point of view insofar as the secrecy of such notes makes them look as if they were not acts of communication, at least as long as they remain sealed. However, since the note is to be unsealed at some future date, it presumably contains a message, namely, what the author wants to convey at that later date. Then the question arises as to whether the message that would be conveyed at that future date is one that could have been communicated at the time of writing. This question arises because the relevant situation is one where new knowledge is being acquired or created, and the possession of this knowledge can be expected to allow a subsequent interpretation of the note that was not possible at the time of writing, when that knowledge was lacking.

Professor Agassi has suggested that the practice of sealed notes has both philosophical and sociological roots.[9] Philosophically, it is the expression of the inductivist epistemology according to which ideas and speculations are less valuable than facts and observations, and hence the possession of unconfirmed speculative ideas is methodologically unsound, and hence one should not acknowledge them publicly but can record possessing them in secret documents. Sociologically, it tends to ensure priority claims, and hence it fosters research by making it psychologically profitable for an individual to engage in it. Since Agassi does not, however, comment on the rhetorical aspects of sealed notes, I shall do so. My inquiry, besides being a contribution toward a rhetoric of science, will also be a study of the interdependence of logic and rhetoric, specifically of the dependence of rhetoric on logic. In fact, the following analysis of Lavoisier's sealed note shows that its rhetorical content depends on the peculiarities of its logical structure; we might say that the note achieves a certain rhetorical success as a result of a certain logical lack of success.

[9] Agassi 1971, 41, 106, and 103–7.

2. Logical Analysis: A Four-fold Ambiguity

On November 2, 1772, Lavoisier deposited with the Secretary of the Academy of Science in Paris a sealed note, dated the previous day, which reads as follows:

> It is about eight days since I discovered that sulphur while burning, far from losing weight, instead gained some, that is to say that from a pound of sulphur one could get much more than a pound of vitriolic acid, setting aside the humidity of the air. It is the same with phosphorus. This increase in weight comes from a prodigious quantity of air which is fixed during the combustion and which combines with the vapors.
>
> This discovery, which I have established by experiments which I regard as decisive, made me think that what is observed in the combustion of sulphur and phosphorus could well happen with regard to all bodies which gain weight by combustion and calcination, and I became convinced that the weight increase of metallic calces is related to the same cause. Experiment has completely confirmed my conjectures. I performed the reduction of litharge in closed vessels with Hales' apparatus, and I observed that at the moment of change from calx to metal a considerable quantity of air is released and that it makes up a volume at least one thousand times greater than the litharge used. This discovery seemed to me one of the most interesting that has been made since Stahl, and because it is difficult not to let one's friends in conversation catch a glimpse of something that might put them on the road to the truth, I deemed it necessary to make this deposition into the hands of the Academy's secretary, while waiting till I make public my experiments.[10]

The first thing to note about this note is that there are four main conceptual elements: a so-called "discovery" described in the first paragraph, two so-called "conjectures" stated at the beginning of the second paragraph, and an "experimental observation" mentioned in the middle of the second paragraph. The last is the most easily stated. (A) When litharge changes to lead a great amount of air is released. Of the two conjectures, one is more general than the other. The specific one is that (B) the weight increase of metallic calces is caused by the absorption of air. The general conjecture is that (C) all bodies which gain weight by combustion and calcination, do so because they absorb air. It is a little more difficult to determine what exactly is the discovery of the first paragraph since three main propositions are mentioned in it: one is that sulphur gains, instead of losing, weight when burned; the second says that the same is true of phosphorus; and the third says that these weight gains are caused by the absorption of air. The weight increase of sulphur is obviously being given

---

[10] Guerlac 1961, 227–28. The translation is my own.

more importance than the phosphorus weight gain. It is also being given more importance than the statement about the cause of the weight gain because of the matter-of-fact tone of the causal statement, whereas to the sulphur weight gain the honorific term "discovered" is applied. An illuminating way of formulating the discovery described in the first paragraph would therefore be the following: (D) the absorption of air in the combustion of both sulphur and phosphorus causes them to gain weight. This formulation conveys the idea that what was been discovered is primarily an *effect*, namely the effect part of a cause-and-effect relationship where the cause is relatively less problematic and more easily ascertainable. Such an interpretation makes sense of the order, manner, and tone in which the various ideas in the first paragraph are stated.

Next, one of the first questions that the logical reader of this note feels is: What is the discovery which Lavoisier regards as one of the most interesting since Stahl? That is, what is the referent for the phrase "this discovery," with which the last sentence begins?

One possibility is that the discovery he is referring to is the observation mentioned in the previous sentence, namely that a considerable amount of air is released when a metallic calx such as litharge is reduced to the metal.

On the other hand, the release of air in the reduction of litharge is presented by Lavoisier as an experimental confirmation of some previous conjectures. For this reason, it may be these confirmed conjectures that constitute the alleged discovery. But the conjectures are two: one is an explanation of the calx weight gain effect, the other is a general casual relationship between absorption of air and weight gain in combustion and calcination. The claimed discovery could be the former since that is the one conjecture more directly confirmed by the experiment; but it could also be the latter since that is the more general idea.

Finally there is a further possibility. This derives from the fact that the discovery intended at the beginning of the last sentence could be the same one referred to by the same phrase at the beginning of the second paragraph, namely that sulphur and phosphorus gain weight in combustion because of the absorption of air.

Thus the initial impression is that it is not clear what is the discovery that Lavoisier is so proudly announcing and that there are reasons for thinking it is any one of the four propositions previously labeled (A), (B), (C), and (D).

Let us see whether the ambiguity can be eliminated by logical considerations, that is, by considering the explicit or implicit logical interrelationships among the four distinct propositions. For it might be that these four propositions naturally arrange themselves in such a way as to constitute a logical justification of only a particular one out of four. Then, insofar as the other three would be providing the basis for it, we might conclude that it is the reported discovery. Unfortunately this is not possible, for one can arrange the four propositions in four different ways, each equally plausible, and such that each of the four propositions is in turn the final conclusion in each of the four logical arrangements.

Let us consider first this arrangement:

(D) The absorption of air in the combustion of both sulphur and phosphorus causes them to gain weight. Therefore,
(C) all bodies which gain weight by combustion and calcination, do so because they absorb air. Therefore,
(B) the weight increase of metallic calces is caused by the absorption of air. Therefore,
(A) when litharge changes to lead a great amount of air is released.

The step from (D) to (C) would here be an inductive generalization step, from the cases of sulphur and phosphorus as instances which gain weight by burning. The step from (C) to (B) would be a deductive instantiation step, applying the generalization (C) to the special case of metallic calces. The step from (B) to (A) involves partly a deductive instantiation step, to get that (B-1) the weight *increase* of litharge (over lead) is caused by the *absorption* of air; the other step would involve a causal inference from (B-1) to saying that (B-2) a weight *decrease* of lead (from litharge) will be caused by a *release* of air; then (A) would be merely another way of stating (B-2).

The second arrangement would be: (A), so (B); so (C); so (D). Here, all the steps would be the inverse of the ones in the previous arrangement. (A) to (B-2) would be mere reformulation; (B-2) to (B-1) would be the same type of causal inference as before; (B-1) to (B) would be inductive generalization; (B) to (C) would also be inductive generalization; and (C) to (D) would be deductive instantiation.

The third arrangement is: (A), so (B); but (D); so (C). Here the steps from (A) to (B) would be the same as in the second arrangement. Then (D) would be merely asserted, though on the basis of experimental evidence; but this need not concern us here. The only other step in the argument would be from (B) and (D) to (C), and it would be an inductive generalization step, from the cases of metallic calces and sulphur and phosphorus as instances of bodies which gain weight by burning. The final conclusion here would obviously be (C).

The fourth arrangement is: (D), so (C); but (A); so (B). Here the step from (D) to (C) would be an inductive generalization, as in the first arrangement. The only other step would be from both (C) and (A) to (B); now one can go from (C) alone to (B) by deductive instantiation as in the first arrangement, and from (A) alone to (B) by reformulation, causal inference, and inductive generalization, as in the second arrangement; hence the soundness of this subargument from (C) and (A) to (B) would be greater than any of the other subarguments considered so far.

Now, one might argue that the first reconstruction is the most accurate because it reflects the reported sequence of ideas. To do this would be to assume that the reported sequence is a logical one; however, the sequence could be a chronological one, as is generally regarded by historians of science, by those who accept as well as by those who reject the accuracy of the reported chronology. But whether logical or chronological, the reported sequence is unambiguous, and this contrasts with the ambiguity of the announced discovery and of the logical structure in the note. Thus the ambiguity of the announced discovery cannot be resolved by logical analysis, that is by consideration of the note's logical structure.

3. Rhetorical Analysis: Historiographical Confirmation

Is there any other way of solving the problem? I believe there is. To do so one must, however, leave the logical point of view and abandon the attempt to eliminate the ambiguity. If we accept the logical ambiguity as a fact, we can then ask what rhetorical consequences follow. It so happens that the ambiguity makes good rhetorical sense. For Lavoisier may have had in mind the following as he wrote the note. If the theory of combustion and calcination (C) should turn out to be generally true, as it did, then Lavoisier could claim, as he did, that he had conceived it as early as the sealed note, as he did claim. If this general theory should turn out to be incorrect, then the explanation of the calx weight augmentation effect (B) might still be true, and Lavoisier might have claimed that it was this explanation that he had discovered in November, 1772; and the general theory (C) was merely an idea that made him think of (B). If even (B) should have turned out to be incorrect, then this need not have invalidated factual discovery (A), and so Lavoisier could have claimed that it was the latter that he had discovered, and the worst that could have happened to him would have been that his judgment about the significance of this factual discovery would have been wrong. If (A) had turned out to be wrong, then he could have claimed that his discovery had been (D), about which he was pretty confident.

All of these considerations support the historical thesis that on November 1, 1772, though Lavoisier thought he had made an important discovery, he did not know exactly what he had discovered. However, he did know exactly what to say in order that, when the note would be unsealed, he could claim that he had discovered something. Hence it is no surprise that the question of what Lavoisier really meant in the sealed note was never resolved. In fact, even today, we find historians of science opting for each of the four possibilities. They make their choices somewhat uncritically, that is, without awareness or discussion of issues such as the ones discussed here; hence, from this point of view one could criticize their claims. However, from another point of view, that is, from a metalevel, one can regard their claims as the intuitions and judgments of practitioners of the art, and then one can use them as evidence in support of my analysis. Hence it will be useful to produce the relevant evidence.

A search in the writings of Lavoisier scholars yields the following results. McKie is choosing (C) when he says that

in less than two months after embarking on his study of the combustion of phosphorus, Lavoisier was thus able to assert that phosphorus and sulphur on burning combined with air and gained weight, the gain in weight being due to their combination with air; and he had a shrewd suspicion that the long-known gain in weight of metals on calcination was due to the same cause. It was air itself, not any part or constituent of the air, that he supposed had entered into combination with the sulphur and the phosphorus in his experiments, and that combined with the metals to form calces and was given off from them on reduction with charcoal. It was an astonishing conclusion: in another realm of human thought, it would have been treated as extreme heresy, because it utterly contradicted accepted belief. But it was based on facts and facts alone. . . . Toward the end of his life, when his theory had been extended and developed and when it was being accepted by his contemporaries, Lavoisier had cause to quote this note of November 1, 1772, in support of his claim that he has formulated his theory of combustion as early as 1772.[11]

Guerlac is choosing (B) in interpreting the litharge experiment mentioned in the sealed note as a (circumstantially delayed) test for Lavoisier's hypothetical explanation of the calx weight gain effect.[12] Siegfried is also

---

[11] McKie 1952, 102–3.
[12] Guerlac 1961, especially pp. 194–95.

choosing (B) when he says that in the note "Lavoisier argued, rather typically, for more than was literally true. He stated that 'experiment has completely confirmed' that the increase in the weight of the calcined metal is owing to the fixation of air, but he offered as evidence only the reverse process, that air was liberated when the calx was reduced to the metal. This was strong evidence nonetheless, and he saw it as 'one of the most interesting discoveries that had been made since Stahl.'"[13] Kohler seems to be choosing (A) when he says that "in the sealed note Lavoisier characterized the experiment on lead calx as 'the most important since Stahl.'"[14] Finally, Crosland may be interpreted as choosing (D) when he says:

Lavoisier's interest and ambition for priority fully aroused, he deposited with the secretary of the Paris Academy of Science his famous sealed note which attributed the gain in weight in combustion and calcination to "air." The new experiment on which he based this far reaching conclusion was a quantitative one with sulphur. Far from finding that it had lost weight as would be expected by the phlogiston theory, he recorded a gain in weight, which he attributed to "a prodigious quantity of air which is fixed during the combustion." Lavoisier realized that he had discovered something of great significance and immediately began a systematic study of the calcination of metals.[15]

4. Two Conclusions

This analysis of the logical and rhetorical aspects of Lavoisier's sealed note has shown that from the logical point of view there exists in it a four-fold ambiguity, but that from a rhetorical standpoint a definite message is being conveyed by this very ambiguity. It would be wrong to generalize this result to conclude that logical ambiguity is rhetorically effective in science; rather, I believe that the correct generalizations are that (1) rhetoric has a function to play in science, and (2) rhetoric, though distinct from logic, is to be grounded on logic. Additional evidence for these conclusions is to be found not only in Galileo's work, and in the insufficiency of purely logical motivations for basic scientific changes, which I suggested above, but also in controversies such as those between Leibniz and Clarke, Boltzmann and Mach, and Einstein and Bohr. It should be noted that I have stated the second conclusion in a quite general manner,

[13] Siegfried 1972, 71–72.
[14] Kohler 1972, 355.
[15] Crosland 1973, 312.

not restricted to science; for the present investigation is intended not only to draw attention to the rhetorical dimension of science, but also to study the interplay between logical and rhetorical factors in general. Of course, a complete study of this interconnection would include a precise definition of "logical" and of "rhetorical"; however, the proper place for such definitions is at the end of such a series of investigations, not at the beginning, which is what we have here. Nevertheless, I wish to note that the notion of a logical factor I have used is one broad enough to include any process of reasoning and of evaluation of evidence, not merely demonstrative deductive inference. The interesting thing is that even when "inductive reasoning" is subsumed under the logical, there is still an interesting and important aspect of human reality which it is not improper to label "rhetorical."

21

The Concept of Judgment and Huygens' Theory of Gravity (1980)

1. Judgment in Science and in Philosophy of Science

The concept of scientific judgment has been constantly gaining currency in the philosophy of science. Though not yet so current as to have found its way into the main metascientific topics of *Current Research in Philosophy of Science* (Asquith and Kyburg 1978), the neglect is hardly surprising since the inclusion (to use Kant's beginning words in the *Prolegomena*) "must wait till those who endeavor to draw from the fountain of reason itself have completed their work; it will then be the turn of these [collections] to inform the world of what has been done" (Kant 1950, 3). Among those who are presently endeavoring "to draw from the fountain of reason" are Marx Wartofsky (1978), who regards the concept of judgment to be the key to the understanding of scientific discovery and creativity; Thomas Kuhn (1977), who regards it as essential in the process of theory choice; Harold Brown (1977, 145–51), for whom judgment is the central feature of scientific rationality; Thomas Nickles (1980, 39, 43–44), who takes it to be one of the main points of the transition from logicality to rationality; the present author (1977a, 95–96), for whom judgment is the positive, constructive, and defensible side of Feyerabend's move from method to anarchism; Joseph Weizenbaum (1976), whose critique of computer technology suggests a move from calculation to judgment; and Gerald Holton (1973; 1978), whose thematic analysis of scientific thought will be seen below to be intimately related to judgmental analysis.

The aim of the present chapter is to pursue this problematic further by exploring whether there is a common conceptual core in all these discussions of judgment and by analyzing a concrete instance of scientific work in its terms. It will turn out that the basic characteristics of judgment according to these discussions are judiciousness and synthesis, so that scientific judgment is being conceived as the judicious synthesis of opposite methodological ideals and of distinct methodological requirements. It will also turn out that judgment so conceived is constitutive of scientific thought in the sense that it inheres in the very contexts of discovery, pursuit, justification, and clarification of scientific ideas, and not merely in the contexts of philosophical, metaphysical, epistemological, and ethical reflection upon scientific results, or of their practical application. Moreover, such judgment will be shown to occur in the most unexpected works; in fact, my example will be Huygens' theory of gravity, which is usually regarded as a paradigm example of injudicious extremism for its alleged excessive mechanism and excessive Cartesianism. What this means is that the study of scientific judgment presupposes in a certain sense an awareness of and sensitivity to judgment, so that in our case the analysis of Huygens' judgment must be preceded by a historiographical critique of the methodological weakness (or lapses in judgment) found in studies of Huygens' theory of gravity.

2. The Literature on Judgment

In a critique of recent and widespread philosophies of science, Wartofsky (1978) argues that creativity and discovery are an undeniable and important fact of scientific thought (though neglected by recent philosophies of science), that the concept of (deductive, covering law) explanation is incapable of rendering comprehensible (of "explaining"!) scientific creativity and discovery, and that in order to understand such processes we need the category of "scientific judgment." Thus one of Wartofsky's main acceptable points is that judgment plays an important role in science and ought to do so also in the philosophy of science.

A second main point to be accepted is that the judgmental analysis of science is a type of methodological analysis. In fact, Wartofsky claims that this concept "is analogous to that of aesthetic judgment in the arts, clinical judgment in medicine, judicial judgment in law, technological judgment in engineering and applied science, and practical judgment in moral, social and personal contexts" (1978, 35); it involves an analysis of "the strategies or rules of art that were involved in the creative thought processes in science … not … a step by step sequence of thoughts which follow each other in accordance with the rules of inference, i.e. deductively" (Wartofsky 1978, 40). In such a judgmental way of understanding science, one gives "*a heuristic* account, i.e. one which guides us in understanding the creative process by reconstructing the strategies, the methodological rules, the modes of judgment that were involved in a given process of discovery or invention in science" (Wartofsky 1978, 41).

Third, we find Wartofsky claiming that "the category of judgment, in general, is one which suggests the synthesis, the bringing together of things – ideas, concepts, the subject and predicate of a proposition – in such a way that a relation among them is brought to light" (1978, 44). The crucial point here is the reference to synthesis or to bringing together in general; the items mentioned as susceptible of synthesis are merely illustrative. The fruitfulness of such a synthetic judgment will be seen presently.

A fourth insight of Wartofsky's concerns the practical and casuistical nature of scientific judgment: "its quality lies in the ability to interpret general maxims in specific instances, where the interpretation is not given by a rule, or a definition. It is eminently a matter of learning *in practice* how to make such judgments: but not simply a matter of learning inductively from past practice" (1978, 46).

Finally, Wartofsky hints at how one (in philosophy) can use judgment to learn about judgment in science when he says that "the paradigmatic mode of giving an account of scientific judgment is the same as the mode of acquiring it: by example . . . the account would be an account of examples, of actual exercises in judgment given specific boundary conditions, or problem situations, or a reconstruction of historical cases" (1978, 46). The importance of this principle in the present context ought to be emphasized; it is what gives full philosophical status to the investigation undertaken below.

In a recently published essay Kuhn (1977) discusses explicitly the importance of judgment for theory choice. This represents a significant clarification of his earlier remarks that "paradigm choice can never be unequivocally settled by logic and experiment alone" (1962, 93; 1970b, 94) and that "paradigm change cannot be justified by proof " (1962, 151; 1970b, 152). It also is clearly what he was groping toward when, in another intermediate essay, he had analyzed theory choice in terms of individual decisions in the light of certain shared scientific values (1970a, 235–41, 259–66).

Kuhn's latest essay begins by supporting the claim that theory choice "depends on a mixture of objective and subjective factors, or of shared and individual criteria" (1977, 325). He argues cogently that the

subjective or individual criteria are an undeniable fact of scientific inquiry (1977, 321–25), and that their dismissal by recent philosophers
stems from a confusion of the context of justification with the context
of pedagogy (1977, 326–28) and from a failure to appreciate the importance for justification of the context of discovery, which they admit
contains "subjective" elements (1977, 328). Moreover, he interprets the
eventual unanimity of choice characteristic of "normal science" in terms
of a convergence of *answers or concrete choices* based partly on different
individual criteria and decision *processes*, rather than as evidence of the
non-existence of such differences (1977, 328–29).

The more important part of Kuhn's argument deals with the "objective" or shared criteria. He shows that methodological criteria such as
accuracy, consistency, simplicity, scope, and fruitfulness "function not as
rules, which determine choice, but as values, which influence it" (p. 331).
Once more, for him this is both an historical fact about science and a
philosophical desideratum; otherwise scientific progress would be impossible since the introduction of new scientific theories "*requires* a decision
process which permits rational men to disagree" (p. 332) without ceasing
to be scientists (p. 331).

This idea of the indeterminate but influential nature of methodological criteria is crucially important and deserves some elaboration. Kuhn
speaks of the imprecision (p. 322) and "ambiguity of application" (p. 331)
of each criterion by itself, and of the mutual conflict (pp. 322, 330)
among the criteria collectively. What Kuhn means is explained by him
with the help of an analogy to proverbial maxims and to social values.
Each methodological criterion presumably contains an internal opposition or contrast between two polar extremes analogous to proverbs:
"Contrast 'He who hesitates is lost' with 'Look before you leap,' or compare 'Many hands make light work' with 'Too many cooks spoil the broth'"
(p. 330); for example, scope is "an important scientific value, but important scientific advances have repeatedly been achieved at its expense"
(p. 335). Moreover, different methodological criteria usually suggest different choice of theory analogously to the situation with social values:
"improving the quality of life is a value, and a car in every garage once
followed from it as a norm. But quality of life has other aspects, and
the old norm has become problematic. Or again, freedom of speech is
a value, but so is preservation of life and property" (p. 330); for example, "the consistency criterion, by itself, therefore, spoke unequivocally
for the geocentric tradition. Simplicity, however, favored Copernicus"
(pp. 323–24). In view of such internal ambivalence and external

conflict, methodological criteria thus need arbitration similar to that of "judicial soul-searching" (p. 330). Here the category that naturally comes to mind is that of scientific judgment,[1] which may therefore be conceived as the synthesis of opposite methodological ideals (such as generality of scope and specificity of reference), and of distinct requirements (such consistency and simplicity).

One of the most explicit proponents of judgment is Harold I. Brown. In his sketch of a "new philosophy of science" he argues that "it is the case in which we must rely on human judgment that I propose to take as the paradigm of a situation in which reason is required" (Brown 1977, 148). This is contrasted to the traditional philosophy of science, one of whose main goals "has been to remove the scientist from the decision making process and replace him with a set of algorithms" (Brown 1977, 146). Not that Brown denies the importance of algorithms; but he thinks that the reason for their importance has not been properly appreciated; it is that "when we establish one [algorithm] for dealing with a problem it is no longer necessary to devote human thought to that problem and our efforts and reason are freed to work in other directions" (1977, 148). Thus one element of Brown's concept of judgment is the common one that stems from the contrast with computability or calculability, and it is thus analogous to that suggested by Weizenbaum (1976), as will be seen below.

A second element in Brown's concept is claimed by him to derive from Aristotle's discussion of the man of practical wisdom. From this point of view, judgment is something that "require[s] deliberation, the ability to weigh information and make decisions in cases in which there is no necessary knowledge" (Brown 1977, 148). The third component of Brown's "judgment" is adapted by him from Aristotle's discussion of equity: "it is the ability to decide how an exceptional case should be treated" (1977, 149). Finally, for Brown too judgment involves what was called above the synthesis of opposites; he is expressing this idea when he speaks of judgment as the arbitrator of conflicts and discrepancies, such as that between theory and observation (1977, 147–67).

In a critique of the moral abuses of computer technology, Weizenbaum (1976) has made a plea for more emphasis on judgment and less on

---

[1] Though it is obvious that this is the *concept* in Kuhn's mind, as far as the *word* "judgment" is concerned, Kuhn uses it in another sense and in another context, rather than this one. There a judgment is a statement of opinion subject to potential dispute and discussion, and he contrasts that to an indisputable expression of taste (1977, 336–37).

calculation, both in science in general and in computer science in particular. He considers the concept of judgment so important that he refers to
the computer-fed trend he criticizes as a movement "from judgment to
calculation." His critique is based on a judgmental philosophy of science
to the effect that "all empirical science is an elaborate structure built
on piles that are anchored, not on bedrock as is commonly supposed,
but on the shifting sand of fallible human judgment, conjecture, and
intuition" (Weizenbaum 1976, 14–15). He supports this thesis with the
generalization that "scientific demonstrations, even mathematical proofs,
are fundamentally acts of persuasion" (Weizenbaum 1976, 15). The reason he gives for this is, in turn, that "scientific statements can never be
certain; they can be only more or less credible. And credibility is a term
of individual psychology, i.e., a term that has meaning only with respect
to an individual observer. To say that some proposition is credible is,
after all, to say that it is believed by an agent who is free not to believe
it, that is, by an observer who, after exercising judgment and (possibly)
intuition, chooses to accept the proposition as worthy of his believing
it" (Weizenbaum 1976, 16). I welcome the general direction of these remarks and have elsewhere expressed similar ideas (Finocchiaro 1977b;
1978b; 1980b). Here I wish to make some qualifications to, and elaborations of, Weizenbaum's arguments. First, the concept of judgment can
be explored at the methodological level, besides the scientific-statement
level mentioned by him. That is, we must recognize that rules of scientific
procedure can never be absolutely binding; they can only be more or less
fruitful, as Feyerabend (1975) might say. Judgment is required to choose
the time, place, and extent of application. Second, such a judgmental
philosophy of science can be also supported by empirical arguments, as
it were; that is, with evidence from the history of science. I do not wish to
be misleading in calling such arguments "empirical," and so I hasten to
add that the detection and retrieval of judgment from scientific practice
may require a certain amount of commitment to or sensitivity about the
concept in the first place. The case study given below provides a good illustration in this respect, for it involves Huygens' theory of gravity, which
is often taken as a paradigm example of injudiciousness in the sense of
extreme and exaggerated mechanism. However, it turns out that such interpretations are themselves injudicious, in that they violate or misapply
a number of plausible methodological principles.

　　Finally, one of the most fruitful and insightful recent approaches to
the understanding of science is what Holton calls the "thematic analysis of scientific thought" (1973, 11–44; 1978, 3–24). Themata are "those

fundamental preconceptions of a stable and widely diffused kind that are not resolvable into or derivable from observation and analytic ratiocination" (Holton 1973, 24). In saying that they are not so resolvable Holton means that themata operate in a dimension of science outside the plane in which effective and decidable verification and falsification can take place (1973, 23; 1978, 9). Though he does not use the *term* "judgment," since a clear element in this concept is its contrast to algorithmic decidability, it is obvious that Holton is talking about the judgmental features of scientific thought.

According to Holton, an extremely important

finding of thematic analysis that appears to be related to the dialectic nature of science as a public, consensus-seeking activity is the frequent coupling of two themata in antithetical mode, as when a proponent of the thema of atomism finds himself faced with the proponent of the thema of the continuum. Antithetical (Θ, $\neg\ \Theta$) couples – such as evolution and devolution, constancy and simplicity, reductionism and holism, hierarchy and unity, the efficacy of mathematics (for example, geometry) versus the efficacy of mechanistic models as explanatory tools – are not too difficult to discern, particularly in cases that involve a controversy or a marked advance beyond the level of common work. [Holton 1978, 10]

This corresponds to what above I called the synthetic nature of judgment. In discerning such "thema-antithema" pairs Holton (1978, 11) is trying to detect what I would call judgment at work.

Three types of themata are distinguished by Holton (1978, 9): conceptual, methodological, and propositional. This distinction is valid and important, and he deserves credit for not restricting himself to methodological themata only. However, my own interest is in the latter. Thus the judgmental analysis given below may be regarded as a type of what Holton would call "thematic analysis."

3. Huygens Scholarship

Almost all accounts of Huygens' theory of gravity are rather negative in the sense that the consensus seems to be that it had little if any scientific or philosophical significance. For example, Koyré sees it as an instance of excessive Cartesianism, when he says that "Newton had achieved something that Huygens, having discovered the law of centrifugal force, could have done . . . but did not. . . . Huygens paid a tremendous price for his fidelity to Cartesian rationalism *à outrance*" (Koyré 1965, 116). Similarly, Dijksterhuis (1961, 463) views it as a sign of excessive mechanicism. These interpretations are not unfounded. In fact, Cartesianism is confessed in the *Discourse on the Cause of Gravity* when Huygens (1690, 16)[2] explicitly tells us that before Newton's *Principia* he had had the idea that the sun's spherical shape might be due to the same cause that produces terrestrial sphericity, but that he had not extended the action of gravity to interplanetary distances because Descartes's vortices which he accepted at that time had been in the way. Similarly, Huygens is confessing his mechanicism when he tells us, in the opening paragraph of that work, that in order to find the cause of gravity one must explain it in terms of bodies which possess only shape, size, and motion (p. 129). Though not unfounded, these interpretations are problematic because the weight of supporting evidence is of the order required for positive interpretations, namely those which identify a value, a meaning, or a good feature in the work being considered. In short, I am suggesting the adoption of a principle analogous to the one required in jurisprudence, where the standards of proof in criminal cases are stricter than for civil cases; that is, the principle that negative, critical interpretations must be supported with stronger evidence than positive, appreciative ones. Moreover, I am asserting that the usual attributions of excessive Cartesianism and mechanicism to Huygens violate that historiographical principle, when they are contrasted with more appreciative interpretations.

In fact, it is not impossible to find a few positive interpretations. For example, in his book *The Science of Mechanics* Ernst Mach emphasizes Huygens' noticing and correct explanation of the apparent decrease in gravitational acceleration near the equator, and his correct argument that Descartes's rotating cylinder experiments (with wood and lead or water) were misconceived since they would imply that lighter bodies would move toward the center more easily than heavier ones (Mach 1960, 188–89). A. E. Bell in his book *Christian Huygens and the Development of Science in the Seventeenth Century* emphasizes Huygens' distinction between mass and weight in the *Discourse* where he discusses how "the weights of bodies keep the same proportion as the quantity of matter which is in them" (Bell 1947, 162–63). More recently, in an article in *Physis*, Riccardo Bogazzi (1977) has undertaken a philosophical appreciation of the *Kosmotheoros* which places it in the tradition of Reformation freedom of thought and among the precursors of the Enlightenment; though Bogazzi makes only incidental references to the *Discourse*, the implication is clear that it too could undergo a similar type of re-examination, though his

---

[2] Further references to Huygens' *Discourse* of 1690 are so numerous that they will be given by merely writing the page number(s) in parentheses.

historiographical analogy applies only at the level of general method to be followed, rather than substantive result obtained.

And this brings me to the distinction between method and result. For it may be that it is the failure to maintain this distinction that is at the root of the negativity of the usual accounts of Huygens' theory of gravity. The reasoning here would be that since the basic idea of that theory is physically false, Huygens' method must also have been basically incorrect; and then excessive Cartesianism or mechanicism emerges as the most obvious candidate for the method-cause. The part of this argument that infers methodological incorrectness from physical falsehood is clearly wrong, and we may let Huygens himself speak against it. This occurs in the Preface to the *Discourse* where he explains his relationship to Descartes as one of substantive opposition but methodological agreement: "I acknowledge that his [Descartes's] experiments and his view, though false, have served to open to me the way to what I have discovered on the same topic" (p. 127).

This quotation also leads to another historiographical distinction which pertains to the part of the above-mentioned argument that infers Cartesianism and mechanism from methodological incorrectness. For one may now ask, Doesn't this quotation (plus the others one may compile) prove Huygens' Cartesianism, indeed his methodological Cartesianism? I would answer this question by saying that such quotations only prove that Huygens *thought* he was a Cartesian,[3] that is, that Huygens' awareness, self-conception, or philosophy of science was more or less Cartesian, not that his actual science was. To see this we need what may be called the theory/practice distinction. The operative principle here must be that an examination of what someone *says about* his science yields conclusions about the character of his theory of science, while to arrive at a view about the character of someone's actual method one needs to examine what the subject actually does, namely his scientific practice. Thus we need to study the details of Huygens' actual procedure in the *Discourse*. We need to do this in addition to the other two tasks derived from the earlier desiderata, namely we need to distinguish substantive scientific results from methodological procedures and refrain from simple inferences from the incorrectness of results to the incorrectness of

---

[3] Interesting and important qualifications and limitations to Huygens' Cartesianism have also been discussed by Westman (1980) in a paper presented at the Huygens 350th Anniversary Symposium, Amsterdam, 22–25 August 1979. He concentrates on the cultural, psychological, and sociological aspects of the problem.

methods, and we need to counterbalance the excessive negativism that characterizes scholars' accounts of Huygens' method in his theory of gravity by searching for some positive meaning in it.

Before we examine the details of Huygens' methodological practice in the *Discourse*, methodological duty demands and my inclination relishes saying a word about what is perhaps the most sophisticated recent study of Huygens from a philosophical viewpoint, by Aant Elzinga (1971; 1972a; 1972b).[4] I have little hesitation in placing my analysis in the tradition of his approach to Huygens, insofar as his study is positive and appreciative and mindful of the above distinctions; in fact, the distinction between theory and practice is made by him in terms of "research practice" and "theory of research" (Elzinga 1971, 175ff.); and the distinction between method and result is referred to by him when he speaks of cognitive processes for the production of knowledge versus final products of those processes (Elzinga 1971, 176ff.). I would also approve his distinctions between context of discovery and context of presentation, and between theory of scientific research and general theory of knowledge, which he skillfully uses in his study, even though I will have no occasion to apply them in my present analysis. Finally, I do not shy away from presenting my own main result as a refinement and deepening of his own, which I take to be as follows: Elzinga interprets Huygens generally as an opponent of both Cartesian intellectualism and Baconian empiricism (1972a, 26), and as a follower of the Galilean synthesis of theory and experience (1972a, 9); a few specific insights attributed to him are (1972a, 26) the abandonment of the certainty ideal and the awareness of the fallibilism, probabilism, and improvability of science; Archimedean rigor with respect to the reasoning from principles to conclusions; and an awareness of the need of mere persuasion in the justification of principles. My own elaboration of Elzinga's central thesis is that Huygens displays a judicious synthesis of not merely theory and experience, but also of such other opposites as mathematical quantification and qualitative considerations, precision and approximations, criticism and understanding of others, etc. In other words, the theory/experience dichotomy is not rich enough and needs to be supplemented by such other ones. Moreover, my analysis exhibits Huygens' synthetic judiciousness in his research practice, whereas

---

[4] I will discuss only Elzinga 1971 and 1972a since this pair of articles make up chapter II of his book (1972b), and since the additional material in the latter is relevant primarily to Elzinga's own research program stemming from *Criticism and the Growth of Knowledge* (Lakatos and Musgrave 1970).

Elzinga tends to emphasize the theory of research, with respect to which the case for the judiciousness thesis cannot be very well made on the basis of the *Discourse*. Third, Elzinga shows a correct understanding of the Galilean method when he eloquently says that "Galileo's theory of research does not prescribe any set of rules of procedure which might help to 'automatize' research work . . . [but] leaves the decisive work, that of interpretation of the abstract model constructions arrived at, to the judiciousness of the research-worker" (1971, 190). However, the evidence he gives in support of this interpretation often betrays a misunderstanding of Galileo's particular procedures and views, e.g., in his reference to Galileo's alleged belief in "circular inertia" (Elzinga 1971, 186–88), and alleged practice of thought experiments rather than actual experiments (Elzinga 1971, 186).[5] But these are minor matters, which ought not to obscure the considerable meta-methodological, methodological, and historical affinities between his studies and the one attempted here.

4. Judgmental Analysis of Huygens' *Discourse on the Cause of Gravity*

Let us now turn to Huygens' *Discourse on the Cause of Gravity*. Aside from the Preface, the *Discourse* has three main parts: a basic theory of gravity written in Paris for presentation at the royal academy in 1669 (pp. 129–45); a discussion of pendulum deviations due to terrestrial rotation (pp. 145–52); and an appendix occasioned by Newton's *Principia* (pp. 152–80).

The Preface starts with a brief critique of past explanations of the fall of heavy bodies. Since the cause of gravity is not apparent to the senses, Huygens finds it understandable that it has been traditionally attributed to an internal and inherent quality of bodies; however, he objects that this explanation assumes principles that are obscure and not understood. He then criticizes the atomists for being somewhat inconsistent when they attempt to explain all phenomena in terms of atoms, but for the case of gravity they give atoms themselves this property. Contemporary explanations in terms of some external cause are said to be more nearly right, but none is deemed acceptable. Some postulate a subtle and heavy fluid that makes the bodies descend by pressing on them; these explanations are circular since the alleged cause has the property being explained, and they are mechanically misconceived since such a fluid would make

---

[5] After the completion of Elzinga's work, Stillman Drake (1978) discovered new documentary evidence proving beyond a reasonable doubt Galileo's extensive practice of actual experimentation.

bodies go up rather than down. The explanations in terms of immaterial
spirits and emanations are contemptuously dismissed as failing to clarify
anything.

The most striking feature of these critiques is Huygens' judiciousness:
his contemptuous dismissal of the immaterial theory is balanced by his
understanding attitude toward the internal-quality explanation; while his
obvious preference for his own kinetic theory, presently to be expressed,
does not prevent him from giving an essentially internal criticism of the
atomistic theory and of the fluid explanation.

Next, Huygens clarifies his attitude toward Cartesian mechanism.
Here, though he praises Descartes for having recognized that physical explanations must be formulated in terms of the motion of bodies, Huygens
also clarifies that his own commitment to this principle stems from his
wish to restrict himself to "principes qui n'excedent pas la portée de notre
esprit" (p. 126), which I take to be neither a metaphysical nor a dogmatic
principle, but a respectable methodological one. His sense of balance is
further shown when he goes on to express, as remarked above, his rejection of Descartes's substantive thesis coupled with an adherence to the
method followed. Finally, on the one hand Huygens is of the opinion that
if his principal hypothesis is not true, then there is no hope for the true
and healthy philosophy; on the other hand, he confesses that he does
not regard it as exempt from all doubt or objection. Thus we see that the
preface is pervaded by a sense of compromise and of balance between
extremes (which I am here terming judiciousness) in his attitude toward
alternative theories of gravity, toward Descartes, and toward mechanism.
Since this will be seen to be the leading feature of the whole *Discourse*, it
has been instructive for us to give such a relatively lengthy analysis of the
short Preface.

The first few paragraphs of the *Discourse* elaborate the following
argument: gravity must be explained in terms of only the sizes, shapes,
and motions of bodies; it obviously has nothing to do with size and shape;
hence it must be due to some motion; now, motion is naturally straight or
circular; but straight motion cannot produce a tendency toward a center,
which is the main and most common feature of gravity; thus, it must be
explained in terms of circular motion (pp. 129–30).

One cannot deny that this argument may be taken as evidence of Huygens' mechanicism. However one must admit that we also have a plea
for utilizing the concept of circular motion. Now, if we remember that
the theory of circular motion is Huygens' prized discovery and invention,
then the argument also becomes evidence of a desire to apply, extend, and

elaborate one's previous accomplishments. Psychologically speaking this might be described as self-centeredness, but I do not wish to suggest that it was improper, for a certain amount of self-regard may be good. Indeed, perhaps Arthur Koestler's theory elaborated in his book *The Act of Creation* is right; perhaps, as he says, "the sublime balance between self-asserting and self-transcending motives . . . [is] the true scientist's hallmark" (1964, 679). Thus, the question for the present investigation would become whether Huygens shows self-transcendence besides self-centeredness. It seems that he does, the supporting evidence being that the whole discourse is in one sense a discussion of the views of Descartes and of Newton. I do not wish to give the impression that I accept Koestler's theory *in toto*. Rather I am discussing this particular dichotomy (between self and other) merely as the one which is relevant at this place in the *Discourse*, in accordance with my main project of detecting and analyzing Huygens' judgment at work.

At any rate, independently of Huygens' personal involvement with the theory of circular motion, what we have here is an attempt to apply it to a new phenomenon, which becomes especially significant in the light of the prima facie absurdity (mentioned by Huygens himself) of deriving motion toward the center from the tendency away from the center that characterizes circular motion. If such an apparent paradox can be shown to be merely apparent and not real, then the theory of circular motion would receive a spectacular and impressive confirmation. In short, by focusing on the circular motion and centrifugal force aspect of Huygens' research program, then it becomes easier to see him acting in accordance with the methodological requirement that it is good to try to expand the explanatory power of a theory as much as possible. If we then ask whether Huygens is doing this excessively, namely past the point of diminishing returns, and thus showing injudiciousness, the answer is that he is doing so only from the point of view of the general mechanist program, not from our chosen point of view of the theory of circular motion. In fact, the kinetic theory of gravity deriving from the former does represent a diminished return for Huygens' effort in the *Discourse*, whereas his detection of the mass/weight distinction and of latitudinal weight variations represent rich returns deriving from the circular motion program.

The *Discourse* continues with the following critical appreciations of Descartes. Descartes deserves the credit for having been the first to have had, in general, the idea of explaining gravity by circular motion, however his explanation is defective in its details (p. 130). For one of the experiments he proposes involves a cylinder full of a mixture of small wood chips and lead balls, the effect being that during the rotation the wood goes to the middle; this is wholly inappropriate since the experiment implies the contrary of the truth, namely that bodies with less matter weigh more (p. 133). Another experiment proposed by Descartes involved dropping some wood bits onto a rotating cylinder full of water, the alleged effect being that the wood goes toward the middle; however, if he means wood that floats, the alleged effect will not happen, whereas if he means wood that sinks, then the effect does happen but the cause is the wood's slower circular motion due to its touching the bottom of the cylinder (pp. 133–34). In fact, the theory of centrifugal force tells us that in a fluid rotating in a round space from which it cannot escape, a body rotating slower than the fluid will be pushed toward the center as the neighboring fluid closer to the center experiences greater centrifugal force (pp. 131–32). This is confirmed by an experiment with a closed cylindrical vessel containing water and pieces of Spanish wax: before rotation the wax, being heavier than water, sinks to the base; upon starting the rotation, the wax moves toward the circumference, since its friction with the base allows it to follow the rotation more easily than the water; if the rotation is stopped, the wax collects at the center by spiral paths, since that same friction slows it down more easily than the water; if a ball is constrained by strings attached to the vessel to move only along a diameter at the base, then it follows a straight path toward the center once the cylinder is stopped, even if it weighs the same as the water (pp. 132–33).

Huygens' balance here is shown from the fact that he can both appreciate and criticize Descartes. This is obvious from the way I have reconstructed the passage. Less obvious perhaps, but more interesting, and at any rate equally real, is Huygens' synthesis between the two standard and commonly mentioned polarities of theory and observation. We do not have a mere juxtaposition here, but a real synthesis, since Huygens is explicit that first (pp. 131–32) he is describing an abstract situation conceivable within the theory of circular motion, and then (pp. 132–33) he describes an experimental situation where certain phenomena are observed. As these observations are reported in turn, they are then explained in conformity with the theory.

Before proceeding further, it may be useful to summarize our results so far. We have found Huygens to proceed in such a way as to reconcile such opposites as: forgiving understanding of error and arrogant assertion of the truth, Cartesianism and anti-Cartesianism, self-confidence and skepticism, self-centeredness and self-transcendence, vigorous exploitation of novelties (circular motion) and attachment to older views (kinetics), and lastly, theory and observation.

Next comes one of the best known parts of the *Discourse*, Huygens' basic theory of gravity. The theory is introduced by him with the analogy argument that, since the Spanish-wax experiment provides an effect which is similar to terrestrial gravity, the unknown cause of the latter should be similar to the known cause of the former (p. 134). Thus the important thing for us to analyze is how Huygens handles the analogy. First of all we should note that he is well aware that an argument from analogy does not produce certainty, for when he comes around to stating his conclusion he qualifies it with the word "vraisemblablement," saying that gravity probably consists in the effort, by the postulated fluid matter circling the earth in all directions, to move away from its center and to push in its place slower-circling bodies (p. 137). As for the extent of the analogy itself, Huygens seems to have the right idea about how far to carry it and how far not to carry it: the unidirectional cylindrical motion of the experiment is replaced by a spherical motion in all directions, since gravity is *not* perpendicular to the earth's axis (pp. 134–35); to the water in the experimental model there corresponds an hypothetical fluid matter of very small particles and very great speed, since all known substances have weight (pp. 135–37); and the retarding agent, which in the experiment was the bottom of the cylinder, now becomes an hypothetical second fluid matter whose particles are bigger than the first but smaller than air (pp. 137–38). The features that are the same are the circular motion, of course, plus the inability of the rotating fluid to escape from its area of operation, which is postulated for the space surrounding the earth (p. 135). Huygens tries to balance the unfamiliarity of some of the entities and processes he postulates by referring to familiar situations: the (first) fluid matter's circular motion in all directions is compared to the turnings of the little lead drop in the assaying of silver, to the turnings of a candle flame as it is about to be extinguished with a pair of snuffers, and to the agitations of boiling water particles (p. 136); the second fluid matter is said to be the same that Huygens found necessary to explain his vacuum observations (pp. 135–36); while the invisibly minute size of both is said to create no problem since they are probably no smaller when compared to a grain of sand than the latter is compared to a mountain (pp. 138–39). Whatever one thinks of the correctness of these comparisons and contrasts, there is nothing objectionable in the general procedure.

In the last discussion of this first section of the *Discourse* (pp. 139–45), it looks at first as if Huygens is explaining four other features of gravity, besides the primary one of tendency toward the center already accounted for.[6] Accordingly he explains that the reason "why the action of gravity cannot be impeded by the interposition of any known body" (p. 145) is that the matter which causes gravity has particles so small that it "passes very freely through all bodies regarded as solid, with the same facility with which it goes through air" (p. 139). Second, the reason "why the internal parts of each body all contribute to its weight" (p. 145) is that particles of these bodies "have perfect solidity" (p. 140). Third, the reason why "heavy bodies, in falling, always accelerate their motion even when they have already acquired a very great degree of speed" (p. 144) is that the speed of the subtle matter is extremely high, and, to be more exact, about seventeen times greater than the rotational speed of a point at the equator (pp. 143–44). Finally, the reason why the increase in the speed of fall is proportional to the time is that, for cases of fall in ordinary experience, the subtle matter acts continually on bodies with the same force. When so viewed, only the fourth explanation is more or less plausible; in the third the connection between cause and effect is unintelligible, and Huygens may be confusing circular speeds with vertical ones; and the properties postulated in the first two explanations are ad hoc. I would regard this interpretation as giving undue weight to evidence from the context of theory, which in this case consists of Huygens' summary at the end of the discussion (p. 145), and his analysis in the "Table of Contents"; moreover, its supporting evidence is equal to or less than the following interpretation, which is therefore preferable.

In this passage Huygens is discussing the problem of "what produces the different weight of bodies,"[7] criticizing Descartes's theory, and offering the correct explanation that the cause is differences in their respective quantities of matter. Huygens' own view is that the gravity-causing fluid can easily pass through the interstices among the material particles of all known bodies, but not through the material particles themselves; the sum of the volumes of these particles, which defines the quantity of matter in a given body, determines the amount of gravity-causing fluid which is needed to displace the body; the latter amount, in turn, is a measure of the body's weight (pp. 139–140). His criticism is that in certain places

---

[6] Cf. the summary in Huygens 1690, 45, as well as his description in the unpaginated "Table des Matières."

[7] This is Huygens' wording in the "Table des Matières."

Descartes (1644, pt. IV, prop. 20, 22, 27)[8] speaks as if the "gravific" matter is impeded by the earth; this is wrong because bodies do not lose weight inside a mine, or when enclosed by glass or metals (pp. 139, 141). More importantly, Descartes was wrong in emphasizing the weight of the surrounding medium and the agitation of the body's particles, rather than the quantity of matter; for example, he thought that if a piece of gold weighs twenty times more than an equal volume of water, it contains only four or five times more matter (1644, pt. IV, prop. 25). Huygens' criticism here is merely quantitative: though the weight of an equal volume of air must be added to both the gold and the water, this does not appreciably change the ratio of their weights since air weighs about 1/800 as much as water (p. 141); and though the speed of a particle does affect its weight, the relevant speed is circular around the earth (pp. 141–42); moreover, the magnitude of this speed needed to decrease its weight noticeably is probably much more than the speed of agitation of water, since calculations based on the theory of circular motion show that the gravific matter rotates seventeen times faster than a point on the equator (pp. 142–43).

Thus, what we have in this passage, methodologically speaking, is partly some further evidence for Huygens' independence of mind vis-à-vis Descartes. We also see that Huygens is constructive as well as destructive in his criticism, since several positive results emerge. Finally, and this is a new point, but one which will be met again in what follows, Huygens is judicious in his quantitative reasoning, in the sense that he introduces quantitative considerations when really needed, rather than unthinkingly or dogmatically, and he limits himself to qualitative considerations when these suffice.

The second part of the *Discourse* (pp. 145–52) discusses some effects of the earth's rotation. There are two strands in it: one is a synthesis between explanation of known facts and prediction of novel ones; the other consists of mathematical demonstrations impressive for their balance between precision and approximation. Huygens begins by citing the observational report that the length of a pendulum beating seconds has been found to be shorter at the equator than at Paris by $1\frac{1}{4}$ line-fractions of a foot. Qualitatively speaking, his explanation is that this is due to the centrifugal force of the earth's daily rotation, which decreases the felt weight as compared to a motionless earth, so that the period is slowed (p. 146). But he needs a quantitative analysis of the problem because

---

[8] Notice that the Latin text of section IV, 20 is much more revealing than the French translation.

of his interest in using pendulum clocks to determine longitude, so that tables would have to be complied to correct for the deviations in their periods (pp. 150–51). Thus Huygens first uses his previous result of 1/17 (for the ratio of the equatorial speed to the rotational speed of the gravific fluid) to arrive at the figure of 1/289 (which is the square of 1/17) for the weight loss or pendulum-shortening at the equator compared to the pole (pp. 146–47). From this he calculates that the analogous figure for the Paris latitude is 1/668, using the theorem proved here that the equatorial deviation is to the Paris one as the square of the distances from the terrestrial axis to the respective places (pp. 147–49, 151). Changing that figure to line-fractions of a foot, he concludes that the shortening of the seconds-pendulum from Paris to the equator should have been 5/6 of a line (p. 149). Since this is less than the observed value of $1\frac{1}{4}$, Huygens asserts that "one cannot trust entirely these first observations . . . it is to be hoped that with time one will be informed exactly about these periods . . . certainly the matter fully deserves to be researched with care" (pp. 149–50). This attitude, which some might take to be a transgression of an empiricist principle of scientific method, indicates to me judiciousness about when to trust and when not to trust observations; in fact a later report (p. 153) yielded a very good fit. But this is not my main point, which rather concerns the explanation/prediction dichotomy. For at the end of the discussion, Huygens announces the following novel consequences of his theory: that plumb lines are not exactly vertical, the deviation being about 1/10 of a degree at the latitude of Paris; that surveyor's levels do not indicate true horizontal; and that the earth is not spherical but spheroidal.

As regards the mathematical demonstration of the above-mentioned theorem, Huygens' judgment-at-work is shown in the following two approximations. The first occurs at the place in the proof where he equates two triangles by regarding as parallel two of their sides which in reality are not, namely the line from the earth's center to the actual position of the pendulum bob (CHL, p. 148), and the line from that center to the position the bob would be in if the earth were not rotating (CDK, p. 148). The other approximation occurs where he takes the extreme smallness of the actual angle between these two lines (DKH, p. 150) to regard two other lines as perpendicular to each other (HF and GD, p. 150).

The last section of the *Discourse*, entitled "Addition," is said to be occasioned both by Newton's *Principia* and by new data compiled by the Dutch East Indies Company for the purpose of checking the reliability of Huygens' pendulum clock to measure longitude at sea. In analyzing these data, he made corrections based on his calculated variations of the period of a pendulum clock due to terrestrial rotation, and he claimed that for a voyage from the Cape of Good Hope to Holland there was very good agreement between calculated and known longitudes, e.g. an error of only a few leagues in the calculation of the known longitude of a Dutch port. Huygens himself tells us that the company remained unconvinced by his detailed report and ordered another test. The point I wish to emphasize here, however, is his interest in practical applications of scientific ideas and the scientific elaboration of practical problems. This is good judgment with respect to one version of the theory/practice distinction. Huygens is explicit here and he tells us that it is the above-mentioned agreement between observation and calculation that now motivates him to undertake a study of the exact nonspherical shape of the earth (p. 154) which he does next.

The most noteworthy feature of Huygens' analysis of this shape is the use of a method invented by Newton (1934, bk. 3, prop. 19), as Huygens explicitly acknowledges (p. 155). This technique involves thinking of water canals from points on the earth's surface to its center, where they interconnect; the equilibrium maintained in these canals by gravity and by centrifugal force is then exploited to compare the different radial distances from the center to the various surface points. Huygens' main accomplishment in this section (pp. 154–59) is to derive and comment upon a general equation defining the earth's shape, which is found not to be an exact conic section (p. 157), though it reduces to one under certain special but unreal conditions (pp. 157–58), and though its deviation from a conic section can be studied (pp. 158–59). Thus Huygens also computes the excess of the equatorial to the polar diameters, and he arrives at the value of 1/578. He tells us that he is aware that this value differs from the one calculated by Newton, which was 1/231,[9] and which he finds objectionable because it depends on the objectionable principle that all particles attract each other (p. 159). It is difficult to deny that here Huygens' attitude toward Newton is exactly analogous to his attitude toward Descartes, namely methodological agreement coupled with substantive disagreement. There are differences of course: the Newtonian method being adapted is more mathematical, whereas the Cartesian method was the more qualitative idea of explaining natural phenomena in general by motion, and gravity in particular by circular

---

[9] This is the value cited by Huygens from the first edition of Newton's *Principia*; the third edition has the value 1/230.

motion. Nevertheless the analogy is striking, and it should be stressed for the sake of elaborating Huygens' sense of balance between Newtonianism and anti-Newtonianism, and between Cartesianism and Newtonianism.

A similar kind of judiciousness or spirit of compromise is apparent in the next passage (pp. 160–65), where Huygens begins by saying that Newton's *Principia* has convinced him that the centripetal force of gravitation does act at astronomical distances (pp. 160–61), and he then states and solves a difficulty about what kind of substance fills these interplanetary spaces (pp. 161–65). Huygens praises the centripetal force idea for its great explanatory power: not only can it explain the elliptical paths of planets, their variation in orbital speed, and the motion of comets, but it can solve or dissolve difficulties besetting Descartes's vortex theory, namely why planetary orbits have constant eccentricities, why they have different inclinations to the ecliptic, and why their planes all pass through the sun. The difficulty is that, on the one hand, celestial matter must be extremely rare in order not to impede the motion of planets and comets; on the other hand, it is not clear how such a rare matter can allow the action of gravity and of light. To solve the problem, Huygens distinguishes between two kinds of rarity: the first involves particles separated by large empty spaces; the second involves particles which touch each other, but which have a rare texture interspersed with small empty spaces. The first kind of rarity is said to be inconsistent with his explanation of gravity and with the prodigious speed of light. Therefore, Huygens concludes, celestial matter must consist of rare particles that touch each other. Finally, he defends this conclusion from two objections that might be raised from Newton's point of view. First, in line with some considerations made by Newton in proposition VI of book III, one might object that if all space is full of Huygens' particles touching each other, then the pressure near the earth's surface would be so high that even gold would go upwards.[10] Huygens answers that this objection is valid only if weight is an intrinsic property of all matter; but if it is produced by differential centrifugal forces in accordance with his theory, then the celestial matter filling the space near the earth would have no weight and thus would not produce the pressure Newton is talking about (p. 163). Second (pp. 163–65), in line with Newton's proposition XLII of book II, one might object that if interplanetary space is full of Huygens' gravific fluid, then light should not travel in straight lines but bend around obstacles. Huygens does not deny that this happens but claims that the detoured light waves are too

---

[10] Cf. Newton 1934, bk. 3, prop. 6, cor. 3.

weak to be perceptible. He also agrees that in the case of water waves the phenomenon is clearly visible. As regards sounds, he thinks the situation is intermediate between water and light, and he also argues that much apparent evidence of bending may not be relevant; for example hearing a noise from behind a house might be impossible if it were completely isolated and there were no surrounding trees or buildings that might reflect the sound. As mentioned above, this passage exhibits a combination of Newtonianism and anti-Newtonianism. The form that this synthesis takes here is not like the methodological agreement/substantive disagreement of the previous passage. Rather it is more like its reverse, substantive agreement/methodological disagreement; in fact, Huygens here accepts three particular Newtonian propositions (about the rarity of celestial matter, about the pressure this might produce, and about nonrectilinear propagation) in order to strengthen his own theory of gravity by formulating and solving objections to it which those propositions elicit; insofar as the strengthening of Huygens' theory represents a utilization of those propositions for an aim different from Newton's, we might speak here of a methodological disagreement.

It is worth noting that, in these two first main discussions in the "Addition" of the *Discourse*, the primary emphasis is one of appreciation rather than criticism of Newton. It is true that once in each passage (pp. 159, 163) Huygens expresses his opposition to the idea of gravitation as an inherent property, but this criticism is somewhat parenthetical when viewed in context.

If we call such a procedure "critical appreciation," then we may say that the next discussion (pp. 165–68) is another good example of Huygens' critical appreciation of Newton. However, even more striking than this synthesis of appreciation and criticism is the balancing of theory and experience. Huygens now calls attention to Newton's discovery of the decrease of gravity as the square of the distance; he is especially impressed by Newton's demonstration of this law for the case of the moon. Then Huygens applies the principle to terrestrial gravity and pendular vibrations: since the earth is approximately a spheroid, pendulum periods should be affected by a second deviation due to the slightly different distances from the earth's center to various latitudes on the surface, in addition to the deviation deriving from the variation in centrifugal force of rotation; he calculates this second deviation to be equal to the first, which would yield a shortening of the seconds-pendulum by about $1/289$ from the pole to the equator, or a retardation of the period by about $1/578$; both deviations would thus slow a pendulum clock by about five minutes

at the equator compared with the pole. This does not correspond to
the data mentioned earlier which Huygens had from the voyage by the
Dutch East Indies Company. His explanation of the apparent lack of a
second deviation is that the inverse-square distance law probably does
not hold for places in the immediate vicinity of the earth's surface; an
independent reason for this conjecture is that the law obviously cannot
hold below the earth's surface, otherwise gravity would increase without
limit as one approached the center; another independent reason might
be Newton's own calculation that, inside the earth, gravity decreases as
one approaches the center, though in his calculations he assumes the
principle of particle-attraction which Huygens cannot accept. Huygens'
judiciousness here is shown by the fact that he neither rejects Newton's
law in the face of conflicting observations, nor does he dismiss the observations in view of the theory, but he tries to explain the discrepancy
by an hypothesis which is not just ad hoc since it has some independent
supporting evidence. It should be noted that Huygens seems quite convinced of the general truth of the inverse-square distance law, so much
so that in the preceding discussion he had stated that "it is well worth
searching for the reason" (p. 160) for this fact about gravity.

It is thus not surprising that the next passage (pp. 167–68) contains
comments on other consequences of the inverse-square distance law.
Huygens is excited about the fact that by means of this law Newton es-
timated the relative weights of the same body at the surface of the sun,
Jupiter, Saturn, and the earth.[11] He disagrees with Newton's estimates
because he has different values for the earth-sun distance and for the
diameters of the planets, which are used in the computation, but he uses
Newton's method to arrive at his own estimates. In particular the calculation of the gravity on the solar surface, which he finds to be twenty-six
times that of the earth, allows him to reach another conclusion more in
line with his own work. This concerns the circular speed of the gravific
matter near the sun, for which he gives the value of forty-nine times its
speed near the earth, where, as we saw earlier, it already is seventeen times
the equatorial speed. In turn, this "terrible rapidity" (p. 168) of the solar
aether, as Huygens describes it, must be the cause of the sun's light, as the
solar particles rub against the aether ones, in accordance with his own

[11] Cf. Newton 1934, bk. 3, prop. 8, cor. 1. The values given in the third edition of Newton's
Principia are closer to the estimates of Huygens, whose death of course prevented him
from seeing anything but the first edition. I have been unable to consult the latter to see
whether its values correspond to those criticized by Huygens.

theory of light. Besides the obvious synthesis between negative criticism and positive appreciation, and between theory and observation, this discussion shows that Huygens is not altogether uninterested in general systematization (as opposed to particular solutions to particular problems). In fact, he takes the opportunity to establish a connection between the present topic and his theory of light. We need not deny that one of Huygens' fortes is his concrete approach to particular problems (by contrast to, let us say, Descartes, and analogously to Galileo, for example). However, such a concrete approach, to be valuable and effective, must not be dogmatic, mindless, and "mechanical," but must be part of a general awareness of how to strike the proper balance between generalization and systematization on the one hand, and concretism and particularism on the other. From this point of view, the present suggested connection between gravity and light shows that Huygens is not a mindless particularist. Such judiciousness is similar to the one noted earlier when we stressed the connection between the theory of circular motion earlier worked out by Huygens, and the present investigation of gravity.

In the last section of the *Discourse* (pp. 168–80), the synthetic and judgmental character of Huygens' procedure is more explicit than usual. Moreover, since more than one dichotomy is significantly involved, we might even speak of a synthesis of syntheses, as it were. The relevant polarities lie respectively along the axes of mathematization, theory and experience, and Newtonianism. The physical topic is motion in resisting mediums, the mathematical one is the nature of the natural logarithmic curve, and the occasion is book II of Newton's *Principia*. Huygens' penchant for mathematization is so obvious in this passage that little needs to be said: he discusses at least four mathematical consequences of the assumption that a body thrown perpendicularly upwards is resisted by a medium in a simple proportion to the speed (pp. 170–71); at least three mathematical features of a body thrown obliquely upwards in the same kind of medium (pp. 171–73); one property of a body thrown obliquely downwards (p. 173); two specific features of a body thrown upwards when the resistance of the medium varies as the square of the speed (pp. 173–74); one general formula for a body moving under the same conditions (p. 174); one very curious difference between resistance proportional to the speed and resistance proportional to the square of the speed when motion is horizontal (pp. 175–76); and no less than fifteen theorems about the logarithmic curve (pp. 176–80). However, the other side of the coin of the compactness and brilliance of this mathematics is its sketchiness and its lack of proofs, which ought to be positively described as judiciousness of mathematization. This is especially so since in this one case Huygens, besides giving us the benefit of his judgment at work, gives an indication that he is explicitly aware of what he is doing. In fact he gives three reasons for his procedure: first, the study of motion in resisting mediums did not seem to him to be "sufficiently useful, or sufficiently consequential, in proportion to the difficulty one encounters" (pp. 168–69); second, the natural logarithmic function is relevant primarily for resistances directly proportional to speed but this is not true for air or water, "therefore I saw my new theory overthrown, or at least useless" (p. 169), and "I neglected it entirely" (p. 173) until Newton's book came along; third, the analysis of resistance proportional to the square of the speed is "much more difficult" (p. 169), and "it is extremely difficult, if not totally impossible to resolve this problem" (p. 175) in general terms.

The second significant element of Huygens' discussion here – the theory/experience synthesis – is shown by the readiness with which he abandons the assumption that the resistance to motion through a medium varies directly as the speed, since his experiments at the Academy of Sciences indicated a variation in proportion to the square of the speed (p. 169). Lest someone mistake this decision as an instance of naive empiricism, rather than judicious synthesis, we find Huygens assuring us that the observed phenomenon makes a lot of sense "because a body moving, for example, with double the speed is hit by twice as many particles of air or water, and with double the swiftness" (p. 169).

As regards his attitude toward Newton, Huygens does primarily two things. On the one hand, in the analysis of resistance proportional to speed, which Newton also considered abstractly, Huygens reports results from earlier studies where he arrived at the same trajectory of motion that Newton found in proposition IV of book II, but by a simpler construction, which makes use of the logarithmic curve (pp. 169–73). On the other hand, for resistance varying as the square of the speed, Huygens does not hesitate to admit the superiority of Newton's analysis which gives a general solution of the problem of vertical ejection (proposition IX, book II), whereas he had been able to solve it only for two special cases (pp. 173–74). Huygens even frankly confesses that the stumbling block to his approach had been his inability to find the sum of the infinite sequence $a + a^3/3 + a^5/5 + a^7/7 + \cdots$, which, after having seen the *Principia*, he can now compute in terms of a sector of an hyperbola, this being the crucial element in Newton's approach (pp. 174–75). As in previous discussions, Huygens' attitude is one of critical appreciation, the emphasis here being more on appreciation.

To summarize this analysis of Huygens' *Discourse on the Cause of Gravity*, I have argued that its most significant methodological feature is something I call judgment, which in general terms is the synthesis of opposite and of distinct requirements. Opposites are, for example, the requirements of theory and of observation; whereas the requirements of theory and of mathematization are distinct. The most common of such relevant opposites turned out to be: theory and observation, mathematical precision and qualitative considerations, Cartesianism and anti-Cartesianism, Newtonianism and anti-Newtonianism, negative criticism and positive appreciation. Occasionally we also found a synthesis of intellectual pursuit and practical-economic involvement, systematization and piecemeal approach, self-regard and self-transcendence, explanation of known facts and prediction of new ones.

5. Recapitulation

We began with an analysis of the recent philosophy of science literature on the concept of judgment; the conclusions were that judgment plays a very important role in scientific thought, and that the relevant concept of judgment is that of judiciousness and synthesis. We then proceeded to an analysis of judgment as found (or as lacking) in historical practice, specifically the historiography of Huygens' theory of gravity; the methodological weaknesses of this literature were criticized in terms of the distinctions between method and result, between theory and practice, and between the strength of evidence for negative criticism and for positive appreciation. Finally, we undertook a detailed judgmental analysis of Huygens' *Discourse*; besides providing a case study of judgment-at-work in science, this analysis provided overwhelming evidence for the methodological and historiographical significance of this work; this contrasts with its usual one-sided readings from the points of view of metaphysics, mechanism, Cartesianism, and anti-Newtonianism.

22

Empiricism, Judgment, and Argument

Toward an Informal Logic of Science (1988)

The concept of argument has always been of central importance in the philosophy of science. This was true even in the heyday of logical empiricism, since the logical component of the latter in effect meant that great emphasis was being placed on a *particular* conception of argument, which may be called formal, mathematical, deductive, demonstrative, or logicist. More recently, other approaches have displaced logical empiricism from its position of dominance, but it would be as much of a mistake to think that the focus on argument has thereby waned, as it would be to think that the empirical component of logical empiricism really involved that much empiricism, or at least any more than what would be allowed by proponents of other approaches. On the contrary, what has happened is that the concept of argument has become even more central since the nonlogicist conception of argument turns out to be very useful in analyzing features of science that recent empirical-historical research about science has shown to be of paramount importance, such as the phenomena of scientific change and disagreement (e.g., see Pera 1982). Thus, the proper appreciation of the role of argument in science requires a proper appreciation of a nonlogicist, argumentative conception of argument, just as to appreciate that the death of logical empiricism does not mean the demise of any empirical science one must not take the meaning of empiricism for granted. In what follows I should like to explore how the argumentative conception of argument goes hand in hand with the proper understanding of the empirical ideal, and wherein lies the connection. It will be seen in due course that the key link is provided by the notion of what may be called judgment.

1. Empiricism and Apriorism

In some ways empiricism was never alive. Consider, for example, one of its most classic formulations, namely the system in David Hume's *Treatise of Human Nature*. If I may be allowed to give an ironical twist to his own famous remark about the book's failure to win him literary fame (Hume 1955, 4, 10), I would say that Hume's empiricism was stillborn. For, first, the basic principle of his system, that all ideas derive from impressions (Hume 1911, 13–14), does not survive the self-referential test of asking for the impressions from which it itself derives. Second, Hume himself recognizes that his system needs various principles of association of ideas, and that these principles are innate in human nature (1911, 21). Thus, even Hume's classic empiricism contains some apriorist elements.

Indeed, the whole history of philosophical empiricism is less like a cemetery full of corpses, and more like a medical laboratory display of still-births, with specimens preserved in formaldehyde. For Hume's predicament is entirely typical, and to his principles of association of ideas, there correspond Francis Bacon's idols, like the Idols of the Tribe, which he thinks cannot be eradicated from the human mind (cf. Bechler 1981, 64). Analogously, we have Locke's dogma of the *tabula rasa*, Russell's a priori knowledge of general truths such as the principle of induction (Russell 1959, ch. vi, vii; 1960, 51), and Popper's methodological rules as conventions (1959, 49–56). It is thus easy to sympathize with Dudley Shapere when he boasts, with some justice, that his own theory of scientific change may be the first genuine empiricist philosophy of science, free of any presuppositions, ever advanced (1984, 239).

My purpose here is not by any means to defend the apriorist cause. In fact, philosophical apriorism presents us with a similar museum of medical pathology. Consider the classic Cartesian formulation centered upon the principle that all clear and distinct ideas are true. Where did Descartes get this principle? In a recent article, Ronald Rubin (1977) has discussed this question in connection with a different but related problem. He shows convincingly that Descartes arrived at his all-important principle from empirical observation, specifically self-observation or examination of his own experience. The point is that it is simply an observation-report for Descartes that he cannot doubt the truth of that which he perceives clearly and distinctly (cf. also Sakellariadis 1982).

Actually, in the case of Descartes something more unnatural than a stillbirth occurred. For, instead of burying or giving to a medical laboratory the lifeless fetus, he tried to pass it off as being alive. He did this when he made extensive use of his principle of clear and distinct ideas in order to devise a science of nature. As might be expected, his physics and cosmology turned out to be mostly wrong, an instance of a philosophical novel, as some called it.

Again, Descartes is by no means an isolated example. Of course, after Kant anti-empiricism was no longer pure, but rather it took the form of synthetic apriorism. Among contemporaries, the most well-known example of such apriorism is undoubtedly Thomas Kuhn (1970b). This interpretation has been advanced not only by his critics (Bechler 1981), but also by such an acute, sympathetic, and historically well informed follower of Kuhn as Harold Brown (1975). Kuhn's apriorism is evident from the fact that he holds that commitment to a paradigm is the beginning of a science; in other words, for him normal scientific research consists of the attempt to elaborate, articulate, apply, extend, and clarify some a priori commitment, whose role is thus to serve as a presupposition of that research. The apriorism here derives from the alleged methodological primacy of the paradigmatic propositions. How is such apriorism infected with empiricism? First, there is the obvious empiricism of Kuhn's own practice; that is, it is well known that his view of science originated from and is based upon historical evidence (Kuhn 1957; 1970b, ch. i). Second, less obvious, but equally crucial, is the empirical basis of scientific revolutions (cf. Bechler 1981, 75–85); for Kuhn these episodes are changes of paradigm, such changes are responses to crises, crises are the result of the accumulation of anomalies, and anomalies are mostly empirical difficulties faced by the old paradigm; since scientific revolutions are as necessary as normal scientific research, the apriorism of normal science is not really primary, and hence Kuhn's theory is as empiricist as it is apriorist.

In formulating some of my general theses above, I did so with qualifications. It is now time to bring these into the open. I said earlier that empiricism was never alive *in some ways*, and that what constitutes my facetious museum of stillbirth pathology is the history of both empiricism and apriorist *philosophies*. To explain the point of these qualifications, I now turn to some other examples of empiricism and anti-empiricism.

The most famous episode of empiricism in the history of science is perhaps Galileo's inability to bring himself to accept the Copernican cosmology before the observational evidence of the telescope. Certainly his confession to that effect is the most eloquent, though, ironically, it is often taken out of context and misinterpreted as evidence of apriorism. To be able to appreciate the methodology of the situation, a little background is needed.

In 1543 Copernicus published his book *On the Revolutions of the Heavenly Spheres*, in which he explained apparent planetary motions on the basis of the hypothesis that the earth has an annual motion around the sun. This was not the first time that such a view had been conjectured, since it can be found in the Greeks Aristarchus and Pythagoras; but it was the first time that the technical details of an heliocentric theory had been worked out. Copernicus's essential contribution was an original explanation of old observational data by means of an old discarded idea. The idea of a moving earth had been considered and discarded by the ancients and the medievals because of the weight of many philosophical, religious, and scientific objections. Among the latter, there were some theoretical arguments, based on the available laws of physics: for example, it was said that if the earth rotated on its axis it would disintegrate, and also that bodies would not be seen to fall vertically on a rotating earth. There were also more empirical objections: the strongest one was that if the earth moved annually around the sun, then our distance from our two nearest planets – Venus and Mars – would undergo periodic variations, with the maximum distance being six or eight times the minimum; this in turn would entail a variation in apparent brightness and size of the order of the square of these numbers; however, observation revealed no variations in size and much smaller variations in brightness. In order to answer these scientific objections, one needed new laws of motions and qualitatively new astronomical evidence. Galileo's work on the foundations of the science of mechanics contributed to the former, his telescopic discoveries helped the latter. That is why Galileo did not commit himself to the Copernican system until his *Sunspot Letters* of 1613, for by 1609 he had essentially completed his work in mechanics and had begun using the new telescope. This instrument made possible the observation of such phenomena as lunar mountains and Jupiter's satellites, as well as the periodic variations in the appearance of Venus and Mars entailed by the hypothesis of a moving earth. It is in the *Dialogue* of 1632 that Galileo confesses that without the empirical evidence of the telescope he would have been unable to accept this hypothesis (Galilei 1967, 327–28; cf. Finocchiaro 1980b, 128–29).

However, my point is not that Galileo was an empiricist, but only that he acted and spoke as one in this particular episode. In fact, I now want to present another classic example, but one which indicates apriorism. This episode concerns the law of falling bodies. The question is whether or not, and how, the speed of fall is dependent on weight. The Aristotelian answer was that heavier bodies fall faster, and some specified that the variation was in direct proportion to the weight. Galileo countered that, under ideal conditions, that is, disregarding air resistance, all bodies fall at the same rate, independently of weight. What is interesting is that Galileo argued that in this particular case we do not even need to make an experiment to prove the Aristotelian law wrong. The explicit experiment, under the specified ideal conditions, was made in 1969 by the first astronauts on the moon, but not even self-styled empiricists would need to wait that long. Galileo's argument is, in fact, a gem of *reductio ad absurdum*. In it he considers bodies of the same material, so that the larger is heavier. His argument may be reconstructed as follows: if heavier bodies fall faster, then the larger of the two would fall faster than the smaller one; but if one body wants to move faster than another, then if they are tied together the composite body would move slower than the faster one, but faster than the slower one, since one would be slowed down by the other, while the second would be speeded up by the first; therefore, if heavier bodies fall faster, then two bodies of different sizes tied together would fall slower than the heavier one alone; but the two bodies tied together constitute a body which is heavier than each of the two original ones; therefore, if heavier bodies fall faster, then two bodies of different sizes tied together would fall faster than the heavier one by itself; therefore, the view that heavier bodies fall faster implies the contradiction that two bodies tied together would fall both faster and slower than the heavier one by itself (Galilei 1974, 66–67).

Such examples of seemingly opposite methodologies can be multiplied with respect to most of the common dichotomies (Finocchiaro 1980b, 103–4, 145–50, 157–64; cf. McMullin 1978). For example, on the question of mathematical analysis versus qualitative thinking, Galileo is mathematicist in his work on the laws of motion, but qualitative in astronomy; from the viewpoint of causal investigation, Galileo is positivist-oriented in his refusal to seek the cause of accelerated fall, but he is constantly searching for the causes of astronomical phenomena; and concerning the ideal of scientific demonstration, he tends to be a strict rigorist in mechanics, but an hypothetical fallibilist in astronomy.

These oppositions are more apparent than real. For, to go back to the empiricism and apriorism examples, it is obvious that the contradiction would be in the mind of the philosopher who would want to formulate his methodological lessons in an injudicious manner (e.g., Losee 1980, 51–60). This would be the case if he were to conclude from the example of the telescope and Copernicanism, either that all scientific theories are to be rejected when they face direct empirical counterevidence, or that

Galileo preached or practiced this principle. It would be similarly injudicious to infer from the falling bodies episode that, either for Galileo or for ourselves, scientific research can or ought to be conducted by pure speculation without observation. Instead of formulating the methodological lessons as universal generalizations, or even as typical generalizations, we should formulate them as existential ones. That is, in the two cases under considerations the correct conclusions are that *sometimes* one should not accept a theory that clearly conflicts with observation, and that *sometimes* one does not need an experiment to check whether an alleged law is true. We can be more specific and specify the occasion, by saying that we should be empirical-minded on occasions *similar to* that of Galileo and Copernicanism, and that we should have an apriorist orientation on occasions *similar to* that of the Aristotelian law of falling bodies. We can even add that the decision of when to be empirical, and when apriorist, should be left to each individual scientist, and not be dictated by the scientific community (cf. Bechler 1981). But I do not think we can go much further than this sort of lesson.

The position I am moving toward can perhaps be more incisively expressed in philosophical, or perhaps I should say metaphilosophical, terminology. According to a widespread view of philosophical inquiry, philosophy is the study of universals and/or general concepts. From this point of view, there is no philosophical issue about empiricism here. It is as wrong to be always empirically minded, as it is to be always inclined toward a priori analysis. What we can say without fear of error is that scientific inquiry must at all times be judicious. This brings us to the concept of judgment, using this term in the sense in which it refers to judiciousness. The concept of judgment is thus a more fruitful notion for the philosopher of science to study than the meaning of empiricism. But how shall we go about exploring the meaning and structure of judgment and its role in scientific inquiry? I believe that a judicious way to proceed would involve two things: one is to analyze important and clear cases of judgment as we actually find it among scientists, and another is to examine other philosophies of science where the concept has an important metascientific function. In fact, the case of Galileo mentioned above is not an isolated example of scientific work, and among philosophers the kind of examples discussed earlier do not exhaust the field, and there are even cases of self-styled empiricists and of apparent anti-empiricists whose work has a strong judgmentalist component. The prima facie empiricist I have in mind is Paul Feyerabend, the self-styled empiricists are Dudley Shapere and Harold Brown, and the exemplary scientists

are (besides Galileo) Huygens, Boltzmann, and Einstein. It will turn out
that what I call judgment is similar to Einstein's self-styled opportunism,
Boltzmann's pluralism, Huygens' eclecticism, Feyerabend's so-called anarchism, Brown's interpretation of scientific rationality, and Shapere's
middle course between Platonism and relativism.

2. Einstein's Opportunism, Boltzmann's Pluralism, Huygens' Eclecticism

The most self-aware expression of judiciousness in recent science is perhaps Einstein's confession of what he calls opportunism. This is found in
what may be regarded as his most considered and mature methodological
statement, among the comments he makes on the various essays included
in the Einstein volume of the Library of Living Philosophers edited by
Schilpp (1951, 683–84). The remarks I want to focus on were occasioned
by Lenzen's essay on "Einstein's Theory of Knowledge" (Schilpp 1951,
355–84) and by Northrop's essay on "Einstein's Conception of Science"
(Schilpp 1951, 385–408).

To begin to clear the air about Einstein's confession of opportunism,
we should note that he is also the author of another very famous and
much-quoted aphorism, namely that "if you want to find out anything
from the theoretical physicists about the methods they use, I advise you
to stick closely to one principle: don't listen to their words, fix your attention on their deeds" (quoted in Northrop 1951, 388 from Einstein
1934, 30). Thus when Einstein tells us that a good physicist is an epistemological opportunist, should we perhaps disregard such advice? My
answer is that we should not, any more than we should disregard the
just-stated aphorism. Rather, we should be judicious in our attitude toward such methodological *dicta*. For example, in order to avoid obvious
self-reference problems with the just-quoted aphorism, it should be interpreted as meaning that the epistemologist should fix his attention on
scientists' deeds *as well as* listening to their words. Actually, there is no
need even to be too mechanical in the application of this reinterpreted
principle. Hence, on the present occasion I feel free to pay more attention to Einstein's words, since I am also focusing on the corresponding
deeds of other scientists; for example, I have already examined, and am
ready to examine more of, Galileo's deeds in that light.

Einstein's point about opportunism is somewhat weakened by his as-
sociating it with unscrupulousness; moreover, it sounds rather apologetic
vis-à-vis the systematic epistemologist. It can, however, be expressed more

constructively and positively if we think more in terms of the adjective "opportune." In fact, whereas the term "opportunism" has, especially in English, and especially in politics, a negative connotation, the term "opportune" has an almost entirely positive one. However, in its core, and etymologically as well, opportunism is simply the policy of doing what is opportune under the circumstances at hand, without undue adherence to rigid principles; in turn, "opportune" here means simply "appropriate" or "well-suited." Thus one should be an empiricist when it is opportune to be one, and an apriorist when that is the opportune thing, and so on.

Of course, one could object to Einstein that this advice is not very informative, for one would like to know more about when it is opportune to be an empiricist, and when it is opportune to be an apriorist. I have already suggested, when this question arose in my discussion of Galileo, that there is in fact a little more that Einstein could say. He could do this by giving one or more examples, from his own scientific practice, when it was opportune to be an empiricist, and one or more examples of opportunistic apriorism. What more, or how much more to expect, would depend on one's own point of view of the epistemological enterprise. In fact it is here, in his implicit metaphilosophical view that one could criticize Einstein, for his deference to a particular conception of the philosophy of science. He feels that the opportunistic scientist is likely to appear unscrupulous to the epistemologist because the latter aims at being systematic and interpreting scientific practice in terms of a single metascientific concept. It is at this point that one should add a qualification to Einstein's own Kantian statement about the mutual relationship between science and epistemology. He says in effect that epistemology without science is empty, and science without epistemology is blind. The qualification to be added is that science accompanied by a dogmatic and pretentious epistemology risks being doubly blind, while epistemology accompanied by partisan science risks being both blind and empty (cf. Agazzi 1981, 248).

In other words, if and to the extent that scientific practice is opportunistic, then it could be argued that there is no reason why philosophy of science should not also be opportunistic. Why should the philosopher, for example, take the ideal of systematicity any more one-sidedly and dogmatically than it is taken by scientists themselves? (cf. Shapere 1984, 235).

Let us now briefly examine whether Einstein's own scientific work was indeed as opportunistic as he claims science in general to be. For, when I said above that in this context I wanted to pay more attention to his words, I meant this to be taken as a matter of relative rather than absolute emphasis. With respect to the deterministic ideal, Einstein could on the one hand make some of the most original contributions to the nondeterministic foundations of quantum theory; this he did with his explanation of the photoelectric effect and with the elaboration of a quantum statistical thermodynamics; on the other hand, he was one of the most determined believers that the indeterminism of quantum theory is a sign of its incompleteness and unsatisfactoriness. From another point of view, on the one hand his discoveries were intimately related to some of the most abstract mathematics used up to that time in science, such as the tensor calculus; on the other hand, some of them are also susceptible of being stated in a qualitative manner without much loss of meaning (cf. Einstein and Infeld 1938); here one need only refer to the principles that the speed of light is a universal constant, and that the laws of physics are invariant in all inertial frames of reference. Or again, more relevantly for our present theme, on the one hand his relativistic physics can be seen as the outcome of a strict empiricism grounded on the Michelson-Morley experiment; on the other hand, it can be seen as a drawing out of the full consequences of the analysis of such concepts as simultaneity, space, and time.

Finally, Einstein's quest for a unified field theory is more problematic. For it seems to involve an absolute commitment to the ideal of comprehensive systematicity, which is similar to that shown by many philosophers of science in their search for a single all-encompassing epistemological theory. And it might be objected that he is doing in his own favorite field of the physics of forces, what is presumably objectionable when done in the field of the philosophy of scientific methods. However, recall that the objectionable character of a non-opportunistic epistemology was elaborated above as our own thesis, not Einstein's; in fact, we pointed out that he does not seem to object to philosophers following an approach which physicists do not, and we criticized him for this. It follows that Einstein was at least self-consistent, since he may be interpreted as granting as much legitimacy to the unificationism characteristic of much epistemology, as to the one he practiced in field theory. The difficulty arises for our more thoroughgoing opportunism suggested earlier, which holds that philosophy of science should be opportunistic since science characteristically is; the difficulty is that Einstein's unificationism in field theory seems to constitute disconfirming evidence. Two answers can be given to this objection. First, all I need to claim is that, as I just said without emphasizing it, science *characteristically* is opportunistic; such a rule obviously allows for exceptions, and Einstein's unificationism may be regarded as an exception. Second, one would have to point out that he did not in fact succeed in his quest for a unified field theory, hence his attempt may be declared *inopportune*, and perhaps as a first approximation we may say that it is outside scientific practice.

My second example of scientific judiciousness is the work of physicist Ludwig Boltzmann (cf. Hiebert 1981; Feuer 1974, 335–41; Brush 1964; and Brush 1976, 1: 231–48). However, it will not be a mere illustration, any more than Einstein was one in this discussion. For, just as the latter enriched our concept of judiciousness with the notion of opportunism, Boltzmann will add the notion of pluralism.

Boltzmann was born in 1844 and made epoch-making contributions to many parts of theoretical physics, but especially to the kinetic theory of gases and to statistical mechanics. He may be regarded as the main founder of this branch of physics in its present form, a fact reflected by the frequency with which his name is used in contemporary textbooks, to name various equations and physical constants. Although his work was destined to be appreciated better after his death, he achieved a good deal of recognition during his own lifetime, and he came to hold important positions at the Universities of Vienna, Munich, and Leipzig. Despite such success, in the last several years of his life he suffered increasingly from mental depression, attempted suicide more than once, and in 1906 he killed himself.

There is no unanimity on the cause of his suicide, but one persistent view holds that it was the result of depression for the criticism to which his life work – the atomic theory of matter – was subjected in the scientific community (Brush 1976, 1: 247; Feuer 1974, 335–41). In fact, at the time empiricism had become incarnated in the persons of such scientists as Ernst Mach, Gustav Kirchoff, Wilhelm Ostwald, Heinrich Hertz, Georg Helm, and Pierre Duhem. This numerous and vociferous group advocated a purely descriptive and inductive approach based only on macroscopic observable quantities, which was commonly referred to as phenomenological thermodynamics; it was also known as the school of energetics, to signal the fact that they wanted to restrict physics to the study of measurable energy transformations (Boltzmann 1964, 13). Given such empiricist commitments, they naturally opposed atomism, since atoms were not directly observable and the assumption of their existence was allegedly dispensable. By contrast, the atomic hypothesis was the fundamental assumption at the root of Boltzmann's epoch-making work. Aside from the historical and documentary questionability of the

charge, it would be somewhat injudicious to blame his suicide only on
empiricism. Before examining some of the arguments, let us simply conclude this aspect of the story by noting the tragic irony. As Stephen Brush
has written, "this suicide must be ranked as one of the great tragedies
in the history of science, made all the more ironic by the fact that the
scientific world made a complete turnabout in the next few years and
accepted the existence of atoms" (1964, 17).

The grounds of Boltzmann's counterattack against the empiricism of
the phenomenological physicists were not apriorist, but rather centered
on pluralism. For example, in commenting on Hertz's approach in mechanics he states: "I absolutely recognise the advantages of Hertz's picture, but on the principle that it is possible and desirable to set up several
pictures for one and the same group of phenomena, I think that alongside Hertz's picture mine still has its significance, in that it has certain
advantages lacking in his" (Boltzmann 1974, 111; cf. Hiebert 1981, 193).
Here Boltzmann's principle of pluralism is explicitly stated to justify his
criticism of an opponent. On other occasions he argues in support of
the principle with the help of several types of considerations. One reason
stems from the temporal limitations of human life, as we learn when he
says that "in a certain sense experiment is entitled to precedence over
all theory. . . . The conflict of theories, however, is an infinitely lengthy
business, indeed it almost seems as though certain controversies as old
as science itself will live on as long as it does" (Boltzmann 1974, 160;
cf. Hiebert 1981, 179). Another justification involves the imperfection
of physical theory and the existence of personal differences, as shown
in the following argument: "it is still possible to have theories that correctly represent a large number of facts but are incorrect in other aspects,
so that they may have a certain relative truth. Indeed it is even possible
that we can construct a system of pictures of experience in several ways.
These systems are not equally simple, nor represent phenomena equally
well. However, it may be doubtful and in a sense a matter of taste which
representation satisfies us most. By this circumstance science loses its
stamp of uniformity" (Boltzmann 1974, 105–6; cf. Hiebert 1981, 182).
Further, Boltzmann gives the argument that pluralism is a way of avoiding one-sidedness, when he says: "nothing will be lost in certainty, while
perspicuity will be retained, if we strictly separate the phenomenology
of the best-attested results from atomistic hypotheses that serve com-
prehensiveness, both being further developed with equal vigour as being
equally indispensable, rather than assert with one-sided regard for the advantage of phenomenology that one day it will certainly displace current

atomism" (Boltzmann 1974, 49; cf. Hiebert 1981, 183). He also uses practical considerations as when he says that "we regard it as expedient to try as many approaches as possible, each of which has its peculiar advantages but also its drawbacks" (Boltzmann 1974, 115; cf. Hiebert 1981, 193). Finally, Boltzmann has the historical argument that "since the history of science shows how often epistemological generalizations have turned out to be false, may it not turn out that the present 'modern' distaste for [kinetic theory and statistical mechanics] ... will have been a retrogression? ... Let us have free scope for all directions of research; away with all dogmatism, either atomistic or antiatomistic!" (Boltzmann 1964, 26).

In the light of such supporting arguments, and of his using the principle in the debate over atomism, there can be no doubt about Boltzmann's pluralism. Although he apparently does not use the term, nevertheless the label is fairly descriptive, and it is a natural one for philosophers and historians to have used (e.g., Hiebert 1981). His own favorite expression was in terms of being careful not to "overshoot the mark" (Hiebert 1981, 191, 195). This brings the judgmental element into the foreground, since the avoidance of extremism is essential to the concept of judiciousness. Such a connection between Boltzmann's pluralism and judiciousness becomes obvious in some of his critiques. For example, "the more boldly one goes beyond experience, the more general the overview one can win, the more surprising the facts one can discover, but the more too one can fall into error. Phenomenology therefore ought not to boast that it does not go beyond experience, but merely to warn against doing so to excess" (Boltzmann 1974, 96; cf. Hiebert 1981, 190). Finally, the connection with opportunism is clear from Boltzmann's remark that "our aim will not be to establish the truth or falsehood of one or the other world picture, but we shall ask whether either is appropriate for this or that purpose while we allow both pictures to continue alongside each other" (Boltzmann 1974, 69; cf. Hiebert 1981, 181).

Turning now to Huygens, his case is doubly instructive, in the sense of being related to the question of judiciousness both at the level of scientific practice and at that of epistemological reflection. Beginning with the latter, I am referring to the widespread view that he was a Cartesian rationalist, and that his excesses in this direction prevented him from discovering the law of universal gravitation (Koyré 1965, 116; Dijksterhuis 1961, 463). He allegedly could have done this by taking another small step after having formulated the laws of centrifugal force, which he had done with great brilliance. But such an interpretation is itself an injudicious excess (Finocchiaro 1980a, 193–96). The fact is that Huygens was a great eclectic, and his eclecticism may be seen as a form of judiciousness.

It may be useful now to summarize his scientific achievements. Besides the laws of circular motion and centrifugal force, he created an essentially correct wave theory of light. In mathematics he pioneered the calculus of probability, worked out an elegant theory of evolute curves, proved many theorems about transcendental curves and inverse calculus problems, and stated without proof many more. He was also an inventor and accomplished instrument maker, and he can be credited with the first pendulum clock, the micrometer, and an improved telescope. In astronomy he is best known for his discovery and correct interpretation of the rings of Saturn. Finally, he made important contributions to scientific organization and institution by helping to found and by serving as the first director of the French Royal Academy of Sciences.

In all this work, Huygens' eclecticism consists in the fact that his career illustrates a balanced combination of many diverse activities, interests, concerns, influences, approaches, etc. First, what I have already said suggests that he was both a great theoretician and a great experimenter; here I am referring to something more than just the ability to give the proper weight to observational data and to speculative ideas, which can be present even in a pure theoretician like Einstein, that is in someone who does not pretend to make experiments and collect data first-hand; in fact, Huygens did something even more than first-hand empirical work, he often built or invented or improved or designed the instruments he used, besides of course also giving a theoretical interpretation. Second, Huygens had both cognitive and practical interests and motivations; for example, it can be argued quite convincingly (Mahoney 1980) that all his scientific work stems from the problem of the measurement of time and of longitude at sea, and it is no accident that his scientific masterpiece, containing the laws of circular motion, is entitled *The Pendulum Clock* (*Horologium Oscillatorium*). Third, he had as keen a physical intuition as acute a power of mathematical analysis. It is not true that he was an extreme Cartesian, but rather he was both a follower and a critic of Descartes; that is to say, he accepted parts of the Cartesian world view and rejected others. For example, on the one hand, he accepted the program of trying to explain all physical phenomena in terms of matter in motion and the contact action of material particles; on the other hand, it was he who showed that almost all of Descartes's own laws of collision were empirically unfounded and had to be rejected or corrected. Huygens' attitude toward Newton was similar: rather than being a mere anti-Newtonian, he rejected some but accepted other parts of Newton's ideas; the most famous disagreement involved the law of gravitational attraction, which Huygens could not accept either as brute fact or as a principle of force acting at a distance. However, in the context of his criticism, Huygens expressed his appreciation for many of Newton's results by combining them with other ideas of his own to solve problems of his own interest or invention; for example, he used the Newtonian discovery that the action of gravity decreases as the square of the distance to deduce that the rate of oscillation of a pendulum slows down as one moves on the earth's surface from the poles to the equator; and he used Newton's discovery that gravitation extends to interstellar distances to estimate the relative weights of an object at the surface of the sun, of Saturn, and of the earth, in part to see whether the gravitational action at the surface of the sun could account for the generation of the light it emits (cf. Finocchiaro 1980a, 205–13).

Of course, the term "eclecticism" possesses as much of a negative connotation as the term "opportunism" does. Moreover, both attitudes can take undesirable forms that involve superficiality, unprincipled do-nothingness, confusing disjointedness, mindlessness, and so on. But I believe that eclecticism has a positive side and can be judicious. In Huygens' case it seems that, in the pursuit of any activity or interest, however deeply involved he gets, he never forgets that there are other activities and interests. That is, Huygens is not single-minded or one-sided. Judicious eclecticism thus involves the avoidance of single-mindedness and one-sidedness.

We may summarize our examination of these three scientific cases by saying that I have tried to enrich the concept of judiciousness with some empirical content, which suggests further theoretical articulations of the concept. That is, I have practiced empiricism by examining certain features of the work of Einstein, Boltzmann, and Huygens. But since I chose them for their opportunism, pluralism, and eclecticism, respectively, and since these three notions have obvious connections with judiciousness, my account is not that of a mere empiricist, but that of a judgmental one, which in turn is equivalent to being a judgmental apriorist. Three conceptual theses that have emerged, and which can become the subject of further inquiry, are as follows. First, opportunism involves judiciousness with respect to the particular problems or topics being studied, vis-à-vis others; the latter might be called concreteness, and thus we may say that to be opportunistic is to be judiciously concrete. Second, pluralism involves judiciousness with respect to the avoidance of excesses or extremes; if we call the latter moderation, we may say that to be pluralistic is to be judiciously moderate. Third, eclecticism involves judiciousness with respect to the avoidance of single-mindedness and one-sidedness; thus to be eclectic is to be judiciously many-sided. Now, instead of proceeding further with such conceptual analysis and theoretical refinements, here I wish to examine other relevant philosophical accounts, as promised above.

3. Learning from the History of Science

The concept of judgment has not received as much attention by philosophers in their theories as it has undergone usage by scientists in practice. Nevertheless, a few philosophers have dealt with it, and an increasing number are beginning to do so. Feyerabend is one of the most well known. In fact, my injunction to "be judicious" is meant to correspond to the sound and constructive part of his slogan that "anything goes" (Feyerabend 1975). However, since I have elsewhere (Finocchiaro 1986b, 157–201) explained the similarities and the differences between my account and his, I do not need to say much more about the matter. Let me note simply that I interpret Feyerabend as a pseudo-irrationalist and hence scientific practice in general, and Galileo's work in particular, as rational. In my view, scientific rationality ultimately reduces to reasoning, in the sense of the art of reasoning; that is, reasoning or argumentation constitutes the deep or microscopic structure of scientific rationality, though its surface or macroscopic structure consists of the judicious balance of methodological rules; formal logic then becomes *a* theory of reasoning, which has its place, but which is somewhat injudicious as ordinarily practiced or conceived.

If Feyerabend's judgmentalism is implicit in the above sense, Harold Brown has been most explicit on the topic. He certainly deserves credit for having incisively made the following declaration: "it is the case in which we must rely on human judgment that I propose to take as the paradigm of a situation in which reason is required" (Brown 1977, 148). It is also difficult to overestimate the importance of his attempt to connect the concept of judgment with Aristotle's notion of equity and practical wisdom. However, I have also commented on his views elsewhere (Finocchiaro 1978a), and so I do not wish to repeat myself here. The only additional and especially relevant comment I have now is a critical one.

It seems to me that, when all is said and done, Brown's philosophy has an undesirable, indeed injudicious, tendency toward apriorism. For

example, in the introductory chapter of his book on the "new philosophy of science" we find as eloquent and clear a statement of apriorism
as one can find in recent literature, when he says that "most scientific research consists . . . of a continuing attempt to interpret nature in terms of a
presupposed theoretical framework. This framework plays a fundamental role . . ." (Brown 1977, 10). Then in the course of his book, Brown
does in fact argue in support of such apriorist theses as the following:
that all observation is theory-laden; that even the empirical refutation of
a theory is theory-dependent; and that the meaning of scientific terms
changes with the change of theoretical framework. Of course, this is,
as Brown himself admits, a version of Kuhn's account, but I do not see
in Brown's book the latent empiricism which I have argued above characterizes Kuhn's apriorism. Instead, corresponding to Kuhn's empirical
character of crises and origin of revolutions, there is simply Brown's thesis that scientific change is dialectical, in the sense that later paradigms
grow out of the difficulties of earlier ones. My main point here is simply
to criticize Brown for an injudicious excess of apriorism, leaving aside
other criticisms that can also be leveled against such specific theses (e.g.,
see Hacking 1983).

I should add that Brown is also apriorist in his philosophical approach.
That is to say, in the otherwise admirable account he gives in his book, the
new philosophy of science is made to emerge out of logical empiricism. In
other words, in accordance with his presuppositionism, Brown criticizes
the old paradigm of logical empiricism and adopts a new one at the
metalevel. The new philosophical paradigm consists essentially of Kuhn's
philosophy of science, though Brown enriches and applies it in original
ways to scientific practice. To be more specific, the new paradigm consists
of theses such as the ones stated above. All of this is understandable and
interesting, but apriorist nonetheless. It may help to contrast Brown's
approach to Kuhn's own historical-empirical procedure at the metalevel,
or to the one I am following in the present investigation. I am trying to
make my ideas emerge out of the empirical evidence consisting of the
historical episodes of scientific practice discussed above. At the same time,
my empirical approach is not empiricist, because I have the concepts of
judgment and argument to guide me.

Let us now turn to Dudley Shapere's view of scientific change. In his
recent work (Shapere 1984) he has been very explicit that his aim is to try
to reach a middle ground between what he calls Platonism or presuppositionism, which characterized logical empiricism, and the relativism which
characterizes some of the work in the more recent tradition of historically

oriented philosophy of science. I find this general program a paradigm example of the use of judiciousness at the philosophical metalevel. More specifically, the attempt at mediation between extremes, and the concern with the avoidance of their excesses, is a typical instance of judiciousness *à la* Boltzmann, as described above. Of course, especially among philosophers, one could find roots of such an enterprise in Aristotle's ethical theory of the golden mean, but that is another story. Moreover, I also agree with Shapere that the two specific views and approaches which he is trying to mediate are indeed implausible and unproductive extremes. Here an eloquent formulation, well worth committing to memory, is Shapere's thesis that "we learn *what* 'knowledge' is *as* we attain knowledge, [and] we learn *how* to learn in the process of learning" (1984, 185).

Turning now from the metalevel to the object level, Shapere has defended a conclusion whose appeal to me becomes self-evident once it is stated: "it is true that science has learned the importance of observations; but it has also learned that there may be circumstances in which insistence on observability may be an injudicious dogma" (1984, 217). He has two supporting arguments (Shapere 1984, 214–22). One involves historical considerations indicating that the concept of observation has undergone changes in the course of the development of science; the other is the metaphilosophical argument based on the necessary vagueness of philosophical inquiry. Although these arguments are different from my own sketched above, they are mutually reinforcing.

More generally, Shapere has argued in support of theses which, from the point of view of my approach, may be seen as original formulations of opportunism and pluralism. For example, he has asserted that "the knowledge-seeking enterprise is not, nor has it ever been, governed by some *single* sort of consideration like verifiability, falsifiability, or observability" (Shapere 1984, 218). Or again, to appreciate the justice of his self-image as an exponent of what "is perhaps the first truly uncompromising empiricist philosophy ever proposed" (Shapere 1984, 239), consider the following argument of his: "although generalization and systematization are, or rather have become, aims guiding us in our inquiries, their application is hypothesized on the basis of past successes in making such generalizations and systematizations, and on the understanding and practical utility they bring. Any particular generalization or systematization, and therefore the whole aim of generalization and systematization is in principle open to frustration" (Shapere 1984, 235).

Two other points deserve mention. One involves the problem of incommensurability, the other the comparison of the philosophy of science to metamathematics. To begin with the latter, Shapere (1984, 182–88) has been very critical of the dichotomy between science and metascience, which was presupposed by logical empiricism, and which yielded a conception of the philosophy of science as the study of such eternal and unchanging categories as explanation, observation, theory, law, measurement, and so on. As Brown (1977) has pointed out, it is an historical fact that logical empiricists adopted this presupposition from the paradigm of mathematical logic, such as Russell and Whitehead's *Principia Mathematica*. Although Brown's account is sound insofar as it goes, it is easy to get the impression from his book that the new philosophy of science consists of the adoption of history of science as a paradigm. However, the situation is more complex, and this is where Shapere and judgment come in. He has pointed out that there is some irony in logical empiricism's choice of a paradigm. In fact, whatever the situation was at the turn of the century, there is now considerable historical (empirical, if you will) evidence that "metamathematical notions are as subject to revision, rejection, extension, and generalization as are mathematical ones" (Shapere 1984, 224). It follows that metamathematics cannot provide the Platonist, eternal foundations of mathematics which it was once believed to be able to do; but it follows further that, even if the philosopher of science were to try to imitate the metamathematician, he ought to dispense with the eternal, a priori presuppositions of the Platonist approach. In short, the analogy to the mathematical situation can be used, if used judiciously, to support an historical approach.

Finally regarding incommensurability, there is Shapere's very important thesis that radical differences between the scientific beliefs and methods of different ages do not preclude the possibility of progress and rationality. The reason is that there is usually a series of developments connecting the sciences of the two ages, such that each step can be seen as a reasonable change; however, in order to see the reasonableness of these steps, we need concrete, historically informed analysis (Shapere 1984, 212, 185–86; cf. Finocchiaro 1973a, 371). Such an argument is important in order to avoid relativism, and it is judicious insofar as it avoids relativistic excesses.

So far I have discussed the extent to which Shapere's theory of scientific change is doubly judgmental, that is to say, concerning both what he does in his own epistemological inquiry, and what he claims about the way science works. By way of criticism, I should now like to examine what I shall call the evolutionary hypothesis and the historiographical assumption. The latter involves, I feel, an excessively uncritical attitude

toward the work of historians of science. Shapere certainly deserves credit
for being aware of the problem, which he discusses in connection with
the question of whether some a priori definition of what science is, is
presupposed by the historical investigations which his view requires the
philosopher to make. If that were the case, then we would have to admit the primacy of another type of Platonist philosophy of science, of
which logical empiricism was just a special case. In accordance with his
general program, Shapere's program is admittedly empirical. He simply
notes (Shapere 1984, 198–99) that in recent decades the study of the
history of science has made great progress, not only quantitatively, by ac-
cumulating much new information, but also qualitatively, by avoiding the
distorting biases and Whiggish attitudes of previous work in the history
of science; he concludes that such progress shows it is possible to study
the history of science without having to assume circularly the philosophical lessons one wants to derive. My qualms are neither with this final
conclusion about the avoidance of vicious circularity, nor with Shapere's
intermediate claim about the great progress made by recent history of
science. Rather I am objecting to the excessively positive picture he por-
trays of the field. On the contrary, I would argue (cf. Finocchiaro 1973c)
that, first, progress in history of science, like progress in science itself
as Shapere himself so cogently argues, is a never-ending affair; second,
though work in the history of science does not significantly presuppose
philosophical theories of science, it does significantly depend on historiographical principles of inquiry; third, though the earlier Whiggish
excesses have almost disappeared, others have surfaced, not the least of
which are abuses of professionalism. Finally, to be more specific, the problem of the causes of the scientific revolution remains a confusion; work on
the origin of Lavoisier's epoch-making discoveries contains identifiable
deficiencies; the work of Koyré, who is widely regarded as the father of
the discipline in its present form, contains numerous errors of reasoning,
erudition, method, hermeneutics, and substantive excess; and historians'
work on Galileo suffers from such rarified difficulties as ideological and
methodological bias, but also from such pedestrian oversights as mis-
translations, misquotations, decontextualizations, and interdisciplinary
confusions. What this means is that the philosopher, without neglecting
anything which is of value in the work of professional historians of science,
must also become his own historian.

Turning now to the evolutionary hypothesis, by it I mean Shapere's
thesis (1984, 183–88, 208–11) that there has been a significant evolution, not only of substantive scientific beliefs, but also of methodological

principles and of so-called metascientific concepts. This is a crucial claim since it grounds the refutation of any Platonist approach. I think that it is also largely acceptable and well supported. My only qualification concerns a particular metascientific concept, and so I want to explore whether the above-mentioned generalization is perhaps an injudicious exaggeration. The notion I have in mind is the concept of argument. My claim is that, whatever may be the case with other metascientific concepts, there is no evidence that this concept has evolved, and there is much evidence that it has not.

4. Argumentation in Science: Galilean Examples

Let us begin with a number of preliminary clarifications. First, the term "argument" is only a member of a cluster to which I am referring; other cognate terms are: argumentation, reasoning, inference, reason for a claim, premise, conclusion, and so on. Second, I am understanding it in a rather loose way, in the sense of what is sometimes called informal logic (Johnson and Blair 1985), rather than in the sense or formal or mathematical logic; that is, I am taking the term "argument" with a meaning somewhat analogous to the metaphilosophical one, the main difference being the socio-linguistic fact that, whereas the notion is the stock in trade of philosophical discussions, in scientific inquiry it is much less explicit; in short, I am taking the term to mean simply a series of statements some of which are reasons for others. Next, if it is questioned whether the notion should be regarded as a metascientific one, I would admit that philosophers of science have made less use of it (at least explicitly) than they have of such concepts as explanation, theory, observation, confirmation, measurement, and even judgment; nevertheless, I would argue that this underutilization is unfortunate. Fourth, some might admit that the descriptive-analytical concept of argument, non-evaluatively understood, may not have undergone evolution, but then claim that principles for the evaluation of arguments, or rules of sound argumentation, have; I certainly accept this distinction, but I do not think the case has been made; in particular the case cannot be made on the basis of the indisputable fact that there has been a growth in the kinds of arguments that it is possible to formulate in science, since many arguments of later periods would not even be understood in earlier ones; the crucial point that would have to be established is that reasoning patterns have evolved, where the notion of a pattern is understood in a *bona fide* formal sense devoid of substantive content. This is precisely what no one has proved.

On the contrary, it may be argued that the concepts of argument, rules of reasoning, patterns of inference that prevailed in the Copernican debate of the seventeenth century were not significantly different from those of today, or of earlier periods; let me repeat, however, what I have suggested above, namely that these concepts need to be richer than, for example, the symbolic-logic equation of an argument with any non-empty ordered set of sentences; for the same evidence shows that the latter notion had as little applicability to natural language argumentation (including science) as it has today.

These abstract generalities can be illustrated by translating into argument-theoretical terminology the Galilean examples discussed earlier from the point of view of empiricism, apriorism, and judgment. Galileo's inability to accept Copernicanism until the telescopic evidence was given as an instance of empiricism, but empiricism of a judicious sort, and hence a special case of judgment, by contrast to the usual versions of philosophical empiricism. From the point of view of informal logic, the argument in question is the following: (1a) if the earth revolved around the sun, then Venus and Mars would appear to change in brightness and size by factors of the order of thirty-six or sixty-four; (1b) but no such variations are observed; (1c) therefore, the earth does not revolve around the sun. The best analysis of this situation is that Galileo had rejected the earth's annual motion because he felt the denial of this motion followed validly from true premises. Thus Galileo is acting in accordance with an eternal-sounding rule of reasoning. Later, after the telescopic evidence, Galileo became convinced that the minor premise of the above instance of denying the consequent was no longer true. Hence he was in a position to propose the following: (2a) if the earth revolved around the sun, then Venus and Mars would appear to change in brightness and size by factors of the order of thirty-six or sixty-four; (2b) Venus and Mars are indeed observed to undergo these apparent variations; (2c) there is no way to explain these observations, other than by the hypothesis of the earth's annual motion; (2d) therefore, the earth probably revolves around the sun. The principle of reasoning inherent in this argument is, once more, a familiar and recurring one; we may call it the inductive rule of affirming the consequent (to be distinguished, of course, from the deductive fallacy of affirming the consequent).

An additional argument needs to be mentioned at this point. It is well-known, in fact, that even after the telescope Galileo could not observe the stellar parallax entailed by the earth's annual motion. Indeed this phenomenon did not become detectable until the nineteenth century.

Yet Galileo did not reject Copernicanism for that reason. Why not? Was he therefore violating the rule of denying the consequent? Textual evidence (Galilei 1967, 383–87; cf. Finocchiaro 1980b, 132–33) indicates that Galileo was now reasoning as follows: (3a) if the earth revolves around the sun, then various phenomena of stellar parallax should take place; (3b) but no stellar parallax is detectable at all; (3c) this lack of detection is best explained, not by the non-existence of the phenomenon, but by the fact that no one has tried to observe it seriously or systematically enough, or with the appropriate instruments, or with the necessary skill; (3d) therefore, the earth *may* revolve around the sun. Here Galileo is again behaving in accordance with the inductive rule of affirming the consequent.

Let us now examine Galileo's apriorist rejection of the Aristotelian law of fall. We saw earlier that, although this was apriorism of sorts, it did not support an apriorist philosophy but a judgmental one. Since my earlier account was already expressed in terms of a *reductio ad absurdum* argument, I can be briefer here. Galileo is reasoning in accordance with the rule that one must reject propositions which entail contradictions or their own denial. The pattern here is one used and known since ancient Greek times.

This discussion would perhaps be incomplete without a brief analysis of the tower argument, since it plays such an important role in Feyerabend's account and has received so much attention in the literature (e.g., Goosens 1980). The argument was an ancient one against the earth's diurnal rotation on its axis; it held that on a rotating earth bodies could not fall vertically, but since they are seen to do just that, the earth cannot rotate. Galileo tried to answer this argument, and Feyerabend tries to derive methodological lessons from that answer. Galileo's answer is as follows: one must distinguish apparent from actual vertical fall; if the tower argument refers to actual vertical fall, then it begs the question, since the minor premise of actual vertical fall cannot be known to be true unless the earth stands still, which is the conclusion of the argument; if the tower argument is referring to apparent vertical fall, then its major premise (the conditional proposition) becomes questionable, since it conflicts with the principle of the conservation of motion (or inertia), which can be supported independently. Despite his important insights, Feyerabend is wrong in trying to draw counterinductivist lessons, i.e., apriorist ones, and anarchist implications, in the bad, relativistic sense of anarchism. His central error is perhaps that, despite his rejection of the theory-observation dichotomy, he still looks at the situation with the spectacles of that distinction, and thus he thinks that Galileo is trying primarily to analyze that relationship apropos of the observation of vertical fall and the theoretical options of whether or not the earth moves and whether or not motion is relative. On the other hand, Galileo is concerned mostly with the logic of the situation, and his main result in this context is the analysis and evaluation of a geostatic argument, as sketched above.

It is this kind of historical evidence that has convinced me that at the informal-logic level just described, scientific thought seems to exhibit a uniform non-evolving structure. This is not meant to deny by any means either the legitimacy of the methodological level of analysis, which deals with more general macroscopic features, or the existence of an evolution at the methodological level. Similarly, I do not mean to deny in principle the legitimacy of a finer level than the microstructural one of argumentation, for example that of pure deduction, though the usefulness and effectiveness of such formal deductive analysis remains to be proved in practice. Interesting questions arise, of course, about the relationship among these levels, especially between the informal-logic one of argumentation and the methodological-epistemological one of theorizing and observation. One of the most interesting of these questions is how the concept of judgment relates to that of argument. Is argumentation merely a special case of judgment? But this and similar questions cannot be pursued here. For the moment the following connection with judgment will have to suffice, namely that the critique of the science-metascience dichotomy rooted on the evolutionary hypothesis may exhibit the injudicious excess of overgeneralizing, by claiming evolution for all metascientific concepts. We have seen that the notion of argument may be the exception that proves this rule.[1]

[1] Acknowledgments: Various parts and preliminary versions of this chapter were presented at the 12th Annual Symposium in Philosophy, California State University, Fullerton; the Seventh International Congress of Logic, Methodology and Philosophy of Science, Salzburg, Austria; and the Israel Colloquium for the History, Philosophy, and Sociology of Science, Third Annual Series. It was completed while the author held a sabbatical leave from the University of Nevada, Las Vegas, and during his tenure of a Barrick Distinguished Scholar award at the same institution (1986–87), whose support is hereby gratefully acknowledged. I also thank Dudley Shapere, Harold Brown, and Thomas Nickles for helpful comments.

23

Criticism, Reasoning, and Judgment in Science (1995)

1. Bohr: Critical Thinking versus Logical Thinking

In his autobiography, physicist Otto R. Frisch tells the following revealing
anecdote about Niels Bohr. Bohr, we are told, "never trusted a purely
formal or mathematical argument. 'No, no' he would say 'You are not
thinking; you are just being logical'" (Frisch 1979, 95).[1] It would be arbitrary and uncharitable to interpret Bohr's point as implying that being
logical is not a form of thinking. Rather it seems obvious that he is distinguishing between two types of thinking, logical thinking and another kind
which may be appropriately labeled critical thinking. By logical thinking
here Bohr seems to mean a mental activity which progresses from one
thought to another in accordance with strict rules, namely rules that are
clear, distinct, and exact. It might be better to call such thinking formal,
or algorithmic, or deductive, in order not to limit the concept of logic to
a one-sided and prejudicial conception. However, I do not want to focus
on that, but rather on the other type of thinking. It is obvious from the
context that critical thinking is different from logical thinking, not in the
sense of being illogical, but rather in the sense that either it follows no
rules or it follows rules that are not formal.[2] One may speak of informal

[1] This statement by Bohr appears as the epigraph to the Introduction in Margolis (1988,
1), through which it first came to my attention. The relevance of Margolis's book to
the present topic extends, however, beyond this particular detail, for its central thesis
is that human thinking is essentially informal, and this conclusion is supported with
experimental evidence from cognitive psychology and historical evidence from the history
of science.

[2] To prevent misunderstanding, it is useful to reiterate that I am *not* claiming that critical
thinking is not logical (as Bohr may be claiming) or that it is not rule-governed. Such

judgment to refer to this feature of critical thinking being suggested here.

Frisch attributes to Bohr's thinking some other qualities which are directly relevant: an element of comparative evaluation or critical judgment, and an element of reasoning or ratiocination or argumentation. Frisch's formulation is made in terms of an image which is sufficiently eloquent to merit quotation: "when it came to attacking a real problem, a serious problem of physics, [Bohr] was marvellous to watch. I always felt he moved with the skill of a spider in apparently empty space, judging accurately how much weight each slender thread of argument could bear" (Frisch 1979, 94–95).

2. Popper: Criticism in Science

To this intuitive recognition we may add a more theoretical appreciation on the part of some philosophers. Here, I have in mind primarily Karl Popper and his school.[3] The element of critical thinking which they emphasize is what may be called *negative* evaluation, or simply criticism, in a common but more restricted meaning of this term. The Popperians hold that there is an asymmetry between verification and falsification, confirmation and disconfirmation, justification and criticism, and that this asymmetry makes falsification, disconfirmation, and criticism epistemologically viable in a way in which verification, confirmation, and justification are not. Accordingly, an idea is scientific if and only if, and to the extent that, it is falsifiable, disconfirmable, or criticizable. And scientific knowledge consists of those scientific ideas which have survived our best attempts to criticize them. A critical attitude and openness to criticism then become the hallmarks of the scientific method. Let us review some of their arguments.

3. Falsification versus Verification

First, it would seem that laws of nature are not verifiable and cannot be known to be true because and insofar as they are universal generalizations

---

claims would presuppose identifying logic with formal logic and rule with formal rule, and these identifications I find unjustified.

3 See, for example, Popper (1959; 1962; 1963); Agassi (1963; 1968; 1971); Agassi and Jarvie 1987; Bartley (1982; 1984; 1987); Levinson 1982; Miller (1982; 1987); and Schilpp 1974. Other relevant works would be Brown (1979; 1987; 1989) on the role of judgment in science; Pera (1982; 1987; 1988; 1991), on the role of argumentation in science; and Shapere (1984; 1988a; 1988b) on the role of reasoning, though in a slightly difference sense from the one articulated below.

with a potentially unlimited scope, and the supporting empirical evidence can never consist of more than a limited sample (however large) or a finite list of instances (however numerous). These difficulties are well known and stem from the so-called problem of the justification of induction. There is no need to elaborate them here. Examples of universal generalizations to which this argument is meant to apply are: (1) all ravens are black, (2) all emeralds are green, and (3) all particles of matter attract each other with a force directly proportional to the product of their masses and inversely proportional to the square of their distance.

The same point applies to theoretical hypotheses, independently of whether or not they are universal generalizations. Consider for example the claim that the earth rotates on its axis, or the claim that the five continents of the earth have undergone some lateral horizontal movement, or the claim that the human species has evolved from lower species of animals. Such theoretical claims can be tested only indirectly, that is, by checking the truth of their consequences. However, the truth of these consequences does not guarantee the truth of the corresponding hypothesis because the form of argument known as affirming the consequent is formally invalid. That is, it is wrong to reason as follows: if P were true, then Q would also be true; and Q is indeed true; therefore, P is true.

The Popperians go on to add that, on the other hand, both universal generalizations and theoretical hypotheses are falsifiable. That is, if we are testing whether "all A are B," and we can discover a particular A which lacks the property B, then we can be sure that not all A are B. Similarly, if we are testing hypothesis H, and can show that if H were true, then consequence C would have to follow, and then we discover that consequence C does not obtain, we have thereby established that H is false. Therefore, Popperians conclude that falsification is an attainable goal, and survival of attempted falsifications is a more viable epistemological feature than verification.

One objection to this conclusion is that we cannot know with certainty either the truth of any particular counterinstance or of any observational consequence, and therefore such falsifications depend on uncertain premises and so are themselves uncertain. Even if this objection is unanswerable, it does not redeem the impossibility of the verifications in question. And the Popperian point can be expressed by saying that *conditional* falsification is viable in a way that conditional verification is not.

Another objection is to move the discussion from the level of verification to the level of confirmation. The point would be to say that, although positive instances do not verify a generalization, they do confirm it; and although observed consequences of an hypothesis do not verify it either, they too confirm it. Popperians would retort that, although one could easily speak of disconfirmation as a way of referring to the type of conditional falsification just mentioned, it is not clear what is meant by positive confirmation. In particular, if to confirm a generalization means to render it *probably* true rather than certainly true, they find two insuperable difficulties with that.

One of these would be a difficulty which is well known in discussions of the justification of induction. That is, to claim that the observed instances or sample render the generalization probable presupposes some assumption like the following: that it is probable that nonobserved members of a class resemble the observed members. And this principle cannot be justified without circularity or without rendering it tautological.

4. Improbability versus Probability

The other difficulty is that, according to Popper, scientific generalizations are really *improbable*, and, other things being equal, the more improbable the better. His reasoning is based on the claims that (a) scientific generalizations are very informative, and the more informative the better, and (b) the higher the information content the greater the improbability. The latter is a consequence of the conjunction rule for mathematical probability, which states that the probability of a conjunction equals the product of the probabilities of the individual conjuncts, at least in the case when the two conjuncts are independent of each other.

For example, consider a generalization such as that all ravens are black. Now, suppose the class of ravens consists of some number n of specimens, where n is either very large or infinite. Then we may think of the generalization as being equivalent to the conjunction of its n instances. Now suppose we can be 99 percent sure that any one specimen of a raven is black, and suppose $n = 100$; then the probability that all (one hundred) raven are black would be about 0.37.

5. Disconfirmation versus Confirmation

Another Popperian argument is that confirmation is problematic in a way in which disconfirmation is not because confirmation is subject to well-known paradoxes, whereas disconfirmation is not. The best known of these is that if we start with some initially plausible principles of confirmation, we are led to the absurdity that the observation of yellow pencils would confirm a generalization such as that all ravens are black. This has given rise to well-known jokes to the effect that the so-called logical empiricists, who advanced these principles, were committed to allowing the practice of ornithology without leaving the confines of one's study (Brown 1979, 24–36).

The two initially plausible principles of confirmation that lead to the paradox are the following. Nicod's principle states that a generalization such as that "all R are B" is confirmed by the observation of particular instances of R which have the property B, that is, by the observation of objects that have both properties R and B. And the so-called equivalence condition may be stated as follows: if two generalizations are logically equivalent, then whatever observations confirm one also confirm the other.[4] Now, suppose we are testing the generalization that all ravens are black. By the logical principle of contraposition, this is logically equivalent to the generalization that all nonblack things are nonravens. Now, applying Nicod's principle to this latter generalization, we could proceed to confirming it by the observation of things that are neither black nor ravens; all sorts of things easily available and accessible would fit this description, for example a yellow pencil that I may be holding in my hand. Next, given that yellow pencils confirm the generalization that all nonblack things are nonravens, we apply the equivalence condition, and conclude that we have also confirmed that all ravens are black.

Popper's way out of this paradox is to point out that disconfirmation or falsification does not face this difficulty. In fact, to disconfirm that all ravens are black we would need a raven which is not black, that is a non-black raven. Let us now see what observation we would need to disconfirm the equivalent generalization that all nonblack things are nonravens; we would need to find an instance of a nonblack thing which is *not* a non-raven, that is, a nonblack thing which *is* a raven, namely a nonblack raven. And this is the same observation as before. Therefore, there is no difficulty in the *disconfirmation* of equivalent generalizations; the same evidence is needed, and such evidence is relevant in a clear and obvious manner.

6. Critical Rationalism versus Justification by Reasons

Finally, there is another more general argument in favor of the importance of criticism. The argument is basically that skepticism or relativism

---

[4] A plausible instance of this principle would be the pair consisting of Galileo's law of squares and his law of odd numbers. The law of squares states that a body freely falling from rest covers a distance which is proportional to the square of the time elapsed; and the law of odd numbers states that the distances covered by a body falling freely from rest during successive equal times are to each other as the odd numbers beginning with unity. The latter is easier to test experimentally, and that is what Galileo did, thereby establishing the other which is equivalent to it, but conceptually more elegant.

can best be answered by focusing on refutational criticism (Bartley 1982; 1984; 1987). To see this let us begin with what is perhaps the most common definition of rationality: that to be rational is to believe all that can be justified by good reasons, and nothing that cannot be so justified. This definition consists of two parts: if an idea can be justified, then it should be accepted, and if an idea cannot be justified, then it should not be accepted. The difficulty with the principle is a self-referential one. Why should we accept it? How can it be justified?

To see why a justification of this principle is impossible, let us reflect a little on the nature of justification by reasons. To justify a claim means to base it on other claims which are more acceptable and from which it may be derived in accordance with some acceptable rules of reasoning. Therefore, we need premises and rules which are more acceptable than this definition. However, since this principle defines the meaning of rational acceptance, nothing can be more acceptable than it is. And so it is impossible to justify it.

But, if it is impossible to justify this basic principle of rationality, that means that it is in some sense to be taken on faith. And if someone is entitled to take *this* principle on faith, others are entitled to take other principles on faith, for example principles that take as the ultimate authority either the Bible, or the Catholic Church, or the writings of Karl Marx, or the Communist Party.

Moreover, even if it were possible to give a rational justification of this principle, such a justification would motivate only someone who had already accepted it. It could not motivate someone who was inclined to accept some other principle. This means that any justification would necessarily be viciously circular.

To answer the relativists and the skeptics, the Popperians give a different definition of rationality: to be rational means to hold all beliefs open to criticism, and to accept all and only those beliefs that survive criticism. This principle does not oblige the critical rationalist to have to justify it. If we ask him why we should accept it, he replies, Why not? He is bound to listen and answer our criticism, although he will not take it as valid criticism the fact that he does not give a justification of this principle.

The same would apply, for example, to scientific ideas. The critical rationalist does not worry where the idea came from, or whether it has been verified or confirmed, but rather he worries about what might be wrong with it. In particular a scientific theory will be tested by deducing from it some empirical consequence and trying to observe whether this consequence occurs in reality. If it does not, this observation disconfirms or tentatively refutes the theory. But if it does, he will not take this as a verification or confirmation or a sign of its probable truth, but simply as a failure to falsify, as a survival of criticism, and he will tentatively accept it on that basis.

7. The Popperian School and the Critical-Thinking Movement

The Popperians are and have been some of the most strenuous advocates and defenders of the importance and value of critical thinking in science. For example, it is they who have led and persisted in the criticism of Thomas Kuhn's philosophy of science (Kuhn 1962; Lakatos and Musgrave 1970), although this is also a natural target for scholars like Harvey Siegel (1988) who are concerned with both critical thinking and science. However, Popperian ideas are little known and appreciated in the critical-thinking movement so-called. And the reverse is also true: Popperians tend to be unaware of and unconcerned with the critical-thinking movement.

I am not sure of the reasons for this mutual lack of appreciation and communication. I would like to suggest that this is due, on the one hand, to the Popperian failure to appreciate what I regard as one of most important components of critical thinking, namely the activity of reasoning; on the other hand, one may say that for all its talk about critical thinking, the critical-thinking movement has not taken criticism seriously enough. In fact, on the one hand, Popperians tend to be formalists and conceive their falsificationism to be something of a vindication of deductivism; the connection is that the criticism of scientific theories they have in mind focuses on the deduction of observational consequences and depends largely on the logic of the *modus tollens*. Their neglect of reasoning also stems from their tendency to equate reasoning with the "good reasons" approach, and the latter with the verificationist or confirmationist outlook (Miller 1987). On the other hand, scholars active in the critical-thinking movement (Siegel 1988) have a tendency to equate critical thinking to reasoning in general, rather than to a special type.[5] My own aim is to avoid both of these types of one-sidedness, and also to pay proper attention to the notion of judgment, which both groups tend to neglect, with the notable exception of Lipman (1988a;

[5] For a critique of this notion of such a one-sided conception of critical thinking, see Finocchiaro (1989c).

1988b). I plan to do this by reference to some actual scientific practice. The example I have in mind involves selected aspects of the Copernican Revolution and of the work of Galileo Galilei.[6]

8. The Copernican Revolution: Can Everyone Be Wrong?

The Copernican Revolution is perhaps the most significant episode in science for the proper understanding and appreciation of the nature, the power, and the limitations of critical thinking. The label "Copernican Revolution" refers to the sequence of historical developments whose outcome was the replacement of the geostatic and geocentric cosmology by the geokinetic and heliocentric cosmology: the ancient view held that the earth stands still at the center of the universe, whereas according to the modern view the earth moves both by spinning around its own axis once a day and in an orbit around the sun once a year. The process lasted about one hundred fifty years, from about 1543 which is the year of publication of Nicolaus Copernicus's famous book *On the Revolutions of the Heavenly Spheres* to the year 1687 which is the date of publication of the first edition of Isaac Newton's book entitled *Mathematical Principles of Natural Philosophy.*

The episode may be said to have been earthshaking in both a literal and figurative sense. For the key development was the discovery that the terrestrial globe possesses physical motion and is not the center of the universe, and this discovery was so pregnant with consequences in all areas of human culture and life that it precipitated a cultural, psychological, and social upheaval.

One of the things that makes the Copernican Revolution so relevant to critical thinking stems from the fact that it involves some beliefs which today are known with certainty to be false and incorrect, and others which are now established with equal conclusiveness as being absolutely true and

---

[6] Other instructive examples would be Christian Huygens' theory of gravity, as approached in Finocchiaro 1980a, Albert Einstein's "opportunism" (Finocchiaro 1988a), and Ludwig Boltzmann's "pluralism" (Finocchiaro 1988a). Other examples from the social sciences would also be possible, though they would probably be less instructive because, by its very nature, critical thinking would be expected to be relevant in their domain. On the other hand, social-scientific examples would be more instructive from other points of view, as may be seen in Finocchiaro 1988c. Nevertheless, in exploring the connection between science and critical thinking it would be somewhat misleading to pay equal attention to the social and to the natural sciences, given the problematic scientific and epistemological status of the social-scientific disciplines.

correct.[7] That is, no sane person today can question the fact that the earth moves, and if mankind knows anything at all and if human knowledge encompasses any item of information, then the earth's motion is surely one of these things. Conversely, if we know anything to be false, it is the idea that the earth stands still at the center of the universe.

These epistemological facts have two important implications. On the one hand, there is the lesson that knowledge is possible because it is actual, and it is actual because we know at least one thing, namely that the earth moves and is not standing still at the center of the universe; another lesson is that progress is possible because the Copernican Revolution is an instance of it, and this is so because the result was to replace ignorance by knowledge in regard to the question of the location and the behavior of the earth.

On the other hand, there are also lessons that might be called negative, and these are the ones that point in the direction of critical thinking. To see this we must focus on the fact that for thousands of years, until relatively recently in human history, almost everybody was wrong about a very fundamental matter; and the important fact is that this included not just common people but scientists and philosophers as well, that is the so-called experts. What this shows is that it is possible for everyone to be wrong, or at least for everyone to be wrong some of the time, that is for a certain time, and even for a long time; for that was certainly the case in regard to the motion of the earth up until the time of the Copernican Revolution. This opens the door for the would-be critic, no matter how radical, for he is assured that it is possible that he is the only one to see the truth about the topic in question. And so he is not afraid to claim that most people may very well be wrong in their belief that there will always be rich and poor and that differences of wealth and poverty are socially inevitable, or in their belief that there will always be psychological and behavioral differences between men and women and that some sexual stereotypes are natural.

Be that as it may, the point is that, since for a long time almost everyone held the false belief that the earth stands still at the center of the universe, it is always possible that almost everyone is wrong about almost anything. However, this is just one side of the lesson relevant to critical thinking, the

---

[7] It is obvious that this claim commits me to holding that the Popperian theses and arguments elaborated above (sections 2–6) are not completely correct, but rather need to come to grips with facts such as these. From my point of view, however, there is no difficulty here, for I can simply add this point to the other criticism of Popperianism adumbrated in section 7.

one that concerns the element of criticism. If we do not neglect the element of reasoning, then we are led to ask the following questions about the Copernican Revolution. Although factually wrong in the content of their belief, were people reasonable or unreasonable in holding this incorrect belief? In other words, let us focus on the reasoning which led pre-Copernicans to their false opinion. Was this reasoning right or wrong, correct or incorrect, valid or invalid, sound or unsound? A less well-known fact about this matter is that the reasoning of the pre-Copernicans was essentially correct; that is, pre-Copernicans were basically reasonable or rational in believing that the earth stands still at the center of the universe. This will require a rather lengthy demonstration, but the anticipated lesson will be that the Copernican Revolution does not provide us with evidence that it is possible for everyone to be unreasonable; on the contrary, it suggests that if we move the discussion to the level of reasoning, then mankind is essentially reasonable. In short, one lesson of the Copernican Revolution is that it is possible for almost everybody to hold a false belief, but not for almost everybody to be unreasonable.

9. Traditional Geostatic Arguments

To appreciate this point we need to review some of the many arguments and reasons which grounded the acceptance of the geostatic thesis and the rejection of the geokinetic claim.[8]

The most basic and important evidence in favor of the ancient view was taken from direct observation, which testifies to the correctness of

---

[8] A classic source for most of these arguments is Galilei 1967 as well as the documents in Finocchiaro 1989a; for an analysis of many of these arguments, and of Galileo's critiques, see Finocchiaro 1980b. Earlier accounts of such arguments may be found in Koyré 1939 and Kuhn 1957, which remain valuable and indeed may be regarded as classics in their own right. However, my account differs from theirs in a number of ways. For my critique of Koyré, see Finocchiaro 1980b, 202–23. In regard to Kuhn, I would say, first, that his context was that of the structure of scientific revolutions, as Kuhn's later book (1962) explicitly revealed; whereas my context is primarily that of the theory of reasoning, in which I advocate an approach which attempts to provide an alternative to formal logic and which may be labeled informal logic; this was already explicit in Finocchiaro 1980b, but was made even more explicit in Finocchiaro 1984b. Second, Kuhn's account is oriented primarily toward Copernicus and technical planetary astronomy, whereas mine is oriented primarily toward Galileo, physics, and qualitative astronomy. Finally, Kuhn, at least in his early works (1957; 1962) was inclined to despair of the rationality of the Copernican revolution because of the earlier rationality of the geostatic world view, whereas I use the fact of geostatic rationality as evidence against formalism and in favor of judgment and critical thinking in the theory of rationality.

the geostatic thesis: our visual experience reveals that the heavenly bodies move around the earth every day, a point which is most easily observable for the sun whose rising in the east and setting in the west generates the cycle of night and day; further, according to our kinesthetic sense the earth is felt to be at rest. The argument here was simply that the earth must be standing still because our sense experience shows this.

This positive argument in favor of the geostatic thesis was one side of a coin whose other side was a critical objection against the earth's motion. This was the so-called argument from the deception of the senses, which claimed the following. The earth cannot move because our senses reveal that it is at rest, and if it were in motion that would mean that our senses were lying to us; but the human senses cannot perpetrate such a deception partly because the senses are our main instrument for learning about the world, and if they could not be trusted nothing could, and knowledge would be impossible; moreover, the human senses are the work of God, and He did not make them flawed, for He is all-knowing and all-powerful, and so He would have had the knowledge and the power to make them properly functioning.

Several other objections dealt with astronomical details. For example, the problem with the behavior of the planet Mars was that its apparent brightness and apparent size did not change as much as required by the earth's orbital revolution around the sun. In fact, according to Copernicanism, the earth is the third and Mars the fourth planet circling the sun, and they have different periods of revolution; therefore, there are times when both planets are on the same side from the sun and thus relatively close to each other, and there are times when the two planets are on opposite sides from the sun and thus are much further from one another; these changes in distance occur with regularity deriving from the respective periods of revolution of the two planets. Now, the apparent brightness of an object is inversely proportional to the square of the distance from the observer, and the same applies to its apparent size. It follows that if the Copernican system were correct, there should be very significant changes in the apparent brightness and the apparent size of Mars as seen from the earth, and again the amount of such changes could be calculated. However, observation revealed much smaller changes in brightness, and no change in size at all.

Analogous considerations would apply to the planet Venus, which is the second one from the sun, but in its case the more striking difficulty was its lack of phases. That is, if Venus circles the sun in an orbit inside the earth's own, given their different periods of revolution, it follows that there are times when Venus is approximately in a straight line between the earth and sun, other times when the three bodies form another approximate straight line with the sun in between, and then all kinds of intermediate positions. Now, these changes in the relative positions between the sun, Venus, and the earth would produce changes in the appearance of Venus as seen from the earth, such that Venus should go through a cycle of shapes from crescent, to a semicircle, to a full disc, and then back to a semicircle and to crescent, and so on. This would be analogous to what happens to the appearance of the moon in the course of a month, and the essential reason would be the same; the main difference would be the period of the phases. However, observation revealed no phases of Venus.

In regard to the fixed stars, the difficulty was their lack of so-called parallax. That is, if the earth revolved around the sun, then the apparent position of a fixed star should change in the course of a year. For example, one might measure the position of a fixed star by the angle created by the two lines going from the sun to the star and from the sun to the earth; obviously, as the earth moved around the sun, the magnitude of the angle would undergo a corresponding variation. Again, no change in the apparent position of any star had ever been observed.

This group of specific objections pointed to particular non-observed consequences of the earth's annual motion. Another group of specific scientific arguments involved phenomena studied in the science of motion, and dealt with mechanical consequences of the earth's daily rotation which were also not observed.

One of best known of these was an objection based on falling bodies or vertical fall, sometimes also called the tower argument. It was claimed that if the earth rotated, then bodies could not fall vertically, as they are seen to do. The alleged reason was that during free fall there is nothing that would connect the rotating earth and the falling body, and so the falling body would be left behind, and it would follow a slanted path and would land westward of where it was dropped.

10. Pre-Galilean Arguments for Earth's Motion

These arguments are, I believe, sufficient to show that the ancient geostatic, geocentric view was reasonable or rational. However, as mentioned earlier, to attribute reasonableness to it is not to call it true; indeed we know that it is false. This distinction between reasonableness and truth and between unreasonableness and falsity is related to an appreciation of the difference between the two elements of critical thinking which I have labeled criticism and reasoning. In order to appreciate the next point about the Copernican Revolution we need to appreciate the third element of critical thinking, namely judgment. In fact, at this point some people would begin to despair about how the transition to a geokinetic view was ever possible, and they may think that the transition was itself unreasonable or irrational (Kuhn 1962; Feyerabend 1975). However, this interpretation would be injudicious and thus lack judgment, for it is possible to show that the situation evolved in such a way that the geostatic view became unreasonable.

The first step in this process was the construction of a new argument in favor of the geokinetic thesis. Prior to Copernicus the only geokinetic argument was the very weak argument according to which it would be simpler to let the earth rotate daily on its axis than to let thousands of stars revolve daily around the earth because the geokinetic system would have fewer moving parts. What Copernicus accomplished was to show that the observed details about the motions of the heavenly bodies could be explained much more coherently by postulating the earth to be the third planet revolving around the sun. Although the idea of the earth's motion was not new, the argument was. The idea was not new because, as we have seen, the possibility of the earth moving had been considered since the ancient Greeks, but it had been rejected because of the weight of arguments and evidence against it. Further Copernicus's argument was novel because no one had worked out the consequences of the earth's motion around the sun in full detail, and shown that the specific phenomena in the heavens could be explained this way, let alone that they could be explained better.

Next we have to understand in what sense Copernicus's explanation of heavenly motions was better than the geostatic one. The label I have already used is "explanatory coherence."[9] What I am saying is that the geokinetic explanation has much greater explanatory coherence than the geostatic explanation. What I mean by this is that in the geokinetic theory many of the specific facts can be explained in terms of its basic postulates without having to add special assumptions invented specifically for that purpose. Sometimes this point is expressed by saying that the geostatic theory contained many more ad hoc elements. Notice also that I am not

---

[9] This type of interpretation of the Copernican Revolution, though not exactly in these terms, is suggested in Lakatos and Zahar 1975 and Millman 1976, among others.

saying that the geokinetic theory was merely simpler, at least not in any simple sense of the notion of simplicity.[10]

There is no space here to give illustrations of this. The next point that needs to be made in our account is that Copernicus's novel argument did strengthen the geokinetic view vis-à-vis the geostatic one, but not in any decisive way. The Copernican argument is not conclusive because it is a hypothetical and explanatory argument in which the hypothesis is confirmed or corroborated, but not verified, by the observational consequences; these same observations could still be explained by the geostatic hypothesis, however less coherently, less simply, and less elegantly. Moreover, explanatory coherence was not the only, or even the chief criterion, of scientific merit; the other criteria favored the geostatic hypothesis, that is, observation, physics, and the Bible. This is where Galileo comes in.

11. Galileo's Critique of the Vertical Fall Argument

At first, Galileo was primarily interested in physics and mechanics, and was working on a research program designed to understand in general how bodies move. He was critical of ancient Aristotelian physics and was developing a new theory of motion more in line with the work of another ancient Greek – Archimedes. Galileo was aware of the new Copernican argument, but felt its insufficiency and the greater power of the many anti-Copernican and pro-geostatic arguments. He was initially attracted to the Copernican theory because its key geokinetic hypothesis was more in accordance with the new physics he was developing. In effect, his new physics provided him with an effective criticism of the mechanical objections to the earth's motion, and with some physical evidence in its favor. The connection can best be seen for the case of the vertical fall objection.

Recall that the vertical fall objection argued that the earth cannot rotate because on a rotating earth freely falling bodies would have no reason to keep up with the earth's motion, and hence during free fall they would be left behind; this in turn means that they would not be falling vertically; but it is obvious that they do fall vertically. Here the last step in reasoning could be reconstructed as an instance of *modus tollens*: (1) bodies fall vertically; (2) if the earth rotated, then bodies would not fall vertically; (3) so, the earth does not rotate.

[10] In particular, it is not simply a matter of counting which theory uses fewer "epicycles," which can become a rather complicated business; see, for example, Price 1959.

Galileo begins by asking us to focus our attention on the meaning of the proposition that bodies fall vertically. What does it mean? What is meant by vertical fall? Does it mean fall from the point where the body is released to the point on the earth's surface directly below, such as the motion from the top to the base of a tower; or does vertical fall mean fall along the straight line going from the point of release to the center of the earth? In other words, does vertical fall mean fall perpendicular to the earth's surface as viewed by a terrestrial observer, that is an observer standing on the earth's surface; or does it mean fall perpendicular to the earth's surface as viewed by an extra-terrestrial observer, that is an observer looking at the whole terrestrial globe from a distance? Let us call the first apparent or relative vertical fall, and the second actual or absolute vertical fall. These are indeed different.

To explain their difference Galileo points out that on a rotating earth the two would not coincide, though they would coincide on a motionless earth. That is, assume the earth were in rotation and a rock is dropped from the top of a tower. If the rock were to move with actual vertical fall, then it would land to the west of the base of the tower; therefore, to a terrestrial observer its path would appear slanted westward, and thus not vertical. In short, on a rotating earth, actual vertical fall would not produce apparent vertical fall. Similarly, given the same assumption of terrestrial rotation, if the rock appeared to fall vertically to a terrestrial observer, then it would be seen to land at the foot of the tower; but on a rotating earth the foot of the tower would have undergone some rotational motion during the time of fall, and so as viewed by an extra-terrestrial observer the actual path of the rock would be slanted toward the east. In short, on a rotating earth, apparent vertical fall would not produce actual vertical fall. By contrast, for a motionless earth, if the path were from the top to the base of the tower as seen by the terrestrial observer, then it would also be straight and perpendicular to the earth's surface for the extra-terrestrial observer; and conversely.

Having made such a distinction, Galileo applies it to the above mentioned argument having the form of *modus tollens*. Suppose that, when the argument claims that the earth cannot rotate because bodies fall vertically, the vertical fall in question is actual vertical fall; then we would be entitled to ask how you know that bodies do actually fall vertically because observation reveals only apparent vertical fall. In other words, it is undeniable that to us on the earth's surface bodies are seen to fall from the top to the base of a tower; and it is equally undeniable that we have no experience about how they look from an extra-terrestrial viewpoint. How could one answer that question? How could one justify that falling bodies move with actual vertical fall? It seems that one could try only an empirical justification, by basing actual vertical fall on apparent vertical fall. But to do this would presuppose that apparent vertical fall implies actual vertical fall, and in turn this implication amounts to assuming that the earth is motionless, since this is the only condition under which the implication holds. Unfortunately, the motionlessness of the earth is the very conclusion the argument is trying to prove. In short, interpreted in terms of actual vertical fall the objection from vertical fall begs the question because the premise that bodies fall vertically is either assumed gratuitously or supported circularly by reasons which in their turn presuppose the conclusion at issue.

However, perhaps the objection from vertical fall intends apparent vertical fall, in which case the minor premise of the above-mentioned *modus tollens* would be both true and uncontroversial. That is, the argument would now be that the earth cannot rotate because bodies appear to us to go from the top to the base of the tower. In such a case Galileo questions the major premise, namely the conditional proposition that if the earth were in rotation, then bodies would not undergo apparent vertical fall. What are the grounds for asserting this conditional claim? At that time, the justification of this was based on some basic principles of Aristotelian physics: one was the principle that a body can have only one natural motion; another was the principle that the natural state of heavy material bodies is rest, and motion requires a force to sustain it. To understand the connection we have to understand the first answer the Aristotelians would give in this discussion.

They would say that if the earth were in rotational motion, then falling bodies would not exhibit apparent vertical fall (which in fact they do) because if they did then they would simultaneously be moving downwards (towards the center of the earth) and horizontally (around the center); in fact, if the earth rotated and falling bodies fell from the top to the base of a tower, then (as we saw above) in reality (to an extra-terrestrial observer) they would be slanting eastward; but this eastward slant would be the resultant of straight downward and straight horizontal components. Now, according to Aristotelian physics such a mixture or combination is impossible because the horizontal component of motion would be motion under the influence of no force, and so it would have to be natural; but such a second natural motion could not co-exist with the first, downward motion.

The issue then becomes whether or not it is possible for a free-falling body to have an horizontal component of motion. This is where some of the principles of the new Galilean physics come in; they are the principle of the conservation of motion and the principle of the superposition of motions. Conservation of motion is an approximation to such laws of modern physics as the law of inertia, the law of conservation of linear momentum, and the law of conservation of angular momentum. The Galilean formulation relevant to the criticism of the objection from vertical fall is the following: if a body is moving horizontally, it will conserve its motion as long as it is left undisturbed. And the principle of superposition asserts that it is physically possible for a body to have more than one tendency to move, and in these cases the actual motion will be the resultant as defined by the diagonal of the corresponding parallelogram.

These principles can now be applied to answer the objection from apparent vertical fall. If the earth rotated, then it is possible that bodies would undergo apparent vertical fall, because in this case what would be happening is the following. On a rotating earth, a body before being released would be carried eastward by the earth's rotation; after being released this horizontal component of motion would be conserved because of the just-mentioned principle. The body would also start moving downwards; but this motion would not be a disturbance to the other one. Instead they would combine, by the principle of superposition, to produce the actually slanted path which would carry the body directly below the point of release, for example to the base of the tower.

Now, one last piece of reasoning was needed to complete Galileo's criticism. In that context he could not simply assert the conservation of motion without justification. But he had one ready, which reflected the way he himself had arrived at the principle. The argument is an empirical one and it is the following. Observation reveals that bodies which move downwards are accelerated, that is, their speed increases. We can also observe that bodies are retarded when they move upwards, that is, their speed decreases. Therefore, Galileo reasoned, if a body were moving along a path which was neither downwards nor upwards, its motion should be neutral, so to speak; that is, its speed should neither increase nor decrease in the absence of disturbances. But horizontal motion is an instance of motion which is neither upwards nor downwards. Therefore, bodies moving in an horizontal direction will conserve their speed of motion if left undisturbed.

In summary, the vertical fall objection is based on some untenable assumptions if vertical fall means apparent vertical fall; that is, this version of the argument is groundless. On the other hand, the objection begs the question if vertical fall means actual vertical fall. It should be noted, however, that none of this, by itself, supports the earth's motion directly, let alone proves it; here we have simply the criticism or refutation of an argument, not a counterargument justifying the opposite conclusion.

12. Galileo's Judiciousness toward Copernicanism

Galileo's attitude toward the geokinetic idea before the telescope is, in my opinion, a beautiful illustration of that element of critical thinking which I have been calling judgment. That is, we are not merely dealing with questions of reasoning, for it was not merely a matter of reasoning one's way out of an objection like the vertical fall argument; nor was it a matter of criticism, for there was no question of his willingness and ability to challenge authority, as shown by the fact that he was engaged in a program of physical research which was undermining the foundations of Aristotelian physics. Rather we are dealing with questions of proportion, balance, judiciousness, and avoidance of one-sidedness and of extremes.

Galileo did indeed appreciate the novelty of Copernicus's argument, and he had begun to conceive ways of refuting the physical objections, and ways of providing mechanical evidence in favor of the earth's motion. All that this meant was that physics and the criterion of explanatory coherence now favored the geokinetic idea. But observation was still fully on the side of the geostatic view, and Galileo could not bring himself to any one-sided disregard of sense experience.[11] This situation was drastically changed by the telescope.

What did the telescope reveal? It made possible the observation of phenomena which enabled one to answer arguments like the general observational argument and most of the specific astronomical objections. In regard to the latter, the planet Mars could now be seen to vary in apparent brightness and size as required by the hypothesis of the earth's annual revolution. Similarly, the planet Venus exhibited the required phases. And the general observational argument could now be answered by saying that, besides the direct experience of the unaided senses, one should take into account the indirect observations made with the telescope; since almost all indirect observation favored the earth's motion, then according to the criterion of observation the situation was the following: at the very least it was no longer true to say that observation unequivocally

[11] See Galilei 1967, 327–28; cf. Finocchiaro 1980b, 128–29.

favored the geostatic system, and perhaps it was possible to say that it favored the other system. These discoveries may be said to have tipped the overall balance of evidence and argument in favor of the geokinetic and against the geostatic idea. Consequently, Galileo became increasingly outspoken about the issue, and in general an irreversible historical trend was produced which was to result in the eventual triumph of the geokinetic theory. However, the process was slow and gradual. The telescopic discoveries did not completely decide the issue.

One reason was that at least one important astronomical objection could still not be answered, that is the argument from parallax; even the telescope did not reveal any change in the apparent position of fixed stars. Galileo was correct in arguing that stellar distances are so immense that the parallax is very minute, and therefore more powerful instruments were needed to detect it; in fact, the phenomenon was first observed in 1838.

Another reason why the telescope was not immediately decisive was that for some time there were proper concerns about the legitimacy, reliability, and practical operation of the instrument. Some questioned its legitimacy on the grounds that there was no place in scientific inquiry for instruments which make us see things which cannot be seen without them. Obviously this objection could not be dismissed, as we should be able to appreciate today if we compare the situation at that time with the recent issue about whether psychedelic drugs put the user in contact with a deeper level of reality, or merely make him see things that are not there. Others questioned the reliability of the telescope by pointing out that Galileo had not provided a scientific explanation of how and why the telescope worked; moreover, all empirical checks involved terrestrial observation, and there was not even one instance of a test showing that it was truthful in the observation of the phenomena in the heavens. Finally, the practical operation of the instrument required that one learn how to use it and how to avoid aberrant and deviant observations, which were very mysterious at the time, and which are known today to stem from impurities of the lenses, improper lens shape, and other features of poor design.

Here we should not neglect to mention a still different obstacle to the construction of a conclusive case in favor of the earth's motion. That is the existence of biblical and other theological arguments against it. For example, one anti-Copernican passage in the Bible was taken to be Joshua 10:12–13, where God does the miracle of stopping the sun in its course in order to prevent it from setting at a place called Gibeon, and thus to give that region some extra daylight, needed by the Israelites to win a battle they were fighting. Understandably it took some time for Galileo to come to terms with it by declaring that the Bible is not a scientific authority (Finocchiaro 1986b; 1989a); other people, of course, required an even longer time. Moreover, even though Galileo may have won all the arguments on this issue, he personally lost all the actual battles, as the tragedy of his condemnation by the Inquisition shows.

Finally, let me mention one epistemological issue connected with the objection from the deception of the senses which also required time for a full assimilation. The difficulty is that, although deception may be too strong a word, the earth's motion was then and remains today a phenomenon which is not observable either with telescopes or by astronauts from outer space. Do such unobservable processes have any role in science, and if so what is their role? Can they be taken seriously as descriptions of physical reality, or can they be regarded only as useful fictions, useful, that is, for the calculation, computation, and prediction of other phenomena which are indeed observable? The only point I want to make here is that to admit unobservable entities in the scientific description of the world was a giant step for mankind, to be undertaken with great caution and circumspection.

My conclusion here is that the fact that the Copernican Revolution required about one hundred fifty years to complete, and Galileo's own specific tentativeness and circumspection about the matter, both attest to the importance of judiciousness and judgment in science.

13. Conclusions

In summary, I have argued that nothing compares with the Copernican Revolution as a vivid illustration of the possibility and importance of criticism. The lesson here is both specific to science and applicable to knowledge and culture in general, and the content of this lesson is that everyone may be mistaken, and everything is and ought to be open to criticism. However, man is indeed, as Aristotle declared, a rational animal, and so universal human beliefs are normally rational and reasonable, and such was certainly the geostatic belief before Copernicus and Galileo. Therefore, criticism would lack judgment if it did not recognize the importance of reasoning and the need to work at the level of reasoning. However, reasonableness and rationality are matters of degree and they are contextual; thus what is reasonable under certain conditions need not always remain so, but a change will not occur arbitrarily. Rather the change can be consummated only when one prevailing reasonable idea is shown to be less reasonable than another. Again judgment is required to ensure that reasonable ideas are not discarded arbitrarily, but only in the light of more reasonable ones.

These conclusions can in turn be reinterpreted as conclusions about the nature of critical thinking. For if we take my account of the Copernican Revolution as a defining instance of critical thinking in science, then we have seen that and how critical thinking involves three elements: criticism, reasoning, and judgment. These, in turn, are the same elements which, as we saw at the beginning, were also stressed by Bohr and Frisch. It would require further analysis to determine the connection, if any, between critical thinking in the Popperian sense of refutational criticism and corroboration, and critical thinking in the three-fold sense I have elaborated here. Nevertheless, it would have been uncritical and injudicious to have neglected the Popperian contribution to the problem of science and critical thinking. Theirs is certainly not the last word, but neither is ours.

Selected Bibliography

Adamson, W. L. 1980. *Hegemony and Revolution.* Berkeley: University of California Press.

Agassi, J. 1963. *Towards an Historiography of Science.* The Hague: Mouton.

Agassi, J. 1968. *The Continuing Revolution.* New York: McGraw-Hill.

Agassi, J. 1971. *Faraday as a Natural Philosopher.* Chicago: University of Chicago Press.

Agassi, J., and I. C. Jarvie, eds. 1987. *Rationality.* Dordrecht: Martinus Nijoff.

Agazzi, E. 1981. "What Have the History and Philosophy of Science to Do for One Another?" In Hintikka et al. 1981, 2: 241–48.

Angeles, P. A. 1981. *Dictionary of Philosophy.* New York: Barnes & Noble.

Angell, R. B. 1964. *Reasoning and Logic.* New York: Appleton.

Anselm, Saint. 1958. *Proslogium; Monologium.* Trans. S. N. Deane. La Salle, Ill.: Open Court.

Aquinas, Thomas. 1952. *The Summa Theologica.* 2 vols. Chicago: Encyclopedia Britannica.

Aristotle. 1952. *The Works of Aristotle.* 2 vols. Chicago: Encyclopedia Britannica.

Arnauld, A., and Nicole, P. 1717. *Logic; or, the Art of Thinking.* Trans. G. Ozell. London.

Arnauld, A., and P. Nicole. 1850. *Logic, or the Art of Thinking: Being the Port-Royal Logic.* Trans. T. S. Baynes. Edinburgh.

Arnauld, A., and P. Nicole. 1964. *The Art of Thinking: Port-Royal Logic.* Trans. J. Dickoff and P. James. Indianapolis: Bobbs-Merrill.

Arnauld, A., and P. Nicole. 1965. *La Logique ou l'Art de Penser.* Critical edition by P. Clair and F. Girbal. Paris: Presses Universitaires de France.

Arnauld, A., and P. Nicole. 1996. *Logic or the Art of Thinking.* Trans. J. V. Buroker. Cambridge: Cambridge University Press.

Asquith, P. D., and H. E. Kyburg, eds. 1978. *Current Research in Philosophy of Science.* East Lansing, Mich.: Philosophy of Science Association.

Bailin, S. 1988. *Achieving Extraordinary Ends.* Dordrecht: Kluwer.

431

Barth, E. M. 1982. "A Normative-Pragmatical Foundation of the Rules of Some Systems of Formal₃ Dialectics." In Barth and Martens 1982, 159–70.

Barth, E. M. 1985a. "A New Field: Empirical Logic." *Synthese* 63: 375–88.

Barth, E. M. 1985b. "Toward a Praxis-Oriented Theory of Argumentation." In *Dialogue: An Interdisciplinary Approach*, ed. M. Dascal, 73–86. Amsterdam: John Benjamins.

Barth, E. M. 1987. "Logic to Some Purpose: Theses against the Deductive-Nomological Paradigm in the Science of Logic." In Eemeren et al. 1987, 33–45.

Barth, E. M. 2002. "A Framework for Intersubjective Accountability: Dialogical Logic." In Gabbay et al. 2002, 225–93.

Barth, E. M., and E. C. W. Krabbe. 1982. *From Axiom to Dialogue.* Berlin: Walter de Gruyter.

Barth, E. M., and E. C. W. Krabbe, eds. 1992. *Logic and Political Culture.* Amsterdam: Royal Netherlands Academy of Arts and Sciences.

Barth, E. M., and J. L. Martens, eds. 1982. *Argumentation: Approaches to Theory Formation.* Amsterdam: John Benjamins.

Barth, E. M., J. Vandormael, and F. Vandamme, eds. 1992. *From an Empirical Point of View: The Empirical Turn in Logic.* Ghent, Belgium: Communication and Cognition.

Barth, K. 1963. *God in Action.* Manhasset, N.Y.: Round Table Press.

Barth, K. 1964. *God Here and Now.* Trans. P. M. van Buren. New York: Harper & Row.

Bartley, W. W., III. 1962. *The Retreat to Commitment.* New York: Alfred A. Knopf.

Bartley, W. W., III. 1964. "Rationality versus the Theory of Rationality." In *The Critical Approach to Science and Philosophy*, ed. M. Bunge, 3–31. New York: Free Press.

Bartley, W. W., III. 1982. "Critical Study: The Philosophy of Karl Popper." *Philosophia* 11: 121–221.

Bartley, W. W., III. 1984. *The Retreat to Commitment.* 2nd ed. La Salle, Ill.: Open Court.

Bartley, W. W., III. 1987. "Theories of Rationality." In *Evolutionary Epistemology, Theory of Rationality, and the Sociology of Knowledge*, ed. G. Radnitsky and W. W. Bartley, III, 205–16. La Salle, Ill.: Open Court.

Battersby, M. E. 1989. "Critical Thinking as Applied Epistemology." *Informal Logic* 11: 91–100.

Baynes, T. S., ed. and trans. 1850. *Logic, or the Art of Thinking: Being the Port-Royal Logic.* Edinburgh.

Beardsley, M. C. 1966. *Thinking Straight.* 3rd ed. Englewood Cliffs, N.J.: Prentice-Hall.

Bechler, Z. 1981. "What Have They Done to Kuhn?" In Hintikka et al. 1981, 1: 63–86.

Bell, A. E. 1947. *Christian Huygens and the Development of Science in the Seventeenth Century.* London: Edward Arnold.

Bencivenga, E. 1979. "On Good and Bad Arguments." *Journal of Philosophical Logic* 8: 247–59.

Berkeley, G. 1929. *Essay, Principles, Dialogues.* New York: Scribner's.

Beth, E. W., and J. Piaget. 1966. *Mathematical Epistemology and Psychology*. Dordrecht: Reidel.

Beth, E. W., et al., eds. 1962. *Implication, Formalisation, et Logique*. Paris: Presses Universitaires de France.

Black, M. 1952. *Critical Thinking*. 2nd ed. Englewood Cliffs, N.J.: Prentice-Hall.

Blair, J. A. 1995. "Premise Adequacy." In Eemeren et al. 1995a, 191–202.

Blair, J. A. 1998. "The Limits of the Dialogue Model of Argument." In Hansen et al. 1998.

Blair, J. A., and R. H. Johnson, eds. 1980. *Informal Logic: The First International Symposium*. Inverness, Calif.: Edgepress.

Blair, J. A., and R. H. Johnson. 1987. "Argumentation as Dialectical." *Argumentation* 1: 41–56.

Bochenski, I. M. 1961. *A History of Formal Logic*. Trans. I. Thomas. Notre Dame: University of Notre Dame Press.

Bogazzi, R. 1977. "Il *Kosmotheoros* di Christiaan Huygens." *Physis* 19: 87–109.

Boltzmann, L. 1964. *Lectures on Gas Theory*. Trans. S. G. Brush. Berkeley: University of California Press.

Boltzmann, L. 1974. *Theoretical Physics and Philosophical Problems*. Trans. P. Foulkes. Ed. B. McGuinness. Dordrecht: Reidel.

Bos, H. J. M., M. J. S. Rudwick, H. A. M. Snelders, and R. P. W. Visser, eds. 1980. *Studies on Christiaan Huygens*. Lisse: Swets & Zeitlinger.

Braine, M. S. 1978. "On the Relation between the Natural Logic of Reasoning and Standard Logic." *Psychological Review* 85: 1–21.

Brown, H. I. 1975. "Paradigmatic Propositions." *American Philosophical Quarterly* 12: 86–90.

Brown, H. I. 1977. *Perception, Theory and Commitment: The New Philosophy of Science*. Chicago: Precedent Publishing.

Brown, H. I. 1979. *Perception, Theory and Commitment: The New Philosophy of Science*. Chicago: University of Chicago Press.

Brown, H. I. 1987. *Observation and Rationality*. New York: Oxford University Press.

Brown, H. I. 1989. *Rationality*. London: Routledge.

Brush, S. G. 1964. "Introduction" to Boltzmann 1964.

Brush, S. G. 1976. *The Kind of Motion We Call Heat*. 2 vols. New York: North-Holland.

Buchdahl, G. 1970a. "Gravity and Intelligibility: Newton to Kant." In *The Methodological Heritage of Newton*, ed. R. E. Butts and J. W. Davis, 74–102. Toronto: University of Toronto Press.

Buchdahl, G. 1970b. "History of Science and Criteria of Choice." In *Historical and Philosophical Perspectives on Science*, ed. R. H. Stuewer, 204–30. Minneapolis: University of Minnesota Press.

Buchdahl, G. 1973. "Explanation and Gravity." In *Changing Perspectives in the History of Science*, ed. M. Teich and R. Young, 167–203. Dordrecht: Reidel.

Buroker, J. V. 1993. "The Port-Royal Semantics of Terms." *Synthese* 96: 455–75.

Buroker, J. V. 1994. "Judgment and Predication in the Port-Royal Logic." In *The Great Arnauld and Some of His Philosophical Correspondents*, ed. E. J. Kremer, 3–27. Toronto: University of Toronto Press.

Buroker, J. V., ed. and trans. 1996. *Logic or the Art of Thinking*. Cambridge: Cambridge University Press.

Byrne, R. 1983. "Protocol Analysis in Problem Solving." In Evans 1983c, 227–49.

Carnap, R. 1950. *Logical Foundations of Probability*. Chicago: University of Chicago Press.

Cattani, A. 2001. *Botta e risposta: L'arte della replica*. Bologna: Il Mulino.

Chisholm, R. M. 1970. "On the Nature of Empirical Evidence." In *Experience and Theory*, ed. L. Foster and J. L. Swanson, 103–34. London: Duckworth.

Chomsky, N. 1959. Review of Skinner's *Verbal Behavior*. *Language* 35: 26–58.

Clair, P., and F. Girbal, eds. 1965. *La Logique ou l'Art de Penser*. Paris: Presses Universitaires de France.

Clark, M. 1975. "The Patron Saint of the Left." *Times Literary Supplement* (London), 31 October, no. 3842, p. 1280.

Cohen, I. B. 1966. "Hypotheses in Newton's Philosophy." *Physis* 8: 163–84.

Cohen, I. B. 1971. *Introduction to Newton's Principia*. Cambridge, Mass.: Harvard University Press.

Cohen, L. J. 1966. *The Diversity of Meaning*. 2nd ed. London: Methuen.

Cohen, L. J. 1970. *The Implications of Induction*. London: Methuen.

Cohen, L. J. 1977. *The Probable and the Provable*. Oxford: Clarendon.

Cohen, L. J. 1979. "On the Psychology of Prediction: Whose Is the Fallacy?" *Cognition* 7: 385–407.

Cohen, L. J. 1980. "Whose Is the Fallacy? A Rejoinder to Daniel Kahneman and Amos Tversky." *Cognition* 8: 89–92.

Cohen, L. J. 1981a. "Can Human Irrationality Be Experimentally Demonstrated?" *Behavioral and Brain Sciences* 4: 317–31 and 359–67.

Cohen, L. J. 1981b. "Subjective Probability and the Paradox of the Gatecrasher." *Arizona State Law Journal*, pp. 627–34.

Cohen, L. J. 1982. "Are People Programmed to Commit Fallacies?" *Journal for the Theory of Social Behavior* 12: 251–74.

Cohen, L. J. 1986. *The Dialogue of Reason: An Analysis of Analytical Philosophy*. Oxford: Clarendon.

Cohen, L. J. 1991. "Some Comments by L. J. C." In Eells and Maruszewski 1991, 319–42.

Cohen, M. R., and E. Nagel. 1934. *An Introduction to Logic and Scientific Method*. New York: Harcourt, Brace.

Colodny, R. G., ed. 1962. *Frontiers of Science and Philosophy*. Pittsburgh: University of Pittsburgh Press.

Copi, I. M. 1968. *Introduction to Logic*. 3rd ed. New York: Macmillan.

Copi, I. M. 1972. *Introduction to Logic*. 4th ed. New York: Macmillan.

Copi, I. M. 1986a. *Informal Logic*. New York: Macmillan.

Copi, I. M. 1986b. *Introduction to Logic*. 7th ed. New York: Macmillan.

Copi, I. M., and C. Cohen. 1990. *Introduction to Logic*. 8th ed. New York: Macmillan.

Copi, I. M., and C. Cohen. 1994. *Introduction to Logic*. 9th ed. New York: Macmillan.

Crosland, M. 1973. "Lavoisier's Theory of Acidity." *Isis* 64: 306–25.

Cummings, L. 2002. "Hilary Putnam's Dialectical Thinking." *Argumentation* 16: 197–229.

Czapinski, J. 1980. "Positive-Negative Asymmetry on the Group Level." *Polish Psychological Bulletin* 11: 203–5.

Czapinski, J. 1982. "Positive-Negative Asymmetry at Group and Individual Level." *Polish Psychological Bulletin* 13: 153–58.

Czapinski, J. 1986. "Informativeness of Evaluations in Interpersonal Communications." *Polish Psychological Bulletin* 17: 155–64.

Dahl, R. A. 1956. *A Preface to Democratic Theory.* Chicago: University of Chicago Press.

Davidson, D. 1968. "The Logical Form of Action Sentences." In *The Logic of Decision and Action,* ed. N. Rescher. Pittsburgh: University of Pittsburgh Press.

Del Noce, A. 1978. *Il suicidio della rivoluzione.* Milan: Rusconi.

Descartes, R. 1644. *Principia Philosophiae.* Leiden.

Dickoff, J., and P. James, eds. and trans. 1964. *The Art of Thinking: Port-Royal Logic.* Indianapolis: Bobbs-Merrill.

Dijksterhuis, E. J. 1961. *The Mechanization of the World Picture.* Trans. C. Dikshoorn. Oxford: Oxford University Press.

Doss, S. 1985. "Three Steps toward a Theory of Informal Logic." *Informal Logic* 7: 127–35.

Drake, S. 1978. *Galileo at Work.* Chicago: University of Chicago Press.

Eddington, A. S. 1930. *The Nature of the Physical World.* New York: Macmillan.

Eells, E., and T. Maruszewski, eds. 1991. *Probability and Rationality.* Atlanta: Rodopi.

Eemeren, F. H. van. 1987. "For Reason's Sake: Maximal Argumentative Analysis of Discourse." In Eemeren et al. 1987, 201–15.

Eemeren, F. H. van, ed. 2002. *Advances in Pragma-Dialectics.* Newport News, Va.: Vale.

Eemeren, F. H. van, J. A. Blair, C. A. Willard, and A. F. Snoeck Henkemans, eds. 2003. *Proceedings of the Fifth Conference of the International Society for the Study of Argumentation.* Amsterdam: Sic Sat.

Eemeren, F. H. van, and R. Grootendorst. 1984. *Speech Acts in Argumentative Discussions.* Dordrecht: Foris.

Eemeren, F. H. van, and R. Grootendorst. 1992. *Argumentation, Communication, and Fallacies.* Hillsdale, N.J.: Lawrence Erlbaum Associates.

Eemeren, F. H. van, and R. Grootendorst, eds. 1994. *Studies in Pragma-Dialectics.* Amsterdam: International Centre for the Study of Argumentation.

Eemeren, F. H. van, R. Grootendorst, J. A. Blair, and C. A. Willard, eds. 1987. *Argumentation across the Lines of Discipline: Proceedings of the Conference on Argumentation 1986.* Dordrecht: Foris.

Eemeren, F. H. van, R. Grootendorst, J. A. Blair, and C. A. Willard, eds. 1992. *Argumentation Illuminated.* Amsterdam: Sic Sat.

Eemeren, F. H. van, R. Grootendorst, J. A. Blair, and C. A. Willard, eds. 1995a. *Analysis and Evaluation: Proceedings of the Third ISSA Conference on Argumentation, vol. 2.* Amsterdam: Sic Sat.

Eemeren, F. H. van, R. Grootendorst, J. A. Blair, and C. A. Willard, eds. 1995b. *Perspectives and Approaches: Proceedings of the Third ISSA Conference on Argumentation, vol. 1.* Amsterdam: Sic Sat.

Eemeren, F. H. van, R. Grootendorst, J. A. Blair, and C. A. Willard, eds. 1999. *Proceedings of the Fourth International Conference of the International Society for the Study of Argumentation.* Amsterdam: Sic Sat.

Eemeren, F. H. van, R. Grootendorst, S. Jackson, and S. Jacobs. 1993. *Reconstructing Argumentative Discourse*. Tuscaloosa: University of Alabama Press.

Eemeren, F. H. van, R. Grootendorst, and T. Kruiger. 1984. *The Study of Argumentation*. New York: Irvington.

Eemeren, F. H. van, R. Grootendorst, and A. F. Snoeck Henkemans, eds. 1996. *Fundamentals of Argumentation Theory*. Mahwah, N.J.: Lawrence Erlbaum Associates.

Einstein, A. 1934. "On the Method of Theoretical Physics." In idem, *The World As I See It*. New York: Covici Friede.

Einstein, A., and L. Infeld. 1938. *The Evolution of Physics*. New York: Simon and Schuster.

Elzinga, A. 1971. "Huygens' Theory of Research and Descartes' Theory of Knowledge, I." *Zeitschrift für allgemeine Wissenschaftstheorie* 2: 174–94.

Elzinga, A. 1972a. "Huygens' Theory of Research and Descartes' Theory of Knowledge, II." *Zeitschrift für Allgemeine Wissenschaftstheorie* 3: 9–27.

Elzinga, A. 1972b. *On a Research Program in Early Modern Physics*. New York: Humanities.

Engel, S. M. 1976. *With Good Reason*. New York: St. Martin's.

Ennis, R. H. 1962. "A Concept of Critical Thinking." *Harvard Educational Review* 32: 81–111.

Ennis, R. H. 1968. "Enumerative Induction and Best Explanation." *Journal of Philosophy* 65: 523–29.

Ennis, R. H. 1969. *Ordinary Logic*. Englewood Cliffs, N.J.: Prentice-Hall.

Ennis, R. H. 1976. "An Alternative to Piaget's Conceptualization of Logical Competence." *Child Development* 17: 903–19.

Ennis, R. H. 1980. "A Conception of Rational Thinking." In *Philosophy of Education 1979*, ed. J. R. Coombs, 3–30. Normal, Ill.: Philosophy of Education Society.

Ennis, R. H. 1981. "Rational Thinking and Educational Practice." In *Philosophy and Education*, ed. J. F. Soltis, 143–83. Chicago: National Society for the Study of Education.

Epstein, R. L. 2002. *Critical Thinking*. 2nd ed. Belmont, Calif.: Wadsworth.

Evans, J. St. B. T. 1972a. "Interpretation and 'Matching Bias' in a Reasoning Task." *Quarterly Journal of Experimental Psychology* 24: 193–99.

Evans, J. St. B. T. 1972b. "Reasoning with Negatives." *British Journal of Psychology* 63: 213–19.

Evans, J. St. B. T. 1982. *The Psychology of Deductive Reasoning*. London: Routledge.

Evans, J. St. B. T. 1983a. "Introduction." In Evans 1983c, 1–15.

Evans, J. St. B. T. 1983b. "Selective Processes in Reasoning." In Evans 1983c, 135–63.

Evans, J. St. B. T., ed. 1983c. *Thinking and Reasoning*. London: Routledge.

Falmagne, R. J., ed. 1975. *Reasoning: Representation and Process*. New York: Wiley.

Fearnside, W. W., and W. B. Holther. 1959. *Fallacy: The Counterfeit of Argument*. Englewood Cliffs, N.J.: Prentice-Hall.

Feigl, H., and G. Maxwell, eds. 1962. *Minnesota Studies in the Philosophy of Science*, vol. 3. Minneapolis: University of Minnesota Press.

Feigl, H., and M. Scriven, eds. 1956. *Minnesota Studies in the Philosophy of Science*, vol. 1. Minneapolis: University of Minnesota Press.

Feigl, H., M. Scriven, and G. Maxwell, eds. 1958. *Minnesota Studies in the Philosophy of Science*, vol. 2. Minneapolis: University of Minnesota Press.

Femia, J. V. 1981. *Gramsci's Political Thought*. Oxford: Clarendon.

Feuer, L. S. 1974. *Einstein and the Generations of Science*. New York: Basic Books.

Feyerabend, P. K. 1962a. "Explanation, Reduction, and Empiricism." In Feigl and Maxwell 1962, 28–97.

Feyerabend, P. K. 1962b. "Problems of Microphysics." In Colodny 1962, 189–283.

Feyerabend, P. K. 1963. "How to Be a Good Empiricist." In *Philosophy of Science: The Delaware Seminar*, vol. 1, ed. B. Baumrin, 3–39. New York: Interscience.

Feyerabend, P. K. 1965. "Problems of Empiricism." In *Beyond the Edge of Certainty*, ed. R. Colodny, 145–260. Englewood Cliffs, N.J.: Prentice-Hall.

Feyerabend, P. K. 1970a. "Against Method." In *Minnesota Studies in the Philosophy of Science*, vol. 4, ed. M. Radner and S. Vinokur, 17–130. Minneapolis: University of Minnesota Press.

Feyerabend, P. K. 1970b. "Consolations for the Specialist." In Lakatos and Musgrave 1970, 197–230.

Feyerabend, P. K. 1970c. "Problems of Empiricism, Part II." In *The Nature and Function of Scientific Theories*, ed. R. Colodny, 275–353. Pittsburgh: University of Pittsburgh Press.

Feyerabend, P. K. 1975. *Against Method*. London: NLB.

Feynman, R. P., R. B. Leighton, and M. Sands. 1963. *The Feynman Lectures on Physics*, vol. 1: *Mainly Mechanics, Radiation, and Heat*. Reading, Mass.: Addison-Wesley.

Findlay, J. 1964. *Hegel: A Re-examination*. New York: Humanities.

Finocchiaro, M. A. 1964. "An Analysis of Heisenberg's Attempt to Compare Quantum Mechanics and Thermodynamics." B.S. thesis, Department of Humanities, Massachusetts Institute of Technology.

Finocchiaro, M. A. 1969. "The Problem of Explanation in Historiography of Science." Ph.D. dissertation, Department of Philosophy, University of California-Berkeley.

Finocchiaro, M. A. 1973a. Essay-Review of Lakatos's *Criticism and the Growth of Knowledge*. *Studies in History and Philosophy of Science* 3: 357–72.

Finocchiaro, M. A. 1973b. "Galileo's Space-Proportionality Argument: A Role for Logic in Historiography." *Physis* 15: 65–72.

Finocchiaro, M. A. 1973c. *History of Science as Explanation*. Detroit: Wayne State University Press.

Finocchiaro, M. A. 1974a. "The Concept of *ad Hominem* Argument in Galileo and Locke." *Philosophical Forum* 5: 394–404.

Finocchiaro, M. A. 1974b. "Newton's Third Rule of Philosophizing: A Role for Logic in Historiography." *Isis* 65: 66–73.

Finocchiaro, M. A. 1977a. "Galileo's Philosophy of Science, Part I: A Case Study of the Role of Judgment and of Philosophizing in Science." *Scientia* 112: 95–118.

Finocchiaro, M. A. 1977b. "Logic and Rhetoric in Lavoisier's Sealed Note: Toward a Rhetoric of Science." *Philosophy and Rhetoric* 10: 111–122.

Finocchiaro, M. A. 1978a. Review of Brown's *Perception, Theory and Commitment*. *Isis* 69: 602–4.

Finocchiaro, M. A. 1978b. "Rhetoric and Scientific Rationality." In *PSA 1978*, ed. I. Hacking and P. D. Asquith, 235–46. East Lansing, Mich.: Philosophy of Science Association.

Finocchiaro, M. A. 1979a. "Methodological Criticism and Critical Methodology." *Zeitschrift für allgemeine Wissenschaftstheorie* 10: 363–74.

Finocchiaro, M. A. 1979b. "The Psychological Explanation of Reasoning: Logical and Methodological Problems." *Philosophy of the Social Sciences* 9: 277–91.

Finocchiaro, M. A. 1980a. "The Concept of Judgment and Huygens' Theory of Gravity." *Epistemologia* 3: 185–218.

Finocchiaro, M. A. 1980b. *Galileo and the Art of Reasoning: Rhetorical Foundations of Logic and Scientific Method.* Boston: Reidel.

Finocchiaro, M. A. 1980c. Review of Johnstone's *Validity and Rhetoric in Philosophical Argument. Review of Metaphysics* 34: 143–44.

Finocchiaro, M. A. 1981. "Fallacies and the Evaluation of Reasoning." *American Philosophical Quarterly* 18: 13–22.

Finocchiaro, M. A. 1983. "Judgment and Argument in *The Communist Manifesto.*" *Philosophical Forum* 14: 135–56.

Finocchiaro, M. A. 1984a. "Croce as Seen in a Recent Work on Gramsci." *Rivista di studi crociani* 21: 139–54.

Finocchiaro, M. A. 1984b. "Informal Logic and the Theory of Reasoning." *Informal Logic* 6(2): 3–8.

Finocchiaro, M. A. 1984c. "The Labyrinth of Gramscian Studies and Femia's Contribution." *Inquiry* 27: 291–310.

Finocchiaro, M. A. 1986a. "Marxism, Science, and Religion in Gramsci: Recent Trends in Italian Scholarship." *Philosophical Forum* 17: 127–55.

Finocchiaro, M. A. 1986b. "The Methodological Background to Galileo's Trial." In *Reinterpreting Galileo*, ed. W. A. Wallace, 241–72. Washington: Catholic University of America Press.

Finocchiaro, M. A. 1987a. "An Historical Approach to the Study of Argumentation." In Eemeren et al. 1987, 81–91.

Finocchiaro, M. A. 1987b. Review of D. N. Walton's *Arguer's Position. Philosophy and Rhetoric* 20: 63–65.

Finocchiaro, M. A. 1987c. "Six Types of Fallaciousness: Toward a Realistic Theory of Logical Criticism." *Argumentation* 1: 263–82.

Finocchiaro, M. A. 1988a. "Empiricism, Judgment, and Argument: Toward an Informal Logic of Science." *Argumentation* 2: 313–35.

Finocchiaro, M. A. 1988b. "Galileo's Copernicanism and the Acceptability of Guiding Assumptions." In *Scrutinizing Science*, ed. A. Donovan, L. Laudan, and R. Laudan, 49–67. Dordrecht: Kluwer.

Finocchiaro, M. A. 1988c. *Gramsci and the History of Dialectical Thought.* Cambridge: Cambridge University Press.

Finocchiaro, M. A. 1988d. *Gramsci critico e la critica.* Rome: Armando Editore.

Finocchiaro, M. A., ed. and trans. 1989a. *The Galileo Affair: A Documentary History.* Berkeley: University of California Press.

Finocchiaro, M. A. 1989b. "Methodological Problems in Empirical Logic." *Communication and Cognition* 22: 313–35.

Finocchiaro, M. A. 1989c. "Siegel on Critical Thinking." *Philosophy of the Social Sciences* 19: 483–92.

Finocchiaro, M. A. 1989d. "Fetishism, Argument, and Judgment in Capital." *Studies in Soviet Thought* 38: 237–44.

Finocchiaro, M. A. 1990a. "Cognitive Asymmetries and Argumentation Theory." Paper presented at the Second International Conference on Argumentation, University of Amsterdam, The Netherlands.

Finocchiaro, M. A. 1990b. "Critical Thinking and Thinking Critically." *Philosophy of the Social Sciences* 20: 462–66.

Finocchiaro, M. A. 1991. "Induction and Intuition in the Normative Study of Reasoning." In Eells and Maruszewski 1991, 81–95.

Finocchiaro, M. A. 1992a. "Asymmetries in Argumentation and Evaluation." In Eemeren et al. 1992, 62–72.

Finocchiaro, M. A. 1992b. "Logic, Politics, and Gramsci." In Barth and Krabbe 1992, 25–43.

Finocchiaro, M. A. 1994a. "The Positive versus the Negative Evaluation of Arguments." In Johnson and Blair 1994, 21–35.

Finocchiaro, M. A. 1994b. "Two Empirical Approaches to the Study of Reasoning." *Informal Logic* 16: 1–21.

Finocchiaro, M. A. 1995a. "Criticism, Reasoning and Judgment in Science." In *Critical Rationalism, Metaphysics and Science*, ed. I. C. Jarvie and N. Laor 1: 169–91. Boston: Kluwer.

Finocchiaro, M. A. 1995b. "The Dialectical Approach to Interpretation and Evaluation." In Eemeren et al. 1995b, 183–95.

Finocchiaro, M. A. 1995c. "Empirische Ansätze zur Erforshung des Argumentierens: Experiment, Induktion, historische Textanalyse." *Zeitschrift für Semiotik* 17: 257–83.

Finocchiaro, M. A. 1996a. "Critical Thinking, Critical Reasoning, and Methodological Reflection." *Inquiry: Critical Thinking across the Disciplines* 15: 66–79.

Finocchiaro, M. A. 1996b. "Reasoning about Reasoning." In *Practical Reasoning*, ed. D. M. Gabbay and H. J. Ohlbach, 167–77. New York: Springer.

Finocchiaro, M. A., ed. and trans. 1997a. *Galileo on the World Systems: A New Abridged Translation and Guide.* Berkeley: University of California Press.

Finocchiaro, M. A. 1997b. "The *Port-Royal Logic*'s Theory of Argument." *Argumentation* 11: 393–410.

Finocchiaro, M. A. 1999. "A Critique of the Dialectical Approach, Part II." In Eemeren et al. 1999, 195–99.

Finocchiaro, M. A. 2001. "Valid *Ad Hominem* Arguments in Philosophy: Johnstone's Metaphilosophical Informal Logic." *Informal Logic* 21: 11–24.

Finocchiaro, M. A. 2002. "Elementary Logic from an Advanced Standpoint." *Informal Logic*, Teaching Supplement, vol. 22, no. 2, summer, pp. TS9–TS22.

Finocchiaro, M. A. 2003. "Dialectics, Evaluation, and Argument." *Informal Logic* 23: 19–49.

Fisher, A. 1988. *The Logic of Real Arguments.* Cambridge: Cambridge University Press.

Fisher, A. 1992. "Critical Study: *Dialectics and the Macrostructure of Arguments* by James B. Freeman." *Informal Logic* 14: 193–204.

Fisher, A., and M. Scriven. 1997. *Critical Thinking: Its Definition and Assessment.* Point Reyes, Calif.: Edgepress; Norwich, U.K.: Centre for Research in Critical Thinking.

Flew, A., and A. MacIntyre, eds. 1955. *New Essays in Philosophical Theology.* London: SCM.

Fogelin, R. J. 1978. *Understanding Arguments: An Introduction to Informal Logic.* New York: Harcourt Brace Jovanovich.

Freeman, J. B. 1991. *Dialectics and the Macrostructure of Arguments.* New York: Foris.

Frisch, O. R. 1979. *What Little I Remember.* Cambridge: Cambridge University Press.

Gabbay, D. V., R. H. Johnson, H. J. Holbach, and J. Woods, eds. 2002. *Handbook of the Logic of Argument and Inference.* Amsterdam: Elsevier.

Galilei, G. 1632. *Dialogo.* In Galilei 1890–1909, vol. 7.

Galilei, G. 1890–1909. *Le Opere di Galileo Galilei.* 20 vols. National Edition by A. Favaro et al. Florence: Barbèra. Rpt. in 1929–1939 and 1968.

Galilei, G. 1914. *Dialogues Concerning Two New Sciences.* Trans. H. Crew and A. De Salvio. Rpt., New York: Dover.

Galilei, G. 1953. *Dialogue Concerning the Two Chief World Systems.* Trans. S. Drake. Berkeley: University of California Press.

Galilei, G. 1966. *The Controversy on the Comets of 1618.* Trans. S. Drake and C. D. O'Malley. Philadelphia: University of Pennsylvania Press.

Galilei, G. 1967. *Dialogue Concerning the Two Chief World Systems.* Trans. S. Drake. 2nd rev. ed. Berkeley: University of California Press.

Galilei, G. 1974. *Two New Sciences.* Trans. S. Drake. Madison: University of Wisconsin Press.

George, R. 1983. "A Postscript on Fallacies." *Journal of Philosophical Logic* 12: 319–25.

Germino, D. 1990. *Antonio Gramsci: Architect of a New Politics.* Baton Rouge: Louisiana State University Press.

Gettier, E., Jr. 1963. "Is Justified True Belief Knowledge?" *Analysis* 23: 121–23.

Glaser, E. M. 1941. *An Experiment in the Development of Critical Thinking.* New York: Bureau of Publications, Teachers College, Columbia University.

Goldman, A. I. 1994. "Argumentation and Social Epistemology." *Journal of Philosophy* 94: 27–49.

Goldman, A. I. 1999. *Knowledge in a Social World.* Oxford: Clarendon.

Goosens, W. K. 1980. "Galileo's Response to the Tower Argument." *Studies in History and Philosophy of Science* 11: 215–27.

Govier, T. 1982. "Who Says There Are No Fallacies?" *Informal Logic Newsletter*, vol. v, no. i, pp. 2–10.

Govier, T. 1985. "Logical Analogies." *Informal Logic* 7: 27–33.

Govier, T. 1989. "Critical Thinking as Argument Analysis." *Argumentation* 3: 115–26.

Govier, T. 1998. "Arguing Forever?" In Hansen et al. 1998.

Govier, T. 1999a. *The Philosophy of Argument.* Newport News, Va.: Vale.

Govier, T. 1999b. "Progress and Regress on the Dialectical Tier." In Govier 1999a, 223–40.

Govier, T. 2000. "Critical Review: Johnson's *Manifest Rationality*." *Informal Logic* 20: 281–91.

Gramsci, A. 1958. *Scritti giovanili (1914–1918)*. Turin: Einaudi.

Gramsci, A. 1965. *Lettere dal carcere*. Ed. S. Caprioglio and E. Fubini. Turin: Einaudi.

Gramsci, A. 1971. *Selections from the Prison Notebooks*. Ed. and trans. Q. Hoare and G. Nowell-Smith. New York: International.

Gramsci, A. 1973. *Letters from Prison*. Ed. and trans. L. Lawner. New York: Harper.

Gramsci, A. 1975. *Quaderni del carcere*. 4 vols. Critical edition by V. Gerratana. Turin: Einaudi.

Gramsci, A. 1982. *La città futura (1917–1918)*. Ed. S. Caprioglio. Turin: Einaudi.

Gramsci, A. 1985. *Selections from Cultural Writings*. Ed. D. Forgacs and G. Nowell-Smith, trans. W. Boelhower. Cambridge, Mass.: Harvard University Press.

Gramsci, A. 1988. *A Gramsci Reader*. Ed. D. Forgacs. New York: Schocken.

Griggs, R. A. 1983. "The Role of Problem Content in the Selection Task and in the THOG Problem." In Evans 1983c, 16–43.

Groarke, L. 2002. "Johnson on the Metaphysics of Argument." *Argumentation* 16: 277–286.

Grootendorst, R. 1987. "Some Fallacies about Fallacies." In Eemeren et al. 1987, 331–42.

Guerlac, H. 1961. *Lavoisier – the Crucial Year*. Ithaca: Cornell University Press.

Hacking, I. 1975. *The Emergence of Probability*. Cambridge: Cambridge University Press.

Hacking, I. 1983. *Representing and Intervening*. Cambridge: Cambridge University Press.

Hamblin, C. L. 1970. *Fallacies*. London: Methuen. Rpt., Newport News, Va.: Vale, 1986.

Hansen, H. V. 2002. "An Exploration of Johnson's Sense of 'Argument.'" *Argumentation* 16: 263–76.

Hansen, H. V., R. C. Pinto, C. W. Tindale, J. A. Blair, and R. H. Johnson, eds. 2002. *Argumentation and Its Applications*. Windsor: Ontario Society for the Study of Argumentation. CD-ROM. ISBN 0-9683461-2-X.

Hansen, H. V., C. W. Tindale, and A. V. Colman, eds. 1998. *Argumentation and Rhetoric*. St. Catharines: Ontario Society for the Study of Argumentation. CD-ROM. ISBN 0-9683461-0-3.

Harman, G. 1984. "Logic and Reasoning." *Synthese* 60: 107–27.

Harman, G. 1986. *Change in View: Principles of Reasoning*. Cambridge, Mass.: MIT Press.

Heisenberg, W. 1955. "The Development of the Interpretation of the Quantum Theory." In *Niels Bohr and the Development of Physics*, ed. W. Pauli, 12–29. New York: McGraw-Hill.

Hempel, C. 1965. *Aspects of Scientific Explanation*. New York: Free Press. *Read!*

Henle, M. 1962. "On the Relation between Logic and Thinking." *Psychological Review* 69: 376–82.

Henle, M. 1978. "Foreword." In Revlin and Mayer 1978, pp. xiii–xviii.

Henle, M. 1981. "Another Vote for Rationality." *Behavioral and Brain Sciences* 4: 339.

Hiebert, E. N. 1981. "Boltzmann's Conception of Theory Construction." In Hintikka et al. 1981, 2: 175–98.

Hintikka, J. 1974. "Quantifiers vs. Quantification Theory." *Linguistic Inquiry* 5: 153–77.

Hintikka, J., D. Gruender, and E. Agazzi, eds. 1981. *Theory Change, Ancient Axiomatics, and Galileo's Methodology.* 2 vols. Dordrecht: Reidel.

Hitchcock, D. 1987. "Enthymematic Arguments." In Eemeren et al. 1987, 289–98.

Hitchcock, D. 1989. "A General Theory of Good Inference?" Paper presented at the Third International Symposium on Informal Logic, University of Windsor, Canada.

Hitchcock, D. 1994. "Validity in Conductive Arguments." In Johnson and Blair 1994, 58–66.

Hitchcock, D. 2002a. "The Practice of Argumentative Discussion." *Argumentation* 16: 287–98.

Hitchcock, D. 2002b. "Sampling Scholarly Arguments: A Test of a Theory of Good Inference." In Hansen et al. 2002.

Hockenos, W. J. 1968. "An Examination of *Reductio ad Absurdum* and *Argumentum ad Hominem* Arguments in the Philosophies of Gilbert Ryle and Henry W. Johnstone, Jr." Ph. D. dissertation, Boston University.

Holton, G. 1973. *Thematic Origins of Scientific Thought.* Cambridge, Mass.: Harvard University Press.

Holton, G. 1978. *The Scientific Imagination.* Cambridge: Cambridge University Press.

Hume, D. 1911. *Treatise of Human Nature.* London: J. M. Dent & Sons.

Hume, D. 1935. *Dialogues Concerning Natural Religion.* Ed. N. K. Smith. Oxford: Oxford University Press.

Hume, D. 1955. *An Enquiry Concerning Human Understanding.* New York: Liberal Arts.

Huygens, C. 1690. *Traité de la Lumiere avec un Discours de la Cause de la Pesanteur.* Leiden. Facsimile reprint, London: Dawson, 1966.

Ingard, U., and W. L. Kraushaar. 1960. *Introduction to Mechanics, Matter, and Waves.* Reading, Mass.: Addison-Wesley.

Inhelder, B., and J. Piaget. 1958. *The Growth of Logical Thinking.* New York: Basic Books.

Jardine, N. 1976. "Galileo's Road to Truth and Demonstrative Regress." *Studies in History and Philosophy of Science* 7: 277–318.

Jeffrey, R. C. 1967. *Formal Logic: Its Scope and Limits.* New York: McGraw-Hill.

Johnson, R. H. 1981a. "Charity Begins at Home." *Informal Logic Newsletter*, vol. iii, no. 3, pp. 4–9.

Johnson, R. H. 1981b. "Toulmin's Bold Experiment." *Informal Logic Newsletter*, vol. iii, no. 2, pp. 16–27; and vol. iii, no. 3, pp. 13–19.

Johnson, R. H. 1987. "Logic Naturalized." In Eemeren et al. 1987, 47–56.

Johnson, R. H. 1989. "Massey on Fallacy and Informal Logic." *Synthese* 80: 407–26.

Johnson, R. H. 1996. *The Rise of Informal Logic.* Newport News, Va.: Vale.

Johnson, R. H. 1998. "Response to Govier's 'Arguing Forever? Or: Two Tiers of Argument Appraisal.'" In Hansen et al. 1998.

Johnson, R. H. 2000a. *Manifest Rationality: A Pragmatic Theory of Argument.* Mahwah, N.J.: Lawrence Erlbaum Associates.

Johnson, R. H. 2000b. "More on Arguers and Dialectical Obligations." In Tindale et al. 2000.

Johnson, R. H. 2002a. "Manifest Rationality Reconsidered." *Argumentation* 16: 311–31.

Johnson, R. H. 2002b. "More on Arguers and Their Dialectical Obligations." In Hansen et al. 2002.

Johnson, R. H. 2003. "The Dialectical Tier Revisited." In Eemeren et al. 2003, 561–66.

Johnson, R. H., and J. A. Blair. 1980. "The Recent Development of Informal Logic." In Blair and Johnson 1980, 3–28.

Johnson, R. H., and J. A. Blair. 1985. "Informal Logic: The Past Five Years 1978–1983." *American Philosophical Quarterly* 22: 181–96.

Johnson, R. H., and J. A. Blair, eds. 1994. *New Essays in Informal Logic.* Windsor, Ontario: Informal Logic.

Johnson-Laird, P. N. 1983a. *Mental Models.* Cambridge, Mass.: Harvard University Press.

Johnson-Laird, P. N. 1983b. "Thinking as a Skill." In Evans 1983c, 164–96.

Johnson-Laird, P. N., and P. C. Wason, eds. 1977. *Thinking.* Cambridge: Cambridge University Press.

Johnstone, H. W., Jr. 1952. "Philosophy and *Argumentum ad Hominem.*" *Journal of Philosophy* 49: 489–98.

Johnstone, H. W., Jr. 1959. *Philosophy and Argument.* University Park: Pennsylvania State University Press.

Johnstone, H. W., Jr. 1978. *Validity and Rhetoric in Philosophical Argument.* University Park, Pa.: Dialogue Press of Man & World.

Johnstone, H. W., Jr. 1989. "Argumentation and Formal Logic in Philosophy." *Argumentation* 3: 5–15.

Johnstone, H. W., Jr. 1997. "A Bibliography, 1948–1997." *Philosophy and Rhetoric* 31: 6–19.

Jonsen, A., and S. E. Toulmin. 1988. *The Abuse of Casuistry.* Berkeley: University of California Press.

Kahane, H. 1971. *Logic and Contemporary Rhetoric.* Belmont, Calif.: Wadsworth.

Kahneman, D., P. Slovic, and A. Tversky, eds. 1982. *Judgment under Uncertainty.* Cambridge: Cambridge University Press.

Kalish, D., and R. Montague. 1964. *Logic.* New York: Harcourt, Brace & World.

Kalish, D., R. Montague, and G. Mar. 1980. *Logic.* 2nd ed. New York: Harcourt Brace Jovanovich.

Kanouse, D. E., and L. R. Hanson, Jr. 1971. "Negativity in Evaluations." In *Attribution: Perceiving the Causes of Behavior,* ed. E. Jones et al., 47–62. Morristown, N.J.: General Learning.

Kant, I. 1950. *Prolegomena to Any Future Metaphysics.* New York: Liberal Arts.

Kaufmann, W. 1951. "The Hegel Myth and Its Method." *Philosophical Review* 60: 459–86.

Kitchener, K. S. 1983a. "Cognition, Metacognition, and Epistemic Cognition." *Human Development* 26: 222–32.

Kitchener, K. S. 1983b. "Educational Goals and Reflective Thinking." *Educational Forum* 48(1): 7–95.

Kitchener, K. S., and K. W. Fisher. 1990. "A Skill Approach to the Development of Reflective Thinking." In *Developmental Perspectives on Teaching and Learning Thinking Skills*, ed. D. Kuhn, 48–62. Basel, Switzerland: Karger.

Kittel, C., W. D. Knight, and M. A. Ruderman. 1962. *Mechanics: Berkeley Physics Course, vol. 1.* New York: McGraw-Hill.

Klayman, J., and Y.-W. Ha. 1987. "Confirmation, Disconfirmation and Information in Hypothesis Testing." *Psychological Review* 94: 211–28.

Koertge, N. 1974. "Bartley's Theory of Rationality." *Philosophy of the Social Sciences* 4: 75–81.

Koestler, A. 1964. *The Act of Creation.* New York: Macmillan.

Kohler, R. E., Jr. 1972. "The Origin of Lavoisier's First Experiments on Combustion." *Isis* 63: 349–55.

Koyré, A. 1939. *Etudes Galiléennes.* 3 vols. Rpt. Paris: Hermann, 1966.

Koyré, A. 1965. *Newtonian Studies.* London: Chapman & Hall.

Krabbe, E. C. W. 1998. "Comment on J. Anthony Blair's Paper." In Hansen et al. 1998.

Krabbe, E. C. W. 2000. "In Response to Ralph H. Johnson's 'More on Arguers and Dialectical Obligations.'" In Tindale et al. 2000.

Krabbe, E. C. W. 2002. "Profiles of Dialogue as a Dialectical Tool." In Eemeren 2002, 153–67.

Kreyche, R. J. 1970. *Logic for Undergraduates.* 3rd ed. New York: Holt, Rinehart and Winston.

Kuhn, T. S. 1957. *The Copernican Revolution.* Cambridge, Mass.: Harvard University Press.

Kuhn, T. S. 1962. *The Structure of Scientific Revolutions.* Chicago: University of Chicago Press.

Kuhn, T. S. 1970a. "Reflections on my Critics." In Lakatos and Musgrave 1970, 231–78.

Kuhn, T. S. 1970b. *The Structure of Scientific Revolutions.* 2nd ed. Chicago: University of Chicago Press.

Kuhn, T. S. 1977. "Objectivity, Value Judgment, and Theory Choice." In idem, *The Essential Tension*, 320–39. Chicago: University of Chicago Press.

Lakatos, I. 1963–64. "Proofs and Refutations." *British Journal for the Philosophy of Science* 14: 1–25, 129–139, 221–243, and 296–342.

Lakatos, I., and A. Musgrave, eds. 1970. *Criticism and the Growth of Knowledge.* Cambridge: Cambridge University Press.

Lakatos, I., and E. Zahar. 1975. "Why Did Copernicus's Research Program Supersede Ptolemy's?" In *The Copernican Achievement*, ed. R. S. Westman, 354–83. Berkeley: University of California Press.

Lakoff, G. 1970. "Linguistics and Natural Logic." *Synthese* 22: 151–71.

Leff, M. 2000. "Rhetoric and Dialectic in the Twenty-first Century." *Argumentation* 14: 241–54.

Leonard, H., and N. Goodman. 1940. "The Calculus of Individuals and Its Uses." *Journal of Symbolic Logic* 5: 45–56.

Levin, J. 1988. "Must Reasons Be Rational?" *Philosophy of Science* 55: 199–217.

Levinson, P., ed. 1982. *In Pursuit of Truth.* Englewood Cliffs, N.J.: Humanities.

Lewicka, M. 1988. "On Subjective and Objective Anchoring of Cognitive Acts." In *Recent Trends in Theoretical Psychology*, ed. W. Baker et al. New York: Springer Verlag.

Lindsay, B., and H. Margenau. 1957. *Foundations of Physics*. New York: Dover.

Lipman, M. 1988a. "The Critical Thinker: The Concept of Critical Thinking." *Teaching Thinking and Problem Solving* 10(3): 5–7.

Lipman, M. 1988b. "Critical Thinking – What Can It Be?" *Educational Leadership* 46(1): 38–43.

Locke, J. 1959. *An Essay Concerning Human Understanding*. Ed. A. C. Fraser, 2 vols. New York: Dover.

Losee, J. 1980. *An Historical Introduction to the Philosophy of Science*. 2nd ed. New York: Oxford University Press.

Lupoli, A. 1986. "Il *Dialogo* e la filosofia implicita di Galilei." *Rivista di storia della filosofia* 41: 75–89.

Mach, E. 1960. *The Science of Mechanics*. Trans. T. J. MacCormack. Open Court, Ill.: La Salle.

Mahoney, M. S. 1980. "Christiaan Huygens: The Measurement of Time and Longitude at Sea." In Bos et al. 1980, 234–70.

Malcolm, N. 1942. "Moore and Ordinary Language." In *The Philosophy of G. E. Moore*, ed. P. A. Schilpp, 343–68. Evanston, Ill.: Northwestern University Press.

Mancosu, P. 1996. *Philosophy of Mathematics and Mathematical Practice in the Seventeenth Century*. New York: Oxford University Press.

Margolis, H. 1988. *Patterns, Thinking, and Cognition*. Chicago: University of Chicago Press.

Massey, G. J. 1970. *Understanding Symbolic Logic*. New York: Harper.

Massey, G. J. 1975a. "Are There Good Arguments That Bad Arguments Are Bad?" *Philosophy in Context* 4: 61–77.

Massey, G. J. 1975b. "In Defense of the Asymmetry." *Philosophy in Context* 4(Suppl.): 44–56.

Massey, G. J. 1976. "Tom, Dick, and Harry, and All the King's Men." *American Philosophical Quarterly* 13: 89–107.

Massey, G. J. 1980. "Logic and Linguistics." In *Modern Logic – A Survey*, ed. E. Agazzi, 311–29. Dordrecht: Reidel.

Massey, G. J. 1981a. "The Fallacy behind Fallacies." *Midwest Studies in Philosophy* 6: 489–500.

Massey, G. J. 1981b. "The Pedagogy of Logic." *Teaching Philosophy* 4: 303–36.

Massey, G. J. 1987. "Asymmetry, Fallacy, and Indeterminacy." Paper presented at the Symposium on "Informal Logic: Asymmetry and Fallacy," American Philosophical Association, Pacific Division, San Francisco.

Mates, B. 1972. *Elementary Logic*. 2nd ed. New York: Oxford University Press.

Matlin, M., and D. J. Stang. 1978. *The Pollyanna Principle*. Cambridge, Mass.: Schenkman.

Matson, W. I. 1965. *The Existence of God*. Ithaca, N.Y.: Cornell University Press.

McGuinness, C. 1990. "Talking about Thinking." In *Lines of Thinking*, vol. 2: *Skills, Emotion, Creative Processes, Individual Differences and Teaching Thinking*, ed. K. J. Kilhooly et al., 301–12. New York: John Wiley.

McGuire, J. E. 1968. "The Origin of Newton's Doctrine of Essential Qualities." *Centaurus* 12: 233–60.

McKay, T. J. 1984. "On Showing Invalidity." *Canadian Journal of Philosophy* 14: 97–101.

McKay, T. J. 1987. "Shifting the Burden of Proof." Paper presented at the Symposium on "Informal Logic: Asymmetry and Fallacy," American Philosophical Association, Pacific Division, San Francisco.

McKie, D. 1952. *Antoine Lavoisier.* New York: Henry Schuman.

McMullin, E. 1978. "The Conception of Science in Galileo's Work." In *New Perspectives on Galileo,* ed. R. E. Butts and J. Pitt, 209–57. Dordrecht: Reidel.

McPeck, J. E. 1981. *Critical Thinking and Education.* New York: St. Martin's.

Meichenbaum, D. 1986. "Metacognitive Methods of Instruction." In *Facilitating Cognitive Development,* ed. M. Schwebel and C. A. Maher, 23–32. New York: Haworth.

Meisel, J. H., ed. 1965. *Pareto and Mosca.* Englewood Cliffs, N.J.: Prentice-Hall.

Mill, J. S. 1965. *Essential Works.* Ed. M. Lerner. New York: Bantam Books.

Miller, D. 1982. "Conjectural Knowledge." In Levinson 1982, 17–49.

Miller, D. 1987. "A Critique of Good Reasons." In Agassi and Jarvie 1987, 343–58.

Millman, A. B. 1976. "The Plausibility of Research Programs." In *PSA 1976: Proceedings of the 1976 Biennial Meeting of the Philosophy of Science Association,* ed. F. Suppe and P. D. Asquith, 140–48. East Lansing, Mich.: Philosophy of Science Association.

Mosca, G. 1939. *The Ruling Class.* Trans. H. D. Kahn, ed. A. Livingston. New York: McGraw-Hill.

Naess, A. 1966. *Communication and Argument.* Totowa, N.J.: Bedminster.

Naess, A. 1982a. "An Application of Empirical Argumentation Analysis to Spinoza's 'Ethics.'" In Barth and Martens 1982, 245–56.

Naess, A. 1982b. "A Necessary Component of Logic: Empirical Argumentation Analysis." In Barth and Martens 1982, 9–22.

Natanson, M., and H. W. Johnstone, Jr., eds. 1965. *Philosophy, Rhetoric, and Argumentation.* University Park: Pennsylvania State University Press.

Naylor, R. 1990. "Galileo's Method of Analysis and Synthesis." *Isis* 81: 695–707.

Newell, A. 1973. "You Can't Play 20 Questions with Nature and Win." In *Visual Information Processing,* ed. W. G. Chase. New York: Academic.

Newton, I. 1726. *Philosophiae Naturalis Principia Mathematica.* Rpt., Geneva: Barillot, 1767.

Newton, I. 1934. *Mathematical Principles of Natural Philosophy.* A. Motte's translation revised by F. Cajori. Berkeley: University of California Press.

Nickles, T. 1980. "Introductory Essay." In *Scientific Discovery, Logic, and Rationality,* ed. T. Nickles, 1–59. Dordrecht: Reidel.

Nisbett, R., and L. Ross. 1980. *Human Inference.* Englewood Cliffs, N.J.: Prentice-Hall.

Northrop, F. S. C. 1951. "Einstein's Conception of Science." In Schilpp 1951, 385–408.

Novak, M. 1989. "The Gramscists Are Coming." *Forbes,* 20 March, p. 54.

Ogden, C. K., and I. A. Richards. 1946. *The Meaning of Meaning.* New York: Harcourt Brace Jovanovich.

Oliver, J. W. 1967. "Formal Fallacies and Other Invalid Arguments." *Mind* 76: 463–78.

Ozell, J., ed. and trans. 1717. *Logic; or, the Art of Thinking.* London.

Paggi, L. 1984. *Le strategie del potere in Gramsci.* Rome: Riuniti.

Pareto, V. 1925. "Risposta ad una inchiesta." In *Inchiesta sulla massoneria* ed. E. Brodero, 182–85. Milan: Mondadori.

Paris, S. G., and P. Winograd. 1990. "How Metacognition Can Promote Academic Learning and Instruction." In *Dimensions of Thinking and Cognitive Instruction,* ed. B. F. Jones and L. Idol, 15–51. Hillsdale, N.J.: Lawrence Erlbaum.

Pascal, B. 1952. *The Provincial Letters, Pensées, Scientific Treatises.* Chicago: Encyclopedia Britannica.

Passmore, J. 1961. *Philosophical Reasoning.* London: Duckworth.

Paul, R. W. 1982. "Teaching Critical Thinking in the 'Strong' Sense." *Informal Logic Newsletter* 4(2): 2–7.

Paul, R. W. 1984. "Critical Thinking: Fundamental to Education for a Free Society." *Educational Leadership,* September, pp. 4–14.

Paul, R. W. 1985. "The Critical-Thinking Movement." *National Forum* 65(1): 2–4.

Peeters, G. 1971. "The Positive-Negative Asymmetry." *European Journal of Social Psychology* 1: 455–74.

Peeters, G. 1974. "Patterns of Information Implied in Interpersonal Relations." *Nederlands Tijdschrift voor de Psychologie* 29: 505–34.

Peeters, G. 1986. "Good and Evil as Softwares of the Brain." *Ultimate Reality and Meaning* 9: 210–31.

Peeters, G. 1987. "Positivity Bias and Negative Effect in Social Cognition." Paper presented at the Small Group Meeting on Social Judgment, Jena, DDR.

Pera, M. 1982. *Apologia del metodo.* Bari: Laterza.

Pera, M. 1987. "From Methodology to Dialectics." In *PSA 1986: Proceedings of the 1986 Biennial Meeting of the Philosophy of Science Association,* ed. A. Fine and P. Machamer, 2: 359–74. East Lansing, Mich.: Philosophy of Science Association.

Pera, M. 1988. "Breaking the Link between Methodology and Rationality." In *Theory and Experiment,* ed. D. Batens and J. P. van Bendegen, 259–76. Dordrecht: Kluwer.

Pera, M. 1991. *Scienza e retorica.* Bari: Laterza.

Perelman, Ch., and L. Olbrechts-Tyteca. 1958. *La Nouvelle Rhetorique: Traité de l'Argumentation.* Paris: PUF.

Perelman, Ch., and L. Olbrechts-Tyteca. 1969. *The New Rhetoric: A Treatise on Argumentation.* Trans. J. Wilkinson and P. Weaver. Notre Dame: University of Notre Dame.

Perkins, D. N. 1985. "Reasoning as Imagination." *Interchange* 16: 14–26.

Perkins, D. N. 1986. *Knowledge as Design.* Hillsdale, N.J.: Lawrence Erlbaum Associates.

Perkins, D. N. 1989. "Reasoning as It Is and as It Could Be: An Empirical Perspective." In *Thinking across Cultures,* ed. D. N. Topping, D. C. Crowell, and V. N. Kobayashi, 175–94. Hillsdale, N.J.: Lawrence Erlbaum Associates.

Perkins, D. N. 2002. "Standard Logic as a Model of Reasoning." In Gabbay et al. 2002, 187–224.

Perkins, D. N., R. Allen, and J. Hafner. 1983. "Difficulties in Everyday Reasoning." In *Thinking, the Expanding Frontier*, ed. W. Maxwell, 177–89. Philadelphia: Franklin Institute.

Piaget, J. 1972a. "Intellectual Evolution from Adolescence to Adulthood." *Human Development* 15: 1–12.

Piaget, J. 1972b. *The Principles of Genetic Epistemology*. London: Routledge.

Pollock, J. 1986. *Contemporary Theories of Knowledge*. Totowa, N.J.: Rowman & Littlefield.

Popper, K. R. 1959. *The Logic of Scientific Discovery*. New York: Basic Books.

Popper, K. R. 1962. *Conjectures and Refutations*. New York: Basic Books.

Popper, K. R. 1963. *The Open Society and Its Enemies*, vol. 2. New York: Harper.

Popper, K. R. 1970. "Normal Science and Its Dangers." In Lakatos and Musgrave 1970, 51–58.

Popper, K. R. 1972. *Objective Knowledge: An Evolutionary Approach*. Oxford: Clarendon.

Popper, K. R. 1974. "Reply to My Critics." In Schilpp 1974, 961–1197.

Price, D. J. de S. 1959. "Contra-Copernicus." In *Critical Problems in the History of Science*, ed. M. Clagett, 197–218. Madison: University of Wisconsin Press.

Quine, W. V. O. 1961. *From a Logical Point of View*. 2nd ed. New York: Harper & Row.

Quine, W. V. O. 1974. "On Popper's Negative Methodology." In Schilpp 1974, 218–20.

Reed, C. 2000. "Building Monologue." In Tindale et al. 2000.

Reed, C., and D. Long. 1998. "Persuasive Monologue." In Hansen et al. 1998.

Rees, M. A. van. 2001. "Review of Johnson's *Manifest Rationality*." *Argumentation* 15: 231–37.

Revlin, R., and R. E. Mayer, eds. 1978. *Human Reasoning*. New York: Wiley.

Robinson, J. A. T. 1963. *Honest to God*. Philadelphia: Westminster.

Rossiter, C., ed. 1961. *The Federalist Papers*. New York: Mentor Books.

Rowland, R. C. 1987. "On Defining Argument," *Philosophy and Rhetoric* 20: 140–59.

Rubin, R. 1977. "Descartes' Validation of Clear and Distinct Apprehension." *Philosophical Review* 86: 197–208.

Russell, B. 1945. *A History of Western Philosophy*. New York: Simon and Schuster.

Russell, B. 1959. *The Problems of Philosophy*. New York: Oxford University Press.

Russell, B. 1960. *Our Knowledge of the External World*. New York: New American Library.

Ryle, G. 1954. "Formal and Informal Logic." In idem, *Dilemmas*, 111–29. Cambridge: Cambridge University Press,

Sakellariadis, S. 1982. "Descartes's Use of Empirical Data to Test Hypotheses." *Isis* 73: 68–76.

Salmon, W. C. 1973. *Logic*. 2nd ed. Englewood Cliffs, N.J.: Prentice-Hall.

Salmon, W. C. 1984. *Logic*. 3rd ed. Englewood Cliffs, N.J.: Prentice-Hall.

Scheffler, I. 1973. *Reason and Teaching*. New York: Bobbs-Merrill.

Schilpp, P. A., ed. 1951. *Albert Einstein, Philosopher-Scientist*. Evanston, Ill.: Library of Living Philosophers.

Schilpp, P. A., ed. 1974. *The Philosophy of Karl Popper*. La Salle, Ill.: Open Court.

Schwab, J. J. 1962. *The Teaching of Science as Inquiry.* Cambridge, Mass.: Harvard University Press.

Scriven, M. 1956a. "A Possible Distinction between Traditional Scientific Disciplines and the Study of Human Behavior." In Feigl and Scriven 1956, 330–39.

Scriven, M. 1956b. "A Study of Radical Behaviorism." In Feigl and Scriven 1956, 88–130.

Scriven, M. 1958. "Definitions, Explanations, and Theories." In Feigl et al. 1958, 99–195.

Scriven, M. 1959. "Truisms as the Grounds for Historical Explanations." In *Theories of History*, ed. P. Gardiner, 443–75. Glencoe, Ill.: Free Press.

Scriven, M. 1962a. "Explanations, Predictions, and Laws." In Feigl and Maxwell 1962, 170–230.

Scriven, M. 1962b. "The Frontiers of Psychology: Psychoanalysis and Parapsychology." In Colodny 1962, 79–129.

Scriven, M. 1966. *Primary Philosophy.* New York: McGraw-Hill.

Scriven, M. 1968. "Science: The Philosophy of Science." In *International Encyclopedia of the Social Sciences* 14: 83–92.

Scriven, M. 1976. *Reasoning.* New York: McGraw-Hill.

Scriven, M. 1987. "Probative Logic." In Eemeren et al. 1987, 7–32.

Scriven, M. 1989. "The Philosophy of Ordinary Logic." Paper presented at the Third International Symposium on Informal Logic, University of Windsor, Canada.

Settle, T., J. Agassi, and I. C. Jarvie. 1974. "Towards a Theory of Openness to Criticism." *Philosophy of the Social Sciences* 4: 83–90.

Shapere, D. 1964. "The Structure of Scientific Revolutions." *Philosophical Review* 73: 383–94.

Shapere, D. 1984. *Reason and the Search for Knowledge.* Boston: Reidel.

Shapere, D. 1988a. "Doppelt Crossed." *Philosophy of Science* 55: 134–40.

Shapere, D. 1988b. "Rationalism and Empiricism." *Argumentation* 2: 299–312.

Siegel, H. 1985. "What Is the Question Concerning the Rationality of Science?" *Philosophy of Science* 52: 517–37.

Siegel, H. 1988. *Educating Reason: Rationality, Critical Thinking, and Education.* New York: Routledge.

Siegel, H. 1990. "Must Thinking Be Critical to Be Critical Thinking?" *Philosophy of the Social Sciences* 20: 453–61.

Siegfried, R. 1972. "Lavoisier's View of the Gaseous State and Its Early Application to Pneumatic Chemistry." *Isis* 63: 59–78.

Skyrms, B. 1966. *Choice and Chance: An Introduction to Inductive Logic.* Belmont, Calif.: Dickenson.

Smit, P. A. 1987. "An Argumentation-Theoretical Analysis of Lenin's Political Strategies." In Eemeren et al. 1987, 317–26.

Smit, P. A. 1989. "An Argumentation-Analysis of a Central Part of Lenin's Political Logic." *Communication and Cognition* 22: 357–74.

Smit, P. A. 1992. "The Logic of Lenin's Polemics." In Barth and Krabbe 1992, 11–23.

Snoeck Henkemans, A. F. 1992. *Analysing Complex Argumentation.* Amsterdam: Sic Sat.

Staal, J. F., ed. 1969. "Formal Logic and Natural Language Argumentation (A Symposium)." *Foundations of Language* 5: 256–84.

Stich, S. P. 1981. "Inferential Competence." *Behavioral and Brain Sciences* 4: 353–54.

Stich, S. P. 1985. "Could Man Be an Irrational Animal?" *Synthese* 64: 115–35.

Stich, S. P., and R. E. Nisbett. 1980. "Justification and the Psychology of Human Reasoning." *Philosophy of Science* 47: 188–202.

Strawson, P. F. 1952. *Introduction to Logical Theory*. London: Methuen.

Tannen, D. 1998. *The Argument Culture*. New York: Random House.

Tarski, A. 1965. *Introduction to Logic and to the Methodology of the Deductive Sciences*. 3rd ed. New York: Oxford University Press.

Thomas, S. N. 1986. *Practical Reasoning in Natural Language*. 3rd ed. Englewood Cliffs, N.J.: Prentice-Hall.

Tindale, C. 2002. "A Concept Divided." *Argumentation* 16: 299–309.

Tindale, C., H. V. Hansen, and E. Sveda, eds. 2000. *Argumentation at the Century's Turn*. Ontario Society for the Study of Argumentation. CD-ROM. ISBN 0-9683461-1-1.

Togliatti, P. 1979. *On Gramsci and Other Writings*. London: Lawrence and Wishart.

Toulmin, S. 1958. *The Uses of Argument*. Cambridge: Cambridge University Press.

Turing, A. M. 1950. "Computing Machinery and Intelligence." *Mind* 59: 433–60.

Tversky, A., and D. Kahneman. 1971. "The Belief in the Law of Small Numbers." *Psychological Bulletin* 76: 105–110.

Tversky, A., and D. Kahneman. 1973. "Availability: A Heuristic for Judging Frequency and Probability." *Cognitive Psychology* 5: 207–32.

Vignaux, G. 1976. *L'Argumentation*. Geneva: Librairie Droz.

Walton, D. N. 1981. "The Fallacy of Many Questions." *Logique et Analyse* 24: 291–313.

Walton, D. N. 1985. *Arguer's Position: A Pragmatic Study of Ad Hominem Attack, Criticism, Refutation, and Fallacy*. Westport, Conn.: Greenwood Press.

Walton, D. N. 1987. "What Is a Fallacy?" In Eemeren et al. 1987, 323–30.

Walton, D. N. 1989a. *Informal Logic*. Cambridge: Cambridge University Press.

Walton, D. N. 1989b. *Question-Reply Argumentation*. New York: Greenwood Press.

Walton, D. N. 1990. "What Is Reasoning? What Is an Argument?" *Journal of Philosophy* 87: 399–419.

Walton, D. N. 1992. "Questionable Questions in Question Period." In Barth and Krabbe 1992, 87–95.

Walton, D. N. 1996. *Argument Structure: A Pragmatic Theory*. Toronto: University of Toronto Press.

Walton, D. N. 2004. "A New Dialectical Theory of Explanation." *Philosophical Explorations* 7: 71–89.

Walton, D., and E. C. W. Krabbe. 1995. *Commitment in Dialogue*. Albany: State University of New York.

Wartofsky, M. 1978. "Scientific Judgment." *Dialectics and Humanism* 5: 35–46.

Wason, P. C. 1983. "Realism and Rationality in the Selection Task." In Evans 1983c, 44–75.

Wason, P. C., and P. N. Johnson-Laird. 1972. *Psychology of Reasoning*. Cambridge, Mass.: Harvard University Press.

Watkins, J. W. N. 1970. "Against 'Normal Science.'" In Lakatos and Musgrave 1970, 25–38.

Weizenbaum, J. 1976. *Computer Power and Human Reason: From Judgment to Calculation.* San Francisco: W. H. Freeman.

Westman, R. S. 1980. "Huygens and the Problem of Cartesianism." In Bos et al. 1980, 83–103.

Whately, R. 1838. *Elements of Logic.* New York.

Willard, C. A. 1983. *Argumentation and the Social Grounds of Knowledge.* University: University of Alabama Press.

Woods, J. 1980. "What Is Informal Logic?" In Blair and Johnson 1980, 57–68.

Woods, J., and D. N. Walton. 1977a. "Post Hoc, Ergo Propter Hoc." *Review of Metaphysics* 30: 569–93.

Woods, J., and D. N. Walton. 1977b. "Towards a Theory of Argument." *Metaphilosophy* 8: 298–315.

Woods, J., and D. N. Walton. 1982. *Argument: The Logic of Fallacies.* Toronto: McGraw-Hill Ryerson.

Woods, J., and D. N. Walton. 1989. *Fallacies: Selected Papers 1972–1982.* Dordrecht: Foris.

Wyatt, N. 2001. "Review of Johnson's *Manifest Rationality.*" *Philosophy in Review* 21: 185–87.

Index